A LOW DISHONEST DECADE

A LOW DISHONEST DECADE

The Great Powers, Eastern Europe, and the Economic Origins of World War II, 1930–1941

PAUL N. HEHN

CONTINUUM
New York • London

2002   0826414494

The Continuum International Publishing Group Inc.
370 Lexington Avenue, New York, NY 10017

The Continuum International Publishing Group Ltd
The Tower Building, 11 York Road, London SE1 7NX

Library of Congress Cataloging-in-Publication Data

Hehn, Paul N.
    A low dishonest decade : the great powers of eastern Europe and the origins of world war II, 1930-1941 / Paul N. Hehn.
      p. cm.
    Includes bibliographical references and index.
    ISBN 0-8264-1449-4
    1. World War, 1939-1945 – Causes. 2. Europe, Eastern – History – 1918-1945. 3. Europe – Economic conditions – 1918-1945. 4. Depressions – 1929 – Europe. 5. World War, 1939-1945 – Economic aspects. I. Title.
D742.E852 H44 2002
940.53'11 – dc21
                                      2002008015

In memory of my parents,
Paul Hehn and Germaine Gagnon Hehn,
who came to America from Germany and Quebec
in search of a new and better life than they had known
and gave me their unstinting love and devotion.

For Phyllis, without whom this book
might never have been written.

Contents

Photographs and map following p. 244

Part Three:
Germany's 1930s Trade Offensive and the Small Countries of Southeastern Europe

Part Four:
The Struggle for Hegemony in Eastern Europe, 1939–1941. The Shift from Political Conflict to Military Force

Preface

To give the reader some idea of what this book is about, how I went about writing it, and what I wanted to accomplish — as it is long and comprehensive — I provide a short précis to guide the reader through the major themes and subject matter.

As happens with many writers, what I started out to do was not what this work eventually became. I thought of a primarily political and diplomatic history of Great Power relations with Eastern Europe in the 1930s where I thought the origins of the war lay. As a child of the era, like most of my generation, World War II had an overweening influence on my life. In truth, I sometimes think that I never really got from under its mesmerizing effects. This book in a sense probably was an effort to finally exorcise World War II and place it behind me by unlocking the secret of how it happened.

As I researched it, I felt the powerful influence of the untouched history of the 1930s trade wars upon the politics and ideology of the era. The first stage of conscious discovery for me was an urgent September 1939 telegram from the German Foreign Office to its minister in Belgrade pleading for increased shipments of copper: "Copper is a life and death matter," it said. "A life and death matter!" This begged the question: Why was copper so important to Berlin? After that I looked more closely and respectfully upon economic evidence of Germany's growing raw materials problems and their influence upon politics.

The book is divided into four parts with seventeen underlying chapters. Part I contains five discrete chapters dealing with separate themes and countries (1933–1939). Parts II and III, the book's core, contain eight chapters dealing with a mix of subjects focusing on Great Power conflicts and their consequences for the smaller powers (1935–1939). Part IV contains four chapters, the first two of which are a continuation of the conflicts described in the preceding chapters; the last two, and longest, concentrate on the outbreak of war (1939–1941) and the switch to military measures provoked by the unresolved political struggle.

Because this ambitious project, with major themes as well as many minor ones and side eddies contrapuntally reacting with one another, might intimidate and overwhelm the reader, I decided "to lay it all out" — as one of my readers suggested — in the first chapter. Thus chapter 1 provides a brief overview of the most important causes of the war: the 1930s fight for trade markets; Germany's quest for European domination leading to expansion into Eastern Europe in search of export markets, raw materials and foodstuffs for its rearmament program and consumer economy; and the hesitant and gradual opposition to these moves by Britain, France and America leading to war.

Chapter 2 deals with Italy and its historic problems and reasons for entering the war; chapter 3 treats France and Poland and their difficult relationship; chapter 4 covers Germany's bilateral trade relationship with Yugoslavia and its need for Eastern Europe's raw materials; and chapter 5 covers Germany's geopolitical and ideological plans for incorporating Eastern Europe under its leadership and domination, inciting Britain's traditional balance of power opposition to Europe's domination by a single power.

Chapters 6 to 15, the core of the book, deal primarily with Germany's drive first for economic then political supremacy in Eastern Europe, and the British and French decision to appease Hitler and alter the status quo established since 1918. Themes of political and economic frictions among the Great Powers are interwoven with discussion of individual Eastern European countries caught in the struggle.

The last two chapters (16 and 17) deal with the extension of the military conflict into the Balkans after the outbreak of war in September 1939. The final chapter deals with the dramatic Belgrade coup d'état of March 27, 1941. These two chapters are primarily military, political and diplomatic, the forms in which the underlying economic and market struggle were fought out.

The book's approach is both thematic and topical, cutting across geographic regions and individual countries. In a book which deals with five major powers and seven smaller Eastern European countries, not to speak of non-Western areas like Africa and Latin America, settling upon the appropriate approach became a significant preoccupation for which there probably was no completely satisfying answer. A tight thematic format would have been too difficult to follow even for historians, while a country by country approach too tedious to sustain the reader's interest. Therefore, I chose to use a mix of the two as the best solution.

The stylistic format combines narrative and analytic description of interacting trade and market factors and politics. I decided against a purely analytic approach, in favor of the narrative descriptive form whenever possible, to relieve the dry statistical and economic data which even the most patient reader tires of. I hope that the material presented enhances and deepens understanding of the origins of the Second World War. If that occurs, then the many years I spent writing it will have been worthwhile.

In the writing of this book I have a number of large debts of gratitude to repay. First, I would like to thank Professor Earl Smith, formerly a colleague, of Wake Forest College, for having read a first draft during its earliest stage of conception and for having made some particularly cogent comments that aided greatly in dealing with some vexatious theoretical problems.

At the National Archives I was helped by John Taylor and Dr. Robert Wolfe, Director of the German World War II section. Also the many archivists at the National Archives in Washington, who at various times helped me to get through the maze of the Nuremberg Trial materials. I owe thanks to the archivists of the Roosevelt Library at Hyde Park, who directed my attention to the letters and telegrams of Ambassador William Bennett. Also, my thanks to the staff of Sterling Memorial Library at Yale, in particular those in Manuscripts and Archives, who assisted me in my research there.

I owe a great deal to Professor Bill Smaldone, now of Willamette University at Salem, Oregon and one of my former students, who was kind enough to read the final draft of the work and offered a detailed criticism which helped me greatly in getting the manuscript ready for publication. His detailed critique, especially of the German segment of the study, and his many encouraging remarks about the work itself, came at a time when battle fatigue was beginning to set in and I needed some human sympathy.

Also, I have to mention the late Professor Charles Stephanson, a former colleague, of Central Connecticut State University at New Britain, who discussed with me the shoals and reefs of American foreign policy and unfamiliar aspects of American history during the 1930s and who encouraged me during the early and middle phase of this undertaking.

I was also aided financially by a grant from the American Philosophic Society to travel to Europe and defray costs of photocopying documents. Likewise acknowledgement is due for a State University of New York small research grant to pay for the sundry costs of travel and other expenses.

To my editor at Continuum Publishing, Frank Oveis, who decided to publish an oversized and involved work on the origins of the Second World War when others hesitated or refused, I owe a special debt of gratitude. I well remember his comment: "the longer the better." His many years of experience as an editor guided me through the intricacies of preparation, selecting photographs, and other concerns with unfailing good humor and kindness.

Finally, words fail me in thanking my spouse, Phyllis, for the many, many hours of proofreading, photocopying, typing and the many inglorious forms of tedium she endured in the completion of this undertaking, and for relieving me of the chores of daily life that enabled me to spend precious time on the manuscript.

P. N. H.

March 2002
Westbrook, Connecticut

Introduction

A LMOST SIXTY YEARS HAVE ELAPSED since the end of the Second World War in 1945 and despite the mountains of published exegeses on the subject by historians, participants and observers, we have not arrived at a plausible and satisfying explanation for the most horrific and devastating war in modern times which claimed an estimated 55 million casualties. This is in stark contrast to its predecessor, the First World War, with a lesser number of casualties — 35 million — for which a certain consensus has been reached, about which, perhaps, some might demur.

For the first two decades following the war, the bestial misdeeds of Hitler and the Nazis served as a cathartic whipping boy for the unsavory behavior of German business, the bureaucracy and the military. The din and trauma of the conflict still assaulted the war generation's senses and the stench of the crematoriums was still too strong in its nostrils to permit anything else. The universal anger felt over the crimes of Hitler and the Nazis and the participation of many Germans in them can only be fathomed by reading the punitive terms of the 1945 Potsdam Declaration and the 1944 Morgenthau fantasy "Goat Plan" to turn the former Third Reich into an agricultural country. Highly reasoned judgment by the historians of that era was unlikely in such circumstances. The historical record of a cataclysm like the Second World War had to lie cold for a time and the dust allowed to settle before it could be properly considered in the cold light of day.

Few historical figures have drawn such contemporary historical attention as Hitler, the "Bohemian corporal," as Weimar President Paul von Hindenburg contemptuously called him. The harsh-faced German chancellor with his grating voice and comic Chaplinesque mustache fascinated millions and mesmerized the first generation of post-war historians — and continues to do so still — into ascribing to him the blame and responsibility for the war. Although this "intentionalist" interpretation has lost some of its force, it continues to be put forward, most recently by the respected German historian, Gerhard Weinberg, one of its most dogged defenders, in the form of a thousand-page study of the war and its origins.[1]

The watershed work, "The Origins of the Second World War," by A. J. P. Taylor, that perverse demolisher of historical myths and conventions, was the first to cast doubts upon the Hitler devil theory, for which historians owe him an immense debt of gratitude. Relying primarily upon the newly published German and British archival documents, he described Hitler as merely a traditional German statesman. In his opinion Hitler was a rational statesman and "no more wicked and unscrupulous than many other contemporary statesmen." Only in "wicked acts" did he outdo them all. His

greatest gift was an unmatchable ability to wait on events for his opportunities and knowing how to threaten and bluster to get what he wanted.
Taylor erred gravely in minimizing economic determinants by assuming that
armament costs had little to do with Hitler's decision to attack Poland on
September 1, 1939, basing his conclusion on the early rearmament figures of
Howard S. Ellis, now generally believed to be much too low by most historians. Though Taylor's audacious thesis raised a storm at the time, it forced
a salutary reconsideration of the reigning shibboleths about the origin of the
war. However, some of Taylor's statements were either written with tongue
in cheek or to twit his fellow historians ("The greatest masters of statecraft
are those who do not know what they are doing!").

The succeeding generation of German historians (like Broszat and
Mommsen) advanced a new "functionalist" thesis of the primacy of domestic policy and the structure and institutions of the Third Reich. They denied
that Hitler had any pre-determined plan or policy dating back to *Mein
Kampf* and believed he was nothing more than an unscrupulous, Machiavellian opportunist and adventurer. German Marxist historians writing in
the former German Democratic Republic rejected this thesis and blamed an
aggressive, militaristic Nazi imperialism for the war.

The Fischer controversy of the 1960s and the *Historikerstreit* (historian's
quarrel) of the 1970s between the more conservative and the liberal/left
opposing schools of German historical interpretation paved the way for
more multifaceted, diverse and complex analyses of the roots of the Second
World War.[2] These clashes in the arena of recent German historiography did
a service for historical interpretation by questioning whether Hitler alone
bore the major responsibility for the war or was merely *"Der Trommler"*
(the drummer), assembling the German masses to action on behalf of a
German state and system that had been destructive and exploitative from
their very inception. In short, was Hitler puppet or puppeteer? Too much had
been made of Hitler and the Nazi Party and too little of the systemic roots
from which he had sprung. John Lukacs estimates over 100 biographies
have been written about Hitler and adds to the problem by writing another
book about Hitler's biographers.[3]

By the onset of the 1970s newer analyses suggested that the war was
the consequence of internal problems, some inherited from the preceding
Weimar era and some caused by the Nazi rearmament program set in motion by Hitler but concurred in by the German business, bureaucratic and
military elite, i.e., the German upper class. Prominent among these newer
works were Dieter-Petzina's and the pathbreaking articles and books of
Hans-Jürgen Schröder on Germany's trade relations with Southeastern Europe and the United States.[4] The first inspired hint that Hitler's growing raw
material shortages may have moved him to attack Poland came from the
British historian Timothy W. Mason.[5]

Historical investigation of Great Britain in the 1930s, on the other hand,
had to contend less with the problem of Hitler and German fascism than
with the Chamberlain government's motivation in conducting the policy
of appeasement toward the Axis Powers. In this sense British and German
historians shared a dual burden of guilt and remorse before history for the

disastrous policies in the 1930s pursued by the Chamberlain and Hitler governments.

Books and articles on appeasement have become almost a cottage industry beginning with the earlier pioneer works of John W. Wheeler-Bennett and L. B. Namier, written without benefit of the published archival documents and aided only by the official colored books and the memoirs of the leading and lesser known protagonists.[6] As in the German case, the pronounced tendency in the immediate post-war years was to strongly condemn Chamberlain and his supposed craven encouragement of Hitler leading to the fateful Munich Agreement of September 1938 and the headlong rush to repair the damage through the Polish guarantee of August 1939. Two scathing critics from the anti-appeasement school were Martin Gilbert and Richard Cott.[7] Other studies followed by William R. Rock.[8] A recent revisionist work on Chamberlain and his policy by a conservative historian who finds Chamberlain's policy correct under the circumstances is the study of John Charmley.[9] "Appeasement studies" like "Hitlerology" have become a growth industry — to borrow a phrase from the stock market — with no signs of a decline in historical interest, the most recent of which is by R. A. C. Parker.[10]

The veiled but important bystander role of the United States is generally ignored by most historians as America only entered the war in 1941 two years after it began in Europe. However, American trade rivalry with Britain and Germany provided the global avatar within which seethed the political and ideological conflicts. Roosevelt's foreign and trade policy, considered secondary to the other Great Powers, seems maladroit and inconclusive — at least by some American historians like A. A. Offner — but its influence upon British policy and British leaders was often greater than hitherto believed.

As the Second World War grew out of the economic collapse of capitalism in the 1930s, it is surprising how little has been written on the connection between the economic rivalries of the Great Powers on the international market and the war — particularly over the raw materials of Eastern Europe. On the complicated subject of trade conflict between Britain and Germany, standing like a lonely beacon is the older standard work of Bernd-Jürgen Wendt.[11] The political contest over Eastern Europe was primarily a struggle over the raw materials of that region which, had it fallen under German hegemony, would have made Nazi Germany the master of Europe. Thereafter, Britain and France would then have been immediately threatened, as French Premier Daladier warned the British. Partly because of the language and historical problems and partly because of greater interest in German, British, French and Italian history — one is tempted to say a kind of Great Power chauvinism among European historians — any detailed study of the economic problems of the Eastern European countries would be daunting.

A good start is the work of David E. Kaiser and the more concentrated study of William A. Grenzebach.[12] Neither of these authors is a specialist in the region with a reading knowledge of at least some of its languages and their studies are primarily in Western sources. Also, they describe the relations of the Great Powers with Eastern Europe without reference to the relationship between the internal problems of the Great Powers and the struggle for market share on the international market.

Historical research on Hitler as the origin and cause of the Second World War is now, barring the discovery of some hitherto unknown mother lodes of information and materials, petering out into a dry gulch. The same may be said for new studies on appeasement. While the "functionalist" approach to the origin of the war may still have a way to go before completely ceasing to offer interesting insights, it too will soon reach that dead point of conventional history, the "lotus eaters" domain, "a land where all things seem the same." None of these hypotheses either singly or collectively has answered the riddle of the origins of the war. Undoubtedly, there will continue to be "Hitlerologist" and "functionalist" studies as well, but they cannot offer new and far-reaching insights.

The aim of this study is to examine the Great Power, and particularly the British and German, economic and political conflict over Eastern Europe within the context of the global competition for trade and market share during the tariff wars era of the 1930s. The historic collapse and failure of world capitalism in the 1930s stoked the fires of revolution in Europe and North America with each nation desperate to increase exports to solve its own problems of demand and consumption in order to avert social catastrophe. The world colonial system could no longer absorb the increased production of the twentieth century. It was within this context of the failing world colonial system of the 1930s and the struggle for markets that Hitler and the National Socialist regime sought to change the international status quo and to regain Germany's lost position of financial and economic primacy by expanding into Eastern Europe, first by threatening to and finally using its military might against its foes. This study investigates whether, from the standpoint of the Great Power market rivalries, the political and military conflict was an outgrowth of the economic conflict and not, as has been assumed hitherto by most historians, its cause. The hope and expectation are that this approach will lead to some conclusions about the origins of the Second World War. The appearance recently of works like Edwin Black's *IBM and the Holocaust* (New York: Crown Publishers, 2001) connecting the Holocaust and the war with business, as well as forthcoming works dealing with Kodak and other firms are cases in point. Such a study is admittedly an ambitious one. To that end I have consulted the major archival collections and read widely in both Western and Eastern European sources. The conclusions I have reached are my own and the result of much reflection on the subject.

The Second World War is now passing into history and the war generation with it. We continue to read the past and the origins of the war incorrectly into the present and vice versa until it all begins to seem like a bad dream or a hopeless tangle at best. The origins of the war have been distorted by our emotional needs and the need to assign blame. Historians owe it to posterity to try to make some sense out of past history so that the record is at least set straight and we are at liberty to take from it what we wish. The study of history is time consuming and frustrating, yielding its secrets only grudgingly after many layers of the unfathomed and misunderstood have been peeled back. Though we continue to study, reexamine and argue over it, in the end much of it remains simply inscrutable. But I believe that the past is discoverable and to the degree that it enriches and adds poignancy, meaning and understanding to our lives, it is worth writing about. To this end, it is my hope that my small contribution will serve some useful purpose.

Part One

The Roots of War: Great Power Rivalries and the Struggle for Hegemony in Eastern Europe and the World, 1930–1939

Chapter 1

The Trade Wars of the 1930s:
The Struggle for Market Share
and Hegemony

> And 'mid this tumult Kubla heard from far
> Ancestral voices prophesying war!
> — S. Taylor Coleridge, *Kubla Khan;*
> *or, a Vision in a Dream*

POST-WAR HISTORICAL RESEARCH has lagged in placing the origins of the Second World War within the material basis for existence of the Great Powers, particularly Germany, during the 1930s. Hitler, the Nazis and ideological political perceptions continue to mesmerize and preoccupy the present generation of scholars as it had the immediate post-war generation. But this glittering lode is now played out without providing satisfying answers to the origins of the war. This study raises trade and economic conflict in the 1930s and its political and ideological manifestations as a new area of inquiry, particularly Germany's fight to regain its pre-war status on the international market.

Since World War II some German historians have indicted Imperial Germany and the Nazi state as equally involved in aggressive, imperialist expansionism. Historical investigation can no longer be limited to Hitler and the Nazi regime, but must extend to the other Great Powers, their economic interests and particularly international market forces within political contexts. This need not vitiate or deflect the responsibility of the Nazi regime and Hitler as in the historical work of Gerhard Weinberg and others. A. J. P. Taylor's pathbreaking study on the origins of World War II, whatever its merits, at least extended the historic debate beyond Hitler and the Nazi regime.

The distortions and dysfunctions of the peculiar German war economy by 1938 caused tectonic internal shifts and stresses that compelled Germany's expansion into Southeastern and Eastern Europe, exploding into the Second World War. Had Germany not expanded militarily beyond its borders in 1939, it is doubtful whether the Second World War would have occurred. Hitler's decision to rearm forced the other Powers to do likewise, intensifying the struggle for world leadership and power, particularly in the area of trade, the main theme of this study.

German expansionism and the reaction of the other Great Powers can only be explained within the historic context of the inter-war political and economic relations of the dominant states, world market conditions, capital and export-import flows and international trade patterns. International market interests and Great Power rivalries are key to understanding German expansionism.

During the nineteenth century a world trade and market system emerged based upon multilateral trade. Export surpluses from the developed European and North American areas to the developing countries of Latin America, Asia and Africa paid for the raw material exports to Europe and North America. Western Europe and North America, in turn, exported their production surpluses to Great Britain, the world hegemon, and vice versa. Capital flows through long- and short-term loans to the developing areas facilitated and expanded this commerce, though its benefits went largely to the dominant social classes. Unequal trade favored and enriched the core industrialized countries exporting manufactured commodities by draining off the natural resources of the colonial and semi-colonial countries exporting primary materials. The profits from this trade flowed back to the developing world for reinvestment; whenever profits declined, investment also withered.[1]

In his classic study *The Great Transformation*, Karl Polanyi describes four pillars of the international system between 1815 and 1914: the balance of power system; the international gold standard; the self-regulating market and the liberal state. The most important pillar, the self-regulating market, according to Polanyi, "impl[ied] a stark utopia . . . which could not exist for any length of time without destroying the human and natural substance of society." A newly emerging "high finance," dispensing copious amounts of currency, helped calm threatening squalls in relations between states. The balance of power foundered in 1914 and the self-regulating market virtually collapsed in the 1930s.[2]

Before the First World War, Britain exported about $18 billion, France $8.7 billion and Germany $5.6 billion. The United States lent about $2 billion, but borrowed $5 billion, owing $3 billion.[3] Great Power capital exports were as shown in Table 1–1.

Table 1–1. Foreign Investments of Leading Capital-Exporting Countries in Percentage of Total, 1914 and 1930

	1914	1930
United Kingdom	50.3	43.8
France	22.2	8.4
Germany	17.3	2.6
Netherlands	3.1	1.3
Sweden	.3	1.3
United States	6.3	35.3

Cited in Harry Magdoff, *The Age of Imperialism* (1969), p. 56, citing William Woodruff, *Impact of Western Man* (New York, 1966), p. 150.

This skein of relations ended after World War I. The European countries sold their American securities to finance their debts and the United States, which entered the war as a debtor nation, emerged as a creditor. After the war England lost about a quarter of its holdings; France, after losing its Russian holdings, suffered a sharp decline while Germany lost almost its entire foreign holdings. The United States replaced Britain as the leading lender of capital. By the mid-1920s Britain rebounded, surpassed by the United States in capital export volumes.[4]

Germany fell from economic grace, from a dynamic creditor to a debtor nation. The war, the ruinous post-war inflation and the loss of its colonies and national territories cost Germany dearly. Germany became a country without capital and had to make foreign short-term loans with high interest rates to replenish its industry.[5]

The U.S. gradually replaced Britain as the world's leading financial and manufacturing nation and by 1929 produced 40% of the world's manufactures (though rising Soviet production reduced it to 30% later).[6] A notable upsurge of world manufactures production occurred from 1925 to 1929 — 20% higher than 1913 — stimulated by expanded production in the United States and the developing areas. Although Britain again became the leading exporter of capital by 1925, declining manufacturing and export trade weakened its position. This affected the other European nations, particularly Germany, whose considerable exports Britain no longer took, leading to serious problems later.

Britain's economic decline happened because of the post-war shift from heavy industry to the newer and more lucrative production of automobiles, electricity, chemicals and oil. (The United States then produced four-fifths of the world's automobiles.) Oil and other sources of energy replaced coal, and demand for British manufactures slackened, profit rates plummeted and stagnation and unemployment set in during the 1920s, curtailing capital exports. Similar problems afflicted other developed countries like Germany, whose shrinking labor-intensive coal, iron and steel industries produced chronic unemployment by the end of the 1920s and ultimately contributed to the collapse of the Weimar Republic.[7] The failure of the British business class to adapt to the times' exigencies drew the testy comment of the renowned economist, J. M. Keynes, in *The Nation*.

> The mishandling of currency and credit by the Bank of England since the war, the stiff-neckedness of the coal-owners, the apparently suicidal behavior of the leaders of Lancashire, raise the question of the suitability and adaptability of our Business Men to the modern age of mingled progress and retrogression. What has happened to them — the class in which a generation or two generations ago we could take a just and worthy pride? Are they too old or too obstinate? Or what? Is it that too many of them have risen not on their own legs, but on the shoulders of their fathers and grandfathers?[8]

Britain's decline resulted more from economic forces such as decreasing demand in staples like textiles. Since the war, cheaper Indian and other manufactures flooded the market and Britain lost its former markets to

Japan and the United States. During 1900–1913 already British overall production decreased to about half of the pre-1900 figure, in turn, causing a drop in British capital exported to India, its major investment region, from 270 million rupees in 1910 to only 57 million in 1913, according to Paish's figures. Even more consequential, Britain's share in world trade declined from a third in 1870 to a seventh by 1914.[9] Germany, France and the U.S. were expanding their trade faster.

Before the war Britain invested more capital abroad than at home, multiplying earnings rapidly. In 1870 this amounted to about 9% (£35 million) of the national income and more than one-third of total profits. Invisible income from shipping, financial services in trade, banking and insurance came to £168 million more.[10]

Investment both internally and abroad slipped steadily since 1870, prompting some segments of British business, therefore, to welcome the entry of Britain into the war as a golden opportunity to eliminate a business rival. *The Daily Telegraph* (August 19, 1914) declared: "This war provides our businessmen with such an opportunity as has never come their way before.... There is no reason why we should not permanently seize for this country a large proportion of Germany's export trade."[11] The war did, indeed, provide the British economy with the stimulus it needed since profits, uncontrolled, at least during the first two years of the war, soared. The war was largely financed by the working class whose wages declined by about one-fifth during the first three years under the impact of inflation.[12]

However, investment declined in new industry because of war production needs and by 1918, investment in capital equipment fell below the 1870 level.[13] The post-war boom in 1918–1919, from pent up demand and reduced German competition, did not last long enough. By 1920 a serious slump set in, one of the worst in British history. In one year, 1920–1921, production fell by more than a quarter; unemployment rose from 2% to 18%; profits fell by more than one half.[14] Unemployment never fell below 10% during the remainder of the 1920s as British capital fought a class battle with labor to offset falling profits and remain competitive on the world market. Despite a general strike in the mid-twenties, business largely got its way. Nevertheless, investment continued to lag and production declined throughout the decade. But the gathering economic gloom had one saving grace: when the world Depression struck in the 1930s Britain's economy already had gone through the early 1920s economic shakeout and suffered less than the U.S., Germany and France. In Germany and the U.S. it fell catastrophically to almost half of total production as opposed to about 17% in Britain.

In the fifty years before 1914 Britain had been the major investor in the developing world with a quarter of its portfolio going to Asia and Africa — more than it invested in the United States.[15] The decline of British capital investment and exports had immediate repercussions on its overseas markets, particularly in India, the chief recipient of British manufactures. In the 1930s Britain became an importer of capital from overseas, reducing its investments in Asia and Africa, as reflected in Table 1–2.

Post-war market uncertainty and instability curtailed the volume of long-term loans in favor of short-term loans and interrupted the flow of capital

Table 1–2. British Investment in Asia and Africa, 1930 and 1936

	1930		1936	
Country	Pounds (millions)	%	Pounds (millions)	%
India and Ceylon	540	14.4	438	13.5
Malaya*	108	2.8	84	2.5
China	47	1.2	41	1.2
South Africa	263	7.0	248	7.6
British West Africa	46	1.2	37	1.1
Total	1,004	26.9	848	26.1
World Total	3,726	100.0	3,240	100.0

*Including non-British in 1930, but not in 1936.

Source: Royal Institute of International Affairs, *The Problem of International Investment* (London: Oxford University Press, 1937), p. 142; R. M. Kindersely, "British Overseas Investments in 1935 and 1936," *Economic Journal* 47 (1937): 657, quoted in A. J. H. Latham, *The Depression and the Developing World, 1914–1939* (1981), p. 69.

between creditors and debtors.[16] Though European and North American capital exports reached the pre-war figure by the mid-1920s, the volume of capital exports shrank, and changed lending patterns unsettled internal finance.

British manufactures paid for the raw material exports of the developing countries to Europe and the United States. India was the centerpiece and Britain's surplus of $292.2 million there in 1910 was greater than its deficit of $243.5 with the U.S.[17]

India, Britain's major market, and the developing countries produced more staple manufactured products, particularly textiles, and also increasingly received American, Japanese and European commodities. Britain's share of world exports fell from 13.1 in 1913 to 10.6 by 1937. Britain's surplus with India no longer balanced its deficits with the U.S. and continental Europe; its $64 million surplus with India in 1928 failed to make up for a $582 million deficit with the U.S. and $618 million with continental Europe.[18] Similarly by 1938 it had a deficit of $80 million with India, Burma and Ceylon and a somewhat reduced deficit of $258 million with the U.S.

Under pressure from its inner circle of dominions and dependencies (Canada, India, Australia, New Zealand), which had been suffering from mounting agricultural surpluses, Britain, following the 1932 Ottawa conference, agreed to take the exports of those countries under preferential agreements. Keith Hutchison notes: this turnabout "in Britain's trading position was a crucial part in the story of the impact of the Depression on the international trading network and accounts for much of the disintegration of trading relations which marks these years."[19]

Outside of Europe the war stimulated a surge in manufactures and foodstuffs. In the United States, Canada, Australia and Argentina, cereals and livestock expanded during and even before the war. By the end of the 1920s European wheat and cereal production caught up, resulting in overproduction, the collapse of prices and finally a world Depression.

Primary products fell steeply in price. In 1932 world manufacturing fell about one-third below the 1929 volume. In manufactures the decline varied from country to country, depending upon its share in the boom of the 1920s. In the U.S. the index of industrial production for 1932 stood at 54, in Germany 53, and Canada 58, whereas it was 84 for the United Kingdom, 69 for France and 98 for Japan.[20]

In the 1930s the centuries-old system of world capitalism fell into a deep crisis and world trade declined sharply, provoked by many factors: greatly increased output of pre- and post-war primary products; national tariff barriers beginning with the tariff of 1930 in the U.S.; and finally inequities of wealth causing reduced consumption. The "managed capitalism" of the post-World War II era, with its vastly expanded productive forces stimulated by the war and supported by a more broadly based social class structure and a greater capacity to consume and stimulate demand, did not yet exist. Colonialism, then the world market system, badly shaken by the war and hobbled by the Depression's ravages, remained intact.

By the summer of 1932 world production declined to one half of the 1928 level; and world trade volume shrank by one-third.[21] Greatly reduced world trade values tumbled from $58 billion in 1928 to $20.8 billion in 1935.[22]

The foreign trade of Germany, which previously occupied third place in total world trade after Britain and America, fell from 1929 to the mid-1930s by almost one-half. Though Germany's share of world trade during the 1930s held steady at approximately 10% after 1929, its losses in exports and imports measured in national income were well-nigh catastrophic in comparison to Britain and the United States: in Germany from 30% (1929) to 13% (1938), in the U.S. during the same period from 12% to 8%, in England from 40% to 25%.[23] Germany's almost non-existent financial holdings dimmed any prospects of regaining its lost foreign trade. The First World War and punitive reparations drained Germany of virtually all its gold and financial securities; in 1938 it held only 1% of the world's gold and financial resources, compared to the U.S.'s 54%, with France and Britain 11% each.[24]

To revive plummeting home demand, the Great Powers unwisely engaged in an intense struggle for trade and market share. Britain allowed the pound to fall in order to stimulate trade and maintain jobs and wages — while Roosevelt, ardently promoting higher domestic prices to spark recovery, opposed the fall of the pound.[25] This provoked the dislike of Chamberlain for Roosevelt — referred to disdainfully in his letters to his sister as "Master R." — and was reciprocated by Roosevelt's suspicion and mistrust of Chamberlain, the "City" and the British. Recent research suggests market forces caused the pound to fall rather than any deliberate British devaluation for the sake of a competitive edge.[26]

Trade declined and the Great Powers raised tariff walls to keep out the tide of unsalable commodities lapping at their borders. The world market fragmented into a number of commercial blocs: the preferential imperial system of Britain and its empire dependencies created at Ottawa in 1932;

the French franc bloc; the American dollar bloc; and the German "clearing countries."

The clearing agreements between Germany and other countries already existed before 1933, the first Nazi agreements being with Austria and Hungary. By 1935 clearing and barter agreements made up over 80% of German foreign trade, while currency agreements concomitantly fell to only 20%.[27] The Weimar governments first spread the system to European states, besides a smaller number (6) of non-European states.[28] To induce these countries to enter into such an arrangement, Germany, which had not devalued its currency to keep prices high inside the country and out of fear of domestic panic, subsidized its export trade, enabling it to undercut its competitors. Estimates for the rate of export subventions vary between 25% and 40%.

By 1934 the favorable trade balances of the Weimar years tapered off and in 1935 Germany's first unfavorable trade balance forced the National Socialist government to stronger medicine to prevent a disastrous *dégringolade* of the economy. Already in the 1920s and the early 1930s Germany's export and raw material problems encouraged imperialist schemes advanced by, among others, Emile Posse, trade and political department director of the Economics Ministry. Posse believed that a European *Grossraumwirtschaft* (economy of large areas), the "flanking movement of a revisionist policy" (i.e., of the Versailles Treaty), would replace the collapsing trade system. His ideas envisaged Germany as the center of a European trading region encompassing Eastern and Southeastern Europe. Hjalmar Schacht advocated a more ambitious, far more reaching neo-imperialist perspective of a worldwide trading zone for Germany comprising Southeastern Europe, Latin America and the Near and Far East.[29]

Schacht, a tireless exponent of a colonial solution for Germany's economic problems, predicted that without colonies it would be pushed toward war. Germany could neither remain a Great Power nor even continue to function. He painted a graphic picture of this to A. L. Kennedy, a member of *The London Times* working in Berlin in May 1935:

> Germany must have access to more raw materials and have it soon. The standard of living was steadily going down. Nothing can stop this deterioration except much freer world trade, especially the acquisition by Germany of foodstuffs and raw materials. If it is not stopped there would inevitably be an explosion — and the explosion, with the present regime in power, will take the form of war.[30]

Eric Phipps, the well-connected and urbane British ambassador at Paris, formerly at Berlin, rejected Schacht's warning, and predicted concessions to Hitler would be followed by "bigger music" later. But the anti-German Cassandra of the Foreign Office, the powerful Permanent Undersecretary Vansittart and Gladwyn Jebb, the department economic specialist, accepted Schacht's threat as a serious warning.[31] In September 1934, Schacht also told the American ambassador that Germany wanted colonies, preferably without war, but would resort to war if necessary.[32]

The collapse in trade paradoxically had both poisonous and hopeful political consequences. The chief editorial writer for Scripps-Howard publications, Sudwell Denny, in a "journalistic but well documented" book, pictured Britain fighting trade battles with the U.S., and the Hoover administration trying to force through Congress a higher tariff law excluding British products from the American market. "A state of economic war exists between America and Britain," wrote Denny. Diplomatic and naval officials, he claimed, sedulously cultivated "an American hands off policy toward Japanese Imperialism as the price of the growing Japanese-American accord," America's "ace in the hole" in the event of war with Britain. He pictured Britain as destined to go under and eventually become America's colony should war occur.[33]

The advent of the New Deal in the U.S. did not change this atmosphere and, in fact, at first exacerbated it. Roosevelt's desire for higher prices to spark a recovery in the U.S. led him to combat the fall of the pound at the ill-fated London conference of 1933. For the rest of the 1930s Britain shed gold and the U.S. bought it in large quantities to keep the pound high and make American goods more attractive.

The 1932 Ottawa system of preferential tariffs between Britain and the empire dependencies resulted in part from the 1930 Smoot-Hawley tariff barrier against exports to the U.S. Residues of these frictions lingered on in American Undersecretary Phillips's exchange with Lord Lothian (Phillip Kerr) in October 1934. Lothian, a wooly minded pacifist and leading appeaser of Hitler in the 1930s, described MacDonald, Simon and Baldwin as anti-American "for a variety of reasons." "Chamberlain's attitude was of course well-known." He was "not internationally minded," had "a local view" and "although a brilliant man, could not be counted upon to favor cooperation with the U.S." The British public, uninterested in the Japanese problem, focused on Europe, "especially Germany." The "British could not hold the front ranks everywhere" and felt that the Far East "came close to the responsibility of the U.S., but on this point there was a division of opinion in the cabinet." Britain could not, even if it wished, exert force against Japan; therefore, if the Japanese offered some solution guaranteeing peace in the Far East and the "open door," the British might accept it without further ado. He admitted this might drive a dangerous wedge between the British and the American government in the Far East. The Lothian conversation reflected the divided opinion in the British government about the Roosevelt Administration and awareness, as Hitler's intentions became known, that the two countries should collaborate closely.[34]

By 1934 these preoccupations permeated both governments. Atherton, the American State Department's European Division chief, reported already in 1932 that the British-American alignment should continue unbroken.[35] In the fall of 1932, John Simon, a cabinet member not known for his pro-American sympathies, voiced these same sentiments at the General Disarmament Conference: in view of the critical world situation the U.S. and Britain had to work together. Germany's threat to rearm would lead to the breakdown of naval and army limitations.[36]

George Messersmith, the departing American ambassador, arrived at some disquieting conclusions: Germany would try to gain badly needed raw materials either by "negotiation of very favorable agreements with the major suppliers of raw materials" or "through the getting of credits." Germany's imports from other states "do not assure her of the major supplies of raw materials which she needs and do not open to her for her exports the major markets she needs desperately."

The Germans believed that America's eagerness to sell its agricultural surplus would necessitate a favorable agreement. German Economic Minister Schacht wanted credits "for ... propping up a regime which is daily by its acts ... discriminating against American imports and American interests in Germany.... He wants credit from us to help a regime which, by its own acts, is destroying its capacity to pay." The Nazi government perceived the acute raw materials problem "more than any other factor" and "its dangers to the regime." Other "intelligent observers" now believed the Nazi government "cannot survive more than five or six months" and "unless help comes to the regime from the outside which will prop its falling prestige in the country and which will provide the raw materials which they have to have." Business men "who have been rendering lip service to the regime for various reasons are now more outspoken and have lost all confidence." Moreover, "Schacht can hardly agree to pay anything, because if he does, it is practically certain he can't pay anyway." Any agreement would be of little use because the "secondary people" would not permit any exchange to be used for interest payments. "Their only hope is to try to force us into some agreement by which they pay nothing and the bankers promise to use their influence to get credits for raw materials and to add credit or bilateral agreements through which Germany will pay for raw materials or finished goods." This prediction later turned out to be extremely accurate.

Messersmith cautioned: Any aid given "will merely aid to maintain a regime which is beginning to totter." "[T]he only hope for all, is that this regime does fall so that it may be replaced by a Government with which we can deal in the ordinary way...." Messersmith recommended a "policy of waiting" by which "we have everything to gain and nothing to lose."

The Office of the Economic Advisor agreed: German methods of trade (arbitrary quotas, state import monopolies, arbitrary and discriminatory rights to import, restrictions on currency exchanges) deprived the most-favored-nation treaty with Germany of any effectiveness. (Thus, the German lard monopoly had favored other countries with higher quotas at the expense of the United States.) Through "harsh and discriminatory curtailment of shipments of American goods" Germany could demand concessions in the American market and encourage other countries, with unfavorable trade balances with the United States, to do so also. This threatened to "deliberately shut off" much of American trade. Because of the directly competitive German and American markets, the widespread boycott of German goods in America and the unlikely possibility of expanding American trade anyway, further concessions would enhance the Hitler government's prestige, shore it up more for new demands for concessions and credits. Eventually, even within six months, "it would be difficult, if not impossible, for Germany to get along without most of the raw materials now purchased from the United States."[37] Accordingly, Roosevelt later denied American staples like cotton to Germany for credit and even placed restrictions on German trade in the

American market. Roosevelt pursued a contradictory dual track policy of denying Germany trade on the American market and elsewhere while politically appeasing Hitler, which American historians judged muddled and ineffective. In fact it was probably calculatingly deliberate.

The British Foreign Office mulled over these alternatives in a continuous debate over Germany which gathered momentum in the mid-1930s. One alternative was a closer association with the American colossus across the sea, advocated by disparate figures like Davis, the 1935 American Naval Conference delegate, importuning Washington for a statement on Anglo-American cooperation to respond to British parliamentary voices constantly discussing it;[38] or Smuts, the South African leader, who believed the rise of authoritarian fascism and communism and the Far Eastern situation necessitated Anglo-American cooperation;[39] and Simon, a British cabinet member, seeking American support against Hitler.[40] A poignant letter from Charles Strutt to Roosevelt in March 1935 summarized the general feeling:

> I am a great nephew of the late Lord Balfour, and have all his admiration for the United States. Why not an alliance between Great Britain and the USA? Both countries have all to gain and nothing to lose by sticking together. They seem to be almost the only two powers left with any humanitarian ideals. You are the man to carry an alliance through, so why don't you? There are millions who think as I do.[41]

J. M. Patterson, owner of the *N.Y. News,* wrote a lead article, "From Across the Atlantic," calling for a "brotherhood of six hundred million people to keep peace";[42] Prime Minister Stanley Baldwin and the influential British publisher, Lord Beaverbrook, also called for unity;[43] and Winston Churchill suggested an Anglo-American alliance through the pooling of naval and air forces.[44]

British ambassador, Sir Ronald Lindsay, perceived hopeful signs of improved Anglo-American relations despite persistent frictions.[45] Roosevelt's famous message upholding the gold standard at the 1933 Economic Conference "still rankled." Chamberlain and others were anti-American and the British government viewed the Roosevelt administration with "scant sympathy," which plainly discomfited Washington.[46] The German and Italian leaders exploited these dissonances to manipulate British jealousy and apprehension of American economic power.

The "City,"* the Bank of England and its governor Montagu Norman, the major banks and the Treasury Department since the 1920s had become committed to strengthening economic ties to Germany in a community of financial and economic interest to calm nervous world markets. Montagu Norman and the Bank had encouraged penetration of Germany by British capital which "would thwart French and American aspirations to continental hegemony." Following the collapse of the huge Austrian Credit Anstalt Bank that dominated the financial life of Central and Southeastern Europe, the British banks were hard put to recover their loans to German debtors.

---

*The financial section of London.

Only Norman's influence, and other European financial institutions, forestalled the loans from being called in and a general panic. A Standstill Agreement froze existing credits, but allowed interest payments to continue. This 1931 expedient lasted until the outbreak of war.

The Anglo-German Payments Agreement of 1934 barely avoided the threat of a clearing by the banks and seizure of German assets in Britain. Through these agreements Germany traded with Britain while deferring its debt problem, which enabled the Hitler government to carry out its rearmament program. Otherwise Britain's important German trade would have suffered and the world market would have been roiled and impaired. Maintaining Germany's economic viability, and thus countering the bitter seeds of Versailles, later metamorphosed into the policy of economic appeasement in the 1930s. British corporate, financial and governmental institutions favored this policy of pacifying Germany, and protecting the financial interests of the British bondholders, particularly short-term creditors, allowing German traders a credit line almost to the eve of the war, which played a role in causing the Second World War. Otherwise, Britain would have lost the lucrative German trade supporting German rearmament and a possible default by Germany on its debts. The dire effects on Germany and the international market might have been ruinous. There being no great enthusiasm in the Bank of England, the Board of Trade and the Foreign Office to terminate the Standstill Agreement which might jeopardize the bondholders, Britain renewed again before Munich on May 22, 1939. In hindsight, the crass, purposive behavior of these higher commercial interests during Hitler's drive to seize the Czech provinces still leaves an unrelievedly cynical impression six decades later.[47]

When Hitler refused to cease rearming and Britain's own rearmament program in response produced losses in sterling and gold, the trade-off between rearmament and the declining value of the pound became financially unacceptable, threatening the very foundations of the empire. By April 1938 Sir John Simon, then Chancellor of the Exchequer, confirmed to the cabinet that a higher level of defense expenditure would not be possible "unless we turn ourselves into a different kind of nation.[48] Given these facts, the Bank, Treasury and the British government in general decided upon economic and political appeasement of Germany.

To maintain Germany's trade with Britain and obviate further German bitterness, London continued the Anglo-German Trade Agreement, even allowing the Germans to purchase on the British market commodities for the rearmament program not purchasable elsewhere without currency.[49] Contradictorily, Britain occasionally threatened to subsidize its own export trade against Germany's subsidized exports in a trade war to demonstrate that it could drive German exports from the international market.[50] But this would increase strife inside Germany and perhaps cause the collapse of the Nazi government, a prospect from which London shrank.

Lacking the will to restrain the dictators alone, despite differences, the British government felt an apprehensive need for American support. Sir Samuel Hoare, then Foreign Secretary, summoned Atherton during the Italo-Ethiopian conflict and reported the breakdown of negotiations with Mussolini who intended to march into Ethiopia: "It was clear that the man was approaching a form of madness...he was going to reconstruct the old Roman Empire...England had lost its power and...Italy was going to be the new domination force [*sic*] in Europe." Hoare hoped the U.S. would support Britain and France in economic sanctions and condemn Italy at the start of the military conquest of Abyssinia.[51] Instead the U.S. Congress, supported by Roosevelt, passed a neutrality law in August 1935 and, Pilate-like, allowed the oil companies to ignore Hull's "moral embargo" on oil and to sell oil to Italy despite League sanctions.

Having painted itself in the corner by supporting the League of Nations in the successful 1935 election, the Baldwin government could not now be seen as running away from tackling Mussolini over Ethiopia. The Conservative government supported the League, while secretly negotiating a "compromise" through its Foreign Secretary, Samuel Hoare, with the French leader, Laval, to hand over most of Ethiopia to Mussolini. Hoare resigned when the French leaked the plan to the press and his successor, Eden, had to rescind sanctions against Italy. Taking advantage of the Ethiopian commotion and the recently concluded Franco-Soviet Pact as a violation of the Locarno Agreement, Hitler marched into the demilitarized zone of the Rhineland on March 7, 1936.

British and American failure to settle trade differences in time to unite against Hitler must be conceded as one of the major failures that preceded World War II. Believing that Germany, Italy and Japan's lack of raw materials exacerbated economic antagonisms causing the war, Roosevelt and Secretary of State Hull worked to expand the American market and the shrunken Depression markets through the 1934 Reciprocal Trade Agreement. Later Hull pressed Britain to conclude a commercial agreement modifying the Ottawa imperial preferences restricting Britain's import trade to the empire areas, but also with provisions to throttle Germany's trade if necessary. Hull's self-serving demands left unspoken the fact that the United States sold much more to the U.K. than it imported and was adamantly unwilling to lower its own high tariff against British goods. Though the British Minister of Trade, Lord Runciman, held talks in January 1937 with Roosevelt and Hull, the negotiations dragged on interminably. The British suspected that Hull's idealistic rhetoric of expanded trade opportunities and unlimited commercial vistas for all, masked American aspirations to invade Britain's trade markets and replace it as the world hegemon. London also entertained hopes of an economic and political agreement with Hitler.

The inter-war trade disputes and jealousies led directly to the door of war. Hull's memoirs note that the Anglo-American trade agreement of 1938 "reversed the protectionist trend...and made major breaches" in the 1932 British tariff wall removing duties entirely on wheat and other foodstuffs. But, ruefully: "unfortunately it had come too late." Had it come "in 1934, 1935 or 1936, its results would have been far greater." Hull's memoirs elide the suggestion that American trade demands hindered a joint agreement against Nazi Germany and placed a premium on Britain settling its differences with Germany and Hitler in the future.[52]

Failed Western unity and universal dread of war further encouraged Hitler, and the tepid response to the 1936 Rhineland occupation bluff whet his ambition even more. François-Poncet, the astute French ambassador to Berlin, holding conversations in Berlin for a general agreement, noted that "a number of wild men," including Göbbels and Göring, "believe that a policy of rapid action should be followed; but that Hitler at the present time is siding with Schacht, the industrialists and the saner members of the general staff who prefer an arrangement that would enable Germany to live in peace." The French Ambassador thought that the major problem was finding the raw materials Germany needed and an outlet for German finished products if German rearmament ceased. He believed that if Germany had to choose between economic collapse or war it would choose war.[53] At this point Hitler sided with Schacht and the industrialists because Germany was unprepared for war and he thought that Schacht's international credibility and contacts would bring him the raw materials he needed.

Yvon Delbos, Foreign Minister in the Popular Front government of Leon Blum, feared a German attack on Czechoslovakia and the ambiguities it would create. He professed to prefer a direct attack on France, which "would certainly have to march if Czechoslovakia were attacked" even "without the support of either Poland or England."[54] By 1937 French talk of tackling Germany alone became muted or faded altogether as the darkening cloud of defeatism and internecine class conflict fostered a desire to cast off the wearisome burden of defending Eastern Europe.

French and British policy blew hot and cold and showed an appalling defeatism or determined opposition to the expected German expansionist blast which Hitler's pell-mell rearmament program made inevitable. Typical of the era's roller coaster mood swings was the Belgian politician Van Zeeland's April 1937 initial enthusiastic analysis "that for the first time within his knowledge the British had taken an entirely definite and strong line of policy." The British would rearm but maintain their trade barriers until a global settlement occurred guaranteeing their safety. During the next few years Britain "would very nearly control the trend of international affairs and their increasing strength would fully dispose them to use the strong paw of the lion."[55]

Van Zeeland ingenuously thought a "most important" sign of England's changed attitude toward Central Europe was Eden's vague assurance to Czech Foreign Minister Beneš that "Great Britain was not uninterested in the fate of Czechoslovakia." Eden "in the most categorical manner" affirmed British support of the League and "intimated that under the aegis of the League of Nations Great Britain might intervene in case Czechoslovakia should be attacked by Germany." Between Britain, France and Belgium an "absolute accord" existed and "the leader of this trio who called the tune to which the others danced was unquestionably the British Government."[56]

Within days all this fizzled out. Pessimism succeeded optimism when the forceful, authoritarian Chamberlain replaced the slothful, bumbling Stanley Baldwin. French will flagged, then foundered upon the shoals and reefs of Britain's adamant refusal to promise aid beforehand to France if the Germans attacked Czechoslovakia. British diffidence and French repudiation of responsibility toward Czechoslovakia unless Britain did so became a constant bedeviling conundrum down to the eve of Munich. Additionally, defense-gorged budgets, crippling inflation, finally the empire's chaotic decline became self-serving rationalizations justifying a reluctance to do anything to help Czechoslovakia. Growing civil crisis in France — Van Zeeland expected a financial collapse in June or July of 1937 — and a threatened franc devaluation and social unrest sapped French power, feeding a numbing defeatism. Blum glumly ruminated that the gain in all the recent conversations between London and Paris "would be very small."[57]

In the spring of 1937 the witty British ambassador, Sir Eric Phipps, newly transferred from Berlin to Paris, and Foreign Minister Delbos thought peace could be preserved "if England and France should show their teeth to Germany and have behind them the benevolent neutrality of the United States." Both London and Paris agreed that they should play for time by talking about settling the armament question "because it would be desirable to keep Germany talking about something while Britain rearmed." In this strange interlude of heightening tensions in the mid-1930s both Hitler and the Western Powers masked their real intentions by disingenuous peace declarations. Both Britain and France quickly forgot about "show[ing] their teeth to Germany" and agreed that Hitler could take Austria whenever he wanted without creating serious international complications, which German Foreign Minister von Neurath casually confirmed. Eden's tune changed: he told the Austrian Foreign Minister, Guido Schmidt, that "it would be very difficult to persuade the British public to go to war on behalf of Austria."[58]

Hitler determined upon military force to attain Germany's hegemonial and expansionist ambitions, and to relieve the financial and inflationary pressures of rearmament and the unsettling specter of financial debacle — to be discussed later in greater detail. This latter possibility, first raised by the British historian Tim Mason, of a spreading crisis inside the country starting in the mid-1930s and reaching its height in 1939, necessitating a war of plunder to support the rearmament program, must now be considered a serious historical interpretation.[59] Mason called attention to a manpower crisis of one million unfilled jobs caused by the labor-devouring armament program, which necessitated seizing foreign territory with non-German populations, a "plunder of peoples." Otherwise German women would have to be conscripted for long hours of work in the armament program, which might incur the displeasure of the German male working class population. Impressed by working class strikes at the end of the First World War, Hitler and the Nazi government wished to avoid that nightmare.[60] Germany's raw materials and financial problems were well understood in Western chancelleries and constantly discussed by diplomatic officials in their reports and analyses.

Throughout the 1935–1937 period Hitler relied upon his Economics and Reichsbank minister, Hjalmar Schacht, the export sector's representative, to secure the necessary raw materials from the Western countries either through credits or African colonies. Meanwhile, Hitler rearmed and bided his time while waiting for Schacht to solve Germany's economic and financial problems. Anticipating Schacht's demands in May 1937 for the return of Germany's colonies, without an adequate political settlement, French Premier Blum "did not hope for ideal results." In London Delbos considered returning the colonies, but the British rejected this "merely to have Germany make further demands after the colonies were returned." British trade policy denied Germany continental or world hegemony by refusing any colonial concessions or barring access to trade through its Depression-era tariff system. Unfortunately it also curtailed American exports, to Washington's annoyance.[61] The critical absence of the United States in the political equation, and America's refusal to become involved in a European war, which Roosevelt's minister Bullitt repeatedly reiterated to Delbos and to the distraught former premier Chautemps, contributed greatly to sealing the fate of Czechoslovakia.[62]

More knowledgeable of Hitler's intentions than most, Sir Eric Phipps held a very pessimistic assessment of the darkening situation: he thought Hitler "a fanatic" and "did not see the faintest possibility of coming to any agreement with the Nazi leader except through 'military force.' " Hitler's demands for the German-populated Sudetenland would have destroyed the unity, defense and wealth of Czechoslovakia and weakened France's own defensive position. The excellent Czech defense fortifications then would have been handed to Hitler, setting in motion fateful centrifugal forces among the other minorities inside Czechoslovakia. The Western Powers could hardly swallow this without appearing craven before Hitler and losing the support of world opinion.

Intermittently Daladier, the French Premier, seemed willing to fight, and as late as September 26, 1938, at the height of the Munich crisis, he informed Chamberlain that if German troops crossed the Czechoslovak frontier the French army would attack Germany at once and he (Daladier) wanted to be able to tell Hitler that Britain would immediately join France. He believed in the honesty of Chamberlain, who gave him the impression "that in spite of his being a cold and limited man when he shook hands with you and said he was with you, you could count on him." He thought Hitler wanted not only to gain his ends in Czechoslovakia but to humiliate Britain and France. "To fight and die was better than to submit to such a humiliation."[63] But, abhorring war and its horrors, Chamberlain was ready to give in to Hitler's most extreme demands.

At two meetings in 1938 in Germany with Hitler, Chamberlain became naively convinced he had gained Hitler's confidence and he alone could salvage the peace. Arch-appeaser, French Foreign Minister Bonnet, and also Daladier to a lesser extent, quickly fell in with this comforting reasoning. "Chamberlain," declared Bonnet, "had felt that he had established a personal relationship with Hitler and it would be better for all concerned if he should continue to handle the matter on the basis of personal and confidential communications and the French Government had accepted blindly Chamberlain's leadership." Bonnet added that "in spite of the firmness of feeling in the French population he had just received the visit of one hundred Deputies of the Center parties who had asserted that they did not wish France to go to war." American Ambassador Bullitt "doubted the accuracy of this statement," adding that "Bonnet in spite of the firm line which he has been compelled to take by Daladier is *rodently* [Bullitt's emphasis] for peace at any price."[64]

Shortly after the Munich Conference in September 1938, Daladier candidly confessed conflicted feelings: "he felt that Chamberlain had been taken in a bit by Hitler who had persuaded him to remain after the others had left (i.e., at Munich) and had convinced Chamberlain that Germany was ready for peace.... Chamberlain was an admirable old gentleman, like a high-minded Quaker who had fallen among bandits, and he did not think that Chamberlain's last conversations with Hitler had been helpful."[65] Hitler had already determined upon war with Czechoslovakia and only the intervention of Mussolini, whose support he wanted in the event of war, had forced him to the conference table.

What actually happened at Munich can be gleaned to some degree from Göring's account to the Nuremberg psychologist, Martin Gilbert:

> "Neither Chamberlain nor Daladier were in the least bit interested in sacrificing or risking anything to save Czechoslovakia. That was clear as day to me...I was simply amazed at how easily the thing was being managed by Hitler.... We got everything we wanted; just like that." He snapped his fingers. "They didn't insist on consulting the Czechs as a matter of form — nothing. At the end the French delegate to Czechoslovakia said, 'Well, now, I'll have to convey the verdict to the condemned.' That's all there was to it. The question of a guarantee was settled by leaving it up to Hitler to guarantee the rest of Czechoslovakia. Now, they knew perfectly well what that meant."[66]

However, in the unpublished account given by Daladier to Bullitt a few days later on October 3, 1938, we have a somewhat different version in which the French Prime Minister presents himself as a tough, unyielding negotiator, having rejected the more outrageous demands of Hitler, and granting to Germany only the Sudeten-German populated region of Czechoslovakia and little else. Daladier says little about his own self-doubts and the wisdom of the course he and Chamberlain had chosen.

> Daladier lunched with me today. He described in detail the conversations in Munich saying that Hitler had commenced the meeting by a tremendous discourse: that he, Daladier, had then stated that after all the question before them was extremely simple: all four countries represented were prepared to make war at once; the question was whether Czechoslovakia was to be attacked and invaded and destroyed or whether there was to be a reasonable settlement. He suggested that they address themselves to that at once.
>
> Daladier said that after this statement of his, Hitler calmed down and that the discussion proceeded in an extremely orderly manner until he, Daladier, announced that certain terms of the German ultimatum were entirely inacceptable [sic] to him and that he was prepared to make war rather than accept them. I gathered that these terms concerned the demand that the Czechs should leave in the Sudeten region all foodstuffs, cattle, et cetera, et cetera. He said that Hitler began to explode at this point and that he, Daladier, left the room and walked

up and down in an anteroom smoking cigarettes until about an hour later when Hitler appeared and said to him "what you ask is entirely unjust and unfair; nevertheless in the interests of peace in Europe I shall concede it."

Daladier said that after this the conversations were relatively amicable and that Göring especially had devoted a great deal of attention and personal flattery to him saying that he had given France her old warlike spirit.... He said that Mussolini throughout had been most amicable with everyone and had tried to persuade him, Daladier, that Hitler would have no further territorial ambitions after the annexation of the Sudeten, arguing that Hitler's entire interest now would be concentrated on the rebuilding of Germany.

Daladier said that he did not believe a word of this. He thought that within six months France and England would be face to face with new German demands probably in the colonial field and that there might also be more serious Italian demands supported by Germany for Tunis and Syria.[67]

Chamberlain's role before and at Munich is well known. Both he and most of the cabinet agonized excessively that another war would lead to the triumph of bolshevism and "would destroy the rich and idle classes," noted Oliver Harvey, private secretary to both Eden and Halifax. Chamberlain stated in 1939 in Parliament that "we should say quite openly that we have no intention of trying to hamper Germany's *legitimate* freedom of action in Central or Eastern Europe.... I admit that personally I am only too glad that [Germany] should look eastwards instead of westwards."[68] Baldwin bluntly agreed: "If there is to be any fighting in Europe to be done, I should like to see the Bolshies and the Nazis doing it."[69] Britain should acquiesce in this, but only by peaceful means. The search for a "peaceful means" gradually meant abandoning Czechoslovakia to Nazi control at a time when Britain was not yet psychologically prepared for war.

About Daladier the historical record is murkier. A burly and plain-spoken political figure, a "poilu" in the trenches of World War I, the "bull of the Auvergne" was less resolute and tenacious than his popular persona. The Munich document just cited is vintage Daladier: whether he really gave Hitler short shrift, as he claims, may or may not be the case. Whatever the case, Daladier's uncompromising face before Bullitt scarcely conceals the surrender of the Sudetenland and the Czech defenses to Hitler and the betrayal of Czechoslovakia with whom France had an alliance. Therefore, he has been called "the bull with snail horns." He seemed to be personally willing to confront Hitler more than Chamberlain and his friends — or so he comes across in the historical documents — but much of this was convictionless gesture. France's depleted resources, military weakness, sharpening class conflict and its defeatist-riven upper class elite sapped away Daladier's pugnacity. He yielded to Chamberlain's intention to avoid war by satisfying Hitler's demands, lest France end up fighting Germany alone. He had little faith in the Soviets, feared communism and the "reds" more than Hitler and sedulously resisted implementing the Franco-Soviet alliance.

Daladier's unyielding demeanor almost led to a breakdown of relations during the British-French talks in April 1938, but after his September 1938 meeting with Chamberlain, he acquiesced in the Prime Minister's plans. The French and British governments agreed to apply unrelenting pressure on the Czech government for concessions until Prague surrendered the German-populated Sudetenland districts to Germany.

Whether Chamberlain gave Hitler a "free hand in the east" before and during his meetings with Hitler at the Munich Conference may never be satisfactorily established. No definitive written or documentary evidence exists of the meetings that this in fact happened. But Chamberlain undoubtedly gave Hitler the equivalent impression that Britain would not do anything to oppose Germany's domination of Central and Eastern Europe, provided it was done peacefully and legitimately. Certainly this was the sentiment inside the cabinet and in the higher echelons of English society.[70] Constant waffling and flat-out encouragement by British leaders undoubtedly fanned Hitler's belief that Britain in the end would not oppose Germany's domination of Eastern Europe.

How the Great Powers came to such an impasse and ultimately to war will be the subject of the rest of this chapter.

Beginning with the United States, the debates inside the Roosevelt administration, among corporation executives and intellectual elites, reveal by the mid-1930s a growing concern over the paramount need to increase trade opportunities abroad or face social crisis, economic dysfunction and stagnation.[71] A rising chorus of government and business leaders wanted to extend American overseas export markets at all costs, as absolutely vital to the well-being of the American capitalist system. Proponents of a new trade dynamism to counter the Depression rekindled the economic nationalism of the 1920s. Messersmith, Assistant Secretary of State, wanted a new and different approach which "would call for a complete rearrangement of the entire economic setup of the United States." Assistant Secretary of State Francis B. Sayre, a law professor, the son-in-law of President Wilson and chairman of the President's Executive Committee on Commercial Policy, put the matter succinctly: "Unless we can export and sell abroad our surplus production, we must face a violent dislocation of our whole economy." One historian concludes: "that meant Germany, Italy and Japan were defined as dangers to the well-being of the United States," even before the military expansions of those countries in areas vital to its economic system, but rather it "occurred instead as those nations began to compete vigorously with American entrepreneurs in Latin America and Asia."

Some like Treasury Secretary Morgenthau in 1937, alarmed, predicted that one day the Axis powers could be expected to "have taken over Mexico." But it was Asia, "the El Dorado of America's overseas economic expansion" since 1894, on which American business, their commercial juices roiling, expectantly fixed their gaze. Believing "the long awaited opening of China as a market was finally under way," they watched with dismay as Japan invaded China. The American share in the trade of China had surged after slumping in the 1920s. By 1932 it surpassed the Japanese-Chinese trade and in 1935 it reached $22,000,000. By 1937 Asia supplied more than 51.5% of raw and crude materials to the United States and more than 85% to 98% of special commodities like rubber, tin, tungsten, jute, shellac and a third of its mica.

A debate raged within and outside the Roosevelt Administration over whether, once war broke out, the United States should remain strictly neutral and allow its export trade to be lost, or whether it would be driven inexorably to defend its trade abroad or face grave economic and social problems. William Appelton Williams presses the argument to its limit, suggesting: the American leaders "came to accept the necessity of violence" to defend their trade markets even before the Japanese attack on Pearl Harbor and may have been compelled to do so even had that event not occurred. Labor leaders like the monarchical miners' union leader, John L. Lewis, feared business would get the upper hand if war occurred and demanded appeasement and the sharing of raw material markets, while some American business leaders, as in Britain, saw war as bringing in its wake the end of the capitalist system and communism. Other corporate leaders advised fighting the Axis on political and economic grounds. As Hitler invaded country after country, business leaders gradually moved into the New Deal camp and into the government itself to chart the expansion of export markets for a greatly expanded twentieth-century world economy.

In accepting import preferences for the dependencies at Ottawa August 20, 1932, Neville Chamberlain achieved his father, Joseph Chamberlain's, dream of a unified Empire separated from the non-British areas by an encircling tariff wall.[72]

The results benefited the imperial dominions more than Britain. From 1930 to 1938 the Empire increased exports to Great Britain by 22% in value and its share of the British import market rose from 29% to 40%. By contrast the percentage of British exports taken rose only from 43.5% to 50%, but their absolute total fell by 5%.[73] Since import prices fell faster than those of export prices, the terms of trade improved, but at the expense of the export market. A year later in 1934 Neville Chamberlain ruminated glumly on these forebodings:

> The largest problem I see in front of us is what is to be the future of international trade. It has shrunk to ⅓ of what it was in 1929. Is it going to recover, or is the spirit and practice of economic nationalism going to prevail, and each country try to live by taking in its own washing?[74]

The prohibitive Ottawa tariffs meant the effective abandonment of the nineteenth-century multilateral trade system in favor of bilateral agreements, and forcing other countries behind high tariff walls and autarchy. The Darwinian ethos intensified, forcing the strongest nations to survive at the expense of the weaker ones by reversing capital circulation. England went from exporting capital to draining it from the colonial areas, all of which had particularly disastrous consequences for semi-colonial, capital-starved Eastern Europe, dependent upon raw material exports to pay for imports from developed countries.

Germany, lacking colonies, exported its manufactures to England and other European states, and now found itself frozen out of its traditional markets. The Germans joined the feverish scramble for markets to relieve industrial stagnation and unemployment. German trade inevitably expanded into its former Eastern and Southeastern European commercial sphere in search of raw materials. An inflation-stoked, overheated German economy, currency shortages, trade problems and Hitler's imperialist expansionist program and penchant for adventurist gambles made for a devil's brew that could only provoke another war.

Britain's seismic commercial changes at Ottawa drew instant fire: Sir Orme Sargent of the Foreign Ministry's Central Department and Sir John Simon, then Foreign Secretary, warned of the consequences of preferential tariffs in a December 2, 1931, memorandum, but Chamberlain, the Board of Trade and its head, Runciman, prevailed.[75] Notable dissenters were Laurence Collier, head of the Foreign Office's Northern Department, and Sir Hugh Knatchbull-Hugessen, Minister to all three Baltic states and later Turkey. Collier fought unsuccessfully for maintaining British trade connections with Eastern Europe.[76]

In the spring of 1930 at the height of France's power, French Premier Aristide Briand proposed a Pan-European Union, a grandiose plan to counter the trade slump by unifying Europe, expanding markets and encouraging the free flow of goods across borders. The plan replaced Britain's declining pound with France and its gold-backed francs as the new hegemonic power. The Germans reacted negatively, while France's eastern allies, the Little Entente (Czechoslovakia, Romania and Yugoslavia) and Poland were enthusiastic. The Briand project's economic structure underpinned the political organization and territorial boundaries of the Versailles peace settlement.[77] The German Foreign Office viewed this politically unified Europe under the League as a scheme to stabilize the continent under French hegemony. State Secretary von Bülow noted sardonically in August 1930: "Clearly they wish a Pan Europe only if they possess the dominant position inside it."[78]

London also saw the plan as a French ploy "to reinforce France's hegemony in Europe." The inhibiting effect it would have on trade, creating more regional organizations ("European, Pan-America, Russo-Asiatic unions") "might endanger the cohesion of the British Commonwealth of Nations."[79] In retrospect, Briand's grand design, undercut by the cynicism, short-sightedness and mutual jealousies of the Great Powers, may have been a last chance to head off the oncoming Depression and war.

The world Depression struck the Danubian region with powerful hammer blows, leaving ruination and despair in its wake. Disaster and opportunity became close bedfellows and the Great Powers cynically manipulated the economic and social distress of the beggared states of Eastern Europe for their own interests.

After World War I, British and French capital replaced German and Austrian capital in Eastern Europe. France tried to perpetuate its dominant position through large loans and capital investments, primarily in servicing public debt. Britain and the United States did not have major interests in the region, but nevertheless wished to prevent other powers from exercising a stranglehold and denying them access. The two strongest economic powers, they, therefore, clung stubbornly to free trade and the most-favored-nation principle, which fostered a dominant/subaltern relationship with the capital-poor and labor-intensive Danubian countries. For the Great Powers, the Eastern European region represented a vast, densely populated, underdeveloped area whose raw materials and foodstuffs could be extracted through unequal trade — a kind of European India or Africa.

In 1930, France, bolstered by its strong gold reserve, arrived at the pinnacle of its financial power. Realization of their virtual dependence upon the Bank of France jolted the Bank of England and the American Federal Reserve System.[80] Two years later France's luster faded and by 1934, rent by internal strife, it began to slide and England became the strongest of the European powers. From the beginning of the 1930s, France, Germany and Italy fought to secure greater commercial market share and outright hegemonic control of the Danubian countries in order, through lower raw material costs there, to bolster their own declining economic position.

Already in the late 1920s German business and the German Foreign Office pointed to future opportunities in the southeast. Memoranda flowed copiously between German Foreign Office departments and business groups. An unsigned April 1926 Foreign Office note broached the idea of using the German economy ("the consumer power of 60 million people"), as the second greatest consumer country after the U.S., to recover its previous hegemonial position in Eastern Europe.[81] During the 1920s Hjalmar Schacht also put forward the idea of using the consumer power of the Reich as a battering ram to advance German economic and political interests in the region. The German Foreign Office also perceived inviting export possibilities in the southeastern market, but conflicts between German agrarian and industrial interests stood in the way. The newer, influential segments of the export sector, like the chemical industry, in particular I. G. Farben, and the electric industry, supported Stresemann's policy of political reconciliation through a French-led customs union with Germany as "junior partner," while the heavy industries supported a traditional "mitteleuropa" customs union or a return to the Wilhelmian imperialist "border" areas policy of the First World War.[82]

Despite its severely weakened capital position, Germany tried in the early 1920s to counter French and British capital investments in Southeastern Europe. The establishment by the Mannesheim group of the Hungarian-German bank in 1920; the efforts of the Dresdner Bank to preserve German industrial interests in the Balkans; and the abortive efforts of the German industrial tycoon, Stinnes, to acquire leading metallurgical firms in Austria, Czechoslovakia and Hungary represented key moves to gain a foothold in banks, industrial firms and bauxite mines in Hungary and other Balkan states. After the French-German reparations and Ruhr conflict of the early 1920s and the decline of German capitalism in 1923, all these efforts came to naught.[83] The retreat of German capital left the way open to an intensified influx of French and English capital into the region.

In the interwar period foreign capital investment controlled the economies of East Central Europe, amounting to between 50 and 70% — the single exception being Czechoslovakia.[84] Western capital penetrated almost every important area of Balkan industry: the American General Electric firm gained control of the Hungarian electro-technical industry and the telephone sector; the British bought into the Hungarian river transportation system, banks and other enterprises; and in Romania the British and French increased their pre-war grip on the critical oil extraction sector from 5 to 16% respectively by 1931. The high level of foreign capital, primarily Western, in servicing the national debt and share capital of the Danubian countries attests to their tutelage to Western capital: Romania 89.2% of government securities; Yugoslavia 82.5% of government securities and 44% of share capital.[85] Similar figures tell the same story for Poland and Hungary.

In 1930 German heavy industry allied with the bureaucratic-imperialist fraction in pursuit of an expansionist policy designed to economically incorporate the Southeastern European states into the Reich. Germany again exported capital in 1927 to the Southeastern European region for the first time since the end of the war, and German firms (I. G. Farben, Siemens, AEG, Vereinigte Stahlwerke, and some banks) became active in Yugoslavia and Czechoslovakia. Loans flowed in the following year, of 100 million Rm from Vereinigte Stahlwerke; and Vereinigte Glanzstoffabrik participated in constructing a factory in Romania and the Dresdner Bank in the funding of the Romanian Bank.[86] German industrial organizations debated whether to form a customs union "from Bordeaux to Odessa," which included France, or the various schemes of German heavy industry for a new "mitteleuropa" that included Austria and the Southeastern countries, aimed primarily against France, the United States and England. Such schemes of Germany as the new hegemon were premature, given the weakness of German capital. Germany could no longer compete against the stronger economies and financial power of the United States, Britain and France and had to search elsewhere for export markets and cheaper raw materials.[87]

Plummeting internal demand and declining export markets turned German eyes eastward to the lure of limitless markets and boundless raw materials beckoning like the proverbial land of Canaan. To solve the agriculture-industry conflict which hindered the cultivation of the southeastern market, Carl Bosch of I. G. Farben proposed that German agriculture be organized and cartelized with a guarantee of profits through fixed prices and state intervention through the 1930 Mitteleuropäischer Wirtschaftstag (Central European Economic Congress) with Farben playing a key role. "The form for this mediation" (i.e., between business and agriculture), comments a recent writer, "was the Central European Economic Congress (MWT) and the program was one of imperialism."[88]

Farben increasingly depended upon state intervention with subsidies for the hydrogenation of coal-produced synthetic gas. Despite its high cost to consumers, Farben's production of synthetic gasoline at Leuna saved foreign exchange and promised to save more as the currency shortage increased. Stresemann remarked earlier that without I. G. Farben and without coal he had no foreign policy.[89] In its decision to develop the hydrogenation process, Farben was preparing for war.[90] Its later behavior and avaricious thirst for profits certainly indicate this.

As a major spokesman of the more dynamic export sector of the economy, Farben exercised an incestuous influence on the inter-war governments. Carl Bosch of Farben and Chancellor Brüning had a close association, and a Farben managing board member, Professor Hermann Warmbold, entered the Brüning cabinet as Minister of Economics. When world gasoline prices fell and production costs of synthetic gasoline increased, Farben sought help from Brüning. The Brüning government assisted by increasing the duty on gasoline to sixteen pfennigs per liter, the highest gasoline duty in Europe at that time.[91] However, this did not even cover production costs and public hostility towards the high cost of gasoline and the weakening government support forced I. G. Farben to appeal directly to Hitler. The Nazi press had been attacking Farben as an instrument of finance capital and the "Jew Warburg." After the Farben emissaries Bütefisch and Gattineau pointed out the advantages of domestically produced gasoline to Hitler, he agreed to cease the press attacks. The Nazi leader probably saw synthetic gasoline as a way of lessening dependence upon imported gasoline, an Achilles heel for his plans to rearm Germany.

Shortly after, Farben began to support the National Socialist Party through contributions, as it had other leading parties. Heavy industry had already turned against a French-dominated customs union; and the industrialist Schlenker published an article, "Deutschland und Südosteuropa," in February 1932 invoking a German-led customs union with Austria, Romania, Yugoslavia and Czechoslovakia.[92] The expansionist *Lebensraum* ideology enunciated by Hitler in *Mein Kampf* must have been regarded as manna from heaven by the profit-strapped German business class.[93] That Hitler meant a *Lebensraum* in the USSR, i.e., the Ukraine, and not in Southeastern Europe, few noticed.

Already in mid-1931 Berlin created an Austro-German customs union which it thought Czechoslovakia and the Danubian states eventually would be forced to join. The vigilant Permanent Undersecretary of the British Foreign Office, Vansittart, commented: "The French are not altogether wrong in seeing the proposed Austro-German customs union, the first move in a new economic hegemony."[94] Foreign Minister Curtius and State Secretary Bülow conceived of this strategy as a well-aimed response to France's penetration of the southeast through extensive financial loans and credit.

The major Austrian Credit Anstalt Bank collapse enabled the French to short circuit the customs union project through Austrian dependence upon French loans. British financial support temporarily staved off collapse but the dominant French financial position and Austria's dependence in effect scuttled the customs union. The Bank of England's Governor, Montagu Norman, intervened with financial support, purportedly "in the public interest," but actually it was the continuing balancing act performed in order to safeguard British interests. As the dominant imperial power, it was in Britain's interest to maintain international and financial stability.[95] British policy was to move the quarrel to the League of Nations in which it had sufficient influence and could check Germany's imperialist resurgence toward the southeast, where it had trade and investment interests, while also avoiding a direct confrontation between France and Germany.

French power in Eastern Europe reached its apogee in 1931–1932 with the conclusion of preferential trade agreements with Hungary and Yugoslavia and the 1932 Tardieu plan for a Danubian federation under the aegis of France. Berlin viewed the French plan as an effort to seal off the Danubian area from German penetration, under cover of aiding the economically stricken states of the region. German Chancellor Brüning frankly told the British minister at Berlin, Horace Rumbold, that Germany's interest in preventing French hegemony complemented Britain's. The only way to prevent a general collapse in Danubian Europe would be "to float an international loan to help the countries in question.... France was the only country which could provide the necessary credits and there was the danger that, if she stepped into the breach, she might try to create a customs union with Czechoslovakia, Austria, Hungary and Yugoslavia, to the detriment of Germany and England."[96]

The British also offered a Danubian federation plan, suggesting preferential trade between the Danubian states, but protected themselves by insisting upon the most-favored-nation principle for outside powers.[97] Berlin expressed indignation and "surprise" that the British plan closed off Southeastern Europe to German economic influence, hurting its interests there.[98]

Like the United States, Britain championed the most-favored-nation principle and opposed preferences, but this became increasingly difficult and self-serving after the Ottawa conference. While maintaining preferential trade inside the empire, it sought to extend its market share elsewhere. With the involvement of Italy in these rivalries, a rival power in the Mediterranean and Africa, the arena of strife expanded. Italy's hegemonic aspirations in the Balkans collided with both the previous British and French economic and political interests, ensconced there since 1918, and also German hegemonic aspirations.

While the Great Powers vied for the control of the region, the Soviet Union watched nervously from the sidelines as the conflict lapped at its borders, apprehensive that the Western Powers' ultimate aim was to encourage Hitler to launch an attack on it through Eastern Europe. The Balkans and Eastern Europe in the 1930s thus increasingly became a political football over which the Great Powers contended for primacy of place in classical imperialist rivalry. After war broke out Britain and France hesitated whether to strike at the neutral Soviet Union when the Northern War between Finland and the Soviet Union flared up in 1939–1940, or whether to concentrate on defeating Nazi Germany.

The literature of the Nazi period is now extensive enough to assess the results of the National Socialist era. On the face of it, the population as a whole, according to Erbe's figures, did not benefit from the Nazi economic recovery: its share of total production never reached the 1929–1933 level of income, falling from 62%–64% of that period to 57% in 1938.[99] The figures of W. G. Hoffmann shown in Table 1–3 are approximately the same.

German working class gains can be attributed to the rise in number of hours worked from 41.5 in 1932 to 46.5, and 47.8 the last two years before the war. Property and entrepreneurial income in contrast rose from

Table 1–3. The Distribution of German National Income,
1928 and 1932–1939

Year	Wages and Salaries	Property and Entrepreneurial Income	Retained Earnings of Corporations	Income of Government
		As a Percentage of National Income		
1928	65.1	29.2	1.8	3.5
1932	67.3	30.4	–	2.4
1933	66.4	31.2	0.4	2.1
1934	65.1	31.5	1.5	1.9
1935	63.8	31.8	2.4	2.0
1936	62.0	32.3	3.7	2.1
1937	60.6	33.0	4.2	2.1
1938	59.6	33.6	4.9	1.9
1939	58.8	33.8	5.4	2.0

W. G. Hoffmann, et al., *Das deutsche Volkseinkommen, 1851–1957* (Tübingen: Schriften zur angewandten Wirtschaftsforschung, 1959), p. 56.

30.4% to 33.8% and retained earnings of corporations climbed from 0.4% to 5.4% in 1939. Thus, Tim Mason's conclusion that "most Germans, including industrial workers, in 1939 were in a material sense no worse than at the end of the twenties" is true only in a qualified sense.[100] Many, like the unemployed, may have been better off than in 1930–1933 but hardly as well off as in 1929 would be more accurate.

The investment choices made by the Nazi state indicate the critical role of the state as a guarantor of profits for the corporate sector of the economy during periods of crisis. During the 1930s a pronounced disinvestment occurred in the public sector of the economy (public housing, social benefits, etc.). State investment in public housing fell sharply from 1,330 million Rm in 1928 to 250 million Rm in 1939, so that an acute housing shortage existed at the start of the war. Social welfare benefits (*Versorgungsbetriebe*) also registered a decline from 1,023 million Rm in 1928 to 700 million Rm in 1938. In contrast, state investment in rearmament, which benefited heavy industry, stagnating since the late 1920s, jumped from 827 million Rm in 1928 to 15,500 million Rm. Its share of total public expenses, according to Erbe's figures, rose from 49% in 1934 to 74% in 1938 or 19% of the national income in the same year.[101] The chief beneficiary of this shift in public expenditure and investment was private business, particularly the large corporate and industrial sector.

The state debt in Germany more than tripled during the 1933–1938 period, ascending from 12 billion Rm at the end of 1932 to 42 billion Rm in 1938, amounting to 10% of the national income.[102] The German industrial expansion of the 1930s, sparked by rearmament and public works projects of a direct and indirect military character, decreased unemployment and brought the Nazi regime considerable support, but also unleashed a spiraling inflation. While the earlier government policy of subsidies for construction and repairs to private dwellings, highway construction and tax reductions helped cut unemployment from 6 million in 1933 to 3 million in January 1935, the scarcity of goods and raw materials preempted by the industrial sector for rearmament, caused an inflationary spiral. The National Socialist regime had traded off decreased unemployment for inflation.

In the 1930s German business flourished as never before; corporate executive salaries swelled and corporate assets increased. By 1935 German heavy industrial production had passed the 1928 level, but consumer goods in contrast were below the 1926 level. Despite the growth of production and profits in the heavy industry sector, the consumer share in the GNP dropped. The chief beneficiary of the economic recovery and rearmament clearly was the class which owned capital and property. The growth in production was primarily in armaments. The more conservative figures of Carroll, based on German sources, reveal that armament costs jumped from 8% of the German national income in 1935 to 38% in 1940 (see Table 1–4).

Table 1–4. Expenses for German Armament
in Percentage of GNP, 1929–1940

1929	1%
1933	3
1934	6
1935	8
1936	13
1937	13
1938	17
1939	23
1940	38

Taken from Berenice A. Carroll, *Design for Total War* (The Hague, 1968), pp. 184, 266–267[103]

Besides confiscated Jewish-owned property and capital assets, financing of rearmament came from four main sources: corporate profits, taxes, the sale of government securities and expansion of the money supply. Petzina's study of 377 Four Year Plan–associated projects indicated 52.8% came from government securities sold on the stock market, 27.8% from undistributed profits, 13.2% from government sources and 6.2% from the Plan Office.[104] In short, private capital by itself was incapable of financing the industrial expansion of the 1930s. The seizure of Austrian and Czechoslovakian gold and treasury assets as well as plants and corporations seized in Austria, Czechoslovakia, Poland and France, provided a later source of finance.

After 1933 two-thirds of capital investment in new business went to heavy industry. As a contemporary writer noted: "The history of the German economy since 1933 is one of the subjection of every economic interest to the requirements of heavy industry, of armament industry."[105] One third of total national income was expended by the state in the economy, indicating that the state had become an important cog in the capital accumulation process. The deliberately fostered decline of consumer industry is explicated in the statement of Dr. Hjalmar Schacht, disturbing in its implications and candor: "The less the people consume, the more work can be done on armament production. The standard of living and the scale of armaments production must move in opposite directions."[106]

The difficulty of securing raw materials and foodstuffs became more acute with the change in world trade. After 1933 import prices rose on the average of 9%, while export prices declined 9%, forcing Germany to export a fifth more for a corresponding amount of imports.[107] The import volume during the Nazi era improved a little, but remained only about 64% of the 1928 figure.[108] Moreover, much of this commerce remained largely directed toward Europe rather than overseas partly because of apprehension inside the government of action by Germany's enemies. "Without mobilizing a man or firing a shot they can place us in the most serious position while they conduct a covert financial and economic blockade against us," wrote Bülow to Foreign Minister Neurath (August 16, 1934), necessitating raising the European import figure and reducing overseas exports.[109] From 1933 to 1935, Europe took four-fifths of Germany's exports while one-fifth went overseas.[110] German imports were similarly weighted toward Europe, from which in 1935 it took 64.2% versus 28% from overseas.[111] The degree of dependence on sources outside Germany for food had decreased from 35% in 1927 to 19% in 1933; 17% in 1938; and 13% in 1939 at the outbreak of the war.[112] It was only with the annexation of areas outside the Third Reich and the enslavement of conquered peoples that this picture changed.

In the face of almost non-existent financial resources, the demand for raw materials and foodstuffs became increasingly critical. Reichsbank gold and foreign currency holdings fell to 84 million Rm in 1934 and to 74 million Rm in 1938 as opposed to 2,884 million in 1928 — indicating that the Third Reich had come to the end of its rope and either had to cease rearming or to secure its imports in some other manner.[113] The dire need for raw materials and foodstuffs and the inflationary pressures this released advanced Hitler's expansionist ideology from the rhetorical to the active stage. The only clear solution lay in either war or a return to a peacetime economy and decelerated profits, scarcely acceptable to industrial leaders. The German military were divided: some opposed war outright (Fritsch, Beck,) but others, probably the majority, were more malleable (Blomberg) or trusted in Hitler's abilities and leadership (Keitel, Jodl). Thus, unresolvable internal conflicts and pressures, military interests and simple greed for profit and plunder produced a formula for expansion.

The Reich's raw material and foodstuff problems forced it to turn temporarily from trade with the more developed countries to bilateral barter arrangements with the capital poor, agrarian countries of Southeastern Europe and Latin America. At this point its military position was still insufficiently strong to exert pressure on its neighbors or to seize what it needed through military conquest. The German trade offensive in the mid-1930s occurred at an inauspicious time when most countries avidly sought markets to drain off production gluts and stimulate demand. Germany clashed with both the British and the Americans in southeastern Latin America where the United States, rapidly replacing Britain as the dominant foreign investor, saw German economic penetration as a threat to its own hegemonic position. Germany successfully challenged Britain and America in Latin America by willingly taking agricultural surpluses in exchange for German exports delivered without the expenditure of currency under clearing house agreements.[114] For a time Roosevelt considered sending troops into Brazil, the scene of an acute trade struggle between German and American commercial interests.[115]

Berlin looked for accessible sources of raw materials, primarily in Spain and Southeastern Europe, in the event of war. Britain, France, the U.S. and other Western countries held control of Spanish raw materials like copper, iron ore, pyrites, manganese and other non-ferrous metals. From 1936, in payment for German assistance and military support, Franco gave the Germans iron ore from Nationalist-occupied Bilbao province, which Britain imported since the nineteenth century, and copper from the huge Rio Tinto complex, needed by I. G. Farben and the German electro-technical industry. By the end of 1937 British imports of copper from Spain sank to zero. Germany received the lion's share of Spanish exports, roughly 60%; and Spanish ores exported to the British declined to 40%.[116] Hitler admitted on June 27, 1937 that Germany's interest in a Spanish Nationalist victory was more than ideological: "Germany needs ore. That is why we want a Nationalist victory in Spain."[117] In 1937 Germany received from Spain 1,620,000 tons of iron ore, 956,000 tons of pyrites and 7,000 tons of tungsten, copper and bronze.[118] However, Franco's need for credit, which Germany could not offer, and stiff German trade terms forced the Nationalist Government to turn from Nazi Germany back to Britain, France and the U.S. American oil companies contributed signally to Franco's victory through oil exports. The British position improved again in 1938 and 1939 and the Germans began to look for other sources of raw materials.

Southeastern Europe now remained the only European source of raw material available outside of Sweden once war broke out. This was well understood by Hitler and by industrialists like Carl Krauch, a Director of I. G. Farben, and in Göring's Four Year Plan staff. Trade with Southeastern Europe increased steadily in the 1930s moving from 3.5% of total German exports to 9.8% in the period from 1932 to 1938.

Dwindling German financial resources forced introduction in mid-1934 of the "New Plan," the brainchild of Hjalmar Schacht, which undertook through tight trade controls to secure a steady stream of raw materials for the armament program and only secondarily to feed the home population.

By 1936 raw material and foodstuff shortages reached the crisis stage forcing Hitler to decree a Four Year Plan for rearmament "without regard to costs." "The German army must be ready in four years" and "the German economy must be ready for war." Hitler offered a nineteenth-century Malthusian rationale for the coming expansion outside of Germany's borders: "We are over-populated," he wrote "and cannot feed ourselves with our own resources. . . . The final solution lies in the expansion of living space with respect to the raw material and food supply of our people."[119]

The appointment of Göring as head of the rearmament program led immediately to a power struggle with Schacht over the accelerated tempo and direction of rearmament and the economy, and finally with the latter's sidetracking and resignation. German big business split at this point between Schacht, General Thomas, Thyssen, Poensgen and others favoring a slowdown of rearmament and increasing export production and the more aggressive, imperialist-minded industrial sector composed of I. G. Farben, the large banks and the iron and steel barons and industrialists like Flick, Krupp, and Röchling.[120]

The German business community's complicity in the attack on Poland is already well known and has been well documented and established by the Nuremberg Trial. Gustav Krupp, for example, had been informed of the minutes of Hitler's inner sanctum, his Advisory Secret Cabinet.[121] Krupp even agreed to receive strategic information from his agents abroad, and at the suggestion of the OKW (*Oberkommando der Wehrmacht*) to form a committee to carry out sabotage — "disrupting enemy industry and commerce." Krupp already had an organization in the U.S. to do this. Through Otto Wildenfeldt, a former Krupp director and German Ambassador to the U.S., American loans to restore Germany had been funneled to the Krupp-Nirosta Company, operating under Delaware's licensing laws. Later its offices were padlocked by the F.B.I. after Pearl Harbor.

Gustav's son, Alfred, in a Nuremberg affidavit candidly admitted it was "quite clear to me that German policy was not guiltless as far as the outbreak of the war was concerned." A May 17, 1939 phone conversation record in Alfred's files of a direct order from Hitler also indicates foreknowledge: "All exports to Poland are to be stopped immediately." Polish customers were to be given evasive answers.[122] Krupp received the call one full week before Hitler notified the Nazi leadership of his intention to attack Poland. By this time the coffers of Krupp and the other industrialists were fairly bursting with profits as never before — in November 1938 for the current year they banked 5 billion marks (there were only 2 billion in German savings banks).[123]

In September 1933, Carl Krauch proposed in the Reich Air Ministry the investment of 400,000 Rm to be raised to 1.8 billion Rm in fuel production, which later became the basis of the Four Year Plan. The agreement between Farben and the Nazi government later extended to other branches of industry on grounds of defense and economic-political considerations.[124] The Four Year Plan "developed factually into an I. G. Farben Plan." Farben directors entered the Göring plan office and two-thirds of the plan's investment went into the chemical area and the coffers of I. G. Farben. In Petzina's estimate 20% of the Plan's staff came from Farben — rising to 30% by 1944 — giving it the opportunity to eliminate its smaller rivals. The recent study of Peter Hayes disputes these figures, reducing the share of the potash, chemical and oil sector to no more than 25%, and only in the earlier drafts of the plan, including certain other holdings of I. G. Farben, did it come to Petzina's calculations.[125] Even so, the profits to be made from rearmament were much higher than could be made by ordinary commercial contracts during a period of economic downturn, making their acceleration through war very inviting.

Through his position as Plenipotentiary for Chemical Production, later to include mineral oil, rubber, light metals and explosives, Krauch became a dominant figure in the German economy, leading to power struggles inside the Plan organization. In an August 1940 note to Gustav Schlotterer, a Reich Economic Ministry Director in charge of External Economy in the conquered regions, I. G. Farben indicated its desire to regain its pre-war domination of the world chemical market by extending its investments throughout the world.[126] Observing the plundering of the Austrian economy by I. G. Farben, the Nazi economic specialist Wilhelm Keppler asked sardonically "whether the I. G. was intending to swallow the whole Austrian chemical industry."[127] The Nazi Gauleiter of Thuringia, Sauckel, warned Göring that "I. G. Farben must not be allowed to have everything."[128]

The German banks were as avid to share in the plunder as the corporations. The Reichsbank absorbed the Austrian State Bank while the Deutsche Bank took over the majority share of the Austrian Credit-Anstalt and the Dresdner bank swallowed up the Mercurbank.[129] The same fate awaited the hapless Czechoslovak banks, leading competitors of the German banks in Central and Southeastern Europe and holding close ties to British and French financial interests. Representatives of the great German banks moved in the train of the German occupation forces; on the day the Wehrmacht occupied Prague, Baron von Ludinghausen of the Dresdner Bank appeared at the door of the Živno Bank in Prague. On March 21, 1939, at a discussion in the Reich Economic Ministry, after some bickering by the leaders of the leading German banks, Karl Rasche (Dresdner Bank) and Oswald Rosler (Deutsche Bank) agreed that the Bohemian Union Bank would go to the Deutsche Bank while the Bohemian Escompte Bank would pass to the Dresdner Bank.[130] These assimilations, which had already been discussed before the annexations of Austria and Czechoslovakia, placed in German hands key institutions of financial capital with which to penetrate the economies and markets of Southeastern Europe.

The plunder and loot taken from Czechoslovakia were vast and staggered even Hitler. He listed the weapons seized: 1,582 airplanes; 469 tanks; 500 anti-aircraft guns; 2,175 pieces of field artillery; 1,090,000 rifles, 114,000 revolvers — enough weapons to equip 30 divisions, approximately 50% of the German army. The Czech weaponry was of excellent quality and among the finest in Europe in that period.[131]

The Germans took over $100 million worth of gold from the Czechoslovak National Bank, almost $300 million worth of foreign exchange from Czech businesses and investors and about $1 billion worth of raw materials and industrial goods. Of great value were the Czech stockpiles of copper, aluminum, tin and ore supplies for the German steel industry. Enormous amounts of grain, industrial and agricultural products were confiscated and, just as in Austria where individual Germans stripped Austrian shelves bare through their purchases, in Czechoslovakia similar things occurred. The Czechoslovak crown, manipulated to favor the German reichsmark, facilitated this indirect plundering of the Czechoslovak economy.[132] Similarly, I. G. Farben in July 1939, through its position on Göring's staff, moved to take control of the chemical firms of Poland once German forces attacked.

An "Economic Report on Poland" delivered July 28, 1939, by the Economic Department of I. G. Farben to the heads of German firms informed them of the impending booty.[133]

By 1939 Germany had exceeded its 1929 level of production, much of which was armaments. Had armament production continued after 1939 without a significant increase in living standards for the working class, then the National Socialist regime ran the risk of internal disturbances and possible revolt. These contingencies and the ease of the bluff seizure of Austria and Czechoslovakia, and Germany's momentary military superiority, influenced Hitler to move toward war in August 1939, particularly after the non-aggression pact with the USSR.

This seems to have been the meaning of Hitler's explicit statement on May 23, 1939, that "without the entry into foreign states or the attack and seizure of foreign property, the solution of this problem [i.e., the problem of food and raw materials — author] is not possible." Later, on August 22, he candidly declared that war was Germany's only solution: "We have nothing to lose, and can only gain. Our economic situation is, as a result of our limitations, such that we can only hold out a few more years. Göring can confirm this. Nothing else remains for us, we must act."[134] In other words, the economic and social stresses inside Germany might later reach a critical point. To secure access to sources of raw materials, expansion had become necessary. Expansion to the east would also relieve the danger of encirclement by Britain and France since, as Hitler told his military commanders on August 22, 1939, they need "have no [more] fear of [a] sea blockade" as "the east would supply grain, livestock, coal, lead and zinc."[135]

With the conclusion of the Nazi-Soviet Pact this became a reality — at least as long as Germany and the USSR remained friendly. The Soviet Union supplied the Reich from half to two-thirds of Soviet produced phosphorus, asbestos, chrome ore, manganese ore, oil and wool.[136] In non-ferrous metals Germany remained vulnerable and dependent upon the southeast.[137] As the Soviet-German Pact's importance waned and Hitler decided to attack the Soviet Union in 1941, the southeast again became the focal point of German expansion.

Hitherto, Germany had been able to secure through clearing agreements with the Southeastern European states during the 1930s the foodstuffs and raw materials it needed, but after 1938 these were no longer forthcoming even with intimidation and pressure. Information on the clearing side of Germany's foreign trade arrangements was always kept very secret especially in the late 1930s. In his post-war testimony, Dr. Karl Blessing, a Reichsbank Director, stated that Hans Kehrl, an industrialist and economic planner, discovered he was receiving no manganese and other raw materials from abroad. Kehrl tried to find out what was going on and often heard about "blocked clearings" (*verstopten* clearings). Blessing confirmed the source of the grain and raw materials stoppages: "It was connected to the clearings. The things could not be paid for."[138] Germany's available currency no longer sufficed.

There is further evidence from a higher source, Hermann Göring, that Germany could no longer pay for its raw material imports from abroad.

Göring revealed in his post-war interrogation that, although Germany could get additional ore in Salzgitter in Austria and iron supplies from Sweden, bauxite was lacking and copper and tin insufficient. Domestic use of these materials would have to be curtailed and imports increased from Spain. But as Germany was overpopulated, Göring testified, Hitler would be in a better position to get an adequate supply for his people through expansion to the east. "Hitler did not intend to lower the standard of living to meet the food problem, as he could not afford a setback to the 1932 situation. Hitler did not see a solution through international commercial agreements because Germany was not able to fulfill her (barter) obligations to which she would have been committed. Therefore, the only solution was to obtain agricultural living space."[139] Even before the First World War, the German industrialists made no bones about getting their hands on French iron ore. Nitti, the Italian minister of commerce, recalled a conversation with a number of German industrialists in 1913: "They spoke unashamedly of the need to get their hands on the iron ore basin of French Lorraine; war appeared to them as a business proposition."[140] In the interwar period competition between French and German steel cartels and French and German arms manufacturers (Krupp and Schneider-Creuzot) intensified to the point where they fought over control of raw material sources, and the French tried to raise the cost of Swedish iron ore imported by Germany through arrangements with the Swedish industrialists. This caused Nazi members of the steel cartel to press Hitler to do something before the German steel industry collapsed.[141] After the Nazi military victory over Poland a similar policy followed of looting that country of raw materials, private property and industrial goods.[142] This fairly straightforward historical evidence leads to the conclusion that constraint from domestic raw material shortages and lack of currency was pressuring Hitler to attack other countries in Eastern Europe for their economic resources and ultimately led to war.

Further corroboration comes from another source, namely the Japanese leaders accused of war crimes after World War II at the Asian war crimes tribunal. Dower's recent work on the post-war occupation of Japan states the Japanese national imperialist position that these leaders "had been motivated by legitimate concerns for Japan's essential rights and interests on the Asian continent." They saw their country's security as threatened by "truly alarming developments: political chaos, economically crippling anti-Japanese boycotts in China and internal communist revolts there" and elsewhere, but more importantly, "American and European protectionist policies, global trends toward autarchic 'bloc economies' and coercive Western policies in the months prior to Pearl Harbor." Also they contended that "the wartime rhetoric of Pan-Asianism rested on legitimate Japanese and Asian grievances vis-à-vis the 'White Peril' of European and American imperialism."[143]

While the historical evidence offered here for Germany's reasons for moving to war emphasizes economic contributions, it does not exclude other complementary motives for war, some political, some ideological and some purely episodic. There exist a whole range of other determinants: the territorial changes and other mistakes of Versailles, the militarist agenda of World

War I in Eastern Europe, the anti-democratic and anti-socialist hatreds of German nationalism, etc. In conclusion, during the inter-war era no single state had the power to establish its ascendancy and through its economic, financial and military power act as a global policeman establishing certain rules and interdictions to which all the other powers had to adhere. Britain had formerly played this role in the nineteenth century, but it had faltered since World War I and Germany tried to replace it but was opposed by Britain and the U.S. Through coercive pressure, intimidation and suasion, or rewards of certain kinds to recalcitrant powers, a state with overwhelming military strength might have forced or persuaded the other powers to give up their tariffs, imperial preferences, bilateral and clearing agreements and eliminate the ruinous cutthroat competition for limited markets in favor of a freer flowing exchange of trade across international borders. The failure of world capitalism to arrive at some international *modus vivendi* resulted in the outbreak of World War II and the loss of some 55 million casualties. It was a mistake that would not be repeated after 1945.[144]

Chapter 2

Italy, the Powers and Eastern Europe, 1918–1939. Mussolini, Prisoner of the Mediterranean

Italian Minister at Paris: What is the policy?

Count Dino Grandi, Italian Foreign Minister: Do nothing.

Italian Minister at Paris: It won't be easy.

THE BRITISH HISTORIAN Hugh Seton-Watson observed in his classic study of interwar Eastern Europe that Italy had two choices before it: either to throw in with Germany in order to become a large, powerful empire at the expense of Britain and France, or to join the two Western Powers against Germany and eke out a middling existence as a weak, insignificant country.[1]

Italy's relations with Eastern Europe before the fascist era were amicable. In the nineteenth century Mazzini and Garibaldi nobly and generously supported and assisted the Eastern European people's struggle against Hapsburg and Ottoman reaction. Mazzini admired and praised the Eastern European Slavs — particularly the Polish poet Mickiewicz — but in his later years, he unfortunately became an ardent supporter of Italian imperialism.

The warming sun of the Italian Risorgimento inspired the national and literary Risorgimento of the Eastern European peoples. Cavour even defended the Croats against the oppression of the autocratic semi-feudal power of the Magyar nobility.[2] The Venetian lion held the Dalmatian coast in its claws until the French Revolution and Napoleon swept away Venetian rule. French rule invigorated Croatia and Dalmatia with liberal ideas and introduced many of the historical ideas and changes of the French Revolution.[3] The outbreak of the Hercegovina revolt of 1876, against the Ottoman Turks, provoked universal sympathy throughout Italy and groups gathered money for wounded Croats and Serbs and their families. Italian "Garibaldini" journeyed to Dalmatia, Serbia and Hercegovina to fight alongside the South Slavs. Italian newspapers and journals viewed the revolt as a new phase of the Risorgimento in the conflict against the hated Austrians. Garibaldi himself sent numerous exhortative telegrams and letters to the public meetings.[4]

With the advent of the fascist government, Italy pursued an aggressive imperialist policy for an Italian Empire in Africa or by grabbing territory in the Balkans or from Turkey.

Italy arrived at the Versailles peace conference in a divided state: Sidney Sonnino, the Italian Foreign Minister, tenaciously insisted upon the London Treaty and the Allied promise to give Dalmatia to Italy, but the old Italian Socialist Bissolati, the political war horse Giolitti and Italian Premier Orlando had a more benevolent view of the Yugoslavs and other Slav peoples. Bissolati had befriended Slavs in the Austro-Hungarian Empire at the 1917 Rome Congress of Oppressed Nationalities in their struggle for freedom. But, unable to prevail, Bissolati resigned from the government, jeered by a crowd of nationalists and Mussolini, who ironically as a pacifist socialist in one of his many guises had driven him from the socialist party leadership years before. Mussolini, an opportunistic political chameleon, straddled both positions, then later favoring annexation of Dalmatia when the political tide turned right and the Dalmatia question merged with the bourgeois nationalist backlash against factory occupations and land seizures.

The dissolution of its military in 1918 forced Austria-Hungary, fearing chaos and bolshevism, to hastily negotiate for peace. The Italians moved into Istria and Dalmatia as fast as the Austro-Hungarian forces left. Here they confronted deserting South Slav troops from the Dual Monarchy's army, determined to prevent the Italians from seizing purely Slavic populated areas.[5] Ante Trumbić, a Croat representing the new Yugoslav government, ordered its forces to stop the advance of Italian forces. In Boka Kotorska (the Bay of Cattaro) and elsewhere, South Slav crews of the Austro-Hungarian navy revolted, forcing the desperate Hapsburg heir to offer the Austro-Hungarian navy to Yugoslavia, to buy the loyalty of the South Slavs hoping they might hold up the Italian advance.

The Italians landed Bersaglieri at Trieste and Pola, seized Austrian warships there and sailed them to Italy; then they seized Venice for Italy while an Italian naval squadron grabbed Zadar (Zara).[6] General Badoglio, head of the Italian army staff, suggested to Rome insidious ways to play the various South Slavs off against one another by spreading antagonistic propaganda and provoking political and religious suspicions.[7]

Rejected Italian claims to colonies provided the combustible material leading to the rise of Mussolini and fascism. Disparate middle class nationalists, anarchistic youths and *arditi* (wartime shock troops), rabid for adventure, joined Mussolini in a parliamentary bloc. Giolitti, the pre-war liberal icon, hoped to employ the socialists to check the rightists and the fascists to counter the revolutionary socialists and their mass following. Of the fascists: "They are our black and tans," he told a high British official.[8] He planned to buy off the fascist leaders later. Instead the mass of fascist deputies, including Mussolini, forced him to resign on the issue of the Treaty of Rapallo. From 1919 to the early 1920s Mussolini maintained a foot in both the socialist and the fascist camps urging the workers and peasants to seize the landed estates and factories and the squadristi and fascists to attack the latter, uncertain whether the right or left would triumph.[9]

Fascism was not about ideas but feelings, wrote Don Luigi Sturzo, the priest-founder of the Christian Democratic Party.[10] One important aspect of fascism was the generational conflict.[11] Even before the war Italian youth had become embittered against the older, corrupt political class and parlia-

mentarianism. Giolitti, in particular, but also the moderate socialists became
the object of attacks and scorn by the intellectuals and students. Many hoped
that the war would bring social change, and university students demonstrated violently for war. Young people animated by patriotic feelings hoped
to liberate Italian-populated areas still under Austrian rule, but many farm
workers and industrial workers held back.

Many petty bourgeois youth faced hardship upon returning home from
the trenches. Revolutionary upsurges of factory workers and agricultural
farm workers in the socialist leagues threatened their social position.
Widespread unemployment among young intellectuals and declining social
mobility, against which a university degree held no guarantee, created an
inflammatory situation. Students turned violently against those of the older
generation they held responsible for their disillusionment, the failure of the
war to effect change and Italy's humiliation by the other Powers at the peace
conference. They wanted to replace their elders by forcing a "rapid change
within the ruling class but left the social equilibrium essentially unaltered."
The confused post-war era is described by Palmiero Togliatti in 1942:

> The majority of the fascist leaders was young during the war. This
> generation was confronted with a great economic, political and moral
> confusion. A part of it followed fascism, expecting a social revolution
> and a renewal of the nation's life. The best fascists of this generation
> have disappeared.... The others have become bourgeois, rich bureau-
> crats. Once more we have arrived at one of the points which historians
> call a turn of generations.[12]

The fascists fed on resentment over the loss of Dalmatia in the "pro-
Dalmatia" groups and nationalist youths and demobilized veterans looking
for excitement and employment. Probably no incident inflamed and electri-
fied the popular Italian mind more than the seizure of Fiume (Rijeka) by
Gabrielle D'Annunzio, who set up a mock republic on September 12, 1919,
at the head of a few thousand supporters. Mussolini supported D'Annunzio
declaring contemptuously: "face to face with a race like the Slav, inferior and
barbarous, one should not follow the policy of giving sugar, but that of the
club!" His socialism abandoned for nationalism, he declared: "to realize the
Mediterranean dream, it is necessary that the Adriatic which is one of our
gulfs be in our hands."[13] The common people, the workers and peasants,
showed little or no interest in Dalmatia.

Italy had agreed to fight on the Allied side under the 1915 Treaty of
London for the price of Italian annexation of the Dalmatian coast. Nikola
Pašić, the Serbian premier, had been forced publicly to agree in the newspaper, *Corriere della Sera,* to Italian hegemony over the Dalmatian coast.[14]
The South Slav position, as Clemenceau reminded the Croatian and Serbian
leaders Ante Trumbić and Pašić, was compromised by the fact that Italy had
fought on the Allied side while Croats and Slovenes had largely fought with
the Austro-Hungarian forces and that Italy had been promised the Dalmatian district.[15] President Wilson sided with the majority Slavic population
of Dalmatia, abjured the London treaty and gained Dalmatia for the new
Yugoslav state. Italian nationalists felt aggrieved and humiliated by receiv-

ing only niggardly pieces of territory while they watched Britain and France grab the former Ottoman Arab populated areas and German colonies in Africa.

The advent of the Giolitti/Sforza government in 1919–1920 ended the mawkish D'Annunzio interlude. After much haggling between Italian and Yugoslav negotiators, Count Sforza, who opposed an Italian imperialist policy, finally brought the Adriatic question to rest. Both parties signed a treaty on November 12, 1920, at Rapallo which gave Italy all of Istria, the islands of Tessin, Cherso and Zara (Zadar) on the Dalmatian coast, privileges for the small Italian population of Dalmatia and independence for Fiume, a city 52% Italian, which became a free Italian state.[16] Dalmatia went to Yugoslavia. The treaty left half a million Slavs inside Italy while only a few hundred Italians in the fledgling Yugoslav state. It left behind a residue of ill-will and the legend of the *"pace mutilata"* until Italy annexed Dalmatia in 1941 after the destruction of Yugoslavia.

The cult of manly virility and action fed the Italian love of spectacle and offered romantic dreams of glory, empire and overseas adventure. A political opportunistic chameleon, the fascist leader Mussolini, at various times in his career, had been a pacifist, a revolutionary socialist, editor of the militant socialist newspaper, *Avanti,* in Milan before 1914, then a violent leader of pro-war socialists and nationalists. He held few principles for very long except his own self-adulation and thirst for power, and his greatest talent was probably as propagandist in the service of his own interests.

The emergence of a Yugoslav state on the Adriatic — which Mussolini considered *Mare Nostrum* — tied politically to France, threatened Italy's security. As Hungary and Bulgaria nursed enmity to Yugoslavia because of lost territory, Italy actively courted them. Poland also became a cog in Mussolini's anti-status quo and anti-Western policy because of its antipathy to the Czechs and the Little Entente.

To subvert Yugoslavia, Mussolini supplied Hungary and Bulgaria with caches of weapons for their secret camps, harbored on Italian soil Croatian fascist separatists like Ante Pavelić and was paymaster for his Ustasha and the IMRO (Internal Macedonian Revolutionary Organization), whose gunmen in 1934 killed the Yugoslav ruler, King Alexander, and French Foreign Minister Barthou. After Italian aggressive behavior in the 1920s and early 1930s against Yugoslavia and its patron France provoked an international uproar, Mussolini desisted and turned his attention to Ethiopia after 1935.

Yugoslavia cooperated with Great Britain in the League's commercial sanctions against Mussolini for invading Ethiopia, and Italian trade with Yugoslavia plummeted; Germany replaced Italy as that country's leading trade partner.

Overpopulated and without vital raw materials like ores, oil and timber, Italy in the interwar era scarcely qualified as a Great Power. Its major problem was small-scale, uneconomic marginal agricultural holdings. Entire regions of the country suffered from appalling malnutrition and bad housing conditions. *Christ Stopped at Eboli* by Carlo Dolce, an anti-fascist journalist banished to southern Italy, described a remote backwater where nothing had changed since the time of Christ and deeply superstitious peasants believed in werewolves and the evil eye, and lived in pestilential, almost feudal conditions.

In the nineteenth-century political and economic logic of Mussolini, it was easier to seize territory in Africa or the Balkans for raw materials not obtainable in Italy than through trade. It also satisfied the epoch's ideological and psycho-urges for power and mastery. Assuming that the British and French had no intention of giving up their colonial areas to Italy, Mussolini threw in with have-not, humiliated and aggrieved Germany to force a rupture of the status quo through political coercion or war.

Historians have over-emphasized the ideological and cultural roots of Mussolini's expansionist imperialism as arising from a need for self-gratification, theatrical spectacle and the nationalist cult of manliness and virility through conquest and war.[17] The Ethiopian invasion, therefore, supposedly originated in Mussolini's and fascism's psychic and cultural need for prestige and glory through war.[18]

By the mid-1930s, like other countries, Italy entered a period of economic crisis: unemployment in 1932 rose to 1.3 million; and in the winter of 1933–1934, 1.7 million people registered for government food allotments. The government grappled fitfully with the problem by reducing the hours of work to 40, but this reduced profits and many firms fell into bankruptcy. By the eve of the Ethiopian war, Italy's economic and financial position worsened. The war raised the debt level in 1936 after having been sharply decreased the previous year and almost eliminated. It nevertheless stimulated industry and production increased. Mobilization for the army also decreased unemployment. The League of Nations' sanctions worsened Italy's economic position by raising the costs of oil and other imports. The Ethiopian war led to a change in policy: Britain, which led the sanctions fight against Italy, could now be counted an enemy.

The spread of German power and influence down to the Adriatic both frightened and mesmerized Mussolini, who finally moved to join Hitler and the Axis first in 1936 and in the 1939 Pact of Steel. This move toward the stronger German state had been motivated in part at least by economics: the reserves of the Bank of Italy shrank "to almost nothing" by 1939, drained by the cost of sanctions, Italy's sallies into Ethiopia and Spain and the cost of badly needed strategic raw materials.[19] "Her main weaknesses are the dependency of her industry on raw materials imported from abroad and the vulnerability of her coastline to attack," writes Seton-Watson.[20] Mussolini and the industrialists had parted ways, the peasantry lacked interest and Fascist Party local chieftains were interested only in plundering the state's coffers and patronage for their followers. Italy underwent a financial and economic crisis of inertia and creeping stagnation that could be ended by a war-stimulated industry that also enabled Mussolini to flog his demons and to strut and pose before the Italian public. Cultural and psychological imperatives also reinforced the need for economic stimulus through a war of expansion.

Successive Italian governments unsuccessfully tried to grab territory in East Africa, ending in two military defeats in Ethiopia at Dogali and Adua (or Adowa) in the final quarter of the nineteenth century. Mussolini's administration represented one more fling at imperialist adventure; he had also inherited a post-war legacy of failed imperialist enterprises in Dalmatia, then in Turkey which the Italians had to abandon. Another fiasco occurred in Corfu which in 1923 he occupied with troops under a pretext until forced out by the British fleet.

From the beginning Mussolini's East European interests were conflicted by history and geography: Italy lay in the Mediterranean and Eastern Europe mattered less; North Africa had been a granary for imperial Rome after it destroyed its Carthaginian rival. In recent times Italy's more urbanized population needed raw materials and, imperialist apologists argued, a place to send its excess agricultural population.

Early in his career Mussolini advanced the conventional argument of Italy's high birthrate as a rationale for imperialism and overseas expansion. Then, learning that the Italian birthrate, compared to Western countries, had been falling for decades, he became alarmed that Italy might degenerate into a second rate power. After negotiating with Latin American countries to accept greater numbers of Italian immigrants, he was compelled to call back Italian families. Declining immigration and remittances from Italians abroad in the 1930s, increasing demographic stress, inevitably favored strategies to increase birth rates through family subsidies of diverse kinds and a frantic battle for grain to augment the food supply. Mussolini now obsessed that, if the Italian fertility level declined, Italy was in danger of becoming a colony of other states.[21] Therefore, the demographic argument had less to do than previously thought with Mussolini's decision for imperialism and colonial adventure than other imperatives.

Historians are agreed that Mussolini and Italian nationalists believed that the destiny of Italy lay in the Mediterranean and Africa. But Britain's flag implanted at both ends at Gibraltar and Suez held that inland sea firmly in its grasp.

Mussolini's interest in Eastern Europe waxed and waned with his conflict with Britain and France over African colonies. Some historians believe that Mussolini had already decided on an imperialist policy in the early 1920s and perhaps sooner. Imperialism was, he proclaimed in January 1919, "an eternal and immutable law of life."[22]

Mussolini's violent revolutionary impulses influenced by Sorel's revolutionary syndicalism and diverse currents of nationalism shaped his fascist ideology — although Count Sforza claimed that he had not read Sorel, and never read anything but newspaper articles.[23] Historians of Italian fascism agree on its syncretic impulses arising from frustrated imperialist aspirations, hostility to liberalism and bolshevism expressed by contradictory theories and doctrines: anti-modernism, traditional Catholicism and anti-clericalism, revolutionary syndicalism, authoritarianism and naive Rousseauian beliefs. One writer declares in despair: "after sixty years of debate about fascist theories, the scene resembles a desert littered with the burnt-out, rusting hulks of failed theories."[24]

By the mid-1920s fascist revolutionary syndicalism became desiccated and had "lost its main thrust," the leading figures surrounding Mussolini on ceremonial occasions were "tamed" squadristi firebrands and fascist heroes, the leading government ministers were "party hacks" and the system became a dictatorship.[25] Revolutionary syndicalism, a major fascist ideology, as Tannenbaum observes, "substituted national solidarity for the solidarity of the working class, whose goals were to be imposed from above rather than revolution from below."[26]

Fascist expansionism stemmed from a variety of motives: to wipe out "the stain of Adua"; for territory and raw materials; Italian control of the Adriatic and its contiguous territories (including Albania, Northern Greece, Slovenia and Croatia); and hegemony or quasi-hegemony in Central and Eastern Europe (Austria, Romania and Hungary). In the overheated, clichéd hyperbole of fascism, a war of expansion tempering Italians in the cleansing fires of battle would finally prove them a superior race destined to rule over a neo-Roman empire and dominate the world. Mussolini believed an expansionist war would sweep away all the decrepit, corrupt, medieval scaffolding and vestiges of the past: the Catholic Church, the monarchy and nobility, powerful obstacles hobbling his power. The military and bureaucracy's allegiance to the monarchy would be severed and transferred to the fascist state.

Interpretive studies of Mussolini and the fascist regime, while acknowledging the polycratic influences of Fascist leaders like Farinacci, Balbo, etc., have emphasized that Mussolini was the vital force behind the expansionary fascist thrust.[27] Other less visible forces certainly played a role, which begs the question of the social and particularly the economic forces behind the foreign policy of Italy, which has received scant attention and even dismissive disdain.[28]

Fascist Italy in the decade and a half before the Second World War appears economically and financially adrift in a lengthening decline to 1939. Fascism's liberal predecessor regime had failed to save the Banco da Roma and the great concerns like the Ansaldo Steel Company, and the expectation that fascism with its regimentation and controls would usher in an era of prosperity had not occurred. Mussolini undertook numerous large-scale modernization projects, and the figures of the League of Nations for the decade between 1929 and 1938 indicate that Italian manufacturing production doubled, exceeded only by Japan and the USSR, surpassing that of all the other Western Powers.[29] But this picture is deceiving. Italy still remained the lowest of the Great Powers in total share of world manufacturing; its share came to only 2.9% in 1938 (the U.S., 28.7%, USSR, 17.6%, Germany, 13.2%, the U.K, 9.2%, France, 4.5%, Japan, 3.3%).[30] During the interwar years Italy's population grew by only 1% a year but since the gross domestic product grew by only 2%, the per capita average grew by only 1%.[31] Italy, particularly after 1929, was clearly stagnating economically, as suggested by the sketchy figures of the era. Unemployment after 1929 rose steadily and the living standards of the industrial workers gradually declined. Hours of work also fell and employers preferred to discharge employees and re-hire them at minimum wages. These figures, though not perhaps a detailed and comprehensive description of inter-war Italy, are nonetheless far from sparkling.[32]

Living standards as reflected in food intake and total consumption declined in the 1930s in general as compared with the 1920s, and the 1929–

1939 period "did not witness a substantial improvement in the standard of living of the Italian people" as reflected in figures on national income and wages. In 1938 Italian families spent over half of their income on food.[33] As one writer concludes: "Some of us living in this climate of progress may be astonished to learn that the economy was stagnant for more than a decade."[34] National income declined from 1930 to 1936 and the unemployment rolls rose from only 110,000 in 1925–1926, to a million in the early 1930s, to below 700,000 in 1939 due to mobilization, the forty-hour week and defense production. Hours of work increased and, by the eve of the war in 1938, the fascist regime seems, like the Nazi regime, to have restored the Italian worker to little more or even less than its pre-1929 level.[35]

During the early years of fascism in the 1920s, the large landowners in the *Mezzogiorno* (the south) lost out as labor unrest and lack of tariffs forced them to sell out completely or else part of their estates to increasing numbers of small owner operators. With the imposition of agricultural tariffs, lack of cheap credit and mechanization in the 1930s, the large landowners there gained and the small owners were forced increasingly into share cropping.[36] Fascist "ruralization" — encouraging the unemployed to move into rural areas — and the 1930s Depression increased the number of agricultural employees and generally depressed labor. Agricultural tariffs on wheat drove up prices, the highest in Europe, but for a variety of reasons — higher grain prices led to the decline of animal raising, leading in turn to ineffective use of land, raised the cost of manure and animal labor, etc. — the higher tariffs on grains and agricultural machinery had questionable results. In the north, the Po Valley and the center, agricultural conditions were better and the peasantry did not fare as badly as in the south. The much-vaunted fascist syndical corporations, concluded Cohen, citing Schmidt, Welk and Salvemini, "operated in the interest of the employer."[37]

Rates of employment and improvements in real wages were less in Italy under the fascists than in other industrialized countries during the inter-war period.[38] Evidence exists that productivity gains fell below other industrial countries.[39] Investment and output trends between 1926 and 1940 also fell below Italy's pre–World War I figure. Generally speaking, although the evidence is incomplete, the gap between Italy and other industrialized countries, which had been narrowing before 1914, widened under the fascists.[40] Worse still, the average per capita income for the Italians fell and their diet deteriorated. Total foodstuff consumption fell as well as the quality of what they ate. Total daily caloric levels fell from 2,816 in 1921–1926 to 2,643.[41] Consumption of fresh fruits, vegetables, milk, cheese and wheat fell considerably and proteins, carbohydrates and fats as well. Net investment in agriculture decreased from 1920 to 1940.

The fascist regime and Mussolini's relations with the industrialists suggest respect and support mixed with some diffidence and imposed controls. The government taxed industry's dividends at 6% to encourage investment of undistributed profits in 1935–1936 and placed a 10% levy on capital assets of business. Business leaders resented the latter most of all.[42] The fascist government only applied these taxes leniently, nevertheless business complained against government interference and also of the harmful effects of Mussolini's expansionary foreign policy. After war broke out in September 1939, they may also have preferred the economic and commercial advantages of neutrality, but after March 1940, when Britain threatened to blockade Italian shipping to Germany, they changed their mind.

Like Mussolini, the Italian industrialists vacillated opportunistically back and forth between allegiance to Germany or the Western Powers depending on the advantages. Mussolini gladly obliged the industrialists when he joined the 1935 anti-German Stresa Front of the Western Powers. They "lived in perpetual fear of the economic might of Germany" and of the influx of German manufactured articles on the domestic market, and in late February 1935 appealed to Mussolini to protect the Italian market against German manufactured goods, particularly chemicals.[43]

Guarneri's memoirs indicate that the Germans hoped to convert Italy into a colony supplying Germany with agricultural raw materials like the Balkan countries. Walter Funk, the German Economic Minister, actually tactlessly suggested to a shocked Guarneri a division of labor in which Italy specialized in agriculture and Germany in manufacturing. The Italians had no interest in becoming a German colony and curtailed Italian exports of manpower, aluminum products, agricultural foodstuffs, mercury, sulphur and rayon to Germany when the Germans delayed balance of payments credits to Italy.[44]

The industrialists quickly forgot these irritations once Germany decimated Poland and France and seemed likely to win the war. Pirelli and others, including Volpi, the head of the Italian industrial syndical, the CGII (General Confederation of Italian Industrialists), and conqueror of Libya and owner of vast Albanian assets, opted for Germany despite their fear of German domination. The industrialists opted with Mussolini to join Germany in a "parallel war." Volpi wrote in September 1940 that the CGII was planning the economic reorganization of Europe after fascism had triumphed.[45] Thus, the Italian industrialists bear a heavy burden for supporting Hitler and expanding the war.

In the rural areas the struggle for existence worsened for the laboring classes and small proprietors. Owner operators dropped by 500,000 between 1921 and 1931; that of cash and carry tenants rose about 400,000. An earlier observer concluded that fascism protected big agriculture and big industry to the detriment of the agricultural laborer, small peasant and consumer.[46] The claims of social pacification, coupled with pressures for a place to send a surplus population and gain unavailable raw materials for the coming European war, made aggressive expansion whether in Africa, Asia Minor or the Balkans an inviting solution. From 1930 to 1934 imperialist adventures offered a way to reinflate a stagnating economy and at the same time to regain a sense of national purpose and political legitimation.

Natural resource shortages (oil, ores, coal, etc.), chronic unemployment and the lure of business contracts joined fatefully in a bubbling cauldron with fascist, nationalist and ideological frustrations, and Mussolini's impetuous and flamboyant personality made a formula for imperialist aggrandizement. Even before the march on Rome Mussolini learned that bluff and threats accomplished surprising results against timorous adversaries. Already in the late 1920s Mussolini seriously considered attacking in Croa-

tia, Turkey and France.[47] From 1931 on he made plans to seize Ethiopia —
where foreign business interests had already made inroads — regardless of
Western opposition.

The pacification campaign against Ethiopia unleashed a Mussolini at
his most bloodthirsty, urging General Graziani, his military commander,
to shoot, gas and exterminate all those suspected of resistance.[48] Later in
Spain, where he sent tens of thousands of Italian soldiers to fight on the side
of the Franco nationalists, he also ordered the killing of all Italian "reds"
captured, with the sinister admonition that "dead men tell no tales." The
hapless Libyan population experienced similar things for daring to resist
Mussolini's occupation forces.[49]

Though Mussolini stated Italy's imperialist expansion had no specific
limitations, its geographic locus gave its Mediterranean interest primary importance making its European interests secondary. The emergence of a strong
Yugoslav state, a client of France on the opposite side of the Adriatic, decisively influenced Italian foreign policy. Mussolini courted the World War I
losers, Hungary and Bulgaria, who lost territory after 1918 to Yugoslavia, to
counter the latter and gain access to the Aegean. During the 1920s and early
1930s, Italy schemed to destroy Yugoslavia. Mussolini supported Macedonian IMRO activities and Hungarian camps at Janka Puszta and in Italy
for the training of Ustasha Croatian separatists. Ustasha leaders like Ante
Pavelić found safe haven under Mussolini's protection in Italy. Only after
the murder of King Alexander of Yugoslavia and the French foreign minister
at Marseilles on October 9, 1934, and a League investigation revealed Mussolini's involvement with a team of Ustasha and IMRO killers creating an
international scandal did Mussolini relent against terrorist subversion and
fall back on political means.

In 1934 Mussolini moved through the Rome Protocols signed by Italy,
Austria and Hungary to mount a direct response to the Little Entente, a
French-sponsored alliance. The Rome Protocols established a land connection through Austria to Hungary enabling him to put pressure on Yugoslavia
and the Little Entente members. It also opened up the possibility of an
Italian-sponsored customs union in Central Europe and the proposed use
of the moribund port of Trieste to ship goods from Hungary and Austria to the Adriatic. An agreement in the 1920s with Bulgaria kept alive
both countries' irredentist grievances against Yugoslavia. The double-edged
Rome treaty also aimed to block growing German economic domination
and political influence in the Danubian basin.

The reasons for Italy's imperialist aspirations in Eastern Europe and
elsewhere are still a bone of contention among mainstream historians emphasizing cultural influences and Mussolini as the prime mover — like
historians of Nazi Germany who point to Hitler — while left of center historians emphasize internal and socio-economic problems. The former deny
the influence of the industrialist and landowning class as a pressure group
or that Mussolini either listened to or solicited advice from that class, regarding it almost with contempt. The state sequestered entire sectors of
the economy, as in Germany, and the chemical, hydroelectric power, manufacturing and steel corporations enjoyed the bulk of the profits. Reassured

by Mussolini's suppression of the left and social revolution, taming of the unions and the working class and reduction of labor costs, the industrialists, according to some, avoided interjecting their influence into foreign policy.[50] Organizational pillars of fascism like the Fascist Party, the fascist militia and youth organizations and traditional institutions, the monarchy, army, Catholic Church and the bureaucracy exerted a chafing limitation on his power.

This picture has been somewhat overdrawn according to one Italian historian who writes convincingly that "Italian interest groups" in the Ethiopia adventure set in motion vast plans "to gain control of land suitable for settlement, cotton fields, mineral resources, roads and waterways." Employing 400,000 soldiers and 100,000 workers, "it was the largest colonial expedition in history" and quickly changed the economic situation. As mobilization got underway, involving about one million men in Italy and the colonies, "textiles, machinery, heavy industry in general and food processing began to produce once again at full capacity." Metal and machine production and agriculture developed and the net profits of business increased. Fiat, shipbuilders, public works contractors backed by the government made quick profits which only the lack of more Italian capital limited.[51] The economic side of the fascist era is still relatively unexamined and needs further study. Historians have hitherto been too dismissive of economic influences on the regime, particularly during the economically flat years from the late 1920s to the end of the 1930s, when fascism seemed flaccid and a spent force which, in the depressed 1930s, only a war could reinvigorate. Where would such a war be focused? Italy's need for colonies in Africa was greater than its interest in Eastern Europe where the population densely settled the land and could not be easily displaced without unpleasant consequences.

Italy's preparations for war, historians agree, revealed incredible deficiencies in raw materials, machinery, trained manpower and weaponry of all kinds. Shortages existed in everything except aluminum. In the mid-1930s Italy underwent an exchange currency crisis, and somewhat like Germany, to manage it, introduced partial autarchy. After revelations that financial reserves in the Bank of Italy had dwindled from 20 million lire in 1927 to under 3 million at the end of 1939 Felice Guarneri, the Finance Minister, admitted balefully at a Fascist Council meeting: "We are bankrupt." Mussolini used individual raw material inadequacies as an excuse to Hitler in August 1939 not to enter the war. When Hitler volunteered supplies, Mussolini presented him with a list: "it's enough to kill a bull — if a bull could read it," Foreign Minister Ciano gleefully remarked.[52]

Mussolini seemed blithely unfazed about Italian finances and thought Guarneri's fears "exaggerated," but Ciano's doubts encouraged Mussolini's hesitations against joining Germany in a war against Britain and France.[53]

The linchpin of Mussolini's strategy in Eastern Europe was Hungary which shared Italian hostility to the status quo and Yugoslavia, and trepidation over German power in the Danubian basin. Having been despoiled of most of the lands of the Crown of St. Stephan (Transylvania, the Banat, Burgenland, and Slovakia), the Hungarian ruling and middle classes had a simmering hatred for the Trianon Treaty.

A sensational letter of Count Bethlen, a great feudal landowner, former premier and cornerstone of the rightist regime, published in 1934 by *Pester Lloyd*, directly attacked the Versailles treaty and the Locarno Agreement. "All these pacts," Bethlen wrote, "assures for the time being an inconceivable predominance and power in Europe to the policy and to the states which combine for the maintenance of the status quo. This is a hegemony no other group of states have had on the continent since the days of the Holy Alliance." Bethlen demanded the treaty be revised. Bethlen exhorted Hungarian foreign policy to be "watchful" for any opportunity to assert "justifiable Hungarian interests...."[54]

The Hungarian landowner class held a *Herrenvolk* ideology toward their former non-Magyar peasantry over whom they hoped to rule again in the future.[55] The Hungarian middle class professionals, students and the middle echelon officer class also held fervently nationalist, revisionist views and anti-Semitic feelings toward the Jews with whom they vied for scarce jobs during the Depression years. Too minuscule to bring about any effective changes in the Versailles treaty, Hungary had to seek assistance from stronger grievants, Germany and Italy.

After the destruction of the Bela Kun government and the Hungarian Soviet, a new national myth emerged among the upper classes: anti-bolshevism. The major figure in this extreme Magyar nationalism was Szandor Gömbös, a close friend of the Regent, Admiral Horthy, dating to the "Szeged group" overthrow of the Hungarian Soviet after World War I.

Gömbös, already a fascist in the early 1920s — he advocated the founding of a fascist international against the Comintern — maintained early close contacts with the German Nazis and Italian Fascists and visited Hitler in 1934, the first important foreign dignitary to do so.[56] Before Gömbös, Bethlen had laid out the policy to be followed: to seek allies in Rome and Berlin and to split the Little Entente as a prelude to the destruction of the Trianon Treaty.[57] Bethlen led Hungary out of its isolation by signing a treaty in 1927 with Italy, the most significant event of his career, although he held doubts that Italy was strong enough to aid Hungary.

Gömbös tried early in his career to form a Budapest-Rome-Berlin axis, but did not succeed because of Mussolini's suspicions of German designs on Austria and Southeastern Europe.[58] Under Gömbös's successor, Daranyi, and his Foreign Minister, Kanya, a more moderately conservative Hungary became committed to a "free hand" policy of maintaining permanent alliances with neither Germany nor the British and French.

The "Rome Connection" was insurance against Hitler and Nazi Germany's advance into Eastern Europe. Rumors circulated of a secret military agreement between Italy and Hungary aimed against Yugoslavia and the Little Entente.[59] But Mussolini rejected such an alliance as impractical.

Laval, succeeding Barthou, yielding to French tradition and opinion, supported a weakened Franco-Soviet Alliance in 1935, but in his heart of hearts really favored an alliance with Italy. He flattered Mussolini and worked to accomplish this during the Ethiopian affair, asking the Yugoslavs not to make an issue of the murder of King Alexander.

A key player in these maneuvers was Austria, an Italian buffer against Germany. But Mussolini also discouraged talks between Czechoslovakia, Austria and Hungary to create a Prague-directed Danubian confederation directed against Germany. For a time Mussolini ambivalently flirted with a Catholic Hapsburg restoration in Central Europe, centered on Austria and Hungary under Italian auspices, as a bulwark against the rising German tide.

Italian relations with Poland had become embittered by Mussolini's conniving of the failed 1933 Four Power Pact, and his revisionist trumpeting, antagonizing both the Czech leader Beneš and the Polish strongman Pilsudski. Mussolini even dabbled in Ukrainian affairs by contacts with the Organization of Ukrainian Nationalists (OUN). Nazi leader Dr. Rosenberg assured him that the Rome Protocols were no obstacle to a German-Italian alliance that would include Poland.[60] Both Polish Foreign Minister Beck and Mussolini worked jointly against the Little Entente and Czechoslovakia in particular. In Beck's ambitious policy, Hungary was to serve as a "middle piece" connection between Poland and Italy in a "vertical axis" alongside the Berlin-Rome Axis. The "vertical axis" had a broader, more duplicitous aim, namely, "to create an anti-German bulwark along the line of Rome-Belgrade-Budapest-Warsaw with an eventual branching out to Bucharest."[61] Italy offered its support for Hungary's annexation of the Carpatho-Ukrainian region of Czechoslovakia, after the latter's demise, as a connection to Hungary. Astute observers realized that once established in the Austrian and the Czech areas, Germany would have Hungary, Romania and Poland at its mercy and these theoretical alliance fantasies would become meaningless.

Though in contact sporadically during the 1920s, Mussolini and Hitler met for the first time in June 1934 in Venice in private for several hours without an interpreter — Mussolini spoke tolerable German — with Hitler speaking volubly and excitedly and Mussolini listening passively to a torrent of words. Tears came to the Führer's eyes and Mussolini reportedly said of Hitler afterward: "He's a nut." Hitler tried to get Mussolini to give up patronage of his client, the pint-sized Austrian dictator, Dollfuss, but Mussolini ignored the German request. The following month the Austrian Nazis murdered Dollfuss, at a time when the Austrian leader's wife was a guest of Mussolini who had the macabre task of informing her of his death. When Hitler failed to get Mussolini's disavowal of Dollfuss, he went ahead with his plan to stage a palace coup and seize power. The Austrian socialist workers, crushed by Dollfuss several months before, stood by and did little to stop the Nazis then or at the time of the Nazi Anschluss in March 1938 four years later.

The Stresa front of 1935 (Italy, Britain, France) and Italy's agreement with France dashed to pieces on the reefs of the Italian invasion of Ethiopia. The French and Italians had even held military staff talks and Mussolini talked with bravura of destroying Germany if it continued its aggressive policy.

The British attitude immediately before the Italian invasion, in Gaines Post, Jr.'s, apt phrase, was "anxious ambivalence." The Foreign Office leaders Vansittart, Sargent and Hoare and most cabinet members opposed a fall-out with Italy; the Treasury, Board of Trade, Cabinet and other services disliked sanctions and the Admiralty felt unprepared, and despite concern over grandiose Italian territorial ambitions in Africa did not wish to alienate Italy and drive it into the arms of Hitler. Gaines Post, Jr., summarizes: "The Mediterranean crisis presented a conundrum that seemed to resist resolution by coercion, conciliation, or a combination of the two."[62] The refusal of the French and Laval who desired Italian good will and support against Germany to lend adequate military support to Britain led Hoare and Laval to conclude an agreement granting Mussolini considerable concessions in the Ethiopian area. But a public uproar developed when the press exposed secret efforts to mollify Mussolini. A massive poll of the British public revealed overwhelming British support for sanctions. With an election on the way, the prudent Baldwin opted for sanctions.

Hitler saw his opportunity and offered an apology for the murder of Dollfuss and disclaimed any intentions of annexing Austria, aiding Italy with shipments of coal and munitions at a time when Mussolini needed assistance against sanctions. Hitler cynically kept the open wound of Italian-Western relations festering by secretly sending aid and munitions to the Ethiopians.[63] Germany had, in fact, large investments in Ethiopia before the Italian attack and, according to the German scholar Klaus Hildebrand, a strong lobby in Germany wanted to gain a foothold in Ethiopia to spread German influence throughout East Africa. Ribbentrop, his ambassador-at-large, supported this lobby which Hitler could not easily ignore. At the end of 1935 Hitler turned down a proposal by the pro-Ethiopian lobby for a treaty with Ethiopia supplying it with arms in return for Ethiopian agricultural products.[64]

Ethiopia in 1935–1936 became the fulcrum about which the international political rivalries turned, with Germany vacillating uncertainly between allying with Italy or Great Britain. At first Hitler seems to have distanced himself from the Ethiopian affair, content to watch while Italy and the Western Powers got in each other's hair. Finally he saw Britain's preoccupation with Italy's expansion into Ethiopia as a "heaven sent" opportunity to offer German ammunition to the ammunition-strapped British navy. Britain had sent its fleet into the Mediterranean while its minister, Samuel Hoare, and Pierre Laval tried to appease Mussolini with offers of Ethiopian territory. Fearing a German grab for Austria, Mussolini dispatched his best alpine divisions to the Brenner frontier. Italian forces failed to overcome Ethiopian resistance and for a time it looked like Italy might be overcome by the doughty Ethiopians. Both the British and Hitler became frightened that an Italian collapse and the defeat of a white power by an African one would create reverberations throughout the entire colonial world and threaten domination of the white race over the non-white races. Hitler also worried lest an Italian defeat in Ethiopia would gravely undermine the fascist system and bring about the isolation of Germany.

The signing of the Franco-Soviet Pact of 1935 which Hitler declared a breach of the Locarno Agreement — and Soviet support of Ethiopia — moved Hitler and Mussolini toward a rapprochement. Hitler raised the usual amount of coal sent to Italy but contrary to conventional belief sent little else. Hitler now dropped his scheme to aid Britain with military supplies against Italy and sent an emissary to Mussolini, one Strunk, opening the possibility of a German-Italian political understanding.[65]

In January 1936, exactly one year after signing the French agreement, Mussolini made his first move toward the Axis, notifying Hitler that the sanctions had created a breach between Italy and the Western Powers and that he now was prepared to eventually concede Austria to Germany. In fact, he had not completely burned his bridges and continued to maintain connections to France whom he might yet join, "if the price was right."[66] Washington noted Mussolini's tergiversations: the State Department's Pierpont Moffat stated the obvious: "Italy was trying to play both sides of the fence."[67]

But Mussolini's policy of running with the hares and hounds did not advance his grandiose vision for a neo-Roman empire. He had to choose: Hitler or the Western Powers. Mussolini, therefore, slowly inched toward a Rome-Berlin Axis, first approving a German-Austrian agreement, after a final side-glance toward a Hapsburg restoration. While Archduke Otto waited in the wings to be summoned, the leader of the Austrian monarchists travelled to Rome, received Mussolini's benediction, and then went to Budapest. This prompted a hasty visit to Rome on January 15, 1937, of Göring who warned that a monarchist restoration stood in the way of a Rome-Berlin Axis, and Mussolini relented.[68]

As the international atmosphere fairly crackled with tension, the dizzying number of Mussolini's schemes to attack other countries mounted. At one time or another in the 1930s he fulminated, threatening to attack France, Britain, Yugoslavia, Albania, Greece and in Spain.[69] His tactics were always the same: to play off different national groups prior to a general offensive — Croats against Serbs, Albanians versus Greeks, Bulgars against Serbs. In the end, dissuaded by his generals, ministers and fascist leaders — except for a few like the rabid Cremona chieftain, Farinacci — or his own notorious hesitations, he shelved all of these plans. He preferred striking "on the cheap," as in Albania in April 1939, when success favored his enterprise. These outbursts of his political energies in all directions led, in the end, to little positive.

The alliance with Hungary and Austria, the Rome Protocols, Ciano conceded, was becoming "more and more impotent" and because "agreements with a purely economic content necessarily lacked profound vitality," resuscitating efforts remained elusive.[70] In the months before the Munich Conference Italy's nebulous eastern alliance system and influence in Eastern Europe began to fade while Germany's increased. Mussolini refused to protect Hungary from a Yugoslav attack if Hungary became involved in a military conflict with Czechoslovakia. Mussolini scoffed at Polish Foreign Minister Beck's "Third Europe" policy of leaguing the small states of Eastern Europe through a connecting "common border" between Poland and Hungary as "only a cobweb."[71] Hitler's opposition to the "common border" scheme sealed the "Third Europe" plan, primarily because it was not in Germany's interest to allow a policy aimed against it.[72]

During the 1938 crisis, Hungary clung to its "free hand" policy of maintaining itself aloof from any alliance, military or political, with a Great

Power. Chamberlain largely ignored Magyar attempts to gain British support for its territorial claims against Czechoslovakia. The British somewhat duplicitously reassured Hungary its claims would be considered if only it remained patient and neutral. Britain, in fact, may have already written off Hungary as a German pawn, "riddled with Nazism" and "obviously servile" to Germany, in the words of a British Foreign Office official.[73]

Despite Hungary's other commitments, Hungarian Foreign Minister Kanya tried to conduct a policy of staying close to Germany as the only Power interested in bringing about a change in Hungary's borders. He also maintained good relations with Poland and encouraged an alliance between Italy and Britain, the latter still aloof from Central European affairs. In hindsight a British-Italian alliance had no likelihood of success as Mussolini increasingly believed Italy's imperialist destiny lay with Germany, not Britain. As Hungary could not be sure of Italian support if it became embroiled in a fight with Czechoslovakia on the side of Germany, it increasingly preferred a diplomatic solution in which Slovakia fell to Hungary like a ripe fruit.

Mussolini did little to advance Hungary's interests at Munich. Nor did the other three Powers, contenting themselves with an afterthought annex to the principal agreement, granting the other minorities future arbitration meetings if the Czech state failed after three months to conclude separate agreements with them. Hungary repeatedly rejected requests to join Germany in an attack on Czechoslovakia, fearing a Little Entente intervention. An incensed Hitler upbraided Horthy and the Kanya government for forcing him to back down and accept a negotiated settlement.[74] Hungarian military unpreparedness and anxiety that abandonment of the "free hand" policy by joining Germany could lead to a chaotic situation and the triumph of the Arrow-Cross fascists in Hungary, forced Budapest into a more prudent neutral role. Mussolini tried to gain as much territory for Hungary as possible at the post-Munich Vienna meetings to keep alive the Hungarian alliance. But Hitler's refusal to grant Hungary the Ruthenian Corridor linking Hungary to Poland doomed Beck's "Third Europe" plan, and set up Poland for attack in the following year.

Of the two rivals, Hungary and Romania, Mussolini leaned toward Hungary primarily because Hungary like Italy had suffered at the Trianon conference — whereas Romania had gained territory — and its loyalty toward the Axis would be greater. Also, as German need for Romanian oil, wheat and agricultural products grew, Italy lost hope of clientage or economic gain there. Therefore, Hungary remained Italy's last Central European ally.

Berlin finally granted Hungary southern Slovakia and the Sub-Carpathian region without Hungary having lifted a finger during the Munich crisis. Italian attempts to promote a Polish-Hungarian common border failed. Only the "horizontal Axis" lasted, but the German Foreign Office nipped it in the bud too.

Mussolini eagerly grasped the opportunity to play peacemaker at Munich, the only member of that *quadrumvirate* of leaders who knew foreign languages. Befriending all sides, he played his favorite role of holding the balance of power between the two sides. But in actual fact, according to a biographer, he had been in secret contact beforehand with Hitler whom he agreed to support and duplicitously present a prearranged compromise to the German hard demands at the eleventh hour which Hitler would then accept.[75] But he had been too clever by half. Though Italy had emerged from the Munich Conference with increased prestige as a Great Power, Mussolini came back with empty hands, having previously given up Austria and the Sudetenland without a *quid pro quo,* a hard fact which aggrieved him no end. He resolved to seize Albania without consulting Hitler in April 1939, though Hitler may have colluded in the decision for reasons of his own, one month after the Germans marched into Prague.

The Poles ascribed geopolitical factors as the reason for the intricate dance between Italy and the Eastern European states. Szembek noted: "The entire affair of the Anschluss has clearly proved that, for Italy, the Mediterranean interests are infinitely more important than the questions of the Danubian basin and of Central Europe. Italian policy orients itself towards the Mediterranean and it's an error to believe that the affairs of Hungary and Romania could shake up the solidity of the Rome-Berlin Axis. When Germany will have extended its hegemony over Hungary, the fate of Romania will be settled in advance from all points of view."[76]

Mussolini confirmed this on February 4, 1939, to the Fascist Grand Council, described as "a sort of Mussolinian *Mein Kampf,* . . . a geopolitical vision the dictator had entertained since at least the mid-1920s." Italy, he railed,

> is in truth a prisoner of the Mediterranean, and the more populous and prosperous Italy becomes, the more its imprisonment will gall. The bars of this prison are Corsica, Tunis, Malta, Cyprus. The sentinels of this prison are Gibraltar and Suez. Corsica is a pistol pointed at the heart of Italy: Tunisia at Sicily; while Malta and Cyprus constitute a threat to all our positions in the eastern and western Mediterranean. Greece, Turkey, Egypt have been ready to form a chain with Great Britain and to complete the politico-military encirclement of Italy. Greece, Turkey, Egypt must be considered virtual enemies of Italy and of its expansion.

"The task of Italian policy, which cannot have and does not have continental objectives of a European territorial nature except Albania, is first of all to break the bars of the prison." After that occurred then " . . . to march to the Ocean" either the Indian Ocean "joining Libya with Ethiopia through the Sudan, or the Atlantic, through French North Africa." "In either case we will find ourselves confronted with Anglo-French opposition."[77] Despite this disavowal, Italy had not really given up the possibility of securing territory in Yugoslavia; control of the Adriatic remained important.

If Mussolini meekly relinquished hegemony over Hungary and Romania, Yugoslavia was another matter. In early 1939 Mussolini talked of invading Croatia, vowing to fight Hitler if he tried to stop him. Mussolini received some support from industrialists like Alberto Pirelli and "a whole chorus of demands went up for victory, for conquest, for recognition of Italian leadership in the world."[78]

Albania had been an Italian client state since the 1920s, and Italian business held investments in mining, oil wells, finance and banking to gain a foothold there and then expand throughout the Balkans. Talks between the German and Italian military representatives, General Keitel and General Pariani, occurred a few days before the invasion but the Italians gave no clue of the impending event. Mussolini had been planning the Albanian move since February and was startled by the German occupation of Prague and became irrationally alarmed that German power might next move to seize Croatia.

The Albanian campaign can be charitably described as less than brilliant. The Italians were so ill-prepared that Anfuso, Ciano's assistant, admitted that if the Albanians "had possessed a well-armed fire brigade they could have driven us back into the Adriatic."

Mussolini revealed to General Badoglio plans to attack either Greece or Yugoslavia and to "seize Croatia to exploit the considerable resources of that area," underscoring the primary role of raw materials.[79] But the Italian King unexpectedly vetoed these plans: the German alliance was not popular, the army unready, Italy's defenses pitiful. Ciano hoped "to grab ... our part of the booty in Croatia and Dalmatia" without war with Great Britain and France.[80] But General Badoglio had dire forebodings and was not happy with these plans to attack in the Balkans.[81]

Once Mussolini threw in with Germany, he worked to destroy the pro-Western Little Entente by outflanking it through Bulgaria and Hungary. But the timid Balkan states balked: Ciano pressed Bulgaria "which shares our point of view" but "is not completely ready militarily to take a definitive position." Germany and Italy would arm it only when Sofia had defined its international position. Bulgaria received promises its territorial claims would be honored as Hungary's had been for its friendship.[82]

Mussolini informed Hitler of his readiness to seize territory and raw materials in the Balkans and Danubian basin once war broke out. Only Bulgaria and Hungary could be counted on.[83] The Italian move into Albania panicked Turkey, a traditional British ally, into a pact with the British and French in May 1939 aimed against further Italian expansion to the Aegean, greatly complicating the situation in the Balkans.[84] The jittery neutrals, Yugoslavia and Romania, met and coordinated efforts to keep the war out of the Balkans. Both pleaded with the Turks and Western Powers not to include them in the Mediterranean pact[85] pointedly aimed at Italy to avoid irritating Rome and Berlin; the Turks sent many divisions of troops up to the Bulgarian border in Thrace against a possible Italian-Bulgarian attack.[86] The British Minister at Sofia's efforts to cement an anti-Axis Balkan alliance with Bulgaria by bribes of territory came to grief against Bulgarian intransigence and Romanian unwillingness to yield territory.[87]

A too emphatic reading of Mussolini's motivations and idiosyncratic impulses by scholars as the genesis of the Ethiopian, Albanian and Greek campaigns is unconvincing. Great Power envies and rivalries, economic necessity and the stagnation of fascism constrained Italy toward imperialist expansion and the lure of plunder and profits as a quick panacea for Italy's domestic problems. A successful military campaign by Mussolini to rid himself of the palsied and decrepit grip of the monarchy, the military and the Catholic Church may be a probable hidden motive.

On the eve of the war, Italy verged on becoming a quasi-satellite of Germany. Italians paid dearly for German machinery, chemicals and coal in exchange for agricultural products, hemp, silk, rayon and sulphur when Schacht's price control system forced down Italian export prices. Austria's post-Anschluss trade went to the Baltic instead of the Adriatic and the German market became the main one for certain Italian products; and the German bilateral trade system and its coercive trade tactics drove Italian commerce from Balkan markets.

Italy's Achilles' heel, coal, formerly had been supplied mostly by Britain — 60% of its needs — but after the Ethiopian invasion it applied sanctions with other countries and choked off Italian coal imports which Germany quickly seized the opportunity to fill. Government ministers painted a grim picture of Italy's deficiencies in raw materials; coal prices had doubled by 1940 and more coal or oil could not be expected without immediate reimbursement.[88] Italy's wealth had been siphoned off into the madcap Ethiopian and Spanish civil war adventures without an afterthought, creating the "flight forward" (*Flucht nach vorn*) psychology to avoid the chaos noted in Germany on the eve of the war.

Like Hitler, Mussolini disdainfully waved away hard facts by citing dubious countervailing sources of raw materials and finances. Never one daunted by such obstacles, he plunged on determinedly toward will-o'-the-wisp visions of vainglory and empire. Assertive posturing masked his internal psychological turmoil and deep-seated indecision and wavering until the final moments before leaping into the war. Ciano's constant brutal and cynical references to "the booty" and "getting my booty" leaves little doubt that Mussolini and fascism's needs were territory, raw materials and power, preferably through chicanery without burdening the Italian people. Mussolini's trepidation that Italy might degenerate into a second-class power if it remained outside the fight, for all kinds of psychological, ideological and territorial reasons overcame any logic that neutrality might be more beneficial. Beneath everything lay the realization "that his tenure of office would last only so long as he could provide the illusion of bread and circuses." Mussolini and the Italian leadership must be blamed for recklessly engaging in the Ethiopian and other adventures and allying Italy with Germany, encouraging Hitler to unleash the war.

Nationalism represented the *sacro-egoismo* ideology of the Italian bourgeoisie rather than the laboring class which had little to gain from a war in which its blood would be shed; the Fascist Party and its leadership together with the upper classes hoped for a *Herrenvolk* status with the Germans. These elite groups saw in the defeat of Britain and France and parcelling up of their overseas possessions a new opportunity for empire. Mussolini's role as agency dictated the manner and moment of Italy's entry into war. He has been staged as sole decision maker and conveniently saddled with historical culpability by historians who have ignored or understated other realities (raw materials, trade problems, socio-economic imperatives, the decline of fascism). The magnetic draw of Mussolini, like Hitler, remains in post-war historical writing, and other possibilities have received little attention and even a certain dismissiveness. Other determinants must certainly have played a role. To trace the root cause of Italian expansionism primarily to Mussolini and cultural and intellectual influences is not satisfying, unhistorical and reductionist.

In all this, Italy's trajectory in the 1918–1939 period is part of the overarching drama of the hegemonic conflicts of the Great Powers for wealth, markets and raw material sources complicated by the hideousness of fascism and unsettled business from the 1914–1918 previous war.

Chapter 3

France and Poland, 1918–1939.
Poland: French or German Satellite?

Polish Foreign Minister Beck to French Ambassador Noël: If you were attacked by Germany, Poland would march to your aid, because it would be in its interest; but the reverse is not true. . . .
— Leon Noël, *L'Agression Allemande contre la Pologne*

The policy of Warsaw should never be dependent upon Moscow or Berlin.
— Jozef Beck, *Dernier Rapport*

THE PRIMARY DILEMMA in the post-war history of French and Polish relations was that of the eastern border of Germany. France and Britain wished to settle the problem to Germany's satisfaction and revise the mistakes of Versailles, so that Germany would have no reason to rearm. But Poland refused to part with any of its territory — most of which had a Polish majority — and was hag-ridden by historical dread of another partition. Polish territory taken from the USSR after 1921 was many times greater than Germany's territorial losses to Poland and together with Russia's previous occupation of Poland created an almost obsessive fear of the Soviet giant to the east. Poland felt keenly the eighteenth-century partitions and "the dead hand of the past on the living."

France with its empire, greater population and military and economic strength played a Great Power role while Poland, a medium-sized power, did not. But this was deceiving. The Great War had dealt France a debilitating blow.

France's exhaustion after 1918, its lifeblood squandered in the trenches, left a permanent imprint upon its politics and foreign policy. Its decades-long population decline and loss of a million and a half men killed, four million wounded — a million maimed for life — was a staggering blow with grave repercussions. Three decades later Paris metros and buses still had special seats marked: *places reservées aux mutilés de la guerre*, referring to the disabled of World War I, not World War II. France's share of Europe's population dropped from 16% in 1800 to 8% in 1930. The years after did not replenish the stock.

Though France emerged militarily prestigious, paradoxically the blood-letting and psychic exhaustion of war and the nation's actual human and physical resources did not correspond to its extensive political commitments.

France, like Britain, emerged scarred from the war with a soul-searing dread of another conflict.

Social and political cleavages rent France, dating from the French Revolution. Lewis Namier luminously and sympathetically describes interwar France's mindset:

> The more the fruits of victory proved illusory the stronger grew in France the determination to husband that unique treasure, her human material: truly there was nothing worth its sacrifice. Disillusioned and civilized with an intense analytical awareness, the French had lost that primitive élan which carries men into battle. In the spiritual sphere there was a growth of individualism, in the material selfishness. And in the absence of a patent common purpose uniting the nation, social divisions which in the preceding one hundred and fifty years had repeatedly resulted in civil war, became accentuated, inhibiting still further national action. But the creative leaders or servants of a nation merely focus the spirit that is in it.[1]

Hatred of the Republic ("the slut") and betrayal from within by various rightist groups, anti-Republican leagues and veterans organizations emotionally exploded into the Stavisky riots which almost overthrew the Third Republic and later adopted the motto: "rather Hitler than the Republic." A proto-fascist ideology crept into the mid-1930s cabinets. However, some conservative nationalists like Clemenceau's stern bloodhound of 1914–1918, Georges Mandel, opposed the defeatist "Munichois" group after 1938.

After World War II, historians intensely debated inter-war French history, particularly its ignominious military collapse before the Wehrmacht. One historical school immediately following the debacle of 1940 accused the French people and its leaders of moral decay and self-indulgence.[2] Others, like the philosopher Jacques Maritain, denied France was morally delinquent or decadent and lauded the brilliance of French civilization.[3] Recent historical scholarship points to the timidity and fear of politicians like Daladier, Bonnet and Flandin in confronting Hitler, shrinking before an alliance with the Soviet Union, and supporting a hidebound, stodgy French High Command (Generals Gamelin, Weygand, Petain).[4] France's relations with Poland have not drawn much attention in English language historical research, which has petered into a rivulet since the early 1970s.[5] What exists is primarily political history in which decisions unfold in a vacuum, uninfluenced by economic determinants of any sort.

Poland and its relations with France may be considered on two levels: the first as a small power caught in the tides and contentions for dominance between Germany, the Soviet Union and the Western Powers. The second is Poland's material existence after World War I, its economic circumstances and viability as a state and its determination to hold on to the Upper Silesia industrial complex, the Corridor and access to the sea through Danzig awarded it by the Versailles Treaty.

Considering the latter level first, the Versailles Treaty's award of formerly German territory to Poland locked it into permanent conflict with Germany.

Poland received Upper Silesia for a combination of political and economic reasons. After a plebiscite, Germany won possession, but the Poles
seized control after a revolt by the Polish population. German para-military
forces fought back and the whole matter ended up in the lap of the Allied
leaders. After heated debate, the British first backed the German claim then
yielded to the French, who supported the Poles. The decision came down to
a tense and personal confrontation between the two dominant figures on the
Allied Supreme Council, the British politician, Lloyd George, and Aristide
Briand, the French leader.[6] The struggle was hard fought over the Upper
Silesian industrial triangle, the remainder being primarily agricultural and
easier to delineate by population. Its glittering jewel, the highly industrialized southeastern tip, constituted a densely compact region of mines and
factories where a mere couple of miles on either side of the boundary could
be crucial.

The Supreme Council met for five days of bitter haggling between Lloyd
George and Aristide Briand "who fought each other town by town, com-
mune by commune." The French Cabinet rejected the British report that the
Poles had been given too little to be able to survive industrially.

Upper Silesia became a subject of daily debate in the House of Commons and some circles feared that the French might become economically
dominant on the continent. On the Allied Committee, the Italians thought
France might become too powerful and "get her knife into Italy," and therefore supported the British position. A strong German campaign for Italian
support and various promises — Silesian coal among them — and threats to
the Spanish, delivered the Italian and Spanish vote to Germany.

British disinterest in Upper Silesia forced Lloyd George to relent, despite
little support for the French inside the Council. British unwillingness to
break the alliance with France after three years of war decided the matter.

A. J. P. Taylor remarks that in most cases treaties are usually accepted
and, after a certain amount of time, generally forgotten. But the Versailles
Treaty and its deeply felt grievances remained rooted in German minds as
"the slave treaty" or "shackles of Versailles." Hitler later could safely rest
his foreign policy upon this resentment and mask his real intentions of a war
against the Soviet Union for possession of the Ukraine and the destruction
of communism.

The dictatorship established by Jozef Pilsudski after a coup in 1926 and
his personal political attitudes constricted the political vision of his suc-
cessors. The cult of Pilsudskism tied the country unduly to the past and
restricted its development.

After 1926 Pilsudski became increasingly conservative and established a
working concordat with the Polish aristocracy. The Non-Party Bloc headed
by Colonel Slawek in 1935 became the governmental facade behind which
the Pilsudskists ruled the country; and the representatives of the landlords
and big business advanced funds for the elections to support the government
and to protect their interests. Pilsudski's supporters differed from his former
socialist and nationalist comrades in arms. As a contemporary observed, the
government bloc "became more and more deformed" and, Pilsudski himself
later admitted: "The lice crawled over me."[7] Pilsudski metamorphosed from

a pre-war socialist, advocating a federalist Poland leagued to Ukraine and Bielo Russia, to a more conservative, supra-national leader.

Poland's internal political situation following Pilsudski's death foundered in uncertainty and confusion. The opposition parties boycotted the 1935 elections, declaring the electoral laws illegal and the new constitution merely an instrument of the state. Only 46% of those entitled to actually voted according to the official figures.[8]

The country threatened to descend to the pre-1926 anarchy. The minorities were sullen and disgruntled: the Ukrainians seethed with animosity since the 1930s brutal pacification campaign, the Germans sulked unhappily under Polish domination and the Jews resented discriminatory social burdens. To appease the Polish population, President Moscicki appointed one of the more liberal leaders of the bloc to form "the first cabinet of the President of the Republic." But the attacks of the "colonels" in Parliament impeded efforts to liberalize and make the regime more acceptable. Strikes organized by the Peasant Party in the villages and supported by the Socialists in the cities, coupled with the "colonels'" attacks, forced the government to resign. To restore its prestige, the Pilsudskists formed the *Camp of National Unity,* headed by Colonel Koc, a crypto-fascist government party which courted the nationalists and university students by conducting a policy of nationalism, anti-Semitism and clericalism. The Camp received the official imprimatur of Pilsudski's successor, Marshal Śmigły-Rydz.

The Pilsudskist epigone, a clique of "colonels," claiming intimate association with the late dictator, occupied all the positions of leadership, even the Bank of Poland. The "colonels" divided the country between "our camp" and "the rest," in effect declaring: "we don't want recognition from you."[9] The "colonels" adopted the attitude of the *shlachta,* the old Polish nobility: "We are the state."[10]

A curious triumvirate filled the power vacuum left by Pilsudski. The foremost, General Śmigły-Rydz, Pilsudski's heir-designate as Inspector General of the army, distinguished himself against the Soviets, and arrived at a crucial moment with troops during the 1926 Pilsudski coup. Colonel Jozef Beck, the former private secretary to Pilsudski, was foreign minister while President Moscicki, an eminent scientist, became President of the Republic. Real power increasingly devolved upon Śmigły-Rydz and the army. Following Pilsudski's death, quarrels broke out between various groups and leaders.[11] Its image was of a rudderless regime, "a dictatorship without a dictator."

Colonel Beck, intelligent and subtle, a "Mephistophelian" figure — in Professor Henry Roberts's words — rose fast and, groomed by Pilsudski, became foreign minister at the age of 38. Born in Warsaw of Flemish ancestry, he entered Pilsudski's Legion, served in various military diplomatic posts and in military intelligence in the USSR and France. He rose quickly to become the *chef de cabinet* in the War Ministry, later State Secretary with cabinet rank and in 1930 Deputy Minister-President in the Foreign Ministry and finally in November 1932 he became State Secretary in the Foreign Ministry.[12] A historian not unsympathetic to Poland describes Beck thus: His "toughness, dynamism ... went hand in hand with a sharp intelligence and a prodigious memory." "Ambitious and proud. ... Beck's suave manners [had] a certain air of cynicism and mystery." But of the darker side of Beck — "most foreign diplomats regarded Beck as disingenuous, untrustworthy and unscrupulous."[13] Maxim Litvinov, the Soviet Foreign Minister, regarded him simply as "a Nazi pimp."

Neither the new Soviet state nor the new Weimar Republic of Germany greeted the reappearance of Poland, the "child of Versailles," with enthusiasm. The Soviet Union had lost some of its western territories to Poland in 1921 and knew Pilsudski harbored anti-Russian feelings and ambitions to create an Eastern European federation incorporating Poland, Bielo Russia and Ukraine. But for the time being, the USSR did not want a conflict with Poland and a new anti-Bolshevik intervention.

German leaders regarded Poland with derision and contempt as a *"saison-staat"* created by the Versailles Treaty. The monocled army leader General von Seeckt stated this plainly in 1922: "Poland's existence is intolerable, and incompatible with Germany's vital interests. It must disappear and will disappear through its own inner weakness and through Russia with our aid.... A return to the frontiers of 1914 should be the basis for an understanding between Russia and Germany." In a January 24, 1931, speech, von Seeckt declared: "Poland should be regarded as a principal and unconditional enemy."[14]

Brockdorff-Rantzau, later appointed German Ambassador to Moscow, stated emphatically: "Poland has to be finished off."[15] A common border between Germany and Russia and the elimination of Poland should be the political goal of German foreign policy.[16] The German government refused to help Poland against the Bolsheviks after their July 20, 1920 offensive against the Poles, and the Poles in turn supplied the Allied Powers with documentation on German-Soviet military intelligence cooperation.[17]

German and Soviet cooperation started already in the 1920s when Soviet journalist Karl Radek, imprisoned in Germany for his role in supporting the German communists with money, received representatives of the German high command in his cell. Throughout the 1920s and 1930s the Soviet military secretly placed its military bases at German disposal to evade the military restrictions of the Versailles Treaty and helped train and equip German plane and tank forces. A German-Soviet collaboration in a fourth partition of Poland remained a recurrent nightmare for the Polish leadership, against which it designed its entire foreign policy and became the basis for the "policy of balance" — i.e., of not allying exclusively with either one against the other.

The loss of its Upper Silesian natural resources hurt Germany even more. The southeastern tip of Upper Silesia contained one of the largest industrial concentrations in Europe with extensive coal and lignite deposits and also zinc, lead, iron and other ores. The loss of the Upper Silesian industrial region, transferred to Poland, cost Germany 11% of its coal resources. By the post-war settlement, Germany lost 26% of its coal, iron ore, zinc, lead and other raw materials after the loss of Alsace-Lorraine to France, Upper Silesia to Poland, and the Czech Silesian region's coal deposits to Czechoslovakia. John Maynard Keynes, present at the Peace Conference, doubted Germany could survive the loss of Silesian coal.

A predominantly agricultural country, Poland exported coal, wood and foodstuffs to Germany while Germany sent manufactured goods. Historically, Germany had been Poland's creditor, supplying as late as 1930 about 28% of its total short-term credits. German capital investments in Polish enterprises amounted to 541 million złotys in 1930 or 20% of total foreign capital, primarily in formerly German Upper Silesian mining and iron industries. Germany had a lever to commit mischief as its exports to Poland amounted to only 6% of its total exports, while its imports came to only 5% of its total imports. Polish trade with Germany in 1924, in contrast, was 42% and 34.5% of total exports and imports, respectively.[18]

To avoid disruption of Poland's economy, the peace treaty compelled Germany to import from Poland for five years duty-free the same amount of goods purchased before the war from former German areas and for three years an amount equivalent to goods coming from Polish Silesia. Germany retaliated by an undeclared economic boycott against Polish goods. After July 1922 with restored commercial relations, the Polish position weakened as this stipulation was about to lapse. To force the Germans to make concessions, the Poles adopted import restrictions against German goods and the Germans retaliated immediately by unleashing a tariff war against Polish commodities.

Berlin hoped to force territorial concessions by cutting Polish coal deliveries from 500,000 tons to 125,000 tons annually as well as Polish pork exports, despite the misgivings of German foreign office figures like Dirksen, who doubted Germany would benefit either economically or politically by a tariff war to force Poland to its knees "apart from the fact that it would make Poland pliable to our wishes."[19] Others in the Foreign Office favored continued economic pressure on Poland through tariffs, but not if it precluded a trade agreement in Germany's interest. Agrarian representatives inside the German cabinet, who wanted to limit Polish pork and other agrarian products on the German market, complicated matters. The "fatal pigs" and curtailed Polish coal deliveries remained commercial thorns in Polish sides until 1934.

Petitions from German commercial and industrial sectors, who suffered from the loss of the Polish market, "flowed into the Foreign Ministry in torrents" and the influential *Reichsverband der Deutschen Industrie* (National Association of German Industry) gave notice that all industries desired the conclusion of a timely trade agreement with Poland.[20] Curtius, then Minister for Economy and Foreign Minister, recommended that Germany would have to let slide temporarily its political agenda if it hoped to exploit the Polish market; but German Foreign Minister Stresemann avoided abandoning Germany's political interests and offending the government's agrarian interests. This conflict continued to 1934 when Hitler ended it by a treaty of non-aggression with Poland.

Poland stood up to German economic pressure remarkably well, reorienting its coal trade to other countries, particularly Britain where a fortuitous event, the British coal strike of 1926, provided a new market. The net effect was a deleterious decline in German trade. In 1924, Germany accounted for 34.5% of Poland's total imports, but by 1930 this figure had declined to 27%, while its exports declined from 43.2% to 25.8% of Poland's total exports.[21]

To reduce dependency upon trade through Danzig, Poland constructed the port of Gdynia and also built a new merchant fleet. By 1932 Gdynia took almost the same shipping in tonnage as Danzig.[22] Failing to regain Upper Silesia, the Corridor and Danzig by economic measures, Germany resorted to political means.

To obviate the fateful collaboration of Germany and the Soviet Union, which would have meant its demise, Poland after World War I entered into a military accord with France on February 19, 1921, which provided for a mutual alliance against a German attack on either France or Poland. Article III, the most vital part of the Accord, declared:

> if either or both of them should be attacked without giving provocation, the two governments shall take concerted measures for the defense of their territory and the protection of their legitimate interests within the limits specified by the preamble.[23]

Attached to the political part of the accord was an economic convention, which protected the considerable French interests in Poland in the textile, oil and mining industries. The two governments signed an economic agreement granting the French economic concessions first, before the military convention, indicating that French capital sought to replace German capital in Poland, while Germany bogged down in civil war and revolution.

The granting of concessions to French capital was later justified *ex post facto* by French Ambassador Laroche: since Poland had no capital to finance its own industrialization, it had to allow the "inconveniences of foreign capital."[24] A major concern of the French was oil concessions which Briand requested from the Poles before the French would sign the military agreement with Poland.[25] In return for a loan to Poland for its military needs, it agreed to payment in oil and other Polish natural resources and manufactures and through the "partial alienation of the state refinery at Drohobycz" or other concessionary rights. Berthelot, Director of the Political Department of the French Foreign Ministry, also requested protection of French interests from "arbitration action" and the competition of Polish state-owned oil production. The French obtained considerable concessions from the Poles in the commercial agreement that included most-favored-nation status — a status not extended to Polish goods in France — and only minimum tariffs, which did not help Poland, as France, with its important farm sector, could not use Polish agricultural exports. Poland had to accept quantities of unneeded French products such as wines, liqueurs, jewelry, perfumes and cosmetics that it could not afford. French textiles also had to be imported into Poland despite the existence of a Polish textile industry, then ailing from the loss of its traditional Russian market. French firms could establish branches in Poland as Poland could in France, but in practice, because Poland was the weaker power, French firms benefited mostly. The French received important concessions in Upper Silesia, presumably the reason for Briand's fierce fight favoring Poland against Germany.

Resentment over French economic exploitation of Poland later burst out in the Polish press and in the remarks of Vice Minister Szembek to the French Minister about the French-controlled electric company and its exorbitant rates and corruption. The Giraudoux Company with its French and Swiss management became an especial source of friction after the arrest of two French officials, nettling the French and necessitating diplomatic intercession.[26]

The military side of the alliance was strongly supported by the French political leaders, but not the French military, particularly Marshal Foch, who believed Poland a less formidable and reliable power than the Soviet Union, successor to Czarist Russia, its traditional ally. Laroche, then deputy to Phillipe Berthelot, who helped draw up the language of the accord, noted the split. After the banquet reception for Pilsudski and Foreign Minister Prince Sapieha, the French and Polish leaders withdrew into another room, excluding Foch and the French military.[27] Because the latter believed Poland's borders untenable and its position sandwiched between Germany and the Soviet Union to be virtually indefensible, the alliance had less military value.[28] Upon French insistence, Poland and Romania signed a military pact aimed against the Soviet Union.

The 1922 Rapallo Agreement between Germany and the USSR unhinged Franco-Polish relations and raised the hackles of Warsaw. The Locarno Agreement that followed began the slippery slope down what later came to be called appeasement. Germany guaranteed the borders of France and Belgium, but left open the question of its eastern borders, leaving the Poles angry and suspicious, convinced that Stresemann's concessions to France had been made at their expense. Pilsudski summed up Polish feelings in his angry retort that "every decent Pole spits when he hears the word Locarno."[29]

Events in both France and Poland reinforced the drift towards allowing the Franco-Polish Alliance to fade into a historical relic. The Pilsudski regime's imprisonment of opposition leaders in 1930, their exile to Czechoslovakia and the brutal pacification campaign against the Ukrainian minority for the murder of a Polish official alienated the French left.

To silence the revisionist campaign in the West, the Polish dictator Pilsudski affected a brusque confrontational political style and threatened at times to invade East Prussia. A Polish attack in the east accompanied by either a communist or Nazi uprising harried all German governments from 1930 to 1933.[30] Pilsudski's belief that the Papen-Schleicher government of June 1, 1932, was particularly dangerous for Poland, was confirmed at Lausanne, on July 15, when Papen proposed to French Premier Herriot a German-French General Staff merger and a Franco-German Entente in exchange for French consent to German rearmament. Pilsudski delivered a warning to Berlin and Paris by ordering the Polish destroyer *Wicher* (Storm), to sail, without the League High Commissioner's permission, up the Westerplatte in Danzig harbor ostensibly to greet the English fleet, anchor there and, in the event of any insult to the Polish presence, to fire upon the first official building in sight. Although irritated by Pilsudski's display of power, and threatening to stop an impending Polish loan, the French rejected von Papen's demand for equality of armaments.

The *Wicher* affair reflected Poland's increasing sensitivity to being excluded from the Great Power arena, being lectured by the French and having its affairs discussed and settled by others. Henceforth Warsaw distanced itself from the League of Nations. Poland affected the attitudes and symbolic postures of a Great Power, even to seeking colonies for itself. Patriotic and nationalist organizations proliferated.

One of the most active, the Maritime and Colonial League, demanded colonies and overseas possessions. Throughout the 1930s it collected monies, published patriotic materials and promoted mass demonstrations and propagandistic activities. One of these publications, *Morze* (Sea), demanded overseas colonies in blunt, imperialist terms:

> Poland lacks raw materials for economic development. We are every year paying large sums to foreigners who control the sources of raw materials and their trade. Today Poland is fighting in the international arena for free access to overseas colonies and in the direct exploitation of raw materials. We base our demands on the tremendous increase of population and the necessity to develop national industry. . . . We demand free access to raw materials. . . . We demand colonies for Poland.[31]

Polish "latent imperialism," the American minister to Poland believed, undoubtedly stemmed from the successful imperialist expansionism of the fascist powers, and by Poland's own rough handling of Lithuania. Leading government supporters and even the Church participated in the numerous mass processions, "Colonial Days" and "Colonial League" demonstrations. The government itself and its party, the Camp of National Unity, adopted the colonial thesis. Poland demanded the former German colonies in Africa based on the population percentage of the former German Empire entitling it to be regarded as a Great Power. These demands, largely ignored by the Great Powers, were advanced even at the eleventh hour in 1939. Ironically, while ridiculing these colonial demands in his memoirs, Foreign Minister Beck raised the colonial question when Germany prepared to attack Poland and make a colony of it! On the eve of Beck's trip to Britain to seek a British guarantee against Hitler, Halifax gave the request for colonies short shrift: "there is, so far as I know, nothing to discuss," he instructed the British Ambassador to tell Beck.[32]

American Ambassador Biddle revealed another reason, besides raw material sources, for these colonial concerns: the Polish aristocracy, anxious over its vast land holdings, fearing radical and leftist parties intent on land reform for its land-hungry peasant masses, preferred to direct these pressures abroad "as suitable outlets for the surplus farm population as well as for the unwelcome Jewish minority."[33] Ambassador Leon Noël concurred, but believed that enlightened Poles had unreasonable and exaggerated expectations that colonies could benefit a poor country like Poland.[34] Beck broached to French Foreign Minister Delbos in 1937 the possibility of sending part of the excess Jewish population and Poles to Madagascar, considered by commissions and individuals since the 1920s, and which the French supported.[35] Raw material imports, Beck argued, represented over 70% of its imports paid for by currency or exports. Noël believed Beck's colonial interests "created a certain community between German policy and Polish policy permitting him to adopt again a parallel line...for which M. Beck and his intimate collaborators have a certain marked taste."[36]

Colonel Beck candidly set forth Poland's imperialist agenda: "Poland...is looking for places to which her population can emigrate and from which she can procure raw materials for industries."[37] (Beck conveniently forgets this in his memoirs and writes disparagingly of Poland's colonial desires which he pursued in the League and with Halifax in 1939.)[38]

After 1930, the French gradually cooled toward Poland and the politically unpopular Pilsudski dictatorship. Leaders, like Herriot, and military leaders like Marshall Foch spoke openly of loosening the military convention segment of the Franco-Polish Accord.

For both internal and external reasons, the Soviet Union rekindled friendly relations with Poland and Pilsudski reciprocated. Nervousness over a new capitalist encirclement reignited during the Papen-Schleicher cabinets.[39] Needing tranquility during the First Five Year Plan (1928–1933), the USSR mended its fences in Europe.[40]

But Moscow secretly kept the Germans informed of the negotiations with the Poles to allay Berlin's suspicions of a Soviet guarantee of the eastern borders of Poland. Stalin also told the writer Emile Ludwig that the USSR had no intention of guaranteeing the Soviet-Polish border. Despite Soviet assurances, the heyday of German-Soviet friendship was clearly over.[41] The Soviets exhibited a certain glee over both their 1932 pact with Poland and the Franco-Soviet pact three years later, as the USSR's "greatest diplomatic triumph," in breaking up a threatened capitalist encirclement.[42] The Soviet-Polish pact relieved Poland's previous client relationship to France and was the first move toward the Pilsudskian system of "balance" between Russia and Germany. The French alliance system directed against the USSR that had dominated Europe since the Versailles Treaty had lost influence.

The rise of Hitler, the bitterest foe of communism, whose work, *Mein Kampf*, Stalin had read, set off alarm bells in Moscow. National Socialist Germany, for different reasons, represented a threat to both the Soviet Union and Poland.[43]

The Polish Minister in Berlin, Wysocki, told Pilsudski that, when Hitler and the Nazi party "had been reduced to such complete ruin in the opinion of the country, the only way out would be to start a military action...diverting their attention from the internal situation."[44] Wysocki's opinion of Hitler was remarkably low: He was "not a genial nor an exceptional leader," but one who struck "a tone long dead in the German romantic soul." Hitlerism was full of "empty phrases." He erroneously predicted that the Nazi Party would split, the smaller part going to the extreme right, the larger and most powerful going to the Communists. The Nazi Party lacked seasoned politicians and contained many "loud mouths" and "demagogues."[45] The Soviet Minister to Berlin delivered a more realistic prediction: "It is quite clear that with a National Socialist–led cabinet begins the fascist terror against the Communist Party which will be driven underground." But "... it remained uncertain whether some other political figure would be chosen chancellor."[46]

Polish reports from Berlin stress the probable collapse of German capitalism and saw Hitler as a product of the deteriorating economic position, at its worst point since 1918.[47] Wysocki noted the growth of revisionist activity in East Prussia.[48] Moltke, the German Ambassador, reported that most Poles believed Hitler would be too preoccupied with internal struggles and other problems to deal with international matters and that his war on the communists "would lead to a deviation from Germany's Rapallo Treaty." "What everyone here longs for in his secret heart [is] that a Russian-German alienation would remove from Poland the nightmare of revision" and a new partition.[49]

After signing the Soviet-Polish Non-aggression Pact of 1932, Pilsudski confronted German revisionism. In March 1933, taking advantage of Hitler's preoccupation with the Reichstag elections, Pilsudski suddenly struck. Thirty thousand Polish troops marshaled in the Corridor area and the elite border guard troops as well. At dawn on March 6 the Polish troop transport *Wilja* landed a battalion of marine infantry on the Westerplatte, ostensibly to reinforce the Polish garrison there, an illegal act without previously seeking the permission of the League High Commission for Danzig. The German Ambassador, von Moltke, returned to Germany and advised Hitler that Pilsudski planned a "preventive war" against Germany. Whether Pilsudski actually asked Paris to undertake a "preventive war" against Germany has been the subject of an entire historical literature. Despite the favorable moment, Paris did nothing to support Poland.[50]

Secret conversations aimed at revising the eastern borders had been going on since 1931 between German, French, Belgian and Luxembourg industrialists and the semi-official newspaper *Le Temp*'s political editor. By 1933 the French representatives indicated, with the French government's approval, recognition of German interests in Silesia and the Corridor.[51] Jules Laroche, French ambassador to Poland, made similar statements — unreported in his memoir — to the German Ambassador. "Laroche," wrote Moltke, "has repeatedly broached the Corridor question to me of late... such a situation was not really compatible with the modern concept of a state territory. It was clear to anyone who took a map in his hands that the Corridor was not tenable in the long run. It was also in the interest of Poland to reach a rapprochement with Germany and he understood that this was not possible without eliminating the Corridor." The Poles had "a fear bordering on psychosis that if any negotiations were undertaken this could mean the beginning of further partitions of Poland."[52] Von Moltke judged that the time was not ripe for revisionism.[53]

On February 8, 1933, in one of the first conferences of the Hitler government, the new chancellor declared that everything had to be done to make "the German people capable of bearing arms." The German economy would be geared toward that end. It would be dangerous for Germany during that period while it rearmed when France and its eastern allies could be expected to attack.

At a meeting at General Hammerstein's home on February 3, 1933, Hitler suggested that he intended to go beyond simply reclaiming the lost German territories: "Rebuilding of the armed forces is the most important prerequisite for attaining the goal. ... How is political power to be used after it has been won? Not yet possible to tell. Perhaps — and indeed preferably — conquest of new living space in the east and ruthless Germanization of the latter."[54]

The Great Powers believed that once the Disarmament Conference broke down in December 1932 Hitler would leave the League, rearm and then demand Germany's lost territories and colonies. That he intended to seize territory in the Soviet Union occurred to few people. Hitler carefully concealed his real intentions and most Germans believed he only wanted to regain Danzig, the Corridor and Upper Silesia. His ideas about *Lebensraum* in the east only began to be taken seriously after Munich. Up to that point most German nationalists, the military and Foreign Office wanted primarily to regain their lost eastern territory without contesting Poland's right to exist as a state. Even those like Neurath contemplated the destruction of Poland only in connection with regaining the lost territories.[55]

In the spring and early summer of 1933, the revisionist campaign reached its apex in the Four Power Agreement, the first concrete and open move to revise Germany's eastern borders.

Hatched in the mind of Mussolini at Camina del Roche on March 4, the Four Power Pact linked England to Italy and turned German expansionism away from Austria, a virtual Italian dependency, to the Reich's eastern frontiers. Mussolini saw the pact and its proceedings as a *coup de théâtre*. A biographer noted: "The world now recognized the unchallenged authority of the Duce, which would certainly enable Italy to get back the unrequited colonies of 1919."[56] Mussolini told the British, French, Germans and everyone involved different tales of what the pact would accomplish. The whole episode unfolded like a set of Chinese boxes manipulated by Mussolini's deft sleight of hand.

The agreement foresaw a Great Power directory presiding over Europe's affairs. A core agreement with Italy promised Britain continental domination; and the French hoped the pact might head off German rearmament. Rumors Hitler might visit Italy and conclude an Italian-German alliance raised British interest in an arrangement with Germany.[57] Von Hassell, German ambassador to Italy, anticipated the pact's "softening up" of France.[58] Rejecting von Hassell's suggestion of German-Italian cooperation in the Danubian area, the German Foreign Office official Kopke replied: "Our chief concern is the problem of the eastern frontier. Italian policy had only heightened tensions and consolidated the Little Entente,"[59] and Foreign Minister Neurath did not want greater cooperation with Italy.[60]

Baron Aloisi spoke frankly of "revising the boundaries of the treaties," assuring French Foreign Minister Paul-Boncour they "were not directed against France."[61] The French hesitated because of commitments to their eastern allies and a preference for Italian-German hostility over Austria rather than deflecting Hitler's expansion eastward against Poland.

At Geneva, Daladier told the British that French public opinion "would resist making any sacrifices in favor of a Germany that had not honored her signature."[62]

On March 14 Mussolini promised "as bait" recognition of German
claims in the east "through elimination of the dividing Corridor."[63] Two
days before the British arrived in Rome, Mussolini secretly handed the pact's
draft to Berlin and sought their support against France, "who would then
be definitely isolated."[64]

Hitler sent his tentative agreement ("an inspired suggestion") and a few
proposals.[65] The Germans quickly saw Mussolini's casuistic diplomacy went
beyond revisionism. Berlin told von Hassell: "This is a sharp attack against
the French system of alliances, *especially against Poland* and the Little
Entente. It is more than doubtful whether France will accept this."

On March 17, Polish Foreign Minister Beck indignantly told MacDonald
and Simon he objected to Poland's affairs being decided without its consultation and consent.[66] He attacked the plan's "very dangerous clauses" as "a
mortal blow to the League" that "would be a disaster."[67] On March 25,
Beck inveighed against a four power directory "with revisionist tendency as
its real motive."[68]

Czech Foreign Minister Beneš had no brief for the agreement either: "it
aimed to break up Yugoslavia's unity by taking Dalmatia for itself and giving
Croatia to Austria and Hungary and to gain Germany's support by handing
it the Corridor through treaty revision." "Italy wished a free hand from
France for the above settlement, and then Italy would be ready to settle
her relations with France." Beneš thought that "any tampering with [its
ally] Yugoslavia would almost inevitably involve Czechoslovakia in a general
war" and "leave her in an impossibly isolated position.... This would push
her into the arms of Poland, and, as he had already told the British Ministers
confidentially, he had already declined an alliance with Poland."

Mussolini took a different tack with the British: granting Germany equal
rights would be immediately followed by a German drive to rearm, which
it was in the interests of the Great Powers to control. Mussolini pressed the
British for quick assent while the Hitler regime struggled with its internal
problems and the opportunity still existed. Later it would be too late. To
France he promised security and collaboration.[69]

Mussolini proposed that Poland receive a "guarantee of maritime, but
not territorial, outlet to the sea...."[70] The pact also threatened to stir up
a hornet's nest among their eastern allies and offered Paris cold comfort
and doubtful security. Beneš noted French psychic political fatigue: "...in
France the left parties were beginning to think the Little Entente a burden."[71]

The Little Entente and Poland closed ranks, and reportedly were "hysterical" and "doing all they could to prevent French adherence to the Pact."[72]
Patterson at Geneva reported: "You can have no idea of [the] strength of
suspicion here that the outcome of [the] Rome visit is a plot to dish [*sic*] [the]
League of Nations. M. Beneš is deeply disturbed."[73] Erskine, the British Ambassador at Warsaw agreed: "feeling is at present intense, deep-seated and
universal."[74] Beck inveighed bitterly to Ambassador Erskine that the four
powers would "decide what they wanted and then exercise pressure on the
others to accept their decisions."[75]

Titulescu, the Romanian Foreign Minister, "harangued me for an hour
against the Mussolini Pact," complained Lord Tyrrel. "I warned him," Tyrrel

declared, "that an uncompromising attitude against revisionism would not be understood by our public opinion" which "controlled our foreign policy."[76] The Polish press unanimously opposed the Pact.

Tyrrel "was having utmost difficulty in holding at bay [the] Polish Ambassador who was ringing him up day and night to ask for [an] interview."

To draw Poland into an alliance, Beneš offered a pact of "perpetual friendship" with conciliatory arbitration of problems; removal of injurious political attitudes and demilitarizing the frontier between both countries. Taken aback, Beck merely promised to consider it.[77]

Daladier now declared second thoughts about the Pact.[78] At the end of May the British Foreign Office agreed to water down the revisionist clause in the Pact.[79]

Later Paris convinced the Little Entente to sign the eviscerated pact much to the annoyance of the Poles. In his memoirs, Beneš confirmed that the Four Power Pact "was not only revisionist but also in its whole substance directed...against...the USSR."[80] A semi-official Polish newspaper at the time agreed the pact was connected "in the opinion of the average newspaper reader with the anti-Soviet campaign of certain interventionist elements in Europe."[81]

Intense national feeling against the Pact poured out in demonstrations and press attacks. A great wave of unrest seized Poland.[82] Beck complained to the French that the Pact aimed to sever Western Europe and Eastern Europe, revise the borders of Poland and push Hitler to the east. Mussolini's real aim was to draw Hitler's attention from Austria.[83]

Poland, however, held out and drew away from Beneš; and Beck cancelled his projected trip to Prague.[84] Laroche sardonically judged Beck wanted to be the "star" of a constellation, opposing the Four Power Pact, which he really only wanted to associate with but not form.[85] Pilsudski now evinced greater preoccupation with Germany and less with the USSR which Laroche believed stemmed from apprehensions Germany might stir up the Ukrainians.[86] Beck predicted that Hitler would be unable to consolidate his position for "two or three years" and therefore the moment had come to talk as Germany did not wish to risk conflict. An agreement with Germany would purportedly produce an effect sufficiently long that the problem of Poland's borders might disappear from discussions on the international level.[87]

Laroche believed that Poland also wanted to split Western from Eastern Europe, then form a bloc composed of Romania and the Baltic states where Poland had gained some prestige for resisting the Four Power Pact. This necessitated splitting up the Little Entente, "repudiating it because it did not want to allow itself to be led....In sum, it's the *farà da se* of the Polish government." France, Laroche wrote caustically, is looked upon by the Pilsudskists "with a very bad eye: France whom they have never loved and they continue to reproach for its billion in financial aid."[88]

Beck complained that Western Europe considered Poland as "an amorphous state, in some way unfinished, whom they could dispose of as they liked without too much inconvenience." The Polish government had to react vigorously against this specious idea and demonstrate Poland's strong national unity.[89]

The French poured scorn on Poland's new policy: "the Polish policy of prestige," Laroche wrote, "does not appear to have brought more than meager results till now from the practical point of view...this suffices the government to affirm the liberty of action of Poland and its brilliance in order to show that it acts in this part of Europe as a Great Power and does not desire to be in the wake nor even to be second in an alliance.... In all this there is a good deal of bluff."[90] Poland, a nation of 32 million, "proud of its past, but...ferociously patriotic, suffers from being treated at times with disdain and underestimation." In short, "a certain allure of an independent foreign policy does not displease."[91]

Hitler's calculated and bold decision to make peace on Germany's most threatened border enabled him to concentrate on consolidating power and rearmament. Some evidence exists that Pilsudski secretly contacted Hitler already in the fall of 1930 for a ten-year pact with Germany as soon as he came to power.[92] Pilsudski clearly saw the German-Polish Pact did not end Germany's conflict with Poland: "It only means that Hitler has postponed it," he told his wife. "The respite will give us time to organize our lives, but after that we must be ready to defend ourselves. We have no other alternative."[93] As Hitler was an Austrian and not an anti-Polish Prussian, Pilsudski told the French military attaché in November 1933: "I would like him to remain in power as long as possible."[94]

Pilsudski's motive for signing the German-Polish Accord on January 26, 1934, was "the uncertainty of French policy and its incessant concessions under the pressure of England and now of Italy." Pilsudski was candid: "he wanted to drag it out" but the conversations of Ambassador François-Poncet "with Hitler had decided him to hasten matters."

Laroche predicted the temptation might arise in signing the pact not only "to remove the peril, but to enter the path of greater intimacy with Germany." Hitler could not move with impunity against Austria without Polish opposition. But a Polish official expressed indifference: "we will not begin John Sobieski* again."[95] The pact also raised Poland's international self-esteem: in mid-March 1933, Beck confirmed to Laroche that henceforth Poland intended to act as a great European power.[96]

In 1934, a great change came over French diplomacy with the advent of Louis Barthou at the Quai d'Orsay. France shook off a decade of somnolence and bureaucratic decrepitude, displaying an imagination and energy not seen since the days of Poincaré and Clemenceau. Two months later Barthou confided to Titulescu on a visit to Paris his plan for a European alliance to contain Germany in an all-encompassing diplomatic arrangement. This elderly French statesman with his familiar goatee, stooped stance, odd manners and conversational style began to impress the staid European diplomatic corps and restore confidence in France through his eastern travels in the early summer of 1934. He intended to complement the Locarno Agreement with an Eastern Locarno, composed of Germany, France, Poland, the USSR and Lithuania. But neither Poland nor Germany wished to enter

---

*John Sobieski arrived with a Polish army at the gates of Vienna to defend it against besieging Turkish forces in the seventeenth century.

into a political pact with the USSR. Poland could not agree to the passage of Soviet troops across its border to aid another country — France or Czechoslovakia — a stumbling block to appear again in 1939. The Eastern Locarno Agreement of Barthou would reappear in a variety of guises in 1938 and 1939.[97]

Pilsudski's doubts persisted about French firmness on Germany's rearmament. He questioned the Soviet Union's motives for entering the League as insincere and side-stepped French efforts to patch up Polish-Czech relations. Nor did the Poles warm to Barthou's entreaties to enter multilateral agreements with Czechoslovakia and the Soviet Union, which offered few advantages and enfeebled the alliance with France, substituting a complex combination of states Poland disdained. The eastern pact threatened to transform Poland into a battleground between the Soviet Union and Germany.

A closer arrangement with Czechoslovakia might also drag Poland into the morass of Danubian affairs. Poland had reached a *modus vivendi* with Germany which joining the Eastern Pact would undermine.[98]

French and Polish interests were at cross purposes. France had less confidence in Hitler than Warsaw did, while Warsaw mistrusted the pacific intentions of the Soviet Union. General Sosnkowski, Inspector of the Army, repeated Polish dogma on the USSR to the French Military Attaché: "As for the Russian danger, it appears closer than the German threat." He predicted the Russians would throw themselves on the back of the Poles once they became involved in a conflict with the Germans.[99] A Russian guarantee, through an Eastern Locarno Pact, could turn Poland into a satellite of Moscow "or at the least of passing to a subaltern rank, which did not satisfy the two all-consuming requisites of Polish policy: security against a new partition by its two powerful neighbors and the pursuit of its policy of prestige."[100]

A glance at France's internal economic and financial situation during the 1930s is necessary at this point to investigate the influence of economics, if any, upon French foreign policy. This may be delineated into several phases: the immediate post-war inflationary era until 1924 under the left bloc, the Cartel des Gauches governments; the rightist government of Poincaré and the stabilization of the franc in 1928; and successive interim governments until 1932–1933 when French adherence to the gold standard caused severe trade deficits; the Popular Front Against Fascism era from 1935 headed by the socialist Leon Blum and the devaluation of the franc; the fall of the Popular Front in 1938 following the collapse of the second Blum government; and finally the rule of the centrist Radical-Socialists under Daladier until the outbreak of the war.

The dire 1920s inflation, a consequence of the costs of the Great War and reconstruction, ended when the conservative Poincaré government stabilized the franc through budgetary cuts and cost reductions. The franc had risen from 18 to the dollar in 1924 to 50 in 1928 before Poincaré pegged it to about 25, one-fifth of its pre-war value. From 1928 to the mid-1930s, France pursued a deflationary policy domestically and led the gold bloc (Belgium, Holland, Switzerland, Italy, Czechoslovakia and Poland) while the Anglo-

Saxon powers, Britain and the United States, abandoned gold. France's gold assets were on a par with the U.S. despite the difference in population and far exceeded those of Britain.

When the Depression struck, France had already gone through the deflationary meat-grinder of the mid-1920s and early 1930s and initially suffered less than the United States and Germany. But France's deflationary policy since the Poincaré era, based on higher interest rates and indirect taxes, struck hardest at the French working class, forcing it to pay the cost of post-war reconstruction and eroding savings and pensions. Fear of inflation frightened the French middle class into accepting deflation. Unfortunately this economic orthodoxy of burning out inflation by deflation meant higher interest rates and taxes and severe budgetary restraints, fewer new investment possibilities and jobs, social stagnation and a decade of *"gagne-petit"* (earn little).

Encouraged by monetary stabilization and the Right's deflationary policy, French industry produced more pig-iron (3.4 million tons in 1920 compared to 10.3 million in 1930), automobiles (from 40,000 to 254,000) and similar leaps in chemicals and dyestuffs, once German market domination ceased. But a decline in foreign trade after 1930 caused by France's rigid gold policy resulted in dismal production figures: the index of French industrial production fell from 140 in 1930 to 96 by 1932, below the 1913 level. But the centrist French governments of the 1930s rigidly held to the gold standard and deflationary "gagne-petit" policy until the Popular Front era in 1935.

The onset of the Depression affected France less because it depended less on trade than Britain and possessed huge gold stocks. France adamantly refused to go "off gold" or to devalue, a solution advanced by Paul Reynaud, the *bête noir* of the ultra right, costing French commerce dearly. French exports had become too expensive and French trade plummeted alarmingly by almost 60% as the figures in Table 3–1 illustrate.

Table 3–1. General Commerce of France (including reexports), 1931–1939 (in millions of francs)[101]

Year	Imports	Exports	Total	Deficit
1931	42601	30878	73479	11723
1932	30235	20035	50270	10200
1933	28794	18776	47570	10018
1934	23397	18126	41523	5271
1935	21075	15732	36807	5343
1936	25788	15745	41533	10043
1937	43961	24490	68451	19471
1938	46336	31210	77546	15126
1939*	32539	23832	56371	8707

*First nine months.

Invisible income (insurance, carrying charges, etc.) from other sources were only slightly positive and therefore do not reduce these figures greatly.[102]

Devaluation of the franc in order to shrink trade deficits and stimulate exports received support from Right and Center figures (Tardieu, Herriot, Reynaud) but was resisted by the Socialists and Communists. Unfortunately, devaluation intensified the crisis that swirled around the Popular Front, which, like the Cartel des Gauches of the 1920s, had the misfortune to come to power in the midst of a financial and economic crisis. Frightened by the municipal election returns in 1935 favoring the left Popular Front government, "a wall of capital" — like the "wall of moneybags" against Herriot in 1924 — arrayed against the Popular Front. Capital poured from France into safer harbors in America and Britain. In 1936 the Popular Front Blum government devalued the franc forcing prices down further, driving unemployment over one million.

These bare statistics do not convey the agitation of the working class during the period shortly before the Popular Front took power: seething with discontent and exhilarated by its new-found power, it engaged in unprecedented numbers of strikes in every sector of the economy, occupying the factories and throwing fear into the French upper class. The major French working class union, the CGT (Confédération Générale de Travail), Socialists and even the Communists could not control the spontaneous strikes led by communists, socialists and anarchists. France seemed to be tottering on the verge of revolution.

If France's domestic financial affairs were in disarray, French investment outside France and in the colonies do not seem too far removed. Investment abroad came to about 60%, of which 40% was inside the empire, with Teichova reporting 16 billion francs in 1930 and Marseilles 38 billion, a considerable discrepancy. After 1930, French investments abroad almost ceased and shifted instead to Europe. This raises the difficult question of business and financial influences on the Quai d'Orsay and French foreign policy.

Before the First World War France floated loans and investments estimated at thirteen to fifteen billion francs, leading Teichova to conclude that "the Quai d'Orsay was closely tied to French high finance...not only by motives of profit, but also by colonial interests and the interests of French political power." Duroselle finds this somewhat "forced" and limits possible financial influences on the Quai d'Orsay to Secretary-General Paleologue in 1920, François-Poncet and his ties to the *Comité des Forges,* and Berthelot through his brother's connection with the Banque industrielle de Chine.[103]

French financial interests in Eastern Europe and particularly Poland were considerable. French capital shifted from the lost Russian area after 1918, into Polish banks which Duroselle estimates to be fifteen billion francs in 1938, about the same as Britain. Polish industrial products — coal, steel, zinc, yarns and woolens, electrical products, crude and refined oil — were transported on French railway lines. The two billion franc Rambouillet loan to Poland came at a point when France desperately needed capital and had to borrow from Britain. These investments and loans had a sub-rosa purpose as the Director of Political Affairs, Cheveriat, noted in an important comment on October 5, 1938, that despite Poland's conduct at the time of Munich "this enormous development of our industry in Poland" will induce "the maintenance of economic and financial collaboration." He emphasized: "What may have to be subjected to revision will be, rather, the political and military ties that connect us to Poland. Thus, this would leave our collaboration a purely *economic and financial* form, infinitely more efficacious and less dangerous than that which we have affirmed to the present."[104] France would continue to maintain its economic and financial interests in Poland and would be free in the future, if it chose, to reduce its political ties to Warsaw. But, comments Duroselle, "the presence of all this French capital [in Poland] has had a great significance (*une grande portée*)."[105] In short, Poland with Beck at the helm would be free to conduct its independent, at times high-wire, personal foreign policy, but economic and financial ties to France would always prevent it from straying too far from the Western fold. Or, as Duroselle suggests, French investments translated into considerable political influence whether intended or unintended.

Historians have frequently commented that France's considerable agricultural sector — almost 50% in the inter-war period — prevented it from creating stronger political ties with its eastern European allies who were unable to export their surplus agrarian products. Although the amount under cultivation in France had decreased from its pre-war level and the number of peasants fallen — from 8,777,000 in 1906 to 7,097,000 in 1936 — it still produced the same amount of foodstuffs or slightly more and thus "tends to increase" the yield, the figures are not impressive.[106]

Table 3–2. Index of French Agricultural Production, 1910–1934

(1913 = 100)

1910–1913	92
1919–1922	77
1923–1926	90
1927–1930	99
1931–1934	105

Thus, French agriculture seems stagnant in the interwar era (see Table 3–2). Although France enjoyed a position exceeded only by Britain as an investor in the Little Entente countries, only Czechoslovakia figured on a list of its first ten trade partners and then only as tenth. France sold ten times more to Belgium and even Sweden's trade was greater than either Czechoslovakia or Poland (see Table 3–3).[107] This probably occurred because of the dearth of French capital and Poland and the Little Entente countries needed credit guarantees from France in order to purchase French exports unlike Sweden. Trade restrictions against agricultural imports worsened Poland's trade possibilities on the French market.

Some believe foreign trade during the thirties exercised little influence on foreign policy.[108] Perhaps, but recent evidence casts doubt upon this belief.

Table 3–3. French Trade with Poland, Czechoslovakia and Sweden,
1931–1939 (in millions of francs)

Year	Poland		Czechoslovakia		Sweden	
	Import	Export	Import	Export	Import	Export
1931	457	299	330	220	523	269
1932	236	322	250	161	306	140
1933	204	173	219	191	342	124
1934	177	159	190	231	321	147
1935	153	128	192	199	282	184
1936	205	142	231	264	342	194
1937	400	138	408	421	822	354
1938	446	356	300	406	651	494
1939	441	346	281	181	683	715

French Foreign Office officials were certainly aware of France's commercial
and economic decline as the March 11, 1935, worried report of its Assistant
Political Director Coulondre reveals.

> The situation is too serious for us to delude ourselves with appear-
> ances, even if we content ourselves with half-measures which would
> at once be overtaken by events. It would be best to recognise that the
> Gold Bloc does not have enough economic potential and complemen-
> tary markets to be self-sufficient.... If we are to maintain the stability
> of our currency, we must necessarily take indispensable measures for
> the protection of our economy: a further strengthening of quota ar-
> rangements, increased duties, increases in trading tax licences. Perhaps,
> thanks to a system of managed economy, we might be successful for a
> while in avoiding the worsening of our trade deficit. We cannot avoid
> the continuing reduction of the volume of trade. That is the danger.
> Little by little France will impose a closed economy on herself, as has
> happened in the case of agriculture.... We will have to close the still
> open doors and so lose our last external outlets without an anemic
> market being able to absorb our production. How therefore do we
> check the crisis, unemployment and the budget deficit.... What will
> be the fate of the capitalist system if it locks itself into this vice?[109]

In effect, Coulondre requested a further tightening of France's trade restrictions to maintain the franc's stability but perceived the calamitous effects of
such a policy.

How did France allow itself to get into this position? One suggestion
is that it occurred suddenly without warning. The problem did not appear
until March 1935; French financial specialists remained convinced to that
time of the rightness of their policy of staying "on gold" and even thought of
aiding *"le pauvre livre sterling,"* which had fallen in value.[110] But France's
monetarist illusions existed long before that. It clung to gold for political

reasons: French politicians and financial specialists feared the wrath of the French bourgeoisie if it devalued.

Having established that the Quai d'Orsay certainly knew about the problem of France's precipitate decline, the question remains: what influence did this have on the conduct of foreign policy and how did the French leaders act upon it. The French government's passive acceptance of leadership by "the English governess" and its appeasement policy indicates that Britain now held the whip hand. Without British financial support, the French government simply would not have had enough money to pay for rearmament. If loans from London were to be forthcoming, France would have to accept British appeasement policy.

On May 21, 1935, the first offensive against the franc occurred, prompted by fears aroused by municipal election returns and the growing power of the left. The newspapers described the event as a warning shot of capital across the bow of the Flandin government. Belgium's desertion from the gold bloc and decision to devalue contributed to the crisis. In ten days 6.3 billion francs fled abroad, primarily to Britain and the United States. Pre-warnings came from Mönick, financial attaché in London, that unless they devalued "the recovery of our internal economy depends less on ourselves than the foreigner." The tocsin of French capital's alarm over a Popular Front victory dinned ever louder: from May 1935 to June 1936, eleven to thirteen billion francs fled France pushing it towards greater dependence on Britain and the United States.

Collapsing French trade and money bleeding from France's financial arteries caused such a dearth of capital that first the hapless socialist Blum, then later the centrist Daladier had to go hat in hand to borrow money from London. Lamenting this sorry state of affairs, Lacroix, now minister at Prague, wrote on December 28, 1938, paraphrasing a Czech article: "The collapse of the French system does not date from the events of September (i.e., Munich). Its origin is the fact that *France neglected too much the economic side of the struggle for influence* [Duroselle's emphasis]."[111]

French appeasement of Hitler, which so unsettled Poland and France's Eastern European allies, stemmed in good part from a precipitate decline in France's trade and financial position. London was unsympathetic to France's financial problem and extended a loan for about four billion francs only after France agreed in January 1937 to refrain from requesting concessions in the forthcoming tariff talks. On January 20 Eden met Blum and proposed joint negotiations with the Germans to help them and other states in economic and financial distress but only if "economic collaboration and financial appeasement went hand in hand." The negotiations concerned Schacht's obtaining raw materials and capital for German industry, about which we will hear later.

Blum decided against restricting capital flight and currency speculation that would "create a contradiction between our policy which seeks a community of action with the great Anglo-Saxon nations and the signing of a monetary agreement aimed at restoring activity and liberty to international trade." Thus began French subservience to the "English governess." The four billion francs quickly vanished and France's financial difficulties uncoiled with frightening swiftness. Responding to British requests, Vincent Auriol, the French Finance Minister, made promises to liberalize its economy through free circulation of gold, reduction of public works, and numerous changes that opened France to British exports.

The third devaluation in May 1938 abandoned the franc's base in gold and adopted the pound sterling or the "Franco-Sterling" rate. French indebtedness and the British refusal to financially support either the franc or France's rearmament played a role in Blum's "pause" in his program of New Deal-like social reforms.[112]

Blum had already received advice from the Bank of France to establish currency controls which he refused to do in an interview with Rueff, the Director of the *Mouvement des Fonds,* on February 12, 1937, "not because of the domestic consequences — they do not frighten me — but because they will have the fatal effect of straining the ties which unite us to the Anglo-Saxon democracies which are essential to the coherent development of our foreign policy."[113] Blum felt sufficiently assured to make his decision the following day for a "pause" in social reforms.

The effects of this appeared first in French policy toward Spain: at British behest, Blum closed the border to all weapons and planes going to the beleaguered Spanish Republic fighting the Franco Nationalists and their German and Italian supporters. Efforts to enlist Soviet aid terminated to avoid upsetting Baldwin; and British ambassador Phipps, to Soviet astonishment, openly interfered in France's internal affairs. Blum's failure to immediately push through devaluation and controls over capital exports, when the strike movement sufficiently intimidated the Radicals in Parliament, and his dilatory actions and vague and imprecise strategy more than anything else caused the fall of the Popular Front.

By December 1937 the French managed to pay off the entire British loan of forty million pounds sterling or six billion francs, which Bonnet called "a heavy mortgage weighing on our finances."[114] Daladier, the representative of the French small bourgeoisie, came to power and dealt the French strike movement a body blow. When the strikers occupied the huge Renault automobile plant in November 1938, Daladier used force to drive them out. The general strike that followed fizzled out and several million workers left the General Confederation of Labor in dismay.

The expatriated francs trickled back, first on July 10, 1937, $10 million or 300 million francs on the steamship Normandy. By the end of six months $12 million had returned to France.[115] The belated devaluation of September 1936 occurred too late to do any good against prices already driven higher by the counter-strike of the employers against the Popular Front reforms. The *Patronat* refused to invest in new infrastructure and experimentation, ignored new demand and resisted increased production, maintaining profits through higher prices. The strike of capital and the seepage of money abroad continued until Blum's departure. His belated attempt during the brief second Blum government in 1938 to repair the damage by introducing currency controls, a tax on capital and the nationalization of key industries passed the lower Chamber but died in the conservative-dominated Senate.[116]

The centrist governments that followed the fall of the Popular Front in 1937 carried out two more devaluations and reinstalled labor discipline by crushing strikes and curtailing reforms but the years lost in the social struggle cost it dearly in armament production. It was the "wall of capital" and the spiteful strike against social and economic reforms by the *Patronat* class, which feared bolshevism first and Hitler only second or not at all, that contributed to France's defeat and not the CGT and the working class as is sometimes mistakenly claimed.[117]

In summary, France's inability to import more from Poland and the other Eastern European states can be traced to a variety of intertwining causes among which were a collapsing international trade market, a rigid outdated monitarist system, failure to carry out a timely devaluation hobbling its export trade and an undynamic and static agriculture. By 1936 France had no more money to support trade or give to Poland and it was fast degenerating to a middle-level power.

After the Popular Front departed, capital gradually returned to France, productivity rose and by 1938 the factories turned out larger quantities of armaments. By then France began to approach a war footing similar to Germany, but still lagged behind. Politically, the country and especially its leaders remained greatly divided between the appeasement-minded *mous* (softs), *demi-durs* (semi-hards), realists (who accepted the inevitable) and *durs* (hards). In the government only Georges Mandel, Paul Reynaud and Champetier de Ribes fought against further appeasement of Hitler. Among the Radicals, Jean Zay, who like Mandel paid later with his life, Cesar Campinchi and Pierre Cot remained opposed to Munich; and the Socialists voted against the Munich Agreement on December 24–25, 1938, by more than a two to one majority.[118]

A similar struggle was being fought inside Poland. The Polish government's internal struggle against the Polish left closely paralleled its support of fascism. Beck commented to Foreign Minister Neurath about the Ethiopian crisis on October 11, 1935, in Geneva: "the forces of the Second and Third International [in the Italian and Abyssinian crisis] are acting in common and trying to master the conflict." Beck thought an Italian defeat dangerous and would aid the Third International.[119]

By 1934 the number of political prisoners mounted from five thousand to sixteen thousand, many from the Polish Socialist Party and Polish Communist Party and subjected to beatings and torture.[120]

After the March 5, 1933, Comintern directive paving the way for a joint collaboration with the Second International against fascism, the latter's internal secretariat two days later called for a common front against fascism in Germany and the Pilsudski regime.

The PPS (Polish Socialist Party) strongly resisted a KPP/PPS united front during its April 1933 congress, but cooperation from below occurred by the workers who ignored these differences among their leaders. At the 1934 PPS congress, supporters of a united front strategy defected to form a Workers' Socialist Party.[121] Differences gradually disappeared only after the June 1935 Seventh Comintern Congress and negotiations on June 3–4 agreed to a series of political strikes beginning on June 19.[122] Strike actions spread in

Poland between 1930 and 1935 provoked by the misery of the workers and peasantry; and in the 1933 Lodz textile strike, workers united in the factories over the heads of the PPS trade union bureaucracy.[123] In 1934, the Pilsudskists retaliated through a government tolerated or patronized paramilitary group committing violence against the left.[124]

French efforts to patch up the Polish-Czech family quarrel down to 1939 bore little fruit. Frictions dated back to the Austro-Hungarian monarchy and the dislike of Pilsudski and Beck for Beneš's Francophile and Russophile sentiments, but a major problem was the Czech seizure of Teschen in 1920.

In 1918 Pilsudski had sent emissaries to Prague with an offer of friendship. The Czechs claimed the largely Polish-populated Teschen region on historical and economic grounds and the Poles on demographic grounds, presenting unforeseen problems. The Czechs had refused Pilsudski's earlier request for a joint commission and, on January 23, 1919, invaded the region, killing some Polish garrison soldiers. "Pilsudski's hand extended in friendship was left suspended in mid-air."[125] In 1920 during Poland's struggle against the Red Army, the Czechs obtained a decision from the Allied Council annexing the region without a plebescite. The Czechoslovak government declared neutrality on August 7, 1920, and irritated the Poles by preventing arms deliveries. In contrast, the Hungarian government in early May 1920 offered military help against the Bolsheviks, a share in French business options and support against Czechoslovakia.

With some animus Ambassador Laroche confirmed this to Paris: Pilsudski's "rancor" over the munitions transit problem, the role "of Beneš at Geneva and the prestige he enjoys in Europe" and "the personal jealousy of Marshal Pilsudski and Beck, plays a considerable role in their attitude toward Czechoslovakia."[126]

Though irritated by Beck's frequent journeys to Berlin and assiduous courting of Hitler, the French questioned how much influence Beck's anti-Czech policy had in Poland, and thought it might be put down as Beck's personal policy with little resonance in the leadership or the country.[127]

Others saw Beck as more than a minor nuisance. Titulescu told the French: "While M. Beck will be at foreign affairs, Poland is lost for us and will make the worst errors." He urged the French to complete the Franco-Russian Alliance before Germany is completely ready.[128]

Most parties favored reconciliation with Czechoslovakia, but the government party did not like the Czechs. Laroche believed Polish public opinion to be probably divided on the Czechs.[129]

Polish anti-Czech feeling, Grzybowski, the Polish Ambassador at Prague, suggested, would terminate once the Czechs handed over the Teschen district to Poland. Beneš and the Prague government, accordingly, recommended the dispute to a League or some other arbitration tribunal, but the Polish government refused.[130] There the subject lay until the Munich crisis of 1938.

Śmigły-Rydz attacked Beck's policies and asked for a change in government policy, in effect, a change of direction in the Ministry of Foreign Affairs, but Moscicki thought Beck's removal might have political repercussions and he retained his post in the new government.

In the French view Beck tried to regain his prestige by promoting immigration of Jews to Africa to open jobs for Poles in the professions, commerce and artisanry.[131] In German imperialist circles, Germany and Poland were considered competitors for African colonial possessions and in the Baltic as "late-arrived and mal-provided states." *Ostland*, a German review, thought Poland saw Germany as paving the way for future colonial changes and "hope[d] that Germany will forget in far away enterprises the questions of Upper Silesia and Poznan (Posen)." Unless Poland agreed to a satellite dependence on Germany, it might clash with Germany in the Baltic, a German lake.[132]

The agreements between Poland and its neighbors the USSR and Germany had succeeded, in the historian Piotr Wandycz's apt words, in prying open the pincer that threatened Poland. In early February 1935 during a hunting trip in Bialowieza, Göring, with precise instructions from Hitler, probed for a military agreement with Poland to attack the Soviet Union. Pilsudski registered "surprise" (*hat gestutzt*) and rejected Göring's proposal: because "they would have to sleep with their guns at their sides." The Polish historian Wojciechowski believes that Pilsudski left the door open for further discussions. Hitler agreed to a "rounding off" of Lithuanian territory in favor of Poland and urged it to expand into the Ukraine while Germany received compensation with Pomerania and Danzig.[133]

The German-Polish agreement of 1934 vitiated the value of the Polish alliance for France and led to the Franco-Soviet Alliance of June 1935, irritating both Warsaw and Berlin. Göring told the Poles that the Franco-Soviet treaty could provoke Germany into denouncing the Treaty of Locarno.[134] Berlin and Warsaw believed the Czechs stirred up the Ukrainians and had prepared secret air bases in Czechoslovakia for Soviet planes and reinforcements, bringing the Communists into Central Europe. The advent of the Popular Front government in France in 1935 in an anti-fascist front of the Communists, socialists and center parties convinced the Pilsudski regime France was the servant of Moscow in Europe.

Relations with France reached their lowest point between 1934 and 1936. Mühlstein, the Polish chargé in Paris, described Poland's repute in France as "very bad." Herriot, the left and the French press were hostile to Poland and Beck, and skeptical of Polish initiatives in Geneva.[135] The Polish Alliance hung by a thread, and Szembek thought that the French might even denounce it. Beck scoffed that this "would be equivalent to suicide on the part of France."[136] Three years later in March 1938, Mühlstein again pessimistically predicted the end of the alliance with France.[137] But the action of Beck in offering Poland's support to France — perhaps duplicitously — at the moment of Hitler's gamble to occupy the Rhineland, demonstrated continuing Polish fidelity to the tottering alliance.[138] Beck believed that the Rhineland occupation did not involve a *casus foederis* but nevertheless pledged Poland's loyalty to France.[139] Promises of a financial loan to Poland by Flandin also figured into the equation of Polish support in the Rhineland affair.

But more pressing matters revived the alliance: the Polish army needed new weapons which could only be financed through French credits. But

Polish finances were shaky and in 1936 Colonel Koc, the head of the state bank, revealed Poland was one step from insolvency.[140]

Germany owed Poland forty million złotys in railway fees for transportation across the Corridor which it could not collect, although Hitler offered instead to pay with goods. Germany was then in the midst of its own currency crisis.

The Bank of England's Governor, Montagu Norman, offered a four million pound loan, encouraging Poland to join the sterling-bloc.[141] But the British loan never materialized. The choice of loaner narrowed down to France, where Beck's opportunistic pro-fascist policy enjoyed little favor.

But France could hardly refuse the Polish request without dire repercussions; Mühlstein concluded that the French would eventually concede the loan, "but with the utmost contempt."[142]

The rehabilitation of Franco-Polish relations coincided with General Gamelin's visit to Poland August 12–16, 1936, initiated by Premier Blum as a direct military contact with Marshal Śmigły-Rydz, circumventing French Ambassador Noël. However, it did not bear fruit. Gamelin claims in his memoirs he could not ascertain, during his visit, why Noël lacked confidence in Beck.[143] Anticipating French intentions, Beck mended fences with Śmigły-Rydz, a partisan of the French alliance.[144] To prevent the French from exploiting their differences, Beck and Śmigły-Rydz agreed that no support would be given to Czechoslovakia, and to confine the discussion to military matters.[145]

The French tried once again to rid themselves of Beck during Śmigły-Rydz's visit to France. Notwithstanding the warm welcome and lavish reception at Rambouillet Palace with Blum, Gamelin, Polish ambassador Łukasiewicz and Delbos present, the French effort failed.[146] Had they been less timorous and categorically insisted upon Beck's removal, Śmigły-Rydz might have acquiesced.[147] Blum and Delbos single-mindedly concentrated upon gaining Polish support against Hitler. Śmigły-Rydz deftly avoided any commitment to Czechoslovakia — Beneš had asked for French mediation efforts — though he promised not to use force to regain Polish territory.[148] Two years later in 1938 Poland issued an ultimatum to Czechoslovakia at the height of the Czech crisis. The Poles received their loan without significant concessions and seemed surprised at the French need for Poland's support. Łukasiewicz told Szembek, with tongue in cheek cynicism, the price of the French loan was Śmigły-Rydz's visit.[149]

At Rambouillet the French heard that Beck had to be retained "to be on good terms with Germany...to rid ourselves of him would risk giving the appearance of desiring to break with Germany."[150]

The Rambouillet Agreement gave the Poles reassurance against Hitler, and the French a positive Polish ally against Germany rather than having to rely upon the Soviet Union in whom, despite the 1935 Franco-Soviet Alliance, they had little confidence for a variety of reasons (fear of bolshevism, uncertainty over Stalin's reliability). Numerous Soviet attempts between 1935 and 1937 to broaden their alliance met with French stalling, notable exceptions being Blum and Pierre Cott, the French Minister for Air.[151]

The 2.5 million franc loan had strings attached: Polish armament had to come from French factories. While a victory for Beck and his policy, no understanding occurred on the important question of French military support immediately following a German attack on Poland. Why this occurred is incomprehensible. Overweening Polish military confidence played a role and also the Poles accepted verbal assurances of military support after receiving sizeable financial and military credits. But Polish policy toward Czechoslovakia remained unfriendly and the French did not trust Poland in general.

The internal social crisis which assailed the Popular Front Government during the entire period of its existence and the possibility of revolutionary disturbances in France exerted pressure upon Blum and Delbos to settle the problem of Polish support against Hitler. At the Hossbach meeting in 1937, Hitler stated his intention to exploit the outbreak of civil conflict in France to move against Austria or Czechoslovakia.

Poland's deleterious internal situation necessitated the infusion of fresh foreign capital to stabilize the threatened złoty and avoid a financial debacle. With the peasantry and working class disaffected and its leaders either imprisoned or in exile, the intelligentsia alienated, and the minorities sullen, only the aristocracy and business class, the military and certain bureaucratic segments could be counted on for support. A stagnating economy in such circumstances provided a dangerous crucible for social conflagration. When the Polish leaders inside their stone citadels heard demonstrators singing the "Internationale" in the streets of Warsaw, it must have sounded like the tolling bell of social revolution.[152]

The shadow of war forced Poland to devote over 35% of its national budget to armaments; pressure on the złoty mounted and financial crisis again hovered over the Polish government.

The French loan and Noël's requirement that Polish weaponry come from French factories had a checkered history. The two billion franc loan was to be disbursed at 500 million francs over a four-year period at 5 to 6.5% interest, 800 million for the purchase of weaponry in French plants — although not set forth in the terms of agreement — and 200 million assigned to military production. The remainder went to sundry projects like the Katowice-Gdynia railway.[153] But Blum's devaluation of the franc forced a renegotiation to 2.6 billion francs through a Delbos-Łukasiewicz agreement.[154] The upshot of all this was that "800 million francs in financial credits contributed substantially to the strength of the złoty and was instrumental in building up a degree of confidence in Poland's finances."[155] The actual payment amounted to between 130 and 200 million francs in war material and the building of the war industry and meant a jolt for the Polish economy. The French press initially exulted over the result as a triumph for French diplomacy.[156] Once Śmigły-Rydz left, reality set in with the realization that there would be little change in Poland's attitude.[157]

The Anschluss crisis over Austria brought French relations with Poland to a head. On March 8 Noël tried without much success to bridge the Polish-Czech feud. The French government, Noël told Szembek, discounted the

League and the pacifist-inclined Czech Agrarian Party as unable to resist German demands. The Polish-Czech quarrel "from the psychological point of view" created uncertainty and disharmony and encouraged German aggression. Szembek argued that the Prague government was a vast network of cells dominated by Moscow and directed a continuous barrage of anti-Polish propaganda from outside of Poland. Noël replied that France would fulfill its engagements toward Czechoslovakia in the event of a German aggression.[158]

In the wake of the Anschluss uproar, Poland moved against little Lithuania which had the temerity to declare Wilno (Wilna, Pol. or Vilnius, Lith.) — seized in 1921 by the Poles — its capital in its new constitution a few months before. Mediation efforts by the French and British persuaded the Lithuanians to reestablish diplomatic relations. Beck later explained this to the Romanian Foreign Minister, Gafencu, as a clever move to avert further expansion of German power "to the Baltic states had I not hastened to tighten the bonds between Poland and Lithuania" in the face of flaccid Western policy.[159] In Paris and other European capitals, suspicions circulated that Poland had become a secret ally of Hitler.

The French entertained few illusions about Poland after Łukasiewicz, the Polish ambassador, on May 22, 1938, flatly told Bonnet that if France moved against Germany in defense of Czechoslovakia: "We shall not move." Łukasiewicz also told an incredulous Bonnet that Poland would oppose any attempt by Soviet forces to aid Czechoslovakia if it were attacked by Germany. Łukasiewicz reminded him that Poland did not have to support France if it became engaged in a struggle over Czechoslovakia. On June 3 Śmigły-Rydz confirmed this to Noël. Worse still, Daladier told Suritz, the Soviet ambassador to Paris: "Not only can we not count on Polish support but we have no faith that Poland will not strike [us] in the back."[160] In response to a query of Litvinov as to France's response if Poland attacked Czechoslovakia, Bonnet, after some evasion, replied that France would consider itself relieved of any obligations toward Poland under the Franco-Polish alliance.[161] Poland's attitude during the Czechoslovak crisis was not forgotten and in fact after Poland entered the Western camp General Gamelin, the French commander, reminded General Kasprzycki of it during military negotiations the following year. One wonders whether the memory of Poland's divisive behavior as viewed by Paris and London contributed to the failure to attack the Germans with greater forces in the west once war broke out in 1939.

Only the Soviet Union remained friendly to Czechoslovakia, but Soviet aid would occur, according to the terms of the Soviet-Czechoslovak treaty, only if the French aided Czechoslovakia first. Whether Soviet aid to the Czechs would have been forthcoming in 1938 is unknown and, in general, Western historians have been skeptical.[162] The Soviets, however, partially mobilized "massive" forces of up to sixty infantry divisions, sixteen cavalry divisions, three tank corps, twenty-two tank brigades and seventeen air brigades along the Polish and Romanian frontiers.[163] The Czechs now requested the Soviets to threaten Poland with the denunciation of the 1932 Soviet-Polish non-aggression pact which they dutifully did.[164] But a recent historical investigation blames the French, not the Soviets, for avoiding joint military staff talks or a French-British-Soviet alliance.[165]

Before and during Munich, Poland and Hungary cooperated in preparing an uprising in Ruthenia, the tail-end province of Czechoslovakia, to create a common border, but fearing Hitler, Regent Horthy of Hungary hesitated against taking independent action. Beck vacillated against recognizing Hungarian control of Slovakia, harboring ambitions of his own to exercise a Polish protectorate and dominate Southeastern Europe. But Hitler also had plans for the Slovak region and had no wish to establish Polish control there.

Miffed at not being invited to Munich, Beck told the other Polish leaders at a conference on September 30 that the moment had come to regain the Teschen district from the Czechs.[166] They agreed to present an ultimatum to Prague, moving to force if necessary.

Some Poles had deep reservations about an ultimatum, but Beck's opinion won out. Encouraged behind the scenes by Mandel — who was threatening to resign from the cabinet — and Reynaud, Beneš at first decided to fight and began mobilizing Czech forces, and a conflict between Poland and Czechoslovakia almost occurred.[167] Germany then would doubtless have attacked Czechoslovakia and the Western Powers would have intervened on the Czech side or maintained their Munich posture of disinterest. For a perilous moment war could have broken out — over Teschen — a year earlier. But the French advised Beneš that the moment was untimely and to yield to the Polish demands.[168] Noël believed that the Polish leadership was split between moderates and hard-liners and advised ceding Teschen to Poland to undermine the hardliners.[169] Through contacts with Witos, the Polish Peasant Party leader exiled in Prague, Beneš prompted by Paris offered to settle the Teschen dispute — too late — in exchange for an improved Polish-Czech alliance. Beneš yielded to the Polish ultimatum at the height of the Sudetenland crisis. Polish troops entered the Teschen district and also seized some important Czech mines and factories essential to the Czech economy and the important rail juncture at Oderberg (Bohumin) to which Hitler feigned disinterest.[170] This action later brought Beck and Poland much condemnation.[171] For Teschen, Beck and the Pilsudski epigone opened the path to Poland's own destruction; it was an immense error for which Poland paid dearly.

Beck egged Hungary into annexing the tail end of Czechoslovakia, the Ukrainian-populated Sub-Carpathian Ukraine, giving Poland and Hungary a common border. He also conducted an "Intermarium" policy as part of his policy of prestige by tirelessly visiting the capitals of Scandinavia, the Baltic countries, the Balkans, Turkey and Italy to build a "Third Europe" of neutrals. But these small states, strung out like beads on a string from northern Europe to the Black Sea with few common interests except neutrality, could not conceivably provide Poland any measure of support.[172]

Pilsudski and Beck's dogmatic belief that Czechoslovakia was doomed and would collapse under German pressure led them to avoid any commitments toward that country, a much discussed policy both condemned and defended. In retrospect, each country failed to unite against a common danger and thought the German revisionist thrust would strike its neighbor, and hoped to avoid a similar fate by not antagonizing Hitler. Beneš later made other offers and there were intermediary offers to solve the Polish and Czech differences by numerous French leaders (Barthou, Laval, Gamelin, Delbos, Bonnet) which Pilsudski and Beck repeatedly rejected.

On October 24 a great change took place in Poland's relations with Germany: Ribbentrop made demands for a "general settlement" (*Gesamtlösung*) to Ambassador Lipski, the Polish ambassador to Berlin, that included the return of Danzig to Germany and an extra-territorial line through the corridor to East Prussia.[173] Hitler repeated these demands to Beck in Berlin on January 5, 1939, papered over with plummy offers of future colonial gifts, territories in the east and a joint crusade against the Soviet Union. Taken aback, Beck later told Ribbentrop he was now "pessimistic" for the first time about Poland's relations with Germany. Realizing that an outright refusal would only irritate Hitler, he opted for a compromise: a Polish-German condominium over Danzig and a non-extraterritorial connection with East Prussia. A final visit to Warsaw by Ribbentrop on January 25, and a tense conference, failed to budge Beck. The Poles "were more stubborn than the Czechs," Ribbentrop reported to Hitler. "Furious with the Germans," Beck decided to tighten his relations with Britain and France.[174]

Even at this late date, Beck encouraged Slovak separatism and worked to make Slovakia either a Polish protectorate, a Hungarian dependency or a joint Polish-Hungarian autonomous condominium. In the end, the Slovaks, after some hesitancy, opted for an independent course.[175]

On October 25, 1938, one day after Lipski's fateful encounter with Ribbentrop, Beck met with Moltke whom he regaled with the historical argument that the Sub-Carpathian region of Czechoslovakia should never have been granted to Czechoslovakia, "an absurdity... traceable to Beneš's Russophile tendencies." It was unreasonable economically, politically and geographically. With "a disdainful gesture" he dismissed Moltke's apprehensions of a potential Ukrainian nationalist "center of unrest" (*unruheherde*) there — by then Hitler had decided against a common border strengthening Poland — and denied working for a common border with Hungary.[176] In reality, Beck ardently pursued his obsession with a Polish-Hungarian common border in Berlin, Budapest and Bucharest.

French feelings toward Beck and his policy had reached the thin edge of patience after Munich, and Noël, in a 14-page summary of Franco-Polish relations, asked for a complete reexamination of the French alliance with Poland in light of Beck's persistently unfriendly behavior. "We cannot," he wrote, "indefinitely remain in the position of an ally who is compelled from one day to the other to take up arms in the aid of partners, but while waiting for such an occasion to arise finds that the latter are almost always in the camp of its opponents, whatever they happen to be."[177]

Other voices called for dropping or modifying the Polish alliance. Coulondre, French ambassador at Moscow, pointed out the difficulty of maintaining alliances with both Poland and the Soviet Union. "It is probable that our alliance with Poland had appeared secondary to our agreements with Russia. The Polish woods have masked the Russian forest. ... I told Georges Bonnet it is a 'political contradiction' (*contrasens politique*) to have eastern alliances which contradict one another and in my opinion the time has come to align Poland in a position of being for or against."[178] Alexis Leger, Director of the Political Department at the Quai d'Orsay, and Beck displayed mutual disdain for one another. Bonnet, like all the Munichois defeatists, also wanted to reduce France's liabilities in the east and encourage Hitler's expansion there rather than toward France and was ready to scrap both the Polish and possibly the Soviet alliance altogether. Mandel and other anti-defeatist members of the French government resisted this defeatism.

Some Poles like the clear-eyed Polish chargé, Mühlstein, perceived the havoc created by Beck's policy and believed that Poland's attitude during the Sudeten affair had been "bad and disagreeable." He thought Poland should have offered to act as a mediator and told the Germans that if they did not accept certain conditions, Poland should then have joined the allies. Mühlstein told Szembek: "We have made a mess of our position in France from top to bottom and the Franco-Polish alliance has ceased to exist."[179] Others told him that the French public believed Poland had entered the German camp.

When Ribbentrop arrived in Paris to sign the December 6, 1938, German-French Treaty of Non-Aggression, Bonnet told him that Germany would have its long sought "free hand in the east." Bonnet confirmed this to Łukasiewicz, who wrote on December 17: "Ribbentrop received a French promise not to oppose German economic expansion in the Danube basin nor could Ribbentrop have received the impression that [German] political expansion in the same region would encounter serious French resistance."[180] According to the anti-Munichois journalist Genevieve Tabouis, when Ribbentrop asked for the free hand in the east, Bonnet "managed to murmur: '...not...just now.'" More on the mark probably was Łukasiewicz's interpretation as an attempt by Paris to reestablish the equilibrium between France and Germany upset by the Munich conference. But the December 6 conference in his opinion had accomplished little: "all attempts by France to arrange appeasement with Germany on a wide European basis...have suffered complete failure."[181] Despite later denials, Bonnet probably gave Ribbentrop some sort of impression that the guarantee of Czechoslovakia by the Western Powers would not be exercised, giving Hitler a green light to seize the remainder of that country.

Already in July 1938, the Poles noticed increased British economic activity in Danubian and Southeastern Europe — about which we shall comment in detail later — particularly in Turkey, Hungary and Greece, which had "without doubt an anti-German character," and had begun "to include Poland in its policy of encircling the Third Reich."* Szembek observed: "In London they show great interest in the Polish market," particularly in electrical works and armaments "not for any anti-French reason but are rather inspired by the desire to replace France — which is breathing its last gasp." Ambassador Raczynski in London received a visit from Sir George Bowle, a financier and representative of English economic circles, "who sounded

---

*On the British encirclement of Germany, see chapter 14.

him on the possibility of replacing French capital by English capital for the financing of our armaments."[182]

Hitherto, Beck's policy of balance inherited from Pilsudski has been examined by historians almost exclusively from the political and diplomatic viewpoint with almost no attention given to economic considerations. By 1926 Pilsudski made his peace with the Polish landowner class after placing a wreath on the grave of Prince Stanislaw at Nieświez, the Radziwiłł family estate. By then his socialist ideals and baggage had long since been abandoned and he became increasingly a kind of supra-national figure. His federalist aspirations for a Poland in league with other states were largely unrealized. Colonel Beck undertook to do this primarily by gaining Teschen and the za Olza district, a region Poland had at least a right to on ethnic grounds. He had correctly concluded the Western Powers would not fight to preserve Czechoslovakia and sought to gain Slovakia — minus the Magyar-populated southern Slovak region — as a protectorate or through some form of condominium with Hungary. Knowing Beck's territorial ambitions, Hitler proposed a condominium for Slovakia as a bribe to Beck during their meeting on January 6, 1939.

Czechoslovakia was the heart of the Little Entente, linking Romania and Yugoslavia against Hungary. Once it had been destroyed, Poland thought to replace it with a new constellation of powers linking Romania and Hungary with Poland at its core. Czechoslovakia was also an important commercial and economic competitor of Germany in Southeastern Europe and the Balkans. Czech industry supplied Eastern Europe with weapons, precision instruments, manufactures, and its financial and banking interests and extensive ties to Western European financial institutions had far reaching commercial and business ganglia in Southeastern Europe and the Balkans. The small but highly efficient and modern Czechoslovak army supplied with weaponry from the Czech Škoda works was formidable and not surprisingly Hitler marvelled at the rich booty of weaponry and military stocks that fell into his hands when he seized control of that country. Karel Sidor and other Slovak nationalists stoked Beck's hopes for Polish control of Slovakia through a political union. Thus both Germany and Poland stood to gain territorially and economically by the fall of Czechoslovakia.

The duplicitous conduct of the Great Powers themselves in grabbing colonial territories through secret treaties — cloaked as mandates — in the Middle East and Africa, or as the Fascist Powers did (Austria and Czechoslovakia), provided bad examples to Poland and the smaller powers. Therefore, the smaller powers had few compunctions about acquiring territory of other peoples. Minority agreements were often not honored and even resented and few of the minorities received autonomous rights.

In hindsight, given Poland's parlous post-war economic and financial situation and its geographic location, inevitably it gravitated toward either France or Germany and became albeit unwillingly a dependent of either — a Soviet option, given its fiercely anti-Russian mentality, being excluded. To avoid a German dependency, which meant an attack on the Soviet Union, only a close relationship with neighboring Czechoslovakia, some kind of bilateral alliance, could create a barrier against Germany. A Czech-Polish alliance within a collective framework of states that included the Western Powers associated in some way with the USSR might have confronted Hitler with a formidable combination of states. It was the only possibility of survival for both Czechoslovakia and Poland.

The determination of the Great Powers to appease Germany at the expense of the small Eastern European powers encouraged the dog-eat-dog atmosphere in which both Czechoslovakia and Poland directed German expansion against each other.[183]

To avoid a fourth partition, Poland needed the support of at least one major power. Britain had little interest in that burden and in fact even told the French as early as 1926 that it would not support France in a war involving Poland. Only France held a tenuous interest in containing German expansion in the east, but after the abortive Four Power Pact and the resultant signature of the German-Polish Pact of January 26, 1934, and continued frictions between Paris and Warsaw, French support seemed uncertain and indeed fraught with danger. Pilsudski noted the difficulty of conducting a policy of detente with both Germany and the USSR: "Having these two pacts, we are straddling two stools. This cannot last long. We have to know from which stool we will tumble first and when that will be."[184]

Polish support of Italy and Germany in the League and its role during the Czechoslovak crisis in 1938 made it increasingly a German camp follower. By massing two hundred thousand Polish troops on Czechoslovakia's border preparatory to invading the Teschen region, Poland facilitated the collapse of Czechoslovakia. "Every Polish division on Czechoslovakia's border was equal to one German division," Hitler declared with satisfaction. The Polish attitude had been "decisive" during the Munich affair, Beck later boasted to his subordinates, gratified by his clever policy and flattered by Hitler's need for Polish support.

In relations with the French, the specter of the Soviet Union played a major role, Beck notes in his memoirs: "... the essential element which created differences between Polish policy and French policy was not the German question but, invariably, the manner of viewing the Russian problem."[185] With Britain there would be no such problem since in Chamberlain, Halifax and the British leaders, Beck would find kindred souls in their suspicions of the Soviet Union and anti-communist outlook. Daladier and Bonnet equally mistrusted the Soviets, constrained only by the need for the traditional Russian alliance against Germany.

What are we to make of Poland's recent history in the light of its tragic defeat and occupation by Germany? Certainly the pre-war Pilsudskist government and its crypto-fascist leadership — a "gang" Seton-Watson repeatedly calls it — is to be condemned for its harsh treatment of the minorities and the opposition, as even Pilsudski's hagiographic biographer admits. Poland demanded colonies in Africa for the usual reasons: raw materials, prestige and immigration. The Great Powers had done this for decades, it may be argued, thus Poland was doing no worse. But this is a shabby argument. Poland's idiosyncratic pursuit of a policy of "prestige" and "greatness" can only be attributed to its need to free itself from Western financial and economic tutelage. The policy of "balance" failed and Beck had to throw himself into the arms of the West to save himself from Hitler and hastily accepted a British and French guarantee.[186] Beck hid the collapse of his policy of "balance" from the British and French until the last moment when he had to admit that it lay in shambles to Erskine, the British Ambassador.

The more armed and assertive Hitler became, the more Beck clung to Hitler's mantle, continuing the policy of "balance" perhaps in the mistaken belief that through a German-dominated continent he would enhance Poland's status and prestige and finally rid Poland of French dependence. That Hitler might one day reclaim Germany's lost territories in Poland itself, and that a Poland barring his way to the Ukraine would no longer be of interest to him once it balked at a fight alongside Germany against the Soviet Union — all this receded before Beck's hubris. This probably was his supreme folly. Hitler had taken his measure, flattered and sedulously seduced him with talk of equality and friendship. Though favoring the French alliance, Śmigły-Rydz and the other Pilsudskist leaders went along with Beck's Germanophile policy.

A particularly grave mistake made by Beck and the Polish leaders was their belief that Hitler was bluffing particularly after the British guarantee of Poland's sovereignty in March 1939. This made the Poles unduly obdurate according to some historians, triggering the war; others believe that Poland had done little more than defend its own interests which it intended to do anyway — with or without the British guarantee. But in believing with almost mulish obstinacy that Hitler was perpetrating still another bluff, down almost to the German invasion and that Poland would force him to retreat, Beck and other Polish leaders made a serious miscalculation, compounded by a purblind belief in the ability of the Polish army to repel a German attack.

Pilsudski's policy of "balance" had become a sanctified dogma and Beck undoubtedly hung on to it too long. Poland's military unpreparedness and its rapid defeat can be blamed on Pilsudki's fixation on light cavalry rather than planes and tanks. But then France with its larger and better equipped army did not do much better against Germany.

France's military debacle in 1940 can no longer be blamed on its decadence, the parliament, the communists and socialists, the workers and unions or unpreparedness. The French tank was the equal of the German, if not superior, but was disseminated throughout the units of the French army rather than concentrated in special motorized divisions. Only in planes might the French be considered inferior to the Germans. The major cause of French defeat lay more in its incompetent leadership and its antiquated strategic ideas dating back to World War I. General Gamelin, his successor Weygand and others held conventional and unimaginative ideas emphasizing defensive warfare that led to France's humiliating defeat.[187]

The history of the Franco-Polish alliance is a checkered one. When the German danger subsided in the 1920s to the mid-1930s the alliance lost its importance. Seeking Polish security, Pilsudski refused to allow the loosening of the military convention. When the German and Italian danger loomed higher, Blum invited Śmigły-Rydz to meet with the French military leaders at Rambouillet in 1936 and for a time the alliance blossomed again. The more appeasement-minded Daladier and Bonnet wanted to divest or at the very least loosen France's previous eastern obligations, and the alliance again fell into desuetude. At this point Poland, cast adrift and seeking guarantees, allied more firmly with Hitler, with whom Beck opportunistically had coquetted since 1934. Beck decided to run with both the hares and the hounds and menaced Czechoslovakia during the Munich crisis.

To French indignation, Beck felt little obligation after accepting the 1936 loan and conducted his Germanophile policy with impunity because the French would not completely sever their pact with Poland which amounted to "committing suicide." Fears of being made a Western sacrificial goat explain much of his policy.

Poland's relations with France blew hot and cold depending on the European political climate. Poland cozied up to Germany when rejected by France, scurried back to France and England when threatened by Germany. French financial investments, later loans, were the mortar binding the military interests of the two nations and in this sense Poland became a quasi-dependent of France, made even more dependent by its financial insolvency or near bankruptcy. This latter factor has been ignored and trivialized by the emphasis on politics.

Poland's history in general has been examined hitherto primarily from the political and diplomatic viewpoint, the economic and financial having been virtually ignored. Most historians are in agreement that Germany in 1938–1939 was in the throes of a crisis brought on by all sorts of pressures caused by rearmament, labor shortages, currency shortages, raw materials and other deficiencies. Mason and Overy are in disagreement as to whether it was deep enough to, as Mason believes, "leave the regime with a choice between military conquest and a curtailment of the rearmament drive."[188]

Poland's rejection of Hitler's last demand in March 1939 for Danzig and an extra-territorial route through the Corridor decided Hitler to attack Poland and he summoned the army leader General Brauchitsch to draw up plans. He told the latter that he did not intend to attack immediately but would wait for the exact moment and left little doubt of his intentions, adding: "I will then knock Poland out so completely that she will not need to be taken into account politically for many decades."

The signing of the Anglo-Polish Guarantee of April 6, 1939, interrupted these plans and infuriated Hitler and he moved to counter it by a non-aggression agreement with Stalin. In April the final draft of *Operation White*, the name for the Polish campaign, provided for "the operation to be carried out at any time from September 1 onwards."[189] Hitler repeated his decision, much as he had in the earlier Hossbach conference, to his assembled military commanders in May 1939 to move against Poland. "Danzig is not the object.... It is a question of expanding our living space in the east, of securing our food supplies.... There is no question of sparing Poland and we are left with the decision: To attack Poland at the first suitable opportunity." Hitler firmly stated that they could not expect "a repetition of the Czech affair. There will be war." The main task would be to "isolate Poland. The success of this isolation will be decisive.... There must be no simultaneous conflict with the Western Powers." He added: if the Western Powers could not be kept out "then it will be better to attack the west and incidentally to settle Poland at the same time." Later he again decided to finish off Poland first, believing that Poland would strike Germany from the east in a general war against the Western Powers.

In the last week before the war a tug of war for influence over Hitler went on between Ribbentrop, who reinforced the German leader's decision to use force believing that the Western Powers would not fight, and Göring, who thought a negotiated settlement could be arranged. Already on August 11 at Fuschl in answer to Ciano's question: "Well, Ribbentrop what do you want? The Corridor or Danzig?" Ribbentrop said: "Not that anymore. We want war."[190] With the failure of efforts through diplomatic channels and the Dahlerus mission to London — a Swedish business acquaintance of Göring acting as middleman — probably the decision for war was sealed. Hitler seemed genuinely taken aback when Britain and France, after delivering an ultimatum to withdraw his troops from Poland, called his last bluff and gamble and declared war on September 3, 1939.

The scurrying to and fro of the diplomats and emissaries between the various European capitals may not have mattered one jot if Hitler had already decided to gamble once more that the Western Powers would not fight and the Polish campaign was confined to a local engagement. The evidence driving that gamble was the relentless pressure of the intensifying "crisis" of the German state and economy, gearing it up for a pirate war to seize the assets of Poland to relieve pressure or divert attention from Germany's worsening internal problems. This certainly was the case in the last week when one political jolt followed another. On August 23 Germany signed the Nazi-Soviet pact, and on August 24 the British–Polish military assistance pact occurred. About this time Mussolini told Hitler that Italy would not join him and offered to mediate. Under the impact of the latter two occurrences, Hitler hesitated and ordered the suspension of the attack timed for August 26 and waited upon further events.

The British pursued a dual plan of both supporting Poland and working for a negotiated peace to include the return of Danzig to Germany, something widely accepted in French, British and European government circles for years. In both Britain and France the expectation for many years was that Danzig would one day return to Germany but only by peaceful means and that while firmly supporting Poland insisted that the Poles would have to negotiate with Germany for a satisfaction of German grievances. Beck agreed accordingly without enthusiasm.[191] Britain and France led the Poles to believe that once war began they would attack Germany from its western border and bomb German cities. Instead the strange interlude of the *"drôle de guerre"* or "phoney war" (or Ger. *"Sitzkrieg"* or "sitting war") occurred in which the opposing armies merely faced one another and the British and French air forces did little to relieve Poland of the Wehrmacht's full fury. A sour and even bitter feeling pervades this subject among Poles, namely, that they were abandoned, "deliberately misled" and even "doublecrossed and betrayed by their Western allies."[192]

In the last analysis, history and geography powerfully doomed Poland to another partition. Few mourned the disappearance of the Pilsudskist epigone and their government after 1939. The Polish people were left to face the terrible brutality of the Nazi occupation — in which 2.5 million Poles perished — the consequences of faulty policies. Ultimate responsibility for the catastrophe even more than Poland lies with the Western Powers for their supine encouragement of Hitler. Perhaps, as Roos shrewdly observed, the gravest mistake made by Pilsudski, Beck and other Polish leaders was less in the penny-wise seizure of Teschen, than in dogmatically believing that Czechoslovakia was doomed to extinction.[193]

This was already evident when Beck told the American Ambassador to Paris, Bullitt, that he expected Hitler to provoke an "uprising" of the Sudeten Germans, which would not constitute a *casus foederis* under the Franco-Polish Agreement. Therefore, "Poland would not march." "Under no circumstances," he continued, "would Poland become involved in protecting French satellites in Central Europe, especially Czechoslovakia." Beneš, he thought, "would not have sense enough to concede some sort of autonomy" to the Sudetens if this were proposed.[194] On the eve of the British guarantee, through the good offices of Bullitt, Łukasiewicz tried to mend fences over "certain misunderstandings" of past Polish policy by Daladier.[195] This was undoubtedly caused by fears in Warsaw that Poland might be thrown to the wolves. In late June 1939, Bullitt wrote that "a second Munich this time at the expense of Poland was in the making" because of French weariness, doubts about a war for Danzig and the Corridor being worth a war, "a deep-seated dislike of Beck in French government circles" and the difficulty of getting military aid to Poland in the event of a German attack.[196]

The plunder Hitler took from Czechoslovakia strengthened him militarily; the plunder taken from vanquished Poland gave him mastery of the continent and enabled him to attack France, then the Soviet Union with massive military power. Besides the confiscation of over 700,000 homes and farms seized from Poles and Jews in the lands incorporated into Germany, in the annexed district of Lodz, the Nazis took over 70 banks, 3,500 textile factories and shops, 800 large firms, 500 wholesale companies and 8,500 retail businesses which went, without compensation, to German companies, "deserving" Nazi party members and resettled Baltic Germans. Hans Frank, chief gauleiter of Poland, condemned the Poles to the most beggarly existence: "Poland shall be treated as a colony; the Poles shall be the slaves of the Greater German World Empire." Poland would also be on the lowest rung of the German *Grossraumwirtschaft* system: "By destroying Polish industry...Poland will be reduced to its proper position as an agrarian country which will have to depend on Germany for importation of industrial products."[197]

Chapter 4

The Search for Raw Materials: Nazi Germany's Imperialist Plans for the Exploitation of Southeastern Europe in the Inter-War Period

"Copper is a life and death matter."
— Emil Wiehl, German Foreign Office
Economic Specialist, to Von Heeren,
German Minister to Belgrade,
September 21, 1939

IN THE NAZI ERA'S FIRST YEARS, it embarked on Schacht's "New Plan" (1934–1936), in many respects a consequence of the protectionist policies pursued by the leading World Powers in response to the Great Depression of the 1930s. Great Britain, the strongest economic power in the world, reacted to the Depression by the economic nationalist device of closing its borders to the imports of other countries and confining its trade as much as possible to its imperial possessions and dependencies. The United States, France and other industrialized countries did likewise. This protectionist policy wreaked havoc with Germany's considerable trade with England to whom it sent about a third of all of its exports.[1] The British share of world imports in 1932 was 16.3%, making it the leading world importer.[2] Since England no longer took a large portion of Germany's exports as well as those of Southeastern Europe and Latin America, it was only a question of time before those excluded from the imperial preferential arrangements of the British and French empires and the American market found ways to adopt the same tactics. The hostile reaction of the British, French and Americans to the restrictive clearing house and preferential arrangements which the Germans later developed with Southeastern Europe and Latin America was somewhat unjustified and a case of chickens coming home to roost. The German attempt to create an "informal empire" in Southeastern Europe which possessed a plethora of raw materials and markets for German exports was no more than the British and French had done.

Hjalmar Schacht, a former Reichsbank president during the Weimar era, spotted Hitler as a possible solution to Germany's economic problems long before other German business leaders and offered his service in 1931 and 1932 by acting as a mediator in at least one meeting between Hitler and the big business *Bonzen* (bosses).[3] In July 1932 he pledged his support to

Hitler and acted as host in the critical March 1933 meeting.[4] German business grasped the role Hitler could play in its future plans and the way was open for a historic compromise between the Nazis and German industry. As the symbol of this partnership Schacht, whom Hitler considered a kind of honorary Nazi, became President of the Reichsbank on March 17, 1933, and held that office until January 20, 1939. He was next appointed Minister for the Economy in August 1934 and Plenipotentiary for the Economy in November 1937. As virtual economic dictator during the first two years of the Nazi regime, Schacht, through his control of German bank credit, safely charted the Nazi state past the reefs of economic recovery through state-financed public works projects and tax incentives to business while wages were held down and strikes forbidden. Under Schacht's management the Reich debt tripled and the profits of German big business soared. The business upsurge, as has been mentioned, was paid for by the working class which worked longer hours for less wages.[5]

During the first years of the Nazi regime, the economy steered a course between satisfying the demands of the middle class Nazi "intransigents" and the more opportunistic "imperialist" Nazis who inclined toward a partnership with the German military and big business with whom they shared pan-German aspirations for empire. The working class had already been sacrificed to the demands of business by the destruction of the trade unions. The conflict between the middle class "intransigents" and the "imperialist" Nazis came to a head in 1936 when Göring, replacing Schacht as the newly appointed economic czar of the Four Year Plan, rejected Gördeler's moderate plan for continued domestic investment in construction and exports rather than rearmament. Göring made the crucial decision when he accepted War Minister General von Blomberg's memorandum requesting increased production of military materials, rejecting that of Gördeler as "absolutely useless because it set forth a considerable limitation of armaments."[6] This was a decision to seek, through the gamble of war, spectacular gains, rather than more modest economic recovery.

Long before his appointment as economic czar and Reichsbank director Schacht had conceived the possibility of using the buying power of the German market to gain control of Germany's import market. However, the Ruhr industrialist Reusch, chairman of I. G. Farben, to whom he proposed his "Import Monopoly" to use the consumption power of sixty-five million Germans, rejected it as economic heresy, favoring maintenance of the free trade principle.[7] It was Schacht who first perceived that Germany, like her affluent neighbors, needed an "informal empire," turning away from its older trade connections to new ones in order to gain markets and supplies of raw materials. During the 1930s Schacht was the foremost champion of the acquisition of colonies for trade and raw material purposes.[8] Schacht conceived the idea of organizing a trading bloc of capital poor nations eager to trade their surplus foodstuffs and raw materials for Germany's exports of manufactured products, machinery and armaments. In this sense Schacht, the pragmatist, and not economic theorists, may have been the originator of the *Grossraumwirtschaft* (economy of large areas) theory.

Schacht's plans were hatched within the framework of a Europe that had undergone an important transformation. Prior to World War I, Western capitalism's most fertile avenue for investment had been Czarist Russia, but the Bolshevik Revolution ended that lucrative source of profit. European and American capital sought a new investment area for its surplus capital in Eastern and Southeastern Europe.[9] One study of the amount and degree of concentration of foreign capital in the Balkan states by the close of the 1920s indicates that seven international banks held a monopoly of the capital invested in over one-half of the largest enterprises with foreign capital.[10] The total amount of their investments in the Balkans — direct and indirect — amounted to 4.7 billion gold francs. The distribution of capital investment in the Balkans (Yugoslavia, Romania, Bulgaria, Greece, Turkey and Albania) was in state loans or public finances for the most part and to a lesser extent in industry, banks, commerce and insurance.[11] Of the 1,255 billion francs invested by this group in private enterprises in the Balkans only .2 billion francs, or 7.8% of the total, was invested in industry, suggesting that foreign capital was less interested in investing in the development of the productive forces of the area. It remained, therefore, in a state of technological underdevelopment and backwardness.[12] Investment did more to siphon out, rather than to develop, the resources and wealth of the region. Balkan industrial development in the 1930s was largely for export purposes rather than for capital formation.

After the war Southeastern Europe became an important market for the investment of capital by the victorious Entente Powers, displacing German and Austro-Hungarian capital. Since France had fallen heavily into debt to the U.S. and its available capital had been considerably depleted, the only two countries in a position to extend credit were England and the U.S.

Germany's plummet from a leading world power left stillborn Friedrich Naumann's grandiose dream of a "Mitteleuropa," an economic and political union of the states of Eastern Europe with Germany as its core.[13] In 1931, Karl Duisberg, founder of the giant I. G. Farben chemical monopoly, resurrected this dream of German business interests when he evoked in inviting terms the possibility of "an economic bloc from Bordeaux to Odessa."[14] Duisberg pointed the way to the realization of this pan-European idea by indicating to German business that for Yugoslavia, Romania and Hungary their agricultural exports were "a question of existence." He believed that nothing could be more natural than an economic understanding with those states. Already in 1929–1930 in their search for markets the Ruhr magnates moved to seek trade in the Southeast. From the early 1930s I. G. Farben strove to carry out Duisberg's suggestion and increase its declining profits by stepping up its chemical export trade with the states of Southeastern Europe. Previously that region figured negligibly in I. G. Farben's chemical export — 3.4% of its total export trade in 1930, leaving the region primarily to the rival Aussiger Verein and the Belgian firm of Solvay & Cie.[15]

For the capital-poor Southeastern European countries, the purchase of I. G. Farben's chemical exports posed a difficult problem. Agricultural tariffs before 1932 inhibited the sale of its agricultural foodstuffs and grains on the German market. To overcome these obstacles Farben organized yearly

trips of German specialists to develop foreign trade possibilities and to establish connections with economic interests and political figures on the highest
level. From August 8, 1932, through August 1935, I. G. Farben directors
and experts, Dr. Ilgner, Dr. Reithinger, von Moellendorff and Flugge visited
the states of Southeastern Europe. The first fruit of these visits occurred in
Hungary where, with the help of the German Foreign Office and Agricultural Ministry, I. G. Farben specialists worked with Hungarian agricultural
interests to increase the exports of foodstuffs, grain, fruits and other agricultural products to Germany. What could not be marketed in the Reich
was resold abroad. Hungary, in turn, agreed to take I. G. Farben exports at
higher prices than competitors. This "compensation policy" received the
unstinting support of the German Foreign Office and other government
agencies, receiving visiting dignitaries from Southeastern Europe through
the mediation of I. G. Farben representatives; in Hungary and the other
countries of the Southeast, Farben agents dealt directly with government
figures and economic interests, offering marketing information, facilitating
the export of agricultural products and generally making themselves indispensable. Farben's "compensation policy," the first stage in the systematic
peaceful penetration of the economy of Southeastern Europe, Schacht later
expanded into a formidable instrument of commercial domination. Hungary
succumbed first, agreeing in 1932 to export grain, fruit, onions, meat and
poultry valued at ten million pengö or 20% of the total value of Hungary's
exports.[16]

I. G. Farben's profits soon reflected the success of these endeavors. In
the period from 1932 through 1938 exports to Southeastern Europe moved
from 15% of total Farben exports to 21% — a total increase of 44% for
its Southeastern European exports.[17] Throughout the 1930s I. G. Farben
and other specialists evaluated the mining, agrarian, banking and financial,
forest and textile production levels and the estimated reserves of Yugoslavia
and other countries of Southeastern Europe, particularly in raw material
resources essential to the heavy industry and rearmament production of
the Reich.

As German rearmament swung into high gear at the end of the 1930s,
these raw material needs assumed major importance if Germany were to
maintain a decisive edge over its adversaries in the size and strength of its
military capability. The reports sent back by these specialists in the Southeast were comprehensive in scope. One of these reports in October 1938,
by Dr. Adolf Kruemmer, a mining engineer, concludes that for Germany's
military production, the non-ferrous exports of "Yugoslavia in case of war
[are] indispensable."[18] Although by 1938 the stranglehold Nazi Germany
had on Yugoslav foreign trade had become threatening, Yugoslavia had not
yet been completely reduced to an economic satellite of Germany and still
demonstrated the capacity for independent action. Its attitude, complains
the report, "brought unpleasant surprises." At the height of the Czech crisis on September 28, 1938, Yugoslavia suddenly emptied its clearing house
account and demanded payment in currency for all ores and metals. Germany was suddenly cut off from ores already ordered in Yugoslavia. Despite
the visit of Göring and a trade delegation, after fourteen days of German

pressure the order was still not rescinded. The report concluded: "Although Yugoslavia sells half its exports to Germany, its financial and political dependency on the West — as this example shows — is decisive (*ausschlaggebend*). That must be a warning to us." Germany's mining prospects in Yugoslavia "at the moment are not favorable."[19] The ability of Yugoslavia to turn off the flow of critical raw materials to the Reich threatened to become an Achilles' heel. A German report on the "Military-Economic Significance of Yugoslavia for Germany" concluded that the question of whether "military means" should be resorted to in order to gain control of critical supplies of raw materials from Southeastern Europe "must be answered in the affirmative."[20] Germany could not reckon with overseas raw materials deliveries once war occurred and only the resources of Southeastern Europe provided "a relatively easy" solution.

In order to continue the momentum of expansion favored by German business and heavy industry and to remove the threatening obstacle, Carl Krauch, an I. G. Farben director on the staff of Göring, urged in a report delivered in April 1939 that "the only promising possibility to insure supplies for the mineral oil economy for many years was to secure the area by means of the Wehrmacht."[21] Southeastern European oil processed in German hydrogenation plants would "almost double profits compared to coal." The demands of the military economy could not be met within the borders of Greater Germany and could only be achieved by making plans based upon expansion (*Grossraumplanung*) which would include the economies and raw materials of Southeastern Europe.[22] Göring also admitted that further rearmament could not be carried out without expansion into Southeastern Europe.[23]

When Schacht decided to put his concept of an "import monopoly" into practice, Germany was still limping along economically and countries like England threatened to cut off credit unless its creditors received satisfaction. Confrontation would have led to withdrawal of credit by British bankers and paralysis of Germany's overseas trade. Expanded spending in 1933 and 1934 produced a price spiral and hoarding. Demand exceeded supply, and fears persisted of a devaluation of the mark which might lead, as in 1923, to a panic and a valueless mark.

A recent writer described Schacht's "New Plan" of September 1934 "as the most radical commercial policy ever adopted by a major trading power."[24] The government literally undertook to control foreign trade in order to bring imports in line with its dwindling foreign exchange. Imported luxury items, manufactured products and non-essentials were sharply curtailed and trade was now carried out with the producers of primary products needed for German industrial and armament production. A system of preferential import and export agreements avoided the use of convertible currency through clearing house arrangements. In a sense Germany had really abandoned the free trade market system in its economic relations with the states of Southeastern Europe and Latin America. These measures were not supported by Karl Duisberg and the dominant liberal group within the powerful *Reichsverband der deutschen Industrie* which favored free trade principles, but these were ousted in 1933 and supplanted by a leadership favoring the new trend.[25]

German exports were still lagging as late as mid-1934 as a result of being shut out of British, American and other overseas markets. Ruhr industrialists like Peter Klöckner, Director of Klöckner Steel Works, prophesied darkly: "If we don't export, we will be finished in a few months."[26] German armament production — only 6% of the national income in 1936 — was still insufficient to revive German heavy industry. Without exports to pay for imported raw materials and foodstuffs the entire German economy was in danger of breaking down due to the shortage of minerals such as copper. Yugoslavia, in this respect, was of prime importance to the German economy; its raw materials, in the opinion of one specialist, had become as important as the much coveted Romanian oil "which it is a fashionable error to permit to over-shadow the value of other raw materials — chrome, lead, nickel, bauxite and copper.[27]

Germany's economic and political weakness necessitated concentrating efforts in an area not requiring capital investment: i.e., trade. In the period of the early 1930s agrarian protective tariffs and competition from the United States, Canada and other producers of agricultural foodstuffs caused a devastating fall in prices on the world market and left the agrarian states of Southeastern Europe in a desperate economic situation. Therefore, they were only too anxious to market their stocks of foodstuffs wherever they could, and became willing partners in the marketing techniques adopted by Germany. The German-Hungarian trade agreement of 1932 preceded a bilateral agreement with Yugoslavia in 1934, designed to make the German market indispensable. Yugoslavs received extremely favorable terms: a secret clause awarded Yugoslav exports certain financial privileges which a German Foreign Office memorandum described as "a heavy burden" necessitated by the special circumstances surrounding the conclusion of the pacts. These treaties "of a special kind" had political as well as economic aims. Notes and circulars by Foreign Office officials, Ritter and Ulrich, candidly state — in the words of Ritter — that "we wish to attempt the creation of a secure foothold within the economic circle of the Little Entente."[28]

Clearing house arrangements allowed Germany to accept a large share of Yugoslavia's agricultural exports for a stipulated amount of German manufactured and semi-manufactured exports without the use of convertible currencies. Similar agreements were later signed with other countries of Southeastern Europe, enabling Germany to move to first place in trade with those countries by mid-1936. Germany's Southeastern European trade came to 9.2% of its exports and 7.9% of its imports in percentages of its total foreign trade in that year. In the case of Yugoslavia, Germany considerably expanded imports from that country through the May 1934 German-Yugoslav Commercial Treaty. In the export of live animals (excluding horses) Germany imported 6,949 metric tons compared to 193 in 1929; meat and meat products 9,949 compared to 766; fruit 22,486 compared to 9,526; flax and hemp 11,845 compared to 2,178. In the importation of minerals Germany's increases in lead ore were 21,796 compared to 2,245; bauxite 217,542 compared to 67,891 and copper 13,000 compared to 8,139.[29] In short, Germany had succeeded in gaining control over a part of the mineral wealth as well as the foodstuffs of Yugoslavia and that country had begun to enter the orbit of Nazi hegemony.

However, the enchantment of the Southeastern European states with Germany was short-lived. Following massive importations of agricultural products, the German side of the clearing house accounts fell into sizeable debt and Berlin failed to rectify matters by shipping equivalent amounts of exports. Growing German indebtedness through its passive accounts forced these states to import increasing amounts of inferior quality goods from Germany to recoup their losses. During the 1934–1936 period the value of German exports to Southeastern Europe had grown from 47.5 million marks in mid-1934 to 174.2 million, but German indebtedness rose by mid-1936 to 40 million marks to Greece, 25 million to Yugoslavia, 25 million to Hungary and 10 million to Bulgaria.[30] A noisy campaign in the Greek press brought out the fact that 1,600 million drachmas frozen in Germany compelled Greece to purchase its war materials in Germany or face financial loss.[31] The value of the German mark fell in Yugoslavia from the pegged rate of 17.6 dinars to 1 mark to between 12.4 and 14.5 in 1936, which, as one observer remarks, amounted to a covert devaluation of the currency of that country.[32] Part of Germany's success in driving the Southeastern European states to surrender their foodstuffs and raw materials was the fact that it purchased their products at 30% above world prices. What the Germans could not consume they resold on the world market, presumably taking advantage of price fluctuations on the world markets — often at higher prices than they had previously paid. However, the disenchantment of the states of Southeastern Europe was such that had the economic downturn of 1938 in the United States and the world market not occurred they may have turned against doing business with Hitler and looked elsewhere, namely to Western business.[33]

One consequence of Germany's trade drive was its dramatic replacement of Italy as the number one customer in the Southeast. In the case of Yugoslavia in the first half of 1935 Italy was Yugoslavia's principal client taking 20.5% of total trade with Germany second best at 16.88%, but by the first half of 1936 Germany had become the major purchaser of Yugoslav goods with 25.44% of the total while Italy shrank to 1.97% — 11th or one of the least significant of Yugoslavia's clients. In percentages of Yugoslav trade in the first half of 1936, Germany took 25.55%, Czechoslovakia 17.35%, Great Britain 11.44%. Yugoslav imports from Italy fell to 300,000 dinars during the first half of 1936 or .01% of total imports.[34]

The German tactic of importing the foodstuffs of Southeastern Europe while delaying payment caused a reaction, but there was little those countries could do to extricate themselves from the jaws of the German boa constrictor. Yugoslavia made attempts to curtail the export of certain items like honey and wheat to Germany but Berlin could always apply pressure to counter attempts to sell elsewhere. In the autumn of 1936 German imports of Yugoslav foodstuffs fell sharply and German negotiators became less accommodating. By the year's end Yugoslavia was in a state of "economic xenophobia" in its dealings with Germany.[35] As in Greece, articles — probably government inspired — appeared in the newspapers urging that wheat and other products be sold elsewhere for exchange currency other than the mark, but immediately drew sharp protests from Berlin.[36] Despite the despoilment of their economies, the countries of Southeastern Europe had no choice but to sell their exports to Germany to avoid economic collapse. The downturn of the international market and a new cycle of depression sealed the fate of Yugoslavia and the other states of Southeastern Europe which by the end of the 1930s were factually transformed into colonies of Greater Germany and the Nazi imperialist *Grossraumwirtschaft.* The area, declared the *London Times,* was "potentially a dominion of Germany."[37]

Some attempts were made by the countries of the Little Entente to escape entrapment by Germany by forming, under the aegis of Czechoslovakia, itself a satellite of England and France, an economic bloc named after its sponsor Milan Hodža, a Czechoslovak political figure. However, the project, which was originally conceived as a Danubian preferential tariff union to promote trade among the states of Southeastern Europe, risked being perceived as anti-Italian, running counter to the Rome Protocols signed by Austria and Hungary. The Hodža Plan also quickly drew the fire of Berlin which perceived it as a counter to its plans for German hegemony in the Southeast. A final blow was the reserve of Yugoslavia toward the plan and assurances by Prince Paul to the German minister in Belgrade that Yugoslavia had no wish to loosen its economic ties to Germany. Czechoslovakia was not in a position to take the export surplus of Romania and Yugoslavia or to satisfy the industrial needs of those countries, Pilja, the Yugoslav Foreign Office economics expert, told Clodius, his German counterpart, and any attempt to convert the Little Entente into an economic bloc would be "completely harmless."[38] Yugoslav Premier Stojadinović gave similar assurances that "nothing would happen that would displease Germany."[39]

In the summer of 1936, Hjalmar Schacht journeyed to the countries of Southeastern Europe to assure the success of his trade policy. An American diplomatic official in Belgrade, Wilson, predicted that the new economic agreements between Germany and Yugoslavia would probably result "in their political dependency."[40] However, the British, French and Americans had nothing to offer the Yugoslavs that could compete with German offers of higher than world prices for unmarketable agrarian surpluses. Stojadinović disregarded the warnings of Wilson; and Pilja told him that Yugoslavia would be unable to buy American goods unless the United States imported an equivalent amount of Yugoslav goods.[41] German exports were, in fact, higher priced than other countries', but the fact that the German market absorbed Yugoslavia's agricultural surplus gave them a magnetic attraction.

At the same time Germany's economic expansion into Southeastern Europe coupled with its rearmament measures made the British uneasy, and they countered by rearming and negotiating trade agreements with the states of that area. In 1936 trade agreements were signed with Hungary, Romania, and Turkey, resulting in an increase in 1935–1936 in exports to Britain from £9.3 million sterling to £12.3 million. Britain increased its exports to the Southeast by almost half from 6.9 million to 9.7 million. In the period from 1936 to 1938 the British share in Southeast European exports came to 8.5%–

9% and imports 7.5%–8%, making Great Britain the second most important trading partner in the region.[42] But the lion's share of the Southeastern trade they left to the Germans and, despite the misgivings of some, as long as Germany did not interfere with the political independence of the countries of the region, the Chamberlain government accepted German economic hegemony there. In short, the British preferred German economic activity in the Southeast, an area less commercially important to them than their other overseas markets, but at the same time they continued to maintain and strengthen their southeastern market to a point which they showed little disposition to abandon completely. Economic appeasement of Germany in the region was a conscious decision made to avoid conflict and eventually war.

Germany was ill-equipped for a long war. In 1939, at the outbreak of war, Germany depended on outside sources for 10%–20% of its foodstuffs, 45% of its fats, two-thirds of its oil, 80% of its rubber. In metals the situation was not much brighter with Germany dependent on world sources for two-thirds of its zinc, 50% of its lead, 70% of its tin and 95% of its bauxite.[43]

At that point, in an address to members of the Foreign Office on May 24, 1939, General Thomas calculated Germany was spending 23% of its national income on armament in comparison to 12% by Britain, 17% by France and 2% by the U.S.[44] The demands of the rearmament program were felt almost from the beginning in 1935–1936 as the need for copper, lead, zinc, antimony and chrome almost doubled.[45] By 1939, the search for raw materials took precedence over everything else and began to influence the direction of foreign policy. Yugoslavia's position as the source of certain key metals, particularly non-ferrous, made it the object of German attention.

In 1939, Yugoslavia stood first in Europe in lead production and second in copper while in bauxite it produced 10% of world production. Yugoslavia had the largest chrome complex in Europe and with the outbreak of war and the difficulty of securing Turkish chrome its holdings became even more important. In copper production Yugoslavia had the largest copper mines in Europe, producing over 40,000 tons of raw copper primarily from the Bor mining complex owned by France. The British-owned Trepća lead mines had a yield of approximately 71,000 tons at the outbreak of war in 1939. At that time Germany was receiving all of Yugoslavia's bauxite. According to German estimates Yugoslavia covered 40% of its bauxite needs, one-third of its antimony needs, one-fifth of its copper demands and 10% of its chrome requirement.[46] Besides Yugoslavia, other Southeastern European states contributed significantly to the German raw material needs.

Southeastern Europe and Yugoslavia after World War I had become an important investment region for Western European capital, particularly British and French investment interests. By the mid-1930s, Great Britain had replaced France as the primary investing power in the area, concentrating investments and loans primarily in Yugoslavia, Romania and Greece. By 1937 British capital in Yugoslavia had achieved first place after France with a total investment of 873.6 million dinars and this increased 100 million dinars by mid-1938, or 25% more.[47] In Romania, the British invested capital in a variety of enterprises relating to communications, in the petroleum area, gold mines on the Romanian-Czechoslovak border, locomotives, rail cars and machine producing plants in Bucharest, textiles, chemical concerns, cereals, etc. In Greece, where the British had already become entrenched in the nineteenth century, British capital concentrated in banks and mining. In Turkey, the British invested capital in communications and textile works as well as some new industries. In Bulgaria, however, British capital investments were negligible.[48]

In Yugoslavia, British and French capital concentrated in the crucial mining sector of the economy. The estimates in Table 4–1 show the degree of British and French control.[49]

Table 4–1. Percent of Foreign Capital in Mining in Yugoslavia, 1937–1938

France	23.7
Germany and Austria	14.5
Czechoslovakia	.9
England	44.7
U.S.A.	3.5
Italy	1.6
Belgium	1.6

Britain had almost 45% of the total foreign capital in mining, the greatest part controlled by the giant Selection Trust Company which held the Trepća lead mines. France held second place through its holdings in the Trbovlje Coal Works (200 million dinars) and the Mines de Bor (112.75 million dinars). The Banque des Pays de l'Europe Central held the first and the Banque Mirabeau held the second. Only in the area of textiles did Germany achieve any degree of entrenchment, holding about one-third of total foreign capital, while Britain held 10.7% and the U.S. 11.5%, Switzerland 15.7%, Czechoslovakia 9.4% and Italy 5.0%.[50]

In the inter-war period Yugoslavia functioned as a colony of Western European capital, its wealth flowing out of the country in the form of raw materials, primarily metals, to be consumed by the heavy industry of the more developed countries of the West.[51] Between 75% and 77% of the total electro-chemical production was exported. In the extractive industry it exported 74% of its magnesium, 75% of its copper, 96% of its lead, 93% of its zinc, and 84% of its antimony.[52]

The vertically integrated giant corporate monopolies contrived not only to gain control of raw material resources for their own needs, but also of all potential sources in order to limit the competition of rivals.[53] By controlling the extractive resources of the Balkans, the British limited the ability of German heavy industry to expand, forcing it to resort to military aggression and seizure, as Carl Krauch suggested. By the eve of World War II the attention of the European powers rested on Southeastern Europe, the only remaining accessible source of raw materials.

German capital investment in Yugoslavia's mining sector in the inter-war period before 1937 was almost non-existent, coming to less than 1%, but between 1937 and 1940 leaped to about 20%. In the inter-war sessions of the *Mitteleuropäischer Wirtschaftstage* (MWT) and the *Südosteuropäischer Gesellschaft* (SOEG), the leaders of German industry expressed in polite but unequivocal terms their desire to replace Britain, France and the United States as the sole possessor of the raw materials of the Southeast.[54] The tentative decision of the Ruhr chemical and electro-industrial magnates advanced further: With the help of a group of electrical firms, investigative work began on raw materials resources with a view to future exploitation, as the first stage in the development of a raw materials policy.[55]

The protracted struggle in the 1920s and early 1930s between German and British and French interests for the raw materials market of the Southeast assumed diverse forms. To convert the region into an "informal empire" of the Reich, the Austro-German Customs Union acted as a bridge to the Southeast — in the words of Karl Duisberg, "a regional introduction to a large middle European economic region."[56] The French industrial and banking interests blocked the move as ultimately resulting in the closing of Southeastern Europe to French exports.[57]

Helmut Wohltat, a close Schacht associate and German Foreign Office economic specialist, suggested at a December 1936 session of the MWT that German industry should penetrate the Southeastern region through purchases of new mines and industrial establishments. At a 1938 meeting of the MWT, von Wilmowsky described how such purchases could complement German heavy industry, citing as an example a German-Swiss consortium's purchase of two antimony mines in Yugoslavia which then delivered the mined ores to cover German import needs.[58] At a November 1938 meeting, Max Hahn, a leader of the MWT, outlined German efforts to gain access to Yugoslav copper, lead, zinc and antimony mines.[59]

Competing sectors of the German bureaucracy and German industry frequently got into one another's hair in the scramble to expand German raw material holdings in Southeastern Europe. Göring's favorite, the sleazy and unscrupulous consul-general in Belgrade, Franz Neuhausen, frequently clashed with Max Hahn, chairman of the MWT, whom he eventually succeeded in removing.[60] Between the MWT representing the Rhine industrialists and the Viennese Nazi-connected *Südosteuropäischer Gesellschaft* (SOEG) headed by Heinrichsbauer and Baldur von Schirach, the Nazi youth leader, a sharp rivalry developed for preeminence in representing German interests in the region. Heinrichsbauer was the confidant of Dr. Walter Funk, Schacht's successor in the Economics Ministry, and von Schirach.[61] Rivalry between private corporate and state enterprises such as the Hermann Göring Works also produced frictions between party and industrial interests.

German efforts to use their growing commercial and political power to expand investments in the Southeast met with resistance from British, American and French capital interests. A clash between the American Standard Oil Company and German capital interests over oil exploitation rights in the Zagreb basin reached into the Yugoslav government itself, with the son of former Premier Pašić supporting the German group while Standard Oil held "excellent connections with the Yugoslav War Ministry." To prevent the oil rights from going to Standard Oil, Neuhausen threatened Minister-President

Cvetković "with a radical restructuring of all orders from Yugoslavia to other countries."[62]

The Hitler government's public works and rearmament programs and Dr. Schacht's "New Plan" provoked food shortages — a "fat crisis" and a grain shortage — and raw materials deficiencies that affected industrial production. By the summer of 1936 acute raw material shortages caused munitions plants to work at only 70% capacity, but Hitler still refused to cut food imports as Schacht suggested, probably fearing the spread of discontent among the German people. Having come to power with the promise of better living conditions for the German masses, a return to the depressed living standards of the early thirties risked the collapse of the Nazi regime. Hitler's decision to continue the rearmament program and his refusal to curtail imports of raw materials was a prescription for expansionary pressures that could lead only to war. In his proposal for financing rearmament, Schacht warned against fueling a price inflation and a fatal circular pattern of "a snake biting its tail."[63] Schacht became frightened as his warning became a reality and a runaway inflation threatened to undermine the economy. Moreover, a hidden inflation and other deleterious erosional effects on the economy were appearing, caused by Schacht's import controls. Besides shortages of butter and fats, there was also a widespread slaughter of livestock for lack of animal fodder in the winter of 1935–1936. When Schacht, supported by Colonel Thomas of the War Ministry, proposed that the pace of rearmament be slowed down temporarily, Hitler refused and Schacht resigned.

Hitler's decree establishing the Four Year Plan in 1936 really intended to produce a short-term stopgap solution designed to solve Germany's increasingly chaotic trade and currency problems and tide the country over until the Reich was in a position to militarily undertake a definitive solution: conquest in the east.[64] However, by the end of the 1930s the Four Year Plan had failed to make Germany self-sufficient in raw materials or to solve Germany's trade problems.

The Anschluss provided little relief to dwindling German foreign currency reserves and a ghastly idea of what was in store for any hapless victims of Nazi aggression. On March 17, two days after the Anschluss, the German Reichsbank absorbed the Austrian National Bank and all its assets — 230 million of gold and foreign currency reserves and uncoined gold bar, gold deposits in the Bank of England, outstanding debts, foreign currency values, and other assets totaling nearly 1,368,000,000 marks. Germany at that time had almost no foreign currency and its gold reserves were fewer than those of a medium-size bank, amounting to 8–12 million marks.[65] But within one year the Austrian gold currency windfall was used up by the voracious demands of the German armament industry.[66] German industrial firms, aided by Berlin, descended like locusts on Austria and seized or bought up everything in sight. The Hermann Göring Works acquired Austrian businesses worth 60 million marks and the giant Krupp firm seized the important Berndorf Metal Ware Factory, Arthur Krupp. The Nazis forced sale to Krupp for 8,424,000 marks — about one-third its real value, while a Kassel syndicate took over the vast Vienna Locomotive Factory. I. G. Farben took over

Austria's largest chemical plant and the Munich firm, Vereinigte Industrie A.G., assumed supervision and the controlling interest in the electrical power area.[67]

From the onset of the "New Plan," copper became a particularly scarce item, which threatened to bottleneck the German war economy. After iron, copper was the most important metal needed by Germany with Yugoslavia the second-largest European producer. Yugoslavia produced in 1935–1937 roughly 37–38,000 tons of raw copper for export of which Belgium, Germany and the United States each took about 12,000 tons (in the latter year Germany took only 10,655 tons). Although sufficient copper existed, the French owners of the Bor mines in Yugoslavia demanded cash for any copper deliveries. The German firm of Stollberg Metallwerk complained that copper was in such short supply that it could not maintain its current level of production and would have to turn to part time production and layoffs.[68] On the eve of the war, Zinwerk Wilhelmsberg, Germany's second largest electrolytic-copper works had to shut down for lack of copper; the Siemens and Opel Werke plants had closed or were about to close for lack of raw materials.[69] Demand for copper virtually doubled under the pressure of armament production. At a 1938 conference of the War Ministry, General von Hanneken, Plenipotentiary for Iron and Steel, reported that maximum production of copper was 24,700 tons per month as compared with a demand of 35,000 tons.[70] Similar gaps between demand and production existed for lead and cement. National reserves of copper and tin had been entirely used up in the spring of 1939.[71] The copper shortage of World War I threatened to repeat itself.[72] Already in the mid-1930s the Nazis were cognizant of the copper problem and the French-owned Mines de Bor in Yugoslavia as the core of the difficulty. Schacht told Göring that German "copper exploitation in Yugoslavia would occur with the elimination of the French who only sell copper for foreign currency."[73]

By early 1940 the shortage of copper became so acute that a conflict occurred between Göring's Luftwaffe requirements and the Wehrmacht over available stocks. Fritz Todt, later Armament and Munitions Minister, succeeded in temporarily solving the problem, but it surfaced again in mid-year. On July 6 Göring again dealt with the problem of copper scarcity, blaming the workers and managers in one plant and threatening to court martial those responsible.[74] The situation did not appreciably improve and in the same year a shortage of copper brought about a limitation of U-boat production.[75]

Other shortages developed which forced dependence on Yugoslavia and other Balkan mineral stocks even more. With the outbreak of war, Turkey ceased shipments of chrome to Germany amounting to 40,000 tons annually.[76] The German Minister reported to Berlin that Britain, France and the United States were preemptively buying up all available Turkish stocks of raw materials.[77] The United States requested 50,000 tons of chrome while France and England also were requesting large amounts. In December 1939 Ribbentrop advised Papen to try to secure at least the amounts that Germany had been previously receiving from Turkey.[78] By early January 1940, in desperation the Germans offered Turkey industrial goods, pharmaceutical products, chemicals and other items important for war purposes in exchange for chrome.[79] Besides chrome, lead, zinc, antimony and other non-ferrous metals were in short supply and oil shortages threatened the mobility of the Wehrmacht. These raw material difficulties were known to the British and undoubtedly influenced their decision to stand firm against Hitler and to seek accommodation in the waning days before the German attack on Poland. On August 26, 1939, Viscount Halifax wrote the British minister in Istanbul, Sir Hugh Knatchbull-Hugessen: "We have positive and entirely reliable evidence that Germany's stocks of certain raw materials essential for war purposes are very low. Indeed her oil supply (including coal-produced oil) and that of certain other essential materials such as copper, is unlikely under war conditions to last more than about five months. Unless, therefore, she can obtain the full production of the Galician and Romanian fields it is difficult to see how she can carry on a campaign into 1940." Halifax discounted the Soviet oil deliveries as too limited and hobbled by transport problems.[80]

The Germans, however, had not yet used their trump card to secure raw materials: the sale of armaments. With the probability of war by the second half of the 1930s the countries of Southeastern Europe desperately sought to purchase weaponry and munitions in the event of attack. Formerly France had supplied armaments to the countries of the Little and Balkan Entente, but with the adoption of a neutrality policy and the unlikelihood of Britain supplying weapons, increasingly turned to Germany to satisfy their military needs. The Germans manipulated the desperation of those countries for armaments in order to siphon off raw materials and supplement their depleted reserves. Throughout 1938 and 1939 the Germans strung the Romanian government and King Carol along with promises of armament credits for purchases of planes, anti-aircraft weapons and guns. By mid-August of 1939 Germany's oil supplies had reached the point of exhaustion and Berlin had to consider selling Romania armaments for oil. Romania retaliated against German delays by holding up a petroleum-laden ship causing Berlin to hurriedly send a Junkers representative to Bucharest who promised immediate delivery of Heinkel 112 fighters. Berlin even volunteered to pay in currency if the petroleum could not be obtained in any other way. For Germany, which now claimed 40% of Romania's petroleum exports, oil had become a life or death matter.[81]

In the case of Yugoslavia, the Germans manipulated Belgrade's anxious desire to secure armaments both to compel a closer alignment to the Axis powers, adherence to the Anti-Comintern Pact and also as a way of gaining control over Yugoslavia's raw materials and foodstuffs. Negotiations for armaments were deliberately dragged out by Berlin before Prince Paul's June 1939 visit to gain Yugoslav alignment with the Axis powers, but this policy failed. As mentioned, the Yugoslavs retaliated in March 1939 by cutting off deliveries of raw materials to Germany. The Germans continued their dilatory tactics into the second half of the year. Göring remained reluctant to sell Yugoslavia armaments during the September campaign against Poland and a "train by train" policy of exchanging weapons for raw materials was adopted by Berlin as a stopgap solution for Germany's shortages.[82] By the autumn of 1939 pressure mounted for the delivery of more copper and Berlin became more accommodating. Warnings of von Heeren and other German officials of Yugoslav frustrations were instrumental in bringing about negotiations by a mixed German-Yugoslav commission which produced the "secret protocol" of October 5, 1939, signed by State Secretary Pilja and Dr. Jur. Friedrich Langfried, and increased deliveries of copper, lead and foodstuffs from Yugoslavia in exchange for armaments. Germany agreed to provide Yugoslavia with 100 fighters, 13 trainer planes, 7 Škoda flak batteries (7.5), 20 Škoda flak guns and 420 Škoda guns (3.7). In return Yugoslavia agreed to deliver 3,000 tons of copper, 500 tons of lead, 1,000 tons of lead concentrate, 100 tons of aluminum and 100 tons of antimony. After November 1939, Yugoslavia agreed to step up deliveries of copper to 3,000 tons monthly, 500 tons of lead, 2,000 tons of lead concentrate, 100 tons of aluminum and 100 tons of antimony. Exchanges would be made on a "train by train" basis.[83]

The French and British took steps to interrupt these deliveries; and René Paix, manager of the Bor mines, told American minister Lane that he was reducing production to prevent the copper from reaching Germany.[84] The German minister complained to Belgrade of sabotage in the Bor copper works and the dismissal of Italian workers. Limitations of production, Premier Cvetković declared, would be grounds for expropriation by the Yugoslav government.[85] German pressures for still more deliveries of copper and other metals resulted in a new agreement of May 12, 1940. Copper was to be increased to 4,500 tons for May 1940 and 2,000 tons monthly from June 1 to December 31, 1940, lead, 2,000 tons for May 1940, 500 tons after June 1, 1940, until back amounts were settled and double thereafter.[86] The bulk of Yugoslav copper and other raw materials were now being delivered to the Germans but Berlin was still not satisfied. Wiehl, the Foreign Office economics specialist, complained that 5,300 tons of copper had been delivered to France in the first four months of 1940, but after France's defeat in June and additional German protests and threats no more deliveries took place.[87]

After the fall of France the scenario of the plundering of Austria reoccurred. At a meeting in Berlin in August 1940 Dr. Schlotterer of the Reichswirtschafthauptamt urged the penetration of German influence in the Southeast through the squeezing out of French and English capital.[88] German attention was first drawn to the Bor copper mining complex. Through purchase of stock held by the major holder, the Banque Mirabeau, the Germans sought control over the Bor mines for private German capital. The French government was not anxious to sell Bor and only the intervention of Premier Pierre Laval and President Petain succeeded in removing the Vichy government's interdiction. The stock of the Bor works were then purchased by the Preussische Staatsbank and the firm passed under control of Germany with Neuhausen as head during the period of occupation.[89] Similar attempts to purchase the Trepća lead mines were less successful and the mines remained under control of the German occupation administration until the end of the war.[90]

From the mid-1930s German industry had been working to overcome the British and French mineral monopoly in Southeastern Europe and especially in Yugoslavia. The profit lure must have been particularly attractive as, for example, the Bor mines which offered a 300% profit in dividends already by 1929.[91] By the outbreak of the war, Germany's hold in the Southeast was no longer limited to the import of grains, foodstuffs and minerals but was already involved in a considerable capital investment which, according to one source, in the case of Yugoslavia rose from 55 million dinars in 1934 to 820 million dinars in 1938.[92] In the mining sector alone Krupp invested 500,000 Rm for a three-sided investment in the chrome production sector, with the Hermann Göring Werke and Berlin and Salzgitter holding 50% of the stock capital and Krupp the other 50% in "Yugochrome" near Skopje.[93] Neuhausen assured Krupp that other German private competitors would be excluded.[94] The largest part of the Yugoslav chrome production lay in the hands of the English-owned "Allatini Ltd." firm with the remainder produced by the Ljuboten pits. Yugoslav chrome production mounted steadily from 1936 and fell in 1939 possibly because of British sabotage efforts but production of chrome concentrate continued to rise (as shown in Table 4–2).

Table 4–2. Yugoslav Chrome Production, 1936–1939 (in tons)[95]

Chrome Production	1936	1937	1938	1939
Chrome ore production	34,346	42,668	44,600	30,547
Allatini-owned mines	27,891	32,789	36,206	26,094
Ljuboten mines	6,455	9,879	8,394	4,485
Chrome concentrate	8,087	11,380	13,997	14,675

With the outbreak of war, Krupp began to take more aggressive steps to eliminate competitors and expand its chrome holdings in Yugoslavia. In September, Sohl, chief of Krupp's ore department, informed Neuhausen, the German consul general in Belgrade, that Germany's chrome requirements could only be expanded if the companies held by foreign capital could be placed in German hands. Neuhausen, in turn, told Sohl that he was doing everything he could to enable the Krupp interests and Yugochrome "to take over." Krupp was unable during the war to purchase the stock of the Allatini-owned mines because of the inability to contact the original owners, the mines having in the meantime passed under the wartime Serbian government's control. Krupp, therefore, concentrated on gaining control of the Ljuboten pits, particularly the stock of Chromasseo owned by the Jewish Asseo family, which Krupp had been trying to secure even before the war. However, the Asseo heirs fled carrying with them 4,993 shares Krupp had been seeking to secure, and transferred them to the Italian company Azienda Italiana Minerali Metallici in Italian territory. According to the Nuremberg records, Krupp did not want to pay the Asseo family for the stock. Negotiations followed between the Germans and Italians for the stock but the Germans in the end seized the mines at Jeserina, Macedonia, and the chrome produced went to Germany.[96]

The German aluminum firms began to show increasing interest in the bauxite deposits of Southeastern Europe by the mid-1930s as well. By 1938 half of the total Yugoslav production of about 400,000 tons came from firms dominated by German capital. Already by 1937 Southeastern Europe accounted for the major part of Germany's bauxite imports, Yugoslavia, Hungary and Greece being major suppliers (as shown in Table 4–3).

Table 4–3. Germany's Most Important Suppliers of Bauxite, 1937[97]

Country	Tons
Hungary	472,000
Yugoslavia	406,000
Netherlands, India	139,000
Italy	111,000
France	95,000
Greece	81,000

Through the former Austrian Credit-Anstalt Bank and the Deutsche Bank AG the Germans established the Yugoslav-owned mines at Lozovac near Šibenik. In the production of antimony, Swiss and German capital established in 1936 the "Montania AG" smelting plant at Zajaca near Krupanj. Other works were started at Lisa, Srebrenica and Olov; by 1940 a quarter of Germany's antimony needs were being met from Yugoslav sources.[98]

German bank capital, bolstered by the addition of the great Austrian Credit-Anstalt Bank, through the Yugoslav Bank Union, the largest credit organization in the country and the leading German bank in Southeastern Europe, financed enterprises in the wood, textile and foodstuff industries.[99] The I. G. Farben monopoly moved to establish control over the entire Southeastern chemical industry, largely through holdings in Nobel Dynamite, Bratislava, and its numerous affiliates in Hungary, Yugoslavia and Romania. Farben succeeded in stripping its arch-rival Aussiger, owned by the Belgian Solvay Corporation, of Aussig and Falkenau, located in the Sudetenland following the German occupation of the Czechoslovak state. A large contribution of 100,000 Rm and later 500,000 to Hitler for *"sudetendeutsche assistance"* was made by Farben to facilitate matters.[100] However, Prager Verein, formerly Aussig, was a formidable competitor for Farben throughout the war in the latter's attempts to gather the Southeastern chemical industry under its control.

The British-owned Trepća mines under the control of the Selection Trust Company continued to be the main European sources of production with most exports of lead and zinc going to Belgium. Germany received barely 1,793 tons of lead as late as 1938. (See Tables 4–4, 4–5, and 4–6.).

Dependence on Southeastern European imports after war broke out is clear from a report of von Wilmowsky: "Germany can hardly reckon on overseas deliveries outside of Europe. For a relatively easy source of supply in all probability only Southeastern Europe stands open. Yugoslavian

Table 4–4. Yugoslav Lead Ore and Concentrate Exports,
1936–1938 (in tons)[101]

Country	1936	1937	1938
Belgium	46,962	76,750	62,433
Italy	11,359	10	2,163
Netherlands	2,386	—	—
France	4,500	5,870	13,528
Tunis	4,192	1,719	—
Germany	—	—	1,793

Table 4–5. Yugoslav Zinc Exports, 1936 and 1937 (in tons)[102]

Country	1936	1937
Belgium	74,401	65,004
France	4,884	—

Table 4–6. Yugoslav Lead and Zinc Ores and Concentrates
Exported, 1935–1938 (in tons)[103]

	1935	1936	1937	1938
Lead ore and concentrates	97,580	70,765	86,900	89,513
Zinc ore and concentrates	90,078	78,628	65,004	60,316

supplies in copper, lead and zinc are so significant that with them an effective lightening of the German supply balance can be attained."[104] Thus, Berlin suspiciously regarded a three-month work stoppage of the Trepča mines as an English "means of pressure on the Yugoslav government" and an "anti-German" measure.[105]

German big business, primarily I. G. Farben and Krupp, pushed the desire for military self-sufficiency and the domination of Southeastern Europe. Significantly, between October 1936 and July 1938 45% of the total investment under the Four Year Plan was in synthetic products.[106] Thus a leading British specialist concluded that a powerful coalition of leading generals in the war ministry, party leaders and officials and I. G. Farben directors existed with a vested interest in military self-sufficiency graduated into the need to prepare for war.[107] Carl Krauch's *Wehrwirtschaftlicher Neuer Erzeugungsplan* (Economic Defense New Production Plan) for increased production of explosives, gunpowder, fuel, aluminum and ores placed Germany on a virtual economic war footing, with I. G. Farben absorbing the largest share of the plan's investment.[108]

The sessions of the MWT underscore the design of German heavy industry was to achieve Duisberg's dream of an economic bloc "from Bordeaux to Odessa," an idea similar to the Nazi imperialist economy of vast areas or *Grossraumwirtschaft*. In German business's plans for the post-war era,

French capital would not be permitted to play a role; and in the export of nitrogen I. G. Farben did not intend to permit French participation.[109] Farben also intended to gain control of the French chemical industry through the creation of Francolor, a corporation in which Farben would hold 51% of the stock.[110] Thus Farben, Krupp and German business became integral partners with Hitler and the imperialist Nazis in plans for military expansion and conquest, and had developed into military as well as economic imperialists, as Arthur Schweitzer states, "because they had become convinced that their economic superiority on the continent could be established only after a German military victory."[111] A glance at the profits made by the Krupp corporation leaves little doubt as to the validity of that statement. In 1935 the net profits of the firm after taxes, gifts and reserves were approximately 57 million Rm; in 1938 Krupp's profits jumped to 97 million and in 1940 they soared to 111 million.[112] The Nazi government stood squarely behind the expansion of German business interests outside the borders of the Reich. In August 1940 Göring announced that the German government supported a policy of increasing German influence in foreign enterprises. Germany would not wait to accomplish this through the peace treaties after the war but would use every opportunity to make it possible for German business to gain a foothold in enterprises of interest in the occupied countries even during the war. The German Foreign Office accordingly notified the governments of the Balkan countries that it would not recognize transfers of holdings in enterprises owned by the Norwegians, Belgians, English and French which took place after the outbreak of hostilities, and requested them to change their laws accordingly.[113]

This aggressively expanding German economic and political thrust into Southeastern Europe collided with expanding British economic interests already implanted in the region. Britain's increasing investment of capital in Yugoslavia, reaching its height in the years 1937 and 1938, making it, as we have seen, the major capital investor. Between 1937 and 1940 German investment in the critical Yugoslav mining sector grew from 1% to 20% of all foreign capital.[114] A similar situation existed elsewhere in the other countries of Southeastern Europe. The political and diplomatic history of these years is largely a reflection of this struggle between Britain and Germany for hegemony in the Southeast, a struggle that had been going on before Hitler and the war-party of generals, industrialists and Nazi officials decided on the option of military aggression.

Chapter 5

An Euphoric Dream: *Grossraumwirtschaft, Lebensraum* and British Indecision before Nazi Germany's Surge for World Power

> But who can live for long
> In an euphoric dream;
> Out of the mirror they stare,
> Imperialism's face
> And the international wrong.
>
> — W. H. Auden,
> *September 1, 1939*

> Ideology oozes from every pore in the body of capitalism.
>
> — Karl Marx

THE ERA OF THE 1930S was in many respects similar to the prelude to the First World War when the Great Powers concluded agreements with one another against other powers. Most historians ascribe the "pactomania" preceding the Great War to imperialist rivalries when each of the great imperialist powers sought to maintain or to extend its control over new colonial areas as sources of raw materials and cheap labor, the means of enrichment and power for national business and ruling elites.

This occurred again in the 1930s aptly described by the British historian Hugh Seton-Watson as the period of "diplomatic war."[1] The diplomatic struggle that preceded the outbreak of war in 1939 resulted from this conflict of economic interests. Ideology as the meeting point between social theory, economics and politics, therefore, plays a special role in the articulation of real, material interests.

In his writings and public and private declarations Hitler focused upon Russia and the Ukraine as a vast granary, an agrarian region for the settlement of industrious German migrants from the overpopulated Reich who would supply Germany with the raw materials and foodstuffs it required and at the same time provide markets for its industrial production. He saw the conquest of *Lebensraum* or living space in the eastern regions in heroic, romantic terms as a perennial struggle of historic apocalyptic dimensions that would decide Germany's fate and continued existence. The incorporation of the Germans of Austria and the Sudetenland was only the first stage in Hitler's racial and spacial ideology; the next phase was the extension of Germany's hegemony into Eastern and Southeastern Europe, as *Lebensraum* and a farrago of protectorates and satrapies, part of a grandiose design for a Greater Germany, a modernized Holy Roman Empire, the inner hub Germany, connected to the outlying provinces by a network of industry and commerce. In reality Hitler's Thousand Year Reich was a monstrously oppressive, imperialist ideology cloaked in the romantic, nationalist trappings and sentiments of a previous era.

Recent historical research locates the roots of this *Lebensraum* ideology in the Leipzig University geographer, Friedrich Ratzel (1844–1904), who first used the term in an essay which sought to apply Darwin's ideas of natural selectivity within a specific geographical spacial context.[2] A recent historian of Hitler's foreign policy, the American writer Gerhard Weinberg, describes Hitler's race and spacial ideology as "a vulgarized version of Social Darwinism" that had its roots in the intellectual elites and masses in nineteenth- and twentieth-century Germany.[3] It was in fact a reaction of the German middle class to industrialization, particularly the lower middle class from which Ratzel stemmed; its idealized agrarianism and anti-modern, anti-industrial ideology reflected the increased anxiety and nervousness of the older *Mittelstand* of shopkeepers, artisans and petty officials with industrialization which threatened their existence in the 1850s. The linking of contemporary ideas of racial purity and national survival with Ratzel's geographical concept of *Lebensraum* was the basis of Hitler's expansionist ideology. By the twentieth century Ratzel's ideas were deeply embedded in the German political psyche.

A member of the conservative right wing of the National Liberal Party, Ratzel took up the cudgel for his pseudo-scientific theories in the tariff debate of the 1890s to fight against free trade which he feared would destroy agriculture and the peasantry. Despite the social differences between Ratzel's middle class followers and the *Junker* landed aristocrats, intellectually Ratzel sided with the latter in their fears of a dispossessed agriculture gradually replaced by industry, the frightful image of the "machine in the garden" which so disturbed and bedeviled the nineteenth century.[4] As the anxious small farmer and *Kleinbürgertum* increasingly looked to the state for protection from the economic ravages of industrialization, the safety valve of immigration became increasingly important for class survival and found expression in strident and emotional nationalism. Lower middle class interest in "emigrationist colonialism" reinforced the upper class nationalist preoccupations of the Pan-German League and the German Colonial Union and support for German imperialism. As part of the deraciné middle class flotsam of Vienna, forced to spend his nights in doss-houses and his days wandering the streets in search of employment, Hitler absorbed this ideology of the rootless. It found expression in his pseudo-historical judgment "that a nation can exist without cities, but history would have taught us one day...that a nation cannot exist without farmers....Lasting successes a government can win only if the necessity is recognized for the securing of a people's *Lebensraum* and thus of its own agricultural class."[5]

These ideas received intellectual support from those disenchanted with the *kleindeutsch Kaiserreich* of Bismarck and its lack of imperialist perspectives and a mystical spiritual mission like the *schwärmer* Paul de Lagarde.

They despised the meanly commercial German *Bürgertum* which lacked their knight errant medieval notions and were devoid of nobility and romantic vision. Like most nineteenth-century believers in the superiority of their respective peoples over other lesser races, Lagarde, in Fritz Stern's classic study, "preached that Germany's destiny lay in the east, that Germany must rule and colonize the vast lands of eastern and southeastern Europe then ruled by a decrepit Austria and contemptible Russia." Indigent and impoverished Germans would be sent to the east and after receiving land and cattle would become a German gentry there to rule over the hapless natives "in Bohemia or Moravia, Hungary or Istria." German settler-frontiersmen would be settled "in eastern Poland from the Vistula to the Pinsk marshes" to guard Germany's eastern borders. Should Russia refuse to surrender Poland, the Balkans and a part of the Black Sea, "it forces us to war," as the Germans are "convinced that they have a mission to perform for all the nations of the world." All this would be accomplished by huge population transfers of Slovenes, Czechs, Magyars and other non-Germans and colonization of Poland and expulsion of the Polish Jews. Lagarde also believed in a "Führer" who would lead and uplift Germany toward a more spiritual destiny above the materialism and moral morass in which it wallowed.

Moeller van den Bruck held similar views in a later period, clinging to them throughout the First World War into the post-war period. One of the first to advance the *dolchstoss* (stab in the back) legend, van den Bruck saw Russia, whether Czarist or Soviet Russia, as the natural ally of Germany to oppose the West which he hated and fervently promoted an alliance between the two countries. In this he differed from Lagarde who tended to see Russia as an obstruction to German will to rule in the east. Van den Bruck is notable for his work *The Third Reich*, which he saw as a successor to the medieval Reich, and like many others of the post-war disillusioned and discontented intellectuals and unemployed officers longed for an end to the Weimar Republic and the founding of a newer, spiritually purified Third Reich. Like Lagarde he favored Germany's expansion to the east, but more in the direction of the *Baltikum* of the Estonians and Latvians which he was tied to by marriage and where he had once lived and believed bore German cultural and historical influences, rather than towards the lands of the Balkans and Southeastern Europe. Although sharing Largarde's desire for a "Führer," when he met Hitler at least once in the 1920s he found his unbridled proletarian passion too ungoverned and alienating. These ideas, particularly those that advanced a German "mission" to expand into and colonize the Eastern European areas were important as precursors; however, they remained idiosyncratic effusions, distillations without form, lacking commercial and economic flesh until the failed imperialism of Wilhelmian Germany and Hitler's Third Reich.

To achieve Germany's *Lebensraum,* Hitler's eyes focused on the limitless vistas of the Ukrainian steppelands. His writings and speeches indicate little interest in colonizing the Southeastern European area. However, in a secret interview in 1932 Hitler spoke to a German journalist of Anschluss, the breakup of Yugoslavia and Czechoslovakia, and the creation of an independent Slovakia and Croatia which would function as tributary dependencies of the Reich. German minorities in Transylvania were to be gathered "at the mouth of the Sava and Danube," perhaps at Belgrade, which "was and still is Prince Eugene's fortress."[6]

Under the impetus of nineteenth-century imperialism from the mid-century on, German nationalist thought took its cue especially from the United States and began to cultivate ideas of *Grossraumordnung* (System of Large Areas) based upon a German adaptation of the Monroe Doctrine as well as "Manifest Destiny."[7] It was deemed Germany's destiny to perform a civilizing function for "the lesser breeds beneath the law." Germany would play the same role in Eastern Europe as the United States did in Latin America. Eastern Europe would be the exclusive domain of German domination where other states' incursions would be unwelcome.

These notions of a German "manifest destiny" were hardly anything new and had appeared in various guises before the First World War. (Fritz Fischer has described German industry and the military and bureaucratic elite's desire for world hegemony in the period before and during the First World War in several studies.) Naumann's idea of "Mitteleuropa" later reappeared in a new form at the end of the 1930s in the economic ideology of *Grossraumwirtschaft* (the economy of large areas) which blamed the commodity gluts and trade imbalances of the Depression era on unbridled competition and trade restrictions. *Grossraumwirtschaft* would obviate this by creating a vast trading region, with Germany at the center, producing manufactured goods in exchange for the raw materials of the Eastern European hinterland. By 1938 *Grossraumwirtschaft* came into official popularity and seems to have for a time replaced the two older imperialist concepts of *Lebensraum* and *Weltpolitik*.[8]

On the subject of Nazi ideology recent scholars are divided. Some state flatly that Hitler, as the chief Nazi propagandist, believed that ideology had to be adapted to political conditions and circumstances and did not weigh greatly.[9] Others believed the hard kernel of his political orientation from his earliest days was racism, anti-Semitism and expansionism (the massive study of German foreign policy by Hildebrand reconfirms this thesis.[10] Hitler manifested this viewpoint from the very beginning in a letter of September 16, 1919, in which he wrote "the first political piece of writing of his life" and demanded "absolutely unshakably the removal of the Jews," to the end of the Third Reich in 1945 when he boasted of "having realistically grasped the Jewish question" and that later generations would "be eternally grateful to National Socialism for having exterminated the Jews from Germany and Central Europe."[11] "Racism and Space" (*Rassismus und Raum*) were at the very heart of his ideology.[12] Hitler's ideological and spatial program was a hodgepodge of much that was familiar and traditional in German life, particularly in right wing German political thought, which upper class bureaucrats and the military-landowner caste could identify with. In Hildebrand's characterization, Hitler's spatial autarchy and *Grosswirtschaft* (large economy) program was a recreation of Ludendorff's 1918 *Grossraum* (large area) idea, a self-sufficient Germany extended into the Ukrainian region ringed by a system of protectorates, semi-dependencies and independent agrarian states which it drew upon for its raw material needs and sold its industrial export surpluses. These areas would be first conquered militarily or voluntarily accept German domination and — depending on their racial affinities to the German *Herrenvolk* — would be repressed into a sleepy, backward colonial status forgotten and neglected by time and history. Pure and simple, it was a formula for an updated version of the older German imperialism of the Wilhelmian age and Ludendorff's border states expansionist design of 1918.[13]

By early 1930, German business believed that the limited existing capitalist market was insufficient to expand business and that demand could only be stimulated by increased export trade outlets to the east. Various schemes were being floated to solve the problem, besides the Briande Plan and 1915 Mitteleuropa plan of Naumann. Another possibility was a restored Austro-Hungarian state which could never be accepted by the Little Entente. Plans to create a Central European Slavic Mitteleuropa in various forms sponsored in the 1930s by either Czechoslovakia or France failed.[14] As these various plans only evoked the jealousy or rejection of one or another of the Great Powers, only one other possibility remained open for the German business class: the imperialist plan.

Previously the Nazi Party had little contact or support in industry and made its first move toward garnering it by the publication of a 1927 pamphlet aimed at the industrialists. But the latter continued to view the Nazi Party as a socialist-type Party. During the 1920s the Nazis had been primarily a lower middle class party seeking to gain support among the socialist-oriented working class. From 1930 onwards Hitler began to shed his "socialist" and leftist image in order to gain the support of the business and landowning/military upper class, and in 1932 defection of Otto Strasser, arguably the most important Nazi Party figure after Hitler and the main "left" Nazi, inadvertently signaled to the business class that Hitler might be their man. Hitler had refused to enter into a parliamentary coalition with General Schleicher as Strasser advised and the latter resigned from the party.

At a point in the autumn of 1932 when the German upper class industrialists began to see an imperialist policy as the only way out of the Depression, the Nazis issued "the Immediate Economic Policy of the NSDAP" (Wirtschaftlich Sofort Program der NSDAP) — "the first concrete expression of the Party's *Grossraumwirtschaft* policy in 1931."[15]

Hitler opposed the contemporary German drives to the west and the south as contrary to the interest of the Reich and replaced it with the *Drang nach Osten,* towards the steppelands of the Ukraine where Germany's historical destiny would be decided. In *Mein Kampf,* he chided the pre-war Imperial Germany for allying itself to the "mummy" state of Austria rather than England which, because of its overseas colonial interests, would not oppose Germany's march eastward and would act as Germany's protective rear guard — presumably against France. Moreover, the conflict between British and French imperialist interests in Africa and Asia would be expected to distance England from an alliance with France whom Hitler saw as the hereditary enemy.

Many scholars acknowledge Hitler's ideology of expansion to the east played a considerable role in his political thinking. Some historians adhere to a "programmatist" or "intentionalist" school (Hillgruber, Hildebrand) and view Hitler as an ideologue with a program for expansion of Germany's borders into the Soviet Union through the defeat of Poland and France. Later, after having driven England from the European continent, Germany would undertake a final contest with the United States for international hegemony. Other historians have rejected the idea that Hitler had a program or timetable for expansion and conquest and view him as merely a traditional German statesman (A. J. P. Taylor) or as a practitioner of Machiavellian opportunist politics (Rauschning, Bullock, Broszat, Mommsen). Important contributions have also been made by East German Marxists and some West German and other Marxist historians stressing structuralist and economic imperatives embedded in German capitalism as engines of expansion.[16]

In his earliest writings Hitler declared that the key to the establishment of German hegemony on the continent lay with England, the strongest power in the world. In the struggle for control of the continent, Hitler anticipated that Germany would be allied with England against France. Emboldened by his successes in Austria and Czechoslovakia and bolstered by the August 1939 Nazi-Soviet Pact of Non-Aggression, he reluctantly decided to go ahead without England, thus violating his own dictum. The idea of an alliance with England preceded the *Lebensraum* concept by several years and was further reiterated in his *Second Book* in 1928 as a fixed idea in his future plans.

With Italy, from whom Germany was separated only by the dispute over the South Tyrol, which Hitler quickly renounced claim to, he sought only friendship. On the subject of Southeastern Europe whose vital raw materials both Germany and Italy coveted, Hitler chose to remain silent or denied interest in the region altogether while pursuing a policy of establishing German hegemony through economic penetration in the mid-1930s. The first glimmers of the German-Italian conflict over the Southeast occurred over the knotty problem of Austria; the potential rivalry of these two powers was not lost on the British.

Italy was the key to containing Germany, some in the British Foreign Office believed. The main exponent of this line and the most outspoken anti-German in the Foreign Office was the Permanent Under-Secretary Vansittart. The latter was particularly aware of the dangers of a German-Italian alliance: "We must do all we can to keep these two beauties apart," he observed. He was none too discriminating in his methods suggesting that Italy be "bought off... in some form or other" by offers of Ethiopian territory or British Somaliland. Anthony Eden mistrusted Mussolini and opposed him, preferring to place his faith in the League of Nations.

Encouraged by French and British supineness during the Rhineland affair, Hitler next moved in the direction of annexing his former homeland. The British looked upon the imminent demise of the Austrian state with mixed detachment and anxiety. Leopold Amery, Winston Churchill and other conservative imperialists regarded the old Hapsburg monarchy with fond admiration, but it was not until after 1935 that the British began to join the French and Italians in considering a Hapsburg restoration. Although bills were introduced into the British parliament to enable Austria to form a monarchy and the British minister in Vienna informed his Yugoslav counterpart that London would soon agree to a Hapsburg restoration, visits to London by Chancellor Schuschnigg and Prince Staremberg in 1935 and 1936 produced no affirmative response.[17] By this time Italy, the chief supporter of Austrian independence, had undergone a change in attitude as a result of the Ethiopian affair and began to withdraw from its role as protector of Austria. Hitler's willingness to drop German claims to south Tyrol, as well as Germany's sympathy during the Ethiopian crisis, all helped to dissipate Italian hostility over Austria.[18]

In the waning months of 1935 the French and Italians supported by the British took steps to unite their respective armies in the event of a German seizure of Austria. The Little Entente states (Yugoslavia, Romania and Czechoslovakia), allied to France, were to be included in a European wide agreement. Though staff talks were held between the Italian and French military and a French army corps was to be placed between the Italian and Yugoslav forces to provide unity, the behind the scenes activities of the British minister to Belgrade, Nevile Henderson, undermined the agreement.[19]

From the advent of the National Socialist regime a steady stream of British upper class visitors arrived in Germany to find out whether it would be possible to do business with Hitler, starting with Lloyd George and ending with Neville Chamberlain. Hitler's visitors candidly suggested restitution for the wrongs of Versailles particularly in the case of the former German colonies in Africa. Hitler frequently mentioned the return of the lost colonies but without pressing the matter. His mind was mainly on colonial areas in Eastern Europe, particularly the Soviet Union, whose population could be expelled to make room for German colonists. Hjalmar Schacht, however, opposed adventures in the east and propagated the need for colonies in Africa as procurement grounds for raw materials. Hitler's racial antipathies opposed a German empire, in which unruly natives outnumbered Germans, as uninviting. The colonial issue for him was only something to be used in bargaining for larger stakes. In March 1938 the British ambassador Nevile Henderson offered Hitler territory in Africa belonging to Belgium and Portugal. The British had no intention of giving up Tanganyika, and South Africa wished to hold South-West Africa. With some indifference Hitler told Henderson that the colonial question "could wait four, eight or even ten years." After the Anschluss the subject was laid to rest, then once again brought up after Munich.[20]

British voices for accommodation became more insistent after the Anschluss. In a note to Halifax, Henderson candidly suggested "that on some favorable occasion in the House of Commons or House of Lords we should say quite openly that we have no intention of trying to hamper Germany's *legitimate* economic freedom of action in Central or Eastern Europe," adding, "I would not suggest this if I thought that we really could hamper it or if I did not realize that a nation of 75 million must be allowed to expand economically somewhere." This "somewhere" Henderson — and many others in the British upper class — were quite explicit about. "I admit," he wrote, "that personally I am only too glad to wish that She should look Eastwards instead of Westwards."[21] In 1938, following Germany's absorption of Austria, this could only mean towards Czechoslovakia.

Halifax's solution to Hitler's demands for the Sudetenland was to press the Czech government to the utmost for concessions to Berlin that would include annexation of the Sudeten German minority and hope that the rump Czechoslovak state might somehow maintain itself in the future. In this way peace would be preserved, Halifax hoped, and German domination of the continent avoided, which would of necessity reduce it to a second-class power. The German desire to dominate Czechoslovakia, the Czech leader Beneš told Sir Basil Newton, the British minister to Prague, "was not so much an object in itself as an essential step toward the realization of greater ambitions in Southeastern Europe. . . . Because she stood in the way of German ambitions toward that area its destruction was a German objective." He thought the Germans would pursue their ambitions in the southeast through peaceful penetration. If France abandoned the Czechs, it would be finished as a Great Power, he predicted. Unlike Austria, the Czechs would fight against German aggression, he told a British correspondent.[22]

Other Czech leaders were less aggressive and more inclined to mollify Germany. Czechoslovak Prime Minister Hodža defined the problem to Newton as "how to give Germany legitimate satisfaction" and yet prevent the states in the southeast "from being converted into mere colonies." Hodža thought that if Germany's need for the foodstuffs and raw materials of Southeastern Europe could be assured, then the problems might be alleviated.[23]

By mid-1938 Britain was less willing to give Germany a special sphere of interest in the region from which British trade and investment would be excluded. The French had similar misgivings about surrendering the natural resources of Czechoslovakia and the Balkans to Germany. Paul Reynaud told Halifax, "he was anxious about the great reinforcement of strength that such action might bring Germany, both in supplies and manpower." The French Foreign Office official Massigli also warned of the danger of removing the Czech barrier to the southeast: Once Germany got the oil and other raw materials it needed, it would avoid becoming embroiled with Russia and would turn west again.[24]

By this time Chamberlain's policy in Eastern Europe had taken shape: he was prepared to sacrifice the German-speaking Sudeten region to the Reich, but would draw the line at any further absorption of Southeastern Europe by Germany and the exclusion of British economic interests in that region. During Chamberlain's visit to Hitler at Godesberg, the German leader stated only that Germany's interest in the Southeast was economic rather than political. In answer to a direct question by Chamberlain about Germany's interest in the area, Hitler replied that Germany's production of industrial goods and consumption of raw materials and foodstuffs exactly complemented the southeastern region whose economy was the reverse of the Reich. In a reference to the United States whose foodstuffs and raw materials Germany was unable to pay for by exports of industrial goods to the already glutted American market, Hitler indicated obliquely that Germany was being driven inexorably to extend its control over Southeastern

Europe as an indispensable source of raw materials and a market for German exports. Hitler evoked what Chamberlain's biographer, Keith Graham Feiling, refers to as "the old vision" and grandiloquently told the leader of the world's greatest power: "You take the sea and we take the land." Hitler's interpreter, Dr. Paul Schmidt, gives a more expansive version of Hitler's desire for an agreement with Britain. "He returned to his old love." Hitler told Chamberlain: "Between us there need be no conflicts . . . we will not stand in the way of your overseas interests, and you can allow us a free hand without fear on the European continent in Central and Southeastern Europe." The colonial question could be settled later, Hitler concluded, and war need not take place.[25]

Under the pressures for markets generated by the 1938 economic depression, the problem of countering German expansion in the Southeast began to assume increased significance by the middle of that year. The British organized efforts to bolster the Southeastern countries while at the same time pursuing a *modus vivendi* with Germany. As Hitler had not moved into ethnically non-German territory until the occupation of Prague in March 1939, for the British, German expansion to the east did not assume an absolutely critical significance. Following the Munich settlement of September 1938, the British position jelled into a grudging willingness to accord Germany a dominant position in the Southeast, but not to permit British interests in the region to be entirely eclipsed. This bitter pill was partially a concession to Germany's growing military and political power as well as a feeling in the British government that Germany could no longer be frozen out of its share of the raw materials available on the world market without fostering a desperate expansion, further military aggression and ultimately war. The Romanian ruler King Carol received this disconcerting news during a visit to London when Halifax told him that "natural forces" made it "inevitable" that Germany should enjoy a predominant position in the economic field, which, however, did not mean that "we are in any way disinterested in any possibilities in Romanian trade that might be found practicable." Halifax denied that Chamberlain had agreed with Hitler at Munich that henceforth Central and Southeastern Europe was "a German monopoly field."[26]

The absorption of Austria and Czechoslovakia did not solve Germany's economic difficulties. A British appraisal indicated that it "will do little to strengthen her at some of her weakest places particularly her deficiencies in industrial raw materials and liquid fuels and her shortage of labor." Moreover, Germany would have to supply Czech industry "with considerable quantities of iron ore, coal and coke, manganese, ferrous alloys, non-ferrous metals, pyrites and sulphur, salt, petroleum and textiles fibres." Of these only coal, coke and salt were found in the Reich in any great abundance. The rich mineral deposits of Southeastern Europe had become even more important for Germany's economy.[27]

German leaders (Ribbentrop, Göring, Göbbels and Rosenberg) told the French minister to Berlin, Robert Coulondre, that Germany's destiny and interests lay in Southeastern Europe. The French should understand, Göring explained to Coulondre, that Germany wanted a field to expand in the Southeast.[28] Coulondre concluded that the Germans wished to cover themselves with an accord with the French in the West preparatory to undertaking new moves in the East and Southeast.[29] Only Schacht, who was now out of favor, expressed his fear of Nazi adventures in the Ukraine. The Franco-German Declaration of December 6, 1938, gave the Germans the green light to move east. Ribbentrop later claimed that French Foreign Minister Bonnet conceded in so many words that henceforth Eastern Europe constituted a German sphere of influence.[30]

To block Hitler from further penetration into the Southeast a "Third Europe," sponsored by Italy and composed of Hungary, Poland, Romania and Yugoslavia, formed to function within the Axis without manifesting overt hostility to Germany. Mussolini conceived of this bloc of states as a "Horizontal Axis" which would bar Germany from the southeast, maintain Italian influence there and give Italy the strength it needed to contain Hitler.[31] The centerpiece of this program was to be the creation of a common border between Poland and Hungary through the Hungarian annexation of the Carpatho-Ukrainian portion of Czechoslovakia, which the Poles hoped would also block the possibility of a Great Ukrainian state. Berlin realized these schemes were aimed against Germany and vetoed the common border project.[32] The Germans used the Carpathian region to bribe the Poles into joining Germany, returning Danzig and granting a railway connection through the corridor to East Prussia under German sovereignty. Poland, Ribbentrop suggested to the Poles, should join the Germans in the Anti-Comintern pact against the USSR; but the Poles rejected the German offer in late October 1938.[33] It would have meant Poland would agree to become a satellite of Germany. The abortive October 1938 Nazi diplomatic offensive against the Poles was the prelude to Hitler's decision to attack Poland in September 1939. By the end of October Hitler had already ordered the Wehrmacht to be prepared to eliminate the remnant of the Czechoslovak state.[34]

British ambassador Henderson, following his return from London for consultations and an operation, began to have premonitions that Hitler had decided to act when the German leader brusquely mentioned, during a diplomatic function, that "it was not Britain's business to interfere in Central Europe."[35] After the Czechs occupied Bratislava and dismissed the pro-German Tiso government in Slovakia giving Hitler his pretext for action, Henderson hurried to see State Secretary Weizsäcker and implored him not to violate the Munich agreement or to do anything until the arrival in Berlin of Stanley, head of the Board of Trade, and Hudson, chief of the Overseas Trade Department for trade talks. Halifax cancelled the forthcoming visit scheduled for March 15, the day German forces occupied Czechoslovakia.

The German invasion of Czechoslovakia caught the British by surprise; Henderson confessed that "up to the last moment I found it difficult to believe Hitler would go quite as far as he did."[36] Chamberlain's foreign policy lay in ruins and the consternation in London was great. The first Foreign Office memorandum after Hitler marched into Prague revealed an end to illusions about Hitler and the great change in policy that had taken place. "The action clearly revealed Germany's intentions and the expectation of eventual war ... there is every reason to suppose that the treatment applied to Czecho-Slovakia [*sic*] will be extended to other countries in Europe, notably Romania and Poland." Germany was expected "to gradually neutralize these countries, deprive them of their armies and incorporate them in the German economic system." After accomplishing this task, it would turn on the West and attack it.[37]

London resolved to create broad ties with those states in the East to prevent that from happening. Chamberlain, who only a few short months before in a now famous comment had described Czechoslovakia during the 1938 Munich crisis as "a far away country ... of whom we know nothing," was now proclaiming that England's interests lay in Eastern Europe. Two days after the occupation of Prague, Chamberlain delivered an address in Birmingham in which he tried to repair the damage by declaring that "we are not disinterested in what goes on in Southeastern Europe" which "will wish to have our counsel and advice."[38] Britain now had a two-track foreign policy of dealing directly with Göring, Wohltat and other German officials for a general settlement based upon British acknowledgement of German interests in the Southeast, and at the same time blocking further German expansion by extending trade credits to the Eastern European countries and taking larger amounts of imports from the region, preventing its conversion into a German colony. A third policy was to negotiate with the Soviet Union in the event that the talks with the Germans failed to produce the desired results. The Australian scholar, Manne, suggests that the British dealt with the Soviets in earnest and that Chamberlain, contrary to the post-war charges of some detractors who believed he really hoped to come to an agreement with the Germans to encourage them to expand eastward, had in fact come around to the view of his cabinet that they would have to at least try to secure an agreement with the Soviet Union in order to contain Hitler. This benign view of Chamberlain's intentions has been challenged by more recent studies which return to the older view of Chamberlain's hatred of the Soviet Union and all its works and his hopes for a German-Soviet clash.[39]

Throughout the summer months the proponents of an arrangement with Hitler rather than the Soviet Union continued to seek an overall accommodation. The real tragedy of Prague, according to Ambassador Henderson, was not the destruction of Czechoslovakia, but that it had interrupted the Stanley-Hudson visit![40] Even before the German occupation of Prague, Henderson was urging an overall agreement with the Germans. Hitler, he advised Halifax, might be depended upon to keep his word as likely as any other statesman! He also advised that Britain should stay out of Germany's hair in those areas of German interests and adopt a neutral attitude if Hitler became involved in the East. In the event of a war between Germany and the Soviet Union over the Ukraine "it seems to me the less we take sides the better."[41] While Henderson was undoubtedly the outstanding pro-German voice in the government who did not conceal his wish to see Hitler turn east and attack the Soviet Union, there is little doubt that it was the unspoken thought of many in the Government, some in the highest circles, which they took good care to conceal in official communications. This is the only explanation of why the British persisted in their efforts to arrive at a general settlement with Hitler in the face of mounting evidence of Germany's intractable inclination toward aggressive expansion.

The British were cognizant of the problem of a rearmed and assertive Germany as early as 1931 when two Foreign Office officials, Orme Sargent and Ashton-Gwatkin, called for a general settlement of certain complaints.[42] Four years later Ralph Wigram, head of the Central European department of the British Foreign Office, joined Sargent and Ashton-Gwatkin to warn against pursuing a policy of drift or encirclement of Germany. Even if an antirevisionist bloc could be constructed, he prophesied, it would probably not hold together.[43] Brigadier Arthur Temperly, British military representative at the League of Nations, argued in a memorandum in May 1933, that Germany was like a mad dog which had to be destroyed or quarantined while there was still time. The memorandum was sent to the cabinet by Vansittart who also considered the possibility only to discard it because it would only drive the German people to support Hitler.[44] At this time the collapse of the Nazi regime from internal contradictions was considered a distinct possibility.

The history of the period between March and September 1939 is replete with voids and imponderables. It is still unclear why the contacts and discussions between various British and German officials, after the occupation of Bohemia and Moravia in March 1939, did not produce an overall agreement.

Hitler may not have been aware of these contacts at all, as A. J. P. Taylor observed, because they were conducted without his knowledge, or if he were aware of them, then only peripherally, as he was totally immersed in planning his next move against Poland.[45] Hitler's tightened grip on the military after 1938 following his triumph at Munich allowed him to act first without fear of the German General Staff before any of these discussions and contacts could come to a head. The conventional view, of "intentionalists" at least, is that Hitler was now completely locked into his *Mein Kampf* fantasies of *Lebensraum* and plunder in the east. The strange lack of correspondence in these continued contacts between the Germans and British down to the eve of the war on the one hand, and Hitler's dogged moves toward war on the other, can only be explained, according to this view, by the fact that Hitler pursued a different agenda than Schacht, Göring and others.

The likely answer to all these historical conundrums is that both Hitler's political successes and his *Lebensraum* imperialist ideology impelled him toward newer expansionary moves and that simultaneously Germany was running out of raw materials and complex economic forces would not be expected to markedly improve in the future. Meanwhile Britain and France were rearming and growing stronger every year. As Hitler himself attested in August 1939, he preferred to take what he needed by conquest while Germany was still militarily dominant than to settle for international agreements which might be less favorable and could later be ignored or violated.

British foreign policy before Munich was erratic and contradictory, reverting for a time to its former strategy of using Italy to control Germany and in April 1938, therefore, the Chamberlain government concluded the Anglo-Italian agreement (Gentlemen's Agreement). But Chamberlain's failure to heed Vansittart's admonition to buy off Italy with offers of territory during his January visit to Rome, determined Mussolini more than ever to throw in his lot with Germany. In the following month, on May 23, 1939, he signed the Pact of Steel with Germany. After Munich the British pursued several lines: rearming for war; friendship with Italy; agreements with Poland, Romania and the East European states for a broad front; negotiations with the Soviet Union; and arriving at an agreement with Germany through cabinet and lesser officials. Official contacts between the British and German governments scarcely existed after March 15, 1939. On March 17 Henderson was recalled to London and did not return until five weeks later on April 24. Between the date of Henderson's return and late August, the British minister had only a brief meeting with Göring, which "led...nowhere."[46]

His first official contact with Hitler occurred on August 23, when Ribbentrop was already in Moscow to sign the Nazi-Soviet Pact. When Henderson — called by Hitler "the man with the flower" for his boutonniere — contradicted Hitler's elated predictions of the great advantages to be gained from the agreement by moralistic reproaches, of the dangers of supping with the Devil, Hitler became flustered and blamed Britain for having driven him into Russia's arms.[47] In Britain the Czech affair and its repercussions in turning public opinion against Germany had not yet been dissipated; Hitler was still intoxicated by his success in absorbing Austria and the Czech region and preoccupied with planning further expansionary moves. British efforts to arrive at a *modus vivendi* with Germany received little encouragement. A wall of silence frustrated Henderson's requests for information about Germany's price for peace, until Göring finally did tell him that the price was British recognition of Germany's primacy in Europe.[48]

Chamberlain and the British ruling elite felt an even greater loathing for Communist Russia, as the world's chief mischief maker, than it did for Hitler and German fascism.[49] Neville Chamberlain undoubtedly wished the Germans would move east into the Soviet Union — in which case Britain presumably would have done nothing to assist the Soviet government. This at least is implicit in a session of the British cabinet held in November 1938 in which Chamberlain reported King Carol's belief that "Germany's intention was to try to start the disruption of Russia by fostering an independent State in the Ukraine which would, in effect, be under German influence." Chamberlain warned against being drawn into war "in some future quarrel between Russia and Germany in which France might take the USSR's side." This appeared to be difficult for Halifax to swallow and he emphasized: "it was in our interest to see a strong Russia, and that we must not take any action which made it appear that we were anti-Russian, or indifferent to Russia's future." "The Prime Minister agreed that this was so. At the same time it was desirable to avoid entanglements arising out of a possible dispute between Russia and Germany."[50]

However much the British wished the Germans would move east into the Soviet Union, Poland remained an obstacle in the path of a German expansionary move. The Chamberlain government eventually decided that it would not allow Poland to follow Austria and the Czech provinces as the next territorial acquisition of Germany. It was also by no means axiomatic that Hitler might strike east first to Poland, then the Soviet Union, rather than to attack France, Belgium and the Netherlands first. Hitler himself confessed to being undecided. London was less constrained to support Poland for moral reasons than because it had made the decision that its major military ally in the east was not the USSR but Poland. The British military and the British government viewed the Polish army as more important in their military and political reckoning than the Red Army.[51] The elimination of Poland would have meant the gravitation of the small countries of Southeastern Europe into the Nazi orbit.

Like most imperialist nations, the British government had no intention of giving up future investments and commercial prospects in Southeastern Europe. A continued British economic presence in Southeastern Europe would have encouraged those states to resist German domination and strengthen the "peace front." German preeminence in the Southeast would be the forerunner of a German-dominated Europe, a prospect which agonized British leaders for whom it meant the decline of Britain, as Halifax had noted, to a second rank power. The "Roosevelt" Depression of 1938 and the critical struggle for world markets to stimulate demand made the loss of Southeastern Europe to exclusive German trade and investment unacceptable. However much Chamberlain and other British leaders believed that balance of power considerations no longer played a role in Britain's foreign policy, it nonetheless continued to play a geopolitical role.[52] The establishment of German preeminence in Southeastern Europe and thereafter on the continent meant the imperilment of Britain and its overseas empire by a resurgent Germany in possession of the resources of Europe. Thus, British policy hovered between the realistic perception that a powerful and assertive German state of sixty-five million would have to be allowed to expand into Southeastern Europe and the uneasy knowledge that this would threaten its own security.

The British also had no desire to surrender their grip over the lucrative Yugoslav mining industry, Romanian oil and other crucial sectors of the Southeastern European economy. London's disinclination to acknowledge German economic hegemony in the Southeast also stemmed from deeply rooted free trade principles which were almost an article of faith. Free trade, upon which British commerce and industry had been based since the nineteenth century, clashed with Nazi *"Grossraumwirtschaft"* economics which would have converted Southeastern Europe into a kind of closed German colonial hinterland, excluding English trade and commerce.

As long as England maintained its commercial interests in the Southeast by offering an alternative option to dealing exclusively with the Reich, it would delay the conversion of the region into a colony of the Reich. Hitler, therefore, paid little attention to any British siren song of a general settlement, which he probably took to be a deflecting maneuver to blunt Germany's hegemonical course.

Thus, Nazi Germany and Great Britain for geopolitical and economic reasons were bent on an imperialist collision course for control of the Southeast and ultimately for Europe and the world. As in earlier struggles the nations and peoples of the Southeastern region were merely pawns in the clash of rival Great Power interests.

Part Two

Great Power Trade and Political Tensions over Eastern Europe, 1935–1939

Chapter 6

British-German Trade Problems. Britain Threatens a Clearing. Schacht's Last Tape: His Unsuccessful Attempt to Gain Raw Materials

> Avert, High Wisdom, never vainly wooed,
> This threat of War, that shows a land brain-sick.
> When nations gain the pitch where rhetoric
> Seems reason they are ripe for cannon's food.
> — George Meredith, *On the Danger of War*

THE SYSTEM OF BRITISH IMPERIALISM, as we have shown previously, suffered a gradual decline from its heyday in the era from 1860 to 1884 to the decade immediately after the Great War, a fact which exercised enormous influence upon British foreign policy in the 1930s. Between 1870 and 1914 Britain's net annual foreign investment was about one-third of its capital accumulation, the highest in the history of any nation to that time. In the 1860s it amounted to 4.0% of the GNP, rising to an average of 5.2% in the period from 1870 to 1914.[1] During this period, of the total new portfolio capital issued in Britain, 34% went to North America, 17% to South America, 14% to Asia, 13% to Europe, 11% to Australia and 11% to Africa.[2]

A recent somewhat statistically dense historical study of a large number of British firms of various kinds states that British capital investments from 1860 to 1880, the golden age of British imperialism, averaged about 13.5% for the United Kingdom, 13.4% for foreign investments and 21.6% for Empire investments.[3] Overall domestic investments in these firms from 1860 to 1912 averaged 10.2%, foreign investments 9.4% and empire investments 13.0%.

In the era after the 1880s, according to the same study, empire investments fell to 7.6%, declining below domestic profits.[4] Imperialist elite groups (i.e., those involved in financial services, the military, agriculture or were peers, gentlemen and squires, land and property owners, capitalists or banks) held a larger share of foreign and empire firms than domestic firms, while the middle class concentrated on domestic rather than foreign and empire investments.[5] The middle class, on the other hand, owned 54% of U.K. shares, 36% of foreign and 30% of empire shares.[6] The social costs of empire, i.e., the imperial bureaucracy, military costs, etc., were borne for the most part by the British taxpayer. Moreover, the independent countries and dependencies knew that if they avoided payment, the British taxpayer would be compelled to assume the costs.

After the trough of the worst period of industrialization had passed, it is generally acknowledged that real wages and living standards for the working class had significantly improved by the final quarter of the nineteenth century. According to the findings of Leone Levi, in the period from 1851 to 1881, working class incomes rose by 59% and the lower middle class had improved by 37%, while incomes of the middle to upper class had declined by 30%. Then, around 1900 everything changed: real wages declined, production rates stalled and Britain's trade balances adversely shifted against her until 1914 when real wages finally caught up to living costs. In the pre-war period from the 1880s low unemployment, which encouraged labor militancy, machine displaced craftsmen, rising prices and static wages raised working class consciousness and increasingly provoked militant strike actions; and the growing difficulties of the casual laborer and the very poor produced riots in the mid-1880s and massive working class demonstrations to the eve of the war.[7]

The decline and stagnation of the period after 1900 reappeared and greatly intensified after the First World War. In contrast to the era from 1880 to 1914 when unemployment averaged 4.5%, during the inter-war era from 1921 to 1938 unemployment was far higher, averaging 14.2%, largely concentrated in iron, steel, pig iron, general engineering, shipbuilding, textiles, construction and the hotel and public houses category. The social squalor and appalling condition of the unemployed and working class in northern England and London during the 1930s, which one reads of with riveting empathy and disbelief in the early writings of George Orwell such as *The Road to Wigan Pier* and *Down and Out in London and Paris*, defy recent historical comparison, except perhaps with the worst period of the industrial revolution of the early and mid-nineteenth century as described in Friedrich Engels's *Condition of the Working Class in England* or the novels of Charles Dickens.[8]

The 1930s — "the hungry thirties" — was a period in which wealth and poverty were strange and uneasy bedfellows, a period of social and economic stagnation as well as prosperity for some in the 75% of the population which was always employed at any given time. It was an England in which the broad middle class and some in the working class experienced higher living standards and reached greater levels of consumption derived from new industries and the service sector of the economy. The literary chronicler of the era, J. B. Priestly, described an England of "arterial and by-pass roads, filling stations, and factories that look like exhibition buildings, of giant cinemas and dance halls and cafes, bungalows with tiny garages, cocktail bars, Woolworths, motor coaches, wireless, hiking, factory girls looking like actresses, greyhound racing and dirt tracts, swimming pools and everything given away for cigarette coupons."[9]

The shift from the older staple industries of coal, steel and textiles to automobiles, construction and electrical components was accompanied by a striking increase in the consumer and service sector of the economy. The

United Kingdom in the 1930s seemed to be shifting from a society of producers to a society of consumers; average real living standards for those employed — the latter being the key qualifying phrase — rose during the 1930s from 15% to 18%.[10] During this period broad segments of the middle class and some privileged strata of the working class acquired property and savings for the first time. Falling prices contributed to the increase in disposable income for those two social groups, but the geographic and social division between a relatively better off "inner England" in the southeastern region and a stagnant, industrialized "outer England" of Wales, Scotland, northern Ireland and northern England persisted unchanged down to the present day.

Investment moved from the production sector into housing and the consumer and service sector where profit rates were high. In general, private investment lagged and, according to the contemporary estimate of Colin Clark, net capital investment in 1935 had fallen to 6.9% of the national income, far less than the 12.2% in 1907 and even the 7.2% in 1929. The lagging rate of private investment in the thirties has been attributed to the riskiness of business investment and — according to Keynes at least — the propensity of capitalists to save. In reality, the malaise of British industry was caused by increased competition in international trade after 1880 from other imperialist countries, particularly the United States after World War I. An additional development was the transformation of Great Britain into a rentier state, as noted by Hobson, Lenin, Schulze-Gavernitz and others, in which increasing numbers lived off the proceeds of investments abroad. A feature of this transformation was the declining size of the working class.

In the century between 1815 and 1901 the absolute number of workers in basic industries remained static while the population almost doubled. Though the population in that period rose from 17.9 million to 32.5 million, the number of workers increased only slightly from 4.1 to 4.9 million, a decline from 23% to 15% of the total population.[11] According to Marx, Hobson and others a major reason for industrial stagnation is the conflict between labor and capital. Low wages and higher profits combined with underconsumption and declining investment possibilities to place greater amounts of money in the hands of property owners and the privileged few, causing money to be invested abroad for maximum returns. Diminishing rates of return for domestic investment, strikes by a militant working class demanding higher wages, and a higher rate of return on capital in the colonial areas where the organic composition of capital was lower (i.e., lower wages, cheaper raw materials in relation to capital) caused surplus capital to be pushed or pulled abroad.

The changing pattern of British investments was reflected in the parliament and cabinets of the inter-war years, dominated for the most part by the conservatives. The post-war parliament contained a solid phalanx of British businessmen, described by Prime Minister Stanley Baldwin as "associated chambers of commerce" and by the conservative imperialist Duff Cooper as nouveau riche who had made their fortunes during the war "often by methods that did not invite close scrutiny." Randolph Churchill bluntly assessed them as "self-made, self-seekers" who represented "the most squalid and acquisitive segment of the [business] community."[12] Business and occa-sional bureaucratic elements dominated the cabinets of the 1920s and 1930s: Bonar Law pursued a career in business before becoming active in politics; Stanley Baldwin, scion of a Worcestershire iron master, had operated the family business before entering the House; Sir Samuel Hoare was a member of a respected banking family; Lord Londonderry, an aristocrat but also a mining baron; and Neville Chamberlain, who had ties to and financial in-vestments in the "City," had been a former Lord Mayor of Birmingham. Much has been made of their crabbed mentality and inclination toward moral superiority and complacency but, in reality, they were the represen-tatives of a hereditary landed aristocracy with business interests, ruling in partnership with a philistine upper middle class elite that had little taste for adventures abroad or at home and wished only for the pleasant comforts of hearth and kin. The "real desire of Great Britain," Lloyd George confided to Briand, "was to get on with business."[13] When the French occupied the Ruhr in 1923 the British told their wartime ally that England wanted the dispute settled "because rightly or wrongly she attributed the greater part of her unemployment to the present disorganization of the world."[14]

In Germany's case the onset of the world Depression in the early 1930s and the National Socialist Revolution of 1933 dashed these hopes of a peaceful reconstruction of the world economy. To reduce the tide of un-employment, almost one-third of the wage earners or six million persons, the Nazis adopted a program of tax cuts and public works which appeared to be the right nostrum. Unemployment began slowly to recede. However, as the Treasury Department official Michael Pinsent, on loan to the British embassy in Berlin, noted, it was not these measures that eliminated un-employment. "It is probable," he wrote, "in actual fact that the economic recovery has been stimulated less by public works properly so-called than by special factors, viz., rearmament and the revival of the motor trade" (the removal of the tax on cars).[15]

Even before the initiation of rearmament, Germany's economic position was parlous and its share of the world export trade had fallen considerably below the pre-war figure, declining from 13.21% in 1913 to 9.88% in 1933 and even lower in the Nazi era two years later to 8.9% in 1935 (see Table 6–1). While both the U.K. and the U.S. had suffered similar declines, they were beginning to revive in comparison to Germany's steady deterioration. In addition both the U.K. and the U.S. possessed currency reserves whereas Germany did not. Moreover, Germany's indebtedness was a particularly onerous burden.

Noteworthy is the continued decline in German trade — particularly exports — during the first years of the Nazi administration, 1933–1935, depriving Germany of the necessary currency to pay for imports, contribut-ing to internal crisis and eventually war (see Table 6–1). In 1933 the German government increased the duty on Lancashire yarns exported to Germany 50% — viewed in Britain as "a movement with an avowed retaliatory aim" — evoking protests to the British government by the Lancashire textile associations; and in the following year the latter were agitated into further protest meetings when the British government negotiated an agreement with

Table 6-1. Shares of the United Kingdom, Germany and the United States in the World Export Trade, 1913–1935 (in percentages)[16]

Year	Gold Values (millions of gold dollars)	U.K.	Germany	U.S.
1913	18,195	14.08	13.21	13.46
1924	25,127	14.01	6.19	17.90
1925	30,030	12.16	6.81	16.03
1926	29,770	10.66	7.82	15.83
1927	31,308	11.01	7.76	15.20
1928	32,738	10.76	8.93	15.37
1929	33,021	10.75	9.73	15.62
1930	26,438	10.51	10.85	14.31
1931	19,908	9.37	12.09	12.58
1932	12,895	9.92	10.60	12.22
1933	11,740	10.37	9.88	10.90
1934	11,364	10.47	8.62	11.03
1935	11,444	10.83	8.90	11.16

Germany for the payment of older loans without making any provision for the payment of outstanding past trade debts.[17] In June 1934 Germany ceased to transfer abroad interest payments on the Dawes and Young bonds, causing a storm of protest in Europe and the U.S. The close connections between the more powerful British financial circles and the government led London to set up on June 28, two weeks later, a Debt Clearing House to seize the profits of German exports to pay British bondholders, while debts owed to the weaker commercial interests remained in abeyance. A week later Schacht accepted the "Anglo-German Transfer Agreement" for payment in sterling of the interest on bonds held by British creditors, and the following week the Debt Clearing House was abolished. Britain could force payment in this manner because German exports to Britain exceeded imports. However, in the case of the United States where the trade balance was unfavorable, U.S. bondholders were not so fortunate.

In 1933 and for the last time in 1934 before his death J. W. F. Thelwell, the respected British Commercial Counsellor to the Berlin Embassy, made a remarkable prediction of Germany's economic future in his report on "Economic Conditions in Germany." Thelwell declared that "the main source of taxation is German industry and its progress is bound up with exports." However, since 1929 German exports and imports had dropped by 16,500,000 marks. In the first five months of 1933 German exports dropped by 18% and the export surplus was 263,000,000 marks as against 460,000,000 in the same period in 1932. Trade with the USSR, Germany's best market, amounted to 181 million marks in the first three months of 1932 compared to 89 million marks in the same period in 1933. In the stimulation of the home market by vast schemes of government-financed public works and the simultaneous fall in Germany's foreign trade due to international restrictions, Thelwell foresaw "two internal dangers":

> One is that Germany's large and efficient industrial apparatus running at high speed absolutely needs an outlet beyond the home market, if it is not to be choked with its own products and the other, that if some means of financing raw material imports cannot be found the machine will run down for want of fuel and the whole scheme for provision of work will be jeopardized.[18]

Germany, the report predicted, would continue to remain a formidable competitor, despite its difficulties "because she will help her exporters with cheap marks on those markets which are of value to her" since its forward drive in production would tend to outrun internal purchasing power and manufacturers would prefer to sell the excess output very cheaply abroad rather than to lock up capital in stocks. At a later date if Germany decided to devalue the mark to the level of the pound and dollar it "would be a formidable competitor." Devaluation then would become the critical point for the Nazi regime in the future. Thelwell's untimely death did not permit him to foresee with exactitude that the first danger would be met through the rearmament program, which would absorb a good part of German production and at the same time gradually by 1938 return Germany to full production, but that insufficient wages paid to the German worker and scarce consumer commodities would lead to a recurrent inflationary problem and threaten a return to industrial stagnation and unemployment. Furthermore, Germany's export decline caused by inability to sell its exports on the stagnating, highly competitive 1930s international trade market would force it to resort to short-term export subsidization, barter methods and other trade stimulation techniques, as Thelwell predicted, to pay for imports without which it would be unable to survive.

These problems surfaced during the thorny British-German trade negotiations held in Berlin in August and September 1934 conducted by Ulrich, heading the German delegation, and Sir Frederick Leith-Ross, the chief economic advisor to the British government, and Pinsent, a Treasury department official. By that time Schacht's policy under the New Plan of only allowing imports to enter Germany for which exchange currency was available replaced the day-to-day "repartition" of currency. Under the new policy, articles and goods necessary for the German economy could be imported only after a special currency certificate (*Divisenbescheinigung*) had been obtained, which guaranteed the necessary funds to pay for the imported goods.

Leith-Ross stated emphatically to the Germans "that it was impossible to overstate the feelings of U.K. traders in regard to the German trade restrictions.... The German regulations were very effective in stopping business." He bridled at Ulrich's suggestion that Britain allow the German government sufficient released currency to pay its frozen debts, which must have seemed a form of economic blackmail. Leith-Ross declared that payment had to be made before further trade could be resumed. Britain, he emphasized, did not like clearings, but once other countries imposed them on a world scale, they were difficult to avoid. At present Britain was being discriminated against as regards exchange, frozen debts and interest payments on loans owed to British bondholders. He dropped polite innuendo of retaliation: if British exports continued to be "damnified" then "there was no question of Germany exporting luxuries to the United Kingdom." He then addressed himself to the growing barter trade agreements with Southeastern Europe, Latin America and other regions which Germany entered into to gain imports without currency. Speaking personally, he could see where the German scheme of negotiations would lead them. They might be able to compel other countries producing raw materials to take German goods "but this would not work with the U.K. and countries similarly situated." He then accused the Germans of violating the 1924 trade agreement not to interfere in the free flow of goods.[19]

British trade with Germany was beginning to recede. Herring and coal exports to Germany, two leading staple items of export to Germany, had begun to decline already by 1934. Leith-Ross estimated that U.K. exports to Germany were £800,000 less than in 1933 while German exports to the U.K. had been maintained. Although the Germans now had additional exchange available to pay for their imports, "frozen debts had accumulated and feeling had grown in the U.K." Up to June 30, 1934, on the eve of the British-German trade negotiations, the German frozen debts figure was about £1.8 million, but by the time of the negotiations was thought to have increased to between £2.5 and £3 million. Nevertheless, Ulrich insisted that "no exchange would be issued except for the imports of food and raw materials necessary for German economic activities." In the matter of the frozen debts the attitude of the Germans "was not promising." A deadlock occurred when Leith-Ross demanded a 60/40 arrangement allocating not less than 60% of the value of German exports to the U.K. for the future payment of British imports to Germany. The German negotiators promptly countered with a 50/50 demand, which necessitated transferring the negotiations to a higher level.[20]

In October and November 1934 Leith-Ross negotiated with the German Minister of Economics, Hjalmar Schacht, once again raising the question of Germany's delinquent accounts and payment for British imports with hard cash. The British government, he insisted to Schacht, had no desire for a clearing arrangement, but the German negotiators had been unable to make any proposals to satisfy British requirements except within the framework of a clearing agreement. The British government had accordingly sent him to Germany to negotiate a clearing agreement. Although "it was very late to reverse their decision" it was prepared to make several proposals. German exports had increased so that the *Reichsbank* should have the necessary sterling to pay for British exports to Germany which "have not only decreased, but they have not been paid for." To avoid a clearing the British government must be assured that not less than 55% of the value of German exports would be allocated for the payment of U.K. exports to Germany.[21]

Leith-Ross turned the screw still further: the possibility of abandoning a clearing, he told Schacht, "is entirely conditional on definite and satisfactory assurances for the liquidation of the frozen trade debts due to the

U.K." To this end a recent German loan request could be utilized to pay off "the whole or as large as possible a part of these debts." The British demanded £400,000 as an "advance payment" by the Reichsbank and a percentage from the proceeds of German exports to the U.K. within twelve months to liquidate "any balance that cannot be discharged by means of the credit operation." In addition, Leith-Ross demanded the liquidation of the *Sondermark* or special marks — a form of payment used by the Germans to avoid expending exchange currency — out of the 55% allocation of U.K. exports. "If we are to avoid a clearing" there was also to be a "full payment of all coupons of the Dawes and Young loans belonging to British holders" as well as other non-Reich loans.[22]

Several weeks later, with the threat of a clearing hanging over his head, Schacht bowed to the inevitable. In a note to Leith-Ross he agreed to make payments, but declared somewhat evasively that he did not know "what amount I can put at your disposal during the next 6 weeks. The figure of £300,000 which you mention is enormously burdensome to me, but I shall try my utmost and hope to be able to arrange for it." Schacht was "still quite willing to arrange for it if I do not find other means to satisfy you." For a Central Bank to have to borrow was "rather inadequate" and he had only brought it up to Berlin in "case of an absolute necessity." But, as the economic historian Harold James suggests, for Germany to trade at all, a British loan was a necessity. The agreed upon formula of 55% of sterling from the proceeds of German exports to Britain, 10% set aside for debt service worked reasonably well and by 1936 credits provided to German banks and industry fell by 30%. This permitted continued Germany trade with Britain, assured the bondholders of steady payments and avoided the possibilities of a German debt moratorium which could only roil financial and trade markets. Irritated at German rearmament, the indignant share-holders protested vociferously but failed to gain a better settlement and the payments agreement remained in effect. Montagu Norman did not wish to jeopardize a situation in which German payments however slow continued to be met rather than risk receiving nothing at all. In any further financial dealings with the Germans the interests of the bondholders remained foremost; and anything that threatened German trade with Britain and its important stimulus for the British home market was studiously avoided. Norman's close relationship to Schacht had succeeded and in the former's words: "An Anglo-German connection had been created." If it suited British interests, it also suited German in that it permitted Hitler to rearm; those who protested against this and demanded an end to the Payments Agreement either were ignored or eventually silenced.[23]

Germany's economic problems continued to plague it, forcing the German government to resort to new measures to increase its exports to gain exchange to pay for imports. The problem of frozen debts began to recede in the face of this new more threatening problem to the eve of the war.

By mid-1936 the Department of Overseas Trade began receiving reports from its overseas officials and other sources that British firms competing for important public contracts had experienced intense competition from German concerns. This had resulted in some cases of contracts being lost or alternatively of U.K. prices being forced down "to an entirely uneconomic and unprofitable level." Competition had also been experienced in other types of businesses and frequently "the competition had been made possible by the subsidization of German export trade." The reports provoked a full-scale policy evaluation resulting in a fifty-two-page study, "German Competition in World Trade," and a flurry of meetings, memos and minutes by Treasury, Board of Trade and Foreign Office officials below the cabinet level.[24]

Germany, the report declared, had to export manufactured goods to maintain employment and obtain essential raw materials. Any denial of these activities would provoke an economic strain leading "to either internal or external political reactions." Germany had failed to attain the economic position it enjoyed in 1913 and had only succeeded in exporting sufficient goods to be able to meet its import requirements. It was a highly industrialized country whose home market did not offer sufficient outlet for the products of its industry. To maintain employment and to keep prices at a reasonable level, it was essential that outlets be secured for the surplus production. If government orders were reduced, pressures for outlets would increase. German prices were higher than U.K. prices and required a reduction of about 40% to bridge the gap.[25]

To solve the financial crisis caused by the problem of declining exports, in 1935 the Germans, as Thelwell had predicted, devised a direct subsidization of exporters through a fund levied upon industry which had originally been voluntary "or ostensibly so." The money was paid into a central pool managed by the Gold Discount Bank, the charges falling on dividends, depreciation and other reserves. The levy varied from industry to industry based upon the turnover tax or income tax. Six hundred million Rms were believed to have been raised in the first year with the chemical and electric industries reportedly among the more highly assessed. As a result the electric industry claimed that it sold its exports practically at a loss. Great secrecy surrounded the exact working of the scheme in Germany and the amount seemed to vary from one exporter to another. The figure of 35% was reported for a machine exporter; 23% of the price to Siemens while another German firm received a 28% subsidy and was pressing for 40%. In general, the subsidy was aimed at counteracting the depreciation of the pound sterling and the U.S. dollar.[26]

Though perturbed by the German decision to subsidize exports, the British declined to take countervailing action for a number of reasons. The Treasury Department official, Waley, indicated that British agreements with the Scandinavian and Baltic states had been partially responsible for depriving the Germans of markets, forcing them to move into the Central and Eastern European markets through direct subsidy or indirect means such as the block mark agreement. Having captured a greater portion of the Scandinavian and Baltic markets Waley noted, "it suits us pretty well to develop these markets and to leave the thorny path of Central and Eastern Europe for Germany."[27] This was a theme repeated down to 1938; namely, that British cultivation of the more lucrative northeastern market more than made up for the neglect of the Eastern and Southeastern European region where Britain did not have any overriding commercial interest. Leith-Ross indicated resignedly that if the Germans were subsidizing their exports there was little that could be done about it.[28] After a meeting of the Treasury Department and Board of Trade, specialists decided against subsidizing British exports; but, the issue remained alive for the next few years.[29]

Besides direct subsidies of exports the Germans opened another line of attack on the export problem that lay at the heart of the financial crisis: in the summer of 1936 Hjalmar Schacht embarked on his *"Rundreise"* to the Balkans in search of trade opportunities. From his vantage point in the British embassy in Berlin, Pinsent viewed the trip as an attempt to "drive the Balkans along the path that suits Germany." Pinsent confided to Ashton-Gwatkin, the British foreign office economic specialist, that he was not far from sharing the latter's views about the building up of a German preferential empire. While Puhl, Retty and some of the other older Reichsbank officials regarded the current situation as temporary, Pinsent admitted ruefully: "I find myself tending more and more to the pessimistic view that the chances of Germany breaking away from her course of exchange restrictions, managed internal economy and managed external commercial relations, are dwindling." Pinsent saw world trade little by little being divided between the countries with trade restrictions and trade through clearings and those with free currencies, with countries preferring to trade within their own group rather than finding it easier to trade with each other.[30]

In retrospect, the decision taken in mid-June 1936 not to counter the German trade thrust in Southeastern Europe began a policy of British economic appeasement of Germany. The preference for exploiting the more lucrative Scandinavian and Baltic trade market was probably only the ostensible reason for abandoning the Southeastern European trade region to Germany. To do so would run the risk, as the 1936 report "On German Competition in World Trade" indicated, of producing strain on the German economy that might lead "to either internal or external political reactions," i.e., an aggressive expansion by Germany in search of raw materials to sustain its economy. A decline in the German export trade due to lack of markets could lead to an economic downturn and a return to the catastrophic unemployment situation which had brought the Nazi regime to power and which it would take vigorous steps to prevent from recurring rather than face being turned out of power by the German people through an internal revolt or explosion. Thus, the decision to allow Germany to move into and dominate the Southeastern European market probably was based both on political and commercial reasons. However, by 1938 a reaction against this policy set in after Munich, as we shall see, and Britain began to take steps for economic as well as political reasons to prevent Germany from converting the Southeastern region into a German colonial hinterland from which its own trade would be excluded. This came about through pressure from Halifax, at first resisted, but later acquiesced in, by Chamberlain, by means of loans, politically expedient trade and arms supplies to the Southeastern countries, particularly Romania and Yugoslavia.

The Germans saw the problem similarly, but expressed it in somewhat different terms. They viewed the current world trade crisis as a consequence of the rise of the U.S., which had promoted indebtedness through improvident loans but had suddenly and inconsiderately withdrawn funds invested abroad and was now refusing to accept payment through the delivery of goods. As a result of international currency devaluations, Germany had reduced its debt by 14 billion Rm between 1930 and 1934, but it still owed 6.5 billion Rm in short-term debts and 6.5 billion Rm in long-term debts which continued to be the greatest obstacle to a revival of trade. Only a clearing up of the debt question could effect that, but there were few signs this would occur.[31] According to many economic historians, at this time the debt was less of a real than a psychological factor.

Germany had moved toward autarchy only in response to the autarchy adopted by Britain, France, the Soviet Union and the United States. Unlike Germany, those countries had at their command raw materials within their currency areas. Nearly half of Britain's trade was with its dominions and colonies, while about a third of French exports was sent to the French colonial areas. Moreover, the trade of those countries with their colonies and dominions was constantly increasing. Before the war Germany had less need to develop its colonies for raw materials. Now with the shrinking of markets, its trade debts and exchange and raw material problems, without colonies it was at a disadvantage—a *bête noire* constantly invoked by Schacht.[32] These problems stemmed from the system of free trade which had been the product of particular social and economic conditions that now were less prevalent. Germany succeeded in gaining markets and breaking out of this vise by entering into clearance agreements with the Balkan states, similarly strapped with an adverse balance of payments and overflowing with raw materials and foodstuffs. In the 1930s a considerable portion of world trade, in response to the departure from the gold standard of several leading states and the devaluation of the pound, was subject to exchange clearings, import restrictions, commodity regulations schemes, barter arrangements, international cartels, trade preferences and high tariffs. Only a small part of world trade remained open to price competition. Karl Polanyi has maintained that it was the attempt to restore the market in the early 1930s that brought on first fascism, then the Second World War.[33]

Germany's export policy resulted in an overvalued market and high employment; and the willingness of Germany to pay higher than world prices for imports, kept prices in both Germany and the Balkans high which "had decided attractions against internal unrest." Since the 1923 inflation, any devaluation of the mark would be certain to be regarded with apprehension by the German public and therefore as politically unacceptable.[34] Thus, from the standpoint of the regime, export subsidization and import selectivity satisfied German big business's production demands and German labor's interest in high employment, locking the Nazi regime into an iron cage of its own making. Any abandonment of rearmament and export subsidies and a return to the free market meant a leap back into the abyss.

The overvalued mark proved less of a boon and made it difficult for German traders to compete in free exchange markets. Germany found it necessary to resort to various roundabout and only partially effective expedients for subsidizing exports in order to obtain the foreign exchange it needed.[35] The Third Reich's constant exchange shortage throughout the thirties and the ever-present danger that its sources of strategic raw materials in the Balkans and elsewhere might be unobtainable or withheld for lack of sufficient exchange currency, threatened to provoke internal difficulties and chaos. Stiffening resistance in the Balkan states to clearing purchasing in the German market, and increased purchasing by Britain and France in the Balkan market, added to the problem.

The Germans did not invent the exchange clearing system which was introduced first in Switzerland and Hungary, followed by other states. By 1932 Germany had clearing agreements with France, Holland and Switzerland. By purchasing unmarketable agricultural products at prices above the world level, Germany, in the view of some, did not exploit the Southeastern European market but, in fact, greatly benefited the agrarian states of the Southeast by enabling them to dispose of their surpluses without expending exchange currency. In fact, the German aim was not primarily to secure advantages for itself by buying cheap and selling dear, but to increase the volume of its trade for its armament industry to prepare for war — in other words, to buy more and sell more.[36] Nevertheless, German exports continued to fall precipitously from 11 billion Rm in 1928 to 4.1 billion Rm in 1935, representing 11.5% of total German production.[37]

The British position was not more sparkling. Britain's balance of trade had declined from a favorable balance in 1935 of £32 million to a deficit in 1936 of £18 million. By the following year, 1937, Britain's share of manufactures in world exports dipped from 22.9% in 1929 to 21.3% in 1937, almost a third less than the 30.9% it had exported in 1913, and 77% of what it had marketed in 1929. Britain's current accounts from 1920 through 1930 had registered a surplus of £1156 million, but from 1931 to 1938 it showed a deficit for every year except 1935, and the cumulative current account deficit was £374 million. (Current accounts represents the balance of foreign trade + other profits.) This, in itself, would not have been decisive if property income from overseas investments had not declined in the 1930s, which might have tipped the scales or at least reduced the impact of Britain's industrial decline.[38]

The added expense of rearmament threatened to play havoc with British finances and plunge the country deeper into economic decline. After 1936 when Britain's surplus disappeared, it began to borrow to pay for defense costs, pushing deeper into debt and subjecting the government to increasing attacks by the Labor opposition — by no means unified — for spending vast sums on rearmament at the expense of social welfare in the depressed areas. Waley notes the gloom in financial circles in February 1937 over the prospect of having to borrow £278 million for defense: "On the question of defense borrowing, the Governor (of the Bank of England) thought that the figure would shock and that it would have a depressing effect upon our credit. He was not prepared to measure the effect."[39] In short, between loses suffered from the declining German market and German export subsidization abroad and the costs of rearmament, the British financial position threatened to slide into a financial bog. British policy narrowed down to persuading Germany to abandon rearmament and economic autarchy in exchange for a financial bailout in the form of a loan to compensate for the necessary devaluation of the mark and the return of some former German colonies to give Germany a source of raw materials. The latter was increasingly seen by Schacht and his friends in the Economic Ministry as an alternative to rearmament and aggressive expansion to the east.

It had become increasingly apparent to the British leaders that it was only a question of time before Hitler would use Germany's new found military power to engage in military adventures in order to restore Germany's primacy in Europe. In January 1935, following the Saar plebiscite, Anthony Eden noted that "Germany is now well on the way to rearmament, she is no longer afraid of a 'preventive war' against her and in a few years—four I am told is the popular figure in Berlin—she will be strong enough to ask, in a tone which will not brook refusal, for the desiderata."[40] At the end of March after seeing Hitler and Neurath and noting the German chancellor's self-assured and commanding demeanor, Eden observed in his diary that he "was strongly against letting Germany expand eastwards: apart from its dishonesty, it would be our turn next." In the course of his meeting with his British visitors Hitler had casually let drop the remark that German plane production had overtaken England's, raising eyebrows.

By 1936 both Germany and England had reached a crossroad. By that time the British leaders had concluded that the way to a comprehensive agreement lay through cultivation of the so-called "moderate" German government leaders like Schacht and Puhl of the Reichsbank, Neurath and the Foreign Office officials and Schwerin von Krosigk in the Treasury Ministry. Hitler and the Party were the cementing element between these diverse ruling class groups. His own position was weakened by the fact that he had not yet completely consolidated his grip over the German military, which did not occur until 1938. The British policy of supporting the German "moderates" persisted into 1939, when Göring replaced Schacht and some German military leaders joined the group. These people, London believed, opposed the war-minded group in the Nazi party of Ribbentrop, Himmler and Göbbels; and some, like Schacht, thought the time had come by the mid-thirties to enter into discussions with Britain and France for a settlement. The civil government leaders were no less desirous than Hitler of regaining Germany's pre-war hegemony in the east and were, for the most part, nationalist to the core.

These nationalist practitioners of an imperialist *Weltpolitik* believed that Germany would first have to rearm in order to make demands for the return of its pre-war colonies and confiscated territories in Europe. They differed from Hitler only in that they did not believe that war would be necessary in order to make the Western Powers concede to Germany a hegemonical position in Eastern Europe and ultimately through its domination of Europe the restoration of its former position as a leader in world markets. These "moderate" imperialists, composed of a segment of the military elite and the German business class and bureaucracy, wanted to use Hitler and a rearmed Germany to frighten its competitors into acquiescence; opposing them were the more aggressive imperialist business sector allied to Hitler and the expansionist elements within the Nazi party which saw war after the annexation of Austria and the Czech provinces as a way to gain profit and world empire.

An ambiguous dividing line between these two groups might be the desire of the "moderate" imperialists to convert the smaller countries of Eastern and Southeastern Europe into client economic and political dependencies within the hegemony of the German orbit, while the more aggressive expansionists preferred either direct annexation of territory with a subjugated population or some combination of protectorates, client states and annexed territories. There was a certain overlapping of the two outlooks, e.g., the "moderate" imperialists shared the feeling of the expansionists *à outrance* that Poland would either have to become a client state, be partitioned or at least disappear as a threatening entity on Germany's eastern flank. How they expected this to occur without war is difficult to fathom. Munich was the time point at which the moderate imperialists (notably Schacht, General Thomas, General Beck and Neurath) drew back, fearing further adventures would result in war — though General Beck and his group had been conspiring to overthrow Hitler even before Munich. This group set themselves apart from the party "madmen" (Ribbentrop, Himmler, Göbbels) urging Hitler toward new adventures.

Even though the opening of new markets in the Balkans and Latin America enabled Germany to sell its exports abroad and to import raw materials and foodstuffs, it did not radically alter Germany's difficult trade position or bring in sufficient exchange currency to purchase vitally needed imports from Europe and the North American area. Germany had to produce those commodities it could not purchase abroad, preparatory to embarking on a war of plunder to solve forever the problem of raw materials.

Schacht, who had formerly been a staunch advocate of rearmament, now perceived that further continuation of accelerated rearmament would fuel an inflationary spiral that could wreck the economy. Hitler rejected Schacht's demand for deceleration of the war economy; and Speer reports overhearing raised voices during a meeting between Schacht and Hitler at Berchtesgaden in 1936.[41] Finally, Hitler, probably sensing his weak position, appears to have relented and agreed to allow Schacht to use his contacts with the Western Powers to try to solve the raw materials crisis. British policy toward Germany supported the "moderates" in the Nazi Regime, continuing to lean in that direction until the eve of the war.

Important segments of German business acquiesced in Hitler's plans for aggression; other segments hesitated to support a war of aggressive expansion. At any rate, what is significant is that German business split on this issue.

The scope and intent of the conversations conducted by Schacht, first with the French in the summer of 1936, then with the English, have been the subject of some attention by scholars. The intensification of the exchange crisis and a threatening shortage of raw materials, provided Schacht with a propitious moment to return Germany to the free market by gaining sufficient concessions from the Western Powers to slow down rearmament and reduce the thrust toward war and at the same time regain his faltering political position. Hitler originally empowered Schacht to deal only with economic questions. Opinionated and self-assertive, Schacht probably represented part of the German business class and the bureaucratic-class fraction apprehensive of the drift toward war, and, under cover of Hitler's assent to negotiate, sought to extend his role into the political sphere. Schacht hoped to persuade the Western Powers to make an offer to return Germany's colonial territory in Africa, or the equivalent — on which he had strong feelings — to obtain raw materials and also to distract Hitler from launching an expansionist campaign in the east. Armed with this concession, he hoped to be able to persuade Hitler to reduce the armament program to manageable limits and to return Germany to a free exchange market, to be eased by a sizeable Western loan.

When Schacht met with the French in August 1936, Blum, Delbos and other French leaders were receptive, hinting at consideration of German territorial claims in Africa if Hitler would agree to a general European settlement.[42] This was, in fact, suggested by British Foreign Minister Eden a month later in September. However, since Hitler had just torn up the Locarno agreement in March 1936 by occupying the Rhineland, the German leader had no interest in seeing Germany's interests decided by a consortium of powers and of allowing himself to be inveigled into a new Locarno. When Blum informed Schacht that the Soviet Union could not be excluded from any general discussions, Schacht pleaded that for ideological reasons Germany could not conclude an agreement with the USSR. Eden was adamant on a general agreement and refused to consider the return of African colonies, believing that Hitler would offer nothing in return.

Schacht reported the French position to Hitler, requesting that Welczeck, the German minister to Paris, should be recalled for discussions, which Hitler agreed to. Later Hitler told François-Poncet, the French ambassador to Berlin, that since the Saar and Alsace question had been settled, there were no outstanding differences between the two countries, an entente was still possible and that he was ready to discuss the matter in detail. Hitler, however, was skeptical that the British or the French would be willing to give up any colonies other than those belonging to other states. He then added that Germany needed raw materials to survive; it wished "to gain the means amicably" but failing that "it will procure them another way."[43]

The French Foreign Minister told American Ambassador Bullitt that besides tariff reductions in Germany's favor, a consortium of all three powers, France, Britain and America, could supply money and machines to develop a colony which would be given to Germany. French leaders suggested the Cameroons, formerly German, divided now between Britain and France. The British, however, had little interest in yielding territory to Germany.

Newton, the Counsellor of the British embassy in Berlin, was skeptical of Schacht's offers which he believed were inconsistent with Hitler's policy; Eden similarly opposed any concessions to Hitler which would only encourage him in the belief that the Western Powers were only too eager to buy him off. However, E. H. Lever, a representative of British bondholders in Berlin, sent word to Sir Fredrick Leith-Ross that if Hitler were not mollified, he might open negotiations for a political accord with the Soviet Union and the peace party of the German "moderates" would lose influence.[44] The latter argument began to have effect upon the influential Federation of British Industries and financial leaders of the "City" like Montagu Norman, then the Chancellor of the Exchequer, Neville Chamberlain and Foreign Office officials like the Chief of the Economics Section of the Foreign Office, Ashton-Gwatkin, Gladwyn Jebb, private secretary of the Permanent Undersecretary of State, and Leith-Ross.

While the British deliberated Schacht's offer, though chastened by "Eden's attitude and the British rebuff to the French approach," Schacht continued to extol the virtues of his offer of peace in exchange for raw material resources through colonies for Germany. He reminded Cochran, an American official at a Bank of International Settlement meeting, of the sincerity of the Hitler government's offer of disarmament and of limiting the army to 300,000 men, which had been either ignored or refused. The Hitler government now was "firmly established and if there is any attempt to humble Germany the German people will be solidly behind it." Urging an American initiative, Schacht proposed the idea of a Washington conference, which American world leadership and wealth would make effective. Cochran countered with a convoluted scheme of Yanagita of Japan, allowing Germany to buy neutral territory from Britain, presumably a colonial dependency, by borrowing money from the United States, with Britain applying the proceeds of the sale to the British war debt to America. Niemeyer, a British official at the conference, pointed out to Schacht that the two raw materials most needed by Germany, rubber and wool, were not commercially available in the colonies Schacht wanted.[45]

In discussions held in Berlin with French Ambassador François-Poncet, the German government indicated its willingness to come to an agreement on the "humanization of warfare" (armaments limitation, poison gas limitation, prohibition of bombardments in towns and fortified places). François-Poncet believed "wild men," including Göbbels and Göring, advocated "a policy of rapid action" but Hitler then was siding with Schacht, the industrialists and the "saner members of the general staff" who wanted a policy enabling Germany to live in peace. François-Poncet believed Germany needed markets for its finished products from heavy industry then producing war materials and hoped that the negotiations between Germany and France would develop an agreement giving Germany raw materials and economic outlets. He cautioned: if Germany in its predicament had to choose between economic collapse or war it would choose war. If an opportunity for peaceful evolution occurred it would choose peace. Bullitt, however, like the British, remained skeptical that Hitler would accept armament limitations in return for market outlets "which would seem... an abandonment of Germany's desire to alter her Polish and Czechoslovakian frontiers." Chautemps, a former French Premier, enthusiastically supported these talks, but apprehensively told Bullitt — also supporting the talks — that Britain might try to interfere with them and asked the United States to block the British from doing this.[46]

Earlier in the year, the Foreign Policy Committee of the Cabinet took up the subject of colonies. The report of Lord Plymouth, Undersecretary of State for colonies, although skeptical of the value of giving Germany colonies, recommended against a blanket refusal to examine the colonial question in the interests of a general settlement. The Committee subsequently rejected the reservations of Vansittart and Eden, adopting the view of Lord Halifax, Lord Privy Seal, and Chamberlain, not to throw cold water on the possibility of opening negotiations for a settlement of outstanding differences with Germany.[47] Eden was won over to the wisdom of that policy and later cautiously defended it in the House of Commons. Both he and Vansittart favored a five-power meeting in which Hitler's demands would be considered as a basis for peace.

In the beginning of February 1937 the British government sent Leith-Ross to see Schacht secretly at Badenweiler to find out what he had in mind. Schacht claimed that "on the economic side (including colonies) he had full authority and could guarantee that Hitler would accept his views." He had informed Neurath that he would make no commitments on political questions. "But he had frequently discussed these questions both with Hitler and with Neurath and what he told [Leith-Ross] represented their views." If the British met his demands on economic matters, he promised that their political demands would be satisfied.[48]

Schacht was "very disappointed" that his proposals to the French had not been followed by joint Anglo-French-German conversations. "He believed the present opportunity might not easily recur again." Schacht recognized that a general settlement would have to cover political as well as economic problems and proceeded to outline Germany's requirements. He claimed Germany had been forced to accept autarchy and to produce artificial petrol, rubber and other raw materials because it lacked exchange currency to pay for imports. This involved a "reduction in the standard of life" [sic] which German industry realized and only accepted as there was no alternative — a somewhat misleading view of reality since German business was reaping huge profits producing Buna, gas and other ersatz materials. Moreover, autarchy had been introduced not just to satisfy Germany's raw material needs, but to build a powerful war machine.[49]

The alternative to autarchy, Schacht stated, was the return to free market relationships and the concession of colonies for raw materials. This depended first upon improving Germany's foreign exchange position through an "adjustment of currency" involving some internal changes which "would enable him to get rid of his export subsidies, provided other countries would undertake not to retaliate against him." This last reference undoubtedly meant the long awaited devaluation of the overvalued German mark. Schacht also hoped for the removal of quotas on German industrial goods and of other trade barriers and pledged to accept the goods of other countries in return. At a later time, after general discussions, he suggested floating a private market loan for "stabilization purposes" (i.e., to shore up the devalued mark), followed by the voluntary conversion at lower interest rates of Germany's debts. Once this occurred, Germany would be ready to relax exchange controls, at least at first, for commercial operations while retaining them temporarily for capital transactions primarily to prevent a too precipitous withdrawal of capital (partly Jewish, partly Christian).[50]

Finally, Schacht arrived at his *idée fixe:* "Germany must have colonies." His main difficulty was the supply of foodstuffs, and particularly oils and fats which could be produced by the German colonies. Germany could not be left permanently in a position where the supplies of these products might at any time be shut off. The colonies must be under German management and use German currency but an "open door" arrangement would be accepted. If Germany did not receive colonies — "particularly Cameroons and Togoland" — it would have "the feeling of being strangled." Besides being a matter of prestige and necessary for the Germany economy, the transfer of colonies was "a vital condition of getting his views on other matters accepted by the insane elements of the party...."[51]

Schacht appealed to the generosity of England "to make a concession which might change the whole atmosphere at no cost to herself....It was a critical time for Europe and the key was in England's hand." Leith-Ross was pessimistic: "No party in England, whether Liberal or Labor or Conservative, favored the surrender of Colonies." But Schacht was not to be deterred: Germany would be prepared to offer cooperation in an agreement for peace not only for Western Europe, but the whole of Europe. Russia would even be covered, though indirectly, despite Nazi party opposition to a direct agreement. "Hitler had personally told him that he would be able to give an assurance of non-aggression towards Russia." Schacht claimed Hitler would allow either a non-aggression pact or a non-interference agreement with Czechoslovakia, and a limitation of armaments "was not impossible." Schacht claimed that Hitler had only rearmed to reassert Germany's position in Europe. "He had succeeded and that was all he wanted." German industry, according to Schacht, desired a respite in armament production which was draining the economy of capital and labor, hence Germany was ready to accept the principle of arms limitation with the details to be worked out by experts. Schacht spoke of opening other contacts and sending messages through Pinsent in Switzerland or Germany or through diplomatic channels through Neurath. He had told Hitler, Neurath, Ribbentrop and François-Poncet that he was seeing Leith-Ross.[52]

Schacht again urged the importance of an understanding.

> It would be a great mistake to suppose that economic difficulties would be an effective means of political pressure on Germany. It would only strengthen the hands of the wild men, who would then work for some "explosion." Hitler was at present open to argument and if he (Dr. Schacht) could show that other means were available that he would be able to get Hitler to take that chance and to give us the guarantees that we wanted.... Otherwise, one of these days Hitler would publish the proposals which he (Dr. Schacht) had sent to M. Blum and everyone would rub their eyes and say "why did England and France not accept this?"[53]

Although contacts continued to occur, since England would not offer colonies without a general settlement, they were inconclusive. Also the British believed that Schacht only had Hitler's support for economic proposals concerning gaining colonies for raw materials and had exceeded his authority in advancing political proposals. Thereafter, as raw material imports from abroad could no longer be paid for by mid-1939, Hitler increasingly must have been pressed to consider war as the only way out of that problem which he expressed during the conferences with the generals (May 23 and August 22, 1939) — and as Göring testified to after the war — all of which probably confirmed his original beliefs about *Lebensraum* expressed in *Mein Kampf*. This did not prevent Hitler from denying that he had any intentions of going to war and on various occasions of issuing pacific pronouncements to gull his opponents into believing that he would seek redress only through peaceful means.

As the Germans considered their own hapless economic position, Britain's seemingly secure and powerful world empire aroused a certain envy. In early 1935 the London *Times* reprinted an article that appeared in the *Frankfurter-Zeitung's* economic survey for 1935: "The Empire of the Fortunate Isles":

> Strewn over five continents the countries of the British Empire and its economic partners in the extended sterling *bloc* rise like islands from a sea of depression. . . . Few other countries are on the upgrade . . . England's deep rooted capital resources form the main source of the revival. In so rich a country there are numerous investors who even in times of crisis have larger incomes than they need and the impulse to invest capital is so strong that the state is able to forego those instructions which ultimately always leads to new difficulties.

> The role of the Bank of England as the motor force since 1932 was viewed with mixed admiration and jealousy.

> The subsequent development in spite of continued policy depreciation and uncertainty about the level of ultimate stabilization, was almost a classic example of economic theory: the spread of money to the capital market, great state loan conversions, continued rise in the rates of stocks and shares, conversion from other public and therefore private loans, new financing of trade and other industry through issues, stimulation of the means of production industries, etc.[54]

This German view of Britain's wealth and power gnawed and rankled at the soul of those in German business, bureaucratic and military elites as well as the Nazi leaders and Hitler, and fueled the *va banque* irrational tendency of the regime much as it had during the Wilhelmian era. Germany, deprived of its rightful patrimony by a scheming, greedy and perfidious Albion, was a satisfying stereotype that remained very much alive in the interwar German psyche. This writer well remembers his German father who had immigrated to the United States before 1914 listening with excitement to a short wave broadcast of Hitler speaking at some rally in the late 1930s reacting to something Hitler said that drew a deafening roar from the audience. When I asked him somewhat sleepily — it was about 3 AM — "What did he say?" he replied, "God Almighty did not make the world for the English!"

A resplendent Britain, enriched by many dependencies and colonies swimming in a sea of riches in contrast to a beggarized Germany unable to find a way out of its debt and trade problems, was, however, far from a reality.

Financial matters were less than rosy in the U.K. as defense borrowing estimates soared from £109 million in 1933 to £278 million in 1937, as already noted. Already in December 1936 Leith-Ross, in a paper prepared at the behest of the Board of Trade, warned that the twin demons of rearmament and internal demand were drawing industry away from the export market which might in the end produce a balance of payments deficit. He cautioned that they should at all costs avoid getting involved in the vicious spiral of increased prices, wages, costs and depreciation of currency.

Chamberlain shared this worrisome prospect and in April 1937 wrote of the harrowing possibility of "a sharp steepening of costs due to wage increases leading to the loss of our export trade, a feverish and artificial boom followed by a disastrous slump, and finally the defeat of the government." Others like Edward Bridges, a Treasury official and later Cabinet Secretary, warned ominously in a comment on a report by Sir Thomas Inskip, Minister for the Coordination of Defense, that "we simply cannot afford another 1931."[55] Alarm over these figures and the prospect of further increases if German autarchy and rearmament continued, coupled with Labor Party attacks over Conservative indifference to the plight of the unemployed in the industrially depressed regions, impelled the Chamberlain government to reopen contacts with Schacht.

In May 1937 Schacht again saw Blum who laid out an agenda for further discussions around a general settlement of European problems; a general limitation of armaments; and the drawing up of conditions of Germany's reentry into the League of Nations. From his discussion with Blum, Schacht realized that the British were the key to a detente and, therefore, sent Carl Gördeler to see Leith-Ross secretly in England. Gördeler was less discreet, blunter than Schacht had been and did not mince words. He was "surprised" at the illusions about Germany, held by many in England, including bankers. He described a Nazi regime rent with economic problems and contradictions: "their financial policy of piling up debts must lead to bankruptcy; the Four Years Plan [*sic*] was entailing a tremendous drain of capital; armaments also; production was falling off, raw materials and even food were difficult to secure. Meanwhile the church and family were being attacked. There was much more widespread discontent than appeared on the surface."[56]

Gördeler described the struggle between the moderates and the extremists around Hitler; Neurath, Schwerin von Krosigk and others had little influence. Schacht, too, was steadily falling in influence. Himmler and the Radicals were gaining ground; he expected the Radical elements to increase their strength during the next year as the difficulties increased.

British policy toward Germany vacillated between three schools of thought, Leith-Ross told Gördeler: (a) against giving any help to Germany in the hope that increasing difficulties would bring a change of regimes; (b) in favor of giving help in the hope that easement of the present situation would make the Nazi regime more moderate; and (c) in favor of giving help but only on condition that the policy of the German government was radically modified. Gördeler thought the third was the right line while Schacht favored the second. "Schacht appeared to believe that [the British] would be prepared to give up some West African colonies without a political settlement but he did not believe it." Leith-Ross told Gördeler "that he was quite right and that a political settlement must be reached before it was any use talking about colonies; but even then, the transfer of colonies raised great difficulties. . . . The clearer we made willingness to help, given better political conditions, and the more clearly we stated what these political conditions were, the better it would be." Behind this reasoning lay the patent British desire to force Germany to abandon further rearmament so that Britain could improve its own weakening credit position, and to compel Germany to return to the free market system where it would be in a markedly inferior competitive position to Britain and the United States. In short, Britain's continued viability as a Great Power was increasingly perceived as tied to Germany's abandonment of autarchy and German disarmament. Unfortunately, Gördeler's direct and frank way of expressing himself raised doubts in the minds of some of the British leaders whether he was an *agent provocateur*. Leith-Ross, however, was convinced of his sincerity.[57]

Gördeler's discussion with Leith-Ross had encouraged the British not to make any economic concessions of colonial territory unless the Germans first offered political concessions. The Germans likewise made no move toward a political agreement until receiving concessions which would alleviate their economic plight. The two countries seemed to be operating at cross-purposes. The delay that ensued, Leith-Ross noted, "was probably fatal."[58] The French were unable to draw up more than a few general guarantees (a standstill in armaments, prohibition of bombing, "humanizing" war) which rested on Hitler's good faith. From the British standpoint nothing short of a general settlement replacing the Locarno agreement would satisfy London. The British and French entrusted the matter to former Prime Minister van Zeeland of Belgium to make a report with proposals while London pondered the next move. Hitler, however, tiring of Western procrastination, moved toward a decision of his own.

On November 5, 1937, at the now celebrated Hossbach conference, Hitler revealed to his assembled generals, Göring and Foreign Minister Neurath — Schacht, who might have argued with Hitler, was pointedly absent or not invited — his plans to launch a war if necessary to seize Austria and dismember Czechoslovakia. Aghast at this revelation, Neurath went to General Beck and General Fritsch and asked them to dissuade Hitler and General Blomberg, the Wehrmacht head. Beck left a memo opposing military expansion and advising the solution of Germany's economic problems through the world market. Neurath claims to have been so emotionally disturbed by Hitler's revelations that he purportedly took to his bed with severe angina pectoris.[59]

The November 5 meeting had originally been solicited by General Blomberg to deal with the question of rearmament. Schacht at that time had become involved in a confrontation with Hitler and had temporarily gained support from the army leaders for a slowdown of the rearmament program which was creating inflation and food shortages. General Ludwig Beck, the army chief-of-staff, in particular, and General von Fritsch, the commander-in-chief of the army, had been ignoring Hitler's directives since 1935 for a surprise attack on Czechoslovakia, but the more sycophantic generals, Blomberg, the war minister, Jodl and Keitel supported him. The military held the pivotal position and Hitler, accordingly, undercut Schacht at the Hossbach meeting, revealing his war plans in order to gain the generals' support for the continued accelerated pace of rearmament. At the conference Blomberg, Fritsch and Neurath objected to the timeliness of Hitler's decision to destroy Austria and Czechoslovakia — not the decision itself.[60] To avoid this happening again, Hitler took care later to remove Blomberg, Fritsch, Schacht and Neurath, delivering a severe blow to the "moderates." Thereafter, the British transferred their attentions from Schacht to Göring, as the representative of the moderates.

If Carl Krauss of I. G. Farben, Krupp and other industrial leaders were supporters of Hitler's aggressive expansionist plans, the financial circles were less enthusiastic. Germany's capital had been used largely to finance the armament program, thereby depleting the financial resources of the banks. In October 1938 Schacht, in a depressed mood, complained to the diplomat von Hassell that Germany was financially bankrupt. The departure of Schacht from the Ministry of Economics in the fall of 1937 and his removal as President of the Reichsbank in January 1939 severed the final hope of financial circles in the "City" and the British government that a *modus vivendi* might be arrived at with Hitler. The British learned from Schacht that Hitler would merely accept a return of the former German African colonies without a cessation of the rearmament program and a promise of good behavior in Central and Eastern Europe.

After considering the signs and portents, Chamberlain decided to send Lord Halifax to visit Hitler to see if an arrangement with Germany could be made.[61] Fearing that the British would try to force him to put his cards on the table and to box him in, Hitler had little desire for the meeting. After various contretemps — press leaks and planted articles by Hitler — Halifax finally saw the German leader on November 17, a short time after the Hossbach conference. After listening to Hitler's diatribe on a multitude of sins and injustices committed against Germany, Halifax threw out the bait: England was only too willing to listen to Hitler's requests, including the issue of colonies. Only the latter remained to divide the two countries. When Halifax indicated that England was willing to discuss the problem of colonies at a general settlement and asked for a written outline of Hitler's views, the latter was taken aback. Hitler countered only with his willingness to accept colonies elsewhere in Africa if it were difficult to return the mandated areas. Nothing definitive occurred; later, at conferences with Göring, Blomberg and other Nazi leaders, Halifax was told directly what Hitler had not spelled out: Germany wanted hegemony in Central and Eastern Europe. Although the colonial issue was floated from time to time thereafter, it began to subside in importance following the Halifax visit. After meeting with the French, Chamberlain, not yet appeasement-minded, summed up the policy to be pursued in the future: "Whatever Germany's ultimate object — and we might assume that this was to gain territory — our policy ought to be to make this more difficult, or even to postpone it until it might become unrealizable."[62]

In summary, Britain pursued an ambivalent policy toward Germany, by turns obstructive and accommodating: against non-payment of their bond creditors and commercial exporters, it threatened to cut off credits and to force clearings; against Schacht's import controls it threatened the same tactics against German imports; but against export subsidies it did not act; and, on the diplomatic level, Britain was conciliatory.

With the arrival of Hitler and the National Socialist regime to power in 1933, the most forceful and imperialist wing of German nationalism, all this changed almost in the twinkling of an eye. Hitler gave notice that Germany would seek its rightful place in the sun. While absorbed initially in uniting Germany under his absolute power by destroying his internal enemies and acting to solve the unemployment and production problem, Hitler immediately asserted, as he had all along, that Germany would no longer be bound by the stipulations of Versailles — reparations ceased to be paid already in July 1932 — or involved in the League of Nations. All arrangements with other states would be on a bilateral basis which would not inhibit his freedom of action and which he could renounce at will whenever it suited him.

Hitler immediately instituted the rearmament program to regain Germany's lost territories and colonies, if need be by force, and to solve the unemployment problem. The failure of the British and French to act may be considered the beginning of the policy of unilateral and arbitrary actions by Hitler and the source of the countervailing appeasement policy later pursued by the Western Powers. By the time of the Halifax visit to Hitler, the die had already been cast.

Chapter 7

Trade Rivalries in the 1930s. The Foreign Office Debate on Whether to Keep Germany Lean or Fat. Britain Abandons the Southeastern Trade

> As the clever hopes expire
> Of a low dishonest decade....
> — W. H. Auden,
> *September 1, 1939*

BY EARLY 1936 two junior British officials, Frank Ashton-Gwatkin, economics advisor to the Foreign Office, and Gladwyn Jebb, the parliamentary secretary, saw the handwriting on the wall and advanced specific suggestions in a memorandum which posed the question: *"Must Germany 'expand' in the sense of securing new external markets?"*[1] One possibility was simply to let matters take their course. If, in fact, the Germans, faced by a declining export trade were nevertheless able to maintain their economic system without revolution or economic collapse, then Britain should "make it increasingly difficult for them to expand" and "let them stew in their own juice." If Germany performed its "mad dog act" then "so much the worse for all of us." If not, it might be possible to delay the war "for ten or twenty years and it may never occur at all." Germany would soon be so strong that it would prefer war even against an Anglo-Franco-Russian alliance to the alternative of general internal bankruptcy, unless it had some kind of "outlet" or "expansion" before bankruptcy became inevitable, Gwatkin and Jebb concluded.

The memorandum was not sanguine about the future of world trade and a restoration of market equilibrium. The possibility of a self-corrective international market was largely ruled out since there was little likelihood of reduced agricultural protectionism; the creditor countries were still disinclined to lend further, and "in fact the essentials for a return to normal conditions simply did not exist."

A number of financial and trade strategies were considered and discarded. A devaluation of the mark by 40 to 60% might raise German business profits and employment and possibly even British-German trade, but the short-term effect would be "unfavorable" to the U.K., which might be forced to take protective action against the importation of German goods, resulting in yet further deterioration of the German standard of living and sharpening of the "expansion problem." There was little likelihood that Britain would take further German exports — the Import Duties Advisory Committee was even then recommending the raising of duties which would hit German exports and reduce existing trade.

The Ashton-Gwatkin/Jebb memorandum further pointed out that there remained, from the German standpoint, the remote possibility of an economic understanding with France, the USSR or Great Britain. These authors quickly ruled out an economic accord with France, despite some "obvious attractions" (the complementary nature of Lorraine iron and Ruhr coal, etc.) because it would result in a gradual transference of economic and political power from Paris to Berlin, and run afoul of vested interests both in France and in Germany. An accord with the Soviet Union, in which the Soviets would utilize German industrial techniques, would result in larger orders for German industry and in the general interest of Europe. Without this trade exchange the future for the east and southeast would be bleak. Conversely, the alternative to allowing Germany an outlet to the east was equally baleful and set forth in prophetic terms:

> But if we are not prepared to pay the price it means that we must either stand aside and watch Germany's efforts to solve her difficulties, perhaps by war; or we must be prepared to intervene in a war to prevent Germany from realizing her ambitions and satisfying her needs. There is also always the considerable chance that the mere threat of force will succeed in giving Germany what she wants.

A long counter-memorandum by the Foreign Office Permanent Under-Secretary, Sir Robert Vansittart, followed the Jebb and Ashton-Gwatkin memo.[2] Considering Vansittart's reputation as the leading German-eater in the Foreign Office, the memorandum is surprising. Vansittart noted the foreboding reality that "Germany is now heavily rearmed and will demand territorial changes." Britain would have to face the fact that it would have to negotiate a settlement while still rearming, but it could not allow Germany to expand in Europe, which it was now insisting on doing. Vansittart believed that Germany, to achieve its political objectives, aimed at being the strongest power in Europe. He had little faith in the ability of the Powers, large and small, to contain Germany's expansionist thrust and foresaw that Britain would be unable to prevent either the absorption of Austria and Czechoslovakia or the economic and cultural penetration of Russia and the Baltic states. Vansittart considered several possibilities: (1) to allow the situation to develop which was patently too dangerous; or (2) to pursue a policy of encirclement as an alternative, which was questionable because of Italy's unpredictability. The moral influence of the League, with Germany's neighbors remaining armed, did not solve the problem of buying time for rearmament. Britain was thus faced with the third alternative, coming to terms with a heavily armed Germany which could be expected to demand territorial changes. Within that context Britain would have to rearm but Germany probably would not wait until that happened. Vansittart clearly foresaw that Germany's increasing economic and financial strain might drive it to war as had already occurred in the case of Italy and Japan. Aggression on Germany's part might be averted by cooperation but not by ostracism.

Vansittart perceived some signs of a beginning of France's desire for an agreement with Hitler based more on fear than reason, backed by Laval but not by Herriot, which might lead France to abandon leadership of the Eastern European bloc. Hitler's Germany had shown similar signs of a desire for friendship from time to time, but since the Ethiopian crisis of 1936 Hitler had grown cool. This desire for friendship was changing and ambivalent and was variously believed to be due to possible hypocrisy while preparing a blow to the West, to keep the West quiet while attention was turned to Central and Eastern Europe, and possibly a dislike of being ostracized from the other Great Powers. Any settlement would have to be as broad as possible, avoiding a separate agreement. Such a settlement had to be at a price "to be honorably paid for by us and not by Germany's unwilling and unconsulted neighbors," and higher than could have been had several years ago. Britain could not allow Germany to expand in Europe, but since Germany insisted on expanding, the only question was "where or when."

Vansittart expected a variety of responses if this happened. The Baltic, Poland and Russia would fight; a majority in Austria favored some kind of union with Germany; while Hungary, Bulgaria, Yugoslavia and Romania were already flirting with Germany. Only Czechoslovakia would take effective steps and Britain and France's power, he thought, would be limited by France's pacifism. Vansittart foresaw that Germany could fulfill its aims without war: Memel could be assimilated; Austria and Czechoslovakia might be disrupted from within; the Baltic states, Russia and the Danubian area might be penetrated economically and culturally; in fact, the Danubian area already had been (a reference to the German trade offensive of the mid-1930s). Strength meant attraction, hence Britain could not prevent a settlement with Germany but only channel Germany's influence. He fully anticipated Hitler's steps to remilitarize the Rhineland. The final large question was colonies, based upon Germany's prestige and alleged economic needs, complementary to and not exclusive of its eastern aspirations.

The British government had previously been uncompromising and unwilling to make concessions to remove problems between Germany and Britain because Britain was uncertain Germany would make the concessions required of it. If Britain did not, warned Vansittart, it would have to fight or else surrender.

Vansittart warned against raising tariffs against German goods and suggested, like Ashton-Gwatkin and Jebb, that Britain should try to help Germany by agreeing to a "special area" in Eastern Europe. But this would not satisfy Germany and it would frighten Eastern Europe. At present Britain enjoyed a moral prestige and Germany was temporarily undecided but might not be for long. Unless Britain went all out for the policy of concessions "Germany would go for it." Germany was resolved to have its colonies back and Britain could not resist this demand, but if Britain gave in there was no guarantee that Germany would be satisfied. Nevertheless, the crisis might be averted by giving back Germany's colonies. War could thus be averted by building a bridge. If this failed, civilization was doomed.

The British tentatively decided to offer to the Germans either colonies in Africa and/or expansion into Eastern and Southeastern Europe — a process already underway with the German bilateral clearing arrangements of the mid-1930s with individual Southeastern European states — to permit Germany to trade its manufactured commodities for raw materials. The colonial concessions advanced by Vansittart, in fact, were dangled before Hitler by Lord Halifax during his November visit and shrugged off by the German leader who by then had already met with the generals at the Hossbach conference and revealed his plans to annex Austria and Czechoslovakia even if war should ensue.

Pinsent vigorously opposed Vansittart's suggestions, urging both rejection of the proposal to return the African colonies and Germany's absorption of Austria and the German speaking areas of Czechoslovakia.[3] Although Pinsent did not enjoy the influential position of the Permanent Under Secretary, his views are nevertheless worth noting. He denied Vansittart's major assumption that Germany suffered from economic poverty and pictured a Germany whose production for the internal market and overseas trade was substantial and whose problems were largely of its own making. The fall in the export market had been checked and an export and import equilibrium had been established for some months. The fat crisis of 1935 he dismissed as, accepting the explanation of Dr. Schacht, the accidental allocation of foreign exchange for war materials, instead of foodstuffs for the population — a "bureaucratic mistake" and "mere breakdown of machinery." Pinsent drew the opposite and, in hindsight, erroneous conclusion that Germany's indebtedness "should make for peace rather than war. An empty exchequer is almost as bad a foundation for starting war as an empty stomach." Pinsent believed the Reich to be in no position to carry out a war which would run the risk of exposing it to the economic sanctions then being applied to Italy.

> She [Germany] has, it is true, a trained army and considerable accumulated war material, but she has little staying power; she has inadequate internal resources and her negotiable external resources are trivial. A bare 7 millions [Rm] of treasure, very little in the war of foreign investments, a small sum in blocked currencies in one or two foreign countries and no possibility, having regard to her recent past record, of raising foreign loans. Even in the absence of sanctions it is doubtful whether her economy would stand the strain of war for any considerable period. In these circumstances Germany has no prospect of success in a war of aggression, except a very rapid success. So far as this country is concerned (i.e., Britain) the rearmament which is now under contemplation will put such a success out of her reach even supposing, contrary to the best estimates, that her own rearmament is close upon completion... it would be madness to start a war with the food queues already in the streets (even though this was due to an accidental breakdown of machinery) and it is difficult to believe that the realists who now govern Germany suffer from that form of madness.[4]

Pinsent's initial description of Germany's thriving economy contradicts his mention of "food queues already in the streets." The fact that the very financial problems and raw material and food shortages he described later would pressure Germany into attacking its neighbors to solve its economic difficulties does not seem to have crossed his mind.

The ideas of Ashton-Gwatkin, Jebb and Vansittart received indirect support from another quarter. In mid-March 1936 Harold Butler, writing from the League at Geneva to Chancellor of the Exchequer Sir Horace Wilson, reported on Germany's worsening economic difficulties, overtures by Schacht and the possibilities they offered for a settlement.

> I had a long conversation with Dr. S[chacht] and with one of his principal assistants and subsequently with Quesnay, the Secretary-General of the Bank of International Settlements. I derived one very definite impression, namely that the economic situation in Germany is extremely difficult and that the impossibility of furnishing both civil industry and armaments with raw materials for any considerable time to come is weighing very heavily on the minds of those who are responsible for [the] German economy. Moreover, any slackening in armaments is bound to mean heavy unemployment unless outlets can be found for the products of civil industry which Germany can hardly hope to obtain through her own unaided efforts. I felt sure that this was so from information derived from private sources which I have managed to obtain here about the real state of Germany, and I am inclined to think the necessity of finding some way out of the present economic and financial situation is one of the principal motives behind the present move [i.e., Schacht's overtures for colonies in 1936 –P.N.H.].[5]

Referring to Hitler's willingness to return to the League and various territorial concessions by Germany in the wake of the international uproar over the German occupation of the Rhineland in early March 1936, Butler thought that "there is no doubt that Hitler has gone much further than anybody would have conceived possible in the way of offering concessions for the future." "German opinion is 'rather staggered' by the complete reversal of policy with regard to Memel, the Corridor and Geneva, as it was intended to do." Quesnay, who had considerable international economic and financial experience, "strongly believed that this was the first chance since the war of straightening out the whole European situation and ensuring economic revival." Butler "got the impression from Dr. S[chacht] that this was about the last chance of averting a major catastrophe, I think he is right."

> If it is true that the root of the German question is economic, no pacts of non-aggression or air pacts will prevent another war unless German industry is enabled to live (note the passages in Hitler's speech pleading against the view that Germany's poverty is to the advantage of her enemies). How that is to be done I do not know, as in many directions it is over-developed. In any negotiations that took place, however, I feel sure that economic questions should play as large a part as political. That it seems to me is the strength of the British position. If, as I believe, the economic question, that is to say, the fear of renewed

unemployment on a large scale, which would be fatal to the regime, is the prime motive of German action we can assume a direction of the negotiations all the easier.[6]

Some in the British government, like Pinsent, did not concur. The powerful Treasury official S. D. Waley did not believe that the economic question was responsible for Germany's diplomatic overtures or that Germany's problems were to be solved by granting it economic assistance. Nor did Sir Eric Phipps, who agreed with Waley that Butler probably exaggerated the extent to which Germany's misfortunes were economic and thought that none of the other countries were inclined to come to Germany's assistance anyway. Germany's plight might, under prevailing circumstances, be "irreversible" and that little could be done in the near future. Germany's export trade had been badly hit by Britain's adoption of protectionism, but, Phipps observed, "we are not going back to free trade." The real question, Phipps thought, was "whether Britain would be willing to bargain with [Germany] by agreeing not to raise tariffs so long as her currency is managed on some orderly principle in which we had concurred." Phipps concluded pessimistically: "If we are willing to bargain along those lines, how is such a policy to be implemented? For some British industries must be hit and as matters stand they are entitled to demand a remedy at the hand of I.D.A.C." (i.e., the International Development Advisory Committee).[7] Thus, the key to Germany's economic problems, its foundering export trade, lay in the hands of Britain, its most important trading partner, which the British were disinclined to solve at the expense of their own industry.

The ambiguity of Britain's policy toward Germany came to a head at a February 1936 meeting of the cabinet to consider British relations with Germany. At this point the British government was uncertain of Germany's ultimate aims: i.e., whether it merely wished for its rightful position among the Great Powers or aimed at world hegemony once it had become economically and militarily stronger. Runciman, head of the Board of Trade, expressed indignation against the recommendations of Ashton-Gwatkin, stating that the government had dealt "generously" with Germany and that further economic concessions to the Reich could only be made at the expense of Britain's trade. Runciman cuttingly referred to Ashton-Gwatkin's suggestions as "Danegeld," the tribute paid to the Danes in the tenth and eleventh centuries. Decisive support for the pro-appeasement position came from Lord Cranborne, who felt that a policy of "keeping Germany lean in the long run" would be "unacceptable." Cranborne argued that Germany's straightened economic circumstances had forced it into autarchy and rearmament. In retrospect, of critical importance was the shift of the "City" from a pro-German position to one which was equally divided between those opposed to Germany and those favoring a softer attitude.

The German occupation of the Rhineland in March 1936 tested these divisions to the breaking point. British financial circles feared a punitive application of sanctions against Germany for violating the Locarno Treaty could lead to repudiation of Germany's short-term debts to British creditors (circa £40 million) and the annulment of the Standstill Agreement* adopted earlier to satisfy British bondholders. This, in turn, could lead to considerable losses to British financial and banking institutions and their possible collapse. Equally, commercial sanctions against Germany also could lead to catastrophic losses for the considerable British trade with Germany, particularly in the fishing, shipping and textile industries, as well as serious losses for Empire countries and dependencies. Influenced by the warnings of the British Minister of Agriculture and Fishing about the grave effects of sanctions on the British economy, the cabinet decided against sanctions.[8]

The Standstill and Payments Agreement had become an iconic symbol for the Bank and its governor, Montagu Norman, the City, the Treasury and Board of Trade, and dire predictions of the effects of its removal on British trade, the British internal economy and world trade now seem in hindsight to have been exaggerated. Of Britain's 12 leading export trading customers in 1938, Germany accounted for only 4.4% of Britain's trading customers — according to the *Statistical Abstract for the U.K.* (1939), Table 281 cited by Scott Preston (table 3.3, p. 66) — not much more than Denmark (3.3%). Had Germany been forced to pay its debts through a clearing, it is doubtful if this would have caused a debacle on the world market. Germany's trade by then had declined and anyway was turning away from the Western European trade market for greener pastures. As a political maneuver to support the moderates, it failed to prevent Schacht from losing his position, which had probably been overestimated from the beginning. So, in the last analysis, it had only two justifications: to protect the British bondholders and to serve as the economic side of the appeasement of Hitler until presumably some general agreement could have been arrived at. However, admittedly, all these interests must have seemed formidable at the time to the conservative business and political interests then in power in England.

Reports reached the British of strains in the Third Reich brought on by the rearmament program and Schacht's policy of import controls. A German businessman told Pinsent that Germany's exchange position "was probably tighter than it had ever been before" because the countries from which Germany had been buying freely through clearing agreements had begun to react against an excessively close association with the Reich. A rise in world prices for primary products in 1937 enabled them to refuse to sell to Germany for reichsmarks which could be applied only to the purchase of German products, and to export their goods to free exchange countries.[9]

Pinsent's informant hoped that a slowing down of "internal activity and the disappearance of the easy home market would have a powerful effect on inducing German manufacturers to seek once again for their old foreign markets." An additional auger was the rising world price level which tended to close the gap between German prices and world prices, stimulating German interest in the world market. In addition, the beginning of rearmament

---

*The Standstill Agreement, arrived at in negotiations between the British and German governments during the early 1930s, permitted the continued orderly conduct of commercial relations despite German financial and trade debts, based upon an agreement to "stand still" on German monies owed to Britain.

in the countries outside Germany would enable the Reich to export to those areas abandoned by the newly arming countries.[10]

To get around the undercutting of British exports by German export subsidies, barter arrangements, clearing agreements and selective import restrictions causing havoc to its trade, the British government encouraged direct cartel arrangements between British and German industries in order to divide and share export markets. Through the Federation of British Industries and its German counterpart *Reichsgruppe Industrie,* individual arrangements between competing industries were encouraged by certain sectors of the British Foreign Office and the Board of Trade. These efforts to counter subsidized German overseas exports and the decline in British exports to Germany because of import restrictions had little success. Since the British had no desire to disavow their own protectionist policies, there remained only two choices: either to fight fire with fire by subsidizing their own exports as the Germans were doing, a policy of confrontation which had some support in the various departments of the government, but not in the cabinet, or to pursue a policy of economic appeasement begun in the 1930s. The latter was ultimately adopted as the least politically perilous and disruptive to conservative economic principles and trade. The German trade market, the third largest mercantile market in the world, was too important to risk a direct challenge and possibly war. As the German historian Bernd-Jürgen Wendt has stated: "To fail in appeasement would be to sign the death warrant of Britain as a Great Power."[11] This threatened to occur anyway as the cost of rearmament and the loss of trade was draining Britain and disrupting its credit system.

As the British effort to reach accommodation with the Nazi regime through Schacht and the German moderates foundered by the middle of 1937, the British turned their attention elsewhere. The German trade drive in the Balkans and especially Latin America also threatened the rising primary imperial power, the United States.

From its advent the New Deal had been disturbed by the stagnation of world trade in the early 1930s and the role in that decline played by the British government. The Roosevelt government's awareness that overseas trade demand was closely connected to America's internal social and economic problems stoked animosity toward Britain — and Germany as well. "We must sell abroad more of these surpluses," Cordell Hull told the 1935 Montevideo Conference.[12] After a struggle between the traditional agricultural interests headed by George Peek of the Agricultural Department, and the internationalists, led by Secretary of State Cordell Hull advocating a drive for trade through the Open Door principle and Reciprocal Trade Agreement, liberal trade principles triumphed.[13]

Roosevelt and the New Dealers viewed with displeasure the British Imperial preferential system and autarchy in Germany as egocentric economic nationalism that ultimately redounded against America's own imperial interests. Hull thought the Ottawa Conference system and its results was a device to save the British Empire at the expense of the United States.[14] American hostility later extended to Germany's plans to convert Central and Southeastern Europe into a semi-colonial hinterland from which American exports would be excluded. When Germany extended its system of export subsidies, barter and clearing arrangements to Latin America, a crucial trading region for American business in overcoming the Depression, the opposition of the Roosevelt administration intensified. By 1935 Latin America was absorbing 54% of America's manufactured cotton exports; 55% of steel mill exports; 33% of leather, rubber, silk, paper, electrical and industrial exports; and 22% of automobile exports. Between 1919 and 1934 American capital investments had almost quintupled from $1,125,000,000 to $5,000,000,000.[15] The inroads into Latin America made by German export products edging out American-made manufactured goods raised the suspicion of Roosevelt and the New Dealers that Germany was ultimately striving for world domination. In the mid-1930s the German trade threat in Latin American and elsewhere had replaced Britain in the American minds as the principal commercial bugbear. By 1938, despite the latent conflict over British trade preferences, bilateral agreements and violations of the Open Door principle, the overwhelming importance of a joint front against the Nazi challenge forced the British and the Americans to put aside their differences momentarily.

Unable to reach an arrangement with the German moderates in 1937, London sought political ballast in a rapprochement with the United States. The vehicle for the conciliation of relations between the two countries was the American-British Trade negotiations of 1938 which the British handled with great caution and sensitivity. London informed the British envoy to the United States of the extraordinary importance of the treaty for the pacification of Europe and the dissemination of an image of cooperation between the United States and the United Kingdom in the area of trade. In fact, the Cabinet and Foreign Office stressed to its representative in Washington that the political side of the treaty far exceeded the economic.[16] From the first, Berlin viewed the treaty as directed against Germany.[17]

The Anglo-American Trade Agreement of 1938 did not diminish Britain's trade conflict with the United States. Roosevelt believed Chamberlain was an agent of the "City" and pro-German financial interests — Chamberlain, Simon, Hoare, the Astors, Lothian, Geoffrey Dawson and Lord Halifax — were preparing to save the Empire by a deal with Hitler to permit German expansion into Central and Southeastern Europe.[18] From other sources Roosevelt heard that Chamberlain "gets his ideology from the City — England's Wall St."

Increased American hostility to Germany beginning in 1934, however, gradually overshadowed U.S. resentment of the British preferential system and British trade monopolies in Latin America. Hull and Roosevelt chafed at German efforts to evade payment to American holders of German bonds. Washington, like London, saw German trade agreements with Swiss and Dutch creditors granting them special favors as a way of forcing American creditors to accept German autarchy and rearmament. Schacht's visit to the United States in the early 1930s, during which he asked for credit to purchase millions of dollars worth of cotton for resale in Europe with which to pay off American creditors and stimulate trade with Germany, drew a "disguised threat of retaliation" from Roosevelt who was irritated by Schacht's sleight of hand. "Germany," Hull declared, "was deliberately trying to get the American creditor to finance her rearmament." The State Department believed that Germany was trying to "blackmail the U.S. into negotiating a trade agreement on terms satisfactory to her, that is, that we should undertake to buy more German goods.... "[19] Selling 800,000 bales of cotton to Germany, Hull told the German ambassador in an angry exchange, would be like paying blackmail and "taking opium."[20] Encouraged by Secretary of Treasury Morgenthau, Roosevelt retaliated by applying duties against German imports, whereupon the Germans relented and abandoned their trade restrictions.[21] American revulsion over Hitler's persecution of the Jews and repression of political groups further compounded Germany's difficulties with the United States.

In Latin America, American trade was not only losing out in Argentina to both the British and the Germans, but as we have mentioned, the State Department and Roosevelt were apprehensive about Nazi economic and political penetration of Paraguay and Brazil, and were ready to intervene with troops. Similar fears of German penetration of the Mexican oil market, particularly after the nationalization of American-held Mexican oil properties, caused the American government to come to terms with the Mexican government sooner than it might have. A split occurred in the American government between Hull, supporting the oil companies, and Morgenthau, who feared the Mexican government might retaliate by selling oil to Germany and Japan. Despite pressures from the oil companies, Roosevelt rejected military intervention and preferred to negotiate. As the Second World War loomed, the United States did not want a hostile Mexico on its southern border and also wished to avoid violating the anti-intervention clause of the 1936 Buenos Aires Pan-American Conference and the preamble of the 1933 Montevideo Pan-American conference. This would have undermined the American Good Neighbor Policy, which had been designed to be the political instrument of the United States for driving the Germans from the Latin American market.[22] When the Mexican government expropriated the oil lands of the foreign companies, Britain broke off relations; the United States abrogated the silver agreement, but avoided any direct confrontation with the Mexican government. Mexico finally agreed to pay the oil countries compensation, and even though Mexican President Cárdenas sold oil to the Axis to pay off Mexico's debts, by 1940 over one seventh of America's imported oil came from Mexico.[23] American commercial rivalry with Germany continued into the 1940s; in 1938 the two countries almost came to an open break in relations.

With the outbreak of World War II, Roosevelt hoped that the cost of financing the war would force Britain to divest itself of some of its extensive investment holdings in Latin America to the United States, thereby improving the American position in Latin America. The conflict over trade between London and Washington may have also resulted in British "appeasement" of Germany. American Undersecretary of State Berle noted on June 28, 1939: "There is at least some ground for the belief that both the French and the British are preparing to 'appease' the Germans, this time on the theory that they were unable to get the necessary assurances from the United States. Of course they cannot get any such assurances, and are not going to."[24] Berle had "mixed emotions" on the matter: while readjustments in Central Europe he conceded were necessary, he feared it would "inevitably be the basis for a still greater imperialist movement," i.e., an expansion of the Central European area under Axis control, and removal from accessibility to American exports. If this resulted in "an intolerably strong German-Italian empire ... it would be only a question of time — two or three years, perhaps — before they undertook to crush England, with whom they must inevitably come into conflict on both commercial and imperial lines." Berle saw Britain as the lesser threat to the United States: "We have no necessary interest in defending the British Empire.... But we do have a very real and solid interest in having the British and not the Germans dominant in the Atlantic."[25] In a startling prophecy Berle predicted a renewed American imperialism.

> ... we shall be meeting imperialist schemes in South and Central America not on a paper basis, as we do now, but backed up by an extremely strong naval and military force. This can only mean that the next phase of the United States will be militarist and no mistake about it; or, still worse, that we shall be forced into empire to preserve ourselves, much as the British were....[26]

Narrow self-interest influenced the decision whether to continue a policy of strict neutrality as the probability of war increased; American trade rivalry with Britain in Latin America remained a constant obstacle to an alliance. Berle was almost hostile to Britain: "Any such foothold, no matter by whom established, would be unfriendly to us: just as the British influence in the Argentine has persistently been directed against the United States, going even to the length of an attempt to break up the Buenos Aires Conference in 1936."[27] Roosevelt, however, moved in the direction of a "biased" neutrality favoring Britain and France because "there was at least an even chance that the Germans and Italians might win. If that occurred they would ... establish trade relations with the South American countries and Mexico, put instructors in their armies and the like." After defeating the British, Germany, Berle believed, would seize the British fleet and together the Japanese and Italians would surround a badly outmatched United States which might then be forced to fight for its Latin American markets and its continued existence.[28] Berle's preference for a British victory was pragmatic: "We have no necessary interest in defending the British Empire, aside from the fact that we prefer the British as against the German method of running an empire."[29] The success or failure of the New Deal in staving off social disruption increasingly depended on the sale of American commodities abroad, in markets where the British and Germans were strong competitors. Berle recognized that German export subsidies and the British preferential system were effectively locking the United States out of its Latin American interest sphere.[30] It was a quarrel within the capitalist family of nations for a diminished amount of trade.

The *Realpolitik* outlook of Roosevelt, Hull, Berle and others makes it clear that England could not count on the certain support of the United States and that except for French support, the British had to face the

German challenge alone. This undoubtedly had a major influence on the further conduct of the policy of appeasement. Another baleful influence was undoubtedly the parlous state of Britain's economy during the 1930s. The difficulties besetting England were legion: industry lagged and unemployment and poverty were widespread. An increase in military expenditures in the face of an $8 billion debt was out of the question for the staid, business-oriented Chamberlain government. Sir John Simon, Chancellor of the Exchequer, feared that participation in the armament race would ruin Britain.[31] Stark social revolution and chaos attended any new military conflict.

An additional determinant was the Empire itself. Since the 1930s almost one-half of Britain's exports were sold in the Empire as opposed to 22% on the eve of World War I. The Empire's members exercised a pervasive influence in pursuit of a policy of avoiding war. Dominion willingness to pay a higher price for peace than the British government and tensions within the empire creating centripetal tendencies have been cited as one of the reasons why Britain sought a settlement with Germany at the expense of the small countries of Central and Eastern Europe. A new war would be received with nightmarish apprehension in the Empire, and British leaders seemed almost hysterical on the subject. Lord Lothian believed that Nehru was eagerly waiting for the next war "to let loose revolution in India." Eden feared a possible "race riot from Cairo to the Cape." Moreover, because of its world wide interests, a maritime conflict with Italy in the Mediterranean, with Japan in the Far East and on the continent with Germany were contemplated with anxiety and dread.[32] Britain's naval and military forces were unequal to the task; its air force had degenerated to several hundred planes and it ranked sixth in world forces. Its fleet had similarly eroded to the point where it could not meet a Japanese threat and still have sufficient forces to defend the Mediterranean. Its tank forces were all but negligible. Despite early intelligence reports that the Germans were rearming, Chamberlain was parsimonious until the mid-thirties in doling out monies for rearmament and defense.

During a cabinet session in late October 1933, the British thrashed out the vexatious Japanese conundrum, with all of its potentially damaging repercussions for Britain's relations with the United States. At this time the dire menace of fascism did not yet exist and Britain was more preoccupied with overcoming the ravages of the Depression.

Britain's difficulties with Japan, lamented the Chancellor of the Exchequer Chamberlain, had been a direct result of the Washington Naval Conference of 1921–1923; "[Britain's] position in the Far East had only been rendered more precarious." "If only we could be free from all apprehensions as to a conflict with Japan[,] the situation (naval limitation of armaments) would be greatly eased." But, although "Japanese feeling had been . . . almost one of resentment," on the political side relations had been "fairly good" primarily because in the Manchurian affair Britain "had steered a fairly middle course."[33]

Britain's trade relations with Japan, however, were not felicitous. The President of the Board of Trade, Runciman, described Japanese opinion as made up of two currents: one was "purely militaristic" and the other "aggressively commercial" with the former "in the ascendant." From the standpoint of Britain's own commercial interests, "Japanese industry had worked to our detriment." Before going off the gold standard, "the Japanese had built up huge stocks, and that position had been used to damage [them]." Commercially they posed a threat: "They had invaded the Indian and African colonial markets, and were severe competitors in South Africa." An allocation of markets as a way out of this dilemma was "dubious." Though the African colonial market was not the most important, "it was rather difficult not to take action there, in view of the feeling that existed."[34]

These problems surfaced again in the late winter of 1934. The government fretted over the political vacuum created by the end of the Anglo-Japanese accord, the Japanese desire for parity (of naval armaments) in the Pacific and the Japanese trade threat. To solve the problem of Japan's amour-propre and isolation, the British proposed a bilateral understanding to restore Japan's "ruffled feelings" and relieve fears that Britain would unite with the U.S. Britain's ambivalent attitude toward Japan was clearly reflected in the belief that "a hostile Japan meant a risk to [its] possessions in the Far East, a menace to India and Australia. What [Britain] risked by good relations with Japan was (1) trade — better relations meant further Japanese trade incursions — and (2) deterioration of [its] relations with America."[35]

The British government hoped that Japanese expansion would get bogged down and flounder in China: "There was something to be said for the view that if Japan was to expand such expansion was preferable on the continent of Asia rather than southward," in the direction of Britain's colonial holdings in Malaysia and the Indian subcontinent. The Foreign Secretary, Anthony Eden, raised the advantage of a non-aggression pact ("We never wished to attack Japan. Our desire was that they should attack us."), and was instructed to prepare a definite recommendation for improving relations with Japan.[36] Nothing came of this, probably because of the growing danger from Nazi Germany in the mid-1930s and Japan's gravitation toward the latter, signing the Anti-Comintern Agreement in 1936.[37]

Britain's desire to mollify Japan was prompted by its struggle for export markets where the U.S. was an aggressive competitor. American competition in China was "almost negligible," but in Latin America and South Africa it had grown. The U.S. was purchasing "large quantities of . . . leather and tin."[38] At the end of November 1934, the British cabinet which had been under pressure by Roosevelt to pay its loan debts, received a summary of Leith-Ross's account of the "confusion and skepticism" surrounding the Roosevelt administration. "There seemed little prospect of any limitation of production" — a forecast that boded ill for British export hopes — and much chaos over unemployment relief. Public works "had been a disillusionment" and there was a tendency to state socialism of the most inefficient and extravagant kind involving state assistance to banking, industry and agriculture.[39] All this, it may be inferred, fed into the imperative of trade to stimulate demand and reduce unemployment.

In the mid-1930s the British were apprehensive over American trade inroads into Latin America, in particular Argentina, a country vital to British interests. British domination of Argentina was almost total; they controlled 60% of all foreign investment in 1942 while the U.S. held only 20%. Britain was the chief buyer of Argentine grain and meat.[40] The 1933 British-Argentine Commercial Agreement — described as "a rigid bilateral trade agreement reminiscent of Spanish colonial mercantilism of the sixteenth century"[41] — had been faithfully carried out by Argentina, cabinet minutes note, "with very great benefits to British trade and industry." Britain pledged to take Argentine chilled beef at the 1932 level while Argentina promised to use the proceeds to purchase British goods.[42] Under the 1933 treaty, reductions of Argentina duties had been secured for 30% of British exports, free entry for 28% and existing duties for about 13%. The value of British goods to the Argentine, which had fallen from £14.8 million in 1931 to £10.7 million in 1932, had risen to £15.3 million in 1935 and all British frozen debts had been paid off in Argentina. "A very hard bargain had been driven with Argentina" in which the British Board of Trade "had intervened in all important questions.[43] Britain could still do this because of the great power of the British mercantile market.

The bargaining had occurred under the shadow of the American competitor, "a matter of first class importance." For some time the U.S. had indicated interest in the Argentine, and Secretary of State Hull had visited the Pan-American Congress at Buenos Aires. London feared Hull might persuade Argentina that the American market could be easily substituted for the U.K., creating a situation in which "the [British] export trade must inevitably suffer." Britain and the Empire had formerly been the sole market for Argentina. London now was apprehensive over the American ability to "make offers as good as, if not better than [Britain] could." It was, therefore, "urgent" and "very important" that Britain should conclude the new trade agreement with Argentina, before the arrival of Hull's mission to Argentina in December.[44]

The significance for Britain of the Argentine trade may be gauged by British trade estimates: of the two-fifths of Argentina's share of world wheat exports, one-third went to the U.K.; of the two-thirds of Argentina's share of world maize exports one-half went to the U.K.; of the 15% of Argentina's share of world exports of mutton and lamb, all came to the U.K.; of Argentina's half of world beef exports, nearly all went to the U.K. Since 90% of all Britain's mutton and lamb exports came from the Empire and only 10% from foreign countries, Argentine meat imports were in conflict with Empire imports and anticipated home expansion. In Australia and the dominions there were apprehensions that meat imports to the U.K. would be cut in favor of Argentina. Conversely, if Argentine exports to the U.K. were cut, Argentina might cut British imports to that country. In the end, the British cabinet agreed that the Argentine agreement was "a very desirable" one and not to cut Argentine imports by more than 10% in principle.[45]

The interplay of politics and economics in the historical documents disguises the central fact of interwar history: the British and French domination of Europe since 1918 and Germany's determination — with the Italians in opportunistic tandem — to upset this control. The end of this comfortable illusion of British and French hegemony occurred within the British government when Sir Eric Phipps relayed the frank assessment of General von Blomberg, Wehrmacht Chief of Staff: "The Germans and Italians both wanted the frontiers of Europe to be altered, whereas France wanted to keep them as at present while [Britain's] view, broadly speaking, was similar to that of France." The League of Nations was inadequate for the task, Italy felt, since frontiers could not be altered except by unanimous vote.[46]

By 1934 this perception began to sharpen and London became increasingly apprehensive of the hydra of German rearmament. In 1934 and 1935 the cabinet grappled unsuccessfully with the problem of German revisionism which emerged first in a January 1934 cabinet discussion about German designs on Austria and Mussolini's inability or unwillingness to block them. The Secretary of State for Dominion Affairs, Thomas, bluntly asserted the besetting problem: "It was no use bluffing the Germans, but the public here would not stand for a war with Germany." In the end, the government, despite misgivings, contented itself with studying the possibility of a boycott of Germany.[47]

In mid-March 1934 the cabinet divided over whether Germany was the "ultimate potential enemy." Uncertainty and illusion still beclouded decisions: The Foreign Secretary, Eden, thought "Hitler's outlook was not aggressive or threatening to [Britain]. His methods rather than an actual threat were menacing."[48]

The Secretary of State for Air, the Marquess of Londonderry, wanted to face the reality of the German threat: "There was every evidence that Germany was going ahead with her armaments, especially in the air. The Chiefs of Staff assumed that Germany might become a menace in five or six years and within that time might make a demand on them for colonies." It would be "highly dangerous" if England had not corrected its worst deficiencies when Germany had rearmed. Chamberlain, then Chancellor of the Exchequer, wanted to secure some general material guarantees that would not cost the estimated £70 million for defense in five years. In the face of pressure by the Secretary for Air and the Secretary for India who feared that "a long delay might be disastrous," Prime Minister Baldwin temporized. In the end the Cabinet agreed that if the forthcoming disarmament conference did not bring an agreement, then Britain would have the alternative of either joining with other powers to assure the peace or it would be facing "very heavy expenditures on armaments."[49]

The international situation remained unimproved in the spring of 1934. The French ambassador reported: "Germany is unwilling to remain disarmed below a certain minimum...unless she receives some satisfaction on security." Germany was rearming and intended to rearm whatever happened. The real question was whether Germany would limit itself for ten years to Hitler's proposals, which Eden thought were not so unreasonable, "or whether there was to be the prospect of unlimited and much greater rearmament by Germany." There was little possibility of modifying the Versailles Treaty without the danger of an "embittered France" with its great military strength, itself rearming and becoming a risk to England which might then also be compelled to rearm. "The general rise in temperature might eventually result in war."

It is surprising how much the British government misread the French in those early pre-Munich days. For the wrong reasons closer relations with France were to be cultivated despite the "blameworthy French attitude." The Versailles borders, which, if uprooted "would upset every nation in Europe," remained a thicket of problems. The British government began to realize that Germany meant to use force unless it could gain its objectives without fighting. While clearly recognizing and supporting France's need for security, the government was "reluctant to accept any commitment that would have the appearance of a military alliance with France." The cabinet, therefore, made another crabwise move and instructed the Foreign Secretary to draw up "proposals for Security designed to induce France to accept the minimum German terms, but without involving a military alliance with France."[50] At least a part of this fear of entanglement and a conflict with Germany may be traced to the "City's" fear that Germany might repudiate its loan debts.

Following the publication of German rearmament expenditures in April 1934, French opinion hardened further against an international convention legalizing German rearmament.[51] By June the British Foreign Secretary reported broadly that the French neither wished a disarmament agreement with Germany nor intended to give up their military superiority. Lacking belief in German veracity, they preferred a situation in which German rearmament would produce a breach of the Versailles Treaty. The "[French] were full of the idea of an 'Eastern Locarno' " and "anticipated the breakup of Hitlerism." They did not believe they had "to pay court" to the British: "Your country is more afraid of Germany than we are," French Foreign Minister Barthou told Anthony Eden at their first meeting. The French thought Britain would eventually have to side with France "by force of circumstances." The continuing lockstep drift toward war was probably best summed up by a laconic comment of the Lord Privy Seal: "The situation is probably beyond mending." In July 1934 the British agreed, without enthusiasm, to recommend an Eastern Locarno scheme to the German, Polish and Italian governments.[52]

The British were slow to act on reports of German rearmament. In late April 1934 the Defense Requirements Committee adopted the ruling that five years would be required to remove British deficiencies to deal with a German attack.[53] The question was to be kept under constant revision. The dramatic division in the government was expressed three months later in the comment of the Secretary of State for War that "the army was not in a condition to fight at the present time and it would not be in readiness until some unspecified date after 1938." Blame lay directly at the door of Chamberlain: "the reason for this was that the Chancellor of the Exchequer could not approve the money, so that the five-year program had to be cut down from £40,000,000 to £20,000,000."[54]

The shadow of what later came to be known as appeasement fell on cabinet sessions at this early date. Chamberlain led the party of caution and settlement of the German problem by diplomatic means through the League rather than outright military action. His overriding concern was to protect the pound and maintain Britain's financial market position. Neither the cabinet nor the country were ready for military confrontation at this early date and preferred to wait until Hitler's intentions were clearer. However, the cabinet did commit itself to a policy of partial rearmament, and the weakening of the British economic position had begun in earnest, anyway.

By November 1934 doubts about Germany's intentions evaporated as the cabinet noted German rearmament was occurring "in an alarming manner." In a short time Germany would have an army of 300,000 men rather than the 100,000 the Treaty of Versailles allowed. Even though the cabinet noted fear among some German officials that the Versailles powers would accuse Germany of violations, nothing was done to confront Hitler.[55] At a special cabinet session on rearmament, November 26, the cabinet only restated the apprehensions of the previous spring that if allowed to develop the German forces might ultimately become a menace to the peace of Europe.[56]

The British government's foreign policy of wariness and half-decision continued into 1935: the Baldwin government resigned itself to parity of armaments and limitation of armaments through a convention signed at Geneva, but with the French still opposed to a policy of doing little to confront Germany. The British were still wary of any open commitment; public opinion was not ready for anything more. "The Prime Minister suggested that great care must be taken that we did not put ourselves in a position where the French were able to bring Great Britain into action automatically as [if] it [*sic*] were pressing a lever."[57] On the eve of the arrival of the French ministers, Premier Laval and Foreign Minister Flandin, the British government still clung to the possibility of a diplomatic settlement — an "accommodation within a regime of security" — in exchange for which, it would accept a system of supervision. Beyond these commitments the British cabinet would not go. On the subject of the Rhineland: "The view of the cabinet, however, was that demilitarization of the Rhineland was not a vital British interest." If the French ministers raised the subject, the British would say "they were bound by the Locarno Treaty and had no intention of repudiating it."[58] The underlying premise of British policy toward Germany was to maintain the status quo, avoid entangling alliances and commitments and bring Germany back to the League where an arrangement, not too violative of this status quo, could be made over armament and borders. This would preserve the preeminent financial and market position Britain had gained by having seized or forced Germany to give up its colonial territories, financial assets and export markets abroad after 1918.

Whether Hitler intended to move east or west preoccupied the British government in 1935 and the Defense Requirements Committee (DRC) commented darkly on a possible German drive into the east or south. British military intelligence thought Germany would be dominant on the continent and Britain should avoid any kind of "life and death struggle." Any alliance with Russia to prevent German expansion to the east would increase "Russia's power for mischief as the main exploiter of the victory." The DRC explicitly spoke of a German-Soviet conflict in which "we have little to lose, and might even gain considerably."[59] General Dill told Liddell Hart, the military historian: "let Germany expand eastwards at Russia's expense," but Liddell Hart disagreed, "that in the long run, this would be like feeding the tiger that might turn on you: we were the ultimate obstacle to Germany's ambition as in the past."[60]

Some of this reasoning continued into 1937: Eden was somewhat ambiguous in May 1937: no commitments but Britain should "make it clear" that it was interested in "events" in Central Europe. In the Foreign Office there was a division of opinion: Strang, Cadogan and O'Malley wanted Britain to disinterest itself in Eastern Europe more than Sargent and Vansittart. O'Malley wanted to sell "the lumber of Versailles" (Austria and Czechoslovakia) while it "would still fetch a price." Vansittart disagreed: handing over Eastern Europe to Germany, wrote Vansittart, was "quite incompatible with our interests. We fought the last war to prevent this." Vansittart thought assisting Germany in grabbing Eastern Europe, as Lord Lothian suggested after seeing Hitler, "would be going against the democratic tide and *the effect on the USA would be catastrophic.*"[61]

Following the Rhineland occupation, Hitler's ultimate objectives were still undiscernible to most. The two major groups, the City and public opinion, sympathized more with Germany than with France and would not support either British economic or military countervailing deterrence and felt risking war was folly.[62] Most cabinet members and experts held this view and only Duff Cooper, an obdurate exception, felt that Britain would not be in a "relatively better off position" against Germany three years later. Baldwin, always hoping for a conflict between Germany and the Soviet Union, feared that any determined action against Germany would unleash "another great war in Europe." If Germany were defeated by France and Russia, it "would probably only result in Germany going Bolshevik," confirming the widely held preference in London for Hitler rather than Stalin. While Ashton-Gwatkin and Lord Cranborne favored giving Germany economic assistance to prevent war, which might even include "a freer hand in Central Europe," Lord Stanhope, Sargent and Eden desired a political settlement first before considering economic assistance. Vansittart, opposed to turning over Central and Eastern Europe to Germany, suspected Germany's ultimate designs and intentions, and Ambassador Phipps also rejected the notion of economically relieving Germany's distress and declared emphatically: "Hitlerism is no longer the symptom but the disease itself."[63] The policy of Munich appeared in outline of abandoning the southeast gradually to Hitler.

Washington was piqued over Britain's departure from the block of states besieging Germany for debt payments, for mollifying the Reich in the 1934 British-German payments agreement and for bilateral payments agreements with other states. Roosevelt and Hull's suspicions of the "City" and its pro-German sympathies, Britain's sabotage of the most-favored-nation principle — the American credo for trade revival — and London's unwillingness to confront Nazi political and economic expansion, created a climate of tension between London and Washington. Intense trade competition from the United States in South America and to a lesser extent from Japan in Asia influenced the British policy of avoiding a confrontation with Nazi Germany in order to use Germany as a counterweight against overwhelming pressure from the United States.[64]

Feeling militarily unprepared and indisposed to confront Germany, the British government sent Foreign Secretary Eden to meet with Hitler in March 1935 to try to get Germany to return to the League to settle matters.[65] Germany's rearmament program was still incomplete and therefore Hitler had to conceal his true intentions from his potential foes. Hitler denied to Eden that National Socialism had an "expansive character." He insisted: "The German people had no interest in pursuing an imperialist policy." His primary problem was to find an economic basis for the life of 60 million people. Annexation would merely add to the political and economic difficulties with which he was faced. Hitler opposed an Eastern Pact as "dangerous and objectionable" and probably to dissemble his true aims from the British and to appear reasonable, proposed instead "a general pact of non-aggression and consultation and an undertaking not to afford assistance to an aggression." The result of these discussions was the 1935 Anglo-German Naval Conference in which Hitler declared that he only wanted 35% of parity with the British fleet; even though the French had 50%, he declared munificently, he would not ask for more even if other states constructed more or Germany received back its colonies. In public statements designed to allay fears, he asked for air parity with Western European Powers through 2,500 first line aircraft — taking the French figure of 2,500 whereas the French only had 1,000 planes, not all of which were modern — which he hoped to attain in 1935.[66]

The partial rearmament program by the Baldwin government in mid-1934 occurred within a context of declining British foreign investments and loans and profits from abroad. It has been suggested by R. Palme Dutt and others that the British continued on in India to offset their declining capital position primarily by siphoning off capital to Britain as a form of "financial imperialism" during the inter-war years.[67] Therefore, given the shaky financial prospects, there were fears both in the government and business circles that the rearmament program could stimulate an artificial economic upswing only to be followed by a disastrous downturn at a later date.

Lord Weir broached this problem in January 1935 in describing the potential conflict caused by the diversion of funds to the armament program and away from domestic production. He informed the ministers on the Defense Requirements Committee (Baldwin, Eden and Chamberlain) that the rearmament program could not be carried out in five years without affecting exports — unless controls similar to those in Germany were imposed. Though the Defense Requirements Committee members all agreed, later when attempts were made to get the policy changed in 1937, Chamberlain and the Board of Trade strenuously opposed peacetime regulation of industry.[68] Leith-Ross, in a cabinet paper drawn up at the request of the Board of Trade, warned that the situation was diverting industrial production away from export markets building up a potential balance of payments deficit. He warned against spiraling prices, higher wages, increased costs and a depreciation of currency.[69] Chamberlain in 1937 expressed similar fears of inflationary conditions leading to a loss of trade and an artificial boom that could bring down the government.[70] Deflationary nostrums were suggested from controlling new issues on the stock market, regulatory price controls and accepting a temporary balance of payments deficit — proposed in October 1938 by Debenham, a young Cambridge economist — to more orthodox proposals for higher taxes by Waley.[71] Concerns about the loss of overseas markets led the Board of Trade President Runciman publicly to warn British businessmen that the heavy orders generated by the defense program were temporary and that they should not allow their export trade to be lost.[72]

Until 1937 the Treasury Department held a firm grip over defense costs. The strong-willed, domineering Chancellor of the Exchequer, Neville Chamberlain, worked closely with the Permanent Secretary of the Treasury Department, Sir Warren Fischer, to hold down defense costs. Up to September 1938 Fischer supported Chamberlain's policy of placating Hitler, but after the Munich Agreement, he broke with Chamberlain, supporting the need for increased defense outlay and resigned in 1939. The threat of war with Germany began to thrust all other considerations aside.

At the beginning of 1937 Chamberlain still believed that war was not imminent and that to follow Winston Churchill's advice "and sacrifice British commerce to the manufacture of arms" would "cripple the revenue." However, Churchill himself had doubts at times and in August 1937 questioned whether or not Hitler would later enter history as the restorer of German prosperity, a Germany returning "serene, helpful and strong to the forefront of the European family circle." But by 1939 the new Chancellor of the Exchequer Sir John Simon reluctantly conceded that the threat of war was crowding out dire apprehensions of inflation and a credit crisis.[73] In 1938 Britain, as the figures in Table 7–1 indicate, was still far behind the German investment in armaments and in 1939 raised appropriations more than two and a half times the previous year. By 1940 British investments in armaments actually surpassed Germany's. In 1937 British defense expenditures reached £254.7 million and, as the figures in Table 7–2 show, fell into the deficit category.

Table 7–1. Percent of Investment in Armaments for the United Kingdom and Germany, 1932–1940

Year	U.K.	Germany (% of GNP)[74]
1932	3	1
1933	3	3
1934	3	6
1935	4	13
1936	4	13
1937	6	13
1938	7	17
1939	18	23
1940	46	38

Table 7–2. British Defense Expenditure
and the Budget Surplus, 1934–1938 (in millions of pounds)[75]

Year	Defense Expenditure	Government Surplus
1934	118.9	50
1935	140.8	23
1936	183.0	14
1937	254.7	−2
1938	473.2	109

By 1936 all sectors of the British political spectrum from the Labor Party to the Conservatives, with the exception of the International Labor Party, had agreed on the necessity of rearming.[76] In the debate on rearmament in July 1936, Chamberlain received unexpected support for the government's intention of borrowing up to £400 million through the Defense Loans Bill from John Maynard Keynes who declared that the loan would not be too inflationary. Keynes wrote a month later in an article ("Borrowing for Defense: Is It Inflationary?") that rearmament two years hence "may be positively hopeful in warding off a depression," particularly in the depressed areas where the multiplier effect of armaments would raise demand as it wound its way through the economy without adding to inflation. Keynes repeated these arguments later in 1939 that a rearmament loan would help to wipe out unemployment and lead to a savings increase of 8% in the national income, which would pay for the increased borrowing. The Treasury, still steeped in the conventional orthodoxy of the times, rejected such arguments in 1936, and even two years later in April 1938 Sir John Simon told the cabinet that increased defense expenditures would be impossible "unless we turned ourselves into a different kind of nation."[77] The inflation concerns expressed by Sir Thomas Inskip, Minister for Coordination of Defense, in a cabinet session at the end of 1937, did not take place and instead a slump and increased unemployment occurred. By 1938 British unemployment climbed above the 2 million figure and Inskip's warning against exceeding the £1,500,000 tax figure was ignored.

Those like Inskip held the conventional belief that the ability of the government to borrow depended upon savings available for investment and financial confidence, both of which would be reduced by a disturbance in the trade balance. Excessive borrowing by the government would result in inflation and a rise in prices "which would have an immediate effect upon [Britain's] export trade."[78] In 1937 and 1938 Britain was running a £50 million balance of payments deficit. A decline in gold holdings with capital increasingly leaving the country in larger amounts compounded its deteriorating trade position. Between April 1 and September 30, 1938, gold reserves fell by £150 million and by July 1939 declined another £150 million, leaving £500 million available and £200 million worth of foreign securities.[79] The value of the pound dropped from $5 to $4.60; and the orthodox economists in the Treasury Department and Keynes both agreed that the combination of the balance of payments deficit and an increased rearmament program threatened a crisis of confidence similar to 1931 when a run on sterling resulted. Britain might then be forced to take the same measures as Germany to staunch the flow of capital abroad, i.e., exchange controls and import restrictions.[80]

Chapter 8

Schizoid British Views of Nazi Germany: German Moderates or German Radicals. "Will Nasty Mr. Hyde Eat Poor Dr. Jekyll?"

> The German nation must export or die.
>
> — Adolf Hitler, Speech on January 30, 1939

NAZI GERMANY'S ABSORPTION OF AUSTRIA in March 1938 disturbed the British. The conservative imperialist Leopold Avery recorded in his diary on March 13, 1938, that "Austria's collapse came to me as a terrible blow." He thought gloomily that this would cause a "falling back with Italian support, on [Britain's] holding Yugoslavia and the Balkans and letting Germany find elbow room in the west of the Danubian area and in Eastern Europe."[1] Henderson, the pro-German British minister to Berlin, went even further: "German hegemony East of the Rhine, down to the Brenner and the Balkans is a fact, however unpalatable it may be to admit it," adding that "Central and Eastern Europe will in general have to dance as Hitler pipes."[2] *The Economist* noted that Greater Germany had made "something uncomfortably like a political-economic sortie" into Central Europe, forcing a whole series of European countries into "varying degrees of economic servitude — a situation from which they cannot now escape by normal, orthodox [methods]. The system is tending towards a gradual freezing-out from those regions of all states whose trade is conducted on orthodox lines." Greater Germany's trade with Central and Southeastern Europe (Hungary, Romania, Yugoslavia, Bulgaria, Greece and Czechoslovakia) was roughly one-fifth of its entire trade. "Germany's penetration of Central and Southeastern Europe has assumed, with the incorporation of Austria, the character of a drive towards a self-sufficient Central and Southeastern Europe under the political and economic tutelage of Great Germany. And Italy emerges as being four or five times more economically dependent on Greater Germany than is Great Germany upon her. The political and strategic implications need no emphasis." However, the article offered no solution and, in fact, expressly advised against doing anything.[3]

To understand how Britain reached this impasse, it is necessary to trace over time the British reaction to the German trade drive into the southeast. Generally speaking, it consisted of several contradictory feelings: on the one hand an increasing disquiet over the rise of a rival German commercial empire and German hegemonic aspirations in Eastern Europe but an inclination not to impede the "natural" and inevitable slide of German economic power into the region as preferable to military adventures in quest of raw materials and markets.

The world Depression and the financial crisis of the 1930s led to virtual incorporation of Southeastern Europe into the German interest sphere. Curtailment of British capital investment abroad hastened the process of German commercial penetration. A 1936 British Foreign Office study of German trade increases in the region notes the problem:

> ...before the war British exports to countries who [*sic*] could not pay for them were continually being stimulated by loans. Since the war the British public had less to lend abroad, and since the crisis of 1931, by an understanding between the Treasury and issuing houses, foreign lending has been definitely prohibited except in a few special cases. This policy has necessarily reacted unfavorably on British export trade....[4]

Establishment of the Export Credit Guarantee Department insured against the risk of default and non-transfer, but the problem could not be eliminated as long as those countries, lacking exchange currency, did not purchase British exports and allow Britain to purchase those of Central and Southeastern Europe. In short, the Germans filled the gap of dwindling British and other foreign loan and investment capital. The British were not entirely unhappy at German trade success: British trade, which might have been expected to decline, had not done so. In fact, with certain countries such as Greece it had increased considerably. Greece had just reduced its adverse balance with Britain, and Yugoslavia had also restricted and licensed imports from non-clearing countries. Nevertheless British trade with 8 of the Central and Southeastern European countries represented in 1935 only just over 2% of total British trade (£26,441,000 as opposed to 1,162,800,000 Rm of German trade); and its exports (£9,487,000 as compared to German exports of 557,800,000 Rm) "[had] on the whole remained steady in the face of intense competition by German goods."[5]

In addition, British trade with the three Scandinavian countries, Finland, the Baltic States and Poland, representing 10.6% of its total trade, had scored signal successes. United Kingdom exports (excluding re-exports) to those eight countries increased from £28,146,000 in 1932 to £41,396,000 in 1935, while German exports to the same countries decreased from 666.9 million Rm to 579.3 million Rm in 1935. The Foreign Office report concluded:

> Even so, this German export is still slightly greater than her export to the Danubian and Balkan countries while the corresponding United Kingdom export is more than four times as great. It will be seen, therefore, that North-East Europe is a much more prosperous trading area (owing to higher standards of living) and a much more promising market for United Kingdom trade than South-East Europe can ever be. German competition in the latter area is a much less formidable danger to United Kingdom trade than it may become in the former; and so

long as we can be predominant in the Baltic, we should not begrudge Germany the extension of her trade in the Danubian and Balkan countries. Further, the regional increase in German exports which forms the subject of this memorandum is, in essence, a diversion of trade from areas into which, for various reasons, German goods cannot easily penetrate. Should Germany, for instance, decide officially to devalue the mark, it is conceivable that British trade might experience increased competition in those areas and suffer accordingly. The development of the clearing system in South-East Europe is in a sense a substitute for an official devaluation of the mark; and some might hold that, in the circumstances, the substitute is not wholly disadvantageous."[6]

Besides this, the large German trade increases did not appear to have transformed the southeast into a zone of German economic hegemony despite the fact that already Germany controlled "over one half of the foreign trade of Bulgaria and Turkey, and a high percentage of that of Hungary, Romania, Greece, and Yugoslavia." Of decisive importance was the fact that "political control...has not yet manifested itself," but "must be regarded as no remote possibility." Germany not only wanted to assure itself of the benevolent neutrality of the southeastern states in time of war, but also to prevent them from falling under the influence of "the Franco-Russian group or of Italy (acting alone or in conjunction with the Powers). In the event of any important conflict of opinion between the Great Powers, it would be the German point of view to which these countries would be primarily responsive." This prospect elicited little British enthusiasm: "The disadvantage and danger of such a situation to Great Britain and to other Powers is obvious."[7]

The British at this juncture viewed the German trade increases almost apologetically as having occurred not by design, but almost as accidental. Lacking the necessary exchange currency to buy needed imports from "good currency" countries, Germany tended increasingly to buy goods from the nearly bankrupt countries whose currencies were artificially raised (like the Hungarian pengö) or those sliding gradually (like the Bulgarian lev). Purchases made from those countries often at artificially high prices and occasionally in order to be resold for foreign exchange "were not, at any rate at first, part of a deliberate policy of 'expansion' at all costs, but were on the contrary, forced on Germany by events." Credits accumulated in Berlin through clearing arrangements created an acute situation which the Germans only then realized they could manipulate for their own advantage. Balkan exporters, fearing they might suffer losses if the mark were devalued, compelled the purchase of increasingly larger amounts of German commodities. Once in the German trap, when the client states tried to resist, Berlin quickly retaliated. When the Bank of Hungary tried to squirm out of the German grip by threatening to raise the surcharge payable on reichsmarks and thus make German goods more expensive, Dr. Schacht retorted that the German frontier would be closed to Hungarian goods.[8]

As the increased German purchase of agricultural and other foodstuffs created a large passive trade balance in favor of the agrarian countries, pressure increased to take more German exports. The governments of the region assisted by granting premiums to importers via a lower mark rate or by allowing them to pay 50% of their indebtedness in marks obtained from creditors of Germany who had to accept a discount in order to cash in on their debt. To counteract these German pressures, Yugoslavia and Bulgaria made efforts to limit the accumulation of "frozen" marks by encouraging direct barter between individual merchants.

The position of the three tobacco exporting countries Turkey, Greece and Bulgaria — for Turkey 14% of its exports in 1934 and the latter 50% and 43% of exports respectively in 1935 — became particularly difficult. British tastes made it hard to increase the importation of tobacco to the U.K. from those countries. German tobacco purchases saved Greek and Bulgarian tobacco farmers from bankruptcy and raised Yugoslav farmers' living standards. The British, therefore, viewed the German trade offensive in a somewhat positive light as contributing to the general economic well-being of the Southeastern European region. More free trade seemed the only solution to the likelihood of German economic hegemony in the Danubian region. In summary, Treasury and Trade officials and Leith-Ross all agreed with this reasoning. It also permitted Germany's peaceful expansion into the southeast and sidestepped the risk of German military adventures in search of markets and raw materials.[9] Two years later the British began having second thoughts about this decision.

A new British assessment in early May 1938, almost two months after the Nazi annexation of Austria, does not differ too markedly from the 1936 one, viewing the German *Drang nach Südosten* with an ambiguous complacency edged with concern. The British Foreign Office was still unable to decide whether the German trade drive had been produced by the vagaries of the international market or by some deliberate expansionist design. The first phase of the German economic penetration of the southeast, the report deduced, was completed. During this stage the large amounts of raw materials purchased by Germany in the markets of the southeast under the block mark barter system threatened to create more passive balances in its favor. The inability of the eight Southeastern European countries to absorb sufficient German imports to balance their exports enabled the Reich to exercise considerable influence "over the politics of creditor governments in so far as the respective national banks were able to influence importers towards placing their orders in the German market." While accepting the fact that Germany was forced to increase its purchases in Central and Southeastern Europe "by her need of their goods and her inability to get them elsewhere, she clearly would not be blind to the advantages to be derived from her hold upon their export markets." London feared that Germany "would encourage the existing trend and allow the frozen balances of the countries in question to increase to the point where they would give her a complete stranglehold over the economies in question," forcing those countries to import greater amounts of German goods to avoid losing their money if they refused to do so and to increase exports of their raw materials to Germany.[10]

This, however, had failed to materialize: "the Germans were not inclined to force the pace to this extent." A change in the international market at the end of 1936 produced a respite that permitted the eight countries of Southeastern Europe to offer their wares at higher prices outside the German market. Yugoslavia, Greece and to a lesser extent Hungary actually had increased their imports from Germany in order to liquidate their frozen balances while Romania and Bulgaria refused to sell more than a set amount of oil and wheat in 1937 for other than hard currency. Similarly, the Turkish share of exports taken by Germany had fallen from 57% in 1936 to 36.5% in 1937. In Yugoslavia and Bulgaria these frozen balances had "virtually disappeared, through placement of orders for war materials." Greece's balance had been reduced from 25 million Rm in June 1937 to 8 million Rm, and Turkey and Romania were similarly thought to be taking steps to reduce their passive balances.[11]

The British correctly concluded that Germany had reached its ability to expand:

> For the moment, however, it looks as though the limit of her spectacular advance has been reached owing to the satiation of the markets in this area with German goods. Germany will no doubt take all the steps open to her to stimulate the capacity of these markets to absorb larger quantities of her exports in the future, and will, in fact, seek to develop them as "colonial" markets have always been developed by capitalist countries. But for the time being she appears to be weak in the chief requisite for colonial development — capital to export.[12]

However, there were certain worrisome factors on the horizon. The annexation of Austria in 1938 added to the percentage of trade enjoyed by Germany with Southeastern Europe, despite the leveling off of German trade with the region. Germany's trade with Hungary was 25% in 1937, but with the addition of Austria's trade, the total trade with the Reich came to 40%. In the case of Yugoslavia, German trade when coupled with the Austrian share rose from 30% to 40% and Romania's trade also rose from 30% to 40% for imports and 20% to 27% for exports. Germany's share of Czechoslovakia's trade in 1937 was up from 15% to 20% for imports and from 13.7% to 22% for exports.[13]

British assessment of the German trade offensive in the southeast wavered between the belief that German trade expansion had peaked and a period of consolidation would follow, and apprehension that German economic ascendancy in the region would lead to political hegemony and they would be frozen out of the region altogether. Germany would then enjoy a dominant position on the European continent.

A memorandum in late May 1938 by Halifax, the British foreign minister, signaled an end to complacency: "Are we prepared to stand by and allow these vast districts to pass completely under German domination?" asked the foreign minister. Whereas before the annexation of Austria they had been inclined to drift and allow matters to take their own course, now they were having second thoughts about Germany's intentions. The Anschluss "meant an intensification of German economic and commercial influence which, in turn, meant the extension of political domination. This process, if it were allowed to continue unchecked, would mean that Central and

Southeastern Europe would tend to become to Germany what, in many respects, and with some obvious reservations, the Dominions are to the United Kingdom." British interests were such that "Germany should not attain a virtual hegemony in Europe." It was all the more important that Germany not achieve hegemony in Europe so that Britain would be in a position to buy Hitler off with "some colonial territory." A Germany with a powerful foothold in Central and Southeastern territory, a dominant position in Spain should Franco win, "and possessing colonial territory would constitute a direct menace to the security of the British commonwealth." In view of this threat a move "to counteract Germany's advance, political and economic, in Central and South-Eastern Europe seems highly desirable, if indeed it is not considered vital to our interests," noted the British Foreign Minister.[14] Halifax's memorandum contained a note of urgency ("there is no time to lose and we should strike while the iron is hot") warning that failure to do something would result in a slide of those countries in the direction of Germany. To prevent this the foreign secretary proposed the formation of an Inter-Departmental Committee to examine requests for aid from those countries and thereby promote British interests in the southeast.

Chamberlain subjected Halifax's memorandum to withering criticism, questioning Halifax's assumptions "that the vast areas would, in fact, pass under German domination; and...that it was possible for us to do something to prevent this happening." The smaller countries "were only too ready" to use the "blackmail" argument that unless they received financial assistance they would inevitably submit to German domination. He cited the Romanian Foreign Minister's report of increased activity by German representatives in the small countries "the results of which were that directly and indirectly Germany was establishing a stranglehold over those countries." Halifax retorted that the small countries needed a *"point d'appui* as an alternative to domination and exploitation by Berlin." Otherwise Germany might establish a *Zollverein* (Customs Union) system with the Southeastern European countries which would be "very damaging to British trading interests."[15]

Britain's changed attitude to Germany's economic expansion undoubtedly influenced by the "Roosevelt" Depression of 1938, caused by the economic downturn in the United States, produced a corresponding fall in production and a rise in unemployment in Britain. In January 1938 *The Economist* crowed happily that the previous year had been "a very good year.... Almost every business index in the country has broken new records in the course of the year."[16] A week later it cautiously noted the fragility of the economy and that, although the revival of business and employment had been strong, "if revival in the basic industries were to falter or to suffer a slight setback, rearmament might take up some or all of the slack."[17] By mid-1938 the tide of economic prosperity was already ebbing and capital investment was declining in comparison to the 1935–1937 period of a more active and flourishing British industry. Its output of new securities ran at a steady rate of £100 million for the first six months of each of those years while during the first six months of 1938 no more than £40 million was raised or less than half the previous rate of investment.[18] At the end of July, Anthony

Eden noted in a speech at Kennelworth following his resignation and perhaps to embarrass Chamberlain: "The problem of the special areas* is not disappearing, it is spreading."[19] In July, *The Economist* noted gloomily the slackening and adverse balance of trade: "the depression has reached crisis proportions in certain districts...in which the classic remedy of public works may have been put out of court by the prior claims of rearmament," and recommended "cheap money" as a remedy.[20]

The business revival in the mid-1930s for the most part had been in the service areas of the economy. Between 1921 and 1935 the population of Great Britain rose 42.7%, or double the expected increase. Employment in the service industries rose 40% between 1923 and 1937 — more than in the production industries, and in manufacturing mostly in industries producing semi-durable consumption goods for the domestic market.[21] *The Economist* remarked on the changed character of the British economy: "An industrial structure erected on free trade and manufacture for export has since the war been transformed by changes in overseas demand and British fiscal support."[22] In other words, increased competition on the world export market, lagging demand, declining overseas capital export and investment, an adverse trade balance, stagnating production and the prohibitive and burdensome cost of rearmament produced a change in traditional investment and production patterns previously concentrated in capital goods, textiles, coal, iron, steel and other staples. Encouraged by lower domestic prices and rising incomes in the interstitial strata — the middle class, skilled and semi-skilled workers — investment grew in production for the consumption and domestic market. According to a special report of the Economic Section of the British Association entitled "Britain in Recovery," the rise in recovery from 1932 to 1937 occurred in the consumer goods industry, and the depression reappeared "when the expansion of the consumer's purchasing power received its first serious check — recession has appeared more clearly in the consumer's than in the producer's industries."[23]

The rise in British incomes for the most part had been due to the great fall in the price of imported food and textile materials and avoidance of price raising schemes in the coal and steel industries. Lowered food prices were, in part, undoubtedly, caused by increased food imports from the empire countries, which went from 30.8% in 1929 to 43.3% in 1938.[24] Cheap food and low coal and steel prices benefited the domestic as well as the external market, the price of which, because of higher unemployment, was continuing misery for the working class in the areas outside of the more prosperous southeastern region. By 1938 this lopsided prosperity edged unemployment up to 2 million persons, and the decline in demand in the export market — which the domestic economy was unable to completely compensate for — made for a menacing situation. A further downturn and deepening of the crisis, aggravated by the expense of armament production, could intensify social discontent.

The German economy was showing similar signs of strain from the consequences of a war economy and the downturn in the international trade

---

*The economically stagnating areas of high industrial unemployment.

market, but the effects took a different form. By late May 1938 the price of manufactured goods and numerous foodstuffs was rising rapidly. A "Price Stop Ordinance" had been put into effect forbidding an increase in existing prices, but could not be maintained. Prices rose, notwithstanding, in vegetables, fruit and other foods. Ready-made clothing, particularly underclothing, was three to five times more expensive than in New York and rents were twice the pre-war costs, but in marks only 20% higher. Foreigners found prices higher and at a level independent of world prices "inordinately high...like prices in Russia."[25] Foodstuff shortages occurred in Berlin in August 1938 and "the complaint [was] heard" that "there is nothing in the market....Vegetables, fruits, and eggs are obtainable only with some difficulty."[26] In addition share prices on the stock market suffered a very steep decline and bonds were also weak. Taxes were also rising: between the period from 1929 through 1937 taxes as a percentage of national income rose by two-thirds (see Table 8–1).

Table 8–1. Rise in Tax Level on German National Incomes, 1929 and 1937 (in millions of marks)[27]

Year	1929	1937
National Income	76,000	68,500
Reich Taxes	9,170	13,960
As a Percentage of Income	12	20
Reich, State and Municipal Taxes	13,520	18,256
As a Percentage of Income	18	27

By September 1938 there was an ominous heavy fall on the Berlin stock exchange which, among foreign sources, arguably somewhat exaggeratedly, "led to suggestions that Germany is marching toward some undefined 'breakdown' or at least towards radical changes in economic policy to arrest the 'breakdown.' " "The main cause of the drop was unquestionably the increasing burdens placed on capital — of which taxes were only a part — and the fear of investors that profits would decline and that the overtaxed shareholder would be allowed to retain still less of what he received for his own consumption." New taxes were rumored but recent corporate taxes — now double 1936 — had been so disastrous in effect that plans for increases had been discontinued. The total Reich debt had climbed to 22,555 million Rm, which came to 5,541 Rm more than the previous year. Germany was thus a heavily taxed nation, which extremely heavy expenditures (i.e., rearmament) forced to borrow still further. However, the ability to borrow further — especially short-term borrowing — depended upon an increasingly uncertain ample supply of savings, as was the certainty of their being regularly deposited with the financial institutions. More importantly, observed *The Economist,* "The other possible weakness in the whole structure lies in foreign trade. Industrial activity at its present level cannot be maintained without imported raw materials....The Reich is not appreciably nearer to supplying itself...." "On the surface, the figures show a substantial deterioration in the course of the present year."[28]

Despite falling raw material prices and invisible shipping sources of income, the Reich had to import 94 million Rm in gold. The Anschluss and the appropriation of Austrian reserves — unofficially estimated as high as one billion marks at the time — had helped ease the financial situation but "these reserves would not last long in a severe depression of international trade." These two weaknesses (finance and trade) "might compel a reduction in the present high activity of industry."[29]

Counterbalancing this was the authoritarian character of the Nazi regime and the policy and other forces at its disposal which could effectively curb manifestations of discontent. "It is in fact quite impossible," observed *The Economist*, "for the National Socialist government to contemplate a return to idle factories and to a host of unemployed," and cautioned "but who bases his calculations upon an imminent economic decline is probably making a mistake."[30]

At the end of 1937 the British moved to reduce their commercial antagonism with Germany by arriving at direct arrangements with their German competitors. The Department of Overseas Trade encouraged British manufacturers and industrialists to meet with their German counterparts to arrive at arrangements to reduce cutthroat trade competition. The British government itself took a hand in stimulating these agreements when the Parliamentary Secretary, then visiting Germany at the same time as the meeting between the Federation of British Industrialists and the German industrialists, requested that a member of the Department of Trade be sent. The results were a qualified success: numerous bilateral agreements occurred between industries, though some fell short.[31] Encouraged, the British pursued this course of action well into 1939 as a way of mitigating trade hostilities. They pursued a policy of side-stepping confrontation and of countering aggressive German commercial activity by indirect action. Hence, at the end of April 1938, Secretary of State Halifax, anticipating a French argument for a Danubian anti-German bloc, stated that "the moment for such a plan was not yet feasible." It amounted to a "tariff war"; Britain would then have to take the exports of the Central European countries and the proposal would be certain to be opposed by Germany. Instead Halifax preferred to handle each East European country separately and to explore the question country by country.[32] But the British did not limit themselves to this policy.

In May 1938, the Board of Trade, anticipating the possibility of war, undertook measures to avoid financing Germany's commercial expansion with their own money. A memo by Hawtrey, the well-known British economist and Treasury official, describes the action as designed "to exert financial pressures on Germany" by taking "any possible steps to prevent this country assisting neutrals to lend to Germany . . . for the purpose of conserving our own financial resources for war purposes." The Treasury asked that any evidence be reported that neutrals were giving "exceptional credit" facilities to Germany or selling goods on credit for the purpose of placing such neutrals on the statutory Black List and to report any attempt by Germany "to obtain foreign exchange by realizing foreign securities on foreign balances."

Hawtrey suggested: "The clearing accounts between Germany and neutral countries would have to be watched: a country which has arrears in its clearing with us or is obtaining credit here outside clearing house arrangements and has frozen balances in Germany is, in effect, borrowing from us and lending to Germany."[33]

Besides being a step in the direction of financially strangling Germany by cutting off its credit facilities — and thus pushing Hitler still further in the direction of war in the following year — this also explains Britain's parsimonious and cautious doling out of commercial credits to the Central and East European countries. Britain's seeming indifference to the plight of these countries has led a recent American historian to mistakenly conclude that Britain's disinterest in trading with those countries was responsible for creating a vacuum in Southeastern Europe into which Germany inevitably entered.[34] This concedes too much to British disinterest in Southeastern Europe, especially after 1938 when trade became increasingly vital to British production and employment. Britain earlier, in 1935–1936, conceded Southeastern Europe to Germany not only to avoid war but also because of commercial gains in Northeastern Europe. By 1938 it was no longer willing to do so not only for economic, but for political and strategic reasons as well. The approaching likelihood of war also forced the British to husband their financial resources and correspondingly to tighten a credit noose around the neck of the Third Reich.

There was an inevitable conflict between the Foreign Office's desire to promote British influence in Southeastern Europe by economic means and the Board of Trade's disinclination to promote "political" trade by granting trade credits to those countries resisting German expansion. To the frustration of British diplomatic representatives in the southeast, the Board of Trade frequently vetoed granting credits to the Eastern European countries and was only overruled when political considerations were overriding, as in the case of Turkey in May 1938. Turkey's importance as an ally of Britain was so great that the rule against granting political credits was waived. However, Hitler also opposed trade for political reasons.

On June 15, 1938, the cabinet decided to set up the Inter-Parliamentary Committee to promote British trade in the southeast. Halifax had been encouraged by his talk with Sir Percy Lorraine, British ambassador to Ankara, who described the effect of the decision to promote more trade with Turkey as "electric in that country and similarly in Greece."[35] The Inter-Parliamentary Committee, which arrived on the scene scarcely a year before the outbreak of war, included representatives of the Foreign Office, the Treasury Department, the Board of Trade and other agencies. Presided over by Leith-Ross, it coordinated economic measures to prevent further German economic penetration of Southeastern Europe.

Several days later, Chamberlain pessimistically concluded that "it was desirable to stop Germany from getting complete economic control of this area and that it was difficult to do so, particularly if we are to avoid the appearance of becoming parties to a policy of encirclement." He doubted that "much progress would be made with this item" and "we ourselves had not been able to formulate any concrete policy in the matter." The effect of this passive stance would be to push Germany to the east. In mid-autumn the committee recommended an inquiry into what action could be taken "towards the promotion of our political influence in Southeastern Europe by economic measures [which] would at the same time be in consonance with the main lines of our foreign policy and in particular with our policy towards Germany."[36]

London grasped at forthcoming British-German trade talks as a way out of the conflict with Germany, frankly viewing the possibilities of the negotiations "as a stepping stone to political appeasement without of course the sacrificing of our political desiderata." There was little in the way of tariff concessions the British were willing to offer Germany on imports into the U.K. while German tariff concessions were of little use to Britain's export trade because of the limited amount of exchange the Reich released for British goods.[37]

There were hopes of an agreement in the area of "uneconomic competition," i.e., German subsidization of their own exports, clearing agreements and the like, in exchange for concessions that Germany wanted in the colonies. In contrast, a Foreign Office minute indicated somewhat pessimistically that Germany's export policy, rooted as it was in clearing agreements with its trading partners, would probably continue as long as it lacked foreign exchange to pay for its exports. A high official in the German Ministry of Economics confirmed that Germany would not be able to discard its clearing house policy for the next ten years![38] The Board of Trade official, Sir W. B. Brown, suggested abandonment of the system of stimulating exports and Germany's entry into such marketing arrangements as the European Coal Cartel.[39] However, to compete with the other Great Powers, Germany would have to devalue the overrated mark, a fearsome step for the Nazi regime. A political agreement between the two countries would first have to take place before the economic Gordian knot could be cut.

In the autumn and winter of 1938 British policy hardened. To German requests, during negotiations over the Anglo-German Payments Agreement, for duty concessions on German exports to the U.K. and in certain overseas territories, the British asked for similar concessions to U.K. trade. Despite British hopes that the negotiations would reduce trade barriers, the results were meager. Schacht's press statement at the end of November 1938 repeated the standard rationale for Germany's trading methods — that they had been forced on Germany as a result of the "war tribute," i.e., reparations, the Young and Dawes loan, and the threat of a clearing by Germany's creditors. When these were removed and Germany's creditors were ready to take action with the Reich, a door would be opened through which Germany could return to multilateral trade.[40]

Intensive trade discussions were held first between the Federation of British Industries and its Director, Guy Locock, and the *Reichsgruppe Industrie* (Locock was almost, by this time, an unofficial emissary of the government) and later through high government officials like Hudson, head of the Department of Overseas Trade, almost to the eve of the war. At the end of December 1938 Locock reported that "the Germans had been more forthcoming than expected." German prices rather than export subsidies would be considered by British industry as long as these prices could be regarded by British industry as "fair and economic." At the same time, the possibility of an arrangement for the partition of markets by zones was raised.[41] At this point both sides appeared to desire the peaceful adjudication of trade disputes. The fact that the results of these negotiations with the Germans were reported directly to the representatives of the Board of Trade the very next day (December 22), which issued a statement to the press, indicates government concern over the talks.

Since the advent of the Nazi regime, two schools of thought contended inside the government on British trade policy toward Germany, with the advocates of a more cautious approach generally winning out over those advancing a tough line. By the end of 1938 the proponents of a tougher stance toward Germany began to be heard more. A minute by a British official in early October expressed the belief that the time had come to speak plainly to the Germans, that they would have to abandon their trading practices or face the consequences of an open trade war, from which Britain would emerge victorious.

I think that we cannot contemplate allowing the present situation to continue, and that we are bound in the near, possibly the very near future to devise some means of countering German export subsidies, either by encouraging our industries to set up export subsidy funds, or, even at the worst, by a temporary system of Government subsidies. If we do this, and do it on a sufficiently big scale, the effect is, I think, bound to be disastrous to Germany, as they cannot hope to win such a competition in export subsidies against our superior financial strength.

I suggest, therefore, that, in fact, we are in a position to say to the Germans that we will abstain from such a disastrous attack on their foreign supplies of exchange, provided that they in their turn will abandon the system of export subsidies which is upsetting established methods of business throughout the world.[42]

Something like this was actually done on two occasions. The first occurred during the summer of 1938 trade payments negotiations when the British, tired of German foot-dragging on transfer payments and payment of the Austrian debt, threatened to introduce a clearing.[43] On the second occasion, during a conversation with the German ambassador at a Japanese Embassy dinner, Locock made the British position clear.

I explained to him what we were aiming at and I expressed the hope that it would be possible to come to an agreement on a fairly wide front with regard to competition in third markets, and I hinted rather delicately at the unfortunate alternative which it might be necessary to adopt if no such agreement proved possible.

The German ambassador agreed that political relations between the two countries would be eased if progress could be made on commercial questions:

No country could indefinitely afford to disregard economic laws and that the system of autarchy which Germany had adopted could not be an enduring feature of her trade policy. He hoped that there would be a gradual return to a more international system of trade on Germany's part, and he felt that our talks might result in some progress being made in this direction.[44]

However, fresh evidence appeared that an accommodating policy toward Germany would only be considered as a further sign of weakness and an invitation to new forms of aggressive behavior. An unnamed German economist and administrator advocated firm action against Mussolini which "would also prove a severe jolt for Hitler." Unless British policy quickly oriented itself in that direction, he warned, and high quarters understood that after the Nazi success "these gangsters are determined to behave as 'beasts,' then terrible happenings will have to be faced by all of us."[45] Similarly, Otto Jeidels, a German banking official and friend of Leith-Ross, reporting on the continuing crisis situation in Germany, noted the astonishing, almost nervous pace of aggressive actions in foreign and domestic affairs and the accumulation of controversies with a large part of the world. Jeidels also observed an aggravation of the weakness in the economic situation in the scarcity of financial exchange. *"Will this new state of emergency in foreign payments,"* he asked, *"result in moderation or some hazardous issue for 1939?"* [Jeidels's emphasis], then added, "I am really entitled to expect the former after six years experience to the contrary and considering the intrinsic aggressiveness of a party-dictatorship."[46]

The exchange crisis was not merely a passing phenomenon, but a crisis of the German fascist state. By stimulating demand through rearmament, the disastrous deflation of the Brüning era had been replaced by an incipient inflation; an ever expanding state debt; declining exports and restricted imports resulting in an adverse trade balance; high domestic prices; scarce consumer goods; and finally the gradual disappearance of certain kinds of foodstuffs and commodities from the domestic market, as had occurred earlier during the "fat crisis" of the mid-1930s. Viewed in its narrowest sense, the exchange crisis resulted from a controlled economy, raising the prospect of a production decline and a renewal of unemployment. This was aggravated by market resistance in Southeastern Europe and elsewhere, encouraged by the temporary prosperity in 1937 to switch to other more desirable hard currency markets. German business, particularly the export sector, grumbled against the loss of its overseas market. Schacht railed against importing raw materials at prices above the world level as too costly and ultimately at the expense of German production and manpower.[47]

The alleviation of these economic miseries through a return to the free market and the abandonment of the system of autarchy and uneconomic trading methods was, from the German viewpoint, becoming increasingly difficult if not impossible. It meant a return to its previous commercial vassalage to Britain, the United States and France, a position it was not likely to accept as long as it believed that it held the high card of military supremacy. At the same time, such an about-face also meant the abandonment by German big business, the military and other elite groups of their dreams of European and world hegemony. A German-British financial deal involving a levered bailout of Germany predicated upon the Reich's future good behavior in the world market and a cessation of its armament program ultimately meant a devaluation of the mark, a step which would frighten the Nazi regime's support base, the German middle class, with its nightmarish memories of the 1923 inflation, a step which Hitler would not be likely to take. Moreover, it would mean an admission of failure and a return to the status quo.

Having said this, we arrive at a central fact: namely, that both Germany and Britain were locked into rigid and increasingly frozen postures from which they could not easily extricate themselves. There is an eerie sense of tragic inevitability in the years before the outbreak of war in 1939 in which the principals seem to be puppets playing out some macabre Chekovian drama whose denouement is foreordained.

By December 1938, it had become obvious that the German economy was in trouble. Despite earlier successes in production and employment, German consumption lagged behind that of the United States and England. The benefits of increased production were not going to the German working class, which could lead to difficulties in the future. The problem had emerged first in 1935 when increased demand caused by rising employment began to conflict with the government's policy of curtailing imports, and Minister of Agriculture Darre's agricultural policy failed to produce sufficient food for the domestic market. Insufficient currency exchange for imports resulted in periodic food shortages in the period after 1935. Only the intervention of Hitler prevented food rationing, but from that point on the German leader began to lose confidence in Schacht. The food crisis and the dearth of foreign currency reduced Hitler's room to maneuver and probably focused his attention in the direction of military expansion to secure raw materials and foodstuffs for the war economy and the population.[48] The introduction of the Four Year Plan and controls on wages and prices solved the problem for the next few years, but by 1938 the exchange crisis reappeared again as unemployment had been largely eliminated and full employment and higher wages accelerated demand more than ever.

After failing to negotiate regaining colonies and raw materials access, in 1938 Schacht grasped at the international market as the only way out of a future crisis, in the words of his biographer, "like the proverbial drowning man's straw."[49] This meant that Germany would have to devalue the overpriced mark which was approximately 40% higher than its real value and one of the reasons exports had to be subsidized to compete on the world market. Schacht would have had to secure a large loan from the British to support the mark until increased exports stimulated internal market demand sufficiently to replace heavy industry and armaments by consumer goods production. Schacht knew that unless he accomplished this his days as head of the *Reichsbank* were numbered.

In December Schacht and Gördeler visited England in hopes of arriving at the long awaited *modus vivendi* with England. Schacht met with Leith-Ross once again on December 1, 1938, for the last time. The trade talks between the British coal cartel and the German government, he revealed, "were not unfavorable," but Leith-Ross asked Schacht to "help to get a move on this." Schacht answered lamely that German industry had "no discretion" in the matter as "they "[i.e., the Nazi government] had absolute control of all their industries." To Schacht's question whether the British were interested in the "restoration of a free system of currency in Germany[,]" Leith-Ross felt this desirable and "in the interests of Germany herself" but Britain "could not be expected to make unreasonable sacrifices for that purpose." "The internal financial machinery in Germany was working well and so long as control was kept over wages and prices, could be maintained indefinitely," Schacht stated. The government would squander any large loans—he wanted only perhaps £500 million "as a cushion." Leith-Ross took a dim view of Schacht's request to reduce the rate of interest, citing previous reductions.[50]

Restoring free exchange, he hinted, had a price: "it was inevitably linked up with wider political problems." Schacht agreed: "one of the reasons for doing this as quickly as possible was that...this was one of the best ways also to work for moderation in political matters." Leith-Ross ended the discussion and asked for a coal trade agreement to stop "cutthroat competition otherwise Britain would have to subsidize our coal exporters."[51]

A few weeks later Carl Gördeler arrived in England and laid out the conditions for a detente: England would allow cession of the Polish Corridor, a colonial territory and a gold loan of 4–6 billion gold marks (£325–500 million) without interest in return for which Germany would cease all rearmament at once, Southeastern Europe would remain open to commercial trade and development and Germany would guarantee the present status quo in the Mediterranean. In addition, "Germany will cooperate in reestablishing fully and promptly the right and position of the white races in East Asia," and "Germany, France and England shall immediately establish the new League of Nations."[52] It is doubtful if any of these proposals were made with the knowledge and consent of Hitler; and it is doubtful if the British took them seriously. Whatever the case, Hitler would have rejected any abandonment of rearmament and it is likely that the proposals originated purely from Schacht and Gördeler as spokesmen for the business class. Up to 1936 Schacht clearly had the support of German finance and industry; thereafter, Schacht's failure to devalue the mark and dispense with the "voluntary" levies on business to subsidize exports probably cost him some of the support of that class.[53] The "voluntary" levies on business and increased taxes began to eat into their profits and they abandoned Schacht for Hitler and military adventure abroad.

The British based their German policy on the belief that the German moderates (Schacht, Gördeler) and German Nazi Party radicals (Ribbentrop, Göbbels) were vying for Hitler's attention. Chamberlain received conflicting information as to whether Hitler or the moderates were making German policy. Schacht, a moderate, told Leith-Ross that Hitler alone decided policy.

British-German relations in early 1939 had reached an impasse over the trade war. A Board of Trade official stated in November 1938 that tariff restrictions against German imports might be eased after Germany ended its discrimination against British exports.[54] Similarly a memo in the Board of Trade, in late December recounts that "German officials had been told that the principal counter concessions which we would want would be arrangements for the avoidance of uneconomic competition in world markets."[55] The memo mentions the desire of the Germans to import iron ore from Newfoundland and the necessary concessions that would have to be made to Newfoundland. Before any of these difficulties could be ironed out, Hitler dismissed Hjalmar Schacht in late January 1939. We can construct what probably led to Schacht's dismissal after his meeting with Leith-Ross.

Since the British offered Schacht little support for returning Germany to the world market, Schacht could either continue to support Hitler's plans for aggressive expansion through rearmament or demand that the brakes be put on the war economy. He chose the latter. As Schacht admitted bitterly, "the wage and price structure totally fell apart" and the economic situation had completely changed.[56] Full employment had been reached by 1937, so Schacht no longer felt obligated to advance Hitler money to finance his war plans. He had advanced Hitler an estimated 12 billion marks since 1933. In March 1937 his term of office was up and he called a halt to further extension of credit, but after accepting an additional year in office, he agreed to grant another 3 billion marks and Hitler had promised not to ask for more. In March 1938 Schacht agreed to act as head of the Reichsbank for another four years. Rearmament was in full swing and the amount of money in circulation had escalated to inflationary proportions from the 1936 level, when production had reached the 1928 level, from 6.6 billion marks — the same as in 1928 — to 7.6 billion in March 1938, 8.4 billion after the Anschluss in June 1938 and by September 1938 following the Munich crisis it was up to 10 billion marks.[57]

Bereft of German big business support and having failed with the British, Schacht laid the groundwork for his dismissal by an angry letter to Hitler on January 7, 1939, declaring that the system of financing rearmament was being shaken to its foundations by the spiraling inflation and that Reichsbank foreign exchange reserves were depleted. What assets the Reichsbank possessed were invested in government securities. Further Reichsbank financing of Hitler's plans was "not compatible with a sound currency policy, but must lead to the road to inflation." Four directors of the Reichsbank signed their names and declared that while they had "gladly cooperated to attain the great goal, it is now time to put a stop to it." Four demands followed which Schacht's biographer, Edward Norman Peterson, hyperbolically conjectured, "must have blown Hitler right out of his chair." Schacht demanded that the government spend only what was covered by taxes; full control of finances must be returned to the Minister of Finance; price and wage controls must be made effective ("the existing mismanagement must be eliminated"); and the use of money and investment must be kept solely in the hands of the Reichsbank. Upon reading Schacht's letter, Hitler is reported to have muttered: "This is mutiny!"[58]

Commentaries confirm that Schacht's opposition to inflation led to his dismissal.[59] With the fall of Schacht the British government's hopes for a peaceful solution of its economic and political difficulties with Germany also evaporated. At the end of January the British minister to Paris, Phipps, responded to an inquiry by Lord Halifax whether "in the light of recent events" [i.e., the dismissal of Schacht] there was any likelihood of the German government "abandoning or modifying their system of stimulating the export trade" and the possibility of reaching an agreement through negotiations on a wide basis. The droll reply of Phipps in what became known as the "Jekyll and Hyde letter" was not encouraging.

> The German Government can at present moment be visualized as a Dr. Jekyll (administrator) and a Mr. Hyde (Party Extremist). Dr. Jekyll whom we are wont to meet in the Reichsbank, the Minister for Foreign Affairs, and in all but the very highest quarters of the Ministry for Foreign Affairs, certainly wants discussions and cooperation between British and German industrialists, thinks that Germany's economic policy should be directed towards friendliness with the Western Powers (with us in particular), and also that political aims should be in consonance with such an economic policy. Mr. Hyde seems to pay no regard whatsoever to economic considerations; his actions cause Dr. Jekyll acute mental distress and increasing physical discomfort; so far as one can judge from actions his policy is sinister. . . . Any concessions which are made to Dr. Jekyll are greedily but not particularly gratefully exploited by Mr. Hyde who continues cheerfully to pursue a course of action which it would be charitable to interpret merely as sublime indifference to mundane matters such as foreign public opinion and economic repercussions of changes therein. The importance of Mr. Hyde in the make-up of the German Government has been forcibly brought home to us in the shape of news of the dismissal of Dr. Schacht, the Jekyll figure par excellence.[60]

Phipps doubted that there was any likelihood of the German government abandoning their present system of stimulating export trade and any attempt to negotiate the general principle would prove fruitless. "It is probably impossible for the Germans to export enough to pay for imports on their present or even lower scale without adjustment of their prices to a level competitive with the goods of the United Kingdom, the United States of America, etc." The export subsidy scheme intended by Schacht "was to be primarily a corrective for devaluation in other countries." The object of the scheme "is essentially the acquisition of foreign exchange. . . ." Any abandonment of export subsidies would bring about a devaluation of the mark then at an artificially high value.

Phipps believed that, despite the purported moderation of Field Marshal Göring, extremists were now in control of the German economy and an export drive by means of subsidized export schemes was being "vigorously pursued." The recent speech of R. H. Hudson in December produced "dismay" in German official and trade circles which "contemplate with anxiety a subsidy war with the United Kingdom." He reminded Halifax that when the transfer payment negotiations were on the verge of a breakdown the previous summer, "the threat of a clearing caused the Germans to reconsider their position." He advised, therefore, that they "make it clear to the Germans that we propose to take active steps in protection of our interests" and they might be willing to negotiate.[61] Pinsent expressed similar sentiments:

> It is a long time since I read the book, but my recollection is that Mr. Hyde was not aware of Dr. Jekyll. On the other hand our Mr. Hyde is fully aware of his Dr. Jekyll; he despises, abuses, blackmails and exploits him at the same time. Our Dr. Jekyll is of course fully aware of Mr. Hyde, but is only too pathetically anxious to make everyone believe, and indeed to believe himself, that a little sympathy from abroad would make Mr. Hyde vanish into thin air. But our Dr. Jekyll is under a dangerous illusion.[62]

Pinsent pointed to the hostility of Hitler toward England in his last speech in which he accused England of having made war on Germany in order to enrich herself by destroying Germany's trade. The German leader had also made a reference to Sir Samuel Hoare as having said at Geneva with a grin on his face "that some countries were 'haves' and some were 'have-nots' and it would ever remain so." The dismissal of Schacht and other events "all point to a fresh advance of the left wing. Mr. Hyde has got so far that he begins to think that he has sucked Dr. Jekyll dry and can throw him out into the gutter." Pinsent reminded the Foreign Office that Ribbentrop has been "frantically anti-British" since he was in London, and has now convinced Hitler that Britain "is really Public Enemy No. 1 ... the principal item on the program is to settle with Great Britain, even if the time-table has not been fixed." Pinsent recommended that the British should now "show our teeth, not indeed in striking and controversial attitudes, but unobtrusively in the general determination to give nothing away and to develop and use all our weapons in small things and large and to make it clear quietly that this is our attitude." He reminded London of what had happened in the case of the coal agreement which had dragged on for years until Hudson made his threatening speech in December.[63] This coincided with a similar communication by Strang to Sir John Simon, Chancellor of the Exchequer, expressing a somewhat more cautious view, but at the same time preparing the government for the possibility of a trade war with Germany.

After the difficulty of negotiating with the Germans on concessions to German trade in the colonies in exchange for reductions of duties on German exports to the U.K., Strang explained that such concessions were impossible because of the system of exchange control and export subsidies in effect in Germany. The goods actually supplied by Germany were very few and the reduction of duties would then have to be extended to other countries as well. "The main objective of Germany is to obtain foreign exchange," declared Strang. Britain had no objection, but felt that assisting trade exports by subsidies obstructed trade. Strang then approached the main point somewhat gingerly:

> There is no doubt that His Majesty's Government will be subjected to increasing pressure to devise some means of countering German export subsidies either by encouraging industries to establish their own export subsidy or by a system of Government subsidies. His Majesty's

Government would be unwilling to embark on such a policy but there is little doubt that the superior financial strength of this country would enable it to win any competition in export subsidies. In the long run, it would clearly be in the interests of both countries to refrain from a subsidy war.... [64]

Strang referred to the European coal cartel negotiations and British industry's request "for the encouragement of exports by means of a subsidy and which His Majesty's Government may well find themselves obliged to accept should the negotiations prove unacceptable."[65] By this time the F.B.I. (Federation of British Industry) and the Reichsgruppe Industrie had met on December 20–21, 1938, on the suggestion of the Germans that negotiations should take place on the subsidies problem and the two sides agreed to continue the discussions at Cologne in February 1939. The trade difficulties between Germany and Britain had now reached the point where, if they were not ironed out through the process of negotiations, beginning with the coal industry, a trade war was a distinct possibility in the future. Leith-Ross remained skeptical of solving the economic problem through negotiations and saw the key to the solution in the political area:

> ... behind everything stand the political difficulties which prevent capital being attracted to the countries that need it. Monsieur Elbel[a] lays down as a fundamental condition of his scheme the acceptance of disarmament. I do not believe there is the slightest chance that the totalitarian states would accept such a condition in return for any economic assistance.
>
> In fact I feel that Elbel tends to put the cart before the horse and that before anything can be done in the way of economic collaboration there must be a better political atmosphere. The German experts like Wiehl,[b] who is over here, take the same view.
>
> I am not surprised that Funk[c] apparently welcomed these ideas. Ribbentrop and Funk show great interest in any proposals about economic collaboration.... [66]

Hitler restated the Hossbach thesis in his January 30, 1939 address that national limitations did not permit the intensification of efforts to increase food production inside of Germany. This could only be overcome in two ways: to increase imports of foodstuffs and increase German exports "which would necessitate the importation of at least some of the raw materials for their manufacture, with the result that only a proportion of imports received would be available for the purchase of foodstuffs." The other alternative was the "extension of our living space so that in our domestic situation the problem of Germany's food supplies can be solved." Hitler rejected the second alternative as "for the time being not yet sensible." The food situation had reached a critical point: "We have to export in order to buy foodstuffs"

---

a. banker and friend of Leith-Ross.
b. economic specialist in the German Foreign Office.
c. Schacht's successor as Minister for Economy.

and raw materials. "The German nation must...export or die."[67] Henderson suggests that Hitler may have used the stresses in the economy, more especially the need for raw materials, as a pretext for a policy of further expansionism. In this way he could then pretend to give in to the arguments of the war party — expansion-minded industrialists, segments of the military and Nazi party leaders. Economic strains became the reason for desperate measures. There is little evidence in the documents Hitler was dissembling; in fact, what evidence exists indicates the contrary — that the deteriorating economic situation really was reducing his ability to maneuver and forcing him in the direction of war or an overall settlement with Britain.

German expansionism possessed a kind of internal dialectic of its own, responding to events as well as shaping them. Its internal momentum fed on and produced further momentum. The desire of German business to end the burden of forced loans, heavy taxation, subsidizing exports, the lure of profits, the economy's internal stresses, the weakness of the Great Powers before Hitler's demands, the perfervid nationalism of bureaucratic, military and Nazi party elite groups — all combined to exercise a powerful impetus for further expansion. Though it may be argued that Germany never hovered on the brink of economic collapse, nevertheless these internal structural pressures could not easily be resisted. Germany's raw material needs remained as voracious as ever. Alone of all the major countries, Germany had to increase its imports in 1937–1938, a boom year, while its exports declined by 10% (610 million marks), increasing its trade deficits still more.

The annexation of Austria and Czechoslovakia did not produce any signal relief. Despite the fact that the Anschluss netted Germany 440 million marks in gold and Czechoslovakia 189 million, German exports fell 40% lower in the last quarter of 1938 than in the same period in 1937.[68] Increased production of synthetic raw materials failed to close the gap in raw materials, leading one study to conclude that the Four Year Plan had only limited success.[69]

The British realized the serious straits the German economy was in and the possibilities for accommodation offered by the situation. In a report by the Foreign Office economic specialist Ashton-Gwatkin, on his discussions with Funk, Göring and Ribbentrop as well as second-level figures, the British official concluded that Germany was in a "blind alley" (*Engpass*) in which economic conditions were deteriorating, though far from the point of economic collapse. "A steady decline of the standard of living seems, however, to be inevitable."[70] While there was no scarcity of food, eggs, butter, fruits and other foods periodically were unobtainable. Communal arrangements in up-to-date factories were "admirable" but private dwellings of even better class workers were "narrow and comfortless." The causes were manifold, but closely connected to rearmament: large numbers of persons drawn from the rural areas into heavy industry; a great deal of waste in time and industry; the large numbers of quasi-officials and party functionaries living as parasites; the absorption of much of current production by industry; difficulties in the export trade; a trade recession caused by the demands of the home market; and the demand for foreign exchange to acquire much needed raw materials.

The dismissal of Dr. Schacht called attention to the need for a consolidation of the economy. Short-term loans to stimulate the economy in anticipation of future profits from industry had produced the "miracle of the mid-1930s." Schacht had anticipated paying off these loans through taxation or consolidation by new loans. But the construction of the Westwall line requiring 300,000 men, rebuilding of German cities, the cost of mobilization, capital expenditure on the Four Year Plan and above all rearmament had placed a great burden on the finances of the state. Schacht could produce no more "magic" and proposed a program of reduced expenditures, a consolidation of the economy and a temporary respite in industrial expansion. His successor as Minister of Economics, Dr. Funk, told Ashton-Gwatkin that rearmament would continue through financing by short-term loans and that there would be no inflation. The Germans gave the impression that they wished British help in dealing with their economic problems: foreign debt conversion to reduce *Divisen* (foreign exchange currency) demands, procurement of raw materials like copper and cotton from Northern Rhodesia and India, entry of German exports into restricted empire markets and the lowering of tariffs in the United Kingdom and the Empire.[71]

Ashton-Gwatkin sketched out plans with Göring, Funk and von Wilmowsky of Krupp for large-scale industrial development projects in Southeastern Europe, South America and Spain in which the British would put up the capital in exchange for a share in the orders. Göring denied any intention of commercially "shutting out" Britain; Germany would not pursue a policy of "monopoly and exclusion" in the southeast. Ashton-Gwatkin admitted to the German leaders that Germany was the natural market for the products of Southeastern Europe, "but we did not think that this should mean exclusion of British trade."[72] Whether Hitler knew of these talks is unknown, but Schacht's demise did not seem to end the German desire for some kind of an arrangement with Britain.

The financial advisor to the British embassy in Berlin, Pinsent, was skeptical about all this and saw little commercial benefit in British-financed schemes to lend credit to German industry which would end up strengthening German rearmament. Moreover, Germany's present straight-jacketed economy was of its own making. "They have severely limited their own capacity to export by their armament program. Their desire for more raw materials is in fact created by their armament program, and not by the intention of raising the German standard of living." Pinsent advised against making concessions to the Germans. "The German mouth is wide open for concessions on debts, trade, etc... we have listened *ad nauseam* to what the Germans want, and it is perhaps time that we told them again in plain terms what *we want*."[73]

The British Military Attaché, Colonel Mason-MacFarlane, thought Germany's economic situation was "critical" and could be relieved only by abandoning the cause of the problem: rearmament. England must not help the Germans until they first gave up their armament program and devoted the saved energy and materials to their export trade. He recommended showing a firm front to force Germany to set its house in order even if Hitler should decide to fight rather than see his economic ideology fail. Mason-

MacFarlane doubted whether Germany could be induced to abandon the rearmament program in return for trade advantages, and even if it were to do so could not be relied upon to keep its word. Given that assumption, he "deplored" concessions, in general. He cited conversations with the American chargé and contacts with the German opposition confirming the belief that further economic concessions to Germany would be construed as signs of weakness and a lack of will or power to stand up to Germany.[74]

These expectations that Hitler would be forced to relent in his rearmament program to overcome his economic problems proved wrong. In fact, rearmament had stimulated the appetite of German heavy industry, now ravenous for greater profits. The solution to Germany's trade problems lay in the raw materials of Central and Southeastern Europe. "Germany had a *right*," Colonel Warlimont, Wehrmacht operations section head, told the British attaché, "to a privileged position vis-à-vis all other countries as regards trade in Eastern and Southeastern Europe, and she intended to get this right acknowledged."[75]

Some in the British government and other political circles like Oliver Stanley, President of the Board of Trade, Paul Einzig, an influential, anti-fascist journalist writing for *Financial News,* and R. S. Hudson, Parliamentary Secretary of the Department of Overseas Trade, were bent on fighting against further German expansion into the southeast and holding Britain's trading position there. The group disliked Germany's barter methods and economic aggression, and forced through Parliament a measure funding ten million pounds to be used to combat further German economic penetration into the region.[76] However, Chamberlain squelched attempts by Hudson, with some support from junior officials in the government, to force out leading appeasers.[77] The accommodationists remained clearly in control of the government in 1938 and almost to the eve of the war. Similarly, the presence of von Wilmowsky, of the Krupp organization, in the discussions with the British, indicates that German industry had not yet decided on supporting military aggression and war at this point. Göring's presence also indicates that he had replaced Schacht as the major "moderate" voice within the regime and the Nazi party.

Nevile Henderson, Halifax and Leith-Ross initiated private discussions for visits to Germany by Lord Stanley and Hudson to buy off Hitler by offers of some kind of general settlement. Henderson notes in his memoirs: "Behind the facade of privacy the real intention of the visit was patent."[78] Henderson and the British Foreign Office hoped to undercut the Nazi extremists and the war party around Hitler (Ribbentrop, Göbbels and Himmler) through Göring and the more moderate German Foreign Office officials. The signing on January 28, 1939, of the Anglo-German Coal Agreement encouraged these overtures.

But Hitler abruptly sidetracked these British efforts to mollify Germany by suddenly occupying the remainder of the Czechoslovak state. Why Hitler decided on aggressive action rather than negotiation with the British, lacking sufficient documents, can only be conjectured. One possibility is that the German business class was split, with Krupp and other industrialists desiring to come to an arrangement with the British whereby they would gain hegemony in Southeastern Europe and access to foreign markets for their goods. On the other hand, as we have seen, Carl Krauss of I. G. Farben, which earlier had played a leading role in the Four Year Plan, in April, one month after the German occupation of Prague, favored aggressive action through the Wehrmacht in seizing the resources of the southeast. It is not certain whether Krupp, whose profits rose as a result of the rearmament program, favored a cessation of the war economy and a return to the uncertainty of the world market and may in fact have been hesitating on which path to take.[79] I. G. Farben, as has been pointed out, was anxious to absorb and eliminate its chief competitor in Czechoslovakia, and elsewhere in Southeastern Europe, the Aussiger Verein held by the Belgian firm of Solvay & Cie.

Over the summer of 1939 various British and German Foreign Office officials endeavored to breathe life into the abortive Stanley-Hudson mission beginning with Henry Drummond-Wolff, a Tory imperialist acting for the extensive network of conservative elements in the parliament, industry and government who feared war and, with the knowledge of Chamberlain, tried to revive the Czechoslovak leader Hodža's previously suggested idea of a partial renunciation of Britain's most-favored-nation right in the Balkans in favor of Germany. This shadowy group of leading politicians, industrialists and aristocrats in the Council of Empire Industries Association, at first operating as a cartel lobby and later as a "pro-peace cabal" — to use British historian Scott Newton's term — through the 200 member Right Club, "an underground pro-Nazi organization" begun in 1939 by the Conservative MP Captain A. H. M. Ramsay, importuned Chamberlain through letters to prevent war. Once war occurred, they adopted increasingly fascist inclinations, fearing a war with Germany would "play into the hands of Soviet Russia, Jews and the Americans," and undertook to end the hostilities through a negotiated effort between Germany and Britain. Secret peace feelers were sent out through Lord Tavistock and others to the Germans with the knowledge of Halifax. In the Tavistock affair and other schemes to contact and make peace with Hitler, Newton blames Halifax for going "much further than Chamberlain doing so and act[ing] alone in doing so." Newton exculpates Chamberlain as rejecting the extreme right but it seems improbable that Halifax would have "connived" to allow the pro-fascists to go as far as they did without the knowledge of Chamberlain. Newton's argument that Chamberlain opted for a limited war policy and rejected the fascist wing of British conservatism cannot be fully accepted. He conducted a policy of shying away from any confrontation with Hitler and continued with Halifax to avoid doing so even after losing the support of the cabinet and eventually his own party. Whatever the case, the Chamberlain government seems compromised and historically besmirched.[80]

Thus, Chamberlain's complete domination of the cabinet and his avid desire to avoid war at any cost led him to pursue the policy of appeasement beyond the point when the broad British public clearly perceived Hitler's aggressive policy had to be challenged. His naiveté in underestimating Hitler's dissembling and cunning and his overweening pride in the belief that he had succeeded in gaining the German chancellor's confidence at Munich led him to carry out a catastrophic policy that initially gained him much support, but was carried on too long.[81] Certainly, by the onset of the summer of 1939 he had largely lost control of the cabinet and played an obstructionist role in continuing to try to come to an arrangement with Hitler at all costs and in the crucial negotiations with the Soviet Union. Hitler gave no indications that he was ready to have the British "buy up" anything. What he wanted, he told League High Commissioner Burckhardt at Danzig, was "a free hand in the east." On receiving Burckhardt's information Halifax commented to Chamberlain that "Hitler's whole line of thought seems to be the familiar one of a free hand in the East, and, if he really wants to annex land in the East on which he can settle Germans to grow wheat, I confess I don't see any way of accommodating him."[82] In the end, Chamberlain's backstairs diplomacy through Wilson and others achieved little more than to reinforce Hitler's determination to prevail, given Germany's military strength, through war if need be.

Chapter 9

On the Eve. German Raw Material Shortages. "No Butter, No Eggs, but a New Reich Chancellery." British and French Intimations of German Collapse

> "I have pledged my word. I will not make inflation. The people will not understand it." — Adolf Hitler, H. Rauschning, *Gespräche mit Hitler*

W HILE THE NEW 1938 DEPRESSION in the United States threw the "City" "almost into a panic," by the end of the year reports were more guardedly sanguine.[1] British imports in the first nine months of 1937 had improved in volume by 6% and exports by 12%.[2] Though the tempo declined thereafter, there was a feeling that the decline had been worse elsewhere and the setback in British industry "was of a moderate extent."[3] The recovery in the U.S. by midsummer 1938 to the end of the year "appeared to come naturally from the exhaustion of the previously depressing forces," but the upturn was of "only moderate dimensions."[4] The *Westminster Bank Review* noted: "The deterioration in international affairs did not merely begin to exert an influence on the course of every branch of finance and industry; it became a dominating factor." Had it not been "for the marked lack of confidence, the latter months of 1938 would almost certainly have seen considerable improvement in trade and industry."[5]

Whether this analysis of the depression of 1938 and 1939 is really accurate is questionable. Certainly, during the waning final months of 1937 the steam began to go out of the international economy at a time when the possibility of a European war still seemed remote. By mid-1938 there were signs of some improvement, but not enough to restore the world economy to the boom levels of 1937. Government spending, particularly in housing and public works, influenced the slight progression of trade and industry in the U.S. rather than any resurgence of expansionary economic forces. Though the U.S. markedly recovered from the trough years 1930–1932, it still had not reached the 1937 levels by the outbreak of war.

Britain, in comparison to the U.S., had not suffered such a sharp decline. Unemployment fell rapidly because of the stepped up pace of the armament program. The calculations Keynes made in the spring of 1939 that armament production would absorb 750,000 to 1,000,000 persons and would abolish unemployment, replacing it with labor scarcity, had proved more or less accurate. By mid-June over 700,000 had been absorbed and the unemployment figure fell to 1,349,579, a little higher than the peak recovery years and the lowest figure in the last ten years.[6] The remainder were officially defined as hard core unemployables and the temporarily unemployed. Optimists now began to speak of full employment — defined now as 5% unemployment. The tremendous jolt of energy supplied the economy by the armament program may be seen by the figures shown in Table 9–1.

Table 9–1. United Kingdom Total Defense Expenditures, 1935–1940 (in pounds)[7]

1935–1936	137,000,000
1936–1937	187,000,000
1937–1938	266,000,000
1938–1939	400,000,000
1939–1940 (estimate)	655,000,000

In the critical category of trade, the 1929 pre-Depression volume of world trade had still not been reached, nor had it even reached the 1937 level, and the new problem of inflation threatened the British economy. The unsettling political climate showed no sign of abating. British business, noted the *Westminster Bank,* "continues to be dominated to a very large extent by political developments in Europe and the requirements of the rearmament program in this country," and Chamberlain fretted and anguished over his decision to avoid curtailing business and especially trade to pay for the armament program.[8] The Anglo-American Trade Agreement of November 17, 1938, which had both political and economic objectives, was designed to remedy the problem of increasing trade volume.

The Agreement offered the possibility of stimulating trade by reducing preferential tariffs against non-empire countries and moving a step in the direction of an open door arrangement between the U.S. and Britain. It was in effect a truce in the unwholesome trade war atmosphere of the early 1930s. While America's trade with Britain was not critical for the U.K. — it was the fourth largest importer of British goods — its trade with empire associated countries was large. The great excess of America's world imports over exports with the dependent Empire countries was paid for by its exports to the U.K. "She pays for Malayan rubber and tin by selling motor cars to Englishmen," in the colorful commercial metaphor of one observer.[9] Before the Ottawa preferential tariff system, 75% of U.S. goods entering the U.K. in 1930 entered duty free; but in 1938 over 40% paid various kinds of duties, reducing trade volume by almost one-half as the figures in Table 9–2 show.

The British government reduced duties against American products as the first step in a political reconciliation with the U.S. Although negotiations began at the end of 1937, it took almost a year to complete. The urgency of the international situation compelled the two English-speaking Powers to bridge their differences to head off the growing danger of Germany and international fascism. Despite mutual antipathies Roosevelt, Hull

Table 9–2. United Kingdom Trade with the United States,
1929 and 1938 (in millions of pounds)[10]

Year	Imports	Exports	Balance
1929	196	62	−134
1938	118	29	−89

and Chamberlain had to rein in their personal feelings before the common danger.

In June 1938 R. A. B. Butler, parliamentary secretary, assured Ministerial-Direktor Wohltat, a Göring confidant, then in London, that what England wanted in the forthcoming economic talks with Germany was a division of world trade between the three Great Powers, the U.K., Germany and the United States, "so that in the struggle over raw materials and trade markets no war need arise." Quintin Hill, the head of the Overseas Trade Department, and other members of that department made similar statements to him.[11] But in August the situation abruptly changed: Halifax notified Henderson, British minister in Berlin, that although Chamberlain and those around him continued to believe in the necessity of an appeasement of the economic problem as the key to a political solution, Hitler's agitation of the Czech question had "blocked" any further attempts at economic appeasement for the time being.[12] Thereafter the British government was no longer willing after the Munich crisis to pursue a singular policy of economic appeasement in hopes of yoking the Nazi ox to the British chariot to lead Europe into stiller, calmer waters. The Anglo-American Trade Agreement of November 17, 1938, was the instrument of this changed policy. Germany's access to raw materials was now to be made more difficult and export markets for Germany would become increasingly tight.

By lowering tariffs for American goods entering the U.K., the British were in effect giving the U.S. preferential treatment and simultaneously discriminating against German exports at a time when Germany desperately sought to expand its trade volume. The fact that the U.S. denied German exports most-favored-nation status on the grounds that Germany practiced trade discrimination further complicated Germany's trade problem.[13] From Berlin's standpoint, Britain had entered into collusion with the U.S. to "encircle" Germany — a constant accusation of Hitler and the Nazi regime. The agreement also contained a clause — obviously aimed at Germany — that if the major benefit of any concession accrued to another foreign country to the detriment of domestic producers it could be modified or abrogated.[14] One observer exulted that the agreement meant "the coordination of trade over the whole area comprised by the British Empire and the United States, with the mutual recognition that trade must be complementary rather than competitive." The Germans now saw themselves shut out of two gigantic world markets from whom they could not expect to gain any much-needed trade or exchange currency. One would, therefore, be entitled to believe that the agreement and the pressures it placed upon Hitler and the Third Reich at the end of 1938 probably contributed toward aggravating the internal tensions inside Germany that led Hitler to take the leap into the abyss in September 1939.

As 1939 ushered in, Germany presented a stark contrast to the rest of the industrialized world. In the latter stagnation prevailed: the American economy limped along unsteadily and only state pump priming devices prevented relapse into deeper depression. Britain, likewise, stagnated industrially and unemployment approached the two million level. Only rearmament prevented the commodity-glutted internal and world market from further collapse.

At the end of 1938 Germany's economy, in contrast, was strained to its utmost; its very success in almost reaching full employment — approximately half a million remained unemployed by mid-1938 — paradoxically undermined its future economic existence. Reduced access to raw material imports threatened to upset National Socialist successes in curtailing unemployment since 1933 by producing inflation and decline. Shrinking world markets, lower prices and internal demand pressures caused a decline in the value of exports from 5,788 million Rm to 5,257 million Rm (for the Old Reich alone).[15] Exchange reserves were dangerously low, hence increasing exports became more and more vital to offset steadily rising imports.

Hitler's January 30, 1939, speech touching upon Germany's trade problems has hitherto eluded the attention of historians and merits some consideration. It was essentially, in many respects, a confession of bankruptcy. Hitler's emphasis on increased trade in his speech was misunderstood abroad. Though aware of the trade bottleneck and the imperative of increasing imports, his qualification in his January 1939 speech that any increase in imports would first go to the armament program meant that Germany's economic problems would be solved by military means.

By 1939 the forces that Hitler had released by introducing the rearmament program in 1933, intensifying it in 1936, gives the impression that he was a man holding a tiger by the tail. The internal tensions that had accumulated within the German economy drove him forward faster than he wanted to go, at least judging by his November 1937 Hossbach memorandum. In addition, forward momentum encouraged newer and more dangerous adventures while Germany still was at the flood tide of its military superiority over the British and French. Each new acquisition of territory necessitated another to satisfy the ravenous appetite of heavy industry, and the war which he planned to unleash by attacking Czechoslovakia and Poland in 1942–1943 now had to be carried out in 1939 at a point when Germany was economically not completely prepared for a long war.

The January 30th speech allayed American and British trepidations. *Business Week* (January 1939) did not believe war would occur despite the belief of the ambassadors to France and Germany that war in Europe was a possibility in 1939; the Fascist countries would not "risk their peacefully acquired gains. The outlook then is for war scares, not war."[16] American business hoped that the decline in automobile production in February and March and the generally poor business climate might be stimulated "by a huge volume of government fostered production and that, if war came it might benefit American trade, necessitating a change in the Neutrality Act to foster Roosevelt's plans to aid England and France in a possible war with everything but manpower." This should be "watched as a possible bullish influence" on the flagging market.[17]

In February 1939 *Business Week* voiced the expectation, following Hitler's January 30th "trade or die" speech, that world business expected "a German trade offensive on an unprecedented scale" in Latin American markets, expansion plans in Eastern Europe and an increase in trade with the Soviet Union. The *Golddiskontbank* would "vastly increase its system of export guarantees." These new endeavors in Latin America and elsewhere, Berlin warned, did not invite "meddling by the U.S."[18]

The British, prior to Hitler's speech, had been skeptical of Hitler's desire for increased trade. An *Economist* article, "Germany after Schacht," stated: "all the evidence suggests that every industrial financial and technological reserve is being depleted in one gigantic effort. Germany's striking power is being deliberately raised to a peak which could not be excelled and could hardly even be maintained in time of war itself."[19] A letter to *The Economist* by Balogh, the British economic specialist on Germany, declared that Germany's decision not to consolidate the gains of Munich by setting free capital tied up in military construction for domestic benefits was a "sinister" policy, not due to "misunderstandings, misadventures or mistakes" or even to " 'totalitarian' " economics. It was the direct consequence of deliberate policy. "There had been no sign of any reduction of armament expenditures in recent months.... The present policy of the German authorities seems to require simultaneously, an increase in armament expenditures, an increase in exports, an increase in building activities and (probably) a rise in the standard of living of the workers. Not one of these things, let alone all of them together, can any longer be accomplished by drawing in unused resources — because there are none."[20]

These British perceptions of little change in Germany's economic policies and its increasing trade problems coupled with the visit of Montagu Norman, Governor of the Bank of England, in early January 1939, may have prompted Hitler's January 30th speech. *The Economist* hinted ominously: "Questions of clearance would be discussed with Dr. Schacht and the Reichsbank Directors," and some in Berlin feared the introduction of a compulsory clearing by the United States and possibly Britain. In fact, attempts to collect on the German debts for British bondholders was brought up, but the main theme became British willingness to grant a loan of sizeable proportions — between 500 million Rm and 1 billion Rm was mentioned in earlier discussions in London (at the rate of 12 Rm to £1) — to assist Germany in returning to the path of economic liberalism. Norman made it plain to Schacht and the Reichsbank Directors that there had to be a reduction in German rearmament if the money were to be forthcoming.[21] The seizure of the Czech provinces six weeks later temporarily deflated these trepidations inside Germany and ended the possibility of German bankruptcy.

Following Hitler's speech the miasma of British pessimism partly cleared and gave way to optimism similar to that prevailing in the U.S., and prognostications about the beginnings of a fierce trade war, a "battle of desperation [in which] the Government was prepared for anything." The British braced for a further expansion of credit through the *Golddiskontbank,* a subsidiary of the *Reichsbank,* greatly intensified dumping through levies to aid exports and a greater application of the bilateral and barter system to achieve long-term contracts for deliveries of foodstuffs and raw materials above world market prices.[22] Lacking any better alternative, Britain continued doggedly to pursue its policy of economic appeasement while quietly rearming.

For a variety of reasons — Germany's parlous export position, the "world's growing desire to refrain from providing exchange to assist a policy of aggression" — the British now believed that Berlin might be ready to strike an economic deal, in return for the long awaited political arrangement. The strains of rearmament and autarchy were lowering the quality of German exports and creating difficulties in meeting deliveries. In addition, the South-eastern European countries, previously the scene of Germany's commercial victories, were now balking at the amount of their total trade with Nazi Germany. The semi-official *Economist* concluded: "In commercial matters, as in political, Germany is faced with the choice between conflict and agreement. Whatever may be the truth on the military and political front, on the commercial she cannot afford a trade war." Expectations were sanguine: "There is thus good ground for believing that we can make a bargain with the Germans if we wish to."[23]

These rosy expectations were quickly shattered with the return of Frank Ashton-Gwatkin from his conversations with the Nazi leaders. Ashton-Gwatkin's trip had ended "on a slight note of discord" ascribed to the British desire to establish a political understanding followed by an economic accord and the German wish to have economic concessions first. Ashton-Gwatkin doubted Germany would make any political concessions (cessation of autarchy, return to the free market, etc.) in exchange for economic concessions (presumably a British-German trade agreement followed possibly by trade credits or a loan).

Germany greatly depended upon British raw materials before 1933, as the figures in Table 9–3 indicate, but British trade fell drastically in the period 1933–1938 to almost a quarter of what it once had been before the war.

Table 9–3. German Trade with the United Kingdom, 1913–1938 (in millions of marks)

Year	German Exports to the U.K.	German Imports from the U.K.[24]
1913	1,438.0	876.0
1929	1,305.0	865.3
1933	405.0	238.3
1937	432.0	308.6
1938	350.0	282.7

Since 1933 German exports to Britain had fallen by 13.5% but imports from England had risen by 18% in the same period. German desperation is reflected in the comments of *The Economist* two days before Hitler occupied Czechoslovakia: "German pressure to get England to make trade concessions in the joint industrial conversations is growing stronger. Should Great Britain begin a trade war, it is said, she would meet an opponent prepared for anything." More ominously, the *Deutsche Allgemeine Zeitung* warned that those who wished to take advantage of the Germans' economic problems and food difficulties and "let them stew in their own juice until they become politically unimportant and ready to sell their rights as a great power and Kultur nation for a mess of lentils" were "war agitators and destroyers of European order." On this threatening note, *The Economist* commented that foreign trade was not political but commercial and Germany's right to trade would have to be implemented by force if other countries were unwilling to recognize it or make concessions.[25]

One can only speculate at this point why Hitler chose to occupy the Czech-speaking remnant of Czechoslovakia on March 15, 1939, instead of trying to solve his raw material and foodstuff problems through a trade offensive — as the British and Americans expected — and consolidate gains already made by absorbing Austria and the Sudetenland. Several factors probably were instrumental in his decision: first, the temporary relief obtained through the plundering of the Austrian gold reserves and the Austrian and Sudeten industrial and raw material assets had been quickly dissipated by the ravenous armament program. By the spring of 1939 new pressures for exchange currency and raw materials resurfaced. Second, the British refused to extend their monetary support unless Germany ceased its rearmament program which gravely affected their own credit, financial and trade positions, pushing them into economic and social crisis. The niggardly British response to Germany's economic problems undoubtedly confirmed Hitler's decision not to seek relief through the international market and to resort to force while his military position seemed unassailable. A final reason was a shift in the diplomatic winds: when the Slovak nationalist leaders, seeking to disengage the Slovak area from the Czechoslovak state, requested that Slovakia be placed under a German protectorate (which Berlin had been encouraging behind the scenes), Hitler seized this pretext and ordered the occupation of Bohemia and Moravia.

Any decision to lessen armament production threatened a loss in profits for German big business and its support for Hitler and the Nazis. In 1935–1938 the net profits of the Krupp Corporation, for example, after taxes, gifts and reserves almost doubled; other corporations reaped big profits as well.[26] Hitler's decision also may have been influenced by the signature of the Anglo-American accord of November 17, 1938, which blocked any German commercial offensive for a greater share of the world export market.

As he surveyed the possibility of mounting the predicted trade offensive, the prospects of successfully competing with the Western Powers for markets — which he had ruled out in 1932 at the Herren Klub — must have seemed bleak, indeed. Arrayed against Germany in the markets outside the Reich were formidable obstacles. In the southeast, the earlier scene of Nazi trade triumphs, these countries, for a variety of reasons — the need for exchange currency, a wish to reclaim old markets, dropped or neglected as the result of barter and clearing agreements made with Germany, and finally growing dissatisfaction with doing business with the Germans for political as well as economic reasons — combined to make the region an unlikely target for further German commercial activity. In Latin America (see Table 9–4) the same problems existed as in Southeastern Europe — coffee shortages resulted from Brazil's decision not to sell its products to Germany — but even more threatening, the 1938 British-American trade agreement barred the way to further German penetration of the Latin American market.

Table 9–4. Germany's Trade with All of South America, 1934–1938 (in millions of marks)[27]

Year	Imports	Exports
1934	440.6	265.5
1935	558.6	309.8
1936	536.5	508.5
1937	850.3	652.1
1938	809.7	622.7

Prospects in the European and American market where the Germans conducted almost two-thirds of their trade looked even less promising in view of British and American disinclination to take any more German exports without receiving exchange currency and perhaps even resorting to clearings to recover current debts. The only real possibility lay in reclaiming the Russian and East European market, formerly an extremely important source of raw materials.

For a variety of reasons, German-Soviet trade had declined: domestic circumstances in the USSR; a change in Soviet trade policies; the elimination of Soviet foreign debts; the lessening of Soviet need to export; increased English and American competition and the inability of German manufacturers to make deliveries (see Table 9–5). Although Poland and the border states now replaced the Soviet area as Germany's most important trading partner in the northeastern region, German exports to Poland had, in fact, declined in 1938, necessitating a credit of 120 million złotys to stimulate Polish demand.[28]

French governmental circles began to notice already in November 1938 signs of a commercial struggle immediately following the signing of the Anglo-American accord. On November 30 the assertive Overseas Trade Department Secretary, R. H. Hudson, went over to the offensive in a statement before the House of Commons, threatening a trade war if the Germans did not revise their method of conducting their commercial activities, particularly their habit of paying higher than world prices in Central and Southeastern European markets. Superior British financial holdings would give Britain "a great advantage" and would enable it presumably to win

Table 9–5. Germany's Trade with the Soviet Union
and Northeastern Europe, 1934–1938 (in millions of marks)[29]

	1934	1935	1936	1937	1938	1938*
Exports to:						
Soviet Union	63.3	39.3	126.1	117.4	31.8	33.6
Poland [and] Danzig	55.1	63.3	73.9	99.7	134.1	155.2
Finland	43.3	49.2	53.6	78.2	82.4	85.3
Estonia	7.3	11.4	17.6	19.9	22.0	22.3
Latvia	18.8	27.9	31.2	28.4	40.8	43.0
Lithuania Memel	14.7	6.7	7.4	20.5	23.5	24.3
Imports from:						
Soviet Union	223.0	201.7	93.2	63.1	47.4	52.8
Poland [and] Danzig	78.1	75.5	74.0	80.7	109.4	140.8
Finland	42.3	41.4	46.1	70.1	88.6	88.9
Estonia	8.2	13.0	13.8	23.7	24.0	24.3
Latvia	21.1	31.1	33.2	45.7	43.5	43.6
Lithuania Memel	15.1	2.0	9.1	17.2	27.6	27.8

*Greater Germany

out. The French embassy in Berlin reported the distress of the German press following the signing of the Anglo-American agreement which had occurred following the arrival of a British trade delegation to stimulate British-German trade.

The British-German trade talks, noted the French, had undergone "a certain regression."[30] The apparent reasons were provisions in the Anglo-American agreement for reductions of commodities supplied by Germany which posed "a new threat" to the exports of the Reich to England. This and the "offensive" unleashed by the remarks of Hudson produced "a deep discomfort" (*un profond malaise*) in Berlin which, nevertheless, wrote the French chargé d'affaires in Berlin, de Montbas, "carefully avoided burning its bridges to 'the City'" and even seized the opportunity to disavow Germany's desire for an "exclusive monopoly" in Central and Southeastern Europe. The *Deutsche Wirtschaft* (December 1, 1938), therefore, questioned with dismay: "Against whom is the Anglo-American Alliance directed?" The alliance between the democracies was thought to have been against the totalitarian states, primarily Germany in Latin American and Japan in the Far East. The German press reaction, Paris believed, revealed that the Third Reich attached the greatest importance to not being excluded from the system of liberal economy of which England, France and the United States remained the last adherents. What sacrifice, the French asked, would Germany make toward that end at a time when its exports indicate a perceptible downturn and for the first time since the advent of the National Socialist regime, its commercial balance has a heavy deficit?[31]

The observant French minister to Berlin, Robert Coulondre, believed that Britain accepted the German seizure of Austria and the Sudetenland because it lacked the means to oppose it. "It pretends to admit that the Reich exercises a predominance in the center and southeast of Europe. But this is only a 'waiting position' there. In reality England has not renounced its traditional position: it is not abdicating; it is not abandoning Europe to German hegemony. It is thinking of organizing, from now on, resistance to the German thrust. The recent speech of Mr. Hudson certainly shows that Great Britain has decided to use the sole arms at its disposal in order to struggle against this thrust: financial resources."[32]

On the eve of Hitler's January 30th speech, French Foreign Minister Georges Bonnet thought the trade rivalry between Britain and Germany sufficiently acute to report it in a note to Prime Minister Daladier: "Our ambassador in London draws my attention to the increasing preoccupation that the German commercial expansion in central Europe is causing in English economic circles." Great Britain, he wrote, "scarcely had illusions any longer on the aims pursued by the Reich."

German industry and commerce did not want to raise German living standards, but rather "to assume at any price Germanic supremacy in Europe." London now "carefully considered" the possibilities of expanding British commerce in Central Europe, in spite of the German commercial advances. "The British economists considered that the game is not yet lost in central Europe" because of the resistance of the states in that area to German hegemony. They were seeking outlets other than Germany for their products particularly with the western democracies in order to maintain their remaining independence. The British now believed that their exporters might arrive at a mutually satisfactory arrangement with the Balkan countries. They viewed the Germans as having, through their trading methods, "gained a temporary superiority" which they could overcome by subventions to Balkan imports and exports despite the mutilation of their liberal (i.e., free trade) principles. These tendencies were already apparent in the Department of Overseas Trade headed by Hudson and "the entire government is agreed upon emphasizing credit facilities in the political as well as economic interests of Great Britain."[33]

However, the French closely watched the efforts of British industry, under the aegis of the government, to arrive at an agreement on prices, and the sharing of markets continued throughout 1938 and into 1939. During Dr. Schacht's visit to London, Oliver Stanley, head of the Board of Trade, made conciliatory remarks before the House of Commons emphasizing Britain's interest in an amicable agreement with Germany on the sharing of foreign markets.[34]

The Germans reacted to the British-German industrial talks, overshadowed by the glutted markets of the 1938–1939 depression, with "a certain reserve." Opinion in Berlin, noted Coulondre, believed that such an accord would be difficult to achieve at a time when Britain, Germany and other powers were doing their utmost to increase exports in a climate in which foreign markets had been buying less and less for several months. Such an agreement, declared the *Textile Zeitung,* would have to be subordinated to English recognition "of the vital interests of the German nation which might be the prelude to similar agreements with other countries."[35]

Whatever the case, in late 1938 and into early 1939, numerous voices on the French side warned that the Germans might be forced to start a war for economic reasons.[36] French ambassadors and military intelligence analysts noted that German exports had increased by only 3% from 1932 through 1937 compared to a 16% increase in imports. Given all the signs of a faltering economy, growing indebtedness, an adverse trade balance and a drained treasury, astute observers like François-Poncet, French Ambassador to Berlin, and Genevieve Tabouis, diplomatic editor of *l'Oeuvre,* believed that Germany's prosperity was a spurious facade and predicted "the end of it all is either war or the collapse of the regime and it is obvious which the two dictators are likely to choose." Six months after the end of Munich, Daladier predicted Germany would be driven to conquer much of Eastern Europe followed by use of the area's resources to conduct a war against the Western Powers.[37] Coulondre reported graffiti on the walls left by Germans waiting in queues for coffee: *"kein Kaffee, keine Butter, keine Eier aber eine neue Reichskanzlei"* (No coffee, no butter, no eggs, but a new Reich chancellery).[38] Both Gamelin, French Chief of Defense, and Colonel Didelet, head of French military intelligence, believed that Germany's extensive commitment to military rearmament and to feeding its population would drive it to conquest.[39] If diplomacy and intimidation failed, then by brutal military conquest. Colonel Didelet saw resources as central to Nazi behavior. Some Ruhr industrialists in their "anger and alarm," reported Didelet, were urging war in the hope that the emergency might permit a more stable and less erratic regime to emerge.[40]

Others like the son-in-law of the Director of I. G. Farben, Herbert Scholz, an early Nazi and friend of Himmler and Hess and other Nazi leaders, on his way to a diplomatic post in Boston confirmed all this in unstintingly dark terms: "The economic situation of our country is bad, frankly bad, we lack butter, eggs, wheat. Germany is obliged to content itself with a black bread. Propaganda can support the morale of a population for a certain time, and that time is not perhaps far off when the peasant will revolt. He wants to satisfy his hunger. In the Berlin food stores you won't find eggs, and I myself, during my stay there, at certain times, had to give up butter."

If Germany failed to obtain colonies, Scholz declared, it would have to undertake "an active economic penetration" in the east. "It is towards the Ukraine that we tend." If France and England would allow Germany "to break through towards the east, Germany would remain a continental power and would not contend England's mastery of the sea."[41] However, this notion had already been presented to Chamberlain at Munich in order to gain the Sudetenland. The French and British now no longer believed that Germany would confine itself to economic penetration in the east, and the British no longer were willing to concede Eastern Europe as a unilateral German colonial preserve.

The continued territorial expansion of the Reich only masked its problems; its eroding economic position made a reduction in capital goods and other expenditures inescapable. At the beginning of April 1939 Germany's total public debt amounted, according to contemporary British estimates, to about 60,000–70,000 million Rm, necessitating further financial devices.[42]

A new scheme (the Reinhardt Plan), based upon tax receipted bonds, was floated in two issues to be accepted as payment for taxes and due six months after their issue: (Type I) for those redeeming them at later dates, (Type II) because of certain benefits attached to their retention. This amounted to a short-term-loan expedient which, in the end, would add to the already saturated money market and only temporarily stave off inflation. By the end of May this plan had failed because the construction and industrial interests, due to the reduction of their own funds, were able to absorb only 15% of the issue rather than the hoped for 40%.[43] "It would be astonishing," commented Coulondre to Bonnet, "under these conditions if inflation did not accelerate ... it cannot be conceived how the German government would succeed in preventing in the long run a rise in prices and how it could avoid the collapse of the unstable edifice constructed by Dr. Schacht."[44] This situation forced the Reichsbank officials to admit that they had exhausted all possibilities and "were reduced to inflation pure and simple" and that "this couldn't last much longer."[45]

German-Polish tensions which had mounted in the previous October 1938 "reached a dead point" in early May. But on May 9, the Germans, the French sources believed, renewed their attempts to convert Poland into a satellite, offering as compensation for Danzig, "and to better draw Poland into their game ... the possibility of a share of the Russian Ukraine." The French minister at Berlin warned that Germany's ultimate aim was "Germanic hegemony in Central and Eastern Europe and, finally the domination of the continent."[46] If Poland had accepted these Hitlerite proposals it would have "converted itself into a vassal of the Reich," in vassalage to the policy of the Axis and it would have been used "as an advanced guard in an aggressive action against Russia."[47]

Dr. Funk continued to pursue the trade policies of his predecessor, Schacht, in the spring of 1939, of increasing the volume of German imports through bilateral, clearing house agreements. An April 1939 speech of Dr. Funk, citing the recently negotiated German-Romanian trade agreement, indicated little change in the German system of trade. In an uncomplimentary reference to the more favorable currency position of Germany's competitors, Great Britain and the United States, he declared that no "silver bullets" would be fired in this trade agreement, i.e., that the currency-less barter relations between the two countries would continue. At the same time Funk hinted that British-German trade negotiations had only been temporarily interrupted by the Czech affair and left the door open for further discussions. "His attitude is significant," remarked *The Economist*.[48]

Germany's food situation may have been actually worsened as a result of its acquisition of territories with new inhabitants, about 29% over the Old Reich borders of 1913, while the acreage of agricultural land increased by only 10%, and production increases fell far short of what was needed.[49] Vegetable and domestic wheat production (including Austria and the Sudetenland) amounted to only 6,240,000 tons, necessitating the importation of one million tons. Domestic fat production amounted to only 55% of demand; and the British believed that Germany's grain stocks would last about six months. The shortage of agricultural labor, estimated to be about 700,000 to 800,000 laborers, was further aggravated by the absence of Polish laborers, 200,000 in 1938, which was not made up by Italians and had to be supplemented by schoolchildren and students. Meat supplies were also dwindling.[50]

None of this, of course, escaped the sharp eyes of the British and French diplomats abroad as the German Achilles heel and the major area where future bargaining efforts could be made. In late February even the most appeasement-minded of British diplomats, Nevile Henderson, warned "that it is really essential to appreciate...the real extent not only of Germany's economic difficulties, but also of her immediate aims.... Can Germany continue her present armaments race and *at the same* time increase her imports? It is at least doubtful if she can."[51]

The British Foreign Office during the 1930s contained formidable congeries of groups, sub-groups and influences of various kinds. The ideas and influence of section heads, deputy undersecretaries and permanent undersecretaries radiated upwards toward the government members. Even before the advent of Hitler, different groups of "economic appeasers" were active in the highest levels of British society and within the cabinet and the departments of the government. Some sought to soften the protectionist policy of Ottawa 1932 and to draw Germany back into the family of nations by expanding world trade and reducing economic competition and economic nationalism (Marquise, later Lord, Lothian, Thomas Jones, Barrington Ward, E. H. Carr); others assented to this in the Foreign Office (Jebb, Ashton-Gwatkin and at times Eden), occasionally joined by Leith-Ross. However, their proposals ran into the resistance of the specialists in the various economic departments, the Treasury, Board of Trade, Agriculture and the government itself, where they were sniped at, derided for being amateurish and their proposals either diluted or ignored.

An additional motive for economic appeasement was the desire of the "economic appeasers" to maintain the social contract and avoid a clash with labor in Britain. Rearmament with its risks of inflation-induced social unrest led these "economic appeasers" to advocate economic concessions to Germany in order to maintain class hegemony and uphold social peace. This brought them into conflict with imperialist elements (Churchill, Amery, Sandys) at times, and at various levels of the government with those sympathetic to their ideas like Leith-Ross, who felt strongly that a political settlement had to precede any economic concessions.[52]

To avoid war, London returned to the policy of working with the German moderates. Conversations were held in June and July 1939 between Wohltat, Göring's confidence man, and members of the Foreign Office (Ashton-Gwatkin) and the British government (Hudson, Sir Horace Wilson). Wohltat indicated that Germany would settle for a "preferential" rather than an "exclusive" position in Southeastern Europe. A Wilson memorandum added parenthetically that "Britain was only interested in keeping her share of the Southeastern European trade." A subsequent non-aggression pact on this basis would have made the Polish and Romanian guarantees "superfluous."[53]

Wohltat believed that economic concerns "to his sorrow" played very little part in the Fuhrer's mind. The Anschluss had some economic justification, but the annexation of Bohemia had been a "grave mistake" from the economic standpoint. Why did Britain oppose Germany's military might, asked Wohltat? Hudson reminded him of England's age-old policy of opposing a dominant military power on the continent. Wohltat pictured Hitler as primarily concerned with "consolidating the race" which only a powerful army "could confer." He was pessimistic and agreed that a conflict was inevitable. On the possibility of an alternative policy, i.e., disarmament and establishing Germany "on a strong economic basis," Wohltat believed that only Göring could bring such an idea to Hitler's attention.[54]

Wohltat fleshed out the subject again with Hudson, painting an even rosier picture of the future than Wilson had.[55] There would be a division of the world market and supplies of raw materials. Britain and the United States would bail Germany out of its current debt problems with a loan. Africa would be exploited through a "colonial condominium" and there would be a German-British agreement on Britain's share in the markets, with a recognition of Germany's newly acquired special position in the Eastern and Southeastern European region. The two parties were agreeing, in effect, that Germany's expansion to the southeast and elsewhere into Eastern Europe would not encounter British resistance. The money advanced to the Germans was to be the most important factor, and Leith-Ross with unmatched arrogant cynicism remarked in anticipation of an agreement: "After the experience which we had had in negotiating with [the Poles], with the Turks, and with the Soviets, I am not at all sure that we could not buy up Hitler plus Mussolini cheaper — and settle accounts with the Japanese without payment."[56]

New addenda were added in talks between the German Foreign Office official, Kordt, and Charles Roden Buxton, of the opposition Labor Party, presumably to avoid government complicity. Besides the recognition of the southeastern area as a German influence sphere and a renunciation of Britain's guarantees to Poland and Romania, the British were to influence France to abandon its ties with the Soviet Union and the Eastern European countries.

All this has been scathingly analyzed in a recent work by Clement Leibovitz, which accuses Chamberlain of having gone behind the back of the cabinet, Foreign Office and parliament to conduct secret negotiations with Hitler, designed to encourage Hitler to seek his *Lebensraum* by an attack on the Soviet Union. Through his emissaries, Horace Wilson and a press official George Steward, the Prime Minister's Press Adviser, who held talks with Dr. Hesse, a D.N.B. news representative, Chamberlain held treasonous discussions with Berlin. "If anything about them were to leak out there would be a great scandal," declared Wilson, "and Chamberlain would probably be forced to resign."

The British Secret Service discovered the contacts and notified Cadogan whose diary confirms Chamberlain's obdurate efforts to appease Hitler ("... [it] looks as if No. 10 were talking 'appeasement' again.") Wilson denied them when confronted by Cadogan who ultimately informed Halifax, forcing Chamberlain to provide the Foreign Office with an account of what had transpired.[57]

News of these meetings leaked to the press — by Vansittart according to a French informant — produced a hubbub that eventually forced the government to scurry for cover.[58] According to the French, these "informal" talks were urged by British "economic and financial circles" disturbed by the increasing burden of armament and the aid given to allies, and the feeling that a positive effort should be made now that Britain had reached a certain level of armed military power to ascertain whether Hitler would be willing to convert Germany's industry and to stabilize its currency problems through "a sort of disarmament loan." The political tension could thus be reduced and the ruinous armament program terminated. If Hitler then rejected this offer, the obloquy of such a step would rest on his shoulders.

On the morning of July 22, 1939, the newspapers broke the story of the talks and a British plan to bail out the German economy in exchange for ending its armament program at a cost of £1 billion according to Gordon-Lennox in the *Daily Telegraph,* or £100 million as stated by the editor of the *News Chronicle.* Ultimately Chamberlain had to make a statement in parliament admitting that discussions had taken place, but denying that the cabinet knew of them. Hudson purportedly had only "expressed a personal opinion" and nothing said constituted a proposal of a loan by Britain to Germany.

When the commotion died down, the German press made hostile references to perfidious Albion's desire to deny Germany its due in Danzig. More importantly, it probably led Ribbentrop and Hitler to believe that Britain and France, in the last analysis, sought to buy off Germany and would not oppose a German attack on Poland, despite the guarantee given by London to that country. The French ambassador in Moscow, with scarcely concealed disdain for the ineptitude of the British, commented on the dreadful impression the exposure of the talks between Hudson, Wilson and Wohltat must have made upon the Soviet leaders, then awaiting the arrival of a British military delegation.

> One can hardly understand how a British minister with diplomatic and parliamentary experience [i.e., Hudson –P.N.H.] who came to Moscow on an official mission last spring, believed he could make such offers to Germany without a mandate, and could have done so at the moment when the cabinet of which he is a member decided to send a mission of experts with the aim of concluding a military convention. We should not be astonished in such circumstances at the mistrust of the Soviet negotiators.[59]

At any rate, both the French and the British were acutely aware of Germany's raw material and financial dilemma by this time. A lengthy French analysis in early June 1939, on the reorganization of the German economy to extricate the Third Reich from the morass of autarchy and rearmament, concluded Germany had two options: "it was obliged to choose between the doctrine of the liberal economy and the thesis of "vital space." Faced with the exhaustion and depletion of its labor force and its financial reserve, the Reich had seized Austria in March 1938 because of "two elements essential to the German economy: the gold of the Bank of Austria and the unemployed of the Ostmark." Despite the institution of forms of obligatory labor and the incorporation of two million women into its active population, three billion Rm as the cost of rearmament had not been relieved by long or medium term loans. The dismantling of the Sudeten region of Czechoslovakia before October 2, 1938, and the falling due of five billion Rm was "striking and merited special attention." Germany quickly exhausted the resources of the Sudetenland which had only "delayed the decision that the masters of the Third Reich would have to make before the end of the year."[60]

The French document speaks of "the ruins accumulated by autarchy" which Hitler indirectly condemned in his speech of January 30. To remedy the economic disaster caused by autarchy, Germany would have "to put to sleep" the vast installations and plants devoted to the production of ersatz materials like buna and gas, the Hermann Göring Hanover works for treatment of low grade ores, etc. This would cost an estimated fifty billion Rm or about one-sixth the value of Germany's total assets in 1933, approximately a 50% replacement in the industries affected. A massive devaluation would also be necessary which would amount to the loss of about two-thirds of the mark's current value. The loans and sacrifices entailed by the other powers were expected to be rejected in the case of the U.S. and the USSR. The alternative to this program of heavy sacrifices for all, by implication, would be further resort to war by Germany.[61]

Throughout most of the 1930s the threat of war had colored the relations of the Great Powers.[62] The "economic appeasers" in the British Foreign Office like Gladwyn Jebb, Ashton-Gwatkin and others in other departments, and influential aristocrats like Lothian outside the government, saw clearly or intuitively that Germany would be forced to expand outwardly unless trade expansion occurred. Germany would not allow a situation in which lack of overseas trade opportunities led to another disastrous inflation, mass unemployment and return to the social conditions of the early 1930s. Britain had to broaden international economic opportunities, particularly for Germany, because as Jebb warned on July 2, 1936: "If we do nothing we are in for war."[63] Eden also in a cabinet paper in the same year sided with the "economic appeasers," pointing out that Germany could be expected to act like Italy when Mussolini's failed policies led to foreign adventures as the sole way out of the impasses.[64]

Most British policy makers agreed, however, on the primacy of a general political settlement with Germany before serious economic concessions could be made. The argument over whether a political solution should precede an economic turned more strongly in favor of a political solution as perceptions that Hitler was bent on expansion and German domination of the continent, strengthened over time and that Hitler would never abandon rearmament and return to the free market whatever concessions were made to Germany.[65] Important voices like the pro-French Foreign Office Permanent Under-Secretary, Sir Robert Vansittart, pressed for a tough stance toward Germany. Vansittart advocated a political solution first as a vital step preceding any policy of economic appeasement. More than any other individual in the government, he represented the view that if Germany was in economic straits it would be better to allow it to simmer in its own juice which would make it all the more tractable and amenable to a general political agreement.[66] In view of the cutthroat commercial atmosphere of the 1930s neither Chamberlain nor many of the other British leaders had any intention of using British resources to assist any country, particularly Germany, out of its economic difficulties.[67]

Considering Britain's own slipping commercial and financial position, with an increasingly commercially assertive American state challenging it in Latin America and elsewhere and a rearmed and galvanized Germany demanding hegemony in Europe and making greater and greater incursions into its foreign trade, pleas to make economic concessions through loans and trade concessions seemed like unrealistic cant to the Chamberlain government. In spite of this, the British government had to appear to be conciliatory and, behind a mask of reasonableness that included occasional cooperative endeavors such as the cartelization talks with Germany over the marketing of coal, to quietly rearm.

None of this escaped Hitler whose offers of friendship, such as the British-German Naval Agreement of 1935, in which Germany agreed to an inferior naval position, were not met by significant concessions from the British, particularly in the area of Eastern Europe. Ribbentrop's mission to Britain for an alliance had ended in failure;[68] and Schacht's efforts to secure colonies had not succeeded. Any return to the world market under circumstances in which Germany possessed no colonies — whether in Europe or Africa — or other assured supplies of raw materials was to play the game of empire with a losing hand. Hitler realized that Britain would never permit Germany, through any general settlement, to regain its pre–World War I market position. Efforts to try and compete with Britain, France and the United States, given Germany's meager financial resources and lack of colonial raw materials, were doomed to fail.

Hitler already clearly realized in his 1932 Herren Klub address to the industrialists that he would not seek to regain Germany's pre-war position by competition on the world market but "through the sword." Schacht and Hitler only differed in that Schacht wanted colonies in Africa while Hitler's colonial dreams of raw materials and *Lebensraum* for the Thousand Year Reich lay in the steppes of Russia. In this respect, the central conflict was a struggle for market dominance and correlative colonial sources of raw materials. Having failed to gain a British alliance and approval prior to undertaking a military attack on Poland and the USSR, Hitler proceeded on his own way, believing that Britain ultimately would not be opposed.[69]

At a session of the cabinet in June 1939, Chamberlain glumly announced that "on the political side we were living in what was virtually a state of concealed war."[70] In a July cabinet session the British tried to ascertain whether Germany's internal financial situation would drive it in the direction of further expansion to avoid economic collapse. A briefing paper informed the cabinet of Germany's darkening economic picture. The Chancellor of the Exchequer commented that Germany had previously relied upon loans and less on taxation of its own people, but was now relying "on immensely heavy taxation of the working classes coupled with a far lower rate of expenditure on the social services." Germany with a population of ninety million spent less on social services than Britain with a population of fifty million.[71]

At that point the cabinet queried Sir Richard Hopkins, Second Secretary to the Treasury Department, on the state of Britain's finances as opposed to Germany's in the event of war. Hopkins presented a pessimistic picture should war break out a year later rather than in the present year. "The situation undoubtedly grew more difficult with every month that passed." Britain's gold stocks would be diminished still more in a year. "So long as we continued on the present course our financial position was being weakened. The adverse balance of trade resulted in a steady loss. This loss would be increased if we stimulated the production of armament goods which involved imports of raw materials."[72]

Hopkins believed that Germany could continue to rearm "indefinitely" but that Germany was in a weaker position than Britain with respect to imports from abroad. "So far as concerned overseas finance, Germany was bankrupt" and only "severe controls" on "necessary commodities" enabled it to keep going. Germany had been able to finance armaments "by lowering the standard of living." British wage earners enjoyed a greater purchasing power than their German counterparts. In Britain wages had risen as compared to 1929, "but the position of German wage earners was much below the 1929 level."[73] A recent report from the Commercial Attaché in Berlin indicated "an increasing strain on the whole German system." There was an "almost complete absence of ordinary consumption goods. The German worker could not spend his money on radios, clothes or furniture. He could only spend his money on beer, food and tobacco or invest." Hopkins was pessimistic on the possibility of a breakdown of the entire Nazi system and the likelihood of a financial breakdown in Germany "at any rate within an early period of time," or that there might be "a drop in industrial production in Germany as would bring about a financial breakdown."[74]

The cabinet papers and the comments of various cabinet members centered also on Britain's inferior financial and economic position if war broke out then as opposed to 1914. Doubt was expressed over Britain's prospects if the war lasted for a long time. Halifax thought the general effect of the cabinet papers "might be to give too gloomy a view. All things were comparative. If our position was difficult, the position of Germany was very likely to be even more difficult in regard to the conduct of a long war. If, notwithstanding all her efforts, Germany was unable to make herself self-sufficient, that militated against the theory of a long war." Halifax added that once the war lasted for some time, "the United States would be sufficiently favorable to us to enable us to win the war." Hopkins doubted whether it "could be assume [*sic*] that the United States would be willing to give us unlimited financial resources in a long war."[75]

Whether or not the crisis had come to a head, there is little doubt that it affected the decisions of Hitler — supplemented by other pressures as well, military, political — pushing him into taking actions against Czechoslovakia and Poland sooner than he had intended to satisfy Germany's need for new sources of raw materials and manpower. Or perhaps despite the flurry of Führer orders and conferences, diplomatic conversations and discussions of Nazi officials in the historical documents, these decisions to attack Czechoslovakia and Poland may never have occurred, at least at that precise time, had not these deficiencies acted as persistent irritants upon Hitler. Tim Mason complements this analysis of the crisis by focusing attention on the manifold domestic forms of the crisis, the failure of the regime's attempts to impose draconian wage cuts, taxes on food, clothing and other necessities on the working class. Mason believes the crisis was perceived only by the upper class elites, high officials, bureaucrats, leading military and political personalities in a position to know but remained masked from the working class mass and the middle classes. Hitler knew and had detailed knowledge of the gathering labor shortages from Göring, Schacht, diplomats abroad, the Treasury and other officials.[76] It is more than likely that all these pressures — ideological, political, economic, labor shortages — upon Hitler in the end certainly played a role in his decisions to attack Czechoslovakia and Poland, but the precise degree which each exercised and how they complemented and played off against one another probably will never be known by historians.

Part Three

Germany's 1930s Trade Offensive and the Small Countries of Southeastern Europe

Chapter 10

Germany as Trading Partner
in Southeastern Europe:
Exploiter or Godsend?

Two nations may exchange according to the law of profit in such a way that both gain, but one is always defrauded.

— Karl Marx, *Grundrisse*

THE EXTENT TO WHICH Nazi Germany despoiled Eastern Europe has become the subject of historical dispute.[1] In the earlier findings of Frederick Benham, Germany's export prices declined relative to import prices of goods from the Southeast European countries. This was challenged by the anti-fascist British journalist and economist Paul Einzig, who accused the Germans of "bad faith and sharp dealings" in their commercial relations with their East European trade partners, which undermined the validity of these price reports.[2] However, the terms of trade for two countries, Hungary and Romania, as shown in Table 10–1, bear out Germany's unfavorable trading position with those countries and the improved commercial position of these two states vis-à-vis Germany in the period of the 1930s.

**Table 10–1. Germany's Terms of Trade
with Romania and Hungary, 1928–1938[3]**

with Hungary

1928	1932	1934	1935	1936	1937	1938
100	70	70	73	51	57	55

with Romania

1928	1932	1934	1935	1936	1937	1938
100	28	33	45	50	43	19

In the terms of trade between Germany and the Southeastern European countries both Kindleberger and Ellis advance the view that Germany lost out to its trading partners (see Table 10–2). Ellis states that German export prices rose relative to rising German employment, and increased internal prices inside Yugoslavia both overtly and covertly in quality deterioration and long delays in delivery, but that this was offset by German offers of extremely low export terms and other advantages. More importantly, Ellis drew attention to the political objectives of Germany and its inevitable

225

Table 10–2. Southeastern Europe's Terms of Trade
with Germany, 1929–1937[3]

Hungary

1929	1930	1931	1932	1933	1934	1935	1936	1937
100	98	93	93	90	102	111	108	102

Romania

1929	1930	1931	1932	1933	1934	1935	1936	1937
100	69	49	52	56	54	63	63	77

menacing influence on the countries of Southeastern Europe. Kindleberger found that Germany's terms of trade with non-industrial Europe — meaning Eastern Europe — increased less than with any other trading region, while British and Belgian terms of trade with non-industrial Europe rose higher than Germany's and that his findings supported Benham rather than Einzig.[4] There is other recent evidence, in the case of Hungary at least, that the terms of trade favored that country rather than Germany.[5] In his recent study Larry Neal believes that Germany established a monopoly position over a four- or five-year period which it did not exploit. Thus, there is a general belief by Neal, Ellis and others that Germany did establish a monopoly position in Southeastern Europe's trade but they deny Germany used its advantages to exploit the southeastern countries. This implies that — although Neal and others do not state this motive — Germany was primarily interested in increasing trade volume and only secondarily in the financial side of its trade with those countries.

Alan Milward is the latest proponent of the view that Germany did not "exploit" the Southeastern European countries in the classic imperialist sense. He objects to the concept of "exploitation" by Nazi Germany of its trade partners in Eastern Europe based upon some narrowly focused economic data similar to that of Ellis, Neal, Benham and others that Germany was, in fact, the loser in its trade relations with the countries of the region.[6] He extends the argument and even claims that those countries exploited Germany, despite Germany's monopolist position in the region. Milward's figures and arguments deduced from them seem forced and designed to fit the procrustean bed of his conclusions. Milward's arguments and some of his evidence are not entirely new or convincing, although he does reformulate the arguments of Neal and others based largely upon the terms of trade and other economic data, but without any historical framework, into a more polished whole.

Milward concludes that the Southeastern European states' trade dealings with Germany were entirely voluntary and self-directed and cites Turkey, which decided to take no further German goods until its clearing debt with Germany had been eliminated.[7] However, Turkey was not in close proximity to the Reich and it was more difficult for Germany to exercise direct pressure on it than on Hungary, Yugoslavia and Romania and there is sufficient evidence of Germany's innuendo and threats of countervailing actions against those states. We have already cited Ribbentrop's difficulties in forcing Turkey to deliver more chrome ore than it wished to in 1939–1940. Therefore, Turkey could be more resolute in dealing with German demands and threats than the frightened, wavering Eastern European powers. Moreover, Turkey was in the British strategic interest sphere at the eastern end of the Mediterranean and could count on British support in resisting the Germans. The British gave Turkey a higher priority in credit and other financial support than to any of the East European states.

Wendt's suggestion that the term "exploitation" might be replaced by "dependent" is merely semantical and makes the more reprehensible German trade practices in the Balkans seem benign, which they were not.[8] Germany's increasingly voracious needs gradually converted the arrangement into a less voluntary and by degrees a more coercive one which the Southeastern European states could not easily escape.

What makes Milward's and similar arguments, based upon economic data, tricky, is that the Germans no doubt did at first offer those countries favorable trade arrangements when the latter had few prospects for their largely agrarian exports. Germany could thus expand and divert its trade from markets it was either shut out of or lacked currency to trade in to those like Southeastern Europe and elsewhere for whose products there were few markets and which were in similar straits.

There is evidence not reflected in the statistics that the Germans did, in fact, bilk the Hungarians in the renewed commercial treaty of 1934. George Peck, the U.S. Agricultural Department's top specialist, notified the American Minister to Hungary of that fact.

> …the commercial treaty which Germany made with Hungary last year has not been working out well for the Hungarians. The money for the goods bought, has been frozen by recent edicts and rulings, and Hungary is now out both the goods and money. Further, the Germans instead of using the goods in Germany, sold them into other markets at cut prices thereby seriously disturbing Hungarian trade in these markets.[9]

The German re-exporting of these goods received from Southeastern Europe, Latin America and elsewhere had become common practice as noted by American commercial officials abroad watching these transactions. The American commercial attaché at Berlin reported "that there was little doubt that Germany was re-exporting compensated products not only from Brazil but from other countries for sale in world markets for valuata or for barter to compensation countries."[10]

The Southeastern European states were not a monolithic trade bloc in the 1930s and their economic circumstances were somewhat different. For most of this period Yugoslavia showed positive trade balances and its trade was primarily with the clearing countries rather than the free currency countries (see Tables 10–3 and 10–4).

Despite these favorable balances, the terms of trade turned dramatically against Yugoslavia in the 1930s. During the era from 1927 to 1930 the terms of trade were quite favorable to Yugoslavia and for most of the years from

Table 10-3. Yugoslavia's Trade Balance, 1935-1938

Year	Exports (dinars thousands)	Imports (dinars thousands)	Differences (excess or deficit)
1935	4,030,360	3,699,774	+330,586
1936	4,376,153	4,077,010	+369,143
1937	6,272,403	5,233,772	+1,038,631
1938	5,047,434	4,975,342	+72,092

Year	Exports (tons)	Imports (tons)	Differences
1935	3,326,883	981,463	+2,345,420
1936	2,868,221	971,328	+1,896,893
1937	4,557,395	1,104,950	+3,452,445
1938	3,702,070	1,269,899	+2,432,171

Figures taken from National Bank of Yugoslavia, No. 10, October 1939, p. 7.

Table 10-4. Yugoslavia's Trade with Clearing Countries, 1935-1938

Year	Exports	Imports
1935	82.8	71.4
1936	76.2	73.3
1937	76.2	75.7
1938	67.0	69.5

Figures taken from National Bank of Yugoslavia, No. 10, October 1939, p. 7.

1919 to 1926; by 1931 they were only slightly favorable, while in the period 1932–1937 the terms of trade turned sharply against Yugoslavia. According to the National Bank of Yugoslavia, measured at the 1926 level (1926=100), the index of exports in 1929 was 114.3 in contrast to imports at 91.4. In 1933 the price index of export products was 58.4 while imports were 74.1. Only in 1938 did the terms of trade favor Yugoslavia — at a point when Germany was taking over half of Yugoslavia's exports of foodstuffs and raw materials — but in the succeeding two years, they were again slightly against Yugoslavia.[11] Thus, in the case of Yugoslavia, the terms of trade argument employed by Neal, Milward and others does not seem to have helped Yugoslavia much.

Already in 1936 the Yugoslav government was forced to decree that certain commodities, representing one-third of the total value of imports, could not be imported from non-clearing countries except through a special license issued by the central bank.[12] Yugoslavia was forced to this extreme step by the costs of imports from hard currency countries which had to be paid in free exchange. When the considerable exports to Germany, which were not paid for and were owed to Yugoslavia for some time, are taken into consideration, Yugoslavia's trade was disadvantageous. Much of the contradiction between the positive trade balances and the unfavorable terms of trade for Yugoslavia during the 1930s can doubtless be attributed to the fact that the Southeastern European countries had to export larger amounts of produce to pay for reduced imports during the 1930s. The object of this policy was to cut imports from the hard currency countries and increase those from the clearing countries, if Yugoslavia were not to lose what was owed to it by Germany. Thus, Yugoslavia was forced into increasing dependence upon Germany.

Doing business with Germany also created drawbacks in Yugoslavia's trade with the non-clearing countries. As a result of being locked into the German trade bloc, Yugoslavia began to experience difficulties in gaining access to foreign currencies other than the mark.

In July 1939 on the very eve of the war, Bolgert, an official of the Bank of France on mission to Yugoslavia to examine the state of its economy and finances, reported that after the "brilliant improvement realized in 1936–37" the monetary situation underwent "an unfavorable turnabout, which continued into the first half of 1939." While the budget and economy improved from 1938 to 1939 and was "relatively satisfying," Yugoslav foreign trade "has become clearly preoccupying. Imports and exports have taken a visible downturn from 1937 to 1938, the latter more than the former."[13]

Table 10–5. Yugoslavia's Foreign Trade, 1937–1938 (in millions of dinars)

	Exports	Imports	Balance
1937	6,272	5,234	+1,038
1938	5,047	4,975	+72
Decline from 1937 to 1938	1,225	259	−966

From the monetary standpoint the import of the figures shown in Table 10–5 becomes clear if the commerce of the clearing countries is compared with those of the free exchange countries. In the latter, during the boomlet of 1937, Yugoslavia had a surplus of 222 million dinars, but in 1938 this positive balance declined to 145 million "despite every effort made to improve the non-clearing trade." However, the contraction of world trade since the previous year continued, stronger in imports than exports, so that in the first five months of 1939 there was a total commercial deficit of somewhere between 219 and 118 million dinars. In trade with the non-clearing countries there was a positive balance of 142 million dinars in 1938 and 168 million in 1939, a small benefit insufficient to pay the public debt and the demands for credit continuing from year to year.

Despite every measure taken, the year 1938 was from the monetary standpoint "the most unfavorable since 1932." Purchases of free exchange currency by the National Bank of Yugoslavia fell from 1,306 million gold dinars in 1937 to 1,015 in 1938 while the demands for financial needs and commercial credits rose from 726 to 1,087 million dinars. Yugoslavia's increasing exports to Germany at higher prices forced a rise in prices inside the country, producing a situation in which the non-clearing countries were less interested in taking Yugoslav exports while favoring exports to Yugoslavia. As shown in Table 10–6, to offset its monetary losses, Yugoslavia had to curtail imports, and "a bilateral restriction of exchanges" occurred which failed to provide sufficient free currency needed to supply the country with raw materials not provided by Germany and the Axis countries, notably textiles, hides and leather, and oil, total imports of which surpassed 2 billion dinars in 1937 and 1,600 million in 1938 mostly payable in currency.

Table 10–6. Index of Yugoslav Wholesale Prices, 1936–1939[14]

Year	1936	1937 (mean annual)	1938	1939 (mean annual for five months)
vegetable products	69.7	74.1	85.8	85.2
animal products	60.0	65.1	65.8	63.7
export products	64.8	72.8	76.2	76.0

Bolgert conceded that "nobody denies that the Greater German market constitutes the principal market outlet for Yugoslav production. But the system of exchange cleverly conceived by the Reich tends to successfully transform this naturally privileged situation into a quasi-monopoly — and in the process detaching Yugoslavia from the world economy, thanks to a systematic augmentation of its national prices."[15]

Bolgert concluded that Yugoslavia had two choices: either deflation or devaluation. If Yugoslavia carried out a deliberate policy of deflation, however, it would allow Germany to buy even greater quantities of Yugoslav goods, strengthening the hand of Nazi economic powers.

After two years of trade with Germany under the clearing system established under the 1934 trade agreement, Germany owed Yugoslavia 520 million dinars for imported commodity deliveries, causing the mark in Yugoslavia to drop 60.7% of its value, offering German importers a 20%–40% premium.[16] Germany also frequently re-exported goods from Southeastern Europe at lower rates than purchased on the international market in order to make use of foreign currency gained by such sales. Moreover, German exporters could sell at whatever price they wished while the Yugoslavs could sell only on the German market at fixed prices. The fact that Yugoslavia was able to run up its largest positive trade balance in 1937 when it was able to take advantage of increased prices and trade in non-clearing countries suggests that Germany's trade offers were advantageous — and that is even doubtful — only in the most desperate circumstances.

The exports of agricultural products from Yugoslavia caused dislocations on the internal market which frequently benefited only the largest firms, while the peasantry had to pay higher prices and work for low wages.

Equally serious was the fact that lower priced German goods wreaked havoc on the domestic industrial market. The leather, metal working and textile industries were particularly hard hit. "The Germans offered dumping prices mainly for products made in Yugoslavia while demanding high prices — often above the world price level — for goods for which there was no Yugoslav competition. The Kordun factory in Karlovac had to reduce prices and lay off workers in consequence. The Mustad factory also had to reduce prices."[17] In the end both Yugoslav and German consumers were the losers.

Another problem was the export to Yugoslavia by Germany of goods not needed in Germany or of useless and valueless commodities particularly after 1938. The markets of the Southeastern European countries were glutted with paper, china and glassware, toys and musical instruments, cosmetics and lacquers. According to one writer, exports of stationery and other paperware from Germany to Yugoslavia increased sevenfold in value as compared with the 1934–1938 average. In 1940 Yugoslavia was obliged to import four times more cosmetics than it had in 1938 while imports of china and glass were increased 2.5 times.[18] In addition the Germans forced the countries of Southeastern Europe, particularly Romania, Bulgaria and Hungary, into cultivating industrial plants and other crops which were important for German industry. Romania and Bulgaria were induced to increase the cultivation of soybeans and Hungary had to produce more flax. Exports of soybeans to Germany increased tenfold compared to 1936.[19]

The economic imbalance produced by the bilateral clearing system often produced ludicrous results. The slump in the price of Yugoslav plums due to Germany's failure to import resulted instead in production of such a surplus of plums that the peasants turned them into sljivovitz, a potent brandy, and the entire country went on a drunken binge.[20] Though stories of German exports of large amounts of aspirin, bird seed and the like dumped on the market of Southeastern Europe may be more apocryphal than real, nevertheless, it did occur. Some of these countries received things that the Germans wished to get rid of rather than what they needed.

However, a Bulgarian writer's investigations revealed that Bulgaria benefited from their trade relations with Germany. German exports to Bulgaria, according to Ljuben Berov, a Bulgarian economic historian, were primarily metal products, machines, agricultural implements, transportation and chemical products (half of which were medical items), textile wares, textile raw materials, rather than luxury and toy articles. Only 2% were toys, cosmetics and other "unneeded" articles.[21]

Some of these experiences also occurred in Hungary. Its balance of trade in the 1930s remained largely positive but on a greatly reduced basis. Like most of the agrarian countries it had lost over 50% of its total trade since 1930–1931, hence these positive balances did not mean much. Germany's increased trade enabled Hungary to barely limp along — Neal's reference to Hungary as being in "receivership" is apt. Although its total trade had increased somewhat by 1939, it still remained about half of what it had been in 1929 before the Depression (see Table 10–7).

Hungarian trade with Germany in the second half of the 1930s clearly helped Hungary to surmount the Depression, but at a price. The terms of

Table 10–7. Hungarian Balance of Trade, 1929–1939 (in millions of pengös)

	Imports	Exports	Total Trade	Balance
1929	1,063.7	1,038.5	2,102.2	−35.0
1930	823.5	911.7	1,735.1	+88.3
1931	549.6	567.1	1,116.7	+17.5
1932	328.5	334.5	663.0	+17.5
1933	314.2	391.3	705.2	+76.8
1934	344.8	405.3	331.1	+60.5
1935	397.4	457.7	851.1	+60.3
1936	436.5	504.1	940.9	+67.9
1937	475.5	588.6	1,063.1	+113.1
1938	410.6	522.4	933.0	+111.8
1939	406.5	605.8	1,012.3	+199.3

Figures taken from Monthly Report of the National Bank of Hungary, Nos. 83–94, 95–97, 99–106, 107–142, 143–154, 167–178. For the two years 1929 and 1938, I am indebted to the Hungarian Statistical Review, vol. 109, 1938, p. 17, cited by Ivan T. Berend and György Ranki, *The Hungarian Economy in the Twentieth Century* (London and Sydney, 1985), p. 141. These figures are slightly different from those of the National Bank of Hungary.

Table 10–8. Hungarian Import and Export Prices, 1929–1938 (1925–1927=100)

	General Imports	Industrial Imports	General Exports	Agricultural Exports	Terms of Trade
1929	103	104	95	95	92
1930	95	93	86	81	90
1931	85	83	73	63	85
1932	71	73	60	53	85
1933	60	64	48	42	81
1934	54	57	51	45	95
1935	56	56	56	52	100
1936	53	51	51	48	98
1937	60	58	55	53	93
1938	59	60	57	52	97

Cited in Berend and Ranki, *The Hungarian Economy in the Twentieth Century*, p. 143, table 3.27.

trade, as shown in Table 10–8, are clearly favorable to Hungary during those years.

During the 1930s the structure of Hungarian trade underwent important changes, shifting from the export of a considerable amount of manufactured and industrial products to proportionately more agricultural commodities. Foreign imports, predominantly finished industrial goods, fell from 62% in 1913 to 27% in 1937 while the proportion of raw materials and semi-manufactured items almost doubled from 38% to 73%.[22] Hungary engaged in industrial import substitution, changing the importance of manufactured goods which decreased in general.

Another structural innovation was a change in Hungary's trading partners. Before the First World War Hungary's trade was primarily with the lands of the Austro-Hungarian monarchy, about 70%. In 1929 it had declined to one-half and in 1937 to only one-quarter with the successor states.

By the end of the 1930s as Germany's power rose, its previous favorable trade terms with Hungary and the other Eastern European states — when Germany was less able to dictate trade terms — were quickly withdrawn. This was facilitated by Germany's appropriation of the considerable Austrian and Czech holdings in Hungary which gave it 12% of Hungary's industrial stock, but approximately one-half of all foreign capital, leading Hungarian Foreign Minister Teleki to comment: "The German Empire possesses such vast and widespread interests in our country that she can control, and what is more, influence it through its interests."[23]

After 1939 Germany intensified its demand that Hungary adapt its economy to German specifications and in effect become a German dependency. Thus, when the joint German-Hungarian committee established by the 1931 trade agreement met in 1939 in Munich to determine what goods would be exchanged, the Hungarian side agreed to German demands for greater Hungarian exports of agrarian foodstuffs — 50% of the wheat surplus, 35% of the rye surplus and 60% of the maize surplus. Fruits, vegetables, animals and animal products were also exported in increased amounts. The Germans now withdrew their more favorable high prices for wheat and declared that Germany's new price would be based on both Hungarian and world market prices, the first step towards the disadvantageous export-import balance of the war years and the withdrawal of the high German import prices of the 1930s.

The Germans also demanded Hungary reciprocate by buying a restricted number of items — motorcars, artificial fertilizer, glass and chinaware, rather than the crude iron and machine tools needed by Hungarian industry, which Hungary reluctantly agreed to as the increased Hungarian agricultural exports weighted the trade balance in Hungary's favor. Hungarian Commission members perceived that "the desire to lower Hungary to the level of a producer of raw materials was quite an obvious trend."[24] The Germans presented a memorandum shortly after to the Hungarian authorities: henceforth, "Hungarian agriculture must adapt itself more strongly than before to the needs of the German market."[25] Hungary was asked to develop only its agrarian sector to avoid conflicting with "the German export interest." The Germans blatantly requested the abolition of the tax and credit benefits enjoyed by Hungarian factories because it made it more difficult for German goods to compete with Hungarian goods in Hungary.[26]

Hungarian industrialists angrily complained against German interference and that Germany was already selling its goods at very low prices in order to destroy Hungary's industry. But GYOZ (the National Union of Industrialists) agreed that "the time of non-compliance on principle is past ... we have to reckon with the existing situation." They agreed upon a temporary expedient: "we might consider the postponement of industrial development; this is the field where we can make significant concessions to the Germans."[27]

Istvan Bethlen expressed what was happening to Hungary even more emphatically: "During the talks we had recently our negotiating partners repeatedly warned us: Don't keep insisting on a Hungarian industry ... you are an agrarian country, be a country of peasants and sell us your agricultural products; we shall supply you with industrial goods. ... This means total economic dependence, total economic penetration by Germany; it can lead to nothing but political dependence."[28]

This was confirmed by A. Szentmiklossy, the Hungarian chargé in Berlin, in a report to Premier Bardossy: Germany desired that Hungary's main products would be cereals and oil seeds; Hungarian-produced raw materials were to be processed in local industry as semi-finished products. Germany desired a "directed cooperation" of Hungarian industry connected to agriculture. Hungarian industry already in existence would be turned over to the Germans, while new industries unsuited to German needs would be discouraged.[29]

Annexations of Sub-Carpathian Ruthenia and part of Transylvania and other areas, later resulting in increased land area, enabled the Germans to demand 35% more imports in one year, 1940–1941, despite the increase in population, which provoked a deficit in the 1940 German-Hungarian trade balance for the first time in years.[30] In the period after 1940 and the outbreak of war with the Soviet Union, Hungarian defense and other industrial production became so important to the Third Reich that the latter relented in its original plan to completely subjugate Hungary to colonial status, for the time being.

The Hungarian minister in Berlin, Sztojay, believed that the economic and political focus had shifted from the southeast to the east and "the political and economic principles formerly in use against us, that Southeastern Europe should dismantle her industry and settle down to agricultural production, have been abandoned, and they are satisfied to have the industrial production of Central and Southeastern Europe supply Germany, at least for the time being."[31] Hungary continued to serve the German war effort after 1941 and during German-Hungarian industrial talks the Hungarian delegation declared: "Hungary would cede a significant part of her industrial capacity to Germany."[32]

However, over the next few years Germany's import demands went beyond the Hungarian surplus and increased year after year, drastically depreciating the Hungarian living standard.[33] The fruits of the 1930s trade agreements were now being gathered.

To make up for its trade losses to Germany, the Hungarians tried to get the Germans to agree not to undercut Hungarian trade in the southeastern region and even to give up German shares in Hungarian industry — the latter scheme in order to pay off the trade balances owed to Hungary, estimated in 1939 to be 120–130 million pengös.[34] This was only partially successful; by 1944 only 34.75 million pengös were returned, offsetting German debts owed to Hungary which in 1942 already amounted to 506 million marks or over 800 million pengös. By 1943 it skyrocketed to 1,035 million marks.[35]

Bulgaria's trade relationship with Germany was somewhat different from the other Eastern European countries, as shown in Table 10–9. In its trade with the Third Reich it had the highest percentage of exports and imports of any Southeastern European country, 71% and 69% respectively in 1939.[36]

Table 10–9. Germany's Trade with Southeastern Europe and Bulgaria, 1937 and 1939

	Exports to Germany (as a percentage of all exports)		Imports from Germany (as a percentage of all imports)	
	1937	1939	1937	1939
Bulgaria	43.1	71.1	54.8	69.5
Hungary	24.1	52.4	26.2	52.5
Romania	19.2	43.1	18.9	56.1
Yugoslavia	21.7	45.9	32.4	53.2

Initially the German capital investment position inside Bulgaria was minimal, totaling 5.2% of all foreign capital before Munich, but with the addition of Austrian and Czech assets it grew to 13.4%, giving Germany third place after Belgium and Switzerland.

Alone of all the Balkan states, Romania stubbornly resisted Nazi economic expansion and succeeded in keeping its exports to Germany down to approximately 25% of its export trade until 1938. Before 1938 Romania was tied with Czechoslovakia and Yugoslavia through the Little Entente and through the Balkan Entente with the French alliance system and the Western Powers. French and British capital held the strongest position in the Romanian economy since 1918. But with the Anschluss of Austria and the piecemeal destruction of Czechoslovakia, Western influence in Eastern Europe declined. King Carol and his confederates saw the handwriting on the wall and tied Romania increasingly to the Axis Powers. Romania more than any other Eastern European country was beset by a multitude of anxieties, foremost of which was the possibility that the Soviet Union and Hungary might seize the opportunity offered by the destruction of the Versailles Treaty to grab its national territories in Bessarabia and Transylvania.

In a word, Romanian trade after 1938 became increasingly politicized and Romania itself, because of its vital oil resources, converted into a German satrapy by 1940.

Romanian export volumes remained high throughout the 1930s, even exceeding the 1920s in some years, but import volumes fell to approximately 40%–50% of its previous level. As in the case of Hungary, export prices fell much more than import prices, forcing Romania to export larger volumes in the 1930s for the equivalent amount of imports in previous years (see Table 10–10).

During the 1930s Romania's trade with the free currency countries was consistently greater than the clearing countries, except for 1935; Germany, the major clearing country, took over one-quarter of Romania's total trade by 1938. Up to that point, trade balances largely benefited Romania but in

Table 10-10. Romania's Trade Balance, 1925-1940

	Quantities (Tons)		Values (1,000 lei)				Differences		
	Imports	Exports	Imports	Mean Value of an Imported ton (lei)	Exports	Mean Value of an Exported ton (lei)	Countries with monetary restrictions	Countries without monetary restrictions	Total
1925	889,925	4,663,892	29,912,645	32,314	29,126,824	6,245	–	–	–785,821
1926	924,442	6,117,781	37,195,415	37,196	38,264,805	6,262	–	–	+1,069,390
1927	1,008,069	7,347,087	33,852,131	33,763	38,110,810	5,131	–	–	+4,258,679
1928	952,808	5,886,405	31,640,956	33,208	27,029,728	4,592	–	–	–4,611,228
1929	1,101,992	7,064,619	29,628,038	27,111	28,960,005	4,099	–	–	–668,033
1930	805,233	9,214,754	23,044,163	29,132	28,522,028	3,096	–	–	+5,477,865
1931	560,366	10,047,003	15,754,569	28,093	22,196,914	2,209	–	–	+6,442,345
1932	449,680	9,056,959	12,011,325	26,693	16,721,593	1,846	–	–	+4,710,268
1933	466,962	8,777,730	11,741,850	25,143	14,170,828	1,614	–	–	+2,428,978
1934	635,868	8,854,096	13,208,543	20,773	13,655,734	1,542	+165,319	+281,872	+447,191
1935	533,268	9,276,009	10,847,530	20,339	16,756,223	1,545	+3,794,582	+2,114,111	+5,908,693
1936	630,443	10,548,913	12,637,698	20,034	21,703,391	2,057	+1,749,170	+7,316,532	+9,065,693
1937	709,415	9,637,497	20,284,748	28,594	31,568,357	3,276	+3,918,030	+7,365,579	+11,283,609

1938	820,603	7,409,084	18,767,830	22,721	21,532,580	2,906	+854,966	+1,909,784	+2,764,750
1938 July	60,977	651,975	1,524,564	25,002	1,694,577	2,599	+49,616	+120,397	+170,013
August	49,394	701,591	1,498,772	30,343	2,139,805	3,050	+331,436	+309,598	+641,033
September	58,823	574,585	1,497,733	25,402	1,674,767	2,915	−55,739	+232,773	+177,034
Total	169,194	1,928,151	4,521,009		5,509,149		+325,312	+662,768	+988,080
October	74,024	671,953	1,283,429	17,338	2,010,248	2,992	+362,009	+364,810	+726,819
November	70,955	824,901	1,539,897	21,702	2,340,550	2,837	+288,981	+511,672	+800,053
December	63,308	681,984	1,471,398	23,242	1,969,186	2,887	−76,712	+574,500	+497,788
Total	208,287	2,178,838	4,294,724		6,319,984		+574,278	+1,450,982	+2,025,260
Total 1938	820,603	7,409,084	18,767,830	22,721	21,532,580	2,906	+854,966	+1,909,784	+2,764,750
1939 January	55,481	628,823	1,463,710	26,382	1,897,834	3,018	+5,056	+429,068	+434,124
February	51,567	625,410	2,073,742	39,449	1,824,217	2,917	−757,386	+507,861	−249,525
March	92,845	642,849	2,436,380	26,241	1,900,129	2,956	−675,090	+138,839	−530,251
Total	200,893	1,897,082	5,973,832		5,622,180		−1,427,420	+1,075,768	−351,652
April	71,050	676,969	2,415,081	33,991	2,097,080	3,098	−510,275	+192,282	−317,993
May	70,954	707,392	1,602,829	22,590	2,345,045	3,315	+498,664	+243,552	+742,216
June	79,178	733,990	2,305,343	29,116	2,420,497	3,298	−11,529	+126,733	+115,154
Total	221,182	2,118,357	6,323,253		6,862,630		−23,190	+562,567	+539,377
July	80,292	697,159	2,091,975	26,055	2,330,276	3,343	+196,554	+41,747	+238,301
August	59,565	608,762	1,488,848	24,905	2,076,981	3,412	+517,065	+71,068	+588,133

1939, when German trade with Romania increased to almost 50% of its total trade, Romania's trade balance with the clearing countries registered deficits in the first six months of that year in comparison to the non-clearing countries which had positive balances. In short, the clearing system after 1938 was much less beneficial to Romania (see Table 10–11).

Table 10–11. Romania's Balance of Trade for Clearing and Non-Clearing Countries, 1934–1938, Values (1,000 lei)

Year	Countries with monetary restrictions	Countries without monetary restrictions	Balance
1934	+165,319	+281,872	+447,191
1935	+3,794,582	+2,114,111	+5,908,693
1936	+1,749,582	+7,316,523	+9,065,693
1937	+3,918,030	+7,365,579	+11,283,609
1938	+854,966	+1,909,784	+2,764,750

Taken from Banque Nationale de Roumanie, Service des Études Économiques, Bulletin d'information et de Documentation, vol. 10, 11th year, Bucharest, October 1939.

Romanian trade balances, except for the years 1925, 1928 and 1929, had been positive, but like the other East European states, trade volume fell sharply after 1930 to about one-half of what it had been in the preceding decade.

After 1938, German efforts to increase their share of Romanian oil, wheat and timber exports prompted repeated pleading from Bucharest to Paris and London, both before and after the Munich conference, to obviate this by increasing the Western share of Romania's trade. Direct appeals by Romanian Foreign Minister Petrescu-Comnen to Halifax and Georges Bonnet in Geneva on May 13, 1938, and by King Carol himself, through Premier Tatarescu, emphasizing Romanian fears of a German trade monopoly, achieved little. In their June 1938 negotiations with the Germans, the Romanians were cagey and doggedly insisted on keeping the treaty language murky in order to avoid becoming inveigled further into the Nazi interest sphere. At this time the German danger had not yet reached its zenith and Bucharest could still risk affronting German ire. The more immediate dangers to Romania were Soviet and Hungarian seizure of Bessarabia and Transylvania taken after the First World War.[37]

At this point Britain was deep into its policy of appeasement and avoided giving Hitler any pretext to invade Czechoslovakia and trigger a war or by doing anything, after Munich, that suggested encirclement of Germany. The Chamberlain government was aloof and unresponsive to Romania's pleas for increased British and French purchases of Romanian exports. Britain's indifference stemmed from its marginal commercial interest in Eastern Europe despite its capital investments in Romania, Yugoslavia and Greece.

British capital investments abroad, even in the favored imperial dependencies, had fallen off in the 1930s in general in favor of domestic investments, and capital investment in general was low. Except for Turkey and Greece, because of their important positions in the eastern Mediterranean, Britain regarded the region as a backwater better left to the Germans and Italians to quarrel over.

Therefore, during most of 1938 Chamberlain resisted any British efforts to shore up Eastern European resistance to Hitler through alliances or trade credits and political trade and only after the German occupation of Bohemia and Moravia in March 1939 did the British do so.

The German seizure of Bohemia and Moravia produced, in the words of Elizabeth Wiskemann, a well-known historian of the area, "in an indirect sense, an economic conquest of Romania." With the Czech and Austrian share of Romania's commerce in its hands, Germany now had more than 50% of its trade which approximately doubled, and "although Romania had previously avoided exporting to Germany upon [*sic*] an overwhelming scale, she is now automatically drawn into the German system." Not only were the considerable Czech and Austrian capital interests in German hands "but with the acquisition of the Škoda factories Germany now controls the bulk of Romania's military supplies."[38]

On October 19, 1938, Colonel Beck met with Carol on the royal yacht in Galatz and tried to induce the Romanian leader to occupy some Romanian populated villages in Sub-Carpathian Ukraine for its "benevolence" in allowing Hungary to absorb the entire Sub-Carpathian region. But this meant, in effect, seizing territory from the stricken Czech state, violating Romania's agreement with Czechoslovakia under the Little Entente, as the Romanian Foreign Minister Petrescu-Comnen ("a perfect imbecile," according to the exasperated Beck) pointed out. Poland would thus have a common border with Hungary and a second railroad connection with Romania.

In the following month, November 1938, Prince Paul, the Yugoslav Regent, visited Bucharest and advised Carol to maintain friendly relations with the Germans and to do nothing that would provoke Hitler. It is probable that Paul advised Carol to stay out of the Sub-Carpathian plans of Hungary which might otherwise bring the Germans into the Balkans in the event of a struggle between Hungary and Romania.[39] Later, in February 1939, Gafencu, replacing Petrescu-Comnen as foreign minister, arrived in Belgrade on February 4 and advised Cadere, the Romanian minister to Belgrade, to refrain from doing anything that might provoke the pro-Axis Stojadinović government which was not liked in Bucharest.[40]

The Romanian minister in Berlin, Djuvara, also advised that Germany was now a neighbor of Yugoslavia and almost of Romania: "It is not then a question of policy but of destiny. Germany needs to be economically satisfied, especially because we are absolutely necessary to her."[41] Göring, he reported, had told the Yugoslav minister that French Premier Daladier purportedly had acknowledged the economic priority of Germany in Southeastern Europe. Seeing the inevitability of increasing Romanian oil and agricultural exports to Germany, King Carol proposed, during his meeting with Hitler in November 1938, economic concessions to Germany provided that Germany did not support Magyar revisionism. Gafencu also was ready to meet the German economic demands, provided that Romania could maintain its economic integrity and did not become a dependency of the Third Reich, i.e., would be free to conduct trade with the Western Powers. But Ribbentrop and Hitler preferred to play off Romania against Hungary, keeping "the two irons in the fire."[42]

Even before he boarded the train for Bucharest after meeting the Nazi leaders, Carol was informed of the excesses committed by the Iron Guard in several Transylvanian towns; Guardists had also assassinated the Rector of the University of Cluj. Purportedly fearing a Guardist coup or else moving to rid himself of a dangerous enemy, Carol decided to behead the movement. Its leader Codreanu and thirteen of his associates were shot "while trying to escape." Incensed at the elimination of his Romanian protegé either during or immediately after his conversations with Carol, Hitler ordered a violent press attack upon the Romanian monarch. Carol's action had the effect of making it look as though Hitler was in collusion with him in the elimination of the Guardist leaders. The "November incident" — as the German Minister Fabricius and Wohltat, Göring's emissary, referred to Codreanu's murder — and the German press attacks may have been contrived to frighten King Carol and the Romanian government into believing a full-fledged German invasion of Romania was impending. It was easier to appease Hitler and the Germans by increased deliveries of oil, grain and other resources than to risk an invasion. This comes through clearly in the German Foreign Office official Heinburg's memo on the anxious entreaties of George Bratianu for the dispatch of Ministerialdirektor Wohltat to Bucharest to negotiate an economic agreement.

Upon his arrival in Bucharest, Carol told Wohltat that Romania would make concessions: "Germany generally shall regain the position of economic predominance in Romania which she had before 1914." But Clodius, Deputy Director of Economic Policy in the German Foreign Office, reminded the two German officials on the spot that, since the most recent agreements of December 10, 1938, "Germany now accounts for 50% of Romanian foreign trade." Beyond that, "No very marked increase in this figure can reasonably be expected...." For the moment, "it would nevertheless be inadvisable to pass up the opportunity offered by the Romanians." Lord Lloyd's arrival in the previous summer and Lord Sempill's visit to Bucharest on February 12, 1939, had frightened Berlin into believing a British economic offensive would follow.

Colonel Gerstenberg, the German military attaché in Bucharest, arrived with a message from Göring who claimed to have defended Carol against Hitler's wrath. Fabricius, the German minister to Romania, advised that the strained relations between Germany and Romania could be improved by Romania's adherence to a new economic agreement firmly binding that country to Germany and enabling it to compete better with Hungary for the Reich's favors.[43]

King Carol accepted these suggestions appointing Ion Bujoiu to replace the pro-Western Constantinescu to conduct the negotiations. However, Romania was then negotiating a guarantee of its borders — Hitler having refused to do so — with the British which gave them sufficient leverage to resist the most extreme Nazi demands.

High drama surrounded the negotiations. In the midst of the treaty discussions, Tilea, Romanian minister to London, in circumstances that have never been definitively explained, either took it upon himself or was prompted by others, to inform the British government that Romania had received "something like an ultimatum" from the Germans to sign the agreement which contained clauses placing it under German domination. Tilea's overkill, which leaked to the British newspapers, had the effect of panicking London into believing Romania was next on Hitler's list and of issuing a guarantee of Romania's independence.

During the German-Romanian treaty negotiations there were fears of a Hungarian attack, and a large number of German divisions concentrated on the Slovak border. Romania mobilized masses of peasants and brought them into Bucharest in anticipation of hostilities. The first proposals in mid-February 1939 for a German-Romanian economic agreement made to Wohltat by the Romanians may have led him to believe that the possibilities for gain were greater than they in fact were — hence the March 10, 1939, German proposals that Romania postpone its industrial development further and that its oil and agricultural resources be placed at the complete disposal of the Third Reich. Tilea's demarche forced Wohltat to amend his proposals and his intentions of implementing them in a secret treaty and instead to negotiate a public agreement.

The outcome is clear: for the time being Romania's oil continued to remain under British and French control and the interpretation of Gafencu that "[the treaty] was definitely favorable to the Reich, but not disadvantageous to the Romanian economy" is largely true.[44] King Carol and his government assuaged German ire and threw Berlin a bone by appearing to have granted concessions to Germany and headed off any precipitous action to overthrow the Romanian government. At the same time they could keep their options open by accepting the Western guarantee of Romanian independence and thereby demonstrate their freedom of action and intimidation by Hitler. Gafencu told the Germans frankly that it was not the British, but the Romanians, who sought the British guarantee.

The Soviet leaders regarded all this with some suspicion. Moscow believed the visit to the Soviet capital of R. S. Hudson ostensibly to discuss economic affairs with the Soviet Government was to cloak the real intentions of the Chamberlain government and designed to create the impression that the British were interested in opposing German expansion into Eastern Europe and the USSR.[45] Soviet historians believed the Ashton-Gwatkin mission and the conversations with German industrialists, Göring and other Nazi officials centered on giving Germany a free hand in Eastern Europe in lieu of concession in the former German colonies, tariff concessions in the empire, etc. and that such encouragement of German expansion into the east was a prelude to the German negotiations with Romania.[46]

The March 23, 1939, economic agreement with Germany hitherto has been presented as a complete Nazi triumph and the virtual conversion of Romania into a Nazi satellite.[47] The new economic minister, Walter Funk, described it as the future model for other East European states and their economic arrangements with Germany. The initial decision was made by King Carol in discussions with Hitler and Göring in Germany and later through Bratianiu, the Liberal Party leader, who met with Göring and Wohltat in the first week of February 1939.

The final agreement that followed the German-Romanian negotiations contains five articles pledging Romania to develop its agricultural and mineral resources to satisfy Germany's economic needs through mixed German-Romanian commissions. Germany agreed to supply Romania with various forms of weaponry, planes and other military commodities. In a secret addition to the treaty the Romanians agreed to export deliveries amounting to 200–250 million marks and to stimulate oil production and refinement through mixed commissions.[48] In actual fact the Germans were unable to increase new oil production: Romania's oil output fell steadily after 1938–1939 from 6,610 to 6,240 tons for those years to about half that by 1944.[49] Though the Germans failed to secure control of the British and French share of Romania's oil in 1939, by the following year the Germans effectively took control of the Romanian oil fields. In 1940 the Germans possessed over half of the reduced total (5,010 tons of crude oil), so, in that sense, the March 23, 1939, economic agreement was really a prelude to complete German control of Romanian oil.[50]

The fears of Daladier that once Germany had secured control of Romania's oil it would be in a position to wage a "war of attrition" against the Western Powers had not yet materialized. Against the possibility of a German invasion of Romania and seizure of the oil wells, the British and Romanians reserved the weapon of razing the wells.

The Romanian slide toward Germany was a direct consequence of the feeble Western efforts to shore up Romania both economically and politically. The Franco-Romanian Trade Agreement signed approximately a week later did not encourage the shipment of oil to France because of the low French price, and the competition of Romanian grain on the French market caused similar results.[51] This was further compounded by the meager results achieved by the mission of Leith-Ross to Romania about which we shall hear further. The British initially promised one million pounds credit in February 1939, which it increased to five million by the time the British-Romanian trade agreement was signed in May 1939, and agreed to take only 200,000 tons of Romanian wheat at a favorable exchange rate. These paltry concessions were insufficient to raise hopes in Bucharest of British and French economic support. Resistance in the British government from the hide-bound, free trade–oriented government departments "against political trade" prevailed.

At his meeting with the British in November 1938 the Romanian ruler inquired whether Chamberlain agreed to recognize Eastern Europe as a German sphere of influence. Chamberlain declared that "natural forces... seemed to make it inevitable that Germany should enjoy a preponderant position in the economic field," but that the British were not "disinterested" in further "political trade" with Romania.[52] This refrain gradually became official British policy. The only real gain in Carol's visit was the British government's agreement to consider sending an economic mission to Bucharest. Promises of British credit were not forthcoming and Leith-Ross seemed to be skeptical of Romania's ability to pay back any credits extended to it.[53]

The literature of the post–World War II era suggests that the Third Reich's policy toward its eastern neighbors was a continuation of policies begun in the Weimar period. It occurred in phases, incrementally unfolding within the political and economic desiderata of the moment.

The early Nazi period (1934–1936) set the stage for the formation of a quasi neo-colonial hinterland in Eastern Europe in which the small countries of Eastern Europe would continue to hold a formal sovereignty and, through the inter-penetration of their economies by a whole panoply of commercial and capital investment organizations, would gradually be drawn into the German economic orbit. As Britain, France and the United States already had commercial blocs of their own, they could hardly object to a Reichsbloc in Central and Eastern Europe. At the root of the growth of these blocs was the collapse of world trade in the 1930s and the struggle for market share overlaid by the continued existence of the colonial system. As long as the world capitalist market was unable to transcend the colonial system that straitjacketed it — which would not occur until long after World War II — it could not resolve the trade constraints at the heart of the world economic crisis.

Advocates of a Reichsbloc in Eastern Europe included Posse, State Secretary for the Economy, Foreign Minister Neurath, Schacht, Bülow, State Secretary in the Foreign Office, the Reich Organization of German Industry, the representatives of heavy industry and other industrial groups and finally the military leaders. In a 1924 memorandum to the Economic Ministry, Posse saw trade policy as a point of departure for a foreign policy with "imperialist horizons."[54] Minister for Economy Dietrich in the Brüning government had urged an arrangement with the Eastern European countries "as perhaps the most important task of German trade policy." Dietrich called for "a new system," once the American trade agreement expired in 1935, in which the constriction of trade could be overcome by extensive bilateral agreements and complementary exchanges of goods with the Soviet Union and South America.[55]

Hjalmar Schacht initially advocated a policy of global dimensions based upon Germany's acquisition of colonies, rejecting expansion into Europe as threatening to Germany's neighbors, but his political opportunism led him to modify his global conceptions to fit Hitler's rearmament program and, in the end, caused his downfall. The sharpening conflict between Schacht's Pan-German colonial plans and the autarchy-driven *Grossraumwirtschaft* was decided in the mid-1930s in favor of the latter. Although Schacht saw South America as a more lucrative area for German trade, he accommodated Nazi plans to expand the Southeastern market and promoted them by trips to the region.

The 1930s German Southeastern trade offensive stemmed primarily from economic and political motives, but also was influenced by perceptions of *"Einkreisung"* (encirclement) by the Western Powers, and the Eastern European area as a region where Western cartels had still not completely penetrated and qualitatively less competitive goods could be marketed without fear of Western competition.[56] German big business generally favored a commercial imperialist expansion to the east, but not at the expense of its Western European and overseas markets. Duisberg, of I. G. Farben, suggested a "double strategy" of pressing overseas trade opportunities "in all the markets of the world" and expansion of the *Mitteleuropa* export market in the event of a decline in the international market.[57] However, there was to be no abandonment of the European market: Why, asked Duisberg, should the chemical industry even with the help of [trade] preferences, for the sake of its 3.4% trade with Southeastern Europe endanger the remaining 96.6%?[58] However, despite conflicts within German business over expansion into Eastern Europe, German elite groups generally favored it. For German business it represented a way out of the problem of a stagnating heavy industry produced by rationalization and overcapacity. By exploiting cheaper sources of labor and raw material abroad and gaining new export markets, German business could restore falling profits.

The German military viewed Germany's dearth of raw materials as an Achilles heel affecting its security in the event of an international conflict, and speculated whether this could be overcome through a policy of conquest by the incorporation of Austria and Czechoslovakia and the Southeastern region's gradual economic and political incorporation into the German sphere. The choices became expansion into the Soviet Union as Hitler advised the generals in 1937 — or a more limited imperialist program, as Wehrmacht head General Beck desired, with the incorporation of Austria and the Sudetenland as a final aim.[59] At any rate, the German elite officer class realized like Hitler that an expansionist *Lebensraum* policy would be absolutely necessary to Germany in order to feed its growing population and at the same time provide the Wehrmacht with essential raw material requirements. These aims, military leaders like General Thomas began to see — given the failure of the New Plan and the growing currency and trade crisis — as only attainable by a policy of expansion into the countries on Germany's borders once war broke out. In April 1939 he declared: "The close proximity of the border to our strength and our weak food basis, in view of currency and gold shortages, could act as external impediments and in the event of a future war places us before the decisive question as to whether at the very beginning of a war[,] military operations for the securing and expansion of our limited economic strength will have to be carried out. The decisive means for this will always remain the offensive of the army as it alone can expand the (German) area (occupation of smaller states, Denmark, etc.)."[60]

Though some officers believed that Germany should pursue trade opportunities in the Scandinavian and Northern European area and viewed the expansion of trade in Southeastern Europe with skepticism, by 1939 many in the German military believed in an expansionary policy, if need be by force. These ideas had been orchestrated and accepted throughout wide sections of the elite groups of the German upper class in big business, the military and the bureaucracy. Hitler, then, recedes as the singular, decisive agent for an expansionist war.

Prince Paul (right), Regent of
Yugoslavia, and Adolf Hitler (left)
after a tense conference in June 1939.

Sir Frederick Leith-Ross (right), chief
economic advisor to the British gov-
ernment, and British Prime Minister
Ramsay MacDonald (left) at the World
Economic Conference of the League of
Nations in June 1933.

Sir Robert Vansittart (left), Foreign
Office Permanent Undersecretary,
and Sir Alexander Cadogan (right),
Foreign Office Deputy Undersecretary,
later Permanent Undersecretary after
Vansittart's removal for opposing
Chamberlain's appeasement policy.

Admiral Nicholas Horthy (left),
Regent of Hungary, and Adolf Hitler
(right) during a wartime meeting.

Marshal Josef Pilsudski, Polish Chief of
State, in 1920, six years before he seized
power and became dictator of Poland.

Eduard Beneš, President of
Czechoslovakia, in July 1941
while in exile in London.

King Boris III of Bulgaria
with his wife, Jeanne de Savoie,
in September 1938.

King Carol II of Romania
in November 1938.

Colonel Jozef Beck (left), Polish Foreign Minister, and Leon Noël (right), French Ambassaddor to Poland, who were often at loggerheads over Polish foreign policy, in 1938.

Montagu Norman (right) Governor of the Bank of England, with his friend Hjalmar Schacht (left), German Minister of Economics and President of the Reichsbank, on a visit to England.

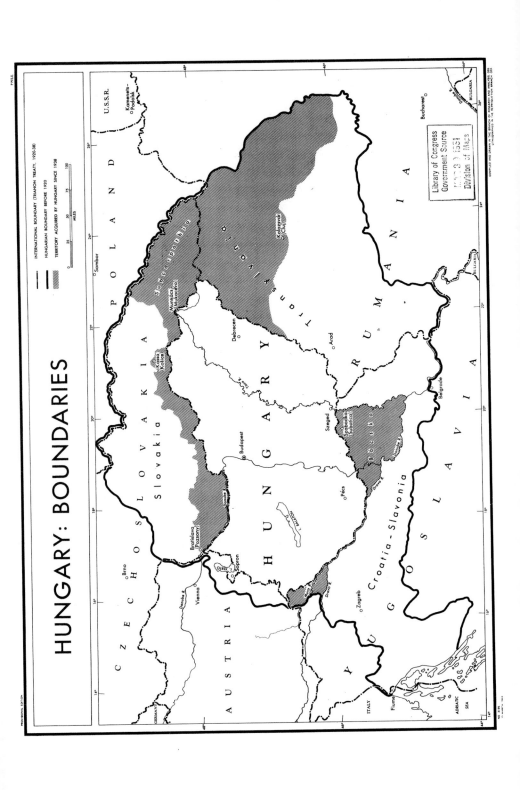

HUNGARY: BOUNDARIES

INTERNATIONAL BOUNDARY (TRIANON TREATY, 1920-38)

HUNGARIAN BOUNDARY BEFORE 1920

TERRITORY ACQUIRED BY HUNGARY SINCE 1938

MILES
0   25   50   75   100

U.S.S.R.

Kamenets-
Podolsk

P O L A N D

C Z E C H O S L O V A K I A

S l o v a k i a

Brno

A U S T R I A

Vienna

GERMANY

ITALY

Fiume

ADRIATIC
SEA

Y U G O S L A V I A

Croatia - Slavonia

Zagreb

Belgrade

R U M A N I A

Bucharest

BULGARIA

Kárpátalja

Munkács
(Mukachevo)

Kassa
(Košice)

Bratislava
(Pozsony)

Sopron

Budapest

Debrecen

Arad

Szeged

Pécs

Erdély

Kolozsvár
(Cluj)

Bácska

Szabadka
(Subotica)

Sombor

Drava R.

Danube R.

Tisza R.

Like Posse and Schacht in the Ministry for Economy, Neurath and Bülow in the German Foreign Office planned a reorientation of German trade policy that would make use of Germany's import capacity by taking advantage of the Depression crisis then in full swing in order to make Germany independent of the constraints of the international market. In practice this meant a departure from the most-favored-nation principle which the trade wars of the 1930s had encouraged. Neurath's outline of foreign trade policy recommended putting aside foreign trade conflicts with England until "other political questions were clarified" and cultivating good trade relations with countries traditionally friendly to Germany (Sweden, Holland, Switzerland) and closer trade connections with Southeastern Europe. Bülow's note of March 13, 1933, articulated fears that Germany would never be able to extricate itself from dependence upon foreign markets, namely, Western Europe and the United States, and anticipating greater trade conflict with the United States and England, saw Germany's future in cultivating trade relations with the Soviet Union and Southeastern Europe. These ideas were expanded upon in detail by Neurath in the April 7, 1933, session of the cabinet, emphasizing the Soviet Union as Germany's greatest export customer and flank cover against Poland. Tariff preferences would be given to Romania, Yugoslavia and Hungary "in order to gain political influence and beyond that, to gain this important market region for our exports." The German thrust into the Southeastern region was also aimed at breaking up the Little Entente and preventing Czechoslovakia from gravitating toward Poland. This could be done, Bülow indicated in his March memorandum, by opening up Germany's import market to these economically distressed countries and "would most likely influence the direction of the foreign policy of Yugoslavia and Romania in their present catastrophic situation."[61] These plans were put into effect in 1934 to counter Italy's efforts to increase its influence in the Danubian region.

The unanticipated decline of the Soviet market after 1933 accelerated Germany's moves to increase its trade with Latin America and Southeastern Europe. Until then the Soviet Union had been the primary market for German goods. Before the Nazi seizure of power, the Soviet Union had been the second most important trading partner of Germany after Holland. As the figures in Table 10–12 show, Germany sent the largest amount of goods to the USSR, reaching 42.5% by 1933.

Table 10–12. Soviet Import Trade, 1933–1935 (in percentages)[62]

	1933	1934	1935
Germany	42.5	12.4	9.0
England	8.8	19.9	18.8
USA	4.8	7.7	12.2
Netherlands	1.7	6.8	8.8
Italy	4.8	5.1	2.3
France	1.5	5.0	7.3

Table 10–13. German Trade with the USSR, 1925–1934[63]

	Imports from USSR		Exports to USSR	
	mill.Rm	% of total imports	mill.Rm	% total exports
1925	209.1	1.7	250.0	2.8
1931	303.5	4.5	762.7	7.9
1932	270.9	5.8	625.8	10.9
1933	–	–	–	5.8
1934	–	–	–	1.5

The Soviet Union's considerable share of German machinery exports fell from 72.3% in 1933 to only 30% in 1935. German exports to the Soviet Union amounted to 10.9% of Germany's total export trade in 1932 but by 1934 it had fallen to 1.5% and had, as Dörte Doering notes, factually almost ceased to exist (see Table 10–13).

High German prices, Hitler's patent dislike of the Soviet Union, German unwillingness to advance sufficient loans, Schacht's insistence in the 1934 trade negotiations that the Soviet Union pay its exchange debts partially in gold and currency and finally German industry's declining interest in the Soviet market once rearmament began — all contributed to the collapse of the Soviet market.[64] In addition, whether for ideological or economic reasons or both, the Soviet Union began to avoid trading with Germany. Large German trade credits offered by Schacht to the Soviet Union also met with stiff resistance in the German Foreign Office and Treasury Department and forced the German Minister for Economy to disavow the German offers.

On the face of it the Eastern European countries benefited by their clearing arrangements with Germany, which after 1938 received roughly about one half of their exports. The overall terms of trade are cited in Tables 10–14 and 10–15 for those countries. Without the increased German trade they would not have been so favorable and declined like Czechoslovakia which did not benefit from a bilateral arrangement with Germany.

However, such an analysis rests on dry, bare bones statistics without reference to and removed from any historical framework and consequently is skewed and drained of dramatic content. In fact, the historical documents reveal that the German chancelleries and governmental departments were persistently engaged during the Weimar and Nazi eras in purposive efforts to bring Danubian Europe into a form of economic imperialism subjugated to the Third Reich which became all the more imperative as Hitler's rearmament program got under way after 1936.

In their lopsided trade with Germany all of the states of Southeastern Europe, with the possible exception of Bulgaria, experienced grave dysfunctions and other difficulties. In the case of Czechoslovakia and Poland, Western European and U.S. capital and trade overshadowed German and they were able to maintain their economic independence. Hence, Hitler had to resort to coercion and military force to subjugate those two countries rather than through the commercial route used against the other Eastern

Table 10–14. Terms of Trade of Various Eastern European Countries, 1929–1934 (1928=100)

	1929	1930	1931	1932	1933	1934
Czechoslovakia	98.4	106.4	116.9	126.9	129.3	131.7
Hungary	90.7	89.1	83.3	83.7	79.7	93.1
Yugoslavia	125.3	121.8	98.3	82.4	95.3	99.8

Taken from M. C. Kaser, *The Economic History of Eastern Europe,* Oxford, 1986, II, p. 217, table 12.21, citing League of Nations, Rev. of World Trade, 1938, pp. 76, 79–81.

Table 10–15. Terms of Trade of Various Eastern European Countries, 1934–1938 (1933=100)

	1934	1935	1936	1937	1938
Czechoslovakia	102	98	95	83	
Bulgaria	100	108	120	117	123
Hungary	118	123	125	113	119
Romania	97	102	112	138	
Yugoslavia	107	117	116	124	135

Taken from Kaser, *Economic History of Eastern Europe,* II, p. 247, table 12.39; cf. Lampe and Jackson, *Balkan Economic History, 1850–1950,* table 12.10.

European states. Similarly Britain's ability to maintain its trade share with the Baltic and Scandinavian regions and even to make slight gains increased pressure for a military solution to solve the problem of raw material and foodstuff shortages. The figures in Tables 10–14 and 10–15 indicate that Czechoslovakia's terms of trade rose in the first half of the 1930s while the Southeastern countries' declined in that period. This situation was reversed in the period from 1934 to 1938 when Czechoslovakia's terms of trade declined and those of the Southeastern countries rose. This probably was due to Western trade dominance in Czechoslovakia plus adverse world market conditions, and German trade dominance in the Southeastern countries.

But the German plans were more far-reaching: for the Southeastern region the initial stage of commercial expansion was to be one of incorporation and integration, followed by outright exploitation and extortion, after 1939, of the region's material wealth. The dim outline of the later fate of those countries could be seen already to some extent in the policy of passive accounts, dumping of unwanted goods on Balkan markets and German pressures to raise the value of the mark against Southeastern currencies. For the countries on Germany's borders — Austria, Czechoslovakia and Poland — Hitler resorted to a formula of military pressure and conquest.

Chapter 11

Germany Seeks New Markets and Some Old Ones. The Czech-German Trade Struggle in Southeastern Europe

> ... The American trade policy is directed toward a growing encircle-
> ment of Germany. ...
>
> —Herbert Gross, "Deutschlands Handelspolitische
> Einkreisung durch USA," *Wirtschaftsdienst* 41, October 18, 1937

LOSS OF THE SOVIET MARKET after 1932 forced the Nazi government to seek new markets in Southeastern Europe, Northeastern Europe (Poland, the Baltic states and Finland) and the Latin American markets. German trade with Latin America grew greatly in the mid-1930s, but German trade imbalances also grew, as the figures in Table 11–1 indicate, from 47.4 million Rm in 1933 to 214 in 1937 and 180.6 million Rm in 1938. In 1935 German clearing debts came to 500,000,000 Rm, but in 1938 fell to half that figure, according to Ellis, aided perhaps by the seizure of Austria and the Sudetenland. (See also the figures in chapter 12, p. 280).

Table 11–1. German Trade with Some Latin American Countries, 1933–1938 (in Rm)

	1933	1934	1935	1936	1937	1938
Total Imports	288.6	325.1	472.5	448.0	732.2	677.0
Total Exports	241.2	226.7	329.6	410.1	518.1	496.4
Total Balance	−47.4	−98.4	−142.9	−37.9	−214.1	−180.6

Taken from: Howard S. Ellis, *German Exchange Control in Central Europe* pp. 386–387. The countries are Argentina, Bolivia, Brazil, Chile, Colombia, Mexico and Peru.

While German exports to Latin America grew, imports grew even more. With the loss of the Soviet market, one of the brighter spots was the Northeastern European region, but this hardly made up for the loss of the Soviet market. The Southeastern European region was fast reaching the end of its ability to export more raw materials and the Germans, by 1938, had concluded that they would have to seek elsewhere for their material needs.

The Scandinavian region, where the traditional practice was to "sell in Britain and buy in Germany," in the inter-war period "became a stage on which

Anglo-German rivalries were played out." In the late 1930s because of its geographic position and raw materials it became a zone of increasingly intense economic competition. Elements in both the British and German governments diffidently entertained notions of drawing the region into a loose connection with either the British Empire or a German *Grossraumwirtschaft*. Britain succeeded in raising its exports to Scandinavia by 18% in the period from 1929 to 1938 representing 9.1% of total British exports against only 5.1% in 1929. Though German exports always exceeded British exports, they amounted to only 12.9% in 1938 of total German exports against 10.2% in 1929. Though British imports were quantitatively greater than Germany's, the Scandinavian share of the German import market grew faster, from 7.4% to 11.4% between 1929 and 1938 as opposed to the British market where its share rose from 9.1% to 10.1% over this same period.[1] The gains were made by Britain and Germany largely at the expense of the U.S., Poland and other states which provoked some bitterness in the American government since the German gains were made through bilateral clearing agreements with Denmark and Finland.[2]

German aspirations to incorporate the Scandinavian countries into the future *Grossraumwirtschaft* had ideological as well as economic motives: in his advice to the newly appointed minister to Finland, Hitler emphasized: "we have to direct our expansion towards the Ostsee-Raum (i.e., the Baltic)." A German report almost on the eve of the war in July 1939 reiterated similar sentiments: "the annexation of the Northern region is indispensable for the *Grosswirtschaftraum*."[3] The Germans did not succeed in outdistancing the British significantly in the region's trade and gains made were more at the expense of other countries' share of the northern European trade. Of greater significance is the increased role the Scandinavian region played in the import trade of Germany, whereas for England the export trade to the area expanded more than ever. Scandinavia and the Southeastern European market exported more raw materials to the Third Reich than ever before, enabling the German war economy to continue functioning without a breakdown. In the last analysis, despite the proposals of Laurence Collier, the energetic head of the Foreign Office's Northern Department, to counter German bilateral agreements with similar British agreements with those countries, both the Board of Trade and the Foreign Office preferred to muddle along in the well-trodden path of free trade. Germany's willingness — as in Southeastern Europe — to pay prices far above the world market made it difficult to compete with.[4]

Similar traditional trade patterns in the Baltic states — sell to Britain, buy in Germany — German clearing arrangements with Estonia and Latvia and German willingness to pay higher than world prices impeded British exports from outdistancing German exports to the Baltic countries. Unlike the British government, which was unwilling to mix politics with economics, the Germans had fewer scruples. Moreover, Hitler's strictures in 1933 that economic objectives would take second place to foreign policy, left little doubt that the ultimate aim of Germany's plans for the Baltic states was not merely to knit them economically closer to Germany, but to impose German political domination.[5] Other contradictions, Britain's adverse trade balance with the Baltic states and the unwillingness of the Board of Trade and elements in the government and Foreign Office to challenge German clearing arrangements with the Baltic states and Denmark enabled the Germans to outdistance the British in the Baltic export trade. In the single case of Lithuania in the 1930s, where the dispute over the Memel area created antipathy towards German exports, Britain was able to step up its exports to Lithuania only when Lithuanian imports from Germany plummeted after 1931 and Britain became the dominant exporter to the Lithuanian market.[6] Considering the desire of Waley in the Treasury Department and others in the British government to "leave the thorny path of Central and Eastern Europe to Germany," and to seek a greater share in the Baltic and Scandinavian trade, why the British did not heed the suggestions of Collier and others to challenge the Germans in the Baltic and Scandinavian area by some vigorous countervailing commercial actions is somewhat puzzling. The reason generally offered is that the established pattern of "selling in England and buying in Germany" was difficult to change. Imperial preference and British stodginess and bureaucratic inertia played a certain role. Uppermost was probably some combination of traditional British belief in free trade and the desire to avoid pushing matters to extremes by denying Germany its natural markets in the northern region, while at the same time claiming enough of the northern market to satisfy its commercial interests and also keep the German wolf from the region's door. British torpor was abetted by declining interest in foreign investment in general in favor of investment in England and to a lesser extent the Empire.

In the case of Poland, its interwar economy was dominated by the penetration of foreign capital estimated to be approximately 40% of total share capital in 1937, reaching 44.8% in 1935. The commanding position of foreign capital enabled it to control roughly two-thirds of all joint stock companies.[7] The largest share of foreign capital initially had been held by the Germans in 1931 at 25%; but by 1937 German-held capital declined to 13.8%, largely due to the deliberate efforts of the Polish government following the German-Polish tariff war (1925–1934) which tried to reduce Poland to a client state of Germany.[8] After 1936 the leading investors of foreign capital in Poland were France (31%), U.S. (20%), Germany (18%), Belgium (10%) and the United Kingdom (5%).[9] The German share in Poland's foreign trade also fell from 43.2% of Polish exports and 34.5% of imports in 1924 to 24.1% and 23% respectively in 1938 (see Table 11–2).

Table 11–2. Poland's Foreign Trade by Country, 1938[10]

Countries	% of total imports	% of total exports
Germany	23.0	24.1
Great Britain	11.4	18.2
U.S.A.	12.2	5.3
Sweden	3.5	6.0
Belgium	4.1	4.8
Italy	2.6	5.5
France	3.6	3.8
Netherlands	2.8	4.6

Poland made up for this loss by considerably increasing its overseas trade. Whereas formerly in the 1920s Polish trade had been almost confined to the continent and the U.K. — 97.7% of total Polish trade — Poland began to expand its overseas trade with the Baltic countries, the U.K., the U.S. and even to Asia and Africa.[11] Although German exports to Poland more than doubled in the period 1934–1938 from 55.1 million Rm to 134.1 Rm (155.2 to Greater Germany) and 78.1 Rm to 109.4 Rm (140.8 to Greater Germany), German imports lagged behind in the same period.[12] Hence, the Scandinavian and Baltic trade, particularly imports, became increasingly more important for Germany as war approached. The precipitate decline of German exports in both the Polish and the Soviet market in percentage figures from the 1920s was a severe blow to German trade efforts. Although Polish imports outran exports in the period after 1933, Germany did not share in this as much as it had in the previous decade.

Greece also experienced the same pattern of trade as Southeastern Europe with Germany, with the latter taking half of Greece's main export, tobacco, which made up 45%–50% of its total exports in 1938. Germany took 50% in 1936 and more than 43% in 1937. Had Germany curtailed its tobacco purchases the consequence would have been catastrophic for Greece. Germany reexported a part of the Greek tobacco product for foreign currency. In 1936 Great Britain took only a very small part of Greek tobacco exports, 337 tons as opposed to 22,212 tons in the same year for Germany. By 1938 Greece sent 38.5% of its exports to Germany, while importing 30.3% of its goods from the Reich.[13]

In addition to tobacco, Germany imported 41,000 tons of bauxite and 8,422 tons of chrome through a clearing arrangement in which the Germans offered more for Greek goods than the world price while selling 20–30% above the world price level.[14] The Greeks were unable to avoid the lure of the German offers while Britain refused to buy more Greek tobacco. In the period from 1936 to 1938, as shown in Table 11–3, Greece's trade balance was unfavorable with imports exceeding exports.

Table 11–3. Trade Balance of Greece, 1936–1938 (in millions of American gold dollars)[15]

	Imports	Exports
1936	5.47	3.34
1937	6.78	4.26
1938	6.51	4.41

As Greece's trade with Germany increased, its frozen funds (payments accumulated in Germany for German purchases of Greek goods for which Greece was unable to receive the equivalent in currency or German exported goods) also increased, standing at:

January 1, 1935	12 million Rm[16]
January 1, 1936	24 million Rm

In January–February 1936 Greece's frozen assets in Germany reached 32 million Rm, more than 60% of Greece's exports to Germany in 1935.[17] Greek frozen funds in Germany accumulated throughout 1938–1939 from month to month.[18] However, the British held dominant positions in the extensive Greek mercantile sector through its insurance of Greek vessels and in advancing credit in the public debt through state loans. The Greek state debt in 1938 was larger than that of any of the Balkan states, amounting to 3.719 billion drachmas of which Britain held 55%, the U.S. 7%, France 5% and Switzerland 3.4%.[19] Also, many in the Greek millionaire class had their money invested abroad in Great Britain, British possessions or mixed Anglo-American enterprises. Of the foreign investments comprising £200 million sterling invested in Greece, Britain held over two-thirds, almost completely controlling financial credit institutions, the mercantile fleet, railroads and light industry. German capital in Greece, however, was only between 2 and 4%.[20]

The annexation of Austria and the Czech provinces only intensified the problem of food and raw materials. In Austria following the Anschluss in 1938 and into 1939, demonstrations, disorders and factory strikes broke out when prices rose, food and consumer goods disappeared from the shelves and a qualitative decline of commodities set in. Disgruntlement spread even to the Austrian National Socialists and pro-Nazi groups, quickly dispelling the initial enthusiasm for the Anschluss.[21]

After absorbing Austria and the Czech provinces, Germany remained dependent on imports for 20% of its foodstuffs — as opposed to about 13% before — and for 30% of its raw materials, much higher for certain products like oil (66%), copper (70%), rubber (85%–90%) and aluminum (99%). A worsening trade balance exacerbated the problem: in 1938 it was adverse with 6,051.7 million Rm in imports against 5,619.1 million Rm in exports, but in 1939 it improved with 5,222.2 Rm in exports against 4,796.5 million Rm in imports, but at a greatly reduced volume level.[22] Other imports had to be paid for out of a greatly reduced amount of available foreign currency. Figures for German exports and imports indicate that both had been steadily falling since 1929. Germany's share of foreign trade fell from 31.9 in 1929 to 11.9 in 1939, according to the figures in Table 11–4. These figures are somewhat different from secret German statistical estimates compiled in 1944 lowering these amounts by approximately 2.4% (1929–1932) and 1.2% to 0.1% (1933–1939). To complicate matters, on the eve of the war, Germany's gold and foreign currency reserves stood at only 500 million Rm.[23]

The most important conclusion of this examination of Germany's trade relations is that the loss of the Soviet market forced Germany after 1933, under the strain of rearmament, more and more into non-traditional areas of trade — Southeastern Europe, Latin America, and to a lesser extent the Baltic and Scandinavian region, and Poland. The division of the world market into trading blocs of the Great Powers accelerated the process. Imperialist expansion, once the Soviet market disappeared, given Hitler's intensified rearmament plans, was a foregone conclusion. The trade possibilities in the Scandinavian, Baltic and Polish market did not make up for the loss of the Soviet market because the British rival was able to hold its own in most

Table 11–4. Import, Export and Total Foreign Trade Share of Germany, 1929–1939[24]

Year	Import Share	Export Share	Foreign Trade Share
1929	15.9	15.9	31.9
1932	10.2	12.5	22.7
1933	8.9	10.4	19.4
1934	8.3	7.8	16.1
1935	6.9	7.1	14.1
1936	5.3	7.1	13.5
1937	7.2	7.8	15.0
1938	7.1	6.6	13.8
1939	5.7	6.2	11.9

of those areas. A *"raub krieg,"* or expansionary war, was then probably inevitable particularly when the Southeast lost its potential after 1938.[25]

Though Hitler's knowledge and disinterest in economics were disparaged by Schacht and others, nevertheless, he was certainly conscious of the German economy's deteriorating condition when he told Schacht at the Berlin train station in 1939: "There will be no inflation, Herr Schacht."[26] A recent historian has commented that of all the Great Powers only Germany wanted war "less because the German economy was fully prepared for war (certainly general and prolonged war) than because Germany was going through a severe economic crisis, of which one possible solution was a war of conquest." The process was a circular one. Once Hitler refused to slacken the pace of rearmament "Germany was in a position where she was arming in order to expand, and then had to expand in order to continue to arm." Or put another way by Peter Hayes, who describes Göring as "strip mining the economy" for the sake of rearmament and having "hardened German economic policy into a self-fulfilling prophesy." "Hitler could increasingly justify a militant drive to the East as the solution to the economic problems he had largely imposed."[27]

Göring admitted in 1938 that without Germany's political expansion into the Southeast he would not be able to achieve the goals of the Four Year Plan.[28] From 1936 on Göring really abandoned any further *Grossraumwirtschaft* plans for incorporating those countries into a loose confederacy with the Reich and concentrated on extracting raw materials and foodstuffs from them for the German economy. This accelerated after 1938 when Hitler's successes in Austria and Czechoslovakia in the face of Western debility intensified his naked bid for territorial conquest in Europe. The more grandiose *Grossraumwirtschaft* design was put aside in favor of the open aggrandizement of the Southeastern region.[29]

After March 15, 1939, Hitler remained uncertain what to do next. Up to that point, as he later told the high command of the Wehrmacht, he knew clearly that he would seize Austria and Czechoslovakia. The Sudetenland annexation had only been a "partial solution."

The decision for the march into Bohemia was taken. Then came the establishment of the Protectorate, and with that the basis for the conquest of Poland was laid, but I was at that point still not clear whether I should move first against the east and then against the west or the reverse. Moltke had to contend in his time with the same problem. As it turned out, it came to a struggle against Poland first.[30]

In his drive towards war it is not entirely clear whether Hitler had the complete support of the traditional German ruling class. The theory of a split in the German upper class comes from both historians of the capitalist Western countries and the former socialist German Democratic Republic. According to this view already in 1936 Schacht's proposal to slow up rearmament and steer production into the export market had been supported by the banks, the steel and coal industries, which wanted to return to production for the world market, and some Wehrmacht officials like Colonel Thomas of the Economics and Armaments section of the War Ministry. The war industries such as the aviation and others like the automobile, machine tool and chemical suggest and elements in the Nazi Party leadership like Göring and Ribbentrop and some Wehrmacht leaders in the High Command supported Hitler.[31] I. G. Farben was heavily involved in the Four Year Plan, although its role may have been less than Petzina's figures suggest, and its representatives in the Nazi regime like Carl Krauch opted for expansionary war.[32]

Two years later in 1938 this situation changed in favor of greater support for the thrust towards war. Hitler had succeeded in emasculating the Wehrmacht High Command by removing Generals Blomberg and Fritsch and finally Beck and appointing the pliant generals Brauchitsch and Keitel. The shift of industrial orders from the private firms to the state-controlled organizations like Hermann Göring Werke and the eagerness of the coal and steel barons and the business interests to share in the spoils from the newly annexed regions weakened their resistance to war. Hitler's success in Austria and Czechoslovakia silenced his opposition in the Wehrmacht or at least made it difficult to mount any effective countervailing force against him.

By the summer of 1939 Hitler's hesitations over whether to attack in the west or the east ended. On the eve of the Polish campaign during his August 22 conference Hitler told his generals:

> I thought of turning against the west in a few years and only afterwards against the east...I wanted to establish acceptable relations with Poland in order to fight against the west first, but this plan could not be realized because fundamental conditions changed. It appeared evident to me that Poland would attack us in case of a conflict with the west.[33]

Hitler's decision to attack Poland was also influenced by his belief that the British would not honor their obligations to Poland undertaken in their guarantee of April 1939, otherwise the British would not have offered only £8 million for Poland's defense to the Polish mission sent to London in the summer of 1939. The British envoy to Warsaw, Kennard, and British military figures like General Ironside failed to overcome the financial objections of the government leaders, Chancellor of the Exchequer, Sir John Simon, and Sir Frederick Leith-Ross.[34] Ribbentrop encouraged Hitler's conviction that Britain would not honor its obligations to Poland; the German Foreign Minister took an even stronger line in dealing with Poland than did Hitler during Beck's sojourn in Berlin in January 1939 and Ribbentrop's visit to Warsaw.[35]

The fate of Poland was also influenced by Germany's loss of trade with the U.K., France and the U.S. in the 1930s which the demands of the internal German market and the rearmament program only made more acute. Attempts to make up for these losses by shifting the focus to the Southeastern European market and Latin America for a time succeeded in raising volume as a short-term expedient. Germany's share of Latin American imports rose from 10% in 1928 to 15% in 1938 and its exports from 10% to 12%. German trade with those two regions is even larger when examined from the standpoint of the mid-1930s (see Table 11–5).

Table 11–5. German Trade with Latin America and Southeastern Europe, 1934–1937 (in marks and percentage of trade)

	Rm millions			% of Trade		
	1934	1936	1937	1934	1936	1937
Imports from:						
Latin America	461	578	915	10.9	13.7	16.8
Six Countries of Southeastern Europe	316	505	672	7.1	12.0	12.3
Exports to:						
Latin America	267	511	663	6.5	10.8	11.2
Six Countries of Southeastern Europe	222	457	667	5.3	9.5	11.3

Figures for percentage of trade taken from: The League of Nations, *The Network of World Trade,* 1942, table 28, p. 55. Figures for Reichmarks taken from: The League of Nations, *Review of World Trade,* 1937, p. 39. The six countries of southeastern Europe are Bulgaria, Greece, Hungary, Romania, Turkey and Yugoslavia.

Though Germany made up for its losses by increasing trade with Southeastern Europe and Latin America, its deficit position with those areas placed a greater burden upon Germany's over-burdened finances and only bolsters the conclusion that Nazi Germany's tradeoff of increased market volume for larger deficits was in the end very costly. Thus, Schacht already in 1935 complained when the terms of trade began to turn against Germany and called for Germany's reintegration into the world market, which meant the end of autarchy and rearmament. In Hitler's view this would not have solved Germany's over-population and food problems, and only Britain could lever such a return to the world market, but it would have been at the price of future German good behavior — a price Hitler would never pay.

These pressures probably already influenced Hitler in 1937 to accelerate his timetable for war in 1939 instead of 1943 as he had originally planned. After the war Göring testified, as we have mentioned previously in chapter 1, that Hitler did not intend to lower the standard of living to satisfy the food situation as he could not accept a setback that would return Germany to the 1932 situation. Nor did Hitler see a solution through international commercial agreements because Germany was not able to fulfill her (barter) obligations to which she would have been committed. Therefore, the only solution was through expansion in order to obtain agricultural living space.[36]

As to the Eastern European countries, they were not monolithic in their trade relations with Germany. Only Bulgaria and Hungary could be said to be firmly in the Nazi trade bloc, for political reasons, as they were revisionist powers, and because they needed German trade to avoid economic calamity.

After 1938 Germany no longer needed to make attractive offers for foodstuffs and raw materials or contend with Austrian or Czech competitors. By 1938 its import surplus from the Balkans had evaporated, forcing Germany to move to military means to maintain the flow of goods or to invade Poland and the USSR.[37]

From a purely statistical standpoint based upon the terms of trade, when judged from the 1920s base (1926–1928=100), Yugoslavia barely gained and may even have lost. A mid-1930s index (1934=100) of trade with Germany, probably a truer index, shows Yugoslavia benefited. But this must be qualified against losses registered with the non-clearing countries, the problems of a skewed trade with Germany, unwanted goods, etc.; the results in this case seem less advantageous.

Hungary shows the same ill effects of its trade with Germany and by 1939 had become, in Göring's words, a "vassal" of Germany. Only Bulgaria could claim to have benefited. The Germans built roads, formed mining companies and sent the Bulgars machinery, medical equipment, technical products and in exchange took Bulgarian tobacco and other imports.

An engrossing postscript to this is the shadowy struggle between Germany and Czechoslovakia for a dominant position in the Southeast that has only recently come to light.[38] The Czechoslovaks quickly realized after World War I that they could not remain a viable state if Germany expanded its economic power in Central and Southeastern Europe to a hegemonic position there to compensate for the loss of its pre-war colonies. In the following detailed discussion of Czechoslovak trade and investment in the other Southeastern European countries, the reader should bear in mind that although Czechoslovakia was not a Great Power, it had considerable investment capital resources and industrial strength. As Germany's eastern expansionist ambitions threatened its very existence, it was to Czechoslovakia's interest to prevent Germany from gaining a commercial stranglehold in Romania and Yugoslavia, a virtual certainty if the Western Powers were unwilling to accept the agricultural surpluses of the Balkan region. The Little Entente would be economically undermined and Czechoslovakia would be politically isolated. To prevent this from occurring the United States, hostile to preferential trade in principle, acted to prevent Germany from gaining an economic foothold in Eastern Europe. The United States deliberately gave Czechoslovakian exports a privileged position on the American market while discriminating against competing German exports, making Czechoslovakia a kind of surrogate of the United States and the Western Powers. Besides this, Czechoslovak banks and industry cooperated with and supplemented Western capital in their efforts to exploit and develop Southeastern European mining, industry and commerce. As Teichova has shown, Czechoslovak banks and industry had close ties with Western European and American capital and was in many ways a surrogate of Western capital.

A *coup d'oeil* should be directed first at Czechoslovakia's inter-war economic and political conditions. The power center in the political economy of Czechoslovakia was the Czech banks, responsible between the wars for a good deal of the economic and social damage and misery in the country. In the opinion of one observer, at least, "Czech bankers, though keeping discreetly in the background, virtually matched the political generals who plagued other countries. Instead of palace coups and putsches, monetary operations and credit management were the principal political weapons in Czechoslovakia."[39] The banks forced the acceptance of a deflationary policy that came in two waves: the first one in the early 1920s purportedly to stabilize the chaotic monetary situation brought on by the greatly inflated Austro-Hungarian currency still in use and also to stabilize currency exchange rates, which in 1923 caused the widespread unemployment of about 450,000 people. It was "a brutal attempt to restore pre-war values" that only half-succeeded in its goals.[40]

This verdict is not entirely shared by the Czech-inclined British historian, Elizabeth Wiskemann, in her classic 1938 study of Czechoslovakia, in which, speaking of the social distress in the German populated areas, she describes the deflationary action of the Czech banks as "partly inevitable and partly the result of a mistaken, but not malevolent policy."[41] But as this policy recurred again in the mid-1930s during which those who benefited from a harder currency policy, namely the banks themselves, came out ahead, the judgment seems questionable.

The economic and social distress which followed the reorganization of the currency in the 1920s ordered by the first Minister of Finance, Dr. Rašin, especially hurt the more vulnerable Sudeten German banks and businesses heavily engaged in foreign trade in Germany and the former lands of the Austro-Hungarian Empire, which collapsed, creating a great deal of social distress and ill-feeling against the Czechs in the German-populated areas. When a wild post-war inflation struck hard in Austria and Germany, the Sudeten Germans had already lost money invested in Austrian and German banks and industries, so that the currency reorganization mishap inflicted even greater suffering and distress. The collapsing German and Austrian currency sent the Czech crown higher and trade plummeted, forcing to the wall many Sudeten firms heavily engaged in the export market. The greater part of the unemployed, as a consequence, tended to be Sudeten Germans. The purchase of bankrupt Sudeten German, Austrian and German firms and banks by the financially stronger Czech banks, at bargain prices, added to the resentment felt by many Sudeten Germans for the Czech Slavs whom they had regarded before the war with a certain disdain and after the war had hoped to be annexed by Germany.[42] Aided by these acquisitions and the bank concentrations of the interwar period, by 1937 six commercial banks held 56.3% of total share capital of all banks and almost half of all deposits, further increasing the political power of the banks.[43]

The second ill-considered deflationary action of the banks during the 1930s provoked by the Czech banks caused even more unemployment — 920,000 people, almost one-third of the entire work force.[44]

Two major Czech banking groups dominated the financial sector of the country and also played leading roles in the direction of the government and foreign trade. The first group headed by Živnostenska Bank controlled the Ministry of Finance, in fact, functioning as the Ministry of the Economy in the early years of the country and through it over the central monetary organization which later became the Czechoslovak National bank. The other, the Prague Credit Bank (Pragobank), allied with the Agrarian Bank. These banks first took over (foreign) German bank holdings which had foundered after the war and later between themselves gradually began to absorb the locally owned banks. The banks shared with the government the direction of foreign trade policy through a special department in the Ministry of Foreign Affairs, always headed by the chairman of Živnobanka, Dr. Preiss. The other group had important connections with the two main power centers, the Agrarian Party and the Castle (i.e., Hradchany Castle, the seat of the government), the latter composed of intellectuals, professionals and trade unionists, with less knowledge of business and finance, and thus beholden to the more hard-headed Czech Agrarianists with their agricultural and business backgrounds.

In 1926 the National Democrats, the party of Živnobanka, left the governing coalition and the Finance Ministry was taken over by Dr. Englis, the leading Czech economist of the time. The Agrarian Party group, previously dominant in the Defense Ministry and in the armaments industry, allied with Pragobank, and the Anglo-Bank carried out a successful deflationary policy which promoted a short-lived boom and recovery from the worst effects of the war. By 1924, Czechoslovak industry reached its pre-war level and by 1929 reached 140% of that figure before being interrupted by the Depression of the 1930s. The conservative Czech governments and banks made matters worse by clinging to the gold standard longer than Britain and the United States and only devalued by 20% in 1934. By 1933 imports rose because of the high exchange rate and exports fell to 60% of their pre-war level. Higher tariff levels in 1930 for agricultural produce from Poland, Hungary and the Southeastern countries brought trade from those countries almost to a standstill.[45]

The banks benefited as the peasantry needed money which only the banks could supply. The Agrarian Party became the strongest party in the country and maintained high protective tariffs for their peasant clients against grains and other agricultural commodities imported from the Southeastern countries. In retaliation, Hungary, the major supplier of agricultural products and the main buyer of Czechoslovak timber and textile products, raised its tariffs and the resultant tariff war reduced mutual trade by 15 and 20% of its previous level. As the Czechoslovak textile industry was a major exporter, the reduction of its exports to a quarter of the 1925–1928 level meant about a 50% cut in the industry's production and newer recruits to the growing ranks of the unemployed.[46] The figures in Table 11–6 give some idea of the decline in trade in Czechoslovakia to the early years of the Depression.

Table 11–6. Czechoslovak Foreign Trade, 1926–1933 (in Czechoslovak crowns)

Year	Imports	Exports	Balance
1926	15,276,601	17,755,025	+2,478,424
1927	17,960,410	20,133,448	+2,173,038
1928	19,190,718	21,205,057	+2,014,339
1929	19,962,258	20,496,921	+534,663
1930	15,712,400	17,471,881	+1,759,481
1931	11,764,187	13,118,574	+1,354,387
1932	7,486,710	7,342,659	−144,051
1933	5,831,091	5,854,696	+23,605

These are the official Czechoslovak trade figures as supplied by Elizabeth Wiskemann, *Czechs and Germans*, p. 165.

As trade with the convertible exchange countries had become extremely limited, it became necessary to resort to the clearing trade increasingly adopted by other countries to make trade possible at all. But the erroneous deflationary policy and dogged adherence to the gold standard hamstrung the economy. When Czechoslovakia finally devalued with respect to the gold standard by one-sixth, it aided trade with the countries using convertible currencies, but made imports from the debtor countries one-sixth more expensive. As the figures in Table 11–7 show, income from exports in 1933 was only 29% of that in 1929. By 1937, export income still lagged 58% below what it had been in 1929.

Table 11–7. Czechoslovak Exports and Imports, Selected Years 1921–1937 (in millions of Czechoslovak crowns rounded to the nearest million)

Year	Imports	Exports
1921	23,685	29,458
1924	15,855	17,035
1929	19,988	20,499
1933	5,831	5,923
1937	10,980	11,983

Official Czechoslovak figures supplied by Zora P. Pryor, "Czechoslovak Economic Development in the Interwar Period," in Mamatey and Luža, *A History of the Czechoslovak Republic 1918–1948* (Princeton, N.J., 1973), p. 193, Table 2.1.

As Pryor concludes, "the ability to control imports was crucial in maintaining a balance of trade surplus," but foreign demand played a less important role in economic recovery between 1934 and 1937 than during the previous decade.[47] More importantly this tight control on imports exercised by the Agrarian Party primarily to keep internal agricultural prices high gravely injured the foreign policy of Beneš in maintaining the cohesiveness of the Little Entente.

Clearing account balances in the Southeastern European countries became frozen. This undermined Czechoslovakia's policy, supported by the United States through its own trade policy, of preventing Germany from penetrating the economies of the Southeast and the Little Entente countries and undermined the entire diplomacy of Beneš.[48] Had Britain not introduced its preferential tariff system in 1932, Czechoslovakia might not have had to introduce higher tariffs against the Eastern European countries. The major beneficiaries of this mistaken policy of devaluation were the Czech banks like Živnobanka into whose hands the bankrupt export firms passed. Thus, the main cause of the trade and industrial problems of Czechoslovakia during the interwar period may be laid at the door of the devaluation policy pursued by the government.

In the 1920s Czechoslovakia repaid debts to other countries and placed its trade on a stable footing, signing commercial agreements in 1921 and 1922 with Germany and Austria who took 47% and 40% of Czechoslovak imports, respectively. Czechoslovakia's first loans for its war-ravaged economy came ironically from Germany, hence Czechoslovakia refused, at the urging of France, to array itself against Germany. In the early 1920s the flow of Czechoslovak trade patterns obstructed its commercial expansion into the Balkans: it bought its raw materials in Western Europe and sold its finished products in Central and Eastern Europe. The Balkan states thus could not sell their agricultural surpluses in the Czechoslovak market. The Depression was even more catastrophic for Czechoslovakia than Western Europe, forcing it to conclude bilateral clearing agreements with Western and Central European, Baltic and Eastern European countries. The powerful Czechoslovak Agrarian Party resisted granting preferences for the agricultural products of the Little Entente states (Romania and Yugoslavia), curtailing further trade with the Balkan region.

By 1930 the Germans gradually moved away from protectionism and notified the Yugoslavs of their intent to grant preferences in exchange for concessions in merchandise. The Yugoslav Foreign Minister and the Yugoslav Minister of Agriculture informed the Czechoslovak minister plenipotentiary in Belgrade that Yugoslavia would have to turn toward Germany if Czechoslovakia did not satisfy its demands, thus driving a wedge between the Little Entente countries. Czechoslovak diplomatic observers in Sofia watched in chagrin as Germany gained a foothold in Bulgarian imports. Beneš, the Czechoslovak Foreign Minister, understood that, without preferences from Western countries, Southeastern Europe would not be able to resist German encroachments; and on April 4, 1931, he submitted a kind of middle European "Danubia" program in which Yugoslavia, Czechoslovakia, Romania, Hungary and Poland would receive preferences from

France, Germany, Italy, Austria and Czechoslovakia for their agricultural products while the Western Powers would not receive any preferences for their industrial products. Beneš noted: "thus, there will disappear in Southeastern Europe the principal cause of the influence of Germany which will no longer be able to utilize its enormous consumption capacity and its economic superiority to win over the agricultural countries to its design." The plan was reworked and submitted to the League of Nations in May 1931 by Briand and François-Poncet, obliging the Western Powers to give preferences to Balkan agricultural wares only to the extent that they received preferences for their industrial products in Eastern European markets. The plan resembled the bilateral clearing system Germany later offered those countries. But French business did not respond sufficiently and the Little Entente countries objected to lowering tariffs on their own agricultural products.

A new plan urged by the Czechoslovaks and named after André Tardieu, the French Minister of Foreign Affairs, envisaged a Central and Eastern European trading bloc similar to the former Austro-Hungarian, in which the small Danubian states could sell their agricultural produce without worrying about purchasing industrial products. The plan also anticipated a future monetary union. But both Germany and Italy feared such a concentration of power in a region vital to their interests and from which their influence would be excluded. Britain was not favorable and the Danubian states were skeptical of their ability to absorb their own surpluses, which they believed only a third market could do. Although France concluded preferential accords with Austria and the Balkan states, good harvests in 1931 and 1932 forced the French to reduce their imports. The French were also parsimonious and grudging in their loans to the Little Entente states in 1932 and the powerful Czechoslovak Agrarian Party obstinately opposed removing tariff barriers for agricultural commodities, facilitating greater German trade success in the Danubian basin. An exception was preferences offered to Yugoslavia and kept secret and paid after 1931 to the Czechoslovak arms factories in order to cover their frozen credits.

In 1932 a new attempt to solve the problem of agricultural surplus through the "Pact of Integration of the Little Entente" immediately ran into difficulties: reorganization of the economic structures needed for the division of labor between those states was too daunting a task. Czechoslovak agrarian interests complained that the plan would mean subsidizing agricultural imports and Czech industrialists thought that their light industry exports would conflict with the desire of those countries to industrialize and produce their own armaments. The Czechoslovak agrarians declared that Romania and Yugoslavia should seek their own trade outlets and imposed customs duties on agricultural products, but conceded a preferential treatment of one-third for such imports. The Little Entente passed a resolution encouraging further exchanges. In 1933 Czechoslovakia gave Romania 16.9 million crowns as preferences for wheat, for reexport to a third market, and a supplement per head of livestock. Yugoslavia received similar preferences; and Czechoslovak producers supplied weapons and industrial products to the Little Entente countries. This had become necessary as the Czechoslovak Agrarian-inspired grain monopoly, established in 1934, kept the price of bread grains well above the world market price so that imports of wheat and wheat flour gradually dwindled. In 1930 these imports still amounted to 290,000 and 190,000 tons, respectively, but by 1938 Czechoslovakia was a net exporter of wheat. Other agricultural imports like meat also suffered. In sum, it was a policy benefiting the "medium stratum of shrewd, money-oriented farmers" while business and industry suffered.

Apart from the Little Entente states, Czechoslovakia concentrated especially upon Bulgaria whose lucrative sales of tobacco, representing 68% of its tobacco sales in 1933, saved the trade position of Czechoslovakia, which had fallen to one-fifth of the previous year. Czechoslovakia held second place following Germany in the Bulgarian trade. In its major export to Greece, sugar, a triangular trade developed involving reshipment to Hamburg, but Greece complained of high-priced Czechoslovak sugar and the Czechoslovak tobacco administration blocked the purchase of tobacco.

In 1932 Italy concluded the Brocchi Accords with Austria and Hungary granting secret preferences to those countries, and in 1934 Germany signed bilateral trade accords with Hungary and Yugoslavia, weakening Czechoslovakia's trade position in the Danubian region by offering subsidies up to 40% on exports and to 25% on imports. In its determination to capture the high priority Yugoslav market German export subsidies reached up to 70%. By 1936, Beneš's worst fears had occurred: Germany had captured a large part of the Yugoslav trade in the southeast. The construction of a large metallurgical plant at Zenice by Krupp, despite the personal intervention of the Czechoslovak Premier Milan Hodža on behalf of Škoda, dealt a hard blow to Czechoslovak hopes.

In mid-1935 Göring journeyed to the Balkans to sell weaponry in exchange for primary materials. Czechoslovakia did not sell weapons in the region on clearing terms because of fierce Czechoslovak agrarian resistance to agricultural imports and to the dogged adherence of the Czech industrialists to free trade principles. Czechoslovakia seemed unwilling or incapable of marketing its industrial goods to buy more primary products or to find channels to reexport products which the internal market could not absorb, and simply could not compete with the more powerful economy of Nazi Germany with its highly centralized state administration.

In 1936 the Czechoslovak government renewed attempts to create a tariff union and unified market which would include Austria and Hungary. Hodža was blunt about its aim: "We would like through this system to elaborate a common program which would be an effective arm against the methods employed by Germany." The plan, however, did not succeed: Germany exerted pressure upon Austria, Hungary feared that it would undermine its revisionist aspirations, the Little Entente countries lacked enthusiasm and Britain and France gave it little support.

Between 1936 and 1938 Czechoslovakia expanded its Balkan imports by increasing the volume and prices for agrarian products; the Little Entente investigated the possibility of expanding imported goods particularly raw materials and semi-finished products. Efforts were also made to improve commercial relations with Greece and Bulgaria; in 1937 Bulgaria received concessions previously granted only to Little Entente states. Czechoslovakia granted loans and credits to exploit the raw material wealth of the South-eastern European countries and to liberate them from the German grip. But these efforts were impeded by the continuing conflict in Czechoslovakia between agrarian and industrial interests: Agrarians blocked the entry of agricultural products from the Balkans, hence also of any exchange of industrial products for agricultural surpluses. Except for Škoda, Bata and a few other corporations, Czech industrialists were unenthusiastic about purchasing Balkan raw materials. There were also problems of ingesting into the internal Czechoslovak market the products from the Balkans. As the tobacco exports of Yugoslavia, Greece and Bulgaria determined the traffic of Czechoslovakian exports — sugar for Greece and heavy machinery and arms for Yugoslavia and Bulgaria — the fact that the Czechoslovak tobacco bureau had enough tobacco for five years, indicates that Czechoslovakia had maximized its import possibilities, notwithstanding the difficulties.

Czechoslovakia had difficulty competing because its exports were 20% to 25% more expensive on the Balkan market. Any move to loosen the Balkans from their dependence upon German trade was immediately checked by Germany with new, more favorable offers, including the payment for some goods in currency. Germany always provided an enormous market for Balkan exports which Czechoslovakia could not match. The case of Greece was illustrative: Germany purchased almost two-thirds of the entire Greek tobacco crop for the German market while maintaining a constant passive account to hold that country in economic fealty.

The export of Czechoslovak capital into Southeastern Europe was even more problematic than its trade relations with the region. It concentrated primarily in Romania and Yugoslavia, less in Bulgaria and was practically non-existent in Greece, Albania and Turkey. Czechoslovak capital was invested in the Danubian area before World War I and was extended from that base. But at that time Czechoslovak bank capital was limited, making it difficult for domestic capital to both establish control of the internal market in Czechoslovakia and at the same time to stake out a sizeable presence in Southeastern Europe. Nevertheless, the leading banks, especially the Živnostenska Bank and the Prague Credit Bank as well as Czechoslovak corporations and industries, participated in exporting capital into the region and, combined with Western European capital, financed a variety of business enterprises and international state loans to Romania, Yugoslavia and Bulgaria.

In Romania the major interest in Czechoslovak investment was in the production of armaments, especially in the second half of the 1930s. On February 6, 1936, Czechoslovakia and Romania signed an agreement to provide Romania with armaments produced by the Škoda and Zbrojovka (Brno) factories for the sum of 2.5 billion lei (or 400 million Cz. crowns). Capital for the financing of armament plants in Romania was to come from a Romanian state loan. Czech armament capital was supplemented by capital from Czechoslovak industry which also invested in establishing a Romanian industrial base and in the Romanian metallurgical industry providing 9 million American dollars, and in the production of agricultural machinery, chemicals, salt and other products. Czechoslovak capital also participated in large international Romanian state loans in 1934 and 1938 for the construction of roads linking the eastern part of the Carpathian Ukraine with the Romanian Transylvanian railroad system amounting to 95 million crowns, 80 million crowns taken from Czechoslovak frozen funds in Romania. Another Romanian state loan of 200 million crowns continued the construction of the roads. In 1931 Czechoslovak banks participated in a loan of $1.4 million to Romania for the purchase of armaments.

Romanian industrial circles welcomed the influx of Czechoslovak capital and the Czechoslovak government, as an ally of Romania in the Little Entente, strove to strengthen the Romanian state's military defenses and industrial base through the support of Czechoslovak industry and banks. A good part of Czechoslovak capital investment was made possible through its frozen funds in Romania. In the 1920s Czechoslovak capital at first was invested in the production of industrial goods in wide demand and only later in the 1930s concentrated in heavy industry and armaments.

Czech capital concentrated primarily in the pre-war Austro-Hungarian Empire (Croatia, Slavonia, Istria, Slovenia and Dalmatia), investing in bank affiliates and in sugar, spirits, machine producing, textile and other industries. A 1922 Yugoslav study situated Czechoslovak capital in the Yugoslav food, construction and cement industries, holding shares in one-sixth of Yugoslav industrial production and probably even more as this did not include post-war enterprises. The high dividends in several areas of Yugoslav industry attracted Czechoslovak capital, e.g., in the chemical industry which reached 40%. Much of this, however, was from pre-war investments.

In the 1920s Czechoslovakian new capital investments in industry, according to one source, were "exceedingly rare," and after a visit of Czechoslovak economic experts in 1923, the latter indicated that there was little interest in investing capital in Yugoslav industry. Yugoslavs criticized the lack of Czechoslovak capital investments in heavy industry and the passive Yugoslav payments account with Czechoslovakia. These reproaches intensified with the outbreak of the Depression. By the mid-1930s one estimate placed the amount of Czechoslovak investments in Yugoslavia at 9.68% of total foreign capital or about 300 million crowns.

The Bata shoe industry of Czechoslovakia organized a network of factories throughout the cities and towns of Yugoslavia; and the Škoda Works armament firm produced weaponry for Yugoslav state orders but, presumably to avoid competition, refrained from constructing a national armaments industry inside Yugoslavia and only after 1940 accommodated the Yugoslav state through credit arrangements for large weapons orders and the expansion of factories in Zenice, Varoš and Sarajevo. Škoda's trade affiliate YugoŠkoda financed Yugoslav trade enterprises as well as business, mining and beer production. But the sole new Czechoslovak capital investment in the 1930s was in antimony production, most investments having been made before World War I or in the 1920s.

Czechoslovak capital investment in Bulgaria originated with the establishment of a sugar beet factory by a Czechoslovak-educated Bulgarian engineer who petitioned the Bulgarian government in 1910 for an industrial concession to build a factory. With the help of Czech capital (approx. 11.324

million gold leva), by 1925 this investment increased to 50 million leva from which two other spinoff enterprises resulted which produced bricks, tiles and fire-resistant materials, as well as other factories producing various industrial products. One factory complex in Gorna Orahovac in the 1920s employed more than 2,900 workers financed by the Prague Credit Bank (later the Anglo-Czechoslovak Bank, renamed the Anglo-Prague Bank). In the 1920s Czechoslovak capital established itself in the tobacco production sector.

Estimates place Czechoslovak capital invested in Bulgaria in 1938 at 119,600,000 leva or 6.8% of foreign capital in the country, but if non-capital firms are included the figure reached almost 8%. Between 1926 and 1940, profits from these Bulgarian investments only amounted to 6%–7%, roughly equaling profits in Czechoslovakia, in the "oversaturated" 1930s light industry sector. But low profits may be accounted for by inordinately high amortization rates masking retained profits, and lower credit costs in Bulgaria transferred to Czechoslovakia where credit rates were much higher, amounting to tens of millions of leva in profits shipped abroad. What percentage of capital imported into Bulgaria made up dividends, interest, high salary rates and price rebates reintroduced back into the country cannot be ascertained.

Czechoslovak investment capital in Turkey amounted to only 0.8% of direct investments in share capital firms in 1927. The total Czechoslovak capital in Southeastern Europe grew significantly as indicated by the figures in Table 11–8.

Table 11–8. Czechoslovak Investments and Loans in Southeastern Europe in the Interwar Era (in millions of Czechoslovak crowns)

	Direct Investment	State Loans
Romania	300	335
Yugoslavia	325	197
Bulgaria	58	14
Turkey	12	–

Zdenek Sladek and Ljuben Berov, "Čehoslovatskii kapital v stranah Jugovostočnoi Evropi v period mezhdu pervoi i vtotoi mirovimi voinami," *Études Balkaniques* no. 4 (1988), p. 39, Tablica 2 and nos. 98 and 99.

However, the level of Czechoslovak investments in the Balkans should not be exaggerated as foreign capital imported into Czechoslovakia, estimated by Teichova at 3.19 billion crowns in December 1937, was four times more than Czechoslovak capital invested in the Balkans. Czechoslovak capital in Romania, Yugoslavia and Bulgaria accounted for less than one-tenth of the total foreign capital invested in those countries. British and other foreign capital was heavily involved in Czech banking concerns from the beginning of the 1920s and early 1930s and the head of the Anglo-International Bank was a leading board member of the Anglo-Czechoslovak and Prague Credit Bank. Thus, Czechoslovak capital in its surrogate capacity in the export of capital to the Balkans cooperated with leading Western European and North American firms like Schneider, Solvay, Mannesmann, Phillips, Rothschild, etc., and in the process sought to shore up the Little Entente countries against the incursion of German capital, trade and industry into the Balkans.

In the 1930s in its struggle against Nazi economic penetration of Southeastern Europe, Czechoslovakia received *sub-rosa* American assistance, and Nazi economic observers believed that the United States exerted pressure upon German exports which amounted to a *de facto* encirclement of Germany.

On October 15, 1935, the United States retaliated against German clearing and other discriminatory trade practices by removing Germany from the most-favored-nation list of states trading on the American market. But American actions did not rest there, giving rise to German suspicions that the United States pursued a policy of economic encirclement and strangulation of Germany on the world market.

These suspicions surfaced when Washington changed the trade status of Czechoslovakia to a quasi-most-favored-nation position in the 1936 Czechoslovak-American trade agreement. Czechoslovakia had previously been denied favored status for giving preferential trading arrangements to Romanian and Yugoslav goods on the Czechoslovak market. Without comment, the U.S. State Department announced the removal of over 100 items from the non-most favored category, an "astounding" situation in the view of one German observer, amounting to $11.483 million, over half of the Czechoslovak export deliveries to the United States.[49] These market concessions placed American goods at a disadvantage on the Czechoslovak market to the goods of Romania and Yugoslavia in the highly competitive market for dried fruits, animal products, wood and mineral oils. Similar German goods on the list of lowered Czechoslovak items amounted in 1936 to $6.4 million, only one-half of the Czechoslovak figure, notwithstanding the fact that Czechoslovakia took only $4.6 million in American goods compared to $100.6 million in American imports on the German market, twenty times more.[50]

A *New York Times* article on September 1, 1937, justified this waiver of Czechoslovakia's non-favored status as "a contribution to the construction of an area of low tariffs inside the Danubian states."[51] The Germans suspected that the move was not purely economic, that it also had political aims.

> The sum of these tendencies allows the conclusion that the American trade policy is directed toward a growing encirclement of Germany in the sense of its exclusion from the American market by making its competitive position more difficult on the world market. The struggle between the "most favored" and "bilateralism" concepts from which the Roosevelt government has long viewed and judged its own political trade principles, in its application to German-American economic relations is increasingly taking on the character of a political anti-fascist front formation which the United States leads and renders more acute by using or withholding its economic reserves.[52]

The stalemate into which an Italian-American trade agreement had fallen in 1935 and the U.S. failure to grant Italian goods most-favored-nation status even though Italy took eight times more American goods than Czechoslovakia, seemed to confirm this. Though Italy eventually received recognition as a most favored nation, probably because Italy's political position was still uncertain and it represented less of a danger than Germany. Though German imports improved their position on the American market in the boomlet year 1937 and total European imports rose about 30%, the overall level of German exports declined.[53]

Yugoslavia had little interest in giving up the trade preference it enjoyed on the German market and Pilja, the Yugoslav economic specialist in the Foreign Office, poked fun at the Little Entente and Czechoslovakia as a substitute for Germany in the Southeast.[54] By this time the clearing house system had tilted heavily in favor of Germany with the value of German products shipped to Yugoslavia falling considerably short of the total value of Yugoslav agricultural products — a fact which worried Belgrade and exercised pressure on Yugoslavia to continue the unfavorable arrangement. Anonymous, officially inspired articles placed in the German press and diplomatic contacts between the two countries prevented the Yugoslavs from straying too far from the fold.[55]

All this greatly influenced the foreign policy of Beneš, the Czechoslovak foreign minister during the critical period of the 1930s. Czechoslovakia's close alignment with France was always anathema in Berlin, but Hitler became particularly incensed over the Franco-Soviet Pact of 1935 which, coupled with Czechoslovakia's alliance with the Soviet Union, he considered bringing Bolshevik influence into the heart of Europe to Germany's very borders. The advent of the Popular Front Governments in France, Spain and elsewhere against the rise of Fascism gave him the pretext for a virulent campaign against Beneš and Czechoslovakia as a direct threat to Germany. Nazi propaganda railed against the Czechoslovak state as the advanced base of bolshevism in Central Europe.

British support for Czechoslovakia began to wane in the mid-1920s following the Franco-Czechoslovak Pact. Thereafter, British documents contain negative comments about the Czechs, supplied mainly by the British minister in Prague, Joseph Addison. Addison arrived from Latvia in the spring of 1930 and prior service in Berlin. After a few months in Prague he took to calling Beneš "the little Jack Horner" of Europe and observed that militarily "the country simply could not be defended." The Czechs purportedly had a centuries-old "inferiority complex" toward the Austrians and Hungarians. In July 1931, Addison wrote, in a private letter to Sargent, stronger anti-Czechoslovak sentiments:

> Czechoslovakia is an injustice — i.e., it is a fictitious country founded on several injustices and maintained by the continuance of injustice and the apparent impossibility of putting an end to it without a convulsion which it is to the general interest to avoid.

Other witless communications followed containing racial comments about most of the peoples of Eastern Europe designed to titillate the British dislike of foreigners.

Can we get back to the state of affairs in which the Slovaks return to their natural job of scrubbing floors and cleaning windows, the Romanians are confined to the exercise of their only national industry (according to Lord D'Abernon's statement in an official memorandum this is fornication), the Poles are restricted to piano playing and the white slave traffic and the Serbs are controlled in their great national activity — organizing political murders on foreign territory? Can we hand Europe back to those who are competent to run it? I doubt it. If this is pessimism, then I am a pessimist.

This so delighted Sargent that he asked mockingly for more such letters because "fireworks which really communicate are always welcome."[56] It was a stone's throw from this growing British wish to retreat into isolation and alienation from Czechoslovakia to the abortive mission of Lord Runciman to that country in July 1938 that undermined London's support of the Czechs and led directly to Munich.

Czechoslovakia's failure to provide a market for the agricultural products of its Little Entente allies, Romania and Yugoslavia, enabled Germany to penetrate the Southeastern markets and isolate it completely. Bereft of Western support, menaced by Poland and isolated from Romania and Yugoslavia, it chose capitulation to Germany rather than resistance.

Chapter 12

The Second Phase of Nazi Attempts to Dominate Eastern Europe

The political line-up followed the economic line-up.
— Cordell Hull, *Memoirs*

THE BRITISH GOVERNMENT remained jittery over Hitler's intentions during the autumn and winter of 1938–1939 and awaited his January 30 speech with nervous expectation. The speech did not justify relaxing precautions, Chamberlain thought, "particularly since we might be dealing with a man whose actions might not be rational."[1] He clung to his belief in Hitler's pledges of no new territorial demands; behind everything was the need to play for time until Britain had reached the German level of armament. In the meantime no umbrage should be given to Germany that might lead it to stumble into war. Also the unexpressed hope — and sometimes expressed, in asides and whispers — persisted that Hitler would attack the Soviet Union and the Western Powers could safely stand aside.

Chamberlain stated that too much attention should not be paid to Hitler's forthcoming speech. He seemed reassured by a recent talk with von Dirksen, the German ambassador, "who had expressed his disbelief in these talks of impending adventure on Herr Hitler's part." Dr. Dirksen "thought that Hitler was devoting his energies to the economic sphere and had expressed satisfaction at the progress of negotiations now proceeding with representatives of certain of our industries, i.e., the coal industry. Furthermore, Dr. Dirksen had recently been in Berlin and had spoken to Herr von Ribbentrop who had seized the importance of increasing German exports." Despite Dirksen's assurances the British government awaited a sudden blow in some direction, either Holland, Switzerland or somewhere else.[2]

The British Foreign Secretary, Halifax, warned that the steadily worsening economic situation inside Germany only fanned Hitler's exasperation during the last quarter of 1938, notably increasing difficulties in obtaining raw materials for armaments and to feed the population. "Hitler had failed to listen to his advisers after Munich to consolidate his position" and, therefore, "would then be forced during 1939, to 'explode' in some direction" to "distract attention from the failure of his system to work in time of peace." Chamberlain cited a report that Dr. Brinkmann, the Technical Head of the Ministry of Economy, gave a speech to a hundred specialists which was critical of the internal situation: the lack of raw materials in Germany was so great that in a few weeks there would be a breakdown in Germany. "The plunder of Germany was exhausted"; this was the "first sign of a coming 'catastrophe' "; and like Schacht, von Krosigk, the Treasury Minister, urged the strictest control of state and Nazi party expenditures. Hitler purportedly replied, "Very well. All this means that the vital decision must come at once, and it is coming at once."[3]

Halifax concluded that an "explosion" by Germany "would be likely" in the near future. Reports arrived at the beginning of January "that in view of the financial position" of Germany, Hitler would order mobilization about mid-February on the Dutch and Swiss frontiers and might try to "terrorize" the western countries with threats and if necessary invade Holland and part of Switzerland, holding them as a "pledge" until his demands were met in full. The British thought "the demands would include measures to solve Germany's financial problem."[4]

In contrast to the vagaries of the free market, military expansion offered an easier and surer way to gain raw materials, buttressed by the belief that Germany could seize newer territories with impunity. In mid-February 1939 Ernst von Weizsäcker confirmed this in his diary: "The thesis England and France would not march in the case of a German war against the Czechs is now the official one."[5] Already on October 21, 1938, Hitler ordered preparations for the destruction of the remnant state of Czechoslovakia. The former German Foreign Minister, Neurath, tried to dissuade Hitler on March 9, 1939, from occupying the Czech area — except in the event the Czechs tried to suppress the Slovak separatists. Germany, Neurath advised, should be satisfied with the control of the Czech economy and foreign affairs in return for guaranteeing a semi-autonomous Czech cultural nation. Germany's important territorial claims were not in the Czech area but in Memel, Danzig and the Polish corridor.[6]

British conciliation efforts toward Germany continued in the area of trade throughout 1938, but German attempts to disavow foreign loan payments and the Austrian loan met with stiff resistance from the "City." After reaching an impasse, a compromise occurred and a payments agreement was signed; but this did not occur before Leith-Ross revived the weapon of a clearing against German imports to England. By this time Germany had lost much of its former sympathy in the "City" and some large British banks believed that it would come "to a struggle with Germany." The "City" supported the hard line position of the British Foreign Office and the government that the loans must be paid.[7] With the signature of the agreement London breathed a sigh of relief.

In 1938 the negative balance between exports and imports, which Schacht succeeded in repairing four years earlier through the "New Plan," reappeared once again. Exports sank by more than half a billion Rm producing a negative trade balance of 192 million Rm, worsening the currency crisis.[8] Despite production increases, the heavy claim made upon raw materials by the rearmament program hobbled the export market and put increasing pressure upon imports. The sharp increase in armaments in 1938 — double the amount of the previous year — also aggravated the currency problem. As rearmament had priority in internal production as well as imports of raw materials, the consumer market inevitably suffered from shortages once again. A worldwide boycott of German goods, following the anti-Semitic excess of *Kristallnacht* in November 1938, complicated the situation and only abated at the beginning of 1939. The foreign trade problem became so critical that State Secretary Brinkmann first urged German firms in a September 5 decree to concentrate upon their export rather than their internal market, then on November 9 ordered them to give their export market the highest priority.[9]

The belief among some historians that economic difficulties would have strengthened the drift away from war, not towards it, flies in the face of contemporary evidence that Germany's increasingly deteriorating trade position and raw materials problems, coupled with the fact that Britain was slowly beginning to catch up to the German armament level, influenced Hitler toward aggressive expansion as a way out of his predicament. Hitler had secretly squirreled away 750 million Rm in foreign currency gained probably sometime in the mid-thirties through a scheme of Schacht's devaluing overseas German holdings held abroad representing reparations in the form of shares, then bought up by intermediaries on the open market at 12% to 18% of their value. These were then forced upon German business which redeemed them at par value. With the 80% profit thus gained, Hitler organized a dumping campaign — as German goods could not move abroad otherwise — which netted the Nazi Government three-quarters of a billion marks in foreign currency. With this windfall, Hitler ordered Minister of the Economy Funk to purchase critically needed raw materials abroad. Thus, if we are to believe Hitler's boastful account of the scheme, Germany was able to stave off immediate economic inflation and bankruptcy in 1938–1939. This would explain, at least partially, Germany's mysterious ability to survive economically in that period. By the end of that reprieve, this nest egg was exhausted and, given Hitler's gambling and adventurist propensities, the only way out was an attack upon either Poland or France.[10]

The only visible sign of activity in the direction of dealing constructively with the trade crisis through a German trade offensive was the visit of Schacht's successor, Walter Funk, to the Balkans in the summer of 1938 to expand German trade in the region. These efforts stretched well into the spring of 1939 and did result in treaties for expanded trade but did not completely satisfy Germany's needs and, in any case, depended on the willingness of those states to continue their subservient economic and political relationship to Germany.

Long before and during the Munich crisis of 1938 the British government, despite the hesitations and objections of some in the Foreign Office (Vansittart, Sargent, etc.) and outside the government, had temporarily and largely written off Central and Southeastern Europe.[11] Throughout most of the 1930s the British studiously avoided any entanglement in Southeastern Europe in a political sense and tried to influence the French to loosen their ties with the area. Before going to meet Hitler at Godesberg in September 1938, Chamberlain had hardly consulted the Foreign Office except for a request for information on the subject of Southeastern Europe through Horace Wilson to Leith-Ross on the purely economic interests of Britain in the region, in the form of remarks on a draft statement the Prime Minister intended to make to Hitler. Chamberlain's statement according to Leith-Ross's recollection pledged Britain "to just about give up any economic interest in Central and Southeastern Europe." Disturbed, the Foreign Office officials, Sir Orme Sargent, Assistant Undersecretary, and Ingram, telegraphed Chamberlain to remind him that "whatever concessions with respect to our economic position in Central Europe they thought of making to Hitler," the danger of "a sudden abdication of our political position in the Balkans, Turkey and Greece" could entail "serious political repercussions." Both of the latter states lay adjacent to the Mediterranean and were "of great strategic importance" for England. Sir Alexander Cadogan finessed the matter, where it lay thereafter.[12] Chamberlain's decision to make concessions to Hitler in Eastern Europe, before the Foreign Office intervened, had been influenced by the unwillingness of the "City" financial circles and foreign export sector — he and Simon held sizeable investments in Imperial Chemical Industries — to risk new investments of money in the Southeastern and Central European region or new investments abroad in general which were halted by the government after the mid-1930s and went instead increasingly into armaments. Nevertheless, Stanley, Minister for Trade, and Halifax showed interest in maintaining a stake in Central and Southeastern Europe.[13]

By 1939 German living standards according to some writers were roughly on the level of 1928. Examined from the perspective of 1933–1939, German workers had purportedly benefited by about a 5%–6% increase in living standards once price increases had been taken into account, a figure one writer describes skeptically as "a phantasy of stability." This must be balanced against the dark clouds of intermittent food shortages, labor shortages, mounting debt, raw material shortages and a steadily encroaching inflation. For many wage increases were not only often wiped out by price increases, but they even lost in earning power. Coal miners, for example, suffered real loss, receiving wage increases which were about half the price increases. Skilled workers fared better than unskilled workers and women in all categories of work received less than men.[14]

Although some German writers seem anxious to vindicate the economic "miracle" of the 1930s brought about by Hitler and the Nazi regime, other recent studies have been skeptical of these claims. German historian Willi A. Boelcke believes that the German upswing by the eve of World War II cannot be attributed solely to the powerful upthrust produced by the enormous expenditures for armaments.[15] Others, like the British writer Harold James, discount the Nazi figures on the rise of national income as "misleadingly high."[16] James believes that the economic problems of both the Weimar system and the Nazi state stemmed from structural problems traceable to the nineteenth century and the rapid conversion of Germany from a middling to one of the great industrial powers. The low growth rates of the Weimar era produced distributional problems which the Nazi state suppressed rather than solved and which reemerged in the form of "clashes within the Nazi party: in 1934, 1936 and later 1943–1944, economic tensions led to profound political upheavals." James concludes: "Fundamentally, the Nazis 'solved' only one economic problem: unemployment. We should be skeptical about other Nazis claims...." He believes most German investment capital was placed not in business but administrative jobs, thus raising employment levels.[17]

Under the Nazi dictatorship, a highly interventionist state faced regular strain and political turmoil as the interventionist mechanism went wrong and as the expectations built around interventionist promises were disappointed. But the tragedy of this story of interventionism was that every breakdown produced yet more interventionism.[18]

As the total amount spent on the Wehrmacht between 1933 and 1939 (till August) equaled the amount spent by the state for civil expenses, approximately 60 billion marks,[19] there can be little doubt of the enormous impact of the outlay for armaments on the unemployment problem, notwithstanding statements to the contrary. In addition, profits for German business during the 1930s according to available evidence exceeded the share of wages in the Nazi upswing.[20] Heavy industry, the more monopolized sector of the economy, benefited the most, going from a profit ratio of 2.10% in 1926 to 6.44% in 1938. The peak years of 1927–1929 for heavy industry average 4.86%, far below the peak years 1934–1938 at 6.47%.[21] Light industry and the financial sector fared well, but in critical consumer areas like clothing, none of the later years of the 1930s exceeded 1927 and 1928 even remotely. Even more to the point, the climb of heavy industry in particular from the trough of the early 1930s to the late 1930s is striking. The same may be said for most other categories.

However, when the buying power and the living standards of Germans at the workplace are compared with the British and Americans, the German standard of living is considerably lower. Thus, the gains made by the Nazi regime in the living standard of the average German do not appear too positive.

Business after 1936 began to become restive over the increasing array of Nazi bureaucratic controls and interference, the loss of its overseas markets and the enforced subsidies it had to pay for exports without which Germany could not compete. Though subsidies enabled Germany to devalue the mark without formally resorting to devaluation, official controls and restrictions undermined business's confidence in the Nazi government and it began to hunger for its old autonomy.[22]

Hitler and the Nazi leaders were always aware of their dependence upon private industry, increasingly selfish and greedy for profits rather than concerned for the German people. German business was expected to move to regain its old export markets in 1938 and 1939, but Hitler and the Nazi leaders had other plans. Announcement of the formation of the Reichswerke A. G. Hermann Göring, a new state-organized iron and steel complex, in July 1937 jolted the industrial leaders who tried to resist, but Göring outsmarted them. Tapped telephones and bugged meetings kept Göring informed of the Ruhr leaders' and Schacht's resistance plans. At first he wanted to arrest them; later he relented and through telegrams laced with threats and cajolery and promises of greater loot for Krupp in future rearmament plans, he undermined resistance.[23] From an initial five million marks in July 1937, the Göring Reichswerke capital increased to four hundred million marks. Having control of a major sector of German industry, Hitler now could conduct foreign policy without fear of contradiction from business. Ruhr production plunged dramatically while Reichswerke output increased: heavy industry went from one-third of total Reich production in 1913 to one-fifth in 1938. Göring refused to export semi-finished products during the boomlet year of 1937 and probably contributed to the trade problem of the succeeding years.

By the middle of the war, the Reichswerke had become a giant state organization with assets of five billion marks, almost twice the size of the rest of the privately owned German steel companies.[24] German heavy industry did not receive the spoils in the Austrian, Sudeten and Czech areas and later in Poland, which went to the Hermann Göring Werke. Krupp failed to get the Škoda works, and its output of steel during the war period fell back from sixteen million tons of steel in 1939 to only eleven million; increased production in steel occurred outside the Ruhr and in the occupied regions. The net result gave Hitler a higher degree of control over business and the economy. With control of the Army and the economy in his hands, Hitler held all the reins of power: "The shift in economic control, away from conservative circles towards the party, was matched by a corresponding shift in foreign policy."[25] Hitler and the war party, therefore, would be more emboldened to expand into Austria, Czechoslovakia and finally Poland after 1938 without fear of repercussions from business and the military elites. However, economic forces outside Germany were another matter.

In the 1930s Germany's foreign trade problem was more a matter of reduced trade volume than of negative trade balances. Between 1928 and 1939 Germany's total foreign trade dropped by almost two and a half times even though only three years out of eleven had trade deficits. Exports fell steadily during the Nazi era, reaching a low point in 1934–1935, the first years with a negative trade balance. At that time 44.8% of raw material imports went to consumer goods while 15% went to production goods.[26] The effects of the 1934 negative trade balance were reflected not only in the internal market but also in the rearmament program in the following shortages of stocks: the cotton industry had only fourteen days' reserves; rubber had only two days' supply; and petroleum reserves covered only three to three and a half months.[27]

We have related already how Britain in 1934 was ready to apply a clearing in order to assure German payment of both outstanding loans and frozen debts. Other countries were anxious lest Germany would be unable to pay its bills in 1934: "The National Socialist economy faced ruin."[28] Only British willingness to grant Germany further loans permitted the Reich to pay for its imports from Britain at all. To avert economic collapse, Hitler released temporary food supplies reserved for the war economy until the expected upswing in foreign trade occurred through drastically restricted imports. Thereafter Germany increasingly resorted to the sale of weaponry abroad as a way of gaining currency for purchasing raw materials and foodstuffs. From 1935 to 1940 Germany contracted to sell 1.25 billion Rm worth of armaments of which one-half billion Rm in orders still remained at the end of 1939.[29] As war approached, the arms trade was cut down as it siphoned off weaponry needed by the Wehrmacht.

The German trade offensive of the mid-1930s and bilateral agreements with Brazil and the Southeastern European countries stepped on American toes at a time when the United States was emphasizing increased trade, reciprocal trade and an "open door" policy as a way out of the Depression. Fear of radical social change in the United States increased pressure for trade to stimulate employment through demand from the very start of the New Deal administration. The atmosphere of intensified trade competition prevalent in the 1930s generated similar pressures upon the Third Reich to escape the vise of the clearing threat by adopting bilateral agreements with other currency-poor countries in similar straits. In numerous articles German officials like Ritter and Schacht emphasized that they really had no interest in the "extreme" trade policy of bilateral trade arrangements but were compelled to because of the Western clearing threat, a form of political pressure to compel debt payment (*Schuldenpolitisches Druckmittel*). Reichsbank Director, Karl Blessing, declared: "...bilateralism is nothing more than the necessary consequence of clearings. We abhor this whole system, because it is economically destructive."[30]

The initial benevolence of the United States toward Germany with whom it conducted a considerable trade — particularly American exports to Germany — turned sour and then to bitter recrimination as Germany switched its trade to the Southeastern European and Latin American states with large agricultural surpluses and little currency for industrial imports. As Germany's trade with Southeastern Europe, Scandinavia, Turkey, Austria, Poland and the Baltic region expanded, its trade with the United States declined. By the late 1930s German imports from the U.S. fell from 598 million Rm in 1932 to 405 million Rm in 1938 — about 30% — while exports fell even more precipitately in the same period from 295 million Rm to 150 million Rm, approximately half. Still more galling for the U.S., German trade inroads into a major U.S. trade region, Latin America, almost doubled in the same era from 353 million Rm to 696 million Rm.[31] As Britain was also under similar competitive pressure from the German penetration of its Latin American market, it was only a question of time before the two English-speaking powers were driven together. As Hull noted in his post-war memoirs: "The political line-up followed the economic line-up."[32]

By 1938 *Grossraumwirtschaft* (economy of large areas) had become a favorite subject of German popular articles and of the academic and scholarly press, which turned out a spate of publications exulting over the "natural" linkage of the Reich and the Southeast. German tourists explored the region and numerous travel articles appeared in the press about the still "primitive" state of the peoples and their customs. The German press increasingly spoke of the two economies — i.e., the industrialized Reich and the agrarian Southeastern region — and the complementary nature of the whole Central and Eastern European area. Some Germans began to speak of a "German Monroe Doctrine"; and Chamberlain spoke of the Southeast as a German "dominion" or "commonwealth."[33] The British expressed a tacit acceptance of this in a range of attitudes towards the area from the traditional "distant good will" to a certain uneasiness over the German trade success which might lead to greater political influence.

However, while the British might have put up with German domination to forestall something worse, they were unwilling to forego future commercial profits in a period of tight economic competition by giving up their most-favored-nation status as the Germans demanded so that the region would, in fact, become a full-fledged German colonial area. This would then insure the Germans of the complete disposal of the region's raw materials without fear of foreign competition. From the German standpoint this was only fair since the other Great Powers had colonial possessions of their own — some taken from Germany in 1918 — and access to raw materials. However, as a British documentary notation indicated in 1933, giving Germany complete control had other unacceptable repercussions: "this is not purely an economic matter. It is, in fact, highly political — a facet of the problem of the mastery of Europe."[34]

As the 1930s recede from living consciousness, it is sometimes forgotten how trade and the struggle for world markets was a life and death matter for the Great Powers, determining national existence and survival itself. History was often pitiless toward the fate of those nations and peoples that fell behind in the race.

In Eastern Europe before the First World War German capital had been dominant. The degree to which Western capital flowed into the area after the war has been the focus of critical examination. Before 1914 Germany accounted for 39.3% and 39% of the Austro-Hungarian monarchy's exports and imports respectively. The United States accounted for 9.5% and 9.1%; Great Britain, 7.0% and 9.1%; and France, 3.4% and 3.0%.[35]

Germany was also the largest investor of capital in the Austro-Hungarian Empire, investing 3,520 million crowns; British investments came to 191.8 million crowns, and French investments were somewhere between 2,090 million and 6,190 million crowns.[36] In the inter-war period this changed as Western capital shifted from Russia to Central and Eastern Europe, partially for political reasons to keep German capital from reentering the region and also as a way of hemming in Bolshevik Russia. The region's raw materials made it a lucrative attraction for Western capital as a source of profit rather than for immediate usage in Western industry. It was the last large colonial region in Europe, after Russia fell away, where the capital loss suffered by the Bolshevik Revolution might be recovered.[37] The French Government, through Paleologue, the Secretary-General at the Quai d'Orsay, did not scruple to use pressure to secure French shareholder participation in the Hungarian General Credit Bank, which the Hungarian government agreed to "as an act of patriotic duty" in the hope that later revision of the peace treaty would bring about a return of Hungary's lost territories.[38] The French Foreign Office also tried to assume "a position of tutelage" in the 1920s over Hungary's railways, iron industry and banks. This was also done to counter British capital positions already entrenched in the country.[39] Similarly, the Czechs invited in French capital to counter the prevalence of German capital in Bohemia after World War I through the intercession of Beneš with the French government.

British capital, hitherto almost negligible in Southeastern Europe before the First World War, began to increase rapidly in the inter-war period. A recent study places British capital investment in pre-war Austro-Hungarian securities at a mere .0004 of its total foreign investment capital.[40] In the inter-war period Anglo-French capital established an almost hegemonical position compared to other foreign investment. In Romania, for example, Anglo-French capital investment enjoyed a "crushing superiority" over German investment: 8 million lei against 550 million.[41] Despite its inferior position, German capital slowly increased during the Weimar era and into the 1930s in Central and Southeastern Europe. By 1937 Germany's capital investment position was as shown in Table 12–1. German capital was most negligible in Romania, which enabled that country to resist German penetration down to almost 1939–1940.

Table 12–1. German Share of Capital Investment in Central and Southeastern Europe, 1937 (in percentages)

Czechoslovakia	Yugoslavia	Bulgaria	Romania	Poland
7.2[a]	6.2[b]	9.3[c]	0.9[d]	13.8

Taken from various sources (Teichova, Marguerat, Berov, etc.)

a. Industry and banks.
b. Private industrial enterprises.
c. All stocks in private possession.
d. Banks, industry, commerce and insurance (in 1938).

After the Austrian Anschluss and the elimination of the Czechoslovak state, the capital investments of Austria and Czechoslovakia were added to the German investments in the Balkans to give Germany a strong foothold for the first time in the foreign capital investment sector of the Balkan economy. After 1939, total German capital in Yugoslavia exceeded British capital, with German capital amounting to 17.8% while Britain held only 14.1%, and France had 17%. Thus, while Anglo-French capital was still predominant, Germany had made considerable gains. The same may be said for Romania: German capital had gained but Anglo-French capital still had the upper hand. In Hungary after 1939 Germany held 125 million out of 900 million pengös in share capital (13%–14%), but 50% of all foreign capital with 25% of Hungarian industry in foreign hands. In Greece, German capital investment grew from 5.2% to 13.47%, placing Germany third after Belgium and Switzerland. In the area of foreign state loans which played an enormous role in Romania, Anglo-French capital investment in April 1939 greatly exceeded German: France and England controlled 43% of the Romanian public debt in contrast to Germany's 10%.[42] In Greece, because of its proximity to British possessions in the Middle East and the Suez Canal, British financial interest predominated, approximately 58% of all foreign capital. (See figures in Table 12–2.)

In Turkey the British invested the largest portion of their capital in private enterprises — £33.5 million — and £3.5 million in state securities, and though German capital investments in Turkey increased, Anglo-French capi-

Table 12–2. Foreign Capital in Southeastern Europe, 1938 (in millions of dollars)[43]

State		England	France	Germany
		Total Capital		
Bulgaria	119	48.9	22.5	1.5
Hungary	369	86.6	32.6	46.0
Greece	486	282.0 (58%)	66.0	55.4
Romania	650	215.0	83.6	75.0 (11.5%)
Turkey	590	185.0	299.0	not given
Yugoslavia	311	25.5	120.0	2.8
Total	2516	843.0	623.7	180.7

tal remained dominant. Some writers have questioned whether the dominant Anglo-French capital position in the Southeast was stagnant capital, i.e., capital in unproductive or the less productive enterprises; and in Bulgaria at least, and to some extent in Yugoslavia, Turkey, Romania and Czecho-slovakia, French and Belgian capital withdrew from some of these states already in the mid-thirties and, in the case of Czechoslovakia, after Munich. Nevertheless, the large amount of British capital investment in Southeastern Europe, despite its negligible figure in relation to total British investments, may have been the reason why Britain refused to give over the region to German economic control.

Thus, Germany had little opportunity because of its lack of capital to penetrate the Southeastern European area other than through its trade inroads. Some writers have called the German trade successes "imperialism without capital" or "commercial imperialism." Trade with the Southeast had become so critical that Göring believed Germany's rearmament depended upon Southeastern Europe's willingness to supply raw materials for the German economy. On the eve of Schacht's trip to the Southeast in 1935 Schacht and Göring discussed how to get hold of Yugoslavia's copper mines for German use.[44] Although the Southeastern trade only amounted to somewhere between 9% and 12% of Germany's trade, it was more than one-half of the entire trade of the countries of the Southeast.[45] The increase in German trade volume in the Balkans came at a time when Western European countries and the United States had a strong lock on world trade. The first stage of Germany's trade offensive in the Southeast occurred in the period from 1934 to 1936. The second stage of German trade increases in the Balkans occurred from 1936 to 1938, at a time when world trade rebounded from the trough of world Depression. The third stage occurred after Munich and November 1938 when the Anglo-American Trade Agreement aimed at preventing further German

Table 12–3. Foreign Trade of Southeastern European Countries
with Germany, 1937 and 1939[46]

Year	1937	1939	1937	1939
	Exports to Germany (% of all exports)		Imports from Germany (% of all imports)	
Bulgaria	43.1	71.1	54.8	69.5
Hungary	24.1	52.4	26.2	52.5
Romania	19.2	43.1	28.9	56.1
Yugoslavia	21.7	45.9	32.4	53.2

trade advances on the world market. By 1939 the Southeast as a purveyor
of raw materials peaked and began to decline except for Romanian oil and
non-ferrous metals, high on the German requirements list (see Table 12-3).

German trade successes in the Southeast came largely at first at the
expense of Italy, whose trade with the area declined dramatically in the
mid-thirties. When Yugoslavia participated in the League of Nations' sanctions against Italy, which had been Yugoslavia's major trading partner, Italy's
trade with Yugoslavia plummeted and Germany moved in quickly to take
up the slack. The Germans had already gained a strong foothold in Bulgarian trade in 1933 when the Weimar Republic already controlled roughly a
third of Bulgaria's export and import trade, and by 1935 about one-half.
In the case of Greece, 23% of its imports came from Germany already by
1934, but Germany received only 14.7% of its exports. By 1935 Greece sent
about 30% of its exports to Germany until the outbreak of war. German
trade with Turkey in the late 1930s had reached the 40%–50% level, second
only to Bulgaria in trade volume until 1940 when it fell suddenly to roughly
10% of Turkey's total trade.[47]

The major losers in the Southeastern trade to Germany were Italy, the
United States and France. France was unable to take the agricultural products of the area, a factor which undermined its political alliances with the
Balkan states. By the end of the 1930s French capital retreated from the
Balkans.[48] The rearmament program forced the British government to curtail new investments abroad in general, thus preventing infusion of British
capital into Southeastern Europe to counter the German economic threat.

British trade, while sometimes stagnating a little, remained steady throughout the 1930s in the countries of the southeast at about 8–10% of Britain's
total trade during the 1935–1938 period. Britain and France did not try to
impede Germany's efforts to gain control of the southeast's trade by increasing their own there because they could get raw materials and foodstuffs from
their own colonies and elsewhere cheaper.

By the late 1930s about 80%–90% of Germany's trade with the Southeastern states was through clearings and only 10%–20% in currency.[49] The
higher prices for industrial goods than for agricultural products on the world
market gave the industrial states like Germany an advantage through this
exploitative system of unequal trade over the agrarian Southeastern Euro-

pean states. Frequent passive balances run up by the Germans once they had received the Balkan exports amounted to granting the Germans a free loan once interest, amortization and other costs are taken into account. Already at the end of December 1934 German debts in all clearing accounts totaled 450 million Rm; in March 1935 they rose to 567 million Rm. At the beginning of May 1936, German debts on clearing accounts to Greece were about 40 million Rm, to Hungary and Yugoslavia 25 million Rm each, to Romania 18 million and to Bulgaria about 10 million. Czechoslovakia's balance was 62 million. In 1937 Yugoslavia's claim rose to 36 million.[50] These countries had to increase imports from Germany as the only way to recoup their export costs. Exports to Germany always outdistanced imports, forcing the Balkan states to export to Germany, and lacking other markets for surpluses, offers of higher than world prices drew them back to German markets like a magnet.

During world market upturns the Balkan countries traded in free currency markets and avoided Germany; when they had no markets for their exports they turned towards Germany in desperation. The problem of excessive passive balances led Yugoslavia and Romania to resort to devices to sell clearing marks on private markets. The mark then sold at lower rates than the officially pegged price. Thus, in Yugoslavia the private clearing rate for the mark fell to 12.50–14.50 dinars although the nominal official rate was 17.42–17.62 dinars, which, in effect, meant a devaluation of the mark had occurred. In Romania it fell from the official rate of 37.5 lei per reichsmark to 33–34 lei.[51] In the interval between the 1937 upturn and the 1938 downturn, the Western Powers did not take the opportunity to strengthen their grip on the area and force the Germans to modify their system of bilateral trade. Britain continued to eschew any economic activity which could disturb Germany's drive to dominate the area, fearing Hitler in desperation would unleash a war. At that time German trade with countries which it did not have a clearing or bilateral system of trade with was only 22.3% of its total imports and 14.2% of its exports.[52] During the period when the Southeastern countries deserted the German market for the free currency countries, Germany increased its sale of weaponry 4.5 times more in 1937 than in 1936 to make up for its loss in sales to the Balkan states, which took 60% of the Reich's sale of weaponry, reducing somewhat Germany's passive balances with those countries and setting the stage for a new trade offensive in 1938.[53]

By using certain sharp practices such as delaying deliveries of weaponry and increasing the prices of the weapons and parts under various pretexts, the Germans were able to commercially skin their trading partners. With the help of these tactics and the pressure of passive balances, Germany was able in 1937 to intensify its trade with the Southeastern European markets.[54] But at the 1938–1939 year-end the export division of the Reich Economics Ministry judged the prospect of further intensified trade with Southeastern Europe "to be completely exhausted. Yugoslavia as well as Romania have shown that they are completely disinclined towards a further dependence (*Anlehnung*) upon Germany."[55] At that point Germany's share in the trade of the Southeastern countries was between 20% and 30%. Much of the increase in trade in 1938 stemmed from Germany's control of the former Austrian Czechoslovak share of the Southeastern trade which amounted to about 2,381 million crowns ($75 million), of which 500 million crowns fell into Germany's hands immediately after Germany annexed the German-speaking regions of Czechoslovakia following the Munich agreement.[56]

Germany also could exploit and manipulate the Southeastern European states' ethnic rivalries and fears of war, and the need for military weaponry following Munich, as a lever to extend its political influence into the region and its grip over trade and thereby increase the flow of badly needed raw materials for its own war economy. Berlin established a priority system for the sale of weapons based upon political and military considerations dividing these states into three groups: Bulgaria and Hungary were classified as "unconditionally friendly"; Greece and Turkey as "conditionally friendly"; and Yugoslavia and Romania as members of the Little Entente (Czechoslovakia, Romania and Yugoslavia) allied to France "in the enemy camp."[57] The first two received almost unlimited consideration as irredentist, former allies of Germany in World War I, and were granted loans with long-term pay-back allowances, with stipulations that a major part of the weaponry would be financed through the shipment of raw materials and foodstuffs and an insignificant portion through currency. In 1936, the first year of Germany's weapons export program, Germany concluded agreements for weaponry with the Balkan states valued at 127 million Rm, which was 57.6% of all agreements, excluding Hungary, to be financed by 45.3 million Rm of exports to Germany with 6% in currency.[58]

In the case of Bulgaria, political considerations prevailed at the behest of the German Foreign Office over the hesitations of the Ministry for Economy and the Bulgarians were granted a loan of 30 million Rm in 1937 to be repaid over a five-year period. In 1938, Bulgaria was given a second loan of 30 million Rm to be repaid in eight years with the possibility of extension to eleven years. The German Foreign Office overruled the Ministry of Economy's protest against the "unreal" terms because the agreement "had to be made out of political considerations."[59]

In the case of Turkey's request for 80 million Rm in weapons credit, only the intervention of Salahhudin Abdul Pasha, a Germanophile Turkish official in Berlin, relieved the doubts of the German Foreign Office sufficiently to permit the granting of credits. He explained away German suspicions about Turkey's friendship with the Soviet Union and the visit of a British Air Force mission to Ankara in 1936 by describing Turkish friendship with the USSR as a necessity, given the size of the Soviet Union and its military forces. Turkey had no real allies in case of an attack by the USSR and, therefore, had to appear to be friendly, but in reality was an enemy of that country. Following this explanation, Berlin promptly approved the weaponry loan. The largest part of the military shipment consisted of artillery, planes, projectors and 4 submarines. However, because of a disagreement over the amount of currency to be paid, Turkey ordered weaponry from Czechoslovakia and destroyers from Germany costing about 50 million Rm.[60]

Similarly, Greece requested 60 million Rm in credit for military equipment to be paid in six years through the Greek clearings balance and 15% through currency or shipments of raw materials for the equivalent in currency. But a bad harvest in 1937 and Greece's inability to ship any more goods via clearings, which ceased in December 1937, prevented payment of more than 40 million Rm to that time. Yugoslavia also placed orders in Germany for various types of planes and weapons which were not always filled; therefore, the Yugoslavs turned to Czechoslovakia and Britain instead.[61]

Bulgaria requested 45 million Rm in credit, placed two days before the Austrian Anschluss on March 13, 1938. Since Bulgaria's ability to make additional deliveries was in doubt, Germany demanded the right to exploit the "Granitoid" mines and new sources of light metals, iron ore and oil. Despite the protests by the Ministry of Economics of the deal's unprofitabilty, the German Foreign Office desired to strengthen Germany's position and to deter Bulgaria from turning to England and France for credit. The German High Command also considered the arming of Bulgaria as extremely important. British and French diplomacy was then working to build up a bloc of neutral states opposed to Germany, and as Bulgaria had been aloof to British and French moves, the Germans approved a new agreement for 45 million Rm in credit, 25 million in weapons deliveries filled from captured Czech supplies.[62] On June 10, 1939, a special agreement permitted Bulgaria 10 million Rm for military aircraft. The arming of Bulgaria and Hungary forced the other states in the Balkan Entente to remain cautious.[63] When Britain extended guarantees against aggression to Romania and Greece on April 13, 1939, and Turkey signed mutual assistance agreements with Britain and France in May and June 1939, Germany ceased deliveries of weapons. But with war approaching in August and September 1939, Berlin reapproved deliveries of weaponry and planes to the Balkan countries on condition that they declare benevolent neutrality and increase the export of strategic raw materials to Germany.

In March 1939 Germany opened negotiations with Yugoslavia for 200–240 million Rm in credit for the purchase of weaponry and aircraft. Berlin laid down specific demands: Yugoslavia would have to leave the League of Nations and sign the Anti-Comintern Pact, which it refused to do. Yugoslavia also had to deliver more raw materials and tobacco and allow Germany geological and exploratory concessions for the exploitation of potential oil resources.

During the Regent Prince Paul's visit to Berlin in 1939, Hitler used the sale of weaponry as a means of pressuring Prince Paul to align Yugoslavia toward the Axis camp. As Germany's alliance with Italy became stronger and Italian aspirations in the Dalmatian littoral and Croatia grew more and more menacing, conversely Yugoslavia's political dilemma became increasingly more acute. Once Mussolini refused Hitler's invitation to attack Yugoslavia after the opening of the Polish campaign in September 1939, Germany renewed offers to supply weapons to Yugoslavia. But as Yugoslavia remained politically doubtful, Göring held up shipments pending a clarification of Belgrade's attitude toward the Axis. Yugoslavia agreed to Göring's limited demands for additional shipments of lead, zinc and hemp. In a secret protocol Yugoslavia placed orders on October 5, 1939, for 100 Messerschmidt 109 fighters, 13 108 Messerschmidt trainers and a number of anti-aircraft and anti-tank artillery from the Škoda works. In return Yugoslavia had to provide Germany by mid-October 3,000 tons of lead, 1,000 tons of lead concentrate and 10,000 tons of hemp, and from November 1 monthly 1,500 to 2,000 tons of copper and 500 tons of lead with a doubling of orders thereafter.[64]

Romania did not initially rely upon Germany for its military needs until mid-1938, placing only 20 million Rm in orders in Germany and 60 million Rm primarily through Škoda in Czechoslovakia. But with the fall of the pro-Allied Titulescu, Germany had the opportunity to contract for weaponry. However, because of Romania's uncertain political attitude, German military circles hesitated to send planes which might be used against it or its Balkan allies, but they agreed to send other weapons.

German pressures for the raw materials of the region increased in 1938 and especially after the outbreak of war when Allied fleets cut off overseas sources of raw materials. The two key countries at the center of German diplomacy in the region were Romania and Yugoslavia because of their oil, non-ferrous metals and foodstuffs. Romania was the fourth largest producer of petroleum in the world after the United States and Brazil, the third largest producer of corn in the world, producing between 1934 and 1938 almost 30% of the total European production, and the fourth largest producer of wheat in Europe in 1938.[65]

An agreement for the purchase of military weaponry was signed between Germany and Romania on July 8, 1939, allowing 60 million Rm in credits, but on July 14 Göring gave instructions for the delaying of deliveries pending clarification of Romania's attitude toward Germany. Hitler's order of June 22 forbade exports of certain types of aircraft like Messerschmidt 109s, but the German minister Fabricius and Gerstenberg, the military representative in Bucharest, insisted that military deliveries should be made because of the critical need for petroleum. "I consider the unimpeded export of petroleum from Romania more important militarily than the weapons being held up," wrote Gerstenberg. Clodius and Wiehl, German economic specialists in the Wilhelmstrasse, agreed to send Heinkel fighters in mid-August. With war looming Fabricius noted the urgency of the situation: every form of railroad carrier, tanker, cistern car and freight cistern were being used to carry to Germany by water or land 660,000 tons of petroleum.[66] Until the autumn of 1938 Romania played an unimportant role in the foreign policy of Germany. But after 1938 when it became clear that the neutrality of Britain could not be relied upon, the possibility of war focused greater attention on Romania's oil reserves. Until 1938 Göring and the German Ministry of Economy believed that German production would almost cover Germany's petroleum needs: 5 million tons normally, 6 million in case of war. But these figures proved to be inaccurate. Göring recalculated Germany's needs from 1938 to 1943 to be approximately double the 5 million tons previously estimated necessary. According to the estimates of a new plan drawn up by Carl Krauch, internal German production would cover only 26% of total needs in 1939, 45% in 1940, 62% in 1941, 72% in 1942 and 79% in 1943.[67] Once war broke out only Romania and the Soviet Union could supply Germany with the large amounts of oil it needed for the Wehrmacht. Between 1934 and 1937 the Soviet Union and Romania supplied the Third Reich with between 8% and 20% of its petroleum; Romania supplied between 7% and 13% of its total. Most of its petroleum came from overseas sources, the United States, the Dutch East Indies, Mexico and Central America. Romania then was the forth and fifth largest producer in the world, producing 8,703,000 tons in 1936 and 7,147,000 tons in 1937 of which Germany took only 453,000 (10%). But Soviet deliveries were slow to arrive after the August 1939 credit agreement in which the Soviets agreed to transfer 161,500 tons monthly plus a hoped for supplement of 2 million tons annually. The Soviets "prudently" reduced this to 800,000 tons per year. The slow delivery of Soviet petroleum made the USSR an uncertain source and placed even greater pressure upon Romania as indispensable.[68]

In 1934 Germany had refused to take Romania's excess agriculture and Foreign Minister Neurath told Petrescu-Comnen flatly that Germany "could only sacrifice for those states whose policy is not like that of Romania which supports our opponents."[69] But Germany's armament needs increased and Romania's exports of petroleum to Germany went from 443,000 tons in 1934 to more than 1 million tons in 1936. By the second half of 1937 world prices fell and the Depression returned. Britain and France suffered trade losses and cut back on imports from Romania, particularly oil and cereals. One million tons of cereals and timber remained unsold on the Romanian market: Romanian export losses resulted in an excess of imports over exports at 11,283 million lei in 1937 and 276 million lei in 1938.[70] In desperation the Romanians began to subsidize exports to Britain and France in order to gain exchange currency which, of course, the Romanian people paid for in the end.

The British economic counter-offensive in Southeastern Europe began with the granting of credits to Turkey and Greece, which were considered the two most important countries in the Southeastern area because of Britain's interests in the Middle East. By March 1938 certain organs of the British government were already galvanized against German commercial power in the Southeast, but the government still had not come around to the view that Germany should be prevented from solving its economic problems by exploiting Southeastern Europe. Thus, on April 28–29, Chamberlain and Halifax rejected French suggestions to cooperate to block Germany from increasing its control over the Southeast by supporting the Little Entente states in establishing a clearing system for the region. Still swayed by the economic appeasers' arguments about allowing Germany to find its raw material needs in the Southeastern region, the British government feared a German reaction against encirclement. Moreover, the British may have believed that Germany would founder increasingly as it became mired in the region and should be allowed to do so.

In April 1939, Petrescu-Comnen, the Romanian foreign minister, approached Halifax to increase British trade with Romania, and Rex Ingram, a Foreign Office official then in Geneva with Halifax, prompted him to take steps to create the Committee on Trade in Central and Southeastern Europe. Halifax brought Ingram's memorandum, "British Influence in Central and Southeastern Europe," before the cabinet which resulted in an interdepartmental committee to get around departmental objections to "political" trade.[71]

In the June 1, 1938, cabinet session, Chamberlain was unenthusiastic and, Hudson, Secretary of the overseas Trade Department — later in November 1938 an opponent of further German penetration into the Southeast — questioned the odious idea of "political trade" to bolster up Balkan economies, as suggested in the Halifax memorandum, effectively scuttling it.[72] The moment was unpropitious as Britain was then moving into the flood tide of appeasement of Hitler. The Chamberlain policy earnestly avoided anything that might arouse German paranoia and anxieties about "encirclement" (State Secretary Weizsäcker even had a special file marked "encirclement").

After Munich, despite all the misgivings of Chamberlain and his supporters, British commercial instincts won out and the Interdepartmental Committee on Trade in Central and Southeastern Europe prevailed. Its members were Leith-Ross (chair), Ashton-Gwatkin, Sargent and Ingram (Foreign Office), Waley (Treasury and Bank of England), with Sir Horace Wilson occasionally attending, probably to keep Chamberlain informed. Thus, as the historian of the committee notes: "In principle the necessity of counteracting German political and economic influence in Southeastern Europe did now seem to have been accepted."[73]

Germany's expansion into Southeastern Europe had been accepted previously because it was believed to be "economic" and not "political." But by the autumn of 1938, with the possible exception of Romania, Germany's commercial position there had become so dominant that the British rightly believed it would shut out British trade and parlay its overweening economic position into political hegemony.

Historians have pointed out that the structure of British, French and other Western capital in Eastern Europe through a whole panoply of state loans, post-war reconstruction aid, private capital investment in the mining and mineral resources of the region, was exploitative in that it extracted wealth without replacing it, which in turn placed those states in a difficult dilemma in the 1930s Depression era when the British and French refused to take their imports.[74] They were then open to German counter-offers and ultimately to German penetration and domination.

British financial interest as opposed to German commercial interest in Southeastern Europe was previously rationalized by the economic appeasers as mutually exclusive. But the entry of more German capital and trade into the region, when Austrian and Sudeten capital and trade passed into German hands in 1938, changed the entire equation. While Chamberlain himself was not enthusiastic about the formation of the Interdepartmental Committee, cabinet and governmental divisions over abandoning the region to Germany forced him to accept it as a hedge against precisely that development. The British thus had never ceased to give up their economic interests in the region, notwithstanding Chamberlain's contrary assertions to Germany. Whereas Germany, lacking colonies, absolutely needed the Southeastern region as a raw material and foodstuffs reservoir, for Britain and most of the other Great Powers with their imperial holdings, dependencies and associations, the Southeast's raw materials were merely a profitable investment either for domestic use or for sale on the international market.

By April 1938 the British began to regard the Southeastern region as something more than an economic sop to contain German military adventures. Halifax's memo of May 24, 1938 ("British Influence in Central and Southeastern Europe") turned away from this view. Ashton-Gwatkin, Leith-Ross and even Chamberlain were interested in garnering any promising new lucrative deals in the Balkans while taking care not to offend German interests or raise the specter of encirclement.[75] The establishment of the Interdepartmental Committee on Trade in Central and Southeastern Europe, while not a "dramatic" change (as its historian Rooke concludes), was nevertheless a "framework for the hitherto piecemeal gestures of support towards the various states of Central and Southeastern Europe."[76]

From this point on, a number of historians are in agreement that British policy wore — in the phrase of the Bulgarian historian, Živkova — "the mark of duality."[77] Openly Chamberlain did not oppose and even encouraged German economic expansion into Southeastern Europe, but covertly the British worked to increase their commercial activity there either through straightforwardly orthodox or "political" trade. The French historian, Marguerat, notes that "since March 1938, the Foreign Office and the Board of Trade supported by the chiefs of staff and by Leith-Ross, the main economic adviser of the government, did everything possible to oppose it (i.e., German domination of the Southeast). The conciliatory declarations of the Prime Minister, whether before Hitler, just after Munich or to the House of Commons on November 1, were simply illusory; they constitute a screen, conscious or not, behind which Halifax, Stanley and Leith-Ross led a British counter-offensive in the Balkans."[78]

Even more significant was the growing pressure from the "City," which had considerable financial interest in the region, and the Association of the British Chamber of Commerce, which asked the British government to take a more active role in British exports and in moving against German economic competition. British newspapers urged the British Board of Trade "to start its own counteroffensive which should be efficient and quick." On the same day — November 1 — Chamberlain reassured Hitler that Britain had no intention of hindering the German penetration of the Southeast or to encircle Germany economically. Stanley also declared on that day, contradictorily, that the British would "preserve some of their positions in that part of the world." On November 30 the House of Commons held stormy debates on the subject of German competition and German methods of infiltration into world markets. R. S. Hudson confirmed that Britain was having difficulty competing with German methods of trade and while recommending continued cartel arrangements with German industries declared that Britain should not retire from trade and other economic opportunities in Southeastern Europe.

The period between the Munich settlement and the following spring was a prelude to the dismemberment of Czechoslovakia with Hitler assessing his opportunities before making his next move. The strings of Slovak, Hungarian and Bulgarian revisionism lay in Hitler's hands to direct as he wished. On

November 1, after having first restrained the Hungarian government, Hitler and Mussolini encouraged Budapest to take control of the Sub-Carpathian Ukraine, by awarding the region to Hungary in the First Vienna Award. In the wake of the Munich Agreement in September 1938, Poland, which took advantage of Czechoslovakia to seize the Tešin district, and Hungary, which occupied the Sub-Carpathian region, began to draw together. Romania feared that its turn had come and that Hungary and Bulgaria would now put forth revisionist claims for Romanian territory in Transylvania and Dobrudja. Rumors circulated that Germany would attack Romania and occupy it, perhaps with the help of its neighbors. On November 5 on the eve of his trip to Berlin and London, King Carol of Romania met with Regent Prince Paul of Yugoslavia to compare notes and to cement their common interest in preventing Bulgarian and Hungarian revisionism and staying out of the Great Power conflict. From Hitler, Carol learned that he intended to support Ukrainian separatism prior to dismembering the Soviet Union and creating a Ukrainian protectorate state. After seeing Carol in London, Chamberlain reported during a cabinet meeting that "King Carol thought that Germany's intention was to try to start the disruption of Russia by fostering an independent state in the Ukraine which would, in effect, be under German influence." Chamberlain made it plain that should war somehow break out between Germany and Russia, Britain would stand aside and let the two fight it out.

> Prime Minister: "Our attitude would be governed by the fact that we did not wish to see France drawn into a war with Germany on account of some quarrel between Russia and Germany, with the result that we should be drawn into war in France's wake."

> Halifax: "emphasized" "it was in our interests to see a strong Russia, and that we must not take any action which made it appear that we were anti-Russian or indifferent to Russia's future."

> "The Prime Minister agreed that this was so. At the same time it was desirable to avoid entanglements arising out of a possible dispute between Russia and Germany."[79]

This exchange raises the likelihood of secret British government hopes of a German-Soviet confrontation closer to a certainty and will be grist for the mill of future historians of the era who seek the locus of British political behavior in upper class hatred of the Soviet Union on the part of Chamberlain and his friends. This same hatred led them to place class survival over the interests of the country which in the end led to the debacle of World War II. Chamberlain and his friends in the government desired to give Hitler at Munich a "free hand in the east" — and probably before Munich — well into the opening months of 1939 and beyond, even after it became apparent that Hitler's aggressive policy and ambitions placed Great Britain and France in mortal danger. Expressed in the most inexplicit and convoluted language, such discussions could later be easily denied as malicious and laid down to misapprehensions and misunderstanding.[80]

The Great Power Struggle for Hegemony in Southeastern Europe, 1935–1940. Erosion of the Little Entente and Balkan Entente

> All these Balkan countries are trash.
> —British Permanent Undersecretary for Foreign Affairs
> Sir Alexander Cadogan, *Diaries*

IN ADDITION TO ITS ECONOMIC OBJECTIVES, German political and diplomatic strategy was to penetrate the economies of the Little Entente countries (Yugoslavia, Czechoslovakia and Romania) in order to loosen their political connection to France. Ministerialrat Willuhn already discussed with Hitler in April and May 1933 the possibilities opened by this policy immediately after the National Socialist rise to power, pointing out the importance of increasing the Southeastern European trade. Germany "would enjoy a preference on the Southeastern European market and secure German economic, cultural and perhaps political influence in the Balkan region."[1]

Foreign Minister Neurath made similar observations in an April 7 cabinet meeting on the economic and political "double strategy" of granting Romania and Yugoslavia preferential trade tariffs.[2] These efforts were capped by the German-Yugoslav agricultural trade negotiations in Berlin in which the Germans agreed to give the Yugoslav agricultural excess production preferential treatment on the German market, and in a secret article to return 7.7 million Rm in German export items, mostly industrial and precision products, which received no preferential treatment on the Yugoslav market. The object of the agreement was to make the German market "indispensable" for Yugoslavia and thus enable Germany to gain a strong economic position in the area and edge out its French, British and Italian rivals.[3] What is significant here is the fact that the avowed aim of Germany's economic policy in the Southeast was from the beginning political hegemony in the region, which Milward, Ellis and others, who insist that Germany's economic exchange with those countries was not exploitative, overlook in their overweeningly mechanistic economic analysis. In the short run it may have been beneficial to the region to open the German market to its trade, but in the long run, particularly after 1938, it ceased to be an advantage. It was only the initial phase in the conversion of the region into a semi-colonial appendage of the Reich.

The results of the German-Yugoslav trade agreement soon became apparent. By 1936 the Yugoslav export and import trade had begun to pass into German hands.[4] The success of the Third Reich is even more striking in that German domination of the Yugoslav trade had been achieved without any significant capital investment. Moreover, as we have seen, the trade agreement had political repercussions. It led to greater Yugoslav economic dependence upon Germany and successfully undermined Czech and French economic and political influence, paving the way for the diplomatic "bomb" of the 1937 Italian-Yugoslav Pact and Yugoslavia's gradual movement away from the Little Entente and toward the Axis.

By 1938, while Germany controlled between 40 and 50% of the total Yugoslav trade, part of the increase stemming from the Austrian trade, in contrast, Yugoslavia's share of the German internal and external market amounted to only 3%. Still more striking is the decline of imports from England, France and Italy from 30% in 1933 to 13% in 1936; similarly exports from Yugoslavia to those countries dwindled from 26% in 1933 to 15% in 1936.[5] Though Hitler told Mussolini that Yugoslavia held no political interest for Germany, which desired only an "open door" in the Southeastern market, these figures, as well as the German Foreign Office statements cited, belie Hitler's assertions of disinterest in the region.[6]

A letter of the Yugoslav Prime Minister Milan Stojadinović to Antić, the Yugoslav Court Chancellor, then in London in 1938 on the occasion of the visit of Prince Paul, indicates a changing situation with the British countering Germany's position in Yugoslavia. "Since 1935," commented Stojadinović, "England has become more interested in Yugoslavia." Trade between the two countries had been increasing, rising from 3% of Yugoslavia's trade in 1933 to 18% in 1937, primarily in agricultural and animal products, meat, bacon, wheat, corn, fruits and wood. "The English government should not permit the economic penetration of Southeastern Europe by Germany," wrote Stojadinović, and instructed the Court Minister to open negotiations if England chose to do so.[7]

Before the Anschluss, Yugoslavia feared Italian ambitions in Southeastern Europe rather than those of Germany which lacked either irredentist claims or a common border with it. Yugoslavia welcomed the Ethiopian crisis as a godsend and both Spaljaković, Yugoslav minister to Paris, and Laval, the French Premier, cynically agreed that it might be best to distract Italy toward Ethiopia "in order that it might be occupied there for half a century and thus turn it away from the Balkans and the Danube."[8] The French did not understand Yugoslavia's greater anxiety over a Hapsburg restoration than Germany's annexation of Austria. From Belgrade's standpoint the latter might be beneficial for Yugoslavia. Spaljaković told Laval that he preferred Hitler being on the Italian border to force Mussolini to throw in his lot with the Little Entente. "We prefer a situation which is dangerous but clear." Laval warned Spaljaković that the situation would become even more dangerous if Germany annexed Austria.[9]

After March 1936 and the Rhineland occupation, Regent Paul noted: "The sole danger are two mad men — Mussolini and Hitler."[10] Support from Britain was equally in doubt. Beneš confirmed this to Paul in the following year: "England's one desire is to make friends with Italy and form an anti-German bloc with that power and France." According to Beneš, Hitler was "a puppet of the German army."[11] Apart from the French left ("Daladier and Blum are against Italy," Turkish Foreign Minister Rushid told Paul), the only possible support in the event of an Italian aggression was the Soviet Union. But Moscow was remote and unpredictable; Yugoslavia had no diplomatic relations with the USSR and was rabidly anti-Bolshevik and still recognized the defunct Czarist government.

After Hitler occupied the Rhineland, Paul feared that the French might try to buy off Mussolini by turning him toward prospects of booty in the Balkans. "Italy," Prince Paul noted, "constantly offers Turkey a pact. Rushid believes that France is in agreement with Italy or rather has yielded to it on this subject, dividing spheres in the [Balkan] area — France would have Yugoslavia as satellite — Italy [would have] Turkey. In this way these two Great Powers would have more than a [foothold] in the Balkan countries which are too powerful en bloc."[12] The main aim of this strategy was to unite Europe against Germany. "Europe must be brought into an accord for a mass attack on Germany if it is the aggressor, but in the contrary case, if someone wanted to attack it, then it would be left alone."[13]

The sole impediment to a German absorption of Austria, given Western supineness, remained the Little Entente Powers, particularly Czechoslovakia and Yugoslavia. When Hitler finally made his move to seize Austria, Yugoslav and Czechoslovak resistance had already been dissipated by trepidations and anxieties over a restored Hapsburg Austria under the aegis of Italy. Yugoslavia feared an enlarged Germany, which had swallowed Austria, less than a monarchist Austria — a possibility when the monarchist Kurt Schuschnigg became Austrian chancellor — once again under the Hapsburg double eagle.[14] A joint action with the other members of the Little Entente against Germany was a rather uncertain possibility and risked intervention by Hungary. Thus, in his meeting with Hitler who indicated his plans to absorb Austria, Stojadinović told him that Yugoslavia would not challenge Germany's ambitions.[15] In a circular note reflecting Germany's strengthened diplomatic position, the Wilhelmstrasse official Benzler warned that Germany would not permit any new economic settlement in the Danubian region that did not take into consideration its interests.[16]

The Germans had hoped that better Yugoslav relations with Hungary would free Stojadinović's hands, enabling him to pursue an agreement with irredentist Bulgaria that would draw it away from the newly created Balkan Entente and place pressure upon Greece and the Aegean.[17] Germany would then not have to choose between Bulgaria and Yugoslavia, awakening mistrust when it moved toward one or the other. This strategy, the German legation in Belgrade believed, "would bring both states into our sphere of influence...in order that we may take over the leadership in Southeastern Europe."[18] When Britain and France did nothing to compensate Yugoslavia for the huge commercial losses suffered when the latter supported sanctions and Italian trade with Yugoslavia declined, Belgrade began to consider its options. There were also other baleful signs: The French President Lebrun indicated that France was no longer preoccupied with security since the Rome accords and if attacked by Germany would not have to concern itself with maintaining troops at the Italian border or in Tunisia and Morocco.[19] As a consequence, after the 1935 Ethiopian affair, Yugoslavia began to adopt the position of neutrality with a tilt toward the Axis which it adhered to down to 1941. When Britain tried to instigate Yugoslavia into making menacing and open statements against Italy in the event of an Italian attack on Britain during the 1935 Ethiopian crisis, Stojadinović then countered by asking the British minister: "Who would then defend us from Italy?" Moreover, such a step could not be taken, he said, without consulting the Balkan Pact states.[20] In addition, the Yugoslav General Staff counseled against doing this given the patent unwillingness of the British and French to take action if Yugoslavia were attacked.[21] Talks between Ambassador Purić and Anthony Eden in London indicated the British had little desire to support the French, adopted an ambiguous attitude toward Italy, and were now moving toward a reconciliation with Germany. The Germans, von Heeren, German minister to Belgrade, told Prince Paul, were delighted with the prospect and if that possibility failed, Hitler would turn to Mussolini.[22]

The French retreat before Hitler during the 1936 Rhineland crisis had even greater repercussions than the Anschluss crisis two years later, leaving Central and Eastern Europe open to the menace of German and Italian power. France was now more committed to defending its borders against Germany and could offer little support against an Italian aggression across the Adriatic. In fact, France was more interested in gaining the friendship of Italy against Germany than in defending the Little Entente states or the Balkan Entente from Italian designs. Laval returned to his plan for a French-Italian-Yugoslav alliance against Germany and recommended that Yugoslavia should overlook Italian collusion in the assassination of the Yugoslav monarch Alexander by Croatian and Macedonian terrorists in 1934 and patch up relations with Italy.[23]

Prince Paul fell in line with the French assessment and two months after Hitler occupied the Rhineland noted: "We have to offer Italy an alliance," and his premier, Stojadinović, was also "rather partial" to the idea.[24] Mussolini previously had assured Paul that he did not want war which Italy, with a considerable debt, could ill afford.[25] He did not believe the Anschluss would happen because France was constantly working with Italy to prevent it. Now, however, the Italians were singing a different tune and since the occupation of the Rhineland ardently desired Yugoslav support against any further German penetration into the Southeast. "The Adriatic Sea should unite not separate them," Ciano, Mussolini's son-in-law and Italian Foreign Minister, told Prince Paul. Germany was not only a dangerous adversary to her enemies but a difficult friend to her friends. He seemed resigned to German expansionism: "The Anschluss is inevitable." Ciano saw a pact between the two countries as a point of departure. "Our pact could draw other countries into our orbit." An entente with Hungary was desirable. Ciano appeared to be apprehensive about facing Germany alone when Hitler, following the Rhineland coup and annexing Austria, would be thrusting into the Southeast. When Vienna became the second German capital, he warned, Budapest must be with us.[26] For mineral and oil-deficient Italy, the natural resources of the Balkans were equally important for its economy, and it too harbored imperialist designs on the area, which had been for centuries an Italian zone of commercial and cultural influence.

All this was not lost on the bluff and opportunistic Yugoslav leader, Milan Stojadinović, who trimmed his sails to the changing winds of international diplomacy. Encouraged by the Germans, Stojadinović protected his eastern flank by signing an agreement with Bulgaria on January 24, 1937, prior to dealing with the Italian threat in the eastern Adriatic. Berlin greeted the news of the Yugoslav-Bulgarian Agreement with jubilation, believing they had weakened the Balkan Entente aimed against Bulgarian revisionism. Stojadinović next moved to improve his relations with Italy. In his negotiations with Italy over Italian hegemony in Albania, Stojadinović failed to get an "open door" agreement and had to recognize Italian preeminence as the price for Italy's friendship. Yugoslav influence in Albania languished and declined in favor of Italy and, in a sense, the pact encouraged later Italian moves to incorporate that country into the Italian imperial sphere of interest.[27]

Ironically both the British and French and the Germans supported the Italian-Yugoslav rapprochement as a step toward drawing Italy closer to them and against Germany. Encouraged, the British and French once again tried to bring about a general accord with the Balkan Powers — an early expression of the "Peace Front," an odd oxymoron adopted by London. The French tried to move in the same sense in Bucharest but failed due to Yugoslavia's refusal. Prince Paul and Stojadinović reported these moves to Berlin and deferentially requested German advice. This kind of sinuous dealing with the Germans made the Regent, Prince Paul, increasingly suspect in the eyes of the British until they decided to get rid of him in 1941. Neurath told Cincar-Marković, the Yugoslav minister in Berlin, to keep his distance from Romania and that "Yugoslavia should in the future maintain a free hand."[28]

The announcement of the Italo-Yugoslav pact of 1937 "came like a bomb," a Czech official lamented. Chvalkovsky, the Czech minister at Rome, reported that "it was an especially great Italian success" and that "the Little Entente is demolished." The Czechs believed that Germany and Italy had divided the Balkans, with Germany conceding Yugoslavia to Italy.[29] The signing of the Bulgarian-Yugoslav Pact had a similar effect on Greece which felt that Bulgaria had improved its position and "the Balkan Pact had lost its real content." As a direct consequence the Turkish Minister-President visited Athens at the request of the Greek strong man and dictator Metaxas and the Greeks moved closer to the Turks "to offset 20 million Slavs."[30] Metaxas had a different reaction to the Italo-Yugoslav Pact which he believed lessened the danger of Greece being dragged into war against Italy if Yugoslavia were attacked and invoked the Balkan Pact.[31]

The pact had a disturbing effect upon Yugoslavia's relations with France whose press attacked Belgrade for its apostasy. When Paul complained to French Foreign Minister Yvon Delbos, he merely shrugged off the matter as "only the scene of a jealous woman." Paul offered no defense for his alliance with Italy to meet French reservations: "I had to look after the interests of my country," he declared dryly.[32]

The Rhineland crisis promoted much diplomatic scurrying about between Vienna-Prague-Budapest to recreate and revive the Hapsburgs as a way of forestalling the Anschluss. Stojadinović and Beneš played a leading role in scuttling these plans and in fact Stojadinović denounced the idea of a Hapsburg restoration hours before Hitler marched into the Rhineland. Even before the Anschluss, Stojadinović had written off Austria and told Hitler that he need expect no difficulties from Yugoslavia. When Hitler and Göring, fearing an intervention by the Yugoslavs and Czechs, brought up the matter during Stojadinović's visit in January 1936, he confided that the Anschluss was "an internal matter in which we will not mix and still less go to war over." Later, Yugoslavia informed Berlin that it would not take part in any sanctions against Germany over the Anschluss.[33]

The Yugoslav High Command met shortly after the Anschluss and decided to give its northwest border first priority in recognition of the fact that Germany and not Italy was the major danger and now shared a common border with Yugoslavia since its absorption of Austria in March 1938.[34] However, the effect of Anglo-French appeasement of Hitler influenced Yugoslavia's ties with the Little Entente. The dismemberment of Czechoslovakia at Munich in September 1938 raised questions about the continued viability of the alliance. When Romanian Foreign Minister Petrescu-Comnen suggested that Stojadinović send a telegram to Göring warning that a Hungarian attack upon the truncated Czechoslovak state would have "unforeseen consequences," Stojadinović refused to do anything unless France first did.[35] Stojadinović questioned whether the Little Entente was still valid if Czechoslovakia had lost a million of its inhabitants by its own decision. Both agreed that the Czech problem rested with the Great Powers and they "would undertake military measures as the situation dictates." If war developed Petrescu-Comnen suggested that their attitude should be "neutrality at first, waiting to see how the fronts develop and who will be our ally militarily, financially, and industrially."[36]

In the early months of 1939 Bulgaria and Italy replaced Germany as the most immediate perils.[37] The British minister, George Rendel, at Sofia, warned that if Bulgarian irredentist demands were not met soon, they would "take the law into their own hands." Rendel's arrival in Sofia and his statements shortly after fanned ultra-nationalist demands for territorial changes, particularly the return of Macedonia. Like Leith-Ross in Romania, Rendel indicated one of his major tasks would be to increase the sale of Bulgarian goods on the British market in order to remove Bulgaria from German economic influence. His mission, he told the Yugoslav minister in Sofia, was to smooth out differences between Bulgaria and its neighbors and "to draw [it] toward Europe as a unified whole."[38]

Prince Paul complained to the British minister of Bulgarian intrigues — inspired, he believed, by the British — to gain an Aegean outlet for Bulgaria at the expense of Greece. Bulgaria, Paul declared, was "playing the Italian game" by sowing discontent among the Balkan states in order to destroy the Balkan Entente. With "a deep touch of bitterness" Prince Paul remarked that a combination of fifty million people which could bar the door to Germany's *Drang nach Osten* was of more value to Great Britain than a nation of four million people which the four Balkan Entente states could crush in a week in the event of war. "If you break up the Balkan Entente," Paul warned, "you will leave me no alternative but to throw myself in the arms of Germany."[39] Campbell believed "Paul's warning was neither a "threat" nor "blackmail" and advised London to cease encouraging Bulgarian territorial demands for the moment against the members of the Balkan Entente, which could only cause disruption in the Balkans from which solely the Axis Powers would benefit.[40] Paul had received more "alarming" news: the Italians intended to depose King Zog of Albania and Ciano would propose a partition of Albania between Italy and Yugoslavia during his forthcoming trip to Belgrade. When Paul questioned him, Stojadinović admitted he found the partition proposal "rather tempting." "Then you must be mad," Paul retorted.[41]

The Prince Regent told Campbell he had persuaded the Croatian Peasant Party leader, Maček, to enter the government with three followers and would shortly drop Stojadinović.[42] Otherwise, Paul would have to take the blame for the continuing quarrels with the Croats and Serb hegemonic centralism, anathema to the Croats and Slovenes.[43] Maček and the United Opposition demanded constitutional changes to provide for more autonomy for the national groups, but did not insist upon it and were willing to put it off until after the King's majority.[44] After a hare hunt, Ciano broached matters to Stojadinović, offering Salonika and its environs in exchange for Yugoslav approval of Italian annexation of Albania. Ignoring instructions from the Prince Regent, Stojadinović countered with a plan to partition Albania, with Yugoslavia receiving northern Albania and Skadar and a long sought secondary access to the Adriatic.[45]

Ciano's visit plunged Prince Paul into an anxious depression. Campbell described the Regent's dilemma:

> I am sorry to say that Prince Paul is in a nervous condition due to the clouds which are darkening his horizon in both external and internal affairs... his position between Germany and Italy who are competing for his friendship, but neither of whom he trusts, is becoming increasingly delicate and difficult. Nor does he seem to be able to throw off his suspicion of King Boris whom he suspects as does King George of Greece of having inspired revisionism in Bulgaria... with Romania threatened from two sides, the position of Yugoslavia becomes disquieting.[46]

To Ciano's chagrin Prince Paul showed little interest in the Italian scheme to partition Albania.[47] The Regent moved against Stojadinović — whom he had once described as a "giant among pygmies" — with a rapidity that startled both his friends and foes alike.[48] Surprised, the self-confident Stojadinović fell gracelessly, without a word, into political oblivion.

Stojadinović and his pro-fascist policies were so unpopular in the country that when news of his downfall spread through the cafés, strangers reportedly got up and embraced one another. He had become an obstacle to the solution of the Croatian question desired both by London and Prince Paul.[49]

The British exerted great political influence in Yugoslavia through its close dynastic connections between the British and Yugoslav royal families. Prince Paul was deeply attached to the British royal family and the British minister at Belgrade enjoyed a predominant position as *éminence grise*. The cordial relations between the British-educated, corvine-faced, suave art-connoisseur, Regent Paul, and the British minister Campbell suffuses the otherwise dry diplomatic correspondence. Prince Paul, referred to by Campbell in the transparently cryptic sobriquet, "our friend," passed much valuable information to the British on Balkan and European political developments.[50] Thus, the British gave unequivocal support to Prince Paul's policies and requests wherever possible in dealing with his adversaries. Even when advising modifications of his policies or lending a sympathetic ear to other internal leaders — like the Croat Maček — it was always with an eye to strengthening the hand of Paul in Yugoslavia.

As the complex negotiations between the Regent and Maček wore on into the summer of 1939, urgent messages from R. W. Seton-Watson, a historian and well-known specialist on Eastern Europe, sent to Yugoslavia by the Foreign Office to make contacts and gather information, warned that chauvinist elements on both the Croat and Serb side might stalemate negotiations and thereby open the door to foreign intervention.[51] Maček was, in fact, also intriguing with Mussolini who hoped to provoke a Croatian revolt and, after the Italians were summoned in for support, to declare an independent Croatian state in personal union with Italy.[52]

In March 1939 Mussolini became suspicious of German political ambitions in Yugoslavia after receiving information that Berlin was fishing in the murky waters of Croatian separatism. Enquiring suspiciously about Germany's Mediterranean interests and intentions, the Italian leader, with "considerable firmness," warned Ambassador Mackensen that German meddling in Yugoslavia might wreck the Axis.[53] Italy had formerly supported the Croatian separatist movement but "that time is past now." Italy now wanted a "strong Yugoslavia." The Croatian question touched upon Italy's Adriatic and Mediterranean interests and it would "react" against any German attitude contradicting this. For Mussolini the Croatian question was *"noli me tangere."*[54]

Von Mackensen assured Ciano that Germany would not abet Croatian aspirations; Hitler had decided that there was to be a clear division of spheres of interest and that Italy had primary interest in the Mediterranean. This would be an immutable law of German foreign policy. Later, Ribbentrop reiterated to German Foreign Office posts abroad that relations with Croatian organizations "are absolutely not to be cultivated."[55]

The British also tried to avoid provoking Mussolini and did not contest the Italian seizure of Albania in April 1939. Britain, however, drew the line at Albania and Halifax told Crolla, the Italian ambassador, that their attitude would be one of the "gravest concern" if Italy tried to extend its power further into Southeastern Europe.[56]

Ciano told his ministers in London and Paris to explain, through third parties, that Italy seized Albania to block German expansion into the Southeastern region.[57] Italy's support in the event of war with Germany prevented London from contesting the Italian invasion of Albania.[58]

Though formally in the German camp through the 1939 Axis agreement, Italy's position remained ambiguous in the split between the Western capitalist powers. Like Germany, it resented the status quo confining its imperialist ambitions, and envied and respected the wealthier Western Powers, Britain and France. Internal economic weakness and fear of Germany and German expansionist designs in the Southeast prevented it from breaking completely with the British. Italy, like Germany, also lacked raw materials without which it could not construct a military machine to realize Mussolini's claims to empire in the Adriatic and Mediterranean.

Once the Italians established themselves in Albania, they were in a position to attack either Greece or Yugoslavia at will. The consequences were immediately noticeable. Foreign Minister Cincar-Marković was servile, reminding the German minister, von Heeren, that Yugoslavia had given "really clear evidence of its loyalty" toward the Axis. It was now Germany's turn to dampen the effects of recent events by expressing its interest in having a strong Yugoslavia. He requested an interview with "his old friend," Foreign Minister Ribbentrop, and asked Göbbels to raise German press coverage on Yugoslavia to fortify his position for its "realistic" policy in the Austrian and the Albanian affairs.[59]

In April 1939 Cincar-Marković visited the Axis capitals. Ciano feared that difficulties in Albania could be anticipated from the Yugoslavs and that friendly cooperation with Yugoslavia was impossible. "Italian mistrust against the English-oriented Prince Paul is great," the German minister at Budapest reported.[60] The Italians, in fact, overestimated Belgrade's desire to do anything about Albania: the Italian lunge into neighboring Albania had, in fact, made the Yugoslav government even more fearful and craven.

Ciano was only half-satisfied with the results of the Yugoslav Prime Minister's visit. On the positive side the Yugoslav delegation to the League of Nations — anathema to Germany and Italy — was "being completely liquidated," but Rome advised Berlin to "nudge" Yugoslavia toward the Anti-Comintern Pact which they were ready to join "but lacked the courage to confess it openly."[61]

Lingering suspicions about Yugoslavia led the Germans to drag out any loans, credits and armaments, especially bombers and fighter aircraft. Göring and the Foreign Office economic specialist agreed to a credit of one hundred million reichsmarks for military armaments pending counter delivery of "vital raw materials."[62]

Following the guarantees given to Romania and Greece, the British considered offering one to Yugoslavia, but as Ribbentrop pointedly reminded Belgrade, they were hardly in a position to fulfill such guarantees. As Yugoslavia avoided Axis commitments and maintained its neutrality, London did not press the matter.

Badly frightened by Italy's invasion of Albania as a prelude to Italian expansion in the Mediterranean, the Turks hastened to sign an agreement with the Western Powers.[63] Though fearing repercussions from the Axis, the Yugoslavs "in their heart of hearts" were pleased and Balkan opinion was relieved.[64] Thus, the "peace front" of states allied with the Western Powers in a broad belt of countries running from the Baltic to the Black Sea had been constructed almost in a breathless haste prompted more by Hitler and Mussolini's actions than anything else.

But after Romanian Foreign Minister Gafencu and Cincar-Marković met to oppose Article VI (of the May 1939 Anglo-Turkish Pact)* in order to avoid irritating the Axis, it was quietly dropped.[65] Romania and Yugoslavia had no wish to be associated too openly with the "Peace Front" encirclement policy of London and Paris. With some Western prodding, as a first step toward drawing Bulgaria into the Balkan Pact, Gafencu and Cincar-Marković agreed to offer Bulgaria territory taken from it by Yugoslavia after World War I, including southern Dobrudja held by Romania since 1918.

The Germans remained suspicious of both Romanian Foreign Minister Gafencu and Yugoslavia's continued adherence to the Balkan Pact, but Cincar-Marković pointedly indicated Romania's rejection of the Romanian-Polish alliance against Germany as well as a Black Sea Pact with the USSR. Gafencu wanted to shore up the Balkan Pact to enable the Balkan states to adopt a neutral position in the event of war. To allay German suspicions, Yugoslav Foreign Minister Cincar-Marković volunteered to exercise "a certain control" over Romania's policy and to undertake further approaches to Hungary.[66] The Yugoslav Foreign Minister insisted to Berlin that Yugoslavia had never been informed of or participated in the British negotiations with Turkey.

British attempts to gain Bulgaria for a Balkan bloc to bar the door to Axis penetration in exchange for southern Dobrudja only whetted the Bulgarian appetite and Sofia now demanded that all the injustices of World War I be redressed (i.e., Macedonia, Pirot and Thrace).[67] The British and Yugoslavs blamed Romania for not offering southern Dobrudja and the failure of negotiations.

The Turks now took matters in their own hands and massed troops on Bulgaria's Thracian border, exercising threatening pressure on Bulgaria in the event of war. Another shadowy participant, hitherto silently observing events from the side, now emerged from isolation.

The British offer of a pact with Turkey jolted the Soviet Union out of its passive role, and in early May 1939 the *Narkomindel* official, Undersecretary Potemkin, visited Turkey to dissuade Ankara from signing, which would have brought British and French power to the door of the Black Sea. Germany also threatened the Soviet Union and a primary object of Potemkin's visit was Bulgaria's price for entering the Balkan Pact. At this point the USSR wished to build up a Balkan bloc as a way of keeping both the Axis and the Western Powers from the Black Sea. After the Nazi-Soviet Pact, the Western Powers became more dangerous to the Soviet Union than the Germans and Italians in the Black Sea area and elsewhere. Ironically, the Soviet Union and Britain pursued the same Balkan bloc policy, but Potemkin had no more success with the Bulgars than the British had. The Bulgarian Minister-President reiterated demands for Bulgaria's 1913 borders, including Greek Thrace; and Potemkin also failed to get Turkey to guarantee Romania's borders.[68]

Bulgaria's position became increasingly perilous in the summer of 1939. Turkey's aggressive action towards Bulgaria probably resulted from Sofia's

---

*Article VI of the Anglo-Turkish Agreement of May 1939 would permit Western military interference in the Balkans if threatened by aggression.

rejection of its overtures to enter the Balkan Pact, fears the Bulgars would now swing to the Axis side and bottle up the Danube, and Turkey's desire to relieve pressure upon Romania which could then concentrate its forces against Hungary in the event of war. In the background the British were undoubtedly supporting if not instigating these moves by Turkey in order to intimidate King Boris of Bulgaria from taking precipitous action against its neighbors.

When Prince Paul and Mushanov, the pro-Allied President of the Bulgarian Parliament, inquired about the extra Turkish forces in Thrace which had "rather frightened the Bulgars," Lord Halifax assured them the Turks had no aggressive intentions. Turkey's motives, he explained, were prompted by a great deal of loose talk about Bulgaria's intentions and the disturbed state of public feeling forcing them to take precautions against any eventuality. An additional motive was Bulgaria's negative attitude toward the Turks whom it would do nothing to help in the event of war between Turkey and the Axis.

Bulgaria played a complicated game of siding with the Germans and remaining outside of the Balkan Pact in hopes of regaining its lost territories, while making occasional overtures to the Western Powers. This meant that Bulgaria had not yet committed itself to the Axis and that King Boris continued to keep open his options.

Frightened of an attack by the Turks and the British, Bulgaria sought armaments from the Germans and also moved closer to Yugoslavia which was also pursuing a neutral course. Besides weapons, Boris asked for two submarines to defend the Black Sea if the Straits were closed. However, because of Bulgaria's continued friendly relations with the British and French, Hitler rejected Boris's repeated requests for arms.[69]

Seeking security through closer association with Yugoslavia, Bulgaria tried to encourage Yugoslavia's withdrawal from the Balkan Pact while keeping Berlin informed of its efforts. Berlin, in turn, encouraged Bulgaria in these moves to undermine the Balkan Pact. Kiosseivanov and Cincar-Marković met at Bled to discuss the possibility of a joint military alliance while maintaining an armed neutrality. To Kiosseivanov's persistent requests to withdraw from the Balkan Pact, Cincar-Marković slyly responded that he could better influence Romania, Greece and Turkey by remaining inside the Pact. Bulgaria agreed to enter the war on whatever side Yugoslavia decided, but failed to dislodge Belgrade from the Balkan Pact. Nor would Yugoslavia guarantee to assist Bulgaria if the Turks attacked. In short, Yugoslavia would not agree to leave the Balkan Pact nor would Bulgaria enter it.

King Boris improved his relations with Yugoslavia and Turkey in order to effectively concentrate on Romania which held the Bulgarian irredenta — southern Dobrudja; Kiosseivanov expected that the Yugoslav-held irredenta (Caribrod and Dedeagatch) would be settled by arbitration.[70] Regaining Macedonia remained a fantasy for many Bulgars and did not fall into the category of Bulgaria's actual policy.

Throughout July and August 1939 the Turkish military buildup on Bulgaria's borders — estimated at two hundred thousand troops by Kiosseivanov — produced paranoia in Sofia. The Bulgarian government believed that the Turkish pressures stemmed from Ankara's fears of an Italian aggression against Greece, especially against Salonika.[71] Boris and the Bulgarian military believed that in the event of a general war, the British and the French, supported by the other Balkan states, would open up a front in Salonika. Kiosseivanov thought that Turkey and Romania had a secret agreement to attack Bulgaria immediately once war broke out, without regard to its neutrality. Sofia saw enemies on all sides. The Germans did not believe an attack on Bulgaria to be imminent, but nevertheless shipped one thousand heavy machine guns in great haste, with fifteen thousand more awaiting shipment in Vienna. Berlin advised the Bulgars that at a time when its full attention was on the Polish war, it did not desire a Balkan war and tried to calm the Bulgarians.[72]

With the collapse of Western negotiations with the Soviet Union, London may have anticipated war between Germany and Poland and may have been preparing a diversionary feint in the Balkans, a later Salonika front as in World War I should circumstances warrant. Part of the reason for the Turkish military buildup was fear of an Italian attack upon Greece, which, however, the Greek military leader Papagos did not believe likely in September 1939. Turkey feared Axis penetration into the Mediterranean and Near East, using Bulgaria as a staging ground. The Turkish move was meant to compel Bulgaria to remain neutral and to prevent this from happening. The Turkish minister to Athens indicated to the Yugoslavs that the Turkish mobilization was designed to prevent an attack upon Turkey from a third power, i.e., Germany or Italy. Kiosseivanov thought that behind the Turkish mobilization were the British whose war plan was to transfer the conflict over Danzig to the Balkans.[73]

Prince Paul was anxious for the opening of a front against Italy and Mussolini, whom he detested. Paul regarded Italy's neutrality as a ruse and demanded that the British solicit guarantees from Rome.[74] Weygand, chief of the French military forces in the Middle East, told General Papagos that a Balkan landing could not be carried out earlier than three months after the decision had been made.[75] Meetings between Weygand and the Greek military from April through December 1939 never went beyond the discussion phase. Weygand asked a great many questions about the Salonika fortifications and believed the western front war would stalemate as in World War I with the Salonika front deciding the outcome. The British and French agreed to send four or five divisions if Greece were attacked while Greece and Turkey agreed to permit transit of these forces through their territory.[76] A year later, when Germany attacked Greece and Yugoslavia, the British fulfilled their obligations.

The attitude of the Balkan states did not offer encouragement. Each Balkan power desired Western aid for itself but was unwilling to aid its neighbor. The Greeks freely conceded that they would not help the Yugoslavs if Italy attacked the latter, nor would they allow Greece to become a base of operations to reinforce Yugoslavia.[77] Yugoslavia's attitude was similar to Greece's, and a year later, when Italy attacked Greece, Yugoslavia remained neutral. Greece had modified its participation in the Balkan Pact years before to meet just such a contingency, relieving it of the obligation of aiding Yugoslavia if that country were attacked by a non-Balkan power, i.e., Italy. The Balkan Pact, thus, continued to be focused exclusively against Bulgaria. Even if a joint Italo-Bulgarian attack occurred against a Balkan power, the invocation of the Balkan Pact was uncertain. When the Greek attaché in Belgrade asked what would happen in just such a contingency, General Simović declared they would support the Greeks, despite the contradictions.[78] Despite these brave words, when the Italians attacked Greece in the following year, Yugoslavia remained neutral. Only a more resolute British and French attitude and the active intervention of Weygand's Syrian army in the Balkans could have brought in any of the Balkan neutrals.

At the end of September 1939, British minister Rendel, dropping "veiled threats," advised Bulgaria to join a neutral front of Balkan states as a bulwark against Germany.[79] However, the lowering war clouds dispersed as quickly as they had come. London extended an invitation to King Boris to England and the Turks now appeared to be desirous of friendship.[80] With the winding down of the Polish war, the exceedingly nervous Bulgarian minister to Berlin, Draganov, reported to Berlin that the danger of war had lessened.

The Soviets also changed their position and now no longer encouraged Bulgaria to enter the Balkan Pact. Bulgaria's neutral position, they now declared, did not contradict Soviet policy and Molotov even offered to conclude a new trade or mutual assistance agreement with Bulgaria. Sofia rejected the Soviet offer and proposed instead a non-aggression or friendship pact to which Moscow did not immediately reply. Schulenberg, the German minister to Moscow, attributed the changed Soviet position to fears that the British and French might gain a decisive position in the Straits area and the Balkan states, and the Soviet desire to exercise an influence in Bulgaria, the only state not belonging to the Balkan Entente. A number of factors were influencing Soviet behavior: the May 1939 British-French Agreement with Turkey which brought a threatening Allied influence into the Straits area; increased British and French hostility toward the Soviet Union following the Nazi-Soviet Pact and the fall of Poland; and the presence of British and French forces in Syria and Palestine poised to invade the Balkans if necessary. For the moment the imminent threat of a British and French invasion overshadowed the danger of Italian and particularly German penetration into the Southeast. The Axis intentions of extending its influence further southward diminished or at least for the moment stalemated while increased danger of a British and French intervention into the Eastern Mediterranean, the Aegean and the Balkans mounted.[81] The conflicts between the USSR and Germany over paramountcy in Romania and Bulgaria in 1940 had not yet occurred.

Soviet fears of an allied invasion of Southeastern Europe and a general military attack against the USSR heightened throughout the winter and spring of 1939–1940. While the Soviet Union had formerly favored a front of Balkan powers including Bulgaria against Hitler's penetration of the Southeast to the shores of the Black Sea and the Straits and had urged Bulgaria to join the Balkan Pact, it now encouraged Bulgaria to remain neutral outside the Pact, which it viewed as an instrument of British power.

As the fall of 1939 waned, Britain became disinclined to extend itself into the Balkans unless forced to, by a German invasion of Greece, to prevent a threat to the Eastern Mediterranean and England's Suez lifeline. Britain avoided antagonizing the Italians into abandoning neutrality, and repercussions from the Soviet Union. Instead the British and French remained satisfied that the Damoclean sword of Weygand's Syrian army dissuaded any Axis move into the Aegean and the Balkans.

British efforts to consolidate Balkan resistance through guarantees to Romania and Greece had achieved a certain effect, but the larger aim of extending the Anglo-French-Turkish Pact to the Balkans and of drawing Bulgaria into the Balkan Pact to create a solid front of Balkan states against Axis aggression had faltered. Bulgaria was now at the disposal of the Axis while Yugoslavia and Romania were in an increasingly difficult position and unable to fend off Axis pressures. The Bulgarian minister to Berlin, Draganov, believed that since the Anglo-French-Turkish Pact, Bulgaria would reject any new plans for accession to the Balkan Pact.[82]

British coolness toward a Salonika front landing was not only on military grounds and a disinclination to extend the war into the Balkans, but also out of vague apprehensions that the French entertained ambitions in the region.[83] Supported by Massigli, the French minister at Ankara, Weygand pressed at the Balkan capitals, Ankara and Paris for the establishment of supply bases in Anatolia, Thrace and Salonika, but British reluctance to risk disturbing Italy undermined these efforts at meetings of the Allied Chiefs of Staff.[84]

Moscow became aware of Allied intentions and moved to neutralize Turkey and frustrate Western preparations for a Salonika landing in an area where they had always been historically sensitive. During the visit to Moscow in October 1939 of Saracoglu, the Turkish Foreign Minister, Stalin proposed to the Turks that their pact with the Western Powers be modified and transformed into a consultative accord in the event of war between the British and French and the USSR. In return the Soviets offered Turkey an assistance pact in case of aggression in the Black Sea. In addition, the Soviets requested a "German clause" — i.e., if Germany and Turkey became involved in war — nullifying the accord in the event of a German attack on Turkey. Saracoglu refused to give way, as did Molotov, and the talks were suspended. The British reluctantly agreed to the Soviet terms, but Daladier "reacted violently," refused to change the text and recalled Massigli to Paris. The Turks returned home empty-handed and in the end they remained loyal to the agreement with the Western Powers, which they had signed in October 1939, several days before Saracoglu left for Moscow.[85]

The outbreak of the Soviet war against Finland at the end of November deflected British and French attention from the war against Hitler and the Salonika enterprise to the northern struggle. The French reacted particularly vehemently against the USSR: French police raided the Soviet trade delegation in February 1940 and on March 15 the French government abrogated the Franco-Soviet trade agreement and declared Suritz, the Soviet ambassador in Paris, *persona non grata*. French communist deputies were expelled from parliament and at the beginning of April 1940 were arrested and sent to prison for four to five years with loss of civil and political rights.[86]

As the Soviet military setbacks against Finland multiplied, French and British interest in aiding the Finns grew stronger through the sending of an expeditionary force across Norway and Sweden, or through an air attack on the Baku oil wells or a landing in the Black Sea. The projected Allied landing in Salonika directed primarily against Germany now began to metamorphose into an attack on the USSR. These plans seemed from the beginning less to aid the Finns than to transfer the war to the Soviet Union, making the conflict against the Germans secondary. The pretext that the USSR was supplying Germany with oil and other raw materials strains credulity, as the amount of oil being sent has been disputed by some scholars. Instead, the real reasons undoubtedly were that the British and French, angry at finding themselves involved in a conflict with Germany while the USSR remained neutral, wanted to use the Finnish war and Stalin's association with Hitler in the Nazi-Soviet Pact as a way of settling scores with the USSR.

The British, previously cool toward an attack in the Balkans, now almost matched the French in their enthusiasm for a confrontation with the Soviet Union. Chamberlain, always anti-Soviet in his outlook, was ready to send British forces across Scandinavia to aid the Finns. Only Swedish obduracy in refusing passage and Finland's apprehension that acceptance of Allied aid would be followed by German intervention and Scandinavia and Finland itself would become a new war front, prevented an Allied intervention.[87] Instead, the Finns decided to accept the Soviet peace conditions when their military situation began to collapse. However, there is little doubt that the Allies would have sent military forces had the Finns wished. Part of Allied indecisiveness lay in doubts over whether to attack the Soviet Union in the south at Baku or a landing in the Black Sea or in the northern theater through Finland. In the end, the British and French backed away from the Baku and Balkan front attack, and in March 1940 the War Cabinet agreed to draw up plans to bomb Baku but did not implement them. The prospect of taking on an additional enemy, the Soviet Union, at a time when all the available forces were needed to defend the western front against a forthcoming German attack, made a side-campaign seem daunting. The repercussions of a defeat, the uncertainties of a Russian campaign and a myriad of other military, diplomatic and political imponderables, caused initial British enthusiasm to subside.[88]

At the Sixth Meeting of the Allied War Council on March 28, 1940, the British procrastinated, insisting that the plans to strike at the Caucasus oil fields be studied further by Allied experts in all their ramifications — i.e., the attitude of Turkey, prospects of success, etc. — even though Finland had capitulated. The fact that the project to attack the Soviet Union in the Black Sea and the plan to aid the Finns through a campaign cutting across Sweden ran in tandem indicates that the compelling idea was to attack the Soviet Union and transfer the war to the eastern front in the hope of reducing the war against Germany. The desired scenario might yet be salvaged. Premier Reynaud's enthusiasm matched that of his predecessor, Daladier, for a strike against the Soviet Union, although he denies it.[89] French politicians and military leaders were exhilarated by the prospects of attacking the USSR, of "breaking the back of the USSR" and "entering the USSR as into butter."

These winter dreams were launched by British and French apprehensions beginning in December 1939 that a Soviet offensive in northern Finland might lead the Red Army to seize the Gallivare iron ore mines in northern Sweden, crucial to the German economy, and provoke a German invasion of Sweden. The British believed that Germany might do this based upon diplomatic evidence, but no evidence exists that Moscow had any such intentions. Numerous conferences in London and Paris throughout the winter of 1939–1940 produced feverish projects to land forces in either Norway in the Narvik area, in Sweden or in Petsamo, Finland. But British plans for an intervention collapsed when the Swedish king threw his weight against bringing the war to Swedish territory.

The British Foreign Office was first concerned about a Soviet-Finnish conflict and, once that occurred, it feared war between Britain and France and the USSR over the Swedish iron ore mines. Later leading Foreign Office officials like Vansittart, Orme Sargent and Collier, cabinet members like Churchill and Halifax, and military leaders like General Ironside became increasingly bellicose and almost pathetically anxious to land forces in Scandinavia. Hoare and others openly spoke of aiding the Finns through volunteers from the regular army. The imagined payoff for aiding the Finns to hold on for some time was heady stuff: the Soviet Union would be expected to disintegrate into economic and political chaos thereby undercutting and eliminating Germany's major supplier of raw materials. Even the ever-cautious Chamberlain spoke of "dealing a mortal blow to Germany" that could be "one of the turning points in the war." Later, Chamberlain and Reynaud saw the unreality of taking on another major enemy at a time when the Western Powers were lamentably weak in war materials of all sorts.

Both the detailed articles of A. J. Bayer on British policy for the northern project and Charles R. Richardson on the French plans for the Caucasus oil field attack jointly agree that there were both fantasy and illusion in the intentions and expectations of the Allied Powers that aiding the Finns through Scandinavia might produce all manner of wondrous things. Bayer concludes: "British policy towards the Russo-Finnish [war] was based on fantasy more than reality." Among the unrealities was believing that Norway and Sweden would allow Allied forces to enter their territory and convert it into a battleground "against an enemy, Germany, whom they clearly viewed as their potential savior against bolshevism." Such "miscalculations, contradictions and fantasies created the grand illusion that the fate of Finland mattered to the outcome of the Allied war against Germany." Chamberlain's belief that Germany could be permanently crippled by economic means lived on to resurface in Plan R4 in late March 1940 to cut off the flow of Swedish iron ore to Germany from Narvik and Lulea, which ended in disaster, forcing him to resign in May 1940. Richardson, on the other hand, is less circumspect on the real aims of the British and French. Like Bayer, he describes the "supreme illusion which the Russophobes and anti-communists eagerly grasped was that the Allies had such military power to spare that they could safely risk war with the Soviet Union in order to deprive Germany of its oil." And more to the point: "This conviction was of great comfort to the defeatists who never wanted to 'die for Danzig.' Having failed to prevent war with Germany, they wanted to avoid military action against her and welcomed substituting Stalin for Hitler as the prime adversary." The French conservative critic, Kerillis, scathingly describes the ironies of the situation:

> Suddenly there was a great demand for war with Russia. Those who had not wished to die for Danzig now wished to die for Helsinki. Those who insisted they could not fight sixty-five million Germans alone could now fight a Russo-German combination of 245 million. Those who preached immobility behind the Maginot Line now pleaded to have an army fight near the North Pole. They ordered the army in Syria, whose mission was to support Turkey against Germany, to prepare an expedition against Baku, thousands of kilometers away from their bases, across deserts and mountains.... They proved that Russia was a colossus with feet of clay which would collapse from the slightest blow. At the foreign affairs commission of Parliament, a deputy spent thirty minutes demonstrating that one could not beat Hitler until having "crushed" Stalin and cut Russia to pieces.[90]

In Britain, some in the upper class dreaded a breach in the Nazi-Soviet Pact, which would face the British and French with coming to terms with Hitler in an anti-Soviet crusade leaving Germany armed to the teeth and morally strengthened or with attacking him when he himself was fighting an enemy whom many considered more venomous than the Nazis themselves.[91] There was also the fear that extension of the war into Russia would arouse much criticism.[92]

The Soviet-Finnish war aggravated British-Soviet relations, at loggerheads since the signing of the Nazi-Soviet Non-Aggression Agreement in August 1939. When R. A. B. Butler insinuated to Maiskii, the Soviet Ambassador to Britain, that the Soviet Union having recently entered into a trade agreement with Germany seemed to be passing into the German camp, Maiskii replied by reading a communication from Molotov laced with acid sarcasm.[93]

But despite the mutual recriminations and bitterness, the reiterated wariness by Butler that Labor was hostile to war with Russia, the frank Soviet wish for a renewal of relations worked for by both Maiskii in London and the new British Ambassador Stafford Cripps in Moscow gradually overcame the suspicions and fears of both countries to some degree.[94] However, a reconciliation did not become a reality until the German attack on the Soviet Union in the following year.

Part Four

The Struggle for Hegemony in Eastern Europe, 1939–1941. The Shift from Political Conflict to Military Force

Chapter 14

German Encirclement Fears. The British Guarantee to Poland, Romania and Greece, March–April 1939. U.S. Trade Relations with Germany and Britain

My poor friend, what have you done? For us I see no other outcome but a fourth partition of Poland.

—Potemkin, Soviet Vice Commissioner for Foreign Affairs, commenting on Munich Conference to Coulondre, French Ambassador

A DETERMINANT THAT INFLUENCED the drift towards war which has not been examined systematically by historians of World War II is the German fear of encirclement by Britain, France and the United States. If the Germans feared political encirclement by their enemies, the Western Powers equally were not reluctant to use German paranoia as a way of controlling the eastward march of German power.

It will be recalled that Ernst Weizsäcker kept an "encirclement" file on his shelf and German Foreign Office officials surveilled any political signs of Western "encirclement" of Germany. As a people in the middle of Europe, the Germans have always been conscious of the peoples around them, particularly in the contemporary period after the formation of the German state. Prussian diplomacy in the era of Frederick the Great in the eighteenth century adeptly concluded alliances with the other Great Powers depending upon its interests at the time. A two-front war through encirclement by Germany's enemies was a nightmare of both Wilhelmian and Nazi Germany. Hitler inherited the problem of the French system of alliances with the Eastern European states and their encirclement of Germany from his predecessor, the Weimar Republic, and shared the aversion of the Weimar government, the Reichswehr and the Wilhelmstrasse for the "poisonous" issues of Versailles, Poland and Czechoslovakia. Shaped like a thorn and lodged deep in Germany's side, the "appendix," as Göring derisively called Czechoslovakia, had alliances with France and the USSR. Therefore, to Hitler and German nationalists, Czechoslovakia was both an instrument of encirclement and the forward base of bolshevism on Germany's border.

In the weeks immediately following the Munich accord, Chamberlain, Halifax and the British Foreign Office were exceedingly loathe to arouse Hitler's "encirclement" anxieties. But when Hitler made no attempt to follow up the declaration of friendship signed at Munich and the soundings of

Leith-Ross, and attacked the British for preventing Germany from achieving its political aspirations in the east, Halifax led Chamberlain and the cabinet into utilizing the previously neglected Eastern European states primarily through financial and economic means, later through political support as well. The opening gambits of this policy were focused on Romania through the Romanian wheat deal, trade credits and "political" trade. Despite this partial turnabout, on October 31, 1938, Chamberlain told the cabinet that appeasement continued to be Britain's policy toward Germany.[1]

But renewed British economic activity in the Southeast and British rearmament aroused German encirclement anxieties. German perceptions of beleaguerment coupled with shortages of currency and raw materials exacerbated internal tensions and the breathtaking pace of Hitler's adventurist gambles. However, the immediate cause of the panther's spring of March 15, 1939, into the Czech provinces was undoubtedly economic.[2]

British wariness of stoking Hitler's paranoia made them chary of too close association with either France or Russia. Halifax enunciated these concerns to a Foreign Policy Committee meeting earlier in March 1938: "the more we produced in German minds the impression that we were plotting to encircle Germany, the more difficult it would be to make any real settlement with Germany."[3]

Daladier scoffed at these misgivings at British-French staff conversations the following month: "As regards the suggestion of encirclement, he did not himself believe Germany was really worried about encirclement. After all who was encircling Germany? In the West she had reoccupied the Rhineland. She had recently occupied Austria. She had forged the Rome-Berlin axis and established satisfactory relations with Poland. She was considering the dismemberment of Czechoslovakia, and if she succeeded in this, she would then succeed in realizing the dream of William II of a Mitteleuropa under German dominance."[4] London avoided any suggestion of encircling Germany even to the point of considering not to support France if it became embroiled in a struggle with Germany or Italy.

Encirclement was part of Hitler's irrational *Weltanschauung,* and he did not scruple to manipulate and exploit German fears of encirclement to achieve his objectives, nor to gull and intimidate the British through fits of rage and displays of temper into believing that any resistance to his will or suggestions of encirclement might unhinge him and propel him into war. Between Munich and March 15, 1939, and even after, British policy in many respects was to tiptoe around Hitler, and in the words of one British writer "to keep the word 'encirclement' out of the German press."[5]

But when Poland was next on Hitler's list of victims, the British acted almost rashly and with stunning speed by giving Poland a guarantee of its independence, including the disputed port of Danzig and the Corridor without asking too many questions. They learned only afterwards that Polish Foreign Minister, Colonel Beck, hid from them his negotiations with Hitler who demanded the return of Danzig and an extra-territorial route through the Corridor. The haste with which Chamberlain and Halifax had offered to guarantee Poland immediately raised fears among some of the conservative supporters of appeasement that Chamberlain, under pressure of the opposition and Labor, would now close with Stalin in an agreement against Germany.

Before the ink had dried on the Polish guarantee, Sir Samuel Hoare warned that the Germans would raise the alarm of "encirclement" and unleash a preventive war.[6] R. A. Butler obliquely cautioned Halifax via notes from Henderson in Berlin that Hitler would be unlikely to declare war unless he believed himself encircled or that Britain was preparing a preventive war against Germany.[7] Henderson tried to exculpate the Polish guarantee by explaining that "what the Germans call encirclement is nothing of the sort but is in fact and simply and solely [*sic*] an attempt to organize resistance to aggression." He feared that the doubling of the territorial army by Britain on March 29, 1939, might cause Hitler to carry out an attack on the premise "better now than later when we will still be more prepared." If Hitler decided to attack Poland "that would probably be the real reason and the fear of an economic collapse and the popularity of the Polish cause" rather than the Polish guarantee and the Anglo-Polish agreement as serious deterrents.[8]

Hitler's demand for the return of Danzig and a corridor-in-the-Corridor met with a level of approval in Germany that the war against Czechoslovakia never did. The German army had done an about face, Colonel Mason-MacFarlane reported: "the German Corps of Officers is absolutely united over the Corridor question, and that most of the senior officers in the War Ministry are now convinced devotees of Herr Hitler."[9]

Dire predictions of disaster came from Eastern Europe and even from Germany's ally, Italy, and some British sources. Agitated and distraught, the Italian ambassador in Berlin, Attolico, told Ogilvie-Forbes, counsellor in the British embassy, that he was "very apprehensive of the effect on Nazi opinion of the present negotiations for an anti-Nazi agreement which, despite all assertions to the contrary would only confirm the German impression of encirclement... the Poles were being unnecessarily aroused against the Germans and also Herr Hitler was in addition infuriated over encirclement."[10] Prince Paul also received reports from Attolico through his minister in Berlin that he expected the Germans to have decided on a " 'preventive war,' i.e., to strike before we had completed their encirclement."[11] The Romanian government demurred against signing a pact with Poland as they were being urged by Britain and France because "it would be regarded by Germany as an attempt at encirclement."[12] The South Africans (General Hertzog) told London a week before the Polish guarantee that "it would have no other result but that of war not because Germany does not necessarily want war, but because such [a] policy of encirclement cannot be taken by her as meaning anything else than a declaration of hostilities differing but little, if at all, from a declaration of war."[13] But these were all arrows shot into the air, as Halifax and Chamberlain knew full well that the Polish guarantee could lead to war.

During talks on the occasion of Bonnet's visit to London on March 21, 1939, Halifax was explicit about British aims: "it was now the question [*sic*] of checking German aggression, whether against France or Great Britain or Holland or Switzerland or Romania or Poland or Yugoslavia or whoever it might be."[14] At the March 27 cabinet meeting Halifax stated that neither France nor Britain could prevent Poland and Romania from being overrun. "We were faced with the dilemma of doing nothing or entering into a devastating war." Doing nothing would mean "a great accession to Germany's strength" and a loss of support from the U.S., the Balkans and elsewhere. "In those circumstances if we had to choose between two great evils he favored our going to war."

When the subject of what to do about the other countries facing the possibility of a German attack came up, Chamberlain observed that Poland would not agree to support militarily any of the Eastern European countries (Romania, Yugoslavia), but only those on the western rim of Europe (Holland, Belgium, Switzerland). A cabinet member — the Chancellor of the Duchy of Lancaster — warned against extending the guarantee to Romania or Greece "or we should lay ourselves open to the charge of trying to encircle Germany." The British government should work toward building alliances between those countries as "such arrangements would not have the same propaganda value for Germany as arrangements similar to the Anglo-Polish agreement."[15] But in the headlong turnaround of the British government to stop further German expansion this was forgotten when Colonel Beck came to London in April 1939. The Polish Foreign Minister had rejected the earlier British plan for a four-power agreement to consult in the event of a new threat of aggression from Germany involving Britain, France, Poland and the Soviet Union and opted instead for one excluding the Soviet Union. The four-power agreement, Beck believed, might bring about a German attack because it threatened Germany with encirclement.

During this period Beck maintained extreme secrecy about his own negotiations with the Germans since 1938, keeping the French and British and even his own ambassador in London, Count Raczynski, in the dark. Raczynski only learned of them later through a conversation with Beck.[16] The negotiations were confided by Beck to Biddle, the American ambassador in Poland, who, as a sympathetic observer representing the neutral American government, had somehow won the Polish Foreign Minister's confidence. As Biddle reported the October 1938 Polish-German talks and those following to Roosevelt and Hull, it is hard to see how the British were not informed.[17] Rumors leaked from various diplomatic and political quarters and the British newspapers eventually got hold of them through German sources. Beck evaded British enquiries during his talks with Chamberlain and Halifax in London and successfully maneuvered them into giving Poland a guarantee and a bilateral pact without first satisfying the British interest in a pact between Poland and Romania against Germany. Beck was playing a double game and probably was reluctant to admit his policy of "balance" between Germany and the Soviet Union had failed and was afraid that knowledge of his talks with the Germans might frighten the British off and they might not give him the alliance he sought.[18]

Long before the British guarantee there was evidence Beck had been entertaining a closer relationship with the British. In a December 1937 analysis Biddle noted that Beck "keeps his eye *on Britain's movements*" and that Britain was important in Beck's long-term policy. "... Beck's fondest aspiration is a close tie-in with Britain."[19] In a later analysis of June 19, 1938, Biddle noted that in "Beck's confusing 'mugwump' policy... he keeps a close eye on British policy." Biddle wrote:

> To my mind, Beck, though mute on the subject, harbors a distinct hope that a potential eventual linking of forceful Polish action with that of Britain and France in countering Germany's expansionist ambitions might prove Poland's best 'out' from the grim prospects of becoming either a potential victim of German expansion, or the potential pathway for a German aggression against Ukraine.[20]

Biddle believed Beck would eventually choose Britain and France mainly because it was "the Polish policy requisite" of "picking the winning horse."[21]

When asked directly by Halifax on two occasions during their meeting in London whether Germany had ever asked for an autobahn across the Corridor, Beck replied evasively that "nothing that had happened had passed beyond the stage of conversations. No written demands had been presented to the Polish Government."[22] The Poles only "came clean" on April 23, almost three weeks later, about the German demands in a conversation between Sir Howard Kennard and Arciszewski, Vice-Minister for Foreign Affairs, when the British ambassador asked "for definite information as to what the German proposals had been and how they had been made."[23] A day later Beck gave Kennard a detailed resumé. In both cases the Poles only admitted to the talks of the previous March but did not go into the conversations of October 1938 or January 1939.[24] Thus the British did not know exactly the gravity of the German demands when they gave their guarantee to the Poles. What they would have done had they had this information — if indeed they did not — must remain the subject of historical speculation.

At first London had been primarily concerned about Romanian oil and keeping it out of Hitler's hands. At the November 1938 meeting between King Carol and his foreign minister, Petrescu-Comnen, and the British in the previous November, Chamberlain had told Halifax: "We must do something for Romania," and the Romanian wheat deal and trade credits resulted.[25] British fears had been stirred up by the "ultimatum" demarche of Vergil Tilea, the Romanian minister in London. It was only later that the British government extrapolated fears of a German attack on Romania into newer alarms over an attack upon Poland.

Up to this time British and French relations with Poland had been cool and distant due to the behavior of "that brute Beck," as Cadogan referred to him, and his treatment of Czechoslovakia during the Munich crisis when Poland menaced Czechoslovakia with an ultimatum demanding some Czechoslovak territory and seemed to be in league with Hitler.[26] The Polish ambassador in London was avoided by the Foreign Office. But it is probably an exaggeration to say that Beck "duped" the British into giving him a guarantee and a bilateral alliance. They had received warnings of Beck's secrecy and dissembling from the French.[27] Moreover, rumors of Beck's talks with the Germans were circulating and Beck's confidences to Biddle probably reached the British. On his way to London Beck stopped at Frankfort-on-the-Oder where he met with Jozef Lipski, Polish ambassador to Germany, who accompanied him to Berlin and underway told him that a British guarantee would only produce a very strong reaction from Hitler.[28] But Beck seemed unperturbed by Lipski's warning. The British probably were somewhat informed of Beck's negotiations with the Germans, knew the Polish Foreign Minister's tendency to dissemble, and certainly his conduct during the Czech crisis was still fresh in their minds. Beck's own Germanophile inclinations were far from over and he probably thought he could use the alliance with Britain to strengthen his bargaining position with Hitler. For the British, dealing with Beck overrode these considerations and both they and Beck preferred an alliance that would exclude the Soviet Union against whom they had strong ideological and — especially in Poland's case — historical antipathies.

Both Chamberlain and Halifax were convinced that "Poland was the key" to controlling Hitler on his eastern flank by the threat of a two-front war.[29] The selection of Poland and not the Soviet Union was partially based upon alleged Soviet military inadequacies and the upper class loathing of Chamberlain and Halifax for the Soviet Union and similar disdain and fear of the landed aristocracies and business classes of Poland, Hungary, Romania and Yugoslavia. Beck rejected an alliance of Britain, France, Poland and the USSR alleging Soviet perfidy and the certainty of a German attack. A Polish-Romanian agreement against Germany encountered similar objections from both Romania and Poland. Nor did London harbor any desire to extend the Polish guarantee to Romania and Yugoslavia at first. The Southeastern states were to be allowed to sputter on in isolation.

All this quickly changed when the French reminded Chamberlain that without Romanian oil Germany's oil supply would not last more than three to six months. The final obstacles to strewing guarantees of states far and wide fell away with Mussolini's occupation of Albania. In April 1939 Romania and Greece now received a British guarantee post-haste.

Writing after the war, Halifax repeated with some dramatic flourish his reason for Britain's decision.

> From month to month evidence seemed to accumulate that Hitler was not interested merely in the re-assembly of racial elements accidentally separated from the parent stock. Something much larger than this was being born and taking shape in that evil mind. After March and the final rape of Prague it was no longer possible to hope that Hitler's purposes and ambitions were limited by any boundaries of race, and the lust of continental or world mastery seemed to stand out in stark relief. Here indeed was the simple explanation a few weeks later of the guarantee given to Poland.[30]

Halifax tried to extend the position he took after March 1939 back to the previous September at Munich by declaring that it was less problematic to enter the war in 1939 when the main commonwealth countries supported the war than in 1938 when South Africa had decided to stay neutral; in Australia there was fierce opposition to war and Canada's attitude was still unknown.[31] Halifax confirmed that the guarantees deliberately put Hitler in a position of facing a two-front war. Neither the Poles nor the Romanians were "under any illusions as to the measure of concrete help they might expect from Great Britain in the event of Hitler choosing war. For them as for us the guarantees were the best, indeed the only, chance of warning him off that decision."[32]

The unconditional guarantee which Beck claimed he had accepted "between two flicks of ash from my cigarette" had temporarily checkmated Hitler. The news of the British action threw Hitler into a wild rage and he pounded the table, witnessed by Admiral Canaris, the chief of the German counter-intelligence bureau, uttering savage curses, and threw out the "venomous threat": "I'll cook them a stew they'll choke on."[33] The "stew" was the Nazi-Soviet agreement enabling Hitler to break out of the checkmate of encirclement less than five months later.

Three days later on April 3 he issued a directive for the attack on Poland to "be carried out at any time from 1 September onwards." Potemkin, the Soviet Vice Commissar for Foreign Affairs, predicted this at the moment of Munich to the French ambassador at Moscow, Coulondre: "My poor friend, what have you done? For us I see no other outcome but a fourth partition of Poland."[34] Coulondre believed that Beck, after his odious behavior at Munich, should have been forced to conclude an agreement with the Soviet Union as the price of the British guarantee as suggested also by Churchill in a speech before parliament. Instead, the British guarantee and alliance with Poland had, as Coulondre astutely observed, consequences not too carefully thought out: "After having pushed Stalin towards Hitler at Munich, it is now Hitler that they pushed towards Stalin."[35]

If Beck had what he wanted in maneuvering Britain into a bilateral alliance, so did Stalin. The British guarantees and alliances given to Poland, Romania, Greece and finally Turkey in May 1939 provided the Soviet Union with the protection it needed from Hitler, for a Nazi attack could only be launched from Poland and Romania. Stalin could now begin the cat-and-mouse game of dealing with the Western Powers and Germany at the same time. Contacts were first made by the Germans through Astakhov, Soviet counsellor in the Berlin embassy, after Ribbentrop telephoned from his castle at Fuschl, near Salzburg, to Peter Kleist, the Eastern European expert on his staff, ordering him to begin improving his relations with the Soviet diplomats in Berlin.[36] Within days Soviet ambassador Merekalov called on State Secretary Weizsäcker, his first visit since his appointment in June 1938.

The British proposal for the Soviet Union to make a unilateral commitment to help any neighboring power on April 14 was followed three days later with a proposal by Stalin calling for a three-power pact with a military convention guaranteeing all states between the Baltic and Black Sea. The British were not ready for such a straightforward and wide-ranging association with Stalin and the Soviet Union, and the proposal was not picked up despite Churchill's pressure from the floor of Parliament to do so. In a cabinet discussion, Malcolm MacDonald, a very anti-Soviet cabinet member, noted that "it would be a serious matter if Russia were neutral and supplying Germany with food and raw materials."[37]

A major stumbling block to the critical alliance with the Soviet Union was Chamberlain's dislike and fulminations against the Soviets. Alexander

Cadogan noted that he "was a man of prejudices which were not easily erad-icated" and his "instinctive contempt for the Americans" was matched by "what amounted to a hatred of the Russians...he was, in a sense, a man of a one-track mind."[38] At one point in May the Prime Minister even consid-ered resigning rather than sign a British-Soviet alliance.[39] Chamberlain even argued that an alliance with the Soviet Union might even provoke German fears of encirclement, "the most devastating product of the German propa-ganda machine."[40] However, this did not work and in the end the cabinet overruled him.

Predictably true to form, Hitler, a man unable to accept defeat, coun-tered the announcement of the British guarantees to Poland, Romania and Greece with a violent diatribe in his speech on April 28 denouncing the German-Polish Pact of Non-Aggression of 1934 and the Anglo-German Naval Agreement of 1935, charging that the guarantees given to those na-tions were the result of plotting to encircle Germany.[41] In the following month Hitler signed the Pact of Steel with Italy as the first step in breaking out of encirclement by his enemies. The next was the Nazi-Soviet Pact of August 1939 which put the final nail in the coffin of Poland.

We have already pointed out that the U.S. placed pressure upon German exports by giving Czechoslovakia most-favored-status advantage, denied to Germany, to preclude German domination of the Eastern European markets.

Although the total American trade with Southeastern Europe did not amount to more than 2%, the New Deal emphasis on trade as a way out of the Depression of the 1930s made the area important for future American trade possibilities. Future markets that might not then have been immedi-ately critical for a nation's economic well-being were often the subject of frictions with other states that led to wars.

Though the negative balances of German-American trade in the Depres-sion years lessened somewhat by the mid-1930s they nevertheless continued through most of the period to 1938, the last year before the war. The Ger-man export trade to the U.S. went steadily down from 5.1% to 2.8% of total German exports from 1933 to 1938. If the broader period from 1929 is considered, the picture is much worse, with Germany failing to recover more than almost half of its former trade in exports with the U.S. Figures for U.S. trade to Germany are not much better (see Table 14–1).

This policy undoubtedly had a political content in giving Germany's com-petitors an edge. In 1944 Sumner Welles confirmed this in speaking of Hull's trade policy: "It helped materially to lessen the stranglehold which Hitler was endeavoring to exercise over the smaller countries of Europe."[42] De-spite the fact that German trade success in Latin America did not come at the expense of American trade but of the U.K., in its shift in emphasis from European trade markets where it was shut out to Latin America, the U.S. in its "anti-European postulate" regarded Germany "as the most uncomfort-able European competitor." From 1934 to the first half of 1937 American exports to Europe only increased from $479 million to $583 million, to Latin America, however, it swelled from $159 million to $583 million.[43] This had been preceded by a series of conferences laying the foundation to the "Good Neighbor Policy" and a visit by President Roosevelt to the

Table 14–1. Germany's Trade with the United States, 1929–1938
(in percentage of total and millions of Reichsmarks)

U.S.A.	1929	1930	1931	1932	1933
Imports	13.3%	12.6%	11.8%	12.7%	11.5%
	1,790.4	1,306.8	791.4	591.8	482.8
Exports	7.4%	5.7%	5.1%	4.9%	5.1%
	991.1	685.2	487.5	281.2	245.9
Balance	−799.3	−621.6	303.9	−310.6	−236.9

U.S.A.	1934	1935	1936	1937	1938
Imports	8.4%	5.8%	5.5%	5.2%	7.4
	372.7	240.7	232.2	281.9	404.6
Exports	3.8%	4.0%	3.6%	3.5%	2.8%
	157.8	169.5	172.0	208.8	149.3
Balance	−214.9	−71.2	−60.2	−73.1	−255.3

Statistisches Jahrbuch für das Deutsche Reich, 1931–1938, cited in Ellis, *German Exchange Control in Central Europe,* p. 384.

region in 1936. Nervousness over the increased German trade presence in Latin America fed a growing anxiety in the U.S. over fascism.

In his September 15, 1938, Berchtesgaden meeting with Hitler, Chamberlain denied to Hitler the often-repeated claim that "England desired not a military but an economic encirclement of Germany," in broaching the question of the future of Southeastern Europe. Hitler replied by explaining the complementary nature of German trade with the region — German industrial exports for southeastern raw materials and foodstuffs — then launched into a further explanation that Germany had "the greatest difficulties with the United States because Germany was willing to import raw materials and food from the United States but the United States could not accept payment in the only form which was possible to Germany, namely, the export of industrial goods, because the United States herself was a producer of these goods, and had 12,000,000 unemployed. That was why Germany had been unable to settle her difficulties with the United States." He suggested that in the future the world economy should be based on the free exchange of goods — industrial goods for primary products.[44] The implication can be easily read into Hitler's statement — although he did not state it directly — that Germany's surge to the southeast, at least commercially, if not politically, was connected to the decline of its trade with the U.S. Faced by threats of a clearing with Britain, a decline of its Russian trade and a boycott against German goods by the U.S. and indirect American aid to Czechoslovakia, in its trade with Yugoslavia and Romania, Germany had good reason to view apprehensively the economic noose tightening around it as a kind of worldwide encirclement by the Western and North American Powers.

Influencing Britain's relations with Nazi Germany was the hovering, wraithlike presence of the U.S. whose role in the origins of World War II is open to tantalizing, if sometimes indeterminate conjecture. Our primary interest here is whether the U.S. encouraged the British guarantee to Poland in March 1939 and, if so, what were the motivations.

For Britain, the decision always was whether to conclude an agreement with an aggrieved Germany over Central and Eastern Europe to stem the power of the rising American colossus or an alliance with the U.S. to curtail the rampaging expansionism of Hitler. In the first year or two of the New Deal, Roosevelt's dynamic solutions to unemployment and the Depression caught the attention and admiration of Hitler and leading Germans like Schacht and Neurath.[45] Despite systemic economic analogies and Roosevelt's evanescent interest in bilateral and barter trade, particularly in the question of the eight hundred thousand tons of cotton needed by Germany, there never was any suggestion of a German-American collaboration along economic, not to speak of political, lines. Trade conflicts particularly in Latin America, cultural and historical differences and American aversion for Hitler and Nazism prevented any real possibility of that occurring.

American foreign policy was largely guided by self-interested considerations of trade, described by a biographer of Roosevelt as "remarkably like the economic and political nationalism of the 1920s."[46] In the frantic search for export markets in the 1930s, the Trade Agreements Act of 1934 promoted the negotiation of numerous most-favored-nation trade agreements. Inevitably, in the trade war atmosphere of the period there were conflicts with Britain and Germany over Latin American trade and with Japan over the China market. To clear away the thicket of tariffs, duties, trade preferences, barter and bilateral arrangements that had grown up in the 1930s and as a way out of the Depression, the U.S. fell back upon the traditional "open door" policy and reciprocal trade agreements.

Initially, Roosevelt, Hull and others viewed Britain's imperial preferences as the arch-hindrance to recovery, but in time anxieties over Nazi Germany's challenge to American trade hegemony in Latin America, Mussolini's seizure of Ethiopia and Japan's depredations in Manchuria and China threatened not only America's markets but also its national security. Hitler's expansionary ambitions also reawakened American and Roosevelt's World War I memories of German militarism when he was Undersecretary of the Navy in the Wilson government.[47]

Roosevelt's policy toward Germany was uncoordinated, by turns conciliatory and assertive. Occasionally it was both at the same time. In its formative stage from 1933 to 1938 it had two objectives: to urge Britain through joint or individual actions to appease Germany's raw materials requirements and after 1937, to negotiate an Anglo-American trade alliance to pry open British markets for American exports and to face the dictators with an alliance of the two strongest World Powers.

Roosevelt's opening gambit in 1936 was to send an emissary, Joseph E. Davies, newly appointed ambassador to Moscow, to Berlin on his way to the Soviet Union to ascertain whether "providing living room for the German people would stop Hitler from making war," and "whether Hitler wanted war or whether he really wanted peace." According to Davies, Roosevelt "sympathized with Germany's need for access to raw materials." Later Roosevelt spoke to Secretary of Treasury Morgenthau about a consortium, which would include Germany, to exploit colonial raw materials to wean it away from producing armaments without causing stagnation and unemployment.[48]

Similarly, he asked Ambassador Dodd on August 5, 1936, about the possibility of "secretly and personally" approaching Hitler to find out whether he would agree to a limitation of armaments and what the limits of his foreign policy were. Dodd could not reach Hitler but met instead with Schacht who advised the U.S. to summon a conference to discuss Germany's demands for colonies.[49] Dodd reported restiveness among German industrialists over production restraints and straitjacketed German trade, and in the German Foreign Office and Army for a return to traditional economic pursuits and a European political settlement.[50]

Davies met with Reichsbank President Schacht on January 20, 1937, and telegraphed to Washington the same day the terms of settlement: international boundaries would be guaranteed; reduction of armaments; the establishment of a new form of League of Nations — all based upon a colonial cession to Germany to relieve the worsening German economic situation. To this the French were agreeable, Davies reported, but the British flatly declined.[51] Chamberlain and Eden both agreed that it would be futile to make concessions to relieve Germany's financial and economic problems before a political settlement. François-Poncet, the French ambassador to Berlin, who spoke fluent German and knew Hitler well, believed Hitler was using Schacht's conversations to conceal his rearmament until he could seize Austria and Czechoslovakia.[52]

In 1936 Roosevelt and Hull met for several long conversations with Lord Runciman, head of the British Board of Trade, to try to arrive at a far-reaching trade agreement as a bridge to a political arrangement. Prior to this, both Chamberlain and Runciman had blocked Eden and the Foreign Office's desire for a political agreement based upon trade concessions to the U.S. and modification of the Ottawa agreements. In his self-convinced, Wilsonian moralistic manner, Hull lectured and harangued his British visitor on what would happen if trade were not liberalized and Germany, Italy and Japan were not given access to raw material markets. Publicly Runciman was an ardent supporter of imperial preferences, but joined Eden in support of trade concessions in the cabinet after he returned to London. Which may have been why he was removed by Chamberlain who succeeded Baldwin as prime minister. Both Oliver Stanley, Runciman's successor, and Chamberlain, who changed his previous position, supported modification of the Ottawa agreements, although Chamberlain's support may not have been the about-face he is alleged to have made. He later confided that his reasons for going "a long way to get this treaty" was "to educate American opinion to act more and more with us" and "to frighten the totalitarians."[53]

Roosevelt's economic appeasement outlook conflicted with Britain's desire for a political settlement and he shifted his focus to assisting the Western Powers through direct political conciliation. He clearly perceived British reluctance to help the Germans economically as long as they continued to rearm, and German unwillingness to cease rearming until they received justice for the wrongs done them. By the end of 1937 Roosevelt's attempts at the economic appeasement of Germany had failed.

Roosevelt's policy at this time was contradictory and muddled, fluctuating between two antipodes of State Department opinion: the appeasement-minded officials like Adolph Berle, Moffat, Phillips and especially Undersecretary Welles, and the anti-fascist critics of the Hitler regime like Messersmith, Undersecretary of State, former minister to Austria and a consul general in Berlin, Ambassador Dodd in Berlin, Morgenthau, and Ickes, Secretary of the Interior. Further compounding the confusion was the split between the internationalists (Hull, Howe, Morgenthau) and the isolationists (Moley, Hopkins, Hugh Johnson, Ickes). The anti-appeasers probably influenced the "Quarantine Speech" of October 5, 1937, in which Roosevelt designated the fascist powers — without naming them — as similar to a pestilence needing international isolation to preserve world health.

The following day a contradictory message was drawn up to appease the German moderates through a plan of Welles granting Germany access to raw materials with vague hints of a revised Versailles Treaty, to be broached at the Conference of the Nine Power Treaty on November 11, 1938. This occurred without any warning to Chamberlain for fear he might scuttle it. After contacts between Eden and John Davis, a State Department emissary, Chamberlain, Horace Wilson and the British cabinet, then deeply involved in the Czech question, blocked any effective agreement between London and Washington on Hitler. Chamberlain had an abiding fear that Roosevelt would only create more problems by intervening in European affairs and was skeptical of the staying capacity of the U.S. Some of this confusion was caused by Roosevelt's overweening preoccupation with the Depression and the "Roosevelt Depression" of 1938. It was only in 1939 that he began to concentrate upon foreign affairs.

The Panay incident in China on December 12, 1937, when Japanese planes attacked an American gunboat on the Yangtze, served up a ready-made opportunity for joint Anglo-American naval action against Japan. Roosevelt seemed ready to pursue action just short of war in reprisal, but Chamberlain feared involvement in Asia at a time when he was fully engaged with Hitler and backed off any full-scale collaboration with Washington.[54] The British cabinet and Chamberlain seemed more interested in an agreement with Germany than with the U.S. Trade conflicts bore a major responsibility: the British refused to abandon imperial preferences in the face of the high American protectionist tariffs and took offense at Hull's preachments about the high tariffs against American goods.[55]

There were many causes for Roosevelt's contradictory shifts between appeasement and anti-appeasement policies: Hitler's concealment of his real aims until 1938; Britain's own conflicted policy toward Germany until 1938; the American State Department's difficulty in assessing any unified strategy toward Hitler; mutual Anglo-American trade rivalries and suspicions; divisions in the Democratic Party between the isolationist and internationalist wing and Roosevelt's unwillingness to move ahead of strongly isolationist American public opinion.

Roosevelt's well-intentioned, evanescent projects arose and evaporated like flecks of foam on a summer pond, but a reworked Welles project bore potential fruit: the ambitious January 1938 proposal for an international conference.[56] To the consternation of Roosevelt and the State Department, Chamberlain turned down the American overture for the international conference despite the enthusiasm of Eden, leading to his withdrawal from the cabinet. The "cold douche of water" from London, in Welles's sour phrase, ended further American mediation efforts, and invites historical speculation. Writing ten years later, Churchill was still "breathless with amazement" at Chamberlain's waving off "the proffered hand stretched across the Atlantic," relinquishing "the last frail chance to save the world from the tyranny of another war."[57] Chamberlain, then in the midst of appeasing Mussolini by *de jure* recognition of the Italian seizure of Ethiopia, feared irritating the dictators. Whether Chamberlain rejected the American offer, preferring an alignment with Hitler against American economic hegemony, or mistrusted an American alliance because previous American offers to cooperate against Japanese encroachments in China always ended in evasion by Washington — or for both of these reasons — is difficult to ascertain.

Hindsight wisdom points to the latter: for political as well as for economic reasons, the loss of German trade to Britain valued at £20.6 million and the deleterious effects on its colonial exports also militated against any abrupt break with Germany which would then make Britain dependent upon the United States.[58]

After September 1938 Roosevelt and the State Department expected an Anglo-German arrangement which would place Central and Eastern Europe under German control and exclude the U.S. from its market. In the spring of 1938 the American embassy in London reported Britain's desperate desire to break up the coalition of three totalitarian powers by detaching Germany. In the days immediately following the annexation of Austria, the State Department's European Division Chief, Jay Pierpont Moffat, noted Britain's flabby response: "British reaction...is, of course, the key to the whole situation and with each day that passes it becomes clearer that England is willing to surrender Eastern Europe to German ambitions."[59]

The news from American diplomatic listening posts in Europe was not good and contradicted Halifax's belief, following his November 1937 visit to Hitler, that the German leader wanted peace — he completely misled Halifax who gave the impression Austria's absorption would not be opposed.[60] Earlier reports from Paris by Bullitt and Welles of talks with Yvon Delbos, French Foreign Minister, and Phipps were much less sanguine: Delbos thought Britain would do nothing to stop the absorption of Austria by Germany, and France could not protect Austria. Beneš would be forced to concede autonomy for the Sudetenland.[61] The Czech minister fanned American suspicions of Hitler's intentions, telling Sayre, Undersecretary in the Trade Division of the State Department, that Germany planned to dominate Central Europe "with a closed door to the trade of every country."[62]

Roosevelt's policy at this point was extremely contradictory: he wanted to avoid war and therefore did not oppose and even supported Chamberlain's appeasement of Germany. At the same time he was disdainful of Chamberlain's unwillingness to confront Hitler's expansionist ambitions and made scathing private remarks about Chamberlain to chosen friends and diplomats, expecting him to make a deal with Hitler permitting the British to retain a modicum of trade in Central and Eastern Europe, but shutting out the U.S. These suspicions and conflicting interests fed into efforts to conclude a trade agreement between the two countries that later had fateful consequences.

The deliberations of the Anglo-American Trade Agreement of 1938 reveal that although both countries ardently wished to conclude an agreement, neither desired to make trade concessions. The problem for the U.S. was primarily Britain's agricultural tariffs. On November 16, 1937, Cordell Hull told the British ambassador, Lindsay, that the U.K. concessions on the American "must list" were "not satisfactory and that the United States expected improvement in some of the concessions...." Hull stressed their joint interests in the political area: "To me time is of the essence," he pointed out: "the world is on fire and unless those who share common desires to protect the precious things of our civilization stand together in some practical program such as the trade agreements program, we may be too late." British press reactions to the negotiations were overly optimistic that Germany and Italy would be forced to abandon autarchy and come to a political agreement on raw materials and colonies and that American isolationism was now over and the U.S. would cooperate with the U.K. in the economic and financial field and eventually in policing the world.[63]

A year later both countries were still at loggerheads. At a cabinet meeting the Chancellor of the Exchequer and the President of the Board of Trade expressed their distress at the American demands for tariff reductions on a number of items (hams, tobacco, maize, lard, planed wood, wheat flour and automobiles). Halifax too was unhappy and the cabinet presented a final list rejecting most of the American demands. Chamberlain did not disguise his feelings: "He had never hoped that we should obtain any great economic or political support from the United States as a result of making this agreement. The advantages to be derived were of a somewhat negative kind." If the agreement failed after such long negotiations "hard things would be said. This was a factor which must appeal to Mr. Hull also."

Although Hull assured Lindsay that the U.S. would not try to capture Britain's trade if war broke out and the British ambassador "seemed much moved and expressed his appreciation," he nevertheless insisted that Britain make more trade concessions. But the British only made some concessions (on ham, lard and tobacco). Afterwards Chamberlain complained that Britain had made too many sacrifices for the political benefits of the treaty. The prolonged haggling and Chamberlain's refusal to journey to the U.S. for the November 17 signing despite the urging of Mackenzie King, the Canadian Prime Minister, subtracted further luster from the agreement. Whether or not the treaty could have lived up to its potential only illustrates Britain's central dilemma of being caught between a Depression-mired, export-conscious American colossus and a rampaging, expansionist Nazi Germany thrusting for European and world hegemony.

The Germans were aware of Britain's discomfort with American competition and were not loathe to suggest that unless Britain acceded to German demands for concessions, it might sink to the level of an American dependency. Trade rivalries in the end undermined the treaty and the Chamberlain government felt itself caught between America and Germany at its trade flanks. The high hopes, that by controlling Germany's access to the two most powerful markets in the world, the Western Powers could stop its imperialist surge, were stillborn. Britain feared German aggression more than the U.S., but it nevertheless also feared American world domination.

At the height of the Sudeten crisis on September 19, 1938, Roosevelt suddenly sent for the British ambassador and expressed his willingness to join with Great Britain and other powers in a blockade against Germany. But Roosevelt's remarks to Lindsay passed as unnoticed in London as did his other overtures. Chamberlain was busy dealing with Hitler whom he saw as the key to the future of Europe and the world. Roosevelt and the State Department then fell back upon the trade agreement with the U.K.

Had the two English-speaking powers not procrastinated in finally concluding the Anglo-American Trade Agreement, Hull lamented in his memoirs, the Second World War might not have occurred.[64] The hard-fistedness of Hull and the State Department upset the British cabinet, and sour feelings prevailed well into 1939, preventing implementation of the agreement.

Roosevelt's policy after the Austrian Anschluss has been described as "opportunist" and "watchful" and his "good man" congratulatory telegram to Chamberlain after concluding the Munich agreement probably indicates his real state of mind, i.e., to appease the dictators but not at American expense.[65] His quarantine speech, blockades, international conferences and the like have been dismissed by historians of American foreign policy during the 1930s as empty gestures which were not serious and quickly forgotten.[66] As to Munich, Undersecretary Berle, at least, believed it would be a good thing if Hitler moved into Eastern Europe and sated his ambitions there, presumably rather than in Latin America where he might claim a greater share of trade and create security problems for the U.S.[67]

Chamberlain was not averse to accepting American support, but he did not believe that it would materialize in a crisis. Roosevelt's failure to confront the Japanese and on several occasions to seek British support in a common front against Japanese encroachment into China, only to scuttle away at the decisive moment, made the British wary of American political initiatives. Britain had no desire to take on another enemy in the Far East, and the U.S., whose trade with Japan was almost ten times that of China, was similarly constrained. Although Britain had, by 1939, $700 million in investments and trade in China, it amounted to only 2.5% of exports and 5% of total trade. For Japan its stake in China was much greater: between 1921 and 1931 China absorbed about one-quarter of Japan's total exports and almost nine-tenths — about $1 billion — of its total foreign investment.[68] For Japan, then, the China market was an imperative while for Britain and the U.S. it was less important, but potentially significant.

Perhaps the most constraining limitation to Roosevelt's freedom of action was the powerful isolationist movement in the U.S. Roosevelt's failure to repeal the Neutrality Act made him appear up to 1939, in the apt description of a German historian, as "a leader without a following."[69] After the German seizure of Prague, the American public became uneasy over Hitler's growing power, and American public opinion influenced Britain's recoil against Hitler's annexation of rump Czechoslovakia. In the cabinet debate (March 15) over whether to recall the British ambassador to Berlin, an important underlying consideration was American opinion. Halifax did not feel drawn to take action, but he felt concerned about the effect of doing nothing upon public opinion in the U.S. and the Balkans.[70]

Through Phipps, Ambassador Bullitt in Paris exercised some influence upon London's decision to guarantee Poland; information of impending Nazi military action against Poland supplied by Biddle in Warsaw and relayed to Ambassador Kennedy figured prominently in the British decision to guarantee the Poles. In the U.S. the British action received widespread attention and approval in the press though there was a residue of suspicion in Washington about the real British motives. Kennedy reported a discussion with Chamberlain on April 4 about "leaving a door open to Hitler."[71]

The Italian seizure of Albania in early April 1939 prompted comments by Vansittart about abandoning Italy for "America who may help us," which Halifax took into a cabinet discussion. American influence through Hull and Kennedy, though indirect, was also felt in the extension of guarantees to Romania and Greece.[72] To relieve French anxieties that Britain would send half its Mediterranean fleet to Asia at a critical time, Roosevelt ordered the American Pacific fleet then in New York back to the Pacific. On April 14 Roosevelt delivered an appeal to Hitler and Mussolini to refrain from attacking thirty-one nations for ten years and preferably for a period of twenty-five years, a move which Chamberlain praised, but which Hitler and Mussolini treated with derision. Nevertheless, it signaled American displeasure with Germany and Italy and placed both in an uncomfortable position before world opinion.

The American decision to raise tariff duties on German products shortly after the Prague coup was a gesture of political disapproval, which hurt the German economy. Nevertheless, there is little evidence that this influenced Hitler any more than the reports of Thomsen, the German chargé in the U.S., branding Roosevelt as an enemy fomenting encirclement of Germany who could be expected to bring the U.S. into the war on the side of Britain.[73] Shortly after, Hull and the State Department refused to recognize Hitler's seizure of the Czech area, calling it an unjust violation of international law. However, Hitler had scant regard for any American counteraction, knowing that military unpreparedness and the powerful isolationist movement hindered any intervention by Roosevelt in European affairs.

Unexpressed American influence upon the British decision to guarantee the independence of Poland is supported by the substantive conclusion of Professor Newman who, although devoting little attention to the American role in the guarantee, intuitively and correctly understands its decisiveness.

...the springs of the British action are to be found not so much in fine calculations of strategic advantage or even vital interests, as in the psychology of British policy makers humiliated by a long series of German successes and stung into action by the realization that Britain would no longer count in the world if she did nothing. To do nothing, as Halifax had pointed out to the Foreign Policy Committee on 27 March, would result in such a loss of sympathy and support in the world, particularly in the United States and the Balkans, and such an increase in German power and influence, that he favored the only possible alternative: "our going to war." Thus the guarantee was a deliberate challenge that would help recover British prestige, end the uncertainty, and allow Britain to abandon at last the narrow dictates of state interests which had driven them to seek agreement with a Germany whose political system they loathed.[74]

Stated more precisely, the U.S. and Britain, previous to 1939, were impelled by economic considerations in their relations with one another and with Germany. The loss of the considerable British export market after the Ottawa agreements — $10.5 million in the empire market after the first year — rankled Washington and Hull, but, stubbornly wedded to this arrangement, Britain showed no disposition to abandon it.[75] Even more important for British business, the German trade market was worth £20.6 million a year. By April 1939 Roosevelt reckoned the likelihood of war 50/50 and these considerations receded in the face of political imperatives.[76]

Roosevelt assisted the British by supporting their efforts to diplomatically separate Hitler from Italy. After a British request for joint action at Rome, Roosevelt decided to use the visit of the new Italian Ambassador to present his credentials in order to warn Italy of Hitler's intentions by giving the unsuspecting and startled diplomat a lecture. An extract from Roosevelt's handwritten note for the occasion reveals his concern that Hitler might be driven to war out of economic necessity and needed Italy for his purposes.[77]

In early 1939 Roosevelt shifted emphasis from economic appeasement of Hitler to finding ways of directly supporting the Western democracies. It was almost ridiculous, he told his cabinet in the summer of 1939, that the U.S. could accomplish anything noteworthy by peddling "a few barrels of apples here and a couple of automobiles there." More importantly, as he grumbled to Henry Morgenthau Jr., "the trade treaties are too goddamned slow. The world is marching too fast." By then Hull had seemed to concede, in a May 1939 cabinet meeting, that events had bypassed economic matters, and predicted Germany's total economic collapse within eighteen months.[78] For Roosevelt, a trade agreement was only an agreement that would lead to a political understanding and partnership with Britain. His support of Hull's policy of expanded free trade opportunities and an end to limited markets, as a way out of the impasse leading to war, was partly sincere and partly, as the British suspected, a self-serving attempt to penetrate the British market and ultimately, at least, replace Britain as the leading hegemonic power. According to Morgenthau, Secretary of State, when he told Roosevelt, "England is really broke," Roosevelt replied "half jokingly": "This is very interesting. I had no idea that England is broke. I will go over there and make a couple of talks and take over the British Empire."[79] The trade agreement as originally conceived by Roosevelt and Hull was to be the first step in this direction by giving the U.S. access to both Britain and its empire market.

However, the British were not quite ready to leave the stage as the dominant World Power, and hoped to use their friendship with the U.S. as a brake on Hitler. Until 1938 and even into 1939 Chamberlain and his friends hoped to gain Hitler's support against the threat of American economic hegemony on the world market and the Soviet threat in Europe. Only in the aftermath of the war would Britain relinquish its leadership to the U.S. under exceedingly different circumstances.

Chapter 15

"Keeping the Pot Boiling" in Eastern Europe. Anglo-Romanian Relations and the Leith-Ross Trade Mission to Romania in April 1939. Erosion of the Munich Settlement and German-British Economic Conflict in the Balkans

> But we don't want the damned stuff.
> — Sir Alexander Cadogan,
> on the purchase of Romanian wheat

Although Romanian trade was insignificant for Britain, paradoxically it became a battleground between Germany and Britain. For Britain, grain and oil imports were of major significance in Anglo-Romanian trade. Other products, including timber, represented less than one-fifth of Britain's imports from the Romanian market. Romania depended very much on its grain harvest — whether good or bad. The principal difficulty in the marketing of Romanian grain in the U.K. was that the sterling price did not give a lei return sufficiently attractive to the Romanian exporter. By 1938 British oil imports had fallen to about half of their previous level due partly to the fall in production and partly to obstacles to exports from Romania. One obstacle was a 12% export tax designed to provide the Romanian government with funds to make up the difference in the official rate of exchange plus a premium of 38% at which the Romanian National Bank bought sterling. Its abolition, Leith-Ross believed, would help exports to the U.K. and strong currency countries.[1]

In the early 1930s inability to pay its trade debts to Britain plagued Romania. Negotiations to remove this problem in 1934 did not progress due to the inadequate offers of Struga, the Romanian negotiator. In a note to Titulescu, the Romanian Foreign Minister, Leith-Ross wrote: "I hope very much that you will do anything to facilitate this, as I cannot exaggerate the strength of feeling in trading circles throughout the country. Runciman is having difficulty in resisting the demands for drastic action."[2] Romania's trade debts a year later forced, through the Anglo-Romanian Payments Agreement of May 1936, a clearing between Romania and the U.K. However, high grain prices and poor international harvests, and Romania's good harvest enabled it to export its grain to the U.K., liquidating much of its indebtedness. A fall in world oil and grain prices and a smaller Romanian harvest in 1937 reduced the level of U.K. imports from Romania and clearing receipts fell short of necessary payments. An increase in Romanian exports to the U.K. was essential. The agreement of September 2, 1938, modified this, allowing Romanian exporters to dispose of a considerable proportion of their sterling for various purposes at a rate fixed by supply and demand. For oil, the situation remained virtually the same. After a trial period, Romanian exports (other than oil) began to move to the U.K. on a satisfactory scale as a result of the higher lei price obtainable by the Romanian exporter.[3]

Britain's trade relations with Romania into mid-1938 continued to be sluggish and irregular. The Treasury official Waley reported that "the Romanian government behave [sic] in a tortuous and dilatory fashion in all their dealings with the Council of Foreign Bondholders...Romania does a lot to hinder the sale of oil here — as it fixes minimum prices above world prices, imposes an export tax of 12%, and charges railway freight concessions."[4]

By mid-1938 Romania increasingly experienced the same problem as Yugoslavia: how to fend off German demands for its raw materials and avoid becoming a German satrapy. Like Yugoslavia, the sole possibility seemed to be increased British and French purchases of Romanian exports. Anxiety had increased in Romania since the Austrian Anschluss and the German minority for the first time in Romanian history had begun to make racial demands. Premier Tatarescu feared that the Germans did not want just a "hinterland" for their trade but a "monopoly." Tatarescu wanted to ensure Romania's freedom by "some trade and economic arrangements with France and Great Britain." He pleaded: "Already there was much English capital invested in Romanian oil fields. Might it be possible to extend such investment to the case of gold mines?" Romania desperately wanted more British capital investments and he asked whether Romanian experts could be sent to the U.K. to discuss these things.[5]

High export prices and export taxes were the main obstacle to greater Anglo-Romanian trade. The oil companies, Leith-Ross told Tatarescu, "had tried and tried again to get the position altered but they were in despair at their treatment." The 12% export tax on oil continued to be an obstacle. Grain exports could only take place aided by a premium extended to exports to the U.K. and other countries which gave them free currencies. He suggested exempting payment to the National Bank of Romania of a portion of the sterling proceeds at the fictitious official rate to encourage trade by side-stepping the Romanian government's need for exchange currency.

Leith-Ross was blunt: British capital was reluctant to invest in Romanian enterprises "until the Romanian administration showed itself more efficient and less corrupt." Tatarescu believed the oil companies might be exaggerating their difficulties. He admitted that the administration had been in a chaotic condition, but he emphasized that the king's policy was to clear it up and to reassure foreign capital. He suggested that Leith-Ross come to Romania "to formulate concrete proposals."[6]

In the same month, Locock, of the Federation of British Industries, revealed that Constantinescu, Minister of Economy and President of the Bank of Romania, had asked a British businessman in Bucharest for an invitation to London to counter "this drift towards Germany and to bring Romania into England's sphere of influence." Locock suggested that, since reports of the Romanian wheat harvest were good, Britain ought to increase its imports of wheat or oil otherwise the Germans would move in and buy.[7] After an exchange of letters between Leith-Ross, Sir William Brown and Orme Sargent and Ashton-Gwatkin of the Foreign Office, Constantinescu was invited to London rather than sending a British representative to Bucharest to avoid giving the Germans the impression of encirclement and raising Romanian hopes of increased trade.[8]

The British had second thoughts on any agreements Berlin might interpret as a planned encirclement of Germany by any Western-sponsored bloc of Eastern European states. Tatarescu held Chamberlain and Stanley responsible for Leith-Ross's failure to come to Romania to conclude a British-Romanian economic and political arrangement.[9] The Inter-Departmental Committee stood for the moment as a symbol rather than a really effective tool.[10] Though Chamberlain's appeasement policy was in its flood tide, opposition outside the cabinet coalesced in the Foreign Office through Vansittart, Oliver Harvey, Rex Ingram, Orme Sargent and lesser officials in other departments. Within the cabinet Duff Cooper and to a lesser extent Stanley were lonely beacons of opposition.

By 1938 Nazi Germany perceived that its oil supply, two-thirds of which came from the U.S. and Latin America, would be jeopardized by blockade once war broke out and that it would have to depend thereafter upon Romania and the Soviet Union as its primary sources. In that year Romania exported most of its petroleum products (74%) through the Black Sea and Mediterranean, which the British largely bottled up once war occurred, 21% up the Danube and 5% by railroad. The German military believed the latter two means of transportation inadequate to accommodate oil shipments, making their need for oil and other raw materials increasingly desperate and undoubtedly leading Hitler to eye Czechoslovakia and its large Balkan assets and trade as a key to the raw materials of the other Southeastern states.[11]

The inability of German industry to satisfy its oil demands by synthetic production intensified Germany's interest in Romania. Whereas most of Southeastern Europe already sent 40%–50% or more of its exports to Germany, Romania only sent a quarter, remaining, in Göring's words, "the sole interrogation point for Germany in Southeastern Europe."[12] German Minister Fabricius complained to King Carol that Romanian economic circles were trying to hinder provisions of the agreement. When Romania had to increase deliveries of oil and cereals in exchange for German armaments, its total trade with Germany was still 25% less in December 1938 than in 1937, although that agreement reckoned on a 30% increase.[13]

But matters had reached a critical point on a higher political level. On August 2, 1938, Theodore Kordt, chargé d'affaires in the German embassy in London, saw Parliamentary Undersecretary Butler and probed whether Britain "would recognize German *Lebensraum* in Eastern Europe" for "some concrete act" from Berlin, insuring that Germany would make no more territorial demands.[14] German contacts warned that Hitler was preparing to attack Czechoslovakia sometime in September.

In late August, Kordt again met with Horace Wilson, the alter-ego of Chamberlain, who delivered something resembling the long-awaited recognition of German hegemony in Eastern Europe, couched in some vagueness.[15] "A constructive solution of the Czech question, by peaceful means, would leave the way clear for Germany to exercise large scale policy in the Southeast," noted Wilson. He disingenuously disclaimed the view that Germany would use the area's resources against Britain, and agreed that the Balkan economy complemented that of Germany. "Neither had Great Britain any intention of opposing a development of the German economy in a southeasterly direction." However, Wilson cautioned that Great Britain hoped to retain its interests in that region. "Her only wish was that she should not be debarred from trade there. There were a number of different products which Germany was not in a position to deliver to the Balkans. Britain wished to have her share in the Balkan trade in these commodities."

The British were by no means writing off further trade and investments in the Southeast and elsewhere in Eastern Europe, notwithstanding the fears of Vansittart and others. This desire to keep their hand in Eastern Europe was not communicated by Chamberlain to Hitler at any of their meetings. In his single-minded pursuit of an agreement with Germany avoiding war, the Prime Minister thought it prudent not to go too deeply into the subject with Hitler either at Berchtesgaden on September 15, 1938, or at Godesberg on September 22, 1938. In between, the Prime Minister met with the French government leaders on September 18, 1938, at 10 Downing Street and again after Godesberg on September 25, 1938.[16]

At the Berchtesgaden Conference, Chamberlain had conceded the necessity of separating the Sudeten-German areas from Czechoslovakia, but in the second conference at Godesberg, the German leader raised the ante by asking for acceptance of the Polish and Hungarian territorial demands against Czechoslovakia and perhaps more, causing Halifax for the first time to oppose Chamberlain, giving the Prime Minister a jolt. Chamberlain's concessions at Godesberg to Hitler's demands were too much even for his defender, the conservative revisionist writer, John Charmley, who comments with some indignation: "Chamberlain and company were, in effect, prepared to make further concessions to preserve peace, even to accepting dishonor."[17]

With the onset of the Sudeten crisis, the Little Entente began to crack at the seams as the Chamberlain and Daladier governments indicated they would permit Germany to expand its political power into Eastern Europe without a struggle. Though this Western policy was not without its zigzags and retreats into defiance, rather than a direct advance, nevertheless its broad goal was always to avoid war by mollifying Hitler through concessions in the east.

After the Anschluss both Romania and Hungary conducted opportunistic policies vis-à-vis both the Western Powers and Germany. As German power grew, Romania abandoned the Titulescu policy of close friendship with the Soviet Union and France and carefully avoided any commitments that would tie them too closely with either power bloc. Romania and the other Eastern European powers tended to tell both sides whatever they thought they wanted to hear. The Romanians deftly dodged a project in the spring of 1938 by France through Emil Krofta, the Czechoslovak Foreign Minister, to link them into a closer alliance with the Little Entente to gain passage of Soviet troops through Romanian territory to aid Czechoslovakia.[18] Romania flatly refused French requests immediately after the Anschluss for passage of Soviet troops and again a few months later, but did allow Czechoslovak pilots to fly over Romanian territory from the Soviet Union in 1938.[19] Petrescu-Comnen told Krofta that the Romanian government in such cases "would close its eyes and limit itself to protests without going any further."[20] This became the official Romanian position into September 1938 as reported by the British minister in Bucharest after an interview with King Carol: Romania would not agree to the passage of Russian troops, but airplanes were another matter. To the Polish undersecretary, Szembek, Petrescu-Comnen "categorically" denied that Romania would permit passage of Soviet troops across its territory, but Szembek agreed Soviet over-flight was "perfectly correct."[21] On September 9, 1938, Djuvara, Romanian minister in Berlin, officially told the Germans that Romania would forbid passage of Soviet troops.[22] But Petrescu-Comnen informed a British cabinet member, Lord de la Warr, in Geneva that, "in case of war, supplies would probably pass through Romania to Czechoslovakia and he thought there would be no difficulty in such a case in allowing transit, especially for aeroplanes." However, the Germans remained doubtful and Erich Kordt, after a trip to Romania, thought that, lacking an air force, it would not be able to repel Soviet troops.[23]

Romania's policy of neutrality by "straddling two chairs" as Victor Antonescu, Romania's former foreign minister, described it, also had an important economic side beyond avoiding a German economic monopoly over Romania: Romania could also earn a tidy profit on orders of oil, coal, grain, fats and other commodities to the two blocs in conflict.[24]

Similarly, the key to understanding Hungary lay in its desire to recover all the territories of "historic Hungary" — two thirds lost after World War I — and its success in getting Hitler to agree to *some* of the Hungarian demands.[25] Upsetting the territorial losses of the Treaty of Trianon was the goal of both the conservative upper class landowners and the nationalist-racialist middle class groups. When French Premier Daladier suggested to Hungarian Foreign Minister Kanya in September 1933 that Hungary should give up its revisionist aspirations and live in peace with its neighbors, Kanya told him that any government which accepted such an idea would immediately fall from power.[26]

Horthy and other Hungarian leaders had been in touch with the German right wing and Nazi Party elements since the 1920s and even offered subsidies solicited by General Ludendorff for the Nazi putschists.[27] Hungary hoped partially to attain its aims through German absorption of Austria, ending the possibility of a Hapsburg restoration, and the eventual destruction of Czechoslovakia. Later Horthy's associate, Premier Gömbös, visited Hitler who blithely informed him he intended to annex Austria and Czechoslovakia after crushing France in a new war. In return for Magyar assistance he was willing to grant Hungary parts of Czechoslovakia and purportedly even promised restitution of German-populated Burgenland formerly belonging to Hungary and given to Austria after 1918. However, Hitler was not willing to support Hungarian revisionism against Romania and Yugoslavia, which could create chaos in the Balkans and disrupt Germany's land access to Greece and Turkey and his supply of Romanian oil and wheat and Yugoslav foodstuffs and metal ores.[28]

Hungary pursued a double policy allowing for a military strategy in a German-Czechoslovak confrontation or a diplomatic solution by Britain, France and Germany in which Hungary would receive all or part of Slovakia and Ruthenia.[29] German policy wavered indecisively over accepting assistance from Hungary which might provoke a war in the southeast between Hungary and the Little Entente states. Ribbentrop concluded that "Hungarian support which brought us new enemies would be no gain."[30]

In two meetings in August 1938 in Germany between Hitler and Horthy, the Regent declined the German invitation to join in an attack on Czechoslovakia on the pretext that Hungary was ill-prepared for war. When the ingenuous Horthy, perhaps put up to it by the German generals and the Wilhelmstrasse, warned Hitler that he would not win in a war with Britain, which might lose battles but seldom lost a war, the exasperated Führer interrupted him, exclaiming: "Nonsense. Keep quiet!" (*Unsinn. Schweigen Sie!*)[31]

News of the non-aggression agreement between the Little Entente powers and Hungary in return for recognition of Hungary's rearmament was further evidence to Berlin of Hungarian perfidy. The subsequent bad feelings of Hitler and Ribbentrop toward the Magyars irredeemably colored relations between Germany and Hungary. The Anglophile Horthy and the other Hungarian leaders preferred a peaceful settlement of their grievances against the Czechs through a British-German agreement to a risky military solution, which the heavily outgunned Hungarians could not win and which might provoke a possible intervention by the Little Entente powers, Romania and Yugoslavia.

Britain and France, in Pilate-like disinterest, left Hungarian territorial demands against Prague to Hitler and Mussolini and abandoned the hapless Czechs to their fate. Germany and Italy then granted Hungarian demands in the First Vienna Awards in October 1938.[32]

In the last analysis, even though the smaller Eastern European countries, cast adrift by the Munich agreement, opportunistically allowed themselves to be neutralized by German and Polish diplomacy, the British and French leaders' decision not to oppose Hitler's demands bore the major responsibility for Czechoslovakia's dismemberment and its later destruction.[33]

On October 19, 1938, Leith-Ross made fresh offers of trade cooperation to Germany designed to ease its trade and financial difficulties, based upon the premise — or at least so he told the Germans — that, if the European Powers did not cooperate with one another, the U.S. would extend its economic hegemony to Europe. He offered the Germans a jerry-rigged plan in which Britain would extend 25% more foreign currency to Germany to purchase Balkan exports enabling the Balkan countries in turn to purchase

British and colonial exports. This maneuver supposedly would help world trade, satisfy the trade demands of both countries and at the same time facilitate Germany's hegemonial ambitions.[34] The Germans were cognizant of Britain's fears of American commercial competition which they used to their advantage in prodding concessions from the British.

The Leith-Ross plan gave Britain more freedom of maneuver in negotiating an Anglo-American trade agreement.[35] London hoped to forestall American demands for trade concessions and relief from tariff restrictions. The British wanted an agreement with Germany, but Hitler's Saarbrücken speech attacking Britain and the rejection of Leith-Ross's offer deflated this effort. It sank from the political horizon, a bribe manqué or misdirected gesture, demonstrating only weakness. Having misfired with Germany, the Chamberlain government now moved toward improving its position with the U.S.

After Munich, British interest in Eastern European and especially Romanian trade perked up but Chamberlain, Cadogan and the Treasury Department continued to look askance at "political trade" and the risk of provoking German encirclement fears. Britain's eroding economic position led the *Westminster Bank Review* to query in early 1938: "Are we heading for a slump?"; and in the spring complained that "Export trade is the most unsatisfactory section of our industrial organization." Between 1937 and 1938 British total exports had fallen £67,632 million. German and particularly Japanese competition were believed partially responsible, but a fall in home market demand once the armament boom fell to more acceptable limits meant "an ever greater need for an expansion of exports to take up the slack."[36]

British business circles favorably regarded the trip of R. H. Hudson, of the Overseas Trade Department, to Northeastern Europe and the Soviet Union to promote British exports and Leith-Ross's trade mission to Romania and the Soviet Union.[37] Britain maintained distant and reduced relations with the Soviet Union and Eastern Europe after Munich, but rumors of Hitler's intention to attack Holland, and a German air bombardment of London sent the British scurrying to open contacts with the Soviet Union and the small Eastern European states.

If falling exports and a ballooning national debt were causing worry and handwringing — Chamberlain spoke of "armament costs breaking our backs" — defense outlays were also solving the unemployment problem, as Keynes had predicted, without any conscious design. By mid-1939 unemployment in the U.K. was at 9.1%, its lowest point in ten years.[38] The rearmament program through its restructuring and expansion of industrial capitalism and employment of large numbers of previously unemployed workers was setting the stage for another post-war surge of capitalist expansion. Through deficit financing it was solving the problem of the Depression of the 1930s. Ironically, the unwilling agent of this historic task was the fiscally conservative Neville Chamberlain and his cabinet.

The central enigma, suspended like a malign incubus of impending doom, remained Hitler's post-Munich intentions. Reflecting in his post-war memoirs on the period between Munich and March 15, 1939, George Kennan—

then an official in the Prague embassy — outlines the probable courses of action open to Hitler.

> Determined not only to regain Danzig and to wipe out the Polish corridor but also to gain dominant political influence and access to raw materials much further to the east, he was faced with three alternative routes of approach to this objective. First he could attempt to play on the national feeling of the Ukrainians and to stimulate demand for an independent Ukrainian state, along the lines of what Germany attempted to do during the occupation of the Ukraine in 1918. This could be done only at the expense of relations with both Poland and the Soviet Union, and at the risk of a simultaneous war against both, into which the Western Powers would almost certainly be drawn. Second, he could pursue the possibility of a deal with Poland at the expense of the Soviet Union — a deal whereby the Poles would satisfy German aspirations with respect to Danzig and Poland's western border and would be compensated at the expense of the Soviet Union. But this, of course meant making war in alliance with Poland against the Soviet Union; and for this the Poles were scarcely to be had. The third alternative was a deal with the Soviet Union at Poland's expense, with at least the possibility that the Western Powers, who had now put up with so much, would remain passive for a further period.[39]

Hitler jointly pursued the first two until the spring of 1939, when, after repeated attempts to gain Danzig and a rail link through the Corridor from Poland prior to attacking the Soviet Union, he desisted and made his decision to occupy the rump Czech state. The decision to ally with the Soviet Union was not made until after the British guarantee to Poland and Romania. As the Polish leaders hid their conferences with Ribbentrop and Hitler (on October 24 and November 19, 1938, and January 5, 1939), the British remained in the dark. Even Ribbentrop's offer of the coveted Polish-Hungarian border through Hungarian annexation of Ruthenia did not tempt the Poles to join the Germans.

What kept Hitler in motion aside from his long-held *Lebensraum* geopolitical beliefs was Germany's deteriorating economy in late 1938. Rubber requirements covered through synthetic rubber production were only one-sixteenth of needs and raw materials such as iron, copper, nickel and even gun-powder production fared little better. Shortages of skilled and unskilled workers existed in most segments of the economy, especially in the coal, munitions and aircraft industries, and the Reich Defense Committee declared that demands placed upon the economy by the construction of the Westwall and the Sudetenland occupation made a continuation of these pressures beyond October 10 an impending catastrophe. In November 1938 Göring admitted that the shortages in manpower and foreign exchange exhaustion had reached the point of desperation.[40] Wearying of his struggle with Ribbentrop for the favor of Hitler and suffering from diabetes, the Reichsmarshal abandoned the field and took an extended vacation in Italy.

Romania and Yugoslavia, in particular, resisted more shipments of oil and other raw materials, further endangering the German war economy.

Cutbacks in allocations for the Wehrmacht resulted. Göring's feverish efforts to negotiate a tariff union with Slovakia, the beginning of a *Grosswirtschaft-raum* that would probably have included the other Southeastern countries, were interrupted by Hitler's decision to solve Germany's economic problems by military means.[41]

In the spring of 1938, France made efforts to block German domination of Central and Eastern Europe but British disinterest there and the Chamberlain government's primary aim of averting a conflict with Germany over the region undercut France's continental interests.

On April 28–29, 1938, Chamberlain, at the insistence of the French, examined a French proposal to coordinate efforts to aid Central and Southeastern Europe avert Nazi penetration. By May these French moves expanded into proposals for the establishment of an Anglo-French consortium to aid the Little Entente countries (Czechoslovakia, Romania, Yugoslavia), but Chamberlain, wary of British commitment there, believed the region would inevitably fall under German economic control and little could be done about it. The French proposal for a consortium handling government-sponsored trade was unacceptable to the orthodox free trade beliefs of the British and by July 1938 the project was dropped.[42]

Hitler claims he actually preferred war with Czechoslovakia — he later called Munich the biggest mistake he ever made — and the British and French capitulation convinced him that they would do little to prevent German expansion to the east. In the months that followed, the British and French did little to disabuse Hitler of that belief: the Leith-Ross offer of cash support, and British and French unwillingness to guarantee the Czech borders, testify to this. Southeastern Europe remained a gray area which Hitler and Chamberlain had barely touched on at Munich nor had they made any formal or informal arrangement about its future. This lacuna enabled Ingram and Sargent, the Foreign Office undersecretary and after Munich an opponent of appeasement, to decide that Britain could legitimately make purchases of Romanian wheat, Greek tobacco or offers of export guarantees to Bulgaria.[43]

Halifax returned to Eastern Europe again after Munich, urging Chamberlain in a round-about way to purchase wheat from Romania "to give evidence" of Britain's presence in Southeastern Europe.[44] Nervous about provoking Hitler, Cadogan opposed this move in testy remarks against Lord Lloyd's request that Britain buy six hundred thousand tons of Romanian wheat: "But we don't want the damned stuff — and the question is are we going to declare war on Germany? (No one can pretend that it is a commercial proposition.)"[45] Despite Stanley's obstinate resistance and Cadogan's opposition, supported by Leith-Ross, Chamberlain decided in Halifax's favor on October 14 to purchase two hundred thousand tons of Romanian wheat, for political reasons.

October 1938, the month after the Munich conference, was one of pessimism and sinking despair. The euphoria that followed Chamberlain's return from Munich and his proclamation of "peace in our time" was soon followed by unease and dismay over Britain's humiliation and Hitler's triumph. Harold Nicolson captured the underlying self-delusion of the House of Commons members in their protestations when Chamberlain confessed that the phrase "peace in our time" had been uttered during the emotion of the moment. "They well know that Chamberlain has put us in a ghastly position and that we ought to have been prepared to go to war and smash Hitler. Next time he will be far too strong for us."[46] This prediction meant the end of the carefree upper class world of gay parties and dinners, the whole social swirl of the insouciant inter-war years, to be succeeded by grimmer more terrible times.

In his darkest and most pessimistic mood, Halifax confided to Ambassador Kennedy that Britain might have to abandon Central Europe to Hitler while concentrating its power in the Mediterranean and the Empire and seek friendship with the U.S. On November 1 he wrote Phipps in Paris glumly of abandoning Europe while holding on to the rim areas of the world.[47] Cadogan held to a policy of trade and appeasement: "We must, of course, keep such markets as we can, and we cannot forego the right to take advantage of any openings. But I believe that any deliberate uneconomic 'encirclement' of Germany will be futile and ruinous."[48] But in November the central reality of Hitler's plans for eastern booty became clearer; Munich had changed little and Leith-Ross's secret follow-up bribe had not succeeded. Harold Nicolson observed portentously: "The Germans pour out attacks on us and completely undo the effect of Munich."[49]

Britain quietly and unobtrusively moved to deny Germany complete economic hegemony in Southeastern Europe through economic rather than any direct political means. In this policy even Chamberlain grudgingly agreed. Direct political support to the beleaguered and threatened East European states, however, did not arrive until after the German seizure of Czechoslovakia.

These important changes were aimed primarily at shoring up those countries which desperately sought British credits for defense weaponry and trade to avoid German economic domination, later euphemistically called the "peace front."

But despite the goal of increasing trade, Britain's export trade was slowly falling. In 1938 Britain's trade deficit was down to £284 million from £339 million in 1937, invisible exports no longer covered these deficits.[50] Dr. Walther Funk's visit to Southeastern Europe in October 1938, to incorporate it into the German sphere, and the British minister in Belgrade's warning of further German economic penetration forced the British government to abandon its scruples against "political" trade and move "hesitantly and pragmatically," in Newman's words, against the German move. During his southeastern tour, Dr. Funk spoke of Germany's *Grosswirtschaftraum* and purchased 400,000 tons of wheat from Romania — unneeded according to Clodius — to get a lock on Romania's oil.[51]

Though the earlier decision not to challenge the German trade drive as long as German trade objectives were primarily economic and not political still held, the November 10 memorandum of Halifax broke with the earlier appeasement policy of "keeping Germany fat." Chamberlain also later conceded the Romanian wheat deal and other later "political" trade and financial credits to the Southeastern countries, on February 8, 1939, in the cabinet, in order to "keep the pot boiling" in Romania.

In reviewing the Interim Report of the Inter-Departmental Committee in his November 10, 1938, memorandum, Halifax advanced a blueprint of nuanced opposition to the previous policy of "keeping Germany fat" in the southeast by conceding Germany's traditional economic interests there:

> Where opinions differ is the point where the line should be drawn, i.e., the degree to which these countries can afford to grant Germany an economic monopoly and thus the degree to which German influence, economic and political, should be allowed to predominate.[52]

Political considerations and overweening German power also had to be weighed:

> ...we may look forward to a time when Germany will again be a colonial Power, in which case her predominance in Europe would be even more dangerous to us than if she were still to be deprived of any colonial territories. The view was therefore that an effort on the part of His Majesty's Government to counteract Germany's advance seemed highly desirable, if indeed, it was not considered vital to our interests.[53]

London also wanted to prevent the door from being slammed in a region where it had an estimated £100 million invested — though only 1%–2% of its total — and its trade frozen out.

> Our object should be to endeavor to ensure that this area of Europe shall look specifically towards the Western Powers rather than feel obliged in default of any other *point d'appui* to allow itself to be exploited in Berlin... there will no doubt be general agreement that these countries should be actively encouraged to realize that a possible *point d'appui* other than Berlin does exist, and that British interest in them, both political or economic will be maintained and developed.[54]

Halifax decided against enabling Germany to grow more prosperous through Britain's financial support in the delusory hope Hitler would then behave. He rejected this logic "as long as the German economic system is maintained" and not conducted along free trade lines but autarchic principles aimed at subjugating the East European countries.

> It seems at present far more likely that any economic dominance that Germany may attain in these countries will result in their economic vassalage to Germany and to German economic doctrine, and that German foreign exchange restrictions and autarchic aims will become factors conditioning and molding the economic life of each of them. This, in fact, seems certain so long as Germany refuses to envisage the depreciation of the mark and to relax her exchange control, and so long as she insists that these countries shall receive payment for their exports in German goods, wanted or unwanted. Moreover, the short-term credits by London to Germany both before and since the

war, have been frozen and provided a source of great embarrassment and, indeed, of danger to the international credit of London. We could not afford to lock up further resources in Germany, so long as she maintains a system of exchange control; nor to advance funds to the Danubian countries so long as their trade with Germany only produces blocked marks. While, therefore, Germany, for one reason or another, is unwilling to lift her exchange control, the arguments in favor of permitting her a free hand in these countries seem largely to fall to the ground.[55]

A week later the Romanian king and his foreign minister arrived in London.[56] Petrescu-Comnen asked for more trade and financial assistance, citing recent trade declines: Romanian trade had plummeted from 2,401,000,000 lei in 1937 to 919,000,000 lei in 1938, coupled with a deficit of 123 million lei with Britain. Halifax complained that Romanian prices were higher than world prices and contrary to British standards of free trade. He reiterated Chamberlain's promise to King Carol for a commission of experts to be sent to Bucharest to examine trade relations. This, he emphasized, "must be handled with discretion and circumspection to avoid giving the least and remotest impression that Britain is seeking to raise a barrier to the German expansion in the east."

Leith-Ross tried to undo the lamentable impression made by Halifax by reassuring the Romanian foreign minister that Britain "was not disinterested in any way in Central and Southeastern Europe," but that all credit would have to be on a sound basis. This was too much for Petrescu-Comnen who lost his composure and, describing himself as just "a peasant from the Danube," warned the British that if they insisted on adhering to the principles of Adam Smith and the Manchester School and not aiding Romania and the other countries of the southeast, then they would be forced into the arms of Germany and the future of Britain itself would be gravely affected. Despite Halifax's assurances that he well understood Romania's predicament, Petrescu-Comnen came away with an unpleasant impression of "this reserved and fear-ridden man."

This calls into question the reality of British policy toward the Central and Eastern European countries. Though the wheat deal was a break with past policies, British commitment to the Danubian basin remained equivocal. Leith-Ross succeeded in getting Romania allotted one million pounds in political credits, moving it from seventeenth in the previous year to fourth on the Strategic Priorities List, just behind Turkey, Greece and Yugoslavia. In February 1939 it moved up to third.[57]

The passage of the Exports Credits Guarantee Bill in December 1938 permitted granting to select countries "political" credits for commercial and even weapons purchases. But the amount, ten million pounds, was not sufficient to mount any kind of sustained counter to the German economic surge in the Eastern European area. In the case of Romania nothing was really done until after the German entry into Prague.

In October the British and French duplicitously shirked their promise to the Czechs to guarantee the borders of Czechoslovakia after the cession of the Sudetenland to Germany. Cadogan reports the British sellout in an October 20 conversation with Henderson: "He told me privately (and I quite approved!) that he had put Göring up to objecting to our guarantee of Czechoslovakia."[58] France also tried to reduce its obligations in the east by loosening its ties to Poland. But after frictions erupted with Italy, France began supporting Balkan resistance to Hitler. From Belgrade, the French minister, Brugère, warned on October 21 that unless France began to massively purchase Yugoslav goods, Germany would do so.[59]

Mussolini, not to be outdone by Hitler, moved toward an "Italian Munich" through the acquisition of French territory. French relations with Italy reached the breaking point when Italian deputies, primed by a Ciano speech, shouted: "Tunis, Corsica, Nice." On December 6, 1938, Bonnet signed the Franco-German Agreement not only giving Germany a free hand in the east but also to enable France to deal with Mussolini.

The French tried to launch an economic counter-offensive, sending trade missions to Bucharest, Sofia and Belgrade, but after working twenty-five days accomplished little. France sought repayment of its loans but refused to buy more goods from Romania or Yugoslavia despite a request from Stojadinović.[60]

British efforts in Southeastern Europe did not yield more results than the French. The Romanian wheat deal became mired in difficulties with British millers, and Greek tobacco exports similarly with British tobacco interests. Halifax's efforts to instruct the other government departments to accept Southeastern European exports met with resistance from Leith-Ross who opposed government trading projects. As the latter had been a great support for political credits, he could not be easily bypassed. But in the end, Hitler's January 30, 1939, "trade or die" speech and Stanley's forthcoming trade talks in Berlin in March led the Board of Trade and Chamberlain to believe that Germany's economic problems had finally forced Hitler to place his expansionist aspirations on hold. To deflect him from that path by sending a trade mission to the Balkans seemed senseless. Therefore, the Romanian trade mission which Leith-Ross had been advancing had to be delayed until April.[61]

On November 10 Leith-Ross, undoubtedly with Chamberlain's approval, renewed his bribe effort of October with Ernst Rüter, a German official then passing through London. Ten days later Wiehl, the German economic specialist, rejected the offer of Ashton-Gwatkin, sent by Halifax, to hold talks with the Nazi leaders. While the Leith-Ross offer may have been designed to increase British trade through an agreement with Germany and kill two birds with one stone, buying Germany's friendship was the better part of the bargain. Leith-Ross's interest in new trade possibilities, as the Economic Advisor to the Government, was a convenient mask for Chamberlain's real intentions.[62]

Leith-Ross complained from Bucharest about bureaucratic stodginess in London regarding trade with Romania.[63] The Committee "and the Prime Minister and other Ministers have declared that, without in any way wanting to encircle Germany, we intended to maintain, and if possible, to develop our trading relations with those countries." Since then King Carol, Halifax and Chamberlain agreed to send a commercial mission. Leith-Ross fumed over the lack of action.

> ...up to the present no decision has been taken even on this comparatively innocuous proposition and when Hudson puts it up to the Secretary of State, somebody at the Foreign Office produces a long draft the whole tenor of which seems to me inconsistent with the instructions given to me by the Ministers. As a result, weeks pass, a great deal of inter-departmental correspondence takes place, and nothing whatever is settled.[64]

Thus, the view that Leith-Ross and the Committee had little interest in promoting trade with Eastern Europe is not correct.[65]

Overton of the Board of Trade objected to Leith-Ross's export credit requests to Romania and the sending of a mission. While the recent Payments Agreement made Romanian exports "highly attractive" and the British now imported heavily from Romania, conversely the demand for U.K. goods exceeded the sterling available or likely to be available in the foreseeable future from imports of Romanian goods. Overton feared failure and thought sending a mission for political purpose "unwise." Similar "penny wise" policy and negative arguments were advanced against sending missions to other countries in the region. Greece, to which Leith-Ross had mentioned sending a mission, had a favorable trade balance with Britain, but like Romania "they have no means to pay for what we export to Greece." If a mission were sent to Bulgaria, this might offend Romania and they might lose more Romanian trade than the total value of Bulgarian trade. "Somewhat similar arguments appl[ied] in the case of Yugoslavia."[66]

Leith-Ross's complaints finally achieved results and in the spring of 1939 he was appointed to head a trade mission to Romania. The Romanians were becoming as desperate for British trade as the Yugoslavs. In 1938, Tilea, the Romanian minister, reminded the British that he had come with special instructions asking them to buy oil. Nothing had been done and the Germans bought the oil Great Britain had refused to buy.[67]

Meeting first with the Romanian Prime Minister, Leith-Ross offered five million pounds "on certain conditions." The Romanian countered that Germany had offered fifteen million pounds and if Britain did not meet that figure or more "it would not look as if Britain was taking a preponderant interest in Romania." Surrounded by a sea of enemies, Romania's priority was first armaments, then commercial interests. He was disappointed that the British could not supply anti-aircraft guns and could provide only old Hotchkiss six-pounder tank guns. The Prime Minister asked that orders be placed "immediately as the position of the country was growing gradually worse."[68]

Bujoiu, the Minister of National Economy, said they were "alarmed" at their situation in the event of war: the Black Sea and the Mediterranean might be temporarily closed; they lacked cotton yarns and steel reserves and therefore asked for credits to buy up stocks, to which Leith-Ross did not object.[69]

On the following day Leith-Roth saw Stoicecu, "a very solemn fellow," who admitted the too complicated Romanian trade system needed to be unified. Stoicecu lamented the five different trade systems: a clearing with Germany and a percentage of free exchange practiced with the U.K., France, Belgium, Switzerland, etc. He preferred to sweep them all away "and get back to a free system, but feared a rise in prices, budgetary and social difficulties and a flight of capital."[70]

Constantinescu met him next "almost with tears in his eyes" because his position "had suffered from the ill success of his efforts in London." Constantinescu asked for raw materials (cotton yarn, steel, zinc, nickel and aluminum) and a framework of general economic collaboration to attract some definite business, and later on Romanian investments. "Otherwise Romania would fall more and more under the control of Germany," followed by Turkey, which depended on Romanian oil. Once Germany controlled the Danube, then the Black Sea, Turkey's northern coast would be difficult to defend.

Constantinescu made suggestions for fostering Romanian exports for the British market: "We ought to organize Anglo-Romanian exporting companies for wheat, timber, etc.," he exhorted. "The Germans had created three for wheat alone. The Romanians were exporting nearly £2 million worth of chemicals for Germany each year. [Britain] was doing practically nothing." Constantinescu reminded that he had proposed bartering imported cotton yarn against wheat, "but nobody seemed interested." He suggested a shipping company with regular sailings between Romania and the U.K.[71]

By May 1939, Leith-Ross's British Trade Commission to Romania and the Romanian government reached agreement, made difficult by the conflict between higher internal prices and lower world prices. "The oil people were particularly difficult. They opened their mouths very wide, and Kessler, the British oil representative, created considerable resentment by appearing to dictate to the Romanian government and threatening to break off discussions if he did not get what he wanted." The Romanian Prime Minister complained to Hoare, the British minister at Bucharest. Leith-Ross wrote: "...the oil companies have really been fooling us.... By manipulating the rate of sterling to lei at much less than it was worth the oil companies made really substantial profits."[72]

The five million pounds credit, in the opinion of Leith-Ross, "was the most important problem." He was patronizingly sympathetic: "No doubt from the Whitehall view they seem persistent beggars...," but the Romanians worked hard to prepare for war and to resist the German demands, and "...it is not unreasonable of them to expect... financial credits." Britain's attitude compared invidiously with the Germans "who are tumbling over themselves to get control of the resources of Romania...." Leith-Ross stressed that to ensure success, credits would have to be issued on non-commercial lines.[73]

These arguments did not dissuade officials with conventional economic views like Treasury official Sir William Brown who opposed bilateral trade: he anticipated Romanian demands and complaints that other nations were receiving more credits, or they would claim a loan because other countries had received one, or the U.K. would be obliged to buy wheat or oil from Romania because it had done so for another country.[74]

These hesitations could be put down only to simple bureaucratic stodginess and lingering appeasement, but also to purblind economic orthodoxy. In addition, the government in 1939 was caught in a dilemma: it wanted to encourage resistance in Eastern Europe, but at the same time avoid handing out precious finances and armaments needed, as the war drew nearer, for the defense of Britain. Plus there was much more than a vestigial distaste for involvement in Eastern Europe from the government elites to the broad general public. Thus Leith-Ross could offer Germany, without qualm, unsolicited credits to unblock its Southeastern trade accounts while the Prime Minister and his government begrudged the Eastern European countries only the most paltry sum in the form of credits and also some increased semi-subsidized trade.

Despite his distaste for war, Chamberlain had to develop a military-political war strategy. In cabinet meetings and in private discussions, he urged a two-front strategy against Germany in which Poland and not the despised Soviet Union would be Britain's major ally in the east.

The February 20, 1939, British Staff Chiefs' incongruously named "European Appreciation, 1939–1940" stated that neither Poland nor the Soviet Union could be given any effective assistance against a German attack. Therefore, no plans were drawn up for a war in the east or of how to offer assistance to the hapless Poles and Romanians in a war on the eastern front. This view steadfastly persisted during meetings of the British and French military and reports of the Chiefs of Staff and cabinet, and even after the guarantees to Poland, Romania and Greece. Neither Poland nor Romania was expected to last more than a few months against a German onslaught. Incredibly, to the date of the German attack on Poland, no plans had been drawn up on how to bring aid to the Poles except for vague talk of air attacks upon Germany once war broke out.

Chapter 16

The Period of Retarded German Hegemony in Southeastern Europe, October 1939–October 1940. The Polish Campaign to Italy's Attack on Greece

> Defenceless under the night
> Our world in stupor lies;
> Yet dotted everywhere,
> Ironic points of light
> Flash out wherever the Just
> Exchange their messages....
>
> —W. H. Auden,
> *September 1, 1939*

ONCE THE WAR BROKE OUT the underlying trade and economic conflicts for the markets and raw materials of Eastern Europe instrumental in causing it increasingly transformed into political and finally military duels. Political and strategic military preoccupations in the Balkans, first Salonika Front fever and later the looming German campaign in the Soviet Union, increasingly fed into clashing Great Power interests. Leaders of the smaller Eastern European powers scurried between the Great Power capitals, jockeying for the best deal they could get and also to exploit the conflict in order to seize neighboring irredentist territories while maintaining their own independence. Their inability to form a common front against Great Power machinations and imperialism, sometimes preferring to assist in mutual destruction, cost them dearly.

Germany's inability to pay the Balkan countries for their raw materials led it to resort to pressure and intimidation to compel delivery. Greater Germany, now bordered on most of the Balkan states, easily manipulated the minority quarrels and native fascist movements (Hungarian Arrow Cross, Romanian Iron Guard, etc.) between and within those countries. Later, after the fall of France, Germany switched to military coercion.

Britain's interest in the region had been primarily as an export market and only secondarily as a source of raw materials, but once war occurred, it was to deny Balkan resources to Germany. After Munich, from 1939 through 1940, Germany's eastern policy consisted in extracting the raw material wealth of the Balkans while British policy, cognizant of Germany's economic predicament, conversely, was to prevent that from occurring. To this end

341

both the Axis and Western Powers harried the Balkan governments, through their diplomats, to gain their ends. Finally in 1940–1941, they resorted to military means. The chapter that follows details this Great Power conflict. With greatly diminished or little capacity to pay for raw materials, Germany could gain this indispensable supply only through credit from the Balkan countries by duress and coercion. While refusing a direct Soviet alliance, Britain worked assiduously to deny Hitler trade and political control of the Danubian basin. The area, thus, increasingly became an imperialist apple of discord over which Britain and Germany struggled for hegemonic power, which eventually led to military conflict. The struggle occurred in two phases: an economic and political conflict from March 1939 to the spring of 1941 and from March 1941 until the end of the Greek campaign when Hitler decided, against his original intentions, to extend the war into the Balkans.

In the case of Yugoslavia, its geographic location left it particularly vulnerable in the event of war. Only 30% of its foreign trade entered across land frontiers, while 50% entered the country by sea and 20% by inland waterway.[1] It could, therefore, be strangled economically as well as militarily if the Aegean and the Mediterranean routes were cut and the Danubian waterway blocked, a distinct possibility in 1939, once Germany annexed Austria and Italy seized Albania. German exports to Yugoslavia were primarily machinery, chemicals, iron and steel, wool and cotton manufactures, 71% of Yugoslavia's anthracite and 62% of that country's bituminous coal at the end of March 1937. In turn, Yugoslavia exported 60.1% of its meat, wheat and corn to Germany. At the end of March 1938, Germany's passive trade debt to Yugoslavia was 13.6 million Rm, constraining it into being a continuing purchaser from Germany.[2] "But to obtain her resources of copper, bauxite, lead, zinc, manganese, chrome and antimony," declared a British memorandum, "will be the chief object of German diplomacy and to transport this within Romania and Southeastern Europe via the Danube."[3] Conversely, the primary aim of British diplomacy was to prevent that from occurring.

The British — and Czechoslovaks — were mainly suppliers to Yugoslavia of textile raw materials: in 1937 Britain exported 47% of Yugoslavia's wool (raw and yarn), 41% of its woolen manufactures, 41% of its cotton tissues, 31% of its cotton (raw and yarn) and 55% of its coke.[4] In return, Britain imported mostly agricultural products. However, British-Yugoslav trade was not a two-way street: the Yugoslavs needed British trade much more than Britain needed Yugoslav goods. The Board of Trade summarized succinctly: "Yugoslavia sends nothing to the British Empire and France which is not capable of replacement from other sources."[5] Other Eastern European countries had similar trade difficulties with Britain.

On the eve of Munich, British public feeling, still in its sleep-walking stage about Hitler, was not averse to seeing German economic power extended into Central and Eastern Europe and, as Winston Churchill told the Danzig Gauleiter, Albert Foerster: "most (English) people...would not resent gradual peaceful increase of German commercial influence in the Danubian basin, but that any violent move would almost immediately lead to a world war."[6] The political mood was to get out of any obligations toward that region rather than getting further into them.

To keep out of the Nazi trade maw, the Yugoslavs placed pressure on the British after 1938 to take more Yugoslav imports and grant loans for defense weaponry. In May 1939 the Yugoslav Finance Minister Djuričić expressed disappointment to two British officials at the meager British loan offer of a half million pounds "and even suggested the offer was derisory." Yugoslavia, Djuričić said, did not need credits so much as measures to help exports.[7] "Her preoccupation was to sell to those countries (i.e., the Western Powers)," the sympathetic British minister, Campbell reported, "for free exchange." Credits in fact created a state of indebtedness.[8] A Board of Trade official's minute on increased Yugoslav bacon exports feared "considerable repercussions" with other states. Britain opposed "favoring one's friends with quotas" rather than the most-favored-nation principle. Moreover, Yugoslavia, a minor supplier, except for poultry, should fulfill existing sales requirements "before we talk of buying more from them."[9] Devaluing the dinar to increase Yugoslav exports could harm U.K. exporters.[10] Waley of the Treasury Department suggested purchasing minerals from Yugoslavia "either for current needs or for war reserves." However, stocks were already filled and "Yugoslav minerals (like zinc) were not of required quality" and "could not be purchased."[11] Equally, Yugoslav wheat purchases could not be increased as Yugoslav wheat was inferior — even to Romanian wheat — for which there was no need in England.[12]

In late June 1939, Subbotić, Yugoslav minister to the U.K., "made a very excited appeal to Leith-Ross for economic assistance to Yugoslavia." To avoid German economic pressure they needed "not credits but increased export outlets." "Did Great Britain realize," he asked Leith-Ross, "that it rested with her to save Yugoslavia from entering the German camp?" Leith-Ross could only suggest that the Yugoslavs should lower their high prices.[13]

Oliver Stanley told Halifax on June 2 the Yugoslav minister of commerce's visit was "pointless" and prospects "insufficient."[14] But in July the Yugoslavs, undaunted, increased pressure to step up British purchases of Yugoslav goods. Subbotić told Sargent, Assistant Under-Secretary of State, that German goods were inferior and Yugoslavia wanted to raise its exports to Great Britain to one-quarter of the export trade to Germany. A one million pound increase "would make all the difference." Yugoslav exporters had received export premiums to sell at world prices and Yugoslavia preferred to buy arms from Britain rather than Germany.[15]

Under intense pressure to join the Axis, Prince Paul prepared to make a trip to Berlin and Rome in July 1939 to see Hitler. Paul was despondent after receiving an intimidating letter from Göring. "I never see the Prince Regent and other Yugoslav officials ... that he didn't express surprise that we do practically nothing to help," Campbell confided. He begged for one million pounds, double the figure assigned, because of the "moral effect."[16] Campbell asked London to step up its offer of twenty-four aircraft, as "lately the Yugoslavs are coming ... to the conclusion that we have lost interest in them and cannot be counted on for any effective help.[17]

To avoid repercussions, Halifax recommended raising the half million pounds for "political credits" to £1 million (£1.5 million pounds in all) on "political grounds," to encourage the Yugoslavs "to fight the Italians vigorously and energetically," but opposed increasing Anglo-Yugoslav trade.[18] H. R. MacLean reported "an impassioned appeal to Nichol (a Foreign Office official) and myself to increase trade between the U.K. and Yugoslavia." Subbotić claimed it had dropped 42% in the last year — an exaggerated figure — and requested doubling the bacon quota from .19 to .38 which "would have a great effect upon the Yugoslav people."[19]

When war broke out, Campbell reported the Yugoslav exports at a standstill — the British would not increase imports and the Yugoslavs would not trade with Germany on the previous basis. The Germans demanded a vastly increased supply on credit of pigs, poultry, etc., and suggested "that the Yugoslav government must, if necessary, support the mark with the dinar, indicating the weakness of Germany's export trade position under war conditions and suggests the possibility that even normal German exports to Yugoslavia will not be maintained. The Commercial Section is of this opinion." Yugoslavia, Campbell thought, would refuse German demands for the supply of goods on credit "and unless Germany exerts pressure Yugoslav-German trade will be reduced in both directions. Since this represents one-half of Yugoslav foreign trade it will suffer unless other outlets can be found."[20] Similar problems occurred in Romania.

Stojadinović had told the American minister, Lane, in April 1938 that Yugoslavia's policy was to diminish as much as possible its trade with Germany.[21]

This evidence from Yugoslavia, only ten days after war began, corroborates Göring's post-war statements that Germany could no longer pay for its requirements from the Southeastern countries and elsewhere through normal trade channels and had to resort to a war of plunder. While not necessarily automatic, had it not done so it faced eventual domestic shortages and, as Göring stated, meant the beginning of the end.

After the Anglo-Turkish Pact blocking his access to the Balkans, Mussolini drew closer to Germany, formalizing the Axis through the Pact of Steel in May 1939. In a memorandum delivered to Berlin by the Italian Chief of Staff, General Ugo Cavallero, in the same month, Mussolini foresaw that a "war between the plutocratic and hence egoistically conservative powers and the populous poor is inevitable." Italy needed three years to prepare for the conflict. Mussolini predicted "a war of usury" in which the Axis would not receive aid from the rest of the world except through its conquests. This meant the seizure of the industrial raw materials and foodstuffs of the Balkans "without regard for neutrality or guarantees" given to Greece, Romania and Turkey. Only Hungary and Bulgaria could be counted upon in that area.[22] Hitler expressed similar sentiments in the same month: Germany had overcome its inferior status since 1933 but had not yet broken into the "charmed circle" of Great Powers. The previous successes in Austria and Czechoslovakia would not be repeated without war, a risk he was prepared to take.[23]

A renegade socialist and *Realpolitiker*, Mussolini viewed the impending clash as an imperialist conflict between the dominant national bourgeoisies of Britain and France ("the plutocratic and hence egoistically conservative powers") and the weaker, less affluent peoples of Germany and Italy ("the populous poor [nations]") for economic and political preeminence in Eastern Europe. His "war of usury" meant that the wealthier Western Powers would utilize their colonies and monetary preponderance to finance the war, compelling Germany and Italy to seize the raw materials they could not purchase, through a war of expansion and conquest in Southeastern and Eastern Europe. Thus, a fateful conjuncture of economic and political pressures ensured aggressive expansion and war.

Besides the major Axis/Western Powers confrontation, there were also contradictions between the Axis powers over control of the Southeast; and internal contradictions between the Balkan states as well. Riven by a farrago of political, social and ethnic problems, the Balkan Powers lacked the ability to face the aggressive imperialist Axis Powers. The Serb-Croat conflict made any unified Yugoslav policy toward the Axis Powers extremely difficult. Similar contradictions existed between the other Eastern European states and their minority nationalities. Once war broke out in September 1939 the bonds formerly connecting these states to the Western Powers loosened and they had to fend for themselves. This last point more than anything else explains the complicated Balkan diplomacy the year before the war and once war erupted.

During his visit to Berlin, Ciano declared Yugoslavia's foreign policy not "satisfactory" (*einwandfrei*) and Ribbentrop warned: "Yugoslavia must be handled toughly."[24] Ribbentrop indignantly rejected Gafencu's neutral Balkan bloc proposal (Yugoslavia-Hungary-Romania) as "a new Little Entente."[25]

Like a tributary vassal, Prince Paul had to journey to Berlin and Rome to pay official obeisance and explain Yugoslavia's recalcitrance. To Campbell's arguments against going, he agonized, "But what [else] can I do?" His whole soul revolted against these visits; he could no longer look at an illustrated paper for fear of seeing "those two horrible faces."[26]

The Regent's unexpected dismissal of the Axis favorite, Stojadinović, had deeply impressed the British and French with a fateful, mistaken belief in the Regent's strength of character which underlies Campbell's comment on Paul's personality after the Albanian affair:

> A pacifist by nature, he recoils with loathing from the idea of war.... But somewhere in his veins runs the Karageorge blood, and I think he is capable of rising to the occasion when his mind is made up. He has given proof of this on several occasions.[27]

By June Prince Paul had recovered from the Albanian affair and surprised Campbell by alluding "suddenly and out of the blue" to a plan to "drive the Italians into the sea" in the event of war. His old hatred of Mussolini revived. "Salonika is his bugbear," Campbell observed. Paul believed the Albanian operation intended to cut off Yugoslavia's only line of communication between the Western democracies and the Balkans, except through the back door of Salonika, the Black Sea and the Dardanelles.[28]

Public sentiment for England and France was growing in Yugoslavia. After his car had been mobbed by hundreds of Yugoslavs shouting pro-British slogans, the British minister, with evident satisfaction, wrote: "I think there is no doubt if they had the chance the whole country would go for [i.e., attack –P.N.H.] the Italians with the greatest joy."[29] However, Campbell warned that the present euphoria could not be sustained without some word from London about Salonika, otherwise Paul would suffer a relapse back to his earlier despair.

But the Foreign Office and British General Staff did not wish to antagonize Italy and it remained a dead letter.[30] Other considerations prevented a full-blown preemptive Salonika front operation: equipment and transportation shortages, commitments elsewhere and financial cost. This would only be considered later. Only when Germany had dangerously extended itself into the Balkans would a Salonika front be reconsidered.

On the eve of the Regent's visit, the German minister, von Heeren, reported Paul desired to act as an intermediary between London and Berlin. Military and political pressures would rule out an overtly pro-Axis policy, in favor of a neutral course. Germany would continue to secure from Yugoslavia essential raw materials even if war should break out.[31]

To impress and intimidate Prince Paul with German might, Hitler held a four-hour parade of massed troops and tanks marching by in a deafening crescendo of noise. Factory and office workers and school children were given the day off.

In a tête-à-tête with Paul, Hitler set forth his demands: Yugoslavia's exit from the League of Nations; Yugoslavia had to join the Comintern Pact and adopt clear language corroborating his close association with the Axis. Hitler had to be certain before his attack on Poland that Yugoslavia would not participate in a Western attack on Germany through a front in Salonika, as in World War I, and spread the war to the Balkans. Paul gained the impression, later undoubtedly passed to London, that Hitler believed the British would not go to war over the Free City of Danzig despite their guarantee to Poland. Hitler confided his fears that Mussolini might precipitate a war through "an act of folly" and, therefore, it might be better if Yugoslavia joined the Axis bloc. He claimed ignorance of the Albanian affair until a few hours before the Italian attack. Paul balked at leaving the Balkan Pact but agreed to leave the League and maintain a neutral position.[32]

The Italian historian Breccia's assessment that Paul had succeeded in maintaining Yugoslavia's neutrality despite Axis pressures is probably correct. He had even gained a German promise of 200 million Rm in credit.

German pressures continued on the Balkan states to join the Axis. The Bulgarian Minister-President expressed mock astonishment and raised a whole raft of objections: fear of Bolshevik propaganda, the danger from Yugoslavia and other Entente members.[33] The Yugoslavs advanced proposals for "a really neutral bloc" including Bulgaria, which collapsed for lack of support.[34]

The Germans recognized Paul's dilemma: Feine, the German consul in Belgrade, noted, "the fact that the foreign policy of the Yugoslav government was in sharp contrast to the mood of a considerable part of the population cannot be contested." The government was endeavoring to please Germany while the people remained unabashedly pro-Western. France and England were spending considerable sums on propaganda and doing everything to draw Yugoslavia into the Western orbit. Yugoslavia, Feine concluded, would maintain its neutrality in the future; General Simović, the Yugoslav chief of staff, desired "strict neutrality" in the event of war, but an Italian thrust through Yugoslavia to Salonika would meet with armed resistance.[35]

Paul again returned to his Salonika obsession. At a private luncheon with the British minister he suddenly "talked with an astounding freedom" of his hatred of Germany and Italy. Paul punctuated his statements with a plea for arms ("I have got a million and a half magnificent fighters but how can they stand up without proper arms against thousands of tanks and armored cars"). The Regent no longer spoke of avoiding war, but of keeping the Germans at bay while he threw the Italians out of Albania into the sea. Believing that Hitler would invade the Balkans and push through to Ankara at an early stage in the war, he urged the British to rush one or two regiments to Salonika to help stiffen the Greeks. Hitler's and Ribbentrop's assertions that they did not know anything about Mussolini's Albanian operation until a few hours before, he believed to be lies.[36]

In February 1939 the British government hardened against appeasement, and London informed Belgrade it opposed German hegemony in the Balkans: "we do not desire that Germany dominate economically in Yugoslavia and become an exclusive client for your raw materials." While conceding Germany's greater interest in the country, at the same time Germany "must content itself with the trade position the region offers and must not extend itself to a monopoly that with time could have political consequences. We could not consent that one day Germany obtains exclusive economic influence in the Balkans. Great Britain cannot and does not want to grant recognition to German industry of a monopoly in the Balkans. In the best of cases it will recognize a privileged position."[37] Thus the British position of the mid-1930s of conceding the exploitation of Eastern and Southeastern Europe to Germany changed by early 1939. All this demonstrates that the struggle for trade and markets — particularly in Southeastern and Eastern Europe — must play a major role in the causes of the Second World War.

At the end of 1938, Yugoslavia had an active balance of 196 million dinars. With war imminent, Prince Paul decided to utilize the excess to purchase 200 million Rm of war materials from Germany, half from the Krupp factory for anti-aircraft guns and other weapons and half from German aviation firms for bombers and fighters.[38] In June 1939, Ambassador Andrić requested 200 anti-tank guns, 50 Dorniers, 50 Messerschmidts and 34 Fuisels. But because of Yugoslavia's uncertain foreign policy, Berlin delayed deliveries.[39] Efforts to trade bauxite with the United States for weaponry failed.[40]

German raw material needs forced them for now to accept Yugoslavia's neutrality. Breccia's assessment is probably true that Prince Paul conducted a "dual policy" (*duplice azione*) while trying to reach an agreement with the Croats and supplying Germany and Italy with raw materials in exchange for weaponry. He conducted a nuanced tightrope policy of cosseting the revisionist powers, Bulgaria and Hungary, and of reassuring Italy and Germany that Yugoslavia intended eventually to join the Axis, while maintaining Western friendship.

Suspicions of British motives in the spring of 1939 produced much cynicism. When Campbell asked what Yugoslavia would do in the event of a German attack on Poland, Prince Paul replied with cutting sarcasm: "You ask me what I am prepared to do, but I would like to know what you are prepared to do."[41] Similarly, Turkish Foreign Minister Saracoglu told the Soviet representative: "If England knew that Poland, Romania, Yugoslavia and Turkey intended to fight Germany it would not raise a finger."[42]

On May 21, 1939, Cincar-Marković, the Yugoslav Foreign Minister, met his Romanian counterpart, Grigore Gafencu, at Turnu-Severin on the Romanian border and affirmed their neutral policy. Since the May Anglo-Turkish Agreement the Germans became hostile to the "fork-tongued" Turks now considered clients of Britain and France and had similar feelings about the devious Yugoslavs and Romanians. Berlin wondered "whether Gafencu was playing a straight game."[43] The Turks irritated Belgrade for compromising the Balkan Pact and Yugoslavia's neutrality through Article VI of the Anglo-Turkish Agreement.

To block any Nazi southeast thrust, Rome ceased supporting a separate Croatian state favoring a strong, centralized Yugoslav state. Mussolini ordered Dr. Ante Pavelić and the Croatian Ustasha in Italy incarcerated on the Lipari Islands.

Ironically, Berlin also favored Axis-inclined Stojadinović's Great Serbia, but after his fall von Heeren suggested supporting Croatian autonomy to prevent the Croats from turning to the Western Powers for assistance.[44]

Maček's lieutenant, Krnjević, advised opting for the maximum solution of the Croatian problem or else Croatia ran the risk of being swallowed by the Germans or Italians.[45] In his post-war memoirs Maček also cites the darkening international situation as his reason for opening negotiations with the Regent Paul.[46] The disturbed state of the economically depressed Croatian masses frightened the predominantly urban bourgeois leadership of the Croatian Peasant Party who saw the formation of a Croatian state as their social and economic liberation. Many spoke of assuming power with or without Maček.[47] The latter's refusal to convoke the long-awaited Croatian Sabor (parliament) and assume jurisdiction over the territories inhabited by the Croats met with widespread disillusionment among the Croatian masses.[48] A radical solution of the Croatian problem offered by the Croatian separatists threatened civil war.

The divisive Croatian problem was a major reason for Stojadinović's dismissal after the 1938 government party's electoral setback. Paul told Ugo von Hassell, former German minister to Belgrade, visiting Yugoslavia in late 1940, that he suspected Stojadinović of having intimate conversations with Ciano and of sacrificing Croatia to Italy. Stojadinović's Serbian centralist policy impeded an accord with the Croats.[49]

Through intermediaries (first Cvetković, later Ivan Šubašić) Prince Paul promised the union of Croatia and Dalmatia including Dubrovnik and northeastern Bosnia, if Maček would accept the existing centralist constitution. Maček agreed, but demanded Hercegovina and part of Srem as well.

But pressure by the Orthodox Church Patriarch, the Serb military and nationalist elements against handing over districts not exclusively Croat forced the Regent to withdraw his concessions. However, moderate Croats and Peasant Party leaders preferred agreement with Belgrade to a partitioned Yugoslavia under Axis rule. A threatened Frankist and Ustasha separatist agenda created a middle ground for preservation of a federalist Yugoslav state.[50] When negotiations with Belgrade languished, Maček appealed directly to Britain as to whether it "would be willing to extend her protection to an independent Croatia...or any kind of protection devised by Great Britain."[51] The Foreign Office lacked interest, and Berlin also refused support for Croatian autonomy, avoiding irritating the Italians. Weizsäcker told von Heeren curtly, "hands off."[52]

Announcement of the Nazi-Soviet Pact, the German minister exulted, "burst like a bomb here.... Friends of Germany are triumphant, its enemies are bewildered and speechless." It spurred Maček to enter the government with four Croatian ministers.[53]

The pact strengthened Yugoslavia's neutral policy more than ever. Anti-German and pro-Western circles also insisted on a policy of "strict neutrality." Von Heeren predicted that even if a military putsch occurred Belgrade would maintain an unswerving neutrality.[54] Subbotić discussed the pact with R. A. Butler and conjectured whether to expect a division into spheres of influence and if Moscow would now enjoy a free hand in the Balkans.[55]

Anti-war demonstrations in Yugoslavia in October and December raised British suspicions: "It appears beyond doubt," wrote Campbell, "that German money and German agents are behind much of the communist propaganda in this country."[56] The British consular official Vibert believed that disturbances in Split — whose exaggerated accounts in the Italian press frightened Belgrade — had been caused by Italian money to create a pretext for intervention.[57]

Overnight, following the Nazi-Soviet Pact, the Yugoslav communists, previously pursuing a "patriotic and defensist" line, reversed position and ardently opposed the war.[58] Only through an alliance with the Soviet Union, the Yugoslav communists maintained, could Yugoslavia be saved and only through a Soviet-British-French alliance, based upon a united peace front, could an imperialist war be prevented. When that could not be accomplished, they postulated, the Soviet Union had to join Germany. By signing the pact with Hitler, the USSR liberated itself from the specter of isolation and the possibility of a united capitalist crusade against it. A Soviet-German pact would localize the war and restrict it for the time being.

The Yugoslav Communist Party now pursued a militant anti-war policy, increasing its participation in political strikes in the coal industry, a bloody strike of six thousand miners, and in the aeronautical and textile industry in Belgrade.[59] The British consul in Belgrade commented:

> Before the signing of the Russo-German Pact the Yugoslav communists were the greatest nationalists in Yugoslavia. Communist students of Belgrade University formed volunteer battalions which were voluntarily trained by army officers. Since the Russo-German Pact these

volunteers have disappeared. Up to 23 August the communists could not wait for the war to begin. Today they are pacifists *à outrance*.[60]

The Yugoslav communists analyzed the clash between Britain and Germany in the Balkans as a zone of imperialist conflict between the two powers.[61] The forces of General Weygand in the Middle East were considered only bait, floated to attract the Balkan states into an anti-Soviet campaign in alliance with the Franco-British imperialists.[62]

In countering Soviet influence in Yugoslavia, the British historian Seton-Watson warned against attacking the Russians rather than the Soviet government because of traditional pro-Russian historical and cultural sentiment. Because of pro-Allied feeling in the country, he thought Yugoslavia offered the easiest Balkan country to extend British influence into and suggested establishing a large British mission in Belgrade similar to the Soviet mission in Bulgaria.[63] These suggestions may have led to the coup of March 27, 1941.

In early August 1939, Ciano met the German leaders at Salzburg where they revealed their plans for an attack on Poland, inviting the Italians to make a dual riposte and occupy Dalmatia and Croatia at the moment of the Polish attack. Ciano noted that Hitler did not mention occupying Slovenia, containing a large German-speaking minority and the object of both German and Italian expansionist plans.[64] After much agonizing, Mussolini pleaded Italian unpreparedness, and declined to enter the war. Despite informing London of Italy's position of non-belligerency, Mussolini had not given up his desire for booty in Yugoslavia.[65]

In a secret handwritten letter to Lord Halifax, delivered personally by his sister-in-law, Prince Paul described Italy's neutrality as "most suspicious," and "without pledges" would result in the destruction of Southeastern Europe. The week before Ciano had made aggressive speeches in Albania promising to unite all Albanians under Italy (more than a half million Albanians in the Kosovo region of Yugoslavia). Paul advised London to clear the Mediterranean as soon as war broke out.[66] Campbell argued that as soon as Hitler was in difficulty, Mussolini would cease to be a problem, but Paul insisted that the Western Powers should "begin by knocking out the weaker of the two partners." The Regent pressed for an Allied base at Salonika, regardless of Italian neutrality, which "would do more . . . to put heart into the Balkans than anything else."[67] Paul's truculent attitude heartened the British and impressed the French minister at Belgrade who confessed to Campbell that he had been wrong about Paul.

The Regent's paranoid apprehensions and mood shifts prompted by his alarmist diplomats abroad and the overwrought, refined, and paper-thin sensitivity of the art esthete revived a few days later. He had "just had the greatest shock of my life," he told Campbell. He had learned that the French and Italians were conducting discussions "with a view to buying Italian cooperation with the Allies at the price of Dalmatia and the Ionian Islands." This news, which had wounded him deeply, arrived suddenly like a hair in the soup at a time when he was prepared to sacrifice a million men.

"He begged with tears in his eyes" that the British government set his mind at ease.[68]

Anxious to build a front of neutral Balkan states barring Axis encroachment, Paul began turning over in his mind a plan to draw Bulgaria into the Balkan Entente.[69] Encouraged by Potemkin, Soviet Assistant Minister of Foreign Affairs, who, during his visit to Bucharest and London, supported the creation of a bloc of neutrals as the best way to frustrate German penetration of the Balkans,[70] Gafencu and Cincar-Marković met September 19, 1939, at Jebel on the Romanian-Serbian border and wove plans to entice Bulgaria into the Balkan Pact by offers of territory pending Saracoglu's return from Moscow.[71] But Molotov told the Turkish Foreign Minister that Russia was disinterested and did not want to endanger its relationship to Germany by an anti-German venture. The plan died when the Bulgarian government turned down the offers after being approached by the Turks.[72]

Answering appeals from the Balkan capitals, Mussolini moved to use Italian non-belligerency as a rallying point for a pied piper leadership of the East European neutrals against Germany and the USSR, both threatening Italy's aspirations.[73] A similar project of Gafencu included absolute neutrality, a treaty of non-aggression among member states and benevolent neutrality if a member were attacked by a non-Balkan power.[74] The British encouraged Italy's leadership and even considered a formal request asking Rome to lead the bloc.[75] However, the French and Yugoslavs, mistrustful of Italian imperialist pretensions, opposed an Italian preeminence in Eastern and Southeastern Europe. Massigli, the French ambassador to Turkey, raised a whole raft of objections, as did Prince Paul. A post-war restored Austria and Italy's preeminence, Paul believed, might induce the Slovenes and Croat Catholics to gravitate toward a Hapsburg restoration.[76]

The Germans clearly saw it as another suspect Balkan neutral scheme to advance Italian hegemony in the Balkans. But Berlin consented, provided it did not assume "a political character," once it learned the Bulgarians would not enter the pact anyway and it would probably collapse.[77] The Turkish connection with England and France had become so strong that an agreement with the Soviet Union was impossible. Therefore, the Soviet-Turkish negotiations collapsed.[78] With the Soviet Union needing Bulgaria more — in King Boris's view — and now supporting Bulgaria's irredentist demands, it became disinterested in a revised bloc of neutrals. The Soviets were as unenthusiastic about Italian hegemony in the Southeast in the guise of a revised bloc of neutrals as they were of British and French. As Germany already had a commanding economic position and full access to the resources of the Balkan area, it therefore did not wish a threatening Italo-Soviet confrontation there. Frictions between Rome and Moscow rankled on into the fall of 1939, until Hungarian reservations toward the Italian-led neutral bloc caused it to fizzle out at the end of November.[79]

The specter of Italian non-belligerency hovered over the military staff meetings of the Anglo-French Supreme War Council at Abbeville (September 12) and Hove (September 22) where the Allied Powers examined for the first time the feasibility of placing forces at Salonika or Istanbul without, however, provoking the Italians. In this and other conferences the French were the more aggressive while the British political and military leaders shrank from large scale projects in the Balkans. The British resisted the French desire to land forces at these points "to act as a cement" to encourage the Balkan states to resist German pressures. Chamberlain flatly declared that the Allies could not prevent a German entry into Yugoslavia. He preferred to let matters take their course and hoped that the various dictators would get into each other's hair in the Balkans. Moreover, a Salonika operation would place an undue strain on Allied shipping and naval facilities. He questioned the wisdom of the plan in view of Turkish and Italian attitudes.[80] A War Cabinet Conference (September 13) concluded: "It would be unfortunate if any steps were taken which gave Italy the impression we were forming a bloc against her."[81]

These attitudes and reservations persisted into the third and fourth meetings of the Supreme Allied War Council (November 17, and December 19). At the November meeting, Chamberlain rejected Daladier's modified request for munitions dumps to be established in Turkey, Thrace or perhaps Syria or Palestine. Such bases, he reasoned, could hardly be established in a neutral Turkey and, in any case, the Allies themselves were short of war materials. Examining the situation from the standpoint of their own interests, the British Chiefs of Staff concluded that Singapore was more important than the Mediterranean, and Turkey and Iraq of greater significance than the Balkans. Chamberlain was not sympathetic to Daladier's exhortations to bolster Balkan resistance. He doubted whether material aid would suffice to hold together a bloc of difficult Balkan states. Chamberlain dismissed the French desire to activate ninety Balkan divisions; he had little faith in the lower quality Balkan forces against the Germans. In the end the British policy prevailed of caution and doing everything possible to avoid disturbing Italy's neutral position. By November 1939, the Italian-directed neutral bloc faded and Italy's need for support against German domination of the Danubian region made Rome less opposed to an Allied-sponsored bloc of neutrals.[82]

To deny the Germans the ores they needed, Campbell again in November 1940, as in the previous June, presented compelling arguments for granting requests made by Prince Paul for armaments: Yugoslavia's exposure was greater than any country except Romania and would not be expected to fight Britain in any case; and its leaders had stated that Yugoslavia would be forced to intervene in the spring on the Allied side, even if Italy joined the Allies, to prevent Italy from being rewarded at Yugoslavia's expense. Pro-Allied feeling was strong and the recently concluded Anglo-French-Turkish accords had evoked popular rejoicing. Moreover, the Yugoslav General Staff influenced the government monopolization of ore deposits as a lever to obtain planes. To deny the Germans ores, Campbell recommended granting the Yugoslav arms requests.[83]

French-owned metal ores of Yugoslavia became absolutely imperative with the paralysis of the sea lanes by the British fleet.[84] To deny access would severely hamper the German war economy, and Hitler would have to occupy Yugoslavia and seize its mineral deposits. This would mean extending the war into the Balkans, which Hitler wanted to avoid; he preferred to gain Yugoslavia's natural resources by diplomatic and political pressure. The latter policy persisted down to the Belgrade coup d'état of March 27, 1941; thereafter Germany resorted to military means.

The pressure for Yugoslavia's minerals had become so great that the Germans decided against not selling Yugoslavia armaments until it aligned itself closer ideologically to the Axis. Fearing Yugoslavia would be unprepared in a Balkan war, Prince Paul offered to sell Yugoslavia's entire copper and lead production for acceleration of the promised deliveries, which Göring and the Wilhelmstrasse official Ritter found "very tempting."[85] Von Heeren also urged acceleration of deliveries fearing a Yugoslav pact with the Western Powers.[86] Wiehl, the German Foreign office economic specialist, declared the need for copper "a life and death matter" for German industry, even forcing Berlin to deny an Italian request for armaments in favor of the Yugoslavs. Once the deliveries were stepped up, Prince Paul nationalized the Bor mines preparatory to handing over its copper production to the Germans.[87] Nevertheless, strong nationalist and pro-Allied feeling particularly among the Serbs meant that any sudden swerving by the government toward a definitive alignment with the Axis could produce an explosion.

Wiehl advised stepping up Germany's anti-tank deliveries to Yugoslavia lest it cut back on its copper shipments.[88] An overriding reason impelling Yugoslavia to sell its copper to Germany was the British and French decision not to open a new front in the Balkans. Ambassador Cincar-Marković warned the German minister "as a friend" that the Western Powers might march their forces through the neutral states to the western front.[89] The flight of the Polish government, the German minister advised, had left a deep impression on the Yugoslav public which felt that Poland had been left in the lurch by the Western Powers. For the present, there would be no change in "the Yugoslav will to remain neutral."[90] To reassure continued raw material deliveries, Paul told the German minister that Yugoslavia would continue to trade with Germany and be a good neighbor, in contrast to a remote England, whatever the outcome of the war.[91]

In September 1939, to allay widespread fears of an attack on Yugoslavia, von Heeren requested Berlin disclaim designs on the Balkans or Yugoslavia with whom Germany wished only mutually beneficial economic relations.[92] Berlin promised Hitler would state Germany's western and southern borders were final.[93]

Anxieties over an Italian attack now arose once the attention of the Western Powers strayed elsewhere. Since the collapse of the Italian-led neutral bloc scheme, Mussolini hoped to gain Croatia and Dalmatia through a World War I Treaty of London arrangement as the price for Italian entry into the war on the Allied side.

These hopes failed by January 1940 and Mussolini, disregarding Ciano's warnings, prepared to seize Croatia and Dalmatia and await the British and French reaction.[94] In late January Ciano interviewed Ante Pavelić, the Croatian separatist leader, to discuss details of the operation.[95] By fomenting internal revolt in Croatia and an intervention by Italian troops, Mussolini hoped to install the Ustasha leader and proclaim the Kingdom of Croatia in personal union with the Italian crown, but General Weygand's French army poised in Syria raised the possibility of an Allied counter-reaction. Mussolini hesitated, then drew back from the abyss until the German attack on France in the spring.

Mussolini's plans reached the ears of Belgrade, and Prince Paul spoke "apprehensively of the designs of Italy in these parts." Sir Percy Lorraine, British ambassador at Rome, thought "a grabbing operation on the part of Italy was unlikely," which Indelli, Italian minister at Belgrade, also denied, but the Regent remained suspicious.[96] Belgrade retreated behind the protective shell of an official neutrality.[97] The Anglo-Italian Trade Agreement, which offered to mollify the Italians, only reignited Belgrade's suspicions.[98] Nichols, a Foreign Office official, reassured Ivan Subbotić and Dr. Cucin that England was not contemplating a deal at Yugoslavia's expense.[99] In his sustained Italianophobia and paranoia, Paul even offered to show Campbell "proofs of a devilish plot" the Italians had prepared: "getting rid" of President Roosevelt! To this Noble dryly noted: "where Italy is concerned Prince Paul is not quite sane. Italy's devilish plot to strike at us by getting rid of Mr. Roosevelt is past all reason."[100] Paul's "increasing state of nerves" flared up again in April when he learned, through an intercepted Pavelić letter to his American lieutenants, that with the help of Germany and Italy he would soon occupy Croatia.[101]

Paul's paranoia and mistrust extended to King Boris and the Bulgars who, he told the British minister, were responsible for the Nazi-Soviet Pact of 1939, having played the role of go-between(!) and now engaged in similar activities for the Axis in the Balkans.[102]

The outbreak of the Soviet-Finnish conflict shifted the war to the northeast. Allied efforts concentrated more on attacking the Soviet Union than Germany, even though the USSR was neutral. London and Paris believed Stalin had cleverly contrived to pit Hitler against the Western Powers and after both sides were exhausted would move into Central Europe and bolshevize the continent. They believed the Soviet Union supplied Germany with oil and other raw materials. Historical evidence reveals allied estimates of Soviet oil deliveries to Germany to be greatly exaggerated.[103]

A hiatus occurred from March 1939 until the summer of 1940 crypto-German occupation of Romania, which the German scholar Martin Broszat called the "period of retarded German hegemony" in the east. Ribbentrop confirmed through the press that German expansion into the region had ceased, giving Prince Paul an opportunity to visit Zagreb and mend fences. The general Yugoslav public held widespread disdain for Prince Paul and his regime's Axis flirtations and hated the repressive, authoritarian regime established by King Alexander, which Paul's eleventh-hour electoral reform and concession of Croatian autonomy did little to change. Paul's unpopularity undoubtedly played a role in his graceless ejection in 1941.

The expected Soviet demand for the Romanian province of Bessarabia, taken from Russia in 1918 and conceded by Hitler to the USSR in a secret clause of the Nazi-Soviet Pact, opened the door to Hungarian and Bulgarian revisionist claims. Anticipating a possible Hungarian and Bulgarian attack, King Carol reversed Romania's Western-oriented foreign policy for a closer connection to Nazi Germany.

Carol's trip to see Hitler on November 24, 1938, was the beginning of a more opportunistic Romanian policy.[104] To avoid any interruption of Romania's delivery of oil, Hitler wanted moderation in the Romanian-Hungarian quarrel. From the outbreak of war the British tried to dry up Hitler's oil supply by the preemptive buying of oil through Lord Hankey's Committee on Preventing Oil from Reaching Germany and sabotage efforts throughout 1940–1941 to either blow up the oil fields or to destroy the barges used to haul oil down the Danube River.[105] But because of bureaucratic problems, uncertainty that choking off Hitler's oil supply might provoke a German invasion of Romania, and the unsuccessful fumbling efforts of their agents in Romania, British efforts enjoyed only a sporadic success. Fearing German retribution, Romania began to cut down on the amount of oil shipped to England and France and increased oil deliveries to Germany.[106] Nevertheless, Romania refused to raise oil deliveries excessively to Germany at the expense of the British and French and turned down the demands of Hermann Neubacher, the German representative in Bucharest.

To buy German support against its revisionist neighbors, the Romanians altered their policy and signed an oil and weapons pact with Germany agreeing to step up their oil production and deliveries to Germany. Carol also dismissed Gafencu, replacing him with Jon Gigurtu and a more pro-German policy. At the end of April, Carol issued an amnesty to the fascist Iron Guard in exile, whose support he now sought, which satisfied Berlin for a time.

After the disastrous Norwegian campaign, England's supply of foodstuffs and raw materials previously coming from the Scandinavian region declined, forcing London to send trade missions to scour Southeastern Europe both to buy what it needed and for preventive purchasing. But the Germans had already a decisive edge and the Balkan states avoided irritating the Germans by obliging the British.

Nazi policy during the first half of 1940 was to extract the natural resources of the region without disturbing the status quo. The German military did not wish to commit any forces in the southeast. Therefore, Yugoslavia could remain neutral as long as it satisfied German economic needs.[107] When Clodius visited the Balkans, Pilja, his Yugoslav counterpart, and Prince Paul assured him that Germany's trade would remain undisturbed. Cvetković complained to Clodius of heavy British and French economic pressure and British efforts to buy up everything in sight in Yugoslavia and Bulgaria.[108] The British Ministry of Economic Warfare conducted the preemptive purchasing of foodstuffs and minerals which Germany needed, through missions sent to Bulgaria, Romania, Hungary and Yugoslavia. The jittery Balkan governments feared repercussions provoking a German invasion of the Balkans for raw materials. The British considered creating a shortage of fats without which Sir John Simon, Chancellor of the Exchequer, believed "it would be impossible for [Germany] to contemplate another winter of war."

Chamberlain admitted to the House of Commons the heavy preemptive purchasing of mineral ores in the Balkans, particularly copper which aggravated Germany's economic problems and became a sore point between

Germany and Yugoslavia.[109] The British historian Medlicott's judgment that the preemptive purchases had accomplished little may be overdrawn in view of constant German copper shortages and German complaints about raw materials being sent to the Allies.

In May 1940, Yugoslavia signed a secret protocol agreeing to meet its arrears to Germany by increasing its ore and metal deliveries.[110] The Germans complained of Yugoslav indifference to stepped up shipments of wood and purchases of eggs by British representatives, whom they deduced were trying to make up for trade losses in the northern countries by increased trade with the southeast, especially Yugoslavia.[111] Learning that Yugoslavia had secretly agreed to supply France with more raw materials, Berlin decided to be less delicate in drawing Yugoslavia into the Nazi *Grossraumwirtschaft*. After the defeat of France, Wiehl instructed its Minister in Belgrade that the Yugoslav government would have to sell all its products to the Axis and to "make particularly clear to the Government there the present economic dependence of Yugoslavia on the Axis powers." By July Berlin achieved the economic subjugation of Yugoslavia: Belgrade agreed to make no deliveries to those countries at war with Germany or which might strengthen their military or economic power.[112]

Germany's growing power aroused the envy of the Italians who anticipated a German entry into Romania. "Germany was preparing to assume a dominant role," wrote Attolico, Italian ambassador to Berlin. Mussolini again contemplated an attack on Yugoslavia. "The Duce talked about Croatia," noted Ciano. "His hands fairly itch." Mussolini did not believe France or England would attack Italy if it struck at Yugoslavia.[113] However, Berlin made plain to Mussolini its disinterest in Italian adventures in the southeast as it already had control of the area's resources.[114] In addition, General Weygand's army, poised in the Middle East, was an additional deterrent. But the British and French shrank from provoking Italy by a Salonika front landing which also risked bringing the Soviet Union into the war. With Turkey's attitude uncertain, it was unlikely troops could be brought across Turkey to Romania at Constanza or elsewhere.[115] Neither the Germans nor the Yugoslavs believed that the Weygand army would attack or land at Salonika, and thus, for the moment, the situation remained dangerously checkmated.[116]

With Hitler's attack on France impending, neither London nor Paris wished to provoke Italy and, in coordinated gestures, they assured the Italians of their peaceful intentions.[117] Throughout April the capitals of Europe seethed with rumors of an impending Italian action at Salonika or in Yugoslavia.[118] The French War Committee shifted defensive responsibility to the Balkan powers: the Allies should "remind them plainly that their individual safety was bound up with that of the Balkan community as a whole."[119] Allied help would depend on their own efforts in collectively resisting aggression: the four Balkan states "should without loss of time create a united military front against aggression." At a War Cabinet meeting Lord Halifax emphasized keeping out of war with Italy, and talked vaguely about what to do if Italy attacked in Dalmatia. An Allied occupation of Corfu might bring about war with Italy.[120] Forcing the Balkan states to disclose their intentions in advance would create misunderstandings of the Allied position.[121] Nattering high level meetings and diplomatic telegrams droned on about the uncertainty of Yugoslav resistance. Sir Michael Palairet, British minister in Athens, warned that British policy would "melt away" if nothing happened following an Italian attack on Yugoslavia. The British pondered whether allowing Yugoslavia to be overrun would outweigh the risk of becoming involved in war with Italy in order to prevent it.[122] The French pressed for use of the "back door to Yugoslavia" through Salonika, but the British rejected a Salonika landing as too risky without anti-aircraft support.[123]

The British Chiefs of Staff took Palairet's advice and recommended war with Italy, if it attacked Yugoslavia. Otherwise Britain might have to go to war against Italy with its Balkan influence gone. Though the British gave Italy a "strong hint" that an Adriatic attack on Yugoslavia would provoke air attacks on northern Italy, they continued to hesitate. The British Chiefs of Staff, the War Cabinet, and Halifax agreed upon an early declaration of war in the Yugoslav case, to "put heart into Yugoslavia" by an immediate attack on northern Italy.[124] The first blow should be struck by Italy rather than Britain to prevent Mussolini from rallying a shocked Italian public which would be more difficult if Italy attacked Yugoslavia first. Uncertainty over Britain's attitude might restrain Italy over the latter course. But during a late April meeting, the War Cabinet waffled against going to war with Italy and agreed only that if Italy attacked Yugoslavia, Britain should not immediately — at least in the following twenty-four hours — declare war; that the reaction of Turkey should be ascertained first; and that the British military attaché should drop a hint to his Italian counterpart that "Italy could not attack Yugoslavia with impunity."[125] The Foreign Office vacillated into mid-May, recommending "a line of action intermediate between a declaration of war and a completely negative attitude."[126] By that time the French campaign was in progress. Italy had lost interest in Yugoslavia and prepared to move against France.[127] At the suggestion of General Carboni, the British decided to open trade talks with Rome as a gesture of appeasement.

The talks engendered dark suspicions in Belgrade of a new World War I London Pact. Butler was evasive to Subbotić's query: the Italian inclination "to draw back" would continue, he believed. But Subbotić warned that if Italy seized offshore islands like Veglia or Cizola, Yugoslavia would fight.[128] Subbotić asked for assurances the British were not contemplating a London Pact type of agreement with Italy. With icy, Jovian condescension Butler replied: "We neither wish to buy peace by giving up bits of other people's territory, nor do we wish to start intrigues in the Balkans."[129] Chamberlain had reservations about aiding Yugoslavia in general and Churchill advised determining whether the Italian attack was upon Yugoslav independence or merely taking some naval bases in the Adriatic.[130]

Smiljanić, the Yugoslav assistant foreign secretary, felt that all the Balkan states were either pro-German or unreliable if the Axis attacked in the Balkans. Since Yugoslavia and Romania would receive the first blow "he did not see the Turkish and Greek armies coming up the line of the Drava [River]." Moreover he did not believe O'Malley, the British minister at Budapest's, assurances that Hungary would fight, but would allow the Germans to pass through, or join them and attack Romania, seize territory and settle old scores. Smiljanić lamented "bitterly" that England had given the Turks forty-five million pounds, but Yugoslavia could hardly obtain a half million pounds further credit to buy weapons. To sustain pro-Allied feeling in Yugoslavia, Campbell urged greater financial support be considered "with the greatest care and sympathy."[131]

British reports on Yugoslav public opinion were sanguine. In the spring of 1940, public opinion believed that as long as it could not resist attack and the Allies were unable to help them it would have to pursue a neutral policy. The effects of the blockade, Allied successes at sea and the reassuring presence of Weygand's force in the Middle East gave the fortifying impression that assistance was near. The 1940 Balkan Entente Conference decided upon mutual support against aggression and Allied assistance to Turkey reinforced these feelings.[132]

Efforts by Prince Paul and Knatchbull-Hugessen, British ambassador to Turkey, to bribe the Bulgarian government into neutrality with some enclaves of territory failed in early May 1940, embittering the Regent even more against the Bulgars and King Boris.[133] Paul angrily recommended seizing the Bulgar airdromes if Germany attacked in the Balkans.[134] His distaste for Boris and the Bulgars hampered British efforts through George Rendel, British minister at Sofia, to reconcile the two rulers.[135]

Desperate for a Great Power protector, the fiercely anti-Bolshevik Prince Paul turned to the Soviet Union with whom Yugoslavia had no diplomatic relations since the Russian revolution.[136] "Paul shows all the fervor of a recent convert," remarked Campbell.[137] Paul even asked the British to relieve Soviet fears of an Allied attack upon Baku or Batum.[138] Moscow offered unlimited war materials, at whatever price Belgrade would care to fix, suggesting that they could be hidden under the wheat cargo on Yugoslav barges sent down the Danube. But by December Soviet interest evaporated leaving Paul to speculate over the "puzzling" Soviet behavior.[139]

Allied failures in Norway and France made the Regent increasingly nervous over his darkening position. The neutral small countries were all for the Allies, he told Campbell, but they could not be expected to "commit suicide" like Czechoslovakia, Poland, Denmark and Norway before them. Paul pointed to the inactive French army under Weygand in Syria and questioned whether it would not have been better to arm the Balkan states instead. The British were skeptical of Yugoslavia's will to act, "unless," Campbell wrote with wry sarcasm, "conceivably to Bulgarian airdromes."[140]

After rejecting a "little war" with Yugoslavia as "humiliating" and attacking France in June 1940, Mussolini dropped his demands for French African territory to maintain Hitler's friendship and passively acquiesced in the Second Vienna Award and the dismemberment of Romania, advising Romania to surrender Bessarabia to the Soviet Union and southern Dobrudja to the Bulgars.[141] After June 1940, to recoup its losses (over one third of its territory) Romania mollified the Germans by denouncing all previous treaties, thus severing connections with the Balkan Entente and Yugoslavia.

The fall of France and Romania's dismemberment effectively gutted and paralyzed the Balkan Entente powers. Yugoslavia, the "most neutral of neutrals" — in the words of Gafencu — retreated further into its isolationist shell. Exuberant talk of "throwing the Italians into the sea" and of "the Karageorge blood" now ceased.

Sensing an eventual Soviet-German clash, Churchill informed Moscow of the British wish for a front of independent Balkan states and "therefore had common cause with the USSR...for this purpose." Molotov expressed "interest" in a Balkan bloc, but Stalin (July 1) refused to be lured into a fight with Hitler and rejected the role of "super-arbitrator" requiring "an army of pacification." Stalin revealed the British alliance offer to the German ambassador as proof of continuing Soviet fidelity to the Nazi-Soviet Pact.[142] But Stalin showed his displeasure over German penetration into the Balkans by establishing diplomatic relations with Yugoslavia on June 24, 1940.

In July and August 1940 Mussolini again returned to a foray into Yugoslavia for territory which Hitler rejected and forbade the German OKH (Oberkommando des Heeres) to give the Italians plans of Yugoslav border fortifications.[143] Thus, when Hitler occupied Romania to protect his oil supply and prepare for the Russian campaign, Mussolini resolved to repay him in kind: "He will find out from the newspapers that I have occupied Greece," exulted the Italian leader.[144]

In April 1940, the Turks, unnerved by the Albanian affair, and probably prodded by London, failed to persuade Yugoslavia to jointly mobilize with them if Italy entered the war.[145] When Italy finally entered the war, Turkey declared itself a non-belligerent, to the chagrin of the British Foreign Office.[146]

As Yugoslavia only had the Aegean escape route through Salonika, the Italians, anticipating a Yugoslav attack, focused a "painful surveillance" upon Belgrade.[147] But the Yugoslavs remained too cowed for bold action: to British dismay the Yugoslav Chief of Staff, Kosić, surprised by the suddenness of the Italian attack on Greece and "in a depressed and nervous state," showed little courage or disposition to fight. "What can we do, we are completely surrounded," he lamented to the British military attaché.[148]

The day of the Italian attack, Prince Paul showed a readiness to fight and recommended to a Crown Council meeting that Yugoslavia should seize Salonika to prevent encirclement. But Prime Minister Cvetković and Minister of War Nedić hesitated and wanted to feel out Berlin first. The Regent assured the nervous Greek minister in Belgrade that he could not permit the Italians to cross Yugoslavia into Greece — "a matter of life or death for the Greeks." "The door was barred," and the Yugoslav Army of the South — three hundred thousand troops — had been fully mobilized ready to attack the Italians if they attempted to pass. Paul hedged on whether Belgrade would refuse a German request for transit, adding, "but it would be the same thing."[149]

The British quickly perceived that they might reap unexpected dividends from the Italian advance into Greece should the strain of conducting a struggle in Africa and Greece prove too much for Italy.[150] At the critical moment, Greece's neighbors remained loyal to their neighbor. Bulgaria refused Mussolini's request to attack the Greeks and share in the plunder, and remained neutral, allowing the Greeks to remove several divisions from the Bulgarian border for use against the Italians. The Turks also told the Greeks to remove their troops deployed in eastern Thrace and promised aid against a Bulgarian attack. Under cover of its neutrality, Yugoslavia funneled large quantities of equipment and arms to the Greeks without which they might not have been able to successfully resist the Italians.[151]

Irritated with the Italians for attacking Greece, the Germans urged the Yugoslavs to seize Salonika, but Rome became aware of Yugoslav probes in Berlin for Salonika and delivered an unmistakable warning: fifteen Italian bombers attacked the Yugoslav town of Bitolj in Macedonia and machine-gunned its airdrome — attacking on two separate occasions. The Bitolj incident led to the War Minister General Nedić's dismissal when he gratuitously recommended to Prince Paul that Yugoslavia should join the Axis and buy neutrality by offering territory to the Italians.[152]

Cvetković questioned whether to accept the German offer to take Salonika: on what conditions would that be — on Romanian conditions? Campbell warned that Yugoslavia would then be in the position of owing something to Germany. Cvetković "emphatically agreed": Yugoslavia would then be reduced to the same state as Romania.[153]

Still nervous over Salonika ("An Italian Salonika is the rope around the neck of Yugoslavia," a Cvetković emissary told the German Foreign Office), Belgrade offered to make territorial concessions to Italy and to demilitarize the Adriatic in exchange for Salonika. These suggestions were later incorporated into Hitler's proposals made during his talks with Ciano.[154]

The threat to the impending campaign against the Soviet Union posed by a sudden flanking movement through Greece overcame Hitler's reluctance to aid the Italians.[155] The landing of RAF units in Greece and the Aegean area in November threatened his Romanian oil supply and evoked all his anxieties. Thus, when Mussolini, *in extremis* over his setbacks in Albania, sent Count Ciano, hat in hand, to beg for assistance against the Greeks, Hitler could only consent. As long as Yugoslavia's position remained uncertain, he felt endangered.

When Ciano arrived to confer with the Germans at Salzburg (November 18–19, 1940), Hitler was at first morose; later his mood brightened and he proposed a pact with Yugoslavia based upon a guarantee of its borders, the demilitarization of the Adriatic and cession of Salonika to the Yugoslavs.[156] Ciano objected that yielding the plum of Salonika would not be easy for the Duce, "who could not suffer the Yugoslavs," drawing the cold rejoinder from Hitler that he too had to cultivate relations with countries uncongenial to him.[157] Mussolini pressed Hitler later for a more positive Yugoslav association with the Axis than a non-aggression arrangement and — after he actually offered Belgrade a non-aggression pact during Cincar-Marković's November visit — Hitler swung around to Mussolini's view and demanded nothing less than Yugoslavia's adherence to the Tripartite Pact.[158] Hitler's change of mind had momentous repercussions for the forthcoming attack on the Soviet Union and upon the future history of Yugoslavia.

London feared that Belgrade would crumble under the pressure.[159] Short of an attempt to force passage, Cvetković admitted to Campbell that Yugoslavia would be conciliatory. While the British wished the Yugoslavs to stand firm against German pressures to enter Yugoslavia or Bulgaria in order to strike at Greece, they refrained from encouraging Yugoslavia's early entry into the war. The Foreign Office was not enthusiastic as it would probably be rapidly overwhelmed and the only advantage might be to force the Turks to enter the war. Dr. Tupaninin secretly enquired of the British Naval Attaché whether the British could supply at least part of the shipping aid and weaponry (anti-aircraft, etc.) in the event that three hundred thousand troops facing entrapment by the Germans had to be evacuated through Salonika or Cavalla, the only sea exits possible.[160]

The British Chiefs of Staff informed Belgrade that through its control of the Aegean it might be able to keep open the supply line through Salonika, depending on the Bulgarian and Turkish attitude. Air assistance to Yugoslavia could only be given at the expense of air assistance to Greece and could only be effective over the southern part of Yugoslavia. "It is not possible," concluded the Chiefs of Staff Committee, "for us to assist Yugoslavia with land forces."[161]

However, the British avoided entirely dampening Yugoslavia's spirit. The Foreign Office instructed British personnel in Yugoslavia to promote governmental resistance and to "urge the Yugoslavs not to think too much of eventual withdrawal." British policy urged resistance without any definite promises of support and assistance. The British War Office correctly believed the Germans would attack Greece through Bulgaria rather than by an inconvenient attack on Yugoslavia.[162] A winter campaign in the Balkans against the Yugoslavs raised all kinds of daunting terrors to Hitler and the Yugoslav military knew this.[163]

Growing German economic and political influence in the Balkans provoked resentment in Rome and divisive consequences inside the Axis. With the conquest of France and the Low Countries, Yugoslav exports formerly bound for those countries were now assigned to Germany. A commission headed by Dr. Kuntze and Neuhausen, German consul-general in Belgrade and named head of the Bor copper company in Yugoslavia on July 26, 1940, exerted pressure for acquisition but the French government rejected it as illegal and a violation of the armistice convention. After some unsuccessful meetings, on October 10, 1940, the Germans delivered a twenty-four-hour ultimatum demanding titular control of the Bor Mines. After meeting with the German ambassador, Otto Abetz, Premier Laval, newly returned from seeing Hitler at Montoire and anxious to collaborate, handed the Bor copper mines to Germany.[164]

Mussolini pressed for the division of the Balkans between the Axis powers and demanded through Riccardi that Yugoslavia be placed in the Italian sphere of influence through a 51% participation and majority share in Bor copper. Minister Funk balked: spheres of influence was a foreign policy question and raw materials issues fell under Marshal Göring's competence. The Bor copper mines and its shares could not be discussed.[165] The rejected Italian demands undoubtedly helped provoke the Italian attack on Greece in the same month.

Since November the British encouraged cooperation between the Balkan powers. King George personally wrote to Prince Paul urging him to discuss mutual cooperation with Greece and Turkey. Prodded by Knatchbull-Hugessen, the British minister at Ankara, the Greeks and London, Campbell suggested staff talks, but Paul's reaction was "not very encouraging."[166] To the Turkish minister's inquiry on Yugoslavia's course if Bulgaria attacked, Paul sardonically replied: what would the Turks do if the Soviets attacked? If both Germany and Russia attacked at once?[167]

Moving closer to the Turks and Greeks appeared too dangerous, so Prince Paul considered other venues. "He seems," wrote Campbell, "to be turning over in his head the possibility of substituting Hungary for Romania whether in a revived Balkan Entente or some other combination I do not know." As Hitler had already advised the Magyars to "relieve [their] southern flank" to bring Yugoslavia into the Tripartite Pact—Hungary had joined the Axis in November but Bulgaria declined fearing Soviet reprisal—the road lay open to a rapprochement with Hungary.[168] After receiving signals from Regent Horthy, Paul opened negotiations; and Budapest kept the Germans informed and received their blessing. In December Hungary signed the "Pact of Eternal Friendship" with Yugoslavia. The Germans had second thoughts about the arrangement as an unwelcome assertion of Hungarian independence.[169]

Hitler held fast to his imperialist goal of hegemonic domination of Central and Eastern Europe and as late as March of 1940 informed Undersecretary Sumner Welles that Germany claimed the right to profit to the fullest extent through trade with Central and Southeastern Europe, and would no longer permit the Western Powers to impair her preferential position. Germany, he told Welles, would obtain recognition for her economic supremacy in Eastern and Southeastern Europe. He demanded the return of Germany's former colonies for raw materials lacking in Germany and for emigration. Welles thought Hitler would not retreat from his demands for continental supremacy and the war would continue.[170]

In November and December 1940, Hitler issued Directives 18 and 20 (*Operation Marita*) for an attack on Greece at assembly points in Romania and Bulgaria. There were certain imponderables: the risk of attack by Yugoslavia, Turkey or even the USSR or a combination of states supported by Great Britain.

During January 1941, eighty thousand to one hundred thousand German troops crossed Hungary and poured into Romania preparatory to striking Greece. Belgrade remained calm, ignoring British efforts to "unscale their eyes," believing the Germans would attack in the spring, yet frightened and relieved that Yugoslavia had escaped the fate of Romania.[171] Concerned over Belgrade's "ostrich policy," the British Foreign Office tried to encourage Subbotić to contact Bulgaria. Subbotić replied with the "usual arguments" that "anything like a Balkan bloc would constitute a provocation to Germany and must be avoided."[172]

Bulgaria now had to decide whether to join the Axis and accept the entry of German troops into the country, risking attack by neighboring states and the British. Before deciding, King Boris sent Premier Filov to Vienna on January 4, 1941, to see Ribbentrop, who regaled him with the awful fate awaiting England whose capital lay in ruins and Germany would invade in fourteen days. Filov did not have to be convinced: Bulgaria agreed with the pact "in spirit." "Our fate," he told Ribbentrop, "is linked to the fate of Germany."[173]

Filov overcame Boris's fears of a national reaction by predicting that war was unavoidable. If they allowed the Germans to simply pass through the country, Bulgaria would suffer Romania's fate, which would be worse than if Bulgaria allied itself with Germany. By then, through the second Vienna Award, Romania had to hand over Transylvania to Hungary. King Carol fled the country, barely escaping under a hail of bullets rained on his railroad car by the Iron Guardists, and the army leader, General Ian Antonescu, assumed power and led Romania into the Three Power Pact with the Axis powers on November 23, 1940. The Conducator (Leader) Antonescu sent agents to his fascist allies and went himself in November 1940 to Mussolini in hopes of playing him off against Germany for Romania's oil.

From an English victory Bulgaria could expect nothing, in Filov's estimation, whereas a German victory would be followed by a bolshevized Bulgaria through a Soviet invasion. Boris agreed with Filov that "it would be best to accept the German offer (of the Pact)."[174] In January 1940 "the four," an inner group of power brokers (Filov, the Foreign Minister, Popov, Gabrovski, Minister of Internal Affairs, and General Daskalov, the War Minister),[175] and the Cabinet approved the pact. The Germans overcame Sofia's apprehensions by promises of Aegean Thrace from the Maritsa to the Mesta giving Bulgaria access to the Aegean Sea.[176]

Nervous and skittish, the Bulgarian leaders complained to the Germans that they were entering Bulgaria with too few troops. But the German minister, Richthofen, soothed these misgivings by deprecating the Yugoslav army and Turkey's lack of serviceable roads. To avoid problems with its neighbors, Filov believed it politic for Bulgaria momentarily to remain outside the war.[177]

The German troop movements strained the fragile relationship between the rightist and fascist groups and the conservative and more moderate wing of the Bulgarian bourgeoisie. While Boris, arbitrator between the factions and the real power, sided with the Germans, he was irresolute and dreaded Bulgaria becoming a battleground and the crown swept away as in Romania.

Expectations rose in Yugoslavia that pro-Western political groups and the Russophile Bulgarian people might oppose and depose the government creating uncertainty in the dynasty. High Yugoslav officials believed that if the Bulgarian opposition could take control at the critical moment, Yugoslavia, Greece, Bulgaria and Turkey could enter into a collaborative arrangement.[178] Why this did not happen in Bulgaria but rather in Yugoslavia some months later is an interesting question.

The Bulgarian bourgeoisie's national and class interests lay with the Germans whose help it hoped to enlist in regaining its lost territories, particularly Macedonia. Bulgaria's adherence to the Three Power Pact produced important defections from its Western oriented leadership such as Momčilov, Popov and Dušanov who were skeptical of a German victory.[179]

In late January, British attention focused on Bulgaria. The British minister, Rendel, tried to counter this "unneutral" drift into the German camp by threats and vague promises to consider Bulgarian interests at the peace conference.[180] Filov caustically retorted that R. A. Butler, the British Undersecretary of State, had offered only preservation of Bulgaria's current borders. Rendel now took off his gloves and threatened a British and Turkish attack and the British fleet's entry into the Black Sea.[181]

In November the Bulgarian government refused a Soviet offer of a non-aggression pact. London urged Rendel to "keep up the pressure" on Sofia. The British reasoned that Bulgaria could not discount an ultimate British victory and losing out in the post-war arrangement. However, resistance to the Germans left Bulgarian cities open to bombardment by the Luftwaffe. Facing a possible Soviet action, Bulgaria risked becoming a battleground of contending forces. The British concluded that Bulgaria would pretend inability to resist German invasion while the Germans slowly filtered down into Bulgaria. The Foreign Office believed Germany had no interest in fighting the Balkan peoples, but only wished to fight the British and draw off British forces in Africa.[182]

To prevent a Bulgarian invasion by Germany, the Foreign Office tried to cobble together a triple agreement between Yugoslavia, Turkey and Bulgaria through a bilateral agreement between two Balkan states.[183] To realize this end they pursued simultaneously a Yugoslav-Bulgarian, a Yugoslav-Turkish and a Turkish-Bulgarian alignment, each of which, if successful, could be joined by a third Balkan power. A Turkish-Bulgarian agreement contained a high risk factor, then insufficiently estimated — namely, that Turkey's hands might be tied in any agreement with Bulgaria. The Italians had been trying similar ploys to draw Yugoslavia into a Rome-Sofia-Belgrade combination. Since the fall of the moderate, Yugoslav-friendly Bulgarian statesman, Kiosseivanov, Belgrade seemed less inclined "to play."[184] Turkish willingness to act also seemed in doubt.[185] The British minister in Belgrade did not expect a Turkish reaction to the German entry into Bulgaria and reckoned at 70% a Turkish intervention into the war if the Germans invaded Greece and Bulgaria remained passive.[186] Von Papen, the German ambassador at Ankara, reportedly told Berlin that Turkey would not act.[187] But some Yugoslav quarters — probably the military — spoke more bellicosely of attacking if the Germans entered Bulgaria.[188]

Belgrade did not share Campbell's optimistic view of the Turkish-Bulgarian talks and feared the Germans would make use of the results. Some in the Foreign Office also doubted the utility of a Turkish-Bulgarian agreement and, in general, believed that the Foreign Office had trusted too much in the loyalty of the Turks.[189] Clearly both the British and the Germans hoped to make use of a Turkish-Bulgarian agreement for their own purposes.

At the end of January 1941, the British concluded that a Turkish-Bulgarian agreement was uncertain and concentrated upon a Yugoslav-Turkish arrangement around which any future Balkan bloc might be built to resist Hitler. A Foreign Office memo by Cadogan hints mysteriously at some "big package."[190] When a Yugoslav-Turkish arrangement foundered, the British shifted to a Belgrade-Sofia accord, advanced by Rendel, who believed Bulgaria might want to do something to preserve its neutrality, and advised the Yugoslavs not to wait for it to come, otherwise Bulgaria would be lost.[191] The arrival of Colonel William Donovan, Roosevelt's troubleshooter, in late January provided the British with the springboard they sought.

Prince Paul told Donovan that Yugoslavia, unlike Bulgaria, would resist the passage of German troops across its borders, but was uncertain about a German entry into Bulgaria. Peasant Party leader Maček was more explicit: "the government wants to avoid war if necessary."[192]

While Donovan informed the Bulgars in Sofia that the British would attack the Germans on Bulgarian territory, the American minister at Belgrade urged Paul to make new overtures to Sofia. Deputy Foreign Minister Smiljanić probed for a visit of Cincar-Marković to Sofia advising that Belgrade had no wish to see them finish like Hungary or Romania. Smiljanić hinted at territorial concessions for a Yugoslav-Bulgarian agreement and Filov immediately relayed the feeler to the German minister in Sofia adding that Cincar-Marković's visit would be "completely unsuccessful" and a non-aggression pact with Yugoslavia could only occur after the Turkish-Bulgarian agreement. Ribbentrop advised Sofia "to handle the matter dilatorily."[193] Later, Smiljanić told the Bulgarian Chargé that Yugoslavia had to go to Berlin for new talks because the Bulgarian government had wrapped itself in silence. "Yugoslavia, at any rate will appear clean before history," he added.[194]

Despite Rendel's warnings of bombings of German bases in Bulgaria, Popov, President of the Council, gave no assurance the Bulgars would not admit German troops into Bulgaria. Rendel threatened that Bulgaria would be "heavily penalized" in the peace arrangements for its "impotence" and "its continued existence as an independent nation would hardly be justified."[195]

But this was already too late: Bulgaria had thrown in its lot with the Germans with whom they held secret staff talks at Predeal on Bulgarian soil in early February. Even before German troops arrived, the Bulgarian minister signed a secret pledge to join the Tripartite Pact.[196] The impending Turkish-Bulgarian treaty of friendship relieved the possibility of an attack upon Bulgaria by the Turks and reduced the probability of an attack from Yugoslavia. Thus, Bulgaria could admit the Germans without danger of attack by its neighbors. The Germans exploited the most glaring defect in the Balkan Alliance: its inoperability in the case of attack by a Great Power upon a Balkan state.

Toward the end of January, Rendel made a last-ditch visit to dissuade Filov several days before his departure for Vienna to sign the Pact. However, his threats to bomb Bulgaria if it admitted the Germans had little impact.[197]

In Vienna Filov fretted over Yugoslavia's "suspicious" conduct, "mobilization, rumors of a military government at Skopje and the words of Smilijanic [*sic*] to Strateiev about an eventual bloc between Yugoslavia, Bulgaria and Turkey." But Ribbentrop radiated confidence: the Yugoslavs had promised not to interfere — "it was one hundred percent certain." The Russians would put up with the new situation and not react.[198] Before the signing, the Germans handed letters to Filov, to be kept secret, giving Bulgaria access to the Aegean Sea from the mouth of the Maritsa once the new Balkan frontiers were arranged.[199]

Hitler revealed to Filov his disenchantment with the Yugoslavs: "He told me what Ribbentrop did not say, that if they tried anything, he will crush them." "The change which has come into his opinion (about Yugoslavia) since our meeting at Berghof is interesting." Hitler previously "considered Prince Paul to be the chief partisan of the Anglophiles" and hoped for some sort of reversal when Peter came of age. He now thought that with the English-educated Peter the Anglophiles would be even stronger. He "winced" when Filov told him of Smiljanić's suggestion and declared: "the Yugoslavs, whatever they did, would never be able to be our friends." Germany had to make concessions to both Bulgaria and Hungary, and Bulgaria should again raise claims for Macedonia.[200]

The Germans and Bulgars were euphoric with the pact. Elated, Hitler broke his strict dietary habits and took two portions of jam! Filov seemed almost fatuously exhilirated: "It appears as if a Great Power and not little Bulgaria has joined (the pact)."[201]

With announcement of the Turkish-Bulgarian Agreement, realization set in that British diplomacy had suffered a defeat. But Campbell thought the Anglo-Turkish Pact "would take precedence with Turkey over the (Turkish-Bulgarian) agreement." Both favored further efforts to align Yugoslavia, but London concluded: Bulgaria was no longer a free agent and a "mere non-aggression" agreement with Yugoslavia was "dangerous" and should not be encouraged.[202] The Foreign Office ruefully admitted the Turkish-Bulgarian agreement was "a German diplomatic triumph."[203] Knatchbull-Hugessen claims to have modified the pact through a Turkish warning to Sofia that if Bulgaria became "soiled" by a connection with Germany, Turkey's attitude would be affected. However, Turkey's inaction when Bulgaria joined the Axis and German forces entered Bulgaria belies the value of the claim.[204]

Alarmed by the prospect of the Germans in Romania and Bulgaria, and ensconced on the Black Sea, Moscow moved to counter the German thrust. Vyshinsky told the Turkish ambassador that the Turkish-Bulgarian agreement created an "unfavorable atmosphere" for the English and was "very serious": the Germans were now at the very door of Bulgaria. The Yugoslav minister to Moscow, Gavrilović, thought the Soviets wanted to see the Germans and Turks clash.[205] If the Turks remained neutral, a possible southern intervention to counter Hitler would be reduced. The previously rejected 1939 and 1940 Balkan front against Hitler, they now urgently tried to organize. Turkey would not fight Germany and Bulgaria combined, the Turkish minister told Vyshinsky, and would act only if Yugoslavia entered the conflict. Gavrilović believed the Turks would do nothing and avoid any possibility of the Russians entering the Balkans. "The key to this [situation] is in the hands of Yugoslavia," he concluded.[206] Later the Soviets told Gavrilović that Yugoslavia would be divided up whether or not it followed Hitler's advice, a prophecy also made by R. A. Butler.[207]

To dispel Turkish fears of Soviet attack, Vyshinsky told the Turkish ambassador that, if Turkey were attacked, the USSR would adhere to its non-aggression pact and not attack Turkey. The British ambassador was summoned and asked for his absolute discretion as Vyshinsky related the same statement before him. Gavrilović mistakenly believed that the Soviet

Union now intended to unite with Turkey and England against Hitler.[208] But Turkish Foreign Minister Saracoglu was suspicious and dissatisfied with the Soviet statement and the "uncertain Russian attitude"; new attempts to arrive at a more definitive statement failed. The Turks believed the Soviets would quickly adjust their policy to take advantage of a Turkish defeat at Turkey's expense.[209]

Soviet entry into the picture raised British hopes of a Turkish-Yugoslav-Greek front against Hitler — Cadogan's mysterious "big package." The collapse of this possibility was the last card the British had to play in their strategy of building a Balkan front. In his post-war memoirs Rendel blames the collapse of the British plan on Belgrade for failing to follow up Turkish action at Sofia in building up a Turkish-Bulgarian-Yugoslav front.[210]

British hope of building an alliance among a group of small, weak and vacillating states against the Axis was probably illusory from the start. Britain's inability to offer military support until the eleventh hour — and then in insufficient amounts — undermined the entire policy. British political diplomacy had reached an impasse and a new phase in the struggle for the Southeastern European region began.

The period of retarded German hegemony over the Southeastern European area ended with the sending to Romania in mid-September 1940 of a motorized division together with tanks and Luftwaffe squadrons, requested by the Romanian military dictator, General Antonescu, who cut a commanding and imposing figure that impressed Hitler. But, in fact, as General Keitel observed, "to protect the oil fields from seizure by a third power and from destruction," Hitler gave Romania an unsolicited guarantee of its independence after Soviet forces occupied Bessarabia and Northern Bukovina. The Germans had agreed to cession of Bessarabia but not Bukovina in the secret arrangements of the Nazi-Soviet Pact. Vowing, "I will not be overrun by the Russians," Hitler violated the consultation clause of the Nazi-Soviet Pact. Hitler's actions in invading the Soviet interest sphere and the landing of German troops in Finland began the erosion of the treaty and forewarned of the German attack on the Soviet Union on June 22, 1941. Romania became a German satellite and in October 1940, Hitler sent thirty thousand German "tourists" into Bulgaria, further exacerbating tensions between Germany and the Soviet Union. The political phase of the conflict for hegemony in Eastern and Southeastern Europe ended and the military phase now began.

Chapter 17

Prince Paul, the Man in the Cage with the Tiger. The March 27, 1941, Belgrade Coup. Prince Paul, the British and the Germans

> Prince Paul's position was like that of the man in the cage with the tiger while dinner time slowly approaches.   — W. Churchill

> Paul petered out and Peter petered in.
> — British Ambassador to Turkey, Sir Hugh Knatchbull-Hugessen

THE OUTBREAK OF THE SECOND WORLD WAR further exacerbated Great Power imperialist rivalries for control of Southeastern Europe. The Italian invasion of northern Greece from Albanian bases transformed these rivalries into armed conflict. Subsequent Italian military defeats encouraged the British to aid the Greeks against the advance of Axis power into the region with the ultimate aim of reinstalling British hegemony. The fateful Belgrade coup of March 27, 1941 must, therefore, be considered as a new phase in the struggle and an intensified effort by the British to frustrate German efforts to convert Yugoslavia into a dependency and to drive Germany from the Balkans.

The dramatic events of the March 27 coup and the role played by the British have deflected attention from imperialist rivalries over the Balkans and focused attention on the coup as a static, historical event unconnected with the Great Power conflict for control of the region's raw materials. Historians have been inordinately mesmerized by the coup and its consequences and have spilled a great deal of ink in exploring the causes and responsibilities for the coup and the British role in that event.

British disinclination to strip their North African armies for a Balkan campaign diminished with every fresh evidence of Greek military successes, and decisively aiding the Greeks against the floundering Italians became increasingly more inviting. Before the Italian attack on Greece the British maintained their influence in Yugoslavia through their Belgrade embassy and contacts with influential Yugoslavs through unofficial and secret agents operating inside the country. In July and August 1940 British intelligence learned that certain dissident Serb groups were leaning toward a coup London considered premature. London believed it could accomplish its objectives best through its influence with the Prince Regent, and side-tracked coup plans, but kept that option open should the situation change.

Historians generally agree that by 1941 London's policy toward Yugoslavia became more demanding and less tolerant of Yugoslavia's difficulties with the Axis. The British were no longer satisfied that Yugoslavia remain neutral and not permit the passage of German forces through its territory to attack Greece. Once British air forces landed in Greece and it seemed certain that war would erupt in the Balkans, the British demanded a more positive attitude on the part of Prince Paul and the Yugoslavs. When the Yugoslavs balked, the British began to entertain the possibility of a coup.

In October 1940 the British toyed with launching a coup which the German minister in Belgrade got wind of and reported to Berlin. After the coup, Simović told the British that young air force officers had been ready to stage a coup in January 1941 and link up with the Turks and Bulgar anti-Axis elements to form a Balkan bloc to support Romania.[1] By mid-February 1941 British efforts to build up a Balkan block began to crumble; and following the German invasion of Romania and the Turkish-Bulgarian Pact, the Great Power conflict in the southeast entered into a new phase.

In January and February 1941, Yugoslav Foreign Office officials noted "a strange lull" in relations with Germany. Prince Paul had taken all the threads of foreign policy into his hands and because of the gravity of the moment avoided normal channels and conducted policy in great secrecy through intermediaries.[2]

On February 4 Stakić and Gregorić, intermediaries selected by Prince Paul, journeyed to Rome and Berlin to sound out the Germans before the onset of spring and the impending German move into Bulgaria or Yugoslavia preparatory to the Greek campaign. To Stakić, Mussolini proposed a population exchange, the Albanians in Kosovo going to Albania while Slovenes and Croats in Istria would move to Italy. Mussolini again brought up the renewal of the Italo-Yugoslav agreement as a way of avoiding adherence to the Tripartite Pact. In exchange for demilitarization of the Adriatic, Yugoslavia would receive Salonika. Prince Paul rejected a population exchange on the grounds that the Slovenes and Croats in Istria had lived there for generations.[3] Paul also had compunctions against despoiling Greece of its territory at a time when it was struggling against the Italians.[4] Stakić again returned to see Mussolini on February 24th and the Italian leader reiterated his request for an Italo-Yugoslav alliance as the only way of avoiding the Tripartite Pact. Mussolini undoubtedly hoped to use an Italo-Yugoslav accord to discourage Greek resistance and avoid a German invasion of Greece to keep the Germans from the Balkans and Yugoslavia's raw materials.

Mussolini reopened talks with the Soviets which had withered several months before. In exchange for an Italian interest sphere in the Balkans, which included Yugoslavia, Moscow demanded Soviet bases in the Straits. But Hitler had no intention of letting the Soviets into the Straits area, nor of recognizing Soviet domination of Bulgaria, rejected during Molotov's November 1940 Berlin visit. He promptly vetoed the Italian-Soviet negotiations. Neither did Hitler intend to recognize Italian aspirations for Yugoslavia or share its absolutely indispensable raw materials with Mussolini.

Prince Paul and the Yugoslav government's major fear was Italy, rather than the Germans. While the Germans were equally imperialistic, they desired only to exploit Yugoslavia's raw materials and had no territorial demands to make against Yugoslavia. Italy, however, hungered to incorporate Yugoslav territory — Dalmatia, the coastal littoral, Slovenia, Montenegro, and Croatia — under the Italian crown.

During these long drawn out negotiations Yugoslavia played for time. A close examination of the Stakić meetings with Mussolini reveals Prince Paul had no intention of signing a pact with Mussolini, was probably playing off the two dictators while drawing out the negotiations and waiting on events. The Yugoslavs knew through their military intelligence Hitler would attack the Soviet Union in the spring. After invading Bulgaria and Greece, they believed, he would bypass Yugoslavia then attack the USSR. Once Yugoslavia became neutralized, Hitler would launch an attack on the Soviet Union which could not be postponed for another year as the Red Army then would be too strong. Otherwise, Germany would have been in an untenable situation with a menacing, powerful Red Army on its eastern border and England stronger and more determined to pursue the war to a successful conclusion.[5]

There is no evidence that Hitler intended to attack Yugoslavia until the fateful events of March 27, 1941. Göring testified at his post-war trial that Hitler desired to bring the Yugoslavs into the Tripartite Pact in order to neutralize Yugoslavia and not to draw it into war. Despite pressures from the Wehrmacht High Command, Hitler expressly ordered that no troop transports should go through Yugoslavia after its entry into the Three Power Pact to avoid compromising its neutrality.[6] This policy was strategic as well as economic. Göring testified at Nuremberg that the Balkans and Yugoslavia's raw materials had become extremely important for the Germans.[7] Hitler wished to keep Yugoslavia out of the war to avoid sharing its mineral wealth and foodstuffs with Italy. This had always been Germany's policy toward Yugoslavia except on the eve of the Polish campaign when he encouraged Mussolini to attack Yugoslavia to draw Allied pressures from the Polish front. Yugoslavia, therefore, was at all times — in the words of General Jodl — treated as a kind of "prima donna" by Hitler.

While Stakić met with Mussolini, Gregorić, a journalist and emissary of Premier Cvetković, once more probed for a meeting between the Nazi and Yugoslav leaders and the possibility of a German-Yugoslav agreement that did not include Italy.[8] This would have placed Yugoslavia under German protection and kept it out of the war, and satisfied Wehrmacht strategic requirements for the Greek and Russian campaigns. The Germans had learned from the Vichy French chargé in Belgrade that the Yugoslavs were playing for time and waiting on events.[9] To avoid more diplomatic jousting, von Heeren proposed that the pro-English Serbs in the government — Čubrilović, Budisavljević and Konstantinović — be removed as a gesture of Yugoslav honesty and resoluteness but Prince Paul did not act on the suggestion.[10]

Frustrated by Bulgaria's rejection of their overtures and mistrustful of the Turks, their margin for choice fast disappearing, Cvetković and Marković journeyed to Obersalzburg to see Hitler on February 14, 1941. After Hitler and Ribbentrop's bombastic predictions of Germany's inescapable triumph, the Yugoslavs suggested their mediating the conflict between Italy and Greece and that a treaty between Turkey, Bulgaria and Yugoslavia could pacify the Balkans. England would then be asked to withdraw its forces from Greek soil; and German fears of English bombing attacks would be allayed by interdiction of the combined Balkan powers. Afterwards Yugoslavia would be free to align itself on the Axis side. Under cover of these proposals the Yugoslavs obviously were playing for time.

As expected, Hitler was skeptical: the English would not leave Greece and the entire plan was "hardly a reality." He pressed the Yugoslavs to align with the New Order in return for an outlet to the sea through Salonika. Germany would recognize Yugoslavia's territorial integrity and not demand aid or obligations after it joined the Tripartite Pact.

For the time being Yugoslavia could retain its neutrality. Paul for reasons of background and family connections — his wife, Olga, was a Greek princess — remained indecisive, but the German infiltration of Bulgaria was forcing him to take a position.

Advanced Wehrmacht mechanized units reached the Serbian border and Bulgarian army forces took up positions along the Turkish border. Badly frightened, the Belgrade government remained demobilized at the crucial moment.

Uncertainty over Yugoslavia was the last deterrent to a German attack on Greece. When Ciano journeyed to Salzburg on March 2 he found Hitler elated: Bulgaria had just signed the Tripartite Pact. Yugoslavia, he predicted, might possibly adopt a more positive attitude. Bulgaria's fears of Yugoslavia were not justified: Yugoslavia would certainly not undertake anything. A bilateral agreement with Yugoslavia, Ciano disclosed, no longer interested Mussolini now that Bulgaria had joined the Tripartite Pact. Hitler, however, was more cautious. Failing Yugoslav adherence to the pact, he was ready to consider an Italo-Yugoslav pact.[11]

Still playing for time, Prince Paul met secretly with Hitler at the Berghof.[12] Paul did not disguise his feelings about the pact and told Hitler "quite plainly" that family ties, his sympathies for England and his attitude toward Italy personally opposed him to it. When Paul suggested an agreement with Italy as a possible first step, Hitler badgered him to agree to the Tripartite Pact. If he followed that course, Prince Paul declared, he would no longer be here in six months. Ribbentrop hinted that the same thing might happen if he did not.

The German accounts of these meetings do not tell the entire story. In a post-war account of his meeting with Hitler, Cvetković noted that "between Germany and Italy there was a certain antagonism in aims in the Balkans. Germany did not want to see Italy installed in this part of the Balkans. We calculated on this difference in views and we thought because of this difference in views that Hitler will remain faithful to the promises he had made us, that is, that he desires a strong and independent Yugoslavia and that he will respect our neutrality."[13]

Even more striking is the omission of certain key phrases in the German account of Prince Paul's meeting with Hitler on March 4. Cvetković noted that "Hitler demanded from Prince Paul that we join the Pact, this being the only way to keep us safe from Italy, and *for egoistic reasons* [author's italics], he needed a strong Yugoslavia."[14] The American writer, Jacob D. Hoptner, without referring to the source as Cvetković, also mentions Hitler's desire for Yugoslavia for economic reasons, but the complete significance seems to have escaped him.[15] Paul also gave substantially the same account to the Yugoslav writer and ex-official Jukić in a meeting on September 27, 1955 in which the Regent repeated that Hitler had explained his desire to spare Yugoslavia *"aus eigenen egoistischen Grunden"* (for my own selfish reasons)." Paul interpreted this to mean that Hitler did not want Yugoslavia drawn into the war because "he wanted Yugoslavia all for himself without war, as a supplier of valuable raw materials and foodstuffs."[16] In addition we also have Göring's testimony at Nuremberg of the overriding need for Yugoslavia's mineral deposits (see chapter 1).

While Bulgarian revisionists held a massive demonstration for Macedonia in Sofia, Prince Paul submitted the results of his talks with Hitler to a Crown Council meeting on March 6. After a lively debate, during which Cvetković predicted a German invasion if Yugoslavia did not accede to the pact, and others gloomily predicted the loss of Croatia and Slovenia in a conflict with little prospect of English support, the Council voted for an emasculated version of the pact and conditional acceptance. Cvetković informed von Heeren of Belgrade's conditions: Yugoslavia's sovereignty and territorial integrity must be respected; neither military assistance nor transit rights could be granted for the duration of the war; the Yugoslav request for egress to the Aegean through Salonika would be considered when the Axis reorganized Europe.[17]

But on March 9, an exasperated Ribbentrop refused to release the Yugoslavs from Article 3, the mutual aid clause of the pact, which exempted Yugoslavia in the case of a conflict with Greece — insisting it would undermine the pact.[18] Belgrade, however, remained adamant; Cincar-Marković told von Heeren the following day of his "very embarrassing position" after previously informing Paul affirmatively regarding Article 3. Within the country anti-German feelings grew, producing "a stiffening with consequent gains by the Serb military who saw the occupation of Salonika as a preventive move, the sole security for Yugoslavia."[19]

The Germans knew Prince Paul was "wavering" but feared British and American influence and the effect of circulating rumors. Public opinion, speculated von Heeren, might cause a very gradual yielding "to spare it the odium of accession" to the pact.[20] Von Heeren reported to Berlin that highly combustible Serbian opposition to the pact mounted hourly, compelling Cvetković to place a number of Serb generals under police surveillance and lay plans to arrest the opposition.

Ribbentrop's insistence on the mutual security clause relented by March 18 and the way was open; Cvetković, however, had already broken the news of Belgrade's impending signature of the pact to Ronald Ian Campbell, the British minister, on March 15.[21]

Though Yugoslavia held the "master geographic position," the invasion of Romania had limited its maneuverability and cowed it into a watchful silence. The entry of British air forces into Greece had not helped to quiet Belgrade's nerves. Prince Paul considered the British air buildup "a clumsy move" and threatened to allow the Germans passage through Yugoslavia if the presence of British troops provoked a German attack. The Yugoslav and Greek governments refused to allow British forces in Salonika and Greek Macedonia until the Germans first entered Bulgaria. Colonel William Donovan, Roosevelt's trouble-shooter, on his trip to Belgrade had failed to budge the Yugoslav government's determination to remain neutral. Internal divisions, in particular Croatian opposition to an aggressive policy towards Germany, made a response unlikely.

Mushrooming reports of an impending German attack on the USSR reaching Belgrade from the well-informed Yugoslav military attaché in Berlin, Colonel Vauhnik, as well as other sources, countered the drift towards accommodation and encouraged the stalling tactics of Belgrade.

Paul's decision to negotiate with the Germans was undoubtedly influenced by British indecisiveness concerning the Balkans. London had been divided on aid to the Greeks; aid to Yugoslavia seemed even more remote. Throughout the winter of 1940–1941 the War Cabinet and Middle East Command favored aiding the hapless Greeks, but the Foreign Office and the Chiefs of Staff were skeptical about securing Turkish or Yugoslav cooperation. The British hedged, claiming their guarantee to the Greeks was something less than an alliance. The British Chiefs of Staff initially had the barest self-interest in responding to the Greek dictator Metaxas's request for aid in August 1940; the British wanted the Greeks to resist without giving them promises that could not be implemented.[22] Metaxas's requests for help in the week preceding the Italian attack left the British cold; the Chiefs of Staff expected the Greeks to quickly "crumple up" under even light attacks on their cities — a grave misjudgment in the light of events.

Pressure from public opinion at home, the desire to help the Italians "make a mess of it," and fears of the effect on Yugoslavia and Turkey if Hitler overran Greece, overcame British scruples against stripping their Egyptian and North African battlefields for weaponry and men.[23] By the beginning of November 1940 Churchill's persistence in War Cabinet meetings and his letters to military and political leaders succeeded in winning over a doubtful Eden and the British military to the Greek gamble. On November 3 the Chiefs of Staff proposed sending several squadrons of planes to Greek airdromes. Churchill told the Cabinet that public opinion in Britain was "most anxious for British intervention in Greece": "Strategically the loss of Athens would be as serious a blow to us as the loss of Khartoum."[24] By the end of the first week in November the Greek commitment had been made.[25]

The Germans on the other hand at first considered invading Greece in connection with their "peripheral" strategy of attacking Gibraltar and in North Africa with the Italians, and Directive 18 mentions Greece almost as an afterthought — "a second rate substitute." Later it graduated to a major operation under Directive 20 (*Operative Marita*) when Hitler substituted the "peripheral" for the "Mediterranean" strategy after canceling the Gibraltar attack.

Hitler and the German military at first were disturbed by the presence of several thousand Englishmen in Greece. Later they seemed satisfied when the Greeks agreed to bridle British attacks against the Romanian oil wells or face Luftwaffe air attacks. But the developing German attack against the USSR, approved on December 5 by Hitler, forced the latter to divert forces to Greece to prevent a new Salonika front.[26]

At the beginning of 1941, the Greeks became alarmed that a German invasion of Greece might be in the offing. Following a flurry of telegrams between London and Athens, General Wavell arrived in Greece (January 15) to confer with Metaxas and General Papagos.[27] Metaxas, however, did not wait for the arrival of Wavell but wrote Prince Paul asking the Regent not to permit German forces to pass through Yugoslavia to occupy Salonika or via the Vardar Valley or Bitolj. Metaxas reminded Paul of Yugoslavia's encirclement problem if Salonika fell to Hitler. On the 17th, through the Yugoslav minister at Athens, Vukićević, Paul assured the apprehensive Greek dictator that he would not permit the passage of German troops through Yugoslavia to attack Greece.[28] There is no indication that Metaxas communicated this to Wavell or that it was made known to the British on later occasions by the Greeks. At any rate the Greek leader died on January 29 and the secret of Paul's assurance with him. In subsequent meetings with the British nothing is mentioned about it. Prince Paul and the Yugoslav leaders reiterated their determination to fight against a German invasion on other occasions, but British policy had already begun to change and this was no longer the primary concern.

British vacillations on the Greek enterprise continued into January and February and even into March 1941. From a strategic standpoint the Balkans were secondary to the more important North African Campaign and Churchill urged Eden and Marshal Dill, sent to North Africa to oversee the military situation, not to feel bound to the Greek project if it showed signs of becoming "another Norwegian fiasco." Britain had "to be careful not to urge Greece into a hopeless resistance" when no British forces could be released which could reach Greece in time. "Loss of Greece and the Balkans is by no means a major catastrophe for us provided Turkey remains honest neutral." Britain's ignominious ejection from Greece would do Britain more harm in Spain and Vichy than the loss of the Balkans.[29] All Britain's efforts to form a Balkan front, Churchill wrote, were based on the secure establishment of its North African position. "The Desert Flank was the peg on which all else hung," and there was little interest "in any quarter of losing or risking that for the sake of Greece, or anything else in the Balkans."

When Eden, Dill, Wavell and other British military figures met with the Greek leaders at the Tatoi Palace outside Athens (February 22), the question of Yugoslavia's support in denying the Germans entry into Greece through the northerly Monastir Gap, outflanking British and Greek forces in Salonika, hung like a specter over the conference. Uncertainty over Yugoslavia and the Turks beclouded the strategy to be adopted. At Eden's suggestion the Greek and British leaders made their decision on defense strategy without respect to whether Yugoslavia would come in or not. Eden promised

100,000 men, 240 field guns, 202 A.T. guns, 32 medium guns, 192 light and heavy A.A. guns and 142 tanks.[30] This was somewhat of an exaggeration of British strength designed to encourage the Greeks to fight. In the end only 74,000 men were sent.[31]

At a meeting (February 24) of the War Cabinet, the British assessed the results of the Tatoi meeting and, prodded by Churchill, approved the decision to send military aid and troops to Greece.[32] Even Cadogan, who had little faith in the Greek project's ultimate success, approved rather than accept the alternative of inactivity. Churchill hoped the British forces in Greece might induce Yugoslavia and Turkey to combine forces with the Greeks against the impending Nazi thrust. Later in 1948 in the jaunty, Churchillian manner, he defended his decision to send British forces into Greece.

> They said that I was wrong to go to Greece in 1940. But I didn't do it simply to save the Greeks. Of course, honour and all that came in. But I wanted to form a Balkan front. I wanted Yugoslavia, and I hoped for Turkey. That, with Greece, would have given us fifty divisions. A nut for the Germans to crack. Our intervention in Greece caused the revolution which drove out Prince Paulsy [*sic*]; and delayed the German invasion of Russia by six weeks. Vital weeks. So it was worth it. If you back a winner it doesn't really matter much what your reasons were at the time. They now say that I went to Greece for the wrong reasons. How do they know? The point is that it was worth it.[33]

However, there were other apprehensions; namely, that Hitler might strike at Britain's Near East jugular vein. Eden believed the Germans wanted to crush Greece and immobilize Turkey as a prelude to a strike at the British position in the Near East.[34] While military considerations appear to have been uppermost at this time, political motives were not far behind. In assessing the results of the abortive Balkan campaign of 1941 the British historian Elizabeth Barker correctly asserts that "what the British did above all . . . was to stake out a claim to an active presence in South-East Europe."[35]

The British continued to pursue the will-o'-the-wisp of the "big package": a Yugoslav-Turkish-Greek front against Hitler. Eden told McVeagh, the American minister at Athens, "that Greece, Turkey and Yugoslavia would all three be fighting against Germany but that there would be lots of shifts and hesitations before that."[36]

Following the Tatoi meeting, Eden journeyed to Ankara at the end of February in quest of the "big package" hoping that the Turks would join hands with the Yugoslavs and Greeks. Up to this time Eden believed that the Yugoslavs might fight if Salonika were attacked "but they are trying to persuade themselves that this will not happen."[37] In Ankara he was disabused of these notions: neither the Turks nor the Yugoslavs were anxious to help the Greeks. The Turks pleaded military inadequacy and the Yugoslavs sent "a lamentable document amounting to a confession that Yugoslavia could not take a definite position and begging that we would not insist on her doing so."[38]

Eden then returned to Athens with the bad news which must have been a decided shock to the Greek leaders. General Papagos, still believing that

Yugoslavia would fight, had not withdrawn his forces from Salonika to the Aliakhmon redoubt and could not be persuaded to do so, concerned that the abandonment of the port city without a fight would have grave consequences for Greek morale. More efforts to gain Yugoslavia ranged from requesting Colonel Miloslav Perišić to come to Athens and discuss military strategy to offers to revise the Italo-Yugoslav border in Istria "as something of a bait for the Croats and Slovenes."[39] Vukičević, the Yugoslav minister to Athens, was "defeatist." Not only was Eden's trip a failure, he told McVeagh, but "Germany had already won the war when France fell and is now master of Europe."[40] Eden admitted to pessimism over placing any hopes in the Yugoslavs who were "unsettled and frightened." Campbell did not offer any reassuring evidence of Yugoslav aid during the Anglo-Greek talks and frankly declared that "they need not despair of Paul, but cannot count on him." Eden continued to half-believe that Greece, Yugoslavia and Turkey would join in the struggle but that there "would be a lot of slippage and sliding before that." McVeagh was more skeptical: the British "had failed to get a lineup."[41] To make matters worse, General Papagos obstinately refused to withdraw his forces from Salonika to the Aliakhmon line. British doubts about the entire Greek project again surfaced, but the timely arrival of Field Marshal Smuts at British headquarters and his advice to go ahead with or without Yugoslav and Turkish assistance bolstered British determination to see the affair through. In retrospect, the entire Greek enterprise seems always to have hung by a thread.

An urgent message from Campbell advising that Yugoslav resolve against signing the pact was crumbling decided Eden in favor of another try with the Turks in hopes of bolstering Yugoslavia. The Yugoslav Premier Cvetković in a letter written in 1953 claimed that it was he who had proposed to Eden "an accord (with Turkey) to defend Greek territory with arms."[42] The Yugoslavs later cited the rejection of these proposals by the Turks and the return of Colonel Perišić from Greece without sufficient British commitments for the defense of Salonika and naval forces to evacuate the Yugoslav army as their reasons for signing the Tripartite Pact.[43] Whenever the Yugoslavs brought up evacuation plans, the British urged them not to think too much about retreat, but to concentrate their attention on resisting Hitler.

General Wavell and the British military were not anxious for the entry of the Turks into the war. Inadequate Turkish military supplies and the need to arm the Turks would strain their own meager resources. Therefore, they would consider a Turkish declaration of war only if it were absolutely necessary in order to bring the Yugoslavs to fight.

The secret talks between Eden and Saracoglu in Cyprus proved another dismal failure with serious consequences for the Yugoslav attitude. Eden suggested to Saracoglu that the Turks and Yugoslavs jointly pledge to defend Salonika. The message "melted in discussion" to an exchange in views about a possible threat to Salonika. In the end the Turks did not even deliver the statement, "protesting the political uncertainties in Belgrade."[44] Eden half suspected that Saracoglu's distrust of Yugoslavia was "a pretext useful to his own diplomacy."[45] All these failures must have been gravely disappointing to Eden at this dark hour in Britain's fortunes. He must have seen clearly that

Yugoslavia and Turkey were frail reeds, that there was little likelihood Prince Paul and his government would join in the struggle against the Germans and that if the opportunity presented itself the Regent and his associates would have to be replaced by leaders more willing to fight.

Under increased Axis pressures the Yugoslavs again sounded London. Subbotić visited R. A. Butler (March 11) and politely inquired whether the British were taking an understanding view of the Yugoslav predicament. Was it true, he asked, that British troops were landing at Salonika? Butler couched his reply in equivocal terms designed to bolster Yugoslav resistance without specifically promising the commitment of British military assistance to thwart a German attack. The British and Greeks, he declared, would put up a strong resistance in the Balkans and Yugoslavia would be best advised to do the same rather than wait until it was too late and suffer the fate of its neighbors. Subbotić indicated to Butler that he was aware of Italy's vulnerable position in Albania and "the great military opportunity" lying within Yugoslavia's grasp. Butler spoke tantalizingly of the possibility of ports in the south of Greece where British assistance could be sent, and asked Subbotić "to inject a tone of resolution" into the messages to Belgrade.[46]

When the Yugoslav Crown Council met March 20 and voted to accept the Tripartite Pact, the three representatives of the Serb parties in the government (Agrarians and Independent Democrats) resigned, precipitating a political crisis. The absence of Serb support for the government "can cause serious difficulties," von Heeren warned Berlin. The "side-tracking" (*Ausschiffung*) efforts of the anti-Axis elements in the cabinet were tolerated up to then because the more conservative Old Radicals refused to enter the government.[47]

Weary of Yugoslav procrastination, Ribbentrop issued an order (March 22) that Belgrade must sign by the 25th at the latest to remove the Yugoslav question from the agenda before the arrival in Berlin of Matsuoka, the Japanese Foreign Minister. Rumors circulating of a German ultimatum heightened the crisis begun by the Serb ministers' resignations; Anglo-American pressure countered that of the Germans.[48] Von Heeren advised Berlin to tone down the German press and to emphasize the friendship of the Reich to Yugoslavia because of the "disorientation of the public" and "a certain psychosis arising from an alleged danger to the interests" of Yugoslavia.[49]

Nationalist and Anglophile segments of the population, like the Serbian politician Trifunović and the influential orthodox prelate, Metropolitan Gavrilo, visited Prince Paul and predicted dire consequences if the pact were signed. The bishop of Požarevac and Metropolitan Nikolaj saw Paul on March 20 and urged him not to sign the pact because the Serbian people "were not ready for it." A later German investigation of the role of the Orthodox clergy in the events of March 27 described Nikolaj as "a crafty Balkan type" who exercised enormous charismatic appeal among priests and peasants who, after visiting him, talked "as if they had just seen God."[50] Both Gavrilo and Nikolaj were later banished to Montenegrin monasteries where they continued their anti-German activities.[51] General Simović, the Air Force Chief and Former Chief of General Staff, also delivered warnings to Paul that his fliers might be difficult to constrain if the government signed the pact and might even bomb "Your Highness in the Palace."[52] According to the journalist Gregorić, Simović reminded Paul of the fate of Alexander Obrenović and the events of 1903 (i.e., the murder of Prince Alexander and his wife by Serbian army officers).[53]

Tempers were growing short. When Cvetković broke the news of Yugoslavia's impending signature of the pact to Campbell on March 15, the British minister in chagrin prodded him to adopt a more positive stand. "Do you want us to attack Germany," Cvetković snapped back sarcastically. Prince Paul ruled out an aggressive policy: "soft" army leaders and the Croats and Slovenes opposed taking the offensive and seizing Salonika. The Croatian leaders were, in fact, less frightened of an Axis encirclement than of war with Germany. Salonika was a Serb problem, not a Croatian.[54]

Prince Paul and Cvetković candidly admitted to the American minister, Lane, that a German occupation of Salonika would not be challenged. Lugubriously, Paul asked Lane what he would do if he were in his place. "Refuse every German demand," was the comfortless reply.[55] Gambling desperately for survival, Belgrade continued to play for time by prolonging the negotiations; each time Berlin accepted their demands the Yugoslavs were surprised. German willingness to accept such "absurd" conditions, argued the British with reverse logic, proved Hitler's weakness.[56] In their policy toward Yugoslavia, in March the British applied measured cajolery on the diplomatic level and behind the scenes pressure through BBC radio broadcasts to Yugoslavia whose tone and content the British minister in Belgrade directed. In this respect the latter bears some responsibility for the coup. This was probably the first time in history that the media — in this case, radio — prepared and provoked a revolution. If the British did not carry out the actual coup that deposed Paul and his government, they certainly did their utmost to manipulate and prepare Yugoslav public opinion for the overthrow. Without the encouragement of the BBC and the activity of British agents and diplomatic personnel inside Yugoslavia, the coup would have been more difficult. The resignation of the three Serb government ministers and the official announcement of Yugoslavia's impending signature of the pact provided the British the opportunity they sought and Campbell quickly alerted London instructing it how to exploit the developing situation.

> I suggest that B.B.C. Serb Croat broadcasts should now adopt [a] stronger line, working on the feelings of Serbs in particular with a view to (a) increasing mass opposition in Serbia to [the] signature of any agreement with Germany and (b) ensuring [a] vehement reaction in Serbia (and so far as possible in the rest of Yugoslavia) if [the] agreement is signed. [The] Croats and their history should not, however, be left out of the appeal.
>
> 2. I suggest the following line: [The] time of decision approaches, Yugoslavia must decide now or very soon whether she is to be just another Romania or true to her glorious past, choose the way of greatness and indicate her belief in freedom and democracy. Yugoslavia is a great nation — her pact with the devil, no encirclement, no betrayal

of your belief. Serbs, Yugoslavs, we know you will be true to the spirit of Kosovo and Kajmakčalan.

3. It would be well, too, if American broadcasts in Serb-Croat should voice the feelings of Yugoslavs in the United States in strong terms.[57]

Campbell telegraphed Eden for instructions (March 21) whether to sever relations with Belgrade "and so encourage the opposition to overthrow the government and annul their signature" to the pact. Eden hesitated, preferring to await the "moment of reaction" and "pending more information on the possibility of success as a result of your soundings." It was more important that Yugoslavia should deny passage, Eden stressed, than that it should declare war if the Germans invaded Greece through Bulgaria. "A German advance through Monastir Gap is the danger we fear most," he emphasized. The Yugoslav commander of the Southern Army was a particularly crucial figure whose attitude had to be ascertained in the event that a split occurred between the Yugoslav government and the military.[58]

London warned against illusions that signing even a modified version of the Pact would stave off a German and Italian occupation. Hitler would not refuse to accept the Yugoslav conditions — why should he? The parliamentary undersecretary and Foreign Office official R. A. Butler told Subbotić that the Germans could be expected to consolidate their position and extend the pledge of cooperation once the Yugoslavs signed the pact. The German promise to respect Yugoslavia's sovereignty would be quickly violated by Hitler as the Germans gradually tightened their stranglehold. The pattern of Romania would be repeated. The British predicted that the Germans would, by stages, first ask for the transport of war materials and troops which would be difficult for the Yugoslavs to refuse, then advise the Yugoslavs to demobilize their army. Under various pretexts they would stop off at key points inside the country while passing through until they had gained complete control. Afterwards, they would foment quarrels and intrigues against the various political leaders and political parties in Yugoslavia to weaken and paralyze the government, army and administration. The offer of Salonika, if Yugoslavia "would come and fetch it," would involve it in an act of treachery and war with England and Greece and would accomplish Hitler's final objective.

Without defending his country's cautious neutrality or denying Butler's gloomy forecast, Subbotić rejected the offer of Salonika and affirmed Yugoslavia's intention to fight if the Germans attempted to force their way through the country. The Yugoslav minister hoped that if the Yugoslav government felt compelled to sign some agreement with Germany, the British would not consider this an abandonment of their basic neutralist position or of their friends. The British sympathized with the "appallingly difficult" position of the Regent and the Yugoslav government and assured Subbotić that if the Yugoslavs signed an agreement with Germany it would not engage in making "useless reproaches and recriminations." However, in such a case Butler foresaw the most serious consequences for its sovereignty and independence.[59]

As the crisis mounted in intensity, London went beyond diplomatic channels and appealed directly to the Yugoslav people to encourage the gathering wave of national indignation against the pact. To counter the government's rationale that it had to sign the pact because the Turks were deceivers and the British were unable to supply war materials, Campbell urged London to broadcast that Britain was helping Greece and to hint "at potential booty in Albania."[60]

All these considerations vanished when Campbell wired Eden of the gathering tension caused by the resignation of the three Serb ministers opposed to the signing of the pact — a crisis provoked by the British who subsidized the Serbian Peasant Party and exercised influence in the other two opposition parties.[61] Eden now underwent a change of attitude and lost whatever scruples he had against overthrowing the Yugoslav government as set forth in his telegram of the previous day to Campbell. Fearing Yugoslavia might "slip by stages into the German orbit" he thought that the Yugoslavs should carry out a coup if necessary and "be prepared to risk precipitating [a] German attack."[62] News of the German ultimatum — an exaggeration of Hitler's somewhat brusque request for a Yugoslav decision on the pact by March 24 — provided the handle Eden had been groping for and he quickly authorized Campbell to give a secret pledge of British support to the plotters for any "further change of government even by coup d'état."[63] A message by Churchill to get Yugoslavia into the war probably contributed to the change of strategy on the part of the British.

As the date of the signature of the pact drew near, prospects for a coup temporarily declined. British communications on March 25 are pessimistic and glum. On that day — or possibly one day later — the putative leader of the coup, Air Force Chief Bora Mirković, held a talk with T. G. Mapplebeck, a private businessman and honorary air attaché in Belgrade and possibly a British agent. Jozo Tomasevich believes that Mapplebeck was the British liaison with the conspirators, while the British historian Elizabeth Barker thought MacDonald, the British air attaché at Belgrade who authored the first dispatch describing the coup on the evening of the 26th and had contact with Mirković, was the key figure on the British side. In a closely reasoned article, David A. T. Stafford, a Canadian historian, writes cautiously that Mapplebeck was "a more important figure" working with the conspirators to launch the coup.[64] In a letter to the *Slavic Review*, R. J. Knezević, a key conspirator, admitted his involvement in the coup but denied any contacts with the British and declared that such allegations stemmed from Dragiša Cvetković, fabricated in order to discredit the coup.[65]

The British minister at Belgrade, Campbell, was less enthusiastic about a coup, considering the SOE (Special Operations Executive) operatives, from the viewpoint of the professional diplomat, as incautious amateurs. He may have believed that the resignation of the Serb ministers from the government made a coup unnecessary and effectively forestalled any signature of the pact for the time being. Fotić, Yugoslav minister in Washington, scoffed at the appointment of new ministers as a "decision to search in the dustbin," demonstrating Serb unity against the pact; Croatian divisions "render them less powerful politically," reflecting the feeling that the government did not have enough support to sign.[66] Accordingly, Campbell notified Eden (March 22) that opposition to the pact had arrested the government's decision to sign "for a day or two." Though the Croat and Slovene ministers favored signing, the British consul in Zagreb, Rapp, reported "the morale of the Croat population is higher and the will to resist the German demands greater than ever in the past."[67]

Earlier on March 20 Jukić, a Croat Foreign Office official, received word from Campbell that something was brewing. Campbell told the Yugoslav diplomat, according to his memoirs, that he was concerned about Paul's fate because of the Regent's personal unpopularity with the Serbs and public agitation over the pact and "he feared a possible coup d'état that might sweep away the Serbo-Croatian agreement along with Prince Paul."[68] The Special Foreign Office official, Shone, also dropped a hint to Paul of possible problems because of the strong feelings against the pact inside Serbia and "the junior ranks of the army."[69]

The British documents do not shed much light on the British minister's relations with the SOE operatives in Belgrade. Whether Campbell did not know that British agents were in close contact with the conspirators and had encouraged the coup is not clear. Recent speculations, based less on documentary evidence than hindsight and statements many decades later, have sought to establish that Campbell played no role in the events of March 27 and had the professional diplomat's innate dislike and distrust of cloak and dagger operators and their methods. Some of his diffidence was no doubt connected with having to bear the blame if the coup failed. Later contentions of Cvetković and others that, had the perpetrators of the coup known the extent of the concessions gained by the government from Hitler, they would never have carried out the coup, seem to be somewhat far from the truth. Some of the leading conspirators — at least according to one source — knew about the German concessions, including access to Salonika, through the participation of the opposition ministers in the Cvetković government, and there is evidence that the Serb military was also informed. At Prince Paul's suggestion Cincar-Marković informed the opposition ministers about the contents of the pact and the qualifying notes but only told Milos Trifunović of the Radical Party "the nature of the notes to be annexed to the pact."[70]

The British had exhausted all their arguments against Yugoslavia's adherence to the pact. Shone, a personal friend of the Prince Regent's, made a final effort to move the Regent before departing for London. Shone advised Paul to mount the wave of popular feeling against the agreement, especially in Serbia, to either avoid or to delay its signature. However, Paul knew that his options had run out and he could no longer delay signing. Whether or not he signed, the country would be split, he declared. He shifted responsibility for the decision to sign, blaming the faintheartedness of the Slovene and Croat ministers. His will failing, Paul argued that if he did not sign the agreement he would be blamed by the Croats and others for not having spared the country the horrors of war by accepting the agreement. Shone replied by quoting the Bible (Second Corinthians, chapter 6, verses

14 and 17).* Allied opinion, Shone declared, would feel that he had made a covenant with the Powers of Darkness. Visibly disturbed, Paul replied: "I know."

Complicating Paul's situation and contributing to his dilemma was the failure of positive support from the Turks which the British had been promising, creating a deplorable impression in Belgrade.[71] Resigned and fatalistic, Cvetković admitted to Lane that the German guarantee was worthless, but insisted nevertheless that his country still needed a guarantee from Hitler. Paul was beginning to crack under the strain: "I am out of my head, I wish I were dead," he lamented, and complained of Bulgarian perfidy, British stupidity and the opposition of the Croats.[72] An eleventh-hour telegram to Paul from Churchill to shore up the crumbling Balkan architecture only elicited skepticism and failed to dissuade the Regent. On March 23 Belgrade published the German guarantee of Yugoslavia's sovereignty; and three days later Cvetković travelled via a side railroad branch to Vienna. Before signing the pact, he received the secret German note on Salonika.[73]

While the BBC blared forth its radio appeals against the pact and British agents worked covertly to prepare the ground, the tension mounted. Leaflets were widely distributed in Belgrade, reminding the Serbs of their glorious past; long-forgotten battles and victories against the Turks were again evoked. One such leaflet circulated throughout Belgrade reflects the emotional climate of dark suspicions, perfidy and apprehensions of treason:

Serbs, Belgradians [sic], the Government is preparing capitulation. In a day or two the tripartite pact is to be signed which means certain shameful death to the country, freedom and the people. For the first time in our history we must bow our knee to tyrants and perish in dishonor and slavery. And this today when the whole people in all districts of all ranks has arisen as in 1912, 13, and 14, and when only one spirit, one wish, one thought [was] to defend its greatest possession with its life and to the death — national freedom and national independence.

The whole nation of 15 million people desires honor and freedom for the fatherland.

The Government of 16 million people wishes the capitulation of slavery and shame.

The people with the greatest patience has waited for the Government and given it time to prepare not capitulation but defence.

Now the cup is full.

These are the last moments when our fate is to be decided. We do not allow capitulation. We'll not lay down our arms. Those who play with the heads of 16 million people play with their own heads.

---

* "You must not consent to be yokefellows with unbelievers ... separate yourselves from them and do not even touch what is unclean."

Serbs, Belgradians, let us show ourselves worthy of our forebears. We dare not be worse than the heroes of Kosovo, the Karageorge rebels or the famous heroes of Kumanovo, Bregalnica, Suvobor, Mojkovac and Kajmakčalan.

Belgrade 1941 must not fail Belgrade of 1915.

Let each fulfill his duty, and the crime which the Government is preparing will be prevented at the last moment.

We want no Tripartite Pact, no instructors, no tourists, no economic experts, no clean up of the enemies of the Axis.

All for honor and freedom. Honor and freedom at any price.[74]

On March 25, Subbotić broke the news to Cadogan of Yugoslavia's impending signature. German troops, he assured Cadogan, would not be permitted to cross Yugoslav territory. The Yugoslav minister was visibly distressed: he had never expected his country would actually sign the pact and had thought they were stringing the Germans along and playing for time. He thought that they might only sign "some innocuous non-aggression pact." Subbotić thought the pact did not amount to much and would be of little use to the Germans in gaining passage through Yugoslavia to attack Greece. He dreaded the disintegrating effect that joining the Axis would produce inside Yugoslavia and suspected that a German threat to support Bulgarian claims to Macedonia, which could involve the loss of all South Serbia and cut off access to the sea, had been a factor in the government's decision. Cvetković was above double-crossing Greece, Subbotić assured Cadogan, and asked that the British refrain from accusing Yugoslavia of treachery in the press which would harm Yugoslav-Greek relations and the solidarity of the Balkan states in their efforts to build a Balkan bloc.

The following day Subbotić tried to put a good face on matters to Butler. The Yugoslav government in his view "thought they would be clever" and gain assurances that Yugoslav territory would not be violated by German forces, but instead "had underestimated the evil machinations of the Germans who would not rest content with the document they had signed." However, it was in Greece's interest to have Yugoslavia's neutrality maintained; the Yugoslav signature to the pact "was not as reprehensible as it might appear." Butler gave him short shrift: besides the fact that Yugoslavia was now the ally of the Italians and Japanese, the government's action had restored the prestige of Italy and Count Ciano, whom the Yugoslavs had professed to loathe. Butler hinted at the impending storm: "Whether the Yugoslav people would be inclined to see things in a moderate light, I doubted."[75]

The storm that Butler alluded to had been gathering since mid-March in the public, in the government and armed forces and diplomatic missions abroad. On the 15th of March, forty-eight patriotic societies presented a petition to the Prince Regent urging resistance to German demands. Letters and telegrams deluged the government urging a firm attitude. Six Senators representing the British-subsidized Serbian Peasant Party addressed a letter to the President of the Council, stating accession to the Tripartite Pact would "sully" the Yugoslav people and threaten the very existence of the country. They threatened to resign their seats in the Senate if the government signed the pact to avoid responsibility for its consequences.[76] "The Serbian Peasant Party under Gavrilović are playing up well," exulted Rose, a Foreign Office official, in a minute to this news.[77] A report from the Washington press stated that the Yugoslav Ambassador Fotić, a Serb, would resign if the government capitulated.[78] On receiving news of the government's signature the Yugoslav Ambassador in Moscow, Gavrilović, immediately resigned and indicated his intention to return home.[79] The decision to accede to the pact had already been made at the March 6 Crown Council meeting and the government ministers were only informed at the last minute as Cvetković prepared to leave for Vienna to sign.

In the aftermath of the coup the deposed leaders blamed one another for what had transpired. The final decision to sign the pact, Prince Paul told Rapp, the British Consul-General in Zagreb, "was due to Matchek's [sic] unwillingness to face up to possible consequences of braving Germany, the attitude of Cvetković being entirely the reverse."[80] Maček in turn blamed Prince Paul whom he was convinced had secretly agreed to the Tripartite Agreement during his five-hour discussion with Hitler. Subsequent events "were simply playing for position on the part of the Prince so that he could justify and carry out an undertaking already given which he did not feel strong enough to repudiate."

Fortifying the rationale to sign the pact were the reports of the Minister of War, "himself a creature of the Prince," citing the absence of assurances of positive help from the Turks and "likewise the insistence on the inability of the British to give immediate effective aid." Rapp related Maček's "real views that the Croats will fight in defense of Yugoslavia if the Serbs are prepared to do the same." Maček pictured himself as powerless in matters of foreign policy and military affairs which lay largely in the hands of the Prince Regent; the decision to sign really rested with the latter.

The minutes of the Foreign Office personnel indicate British disenchantment with Paul. Bowker suspected that "the Prince Regent used the Croat argument to justify what was in reality his own decision not to face up to the possible consequences of braving Germany." Nichol agreed: "Even discounting Mr. Rapp's obviously pro-Croat bias, the part played by the Prince Regent seems to have been a sorry one."[81] This mutual ascribing of blame by the signatories of the pact is in direct contrast to its defense against their mutual enemies of March 27 in the post-war era by Paul, Maček and Cvetković as a realistic decision which preserved Yugoslavia's neutrality without the loss of honor, and extracted maximum concessions from Germany. By this time, of course, Yugoslavia had fallen to Tito and the partisans and those usurped by the coup could claim the pact would have kept Yugoslavia out of the war and prevented the fall of the Royal government.

At the official ceremony in Vienna Hitler complained of the funereal atmosphere; the Yugoslav ministers were uncomfortable and visibly unhappy. But Hitler felt relieved and confided to Ciano that the invasion of Greece would have been "an exceedingly irresponsible operation if Yugoslavia's attitude had been uncertain," adding warily, "internal conditions in Yugoslavia could become complicated in spite of everything."[82]

The complications had, in fact, already begun. Even before the Yugoslav ministers left for Vienna, demonstrations erupted in central Serbia and Cetinje, Montenegro. On March 25 a conspiratorial network led by General Bora Mirković and supported by Air Force Chief Simović, with extensive ganglia in the army and Serbian nationalist circles in the capital and towns, swung into action. After severing the main communications and governmental installations in Belgrade, the conspirators — faking the voice of the heir-apparent Peter — issued a royal proclamation appointing General Simović head of a new government with the prestigious Old Radical, Momčilo Ninčić, foreign minister. In Berlin Simović was thought to represent the Old Serb viewpoint less and ready to compromise on the Croatian question. Simović, a Wilhelmstrasse report notes, was "a sophisticated person, handsome, vain, effeminate, and intelligent."[83]

The conspirators apparently had not worked out what they would do once they came to power. A wrangle broke out among them with Mirković desiring to establish an authoritarian regime while others, led by Professor R. L. Knezević, who together with his brother Colonel Živan Knezević had played important roles in the conspiracy, desired to return to the 1921 centralist Constitution — something which the Croats would have found unacceptable.[84] Churchill was particularly alive to the opportunities which the coup had suddenly and unexpectedly thrown open and urged that a fresh attempt be made to cement a front of Balkan powers against Hitler. He ordered Dill and Eden to go to the Balkans and pressed Inonu, the Turkish leader, to render all possible assistance to Yugoslavia.[85]

The British expected the new Yugoslav government to denounce the pact and join in the defense of the Greeks.[86] Campbell instructed that the BBC be toned down and that press comment be restrained until the success of the coup was confirmed.[87] Later, Cadogan and the Foreign Office officials agreed that Campbell should not withhold diplomatic recognition even if the pact were not denounced. The British learned that the German and Italian ministers had been told the change in government was an internal affair and that Yugoslav policy would be one of neutrality and peace, but that an attack on Salonika would cause it to fight.[88] Early Reuters statements that the new government's foreign policy would not differ from that of the old, London thought, were "merely a blind" to mislead the Germans for a few days while the new government got firmly in the saddle.[89] The presence of the Italophile politician, the Old Radical Momčilo Ninčić, who had negotiated the 1929 "Peace of the Adriatic," also intended to allay German suspicions while the Serb generals and politicians consolidated their hold and prepared for war.

In his first interview with Ninčić, the new minister for foreign affairs, Campbell learned that the government's policy was still under discussion. Salonika, however, "was a question of greatest importance for Yugoslavia." The coup, he told the British minister, "was not due solely to the signature of the Tripartite Pact" but rather to "long discontent with the last regime and all its works."[90] A British foreign office appraisal unflatteringly described

Ninčić as "sixty-five years old, of second-rate ability, and suspected of pro-Italian leanings."

Except for the German minister's vague warning in the previous October of a coup, thereafter nothing appears in the German documents forewarning of the events of March 27, 1941.[91] However, Hitler's allusion to complications in Vienna indicates that they may have known something was brewing. But in all likelihood the coup seems to have caught them by surprise — at least if one is to judge from Hitler's emotional reaction.

Perhaps with the hope of dampening revanchist feelings in Berlin, von Heeren sent a remarkably restrained description of the coup a week later from Berlin, calling it "a typical Serb military putsch" aimed against "the foreigner Prince Paul" and "the gypsy Cvetković" by fanatical Serb patriots who believed that they were being betrayed at Vienna. The popular demonstrations were of "a patriotic nature," greeting the accession of Peter and the entry of popular Serb politicians into the cabinet, and they advanced right up to the German consulate "without a stone having been thrown against a window." Many Serb citizens apologized to him the next day. The German minister warned against discounting the Croats, whose sense of belonging with the Serbs it would be dangerous to underestimate, despite their vehement quarrels, and opposed taking any punitive action against the Serbs.[92]

Paul was in Zagreb at the moment of the coup. Weary of the burdens of office and fearing civil war, he rejected Maček's advice to place himself at the head of loyal Croat troops and lead a march on Belgrade, journeying instead to Zemun (Semlin) where he was conducted to Belgrade and compelled to withdraw in favor of eighteen-year-old King Peter.[93] In the words of the witty British diplomat, Knatchbull-Hugessen: "Paul petered out and Peter petered in."

Hitler at first refused to believe the news of the Belgrade coup which had come "suddenly out of the blue" and at first he thought it was a "joke." His initial nonplussed reaction quickly gave way to elemental rage against the "nest of Serb conspirators" in Belgrade, doubly galling because the Japanese Foreign Minister Matsuoka was in Berlin to witness his contretemps. Summoning the Hungarian and Bulgarian envoys on March 27 Hitler revealed his decision to attack Yugoslavia. The Banat and other former Yugoslav territories belonging to the Crown of St. Stephen inside Yugoslavia, he promised Sztojay, the Hungarian minister, would be returned to Hungary. "Croatia was to be independent possibly in alignment with Hungary, but there must never be another Yugoslavia," he vowed. The Belgrade coup, he told the Bulgarian minister Draganov, "had settled the question of Macedonia."[94] The idea of restoring the old relationship between Croatia and Hungary lingered on. Franz von Papen reported that at the end of the war his cellmate, former Regent Horthy, sent an appeal to Churchill for "some sort of trusteeship" over Croatia by Hungary to preserve Europe from Bolshevism.[95] State Secretary Weizsäcker told von Hassell that "from the hour of the coup d'état in Belgrade, Hitler was set on battle and full of resentment, demands destruction and plans the wildest and most impossible solutions of the South Slav problem: Croatia under Hungarian domination and Dalmatia to Italy."[96]

On the same day Hitler told a meeting of high civil and military leaders including Göring, Ribbentrop, Halder and Keitel that Yugoslavia, "an uncertain factor" since the Belgrade coup, threatened the Greek and forthcoming Russian campaigns and had to be eliminated. He would not wait for loyalty declarations and would "smash Yugoslavia militarily and as a state" by an attack carried out with "inexorable severity." The war would be popular with Yugoslavia's neighbors who hoped for territorial gain.[97] A Führer order "Directive 25" prescribed a three-pronged attack spreading out in concentric circles from bases in Austria, Hungary and Bulgaria.

Despite official blandishments of friendship, the new Yugoslav Foreign Minister Ninčić's statements to von Heeren did not reassure Berlin. The Simović government's policy was to acknowledge the pact but not to enforce it — which, in fact, meant that the pact was a dead letter. The government did not, in fact, notify the German minister of Yugoslavia's adherence to the pact until several days later on March 30. While personally vouching for the maintenance of Yugoslavia's obligations, Ninčić did not rule out a return to neutrality.[98] The Croatian State Secretary in the Foreign Ministry gave similar assurances that the legality of the Pact was beyond question, but that the government hesitated because of the country's mood and the mood in Serbia to admit it publicly.[99] General Mirković also gave his pledge to von Heeren on March 30 of Yugoslavia's continuing adherence to the Pact.[100]

Despite the delirious exaltation released by the overthrow of the Cvetković government, as street mobs chanted *"bolje rat nego pakt"* (better war than the pact), von Heeren predicted that the new cabinet with its Croat wing vouched for the tendency to avoid conflict, but that the Serb members opposed the pact and "a loosening of ties would probably occur."[101] But Yugoslavia's fate was already cast. Hitler secretly ordered the *Volksdeutsch,* the German minority in Yugoslavia, to evade conscription through flight or concealment and ordered all German nationals inside Yugoslavia, except consular officials, back to Germany.

However, the Serb military was more willing to push matters to a dangerous head to reverse Yugoslavia's threatened position. Singling out the weaker Italian partner, General Simović sternly warned the Italian consul Mameli that Yugoslavia could not permit itself to be surrounded and forced to capitulate and would attack the Italians in Albania if the Axis seized Salonika. Simović persisted even when advised that this might lead to war. When von Heeren questioned the Yugoslav foreign Minister about Simović's statement, Ninčić, "evidently shocked" and uninformed, gave the odd explanation reflecting the state of indecision in the new regime, that Simović "could in no way have spoken in the name of the government."[102] The German minister lessened the force of Simović's remarks by reporting that the Simović threat "was shared by some Serbs but few Croats or Moslems." A majority of the cabinet favored unconditional accession to the pact.[103] But Simović made similar threats, according to his *aide de camp,* again on another occasion. The incident increased suspicions in Berlin and Rome that the Serbian military secretly planned a thrust against Albania or Salonika. Von Heeren did not believe the new government yet had command of the situation and was skeptical of Yugoslav motives. "They only want to gain time," he advised Berlin. "After the insane expression of Simović to the Italian consul, a sudden attack in Albania or towards Salonika is within the realm of possibility."[104] Others shared these suspicions. The Romanian military warned the Germans that the Yugoslav General Staff still harbored "the favorite idea" of the old Serb generals to form a front with Greece and, if necessary, to transfer the army abroad as in World War I.[105] A Croat member of the Bern embassy also confirmed the suspicion that "an amateur plan" was being discussed in Old Serb and military circles to strike the Italians from behind in Albania.[106]

While the new government gave every indication of fighting if Salonika were attacked, their attitude toward the pact remained in doubt. There was no certainty that it would repudiate the pact and it might instead even substitute a non-aggression pact. Campbell argued that "there are enough old fogies in the Government to make policy on that line possible." He warned against Yugoslav touchiness about being taken for granted and suggested that London desist from disseminating the notion that they would definitely side with the Western Powers. Attempts to push them closer to the British camp might cause them to "dig in their toes."[107] On March 30 the Simović government informed the Germans and Italian representatives that Yugoslavia wished to remain neutral and by tacit omission would neither cancel the pact nor exercise it. In their efforts to draw Yugoslavia into their alliance with Greece, the British requested that Eden be allowed to come to Belgrade. Simović refused to see Eden but agreed to permit Marshal Dill to come for talks.

In contrast to the emotional catharsis in Belgrade, the Croatian capital remained completely quiet. Public buildings and Serb homes displayed the national colors in honor of Peter's accession, but Yugoslav flags were conspicuously absent from Croat homes. Young Air Force officers had apprehended the Croat ministers in Belgrade and demanded their entry into the new cabinet. After hastily telephoning Maček they assented "to avoid the worst."[108] But Šubašić and Šutej, two of the Croatian ministers, told von Heeren that the situation was serious and that they wished to avoid a conflict with Germany. They felt themselves "almost as prisoners" in Belgrade. While they believed Simović to be "reasonable," the War Minister, Ilić, they thought was "dangerous."[109] The ominous silence in Zagreb attested to the affront felt by Croats over the removal of the Cvetković government in which Maček and other Croat leaders had played an important role. The tactic of Maček, a master of evasion and procrastination, was to gain time to permit his entry into the Simović government without at the same time losing the confidence of Berlin.

Through the Abwehr and a Viennese engineer named Derffler, Maček sounded out Berlin's attitude to the new Yugoslav government. On March 29 Derffler journeyed to Vienna with Maček's proposals. The Croats and Slovenes, Maček warned, were united with the Serbs in opposing the entry of Italian troops into Yugoslavia. He preferred a peaceful solution to war and thought the Simović government "would end in mismanagement" in a few weeks. His entry into the new government with the Croatian ministers would help hasten its demise. Without Croat participation no orderly government would be possible and the country would revert to the chaotic pre-1939 Settlement (Sporazum).[110] Since Hitler had already decided to attack Yugoslavia this was precisely what the Germans wanted.

Through Alfred Freundt, German consul in Zagreb, Ribbentrop advised Maček (March 30) to abstain from any further cooperation with Belgrade, dangling before him the bait of an independent Croatian state as reward for his cooperation "should the Yugoslav state collapse through its own mistakes."[111] Maček, however, declined the German offer: acceptance of the Tripartite Pact by the new government, he told Berlin, was a prerequisite to his entry into the new government. To withdraw the Croat ministers from the new cabinet would be "tactically inexpedient." The Croats would boycott the government only if war would thereby be averted. What Maček did not know or understand was that the Germans no longer cared about the pact and only wished his abstention from the government to create as much disunity as possible at the moment of attack. However, they could not reveal this without forewarning the Yugoslavs of the impending military assault.

Through his chief lieutenant August Košutić in Belgrade, Maček negotiated conditions for entry into the Simović government: recognition of the Tripartite Pact; appointment of two co-regents, one a Croat; and removal of the Serb military from politics.[112] Maček feared a coup by Croatian separatists who sought to exploit the widespread Croat resentment against the Serbs for the March 27 coup and force a break with Belgrade.[113] Disturbing reports from the Croatian leaders in Belgrade warned the Serbian military might send troops to occupy Zagreb, abolish the autonomy of the Sporazum and establish a military administration.[114] Fearing a separatist coup if the Croats joined the Belgrade government, Maček sent three representatives, Šutej, Andres and Smoljan, to Belgrade to gain time and to avoid making a decision.[115]

Košutić's return with full acceptance of Maček's conditions and predictions of war by some Croat leaders decided Maček upon Belgrade rather than Berlin, primarily to avoid a situation in which the Croats would find themselves on the Axis side if war broke out. But Croatian public opinion was divided: the pro-German right wing of the Croatian Peasant Party and the Ustasha separatists opposed a reconciliation with Belgrade while Croatian moderates urged Maček's entry into the Simović cabinet. The American consul in Zagreb, James Miely, described the tense situation in Zagreb: "During this time considerable pressure was brought to bear on Maček by many influential Croats to join the new government. A no less important personage than Stepinec [*sic*], Catholic Archbishop of Yugoslavia, was urging him to return to Belgrade."

"This decision spelled the collapse of the HSS (Croatian Peasant Party). Maček's right-about-face stunned many of his Croat friends — he was no longer their leader."[116] Miely's judgment is probably somewhat exaggerated. Majority opinion, particularly the peasantry, probably favored controlled support of Yugoslavia and the Belgrade government. The radical nationalist intelligentsia and segments of the Croatian town bourgeoisie and officialdom probably represented the minority. The inability of the separatists and radical nationalists to carry out a coup at this time in Zagreb attests to their weakness. The separatists admitted this, claiming that arrests, exile and conscription had depleted their ranks.[117]

Berlin now decided to gain a Croatian defection from Yugoslavia by sending Walter Malletke, the Nazi Party Foreign Office specialist for Southeastern Europe — the organization operated by Ribbentrop's arch-rival, Alfred Rosenberg — and the veteran Wilhelmstrasse troubleshooter, Edmund Veesenmayer, to deal with the Croatian separatists. In a discussion with Maček on April 3, Malletke again offered, without success, the bribe of an independent Croatia. The same afternoon Maček announced his decision, based upon his Christian and humanitarian principles, to enter the Simović government. Maček's decision created a furor and he was immediately branded a "traitor" by the radical Croatian nationalists who believed the hour for the creation of the independent Croatian state had sounded.[118]

Malletke's departure left the field open to Veesenmayer to weld an alliance of radical nationalists, Ustasha separatists and defectors from the right wing of the Peasant Party which proclaimed (April 5) the end of Yugoslavia and a "free, independent Croatian State containing the areas that are Croatian from the historic and ethnic point of view."[119]

This action signified an open split in the Croatian bourgeoisie, a segment of which had now opted for Hitler and fascism while Maček and his followers threw their support to Belgrade. An important element in this decision was Maček's fear of a Serbian military attack on Zagreb and the eruption of a civil war if he did not enter the Simović government. While a segment of the Croatian bourgeoisie in the towns and villages viewed the conflict with the Serbian bourgeoisie as primary and saw in the proclamation of the Croatian state the fulfillment of their nationalist dreams, for the Croatian peasantry the exchange of the Serbian bourgeoisie's overlordship for that of Hitler represented a worsening of their position rather than an improvement. For the Croatian peasantry, fascism could only mean further slavery and degradation. The announcement of the Croatian state and its support by Germany plunged Maček and his followers into gloom and pessimism. "They have betrayed us," the circle around Maček told the Slovak chargé. Maček appeared to be "a broken old man" who could speak only with difficulty, expressing his thoughts more with gestures than words. Maček could no longer find a solution. He now believed that war was no longer avoidable and would lead to the collapse of the state. However, he could not "turn the rudder completely around" because he feared a Serbian attack on Croatia would immediately occur. "Maček's policy and Maček himself has collapsed," the German consul in Zagreb, Feine, concluded.[120] Veesenmayer and Feine reported to Berlin that Maček's influence in Croatia had fallen to zero.[121] While Veesenmayer and Freundt concluded agreements with the Croatian separatists and Peasant Party dissidents recognizing German sponsorship of a Croatian state, Feine requested Berlin to drop leaflets urging the Croats to revolt just before the entrance of German troops into Croatia.[122] The disintegrating political situation influenced the Slovenian leader

Kulovec to send out feelers through the Slovak chargé asking for the creation of a Greater Slovenia or else union with Croatia if war occurred.[123]

While Dill met with the Yugoslavs in Belgrade, negotiations were opened with the Italians through Ninčić and the Soviets through Gavrilović in Moscow with the hope of gaining a military alliance against a German attack. Belgrade had been seeking without success to draw out the Soviets. In the previous year the Soviets evoked pan-Slav solidarity: in the event of a clash with Germany and "of the worst eventuality of a peace between England and Germany in which case it would be isolated," Slav support would be important. Soviet party functionaries told the Yugoslav trade attaché that in a clash with Germany "all our brothers of the same blood will join against Germany." In the meantime they expected England and Germany to weaken while the USSR got stronger.

In the beginning of February, Cincar-Marković asked the Yugoslav minister to Moscow precisely what attitude the Soviet Government would take if German troops entered Bulgaria and "whether the Soviets consider that by this action theirs and our interests would be threatened."[124] But Vyshinsky was evasive. Gavrilović believed that Russia would do nothing and would leave Bulgaria to its own defense.[125] The Turkish-Bulgarian pact drew an immediate Soviet reaction. Vyshinsky twice reiterated that German troops were on the borders of Bulgaria.[126] Gavrilović thought Russia wanted a new Balkan front to weaken Germany while it remained untouched and could intervene at a favorable moment.[127]

Rumors of a postponement of a German attack on Britain and Nazi preparations for an assault on the Soviet Union circulated. Gavrilović believed "the Soviets again feared peace between England and Germany leaving Germany triumphant in the Balkans and in a position to attack the USSR which the United States would be sympathetic to."[128] Notwithstanding, the British continued to work to conciliate Turkey and Russia, but the Turkish minister Saracoglu was suspicious of the Soviets.[129] When the Yugoslav minister inquired what the USSR would do if Yugoslavia signed the pact, Vyshinsky was evasive; later he told Gavrilović that "the question has no purpose as you have already decided to sign the Three Power Pact."[130] The Soviets continued to hold themselves distant from direct talks with the British. Conditions, Vyshinsky told the British ambassador, were still unfavorable. Why, he asked, had Lord Halifax, British minister to the United States, stopped American aid to the USSR? The British ambassador retorted that Britain had proposed economic negotiations but had received no reply. They did not wish the goods to end up in Germany. Gavrilović believed that the Soviets feared that the British were giving them information about the Germans to inveigle them into war with Germany.[131]

News of the March 27 coup delighted the Soviets, while the Germans were in complete consternation.[132] Gavrilović asked Schulenberg to tell Hitler not to ask for a formal renewal of the treaty.[133] In response to the Soviet chargé in Belgrade's proposal for a "military political agreement or alliance," the Yugoslavs sent two military representatives to Moscow. But the Soviets experienced a change of heart when the two Yugoslavs arrived.

Vyshinsky admitted Moscow was still reluctant to break off its relations with Germany, which the agreement with Yugoslavia would do. Instead he proposed a treaty of friendship and non-aggression. The Yugoslavs "received the impression that this was possibly the first step to a military alliance." Vyshinsky inquired several times about the military supplies needed by the Yugoslavs and indicated Soviet readiness to deliver them. At the third meeting Vyshinsky revealed that the Russians had only thought of negotiations on military material and "eventually on some kind of an agreement such as they had proposed." Belgrade had thought it was a question of a military agreement, Gavrilović countered. For an agreement such as Vyshinsky had in mind, a delegation with plenipotentiary powers was not necessary.[134] In the final version of the pact the Soviets altered article 2 to read that in the event of an attack on either of the contracting parties by a third party, the other signatory would remain neutral. This would have had the effect of encouraging the Yugoslavs to resist, without warning the Germans that they would be attacking Yugoslavia, an ally of the Soviet Union — as Stalin later admitted. Gavrilović's request for a postponement, Vyshinsky told him, had placed Molotov in "an uncomfortable position" since he had already informed the German ambassador that the Soviet government would sign a treaty of friendship with Yugoslavia that evening. Gavrilović wondered whether Molotov had shown the German ambassador the earlier text of the agreement with article 2 before it had been changed.[135] Stalin, however, overruled Molotov: the Soviets agreed to the first version of the disputed article 2 and the agreement was signed April 5, 1941.[136]

The following day the Germans attacked Yugoslavia and Greece without warning. The Soviet Government's policy in retrospect was to encourage Yugoslav resistance to Hitler while watching developments in the country. The American ambassador in Moscow, Steinhardt, seemed to confirm this in a post-mortem analysis in May 1941, writing that the Yugoslav minister

> told me yesterday that between the date of the signing of the Soviet-Yugoslav pact and the defeat of the Yugoslav armies the Soviet authorities had promised him armament, munitions, and airplanes and that although there had been sufficient time at least to have discussed the quantities and means of shipment no steps had been taken by the Soviet authorities to implement their assurances. He expressed the opinion that the Soviet Government at the time the assurances were given him contemplated watching developments before commencing deliveries and that had Yugoslavia been able to offer effective resistance deliveries probably would have been made.[137]

Thus ended one of the war's most significant events. Invading Yugoslavia from Bulgaria, Romania and Austrian bases, the Germans overran it swiftly and in equally quick order drove the British out of Greece. Göring testified at Nuremberg that Hitler and the Germans were convinced the Simović coup had been a conspiracy organized by the Soviet Union and financed by Britain. For the Nazi leader it was a final, crucial reason for attacking the Soviet Union in June 1941.[138] Historians have argued since over whether the deflection of German forces to the southeast as a result of the Belgrade coup of March 27, 1941 caused Hitler to alter his timetable for the invasion of the Soviet Union. The Wehrmacht arrived at the gates of Moscow six weeks later at the height of the Russian winter with fatal consequences for Germany, instead of during the milder October fall weather. For Yugoslavia, the coup was even more fateful — opening the country to civil war and revolution, the historical consequences of which are still with us. Yugoslavia regained control of its own natural resources and relieved itself of British, French and German control.

Conclusion

Trade After 1918: The Struggle for Market Share

THE SECOND WORLD WAR first broke out as a quarrel within the bosom of the Western capitalist countries Britain and France, which refused to allow Germany to dominate the continent as the new hegemon. Chamberlain and his friends hoped and even tried to deflect Hitler to the east to attack the Soviet Union, a policy that reached its high point at the Munich Conference in September 1938. This was previously known by the pre-war generation but forgotten by most post-war historians. The perceptive journalist and writer Christopher Hitchens writes in a recent revisionist article on Churchill: "The word appeasement obscures some elements of this realization now, as it did then. It was the vague term chosen by the Tories themselves to mask a collaboration with fascism and also their candid hope that the ambitions of Hitler could be directed eastward towards Stalin."[1] If one considers that World War I also occurred as a quarrel within capitalism with the United States coming in later as in World War II, the first Great War having caused an estimated 35 million casualties and the Second World War about 55 million, totaling 90 million, then capitalism may be credited with generating one of the greatest slaughters in history. The twentieth century was, in all probability, one of the bloodiest in history.

Generally speaking, fascism was merely the brutal face of the World War I program of German imperialist expansion into Eastern Europe to establish its hegemony in that region. The First World War, it is generally accepted, was a struggle between all the European Powers, later joined by the U.S. for the territory, trade and raw materials of Eastern Europe, and the Second World War, in many respects, was a sequel to that drama. The ten-year Great Depression from 1929 to 1939 brought on a crisis within the faltering world colonial system from which it could not recover, and the Second World War was the expression of this crisis. As pointed out throughout this study, economic factors like trade, investment and access to raw materials played a major role, if not a primary one, in bringing on the Second World War as in the First World War. Unlike the historians of the First World War who readily admitted that economic factors, conflicting imperialist interests and the fight for markets played an important role in causing the war, historians of the Second World War have not only been reluctant to acknowledge, but have even denied that these factors had anything to do with the war. Historians such as A. J. P. Taylor, economic historians such as R. J. Overy, and many others have flatly denied that the Second World War was anything more than a political conflict. In view of the foregoing, are we not more than half a century after the conflict really entitled to ask: Was it really the case that the origin of the war is primarily in the political arena, in the primacy of politics? Looked at globally, is not the narrow, constricted view of the *Primat der Politik* no longer tenable?

From the German standpoint, Germany bore no more guilt than the Western Powers for responsibility for the First World War and resented being made to bear the sole guilt for the war, being forced to give up some choice territories and pay huge indemnities. That said, Germany's Versailles-inherited pariah status, a grave but perhaps inevitable error, at first gave Hitler, supported by many Germans, a pretext for expanding German power to recover Germany's stolen lands, then, on less juridical grounds, to expand into areas not previously belonging to Germany but populated by German-speaking peoples like Austria and the Sudetenland.

The tariff wars of the 1930s form the historical arena within which the struggle occurred. The collapse of industrial production and world trade during the Great Depression of the 1930s generated massive unemployment and social chaos and intensified the fight for markets among the Great Powers. To stave off the threat of collapse and social revolution, the European and American Powers sought to assure themselves of internal markets for their industrial and agricultural production by imposing protective tariffs against the exports of other states while seeking external markets for their own surplus commodities. Having lost its colonies and other resource territories after 1918, Germany lacked colonial sources of raw materials at a time when the colonial system was still intact and other countries surrounded themselves by high tariff walls. Only a turn to a policy of rampant imperialism and forceful expansion after 1938–1939 could ward off a return to the economic and financial disaster and social destitution of the Depression.

Germany plunged from a position on the world market before 1914 that was second only to Britain, and threatening to replace it, to almost a second- or third-class power. However, it remained the third greatest trade market in the world, even in its weakened state. The German business class chafed at the loss of its markets and hungered for a return to their previous position of growing dominance on the international market.

The United States, which had been a debtor nation before 1914, emerged from the war as a creditor nation. Up to 1930, at least, the United States was the world's greatest exporter of capital when it was overtaken by the U.K. The collapse of prices and trade volumes during the Great Depression, to almost one-half of their pre-war figures, and the trade wars of the 1930s between the Great Powers that followed in its wake, increased anxiety and tension over markets. As unemployment rose and social chaos threatened, trade took on an even greater importance.

As German trade with Britain foundered in 1934, British traders demanded the seizure of German assets to pay for German debts in the early thirties, but the Bank of England and its pro-German governor, Montagu Norman, the "City," British banks and Treasury Department officials averted a German financial default which could have had devastating consequences for the British bondholders. Protecting the British bondholders and avoiding a collapse of the lucrative British-German trade, and the departure of Germany from international trade, became the major preoccupation of Norman, the "City" and the Bank of England. Loans to Nazi German industry and banks enabled Germany to rearm. This fed into a policy of trying to avoid disturbing Hitler and causing a default by Germany that could destabilize international trade and produce unforeseen consequences. This financial domino theory, resting on the need to protect British bondholders and British-German trade, lacks credibility and merely adds a new dimension to the campaign to rehabilitate Chamberlain and his cronies underway since the conservative 1980s.

By the end of the 1930s, the economic stagnation of the era showed no sign of a letup after the "Roosevelt Depression" of 1938, and world capitalism continued to founder hopelessly. For the world market to overcome its malaise the whole structure of production and trade had to be expanded beyond the confines of the centuries-old colonial order against which it was straining, into the greatly expanded system of production after the Second World War. Whether this could have been done within capitalism without a world war can be debated, but certainly war, with its vastly expanded production capability, would return business to profitability and soak up the unemployed. This was recognized by Hermann Göring just before 1933 in statements to the German aircraft industry and John Maynard Keynes in Britain in 1939.[2] That the war ended the Depression is a truism known to every graduate student. By the end of the 1930s, as a result of the arms buildup in Europe and the United States, unemployment had almost disappeared or dramatically fallen a year or two later.

Eastern Europe as a Semi-Colony of the Great Powers

Already in the nineteenth century, Eastern Europe, particularly the Romanian Principalities and other parts of the Ottoman-held Balkan region, had become an important supplier of cotton, wheat, maize and other foodstuffs for an increasingly industrialized Western Europe and the object of political and economic struggle between the British and the Russian Empires during the Crimean War.[3] Similarly, competing Great Power political and economic nationalisms and meddling in the Balkans had much to do with the cause of World War I. In the 1920s and early 1930s, Eastern Europe became important to the Great Powers as a semi-colonial source of raw materials, particularly non-ferrous metals lacking in Western Europe, and foodstuffs, but also as an export market for their manufactured commodities. After the Bolshevik Revolution, the Western Powers and the United States shifted from investment in Russia to investment in large state loans to Eastern Europe and in the extractive industries such as Romanian oil, Hungarian bauxite, and copper, lead and zinc in Yugoslavia and foodstuffs throughout the Danubian basin. Moreover, the Eastern European region also became important in power-political terms. France after 1918 built a system of political alliances with the countries of the region — the Little Entente (Romania, Czechoslovakia and Yugoslavia) and the Balkan Entente

(Romania, Yugoslavia, Turkey and Greece) — to keep the nations defeated in World War I, particularly Germany and the Soviet Union, under control. By using Hungary and Bulgaria, its former wartime allies who had lost territory to the other states of Eastern Europe, Germany could divide the region and later pick off the "rabbit nations," as Churchill called them, one by one.

France and Germany tried successively to dominate the continent by various schemes to bring the Central and Eastern European countries under their aegis. (Some of these schemes — the Pan-European Union of Briand, the Tardieu Plan — were inchoate forerunners of the post World War II European Common Market.) Britain played its traditional balance of power role by throwing its weight against whichever side threatened to exert a dominating influence, first against France, then Germany, thereby protecting its political positions, investments and market interests in the region.

At first Britain in the mid-thirties tried to avoid an "implosion" inside Germany by not countering the German trade offensive in Eastern Europe but not entirely abandoning its investment interests there, thereby giving Germany's greatly "overripe" industry somewhere to send its exports. The political corollary to this policy was giving Hitler a "free hand in the east," which continued certainly down to March 15, 1939, and the end of the rump Czech state, and arguably beyond. Though cabinet discussions offering Germany a "free hand in the east" may have ceased after 1936, as one British historian (R. A. C. Parker) claims, this was only in a formal sense. Numerous informal meetings between Chamberlain's intermediaries (Leith-Ross, Wilson, among others) and German officials (Dirksen, Wohltat, Kordt) assured Berlin of British acceptance of German dominance in the east and the continuation of the policy of "the free hand in the east." Similar private discussions occurred between Halifax and American Ambassador Kennedy in which the Foreign Minister candidly admitted British acceptance of German predominance in the east, and along the same lines, between Bullitt and the French. The decision to grant Germany something like hegemony in the east was not merely Chamberlain's dissembling to gain time to rearm, but, more especially, to avoid any obligations in the east that could lead to war or that would prevent Germany from accomplishing its goals. After March 15, 1939, and the disappearance of Czechoslovakia, British public opinion and the British political class became frightened that after eliminating Poland, Hitler would turn west and attack France and Britain rather than the Soviet Union.

Later, after Munich, the Chamberlain government secretly hoped for a final German-Soviet Armageddon while seeking insurance in the Polish alliance to prevent German domination of the continent. Neither Chamberlain nor Halifax did anything to advance the critical negotiations during the summer of 1939 in favor of an alliance with the Soviet Union and Chamberlain at one point even hinted that he would resign rather than accept an alliance with the USSR. The latest historical study by Michael Jakara Carley confirms this. Once war broke out, a final ephemeral opportunity occurred during the winter of 1939–1940 to breathe life into the "free hand" policy and launch an anti-Bolshevik crusade with Germany under the guise of rendering assistance to Finland. But this failed to ignite for a whole variety of reasons.

Germany

With the arrival of Hitler and the National Socialists in power in 1933, the most ruthlessly aggressive wing of German imperialism moved to accomplish what it had failed to achieve in the First World War: German imperialism's dream of expanding into the Baltic region and the steppe-lands of the Ukraine. German expansionism and the *Lebensraum* idea did not spring full-blown from the fevered brain of Hitler, but was a part of the ideological stock-in-trade of ideas undergirding the pre–World War I German imperial state and held in common with its business, military and bureaucratic elite. In this sense A. J. P. Taylor's characterization of Hitler "in principle and doctrine" as a traditional German statesman, who simply wanted to make Germany the greatest power in Europe, was correct, but, in his actions and deeds, he was the most brutally aggressive of racialists.

Hitler clearly understood that the instrument of market competition offered little hope of success when the other Great Powers had a virtual lock on foreign trade, raw materials and financial resources against which Germany could hardly prevail. Moreover, this strategy did not fit the Darwinian and racialist martial ideology in which he habitually thought.

The story of German rearmament, through which Hitler sought to place a gun at the head of Germany's erstwhile foes of the Great War and regain the first rank of World Powers, is now well known. The conventional wisdom is that, considering the wrongs done Germany by the Versailles Treaty coupled with the guilt feelings of the British upper class leadership, Hitler's demands did not seem outrageous. He could at first claim that by breaking the Locarno Agreement and occupying the demilitarized Rhineland and later through a plebiscite reannexing the Saarland, he was merely taking back formerly German territory. Later, facilitated by the tortured logic of the era accepted by the British and French leaders, Hitler could justify annexing Austria and the Sudetenland, areas populated by Germans though not previously part of the German Reich. But after Hitler's seizure of the purely Czech provinces on March 15, 1938, this fiction was no longer credible. By then both London and Paris knew that Hitler did not intend to stop there and that either Poland or France would be attacked next.

Undoubtedly British and French naiveté and appeasement of Hitler could be explained by the unspoken hope and expectation that he would ultimately turn east and attack the Soviet Union and destroy Communism. For the Chamberlain government's supporters and the "Munichois" crowd around Foreign Minister Georges Bonnet, Stalin and Soviet Communism rather than Hitler were the chief malefactors of mischief, a fact which was well known to the World War II generation but has been somewhat forgotten since.

What is perhaps less known is that the rearmament program, which Hitler ordered to accelerate in 1936 to prepare for war, had become well-nigh voracious and was consuming roughly about 23% of total national income by 1939, raising apprehensions that only a slowing up of rearmament — which Hitler adamantly rejected — or further aggressive expansion could stave off financial collapse. On the eve of the Austrian Anschluss, Germany's financial reserves were exhausted; again six months later the same problem resurfaced on the eve of the Munich settlement and once again just before the German attack on Poland. Without a slowing of rearmament, the future offered only the unacceptable prospect of inflationary pressures, economic stagnation and a return to the high unemployment and social instability of the final years of the Weimar Republic. But despite the success of the regime in returning the country to higher levels of employment — largely through the rearmament boom and longer working hours — the greatest share of the national income went to industry and the business class rather than the working class. How rife dissatisfaction was against this fact is moot, but according to historians Detlev Peukert and Tim Mason, in the mid-1930s repression increased and 15,000 people were arrested.

Hitler, in fact, admitted in his May 1939 conference and on the eve of the attack on Poland during the August 22, 1939, conference with the Wehrmacht leaders that without breaking into other countries and seizing their resources they could hold out only a few more years at best.

I have documented through sources like Göring and others, as well as copious trade and other economic data, that by the eve of the attack on Poland, Germany could no longer pay for imports of raw materials and foodstuffs from the Southeastern countries and elsewhere and that the Third Reich's parlous economic situation could only be relieved by a *"raub krieg."* We must then conclude that economic forces certainly were instrumental in impelling Hitler to attack Poland, but that these economic pressures and his own imperialist program for expansionist aggression were complementary as the immediate causes of the war. It would be a mistake to dismiss the "programmatic" interpretation out of hand as the "functionalist" historians have done. Hitler did not have a step-by-step plan for conquest, but he did espouse the traditional Wilhelmian nationalist plan of German imperialistic expansionism into Eastern Europe. It is an irony of history with all the hubris and retribution of a Greek tragedy that Hitler's decision to rearm set in motion a whole panoply of forces — economic, financial, political and social — that led to an historical entrapment ending in war.

Germany's economic difficulties were, of course, well known to Britain which arranged for overt and covert bailouts of the German economy by the City, Bank of England and British banks down to 1939 in various forms and guises to protect its investors and maintain market equilibrium and in hopes of future German good behavior toward the Western Powers.

Great Britain

With the advent of Hitler, German demands for a change in the international status quo placed the British on the horns of a dilemma: whether or not to yield to these demands to avoid an implosion inside the Third Reich and accelerating pressures to expand into other states. By the mid-1930s Germany withdrew from the European and American market, where its exports were shut out and it lacked currency to pay for imports, and greatly expanded its clearing agreements with the Southeastern European and Latin American countries, bartering its manufactured goods for raw materials. These successful German trade incursions raised British and American hackles and added to British-American trade rivalries in the Western hemisphere. Britain found itself caught between two fires: a rising American empire and a strident German imperialism seeking retribution and increased market share.

Instead of confronting Germany, Britain shifted from "the thorny path of trade in the Southeast" to competing with Germany for the more lucrative Northeastern European, Scandinavian and Baltic region. Despite indignant cries of "Danegeld!" in the cabinet, the British did not challenge the mid-1930s German trade offensive into Southeastern Europe and by 1938 the region, in the admission of Chamberlain, had become a virtual German "dominion." The British appeared satisfied that Germany had found a market for its export and import needs, sanctioning German economic but not political domination of the region. France, riven by internal problems and defeatism in its upper classes, increasingly became the tail on the British kite supporting Chamberlain's policy of yielding to German demands to avoid war.

In the late 1930s, Chamberlain let the French know that Britain would not support France unless it were directly attacked by Germany or if France, acting under the Franco-Soviet Pact of 1935, became embroiled in a war with Germany.

Throughout the 1930s, a major obsession of the British upper class was hatred and fear of communism, against which Hitler's Germany represented a "bulwark" — that awful cliché — and for whom a war with Germany seemed to mean the bolshevization of Europe and its demise as a class. In the acute observation of A. L. Rowse, they placed the interests of their class above that of the nation.

A steady stream of leading British visitors to Hitler from Lloyd George, Lord Lothian, Halifax and Wilson hinted broadly — and directly at times — that Britain would not hinder German domination of Central and Eastern Europe and German expansion into the Ukraine. Up to the Munich Conference of September 1938, the British people, dreading a new conflict, supported Chamberlain's policy of giving in to Hitler's demands, but after the German annexation of the Czech provinces of Bohemia and Moravia, the British public turned against any new German territorial demands. Halifax led the cabinet into a new policy of encircling Germany by propping up the Eastern European countries through political guarantees, loans and trade, some of it "political trade." However, Chamberlain, his alter ego Wilson and occasionally Halifax continued to pursue a secret counter-policy of assuring Hitler, through various private agents, proposals and projects down to the eve of the war, that they favored the negotiated rectification of Germany's territorial demands in the east and were not, in fact, opposed to German domination of Central and Eastern Europe. Even after 1939 a shadowy group of conservatives, conservative-imperialists and pro-fascists, composed of high industrialists, bankers, government officials and members of Parliament pressed for a negotiated peace and an end to the war.

Thus, British policy after March 15, 1939, was a devious, bifurcated one: Chamberlain's knowing winks and assurances to Berlin over the head of the cabinet — a more open appeasement line would have faced a cabinet revolt or the fall of the government — encouraging Germany's eastward expansion and at the same time reinforcing opposition to German expansion in Romania and the other Eastern European states by political guarantees of trade for unmarketable goods, loans and armament exports.

The hasty British decision to oppose further German expansion in the east through the Polish guarantee stemmed from fear of an eventual German attack in the west and of losing the support of their American and Balkan allies. But the Polish guarantee, despite its shortcomings, may have accomplished more than the British government had really wanted. In one sense it was a paper guarantee designed merely to give the impression of checkmating Hitler while not really intending to do so, as the British military candidly admitted and as Hitler also realized when he scoffed at the paltry loan of eight million pounds for armaments offered to Poland.

In another sense it brought England into the war especially after Hitler broke the checkmate of the Polish guarantee by signing the Nazi-Soviet Pact of August 1939. Similarly, the Leith-Ross mission to Romania in the spring of 1939 offered the beleaguered Romanian government of King Carol a small loan for armament purchases and some trade, barely enough to encourage resistance to the Germans. In neighboring Yugoslavia, Britain continued to maintain trade ties and offered a minimum amount of armaments to the government of Regent Prince Paul against German trade and political pressures.

Once war erupted, the British tried to counter Berlin's efforts to force Prince Paul into the Axis by shoring up the Balkan Pact (Romania, Yugoslavia, Greece and Turkey) against the Axis Powers and by broadening it to include Bulgaria. When Paul, terrified of an Axis attack after the Italian seizure of Albania in April 1939, succumbed to the pressures and agreed to join the Axis by signing the Tripartite Pact, his government was overthrown by a conspiracy of Serb officers on March 27, 1941, with the complicity of British intelligence under circumstances still not completely understood.

The United States

The strong New Deal emphasis on trade and increased market share in the 1930s, as a way out of the Depression, defined American policy in that era. The United States had lost a larger share of trade by the advent of the New Deal than any of the other Great Powers, with the possible exception of Germany. To regain markets for its swollen surpluses, it aggressively pursued a policy of free trade under the Reciprocal Trade Agreements, a seemingly altruistic and benign policy which masked its own ambitions to cut into British and German trade in Europe, Latin America and elsewhere. While complaining about the high tariffs around the U.S., Washington maintained high tariffs against the exports of Britain, Germany and other states. The Roosevelt government took a jaundiced view of both British preferential trade and the German clearing system which excluded American goods from Britain, the empire countries and Southeastern Europe, and moved to undermine both. American distaste for German fascism, its brutal anti-Semitism and Hitler's seizure of Austria and Czechoslovakia further compounded

the trade conflict with Germany. The rearmament-induced financial difficulties of Britain gave the American State Department an opportunity to
press the Chamberlain government for tariff reduction as the price for an
Anglo-American treaty aimed against Hitler and the German clearing system.
Though the treaty was eventually signed, too late to have any real effect, it left
some British embitterment in its wake which may have further determined
Chamberlain and the British government to seek an agreement with Hitler.

The American State Department tried to prevent Southeastern Europe
from becoming a German-dominated trading zone by granting Czechoslovakia most-favored-nation status for its goods on the American market,
while denying it to Germany for allegedly discriminatory trade practices
against American goods. This was done despite discrimination against American goods on the Czechoslovak market. By the end of the 1930s trade relations
between Nazi Germany and the United States had become acrimonious.

In the 1930s Roosevelt at first favored appeasing Nazi Germany; later,
growing impatient and contemptuous of Chamberlain's policy of yielding
Central and Eastern Europe to Hitler, which would have excluded American goods from the region, Roosevelt turned against appeasement. Through
its diplomats abroad and American public opinion, the United States undoubtedly influenced the British decision to guarantee Polish sovereignty.
But American isolationism tied the hands of Roosevelt and prevented any
direct role in the conflict on the side of Britain and France until 1941. In
general, America's attitude toward Britain, France and the other Powers was
generally a concerned watchfulness until 1941.

France

After the First World War, France's position declined both as an exporter of
capital for overseas investment and in trade turnover, paradoxically while
it was the largest holder of gold in the early 1930s. France's prestige after
the war was great but in actuality it was a weak and declining Great Power.
By the mid-1930s internal dissension between capital and labor, the French
right's hatred of the Third Republic and its sympathies for fascism and the
defeatism of its politicians and generals led France to vacillate between bouts
of resistance and apathetic resignation toward Hitler. After the last attempt
to revive the French system of alliances by the visit of Yvon Delbos to Eastern
Europe in 1937, France, its generals clinging to a fossilized defense strategy,
its leaders weak and disaffected, wearied of its ties to Poland and the Balkan
states. France's own considerable agriculture prevented it from absorbing the
agrarian imports of its eastern allies and eroded its trade and influence in
Eastern Europe.

Apprehensive of Mussolini's designs on French territory (Nice, Corsica
and Tunisia) and the possibility of a German attack, and not entirely trust-
ful of its Soviet ally, in the mid-1930s France increasingly sought security
through dependence upon its stronger British ally. France adopted Chamberlain's policy of giving way to Hitler's threats and French Foreign Minister
Bonnet shortly after Munich signed the Franco-German Agreement of De-

cember 6, 1938, arguably recognizing Eastern Europe as a German sphere of influence. Though Bonnet denied this later, his denial is not convincing.

Italy

The weakest of the Great Powers, Italy was barely a Great Power, severely lacking in raw materials, compelling it to pursue an imperialist policy in Africa and Eastern Europe. To counter the lingering economic malaise of Italian fascism in the late 1920s and into the 1930s and to pursue his grandiose dreams of greatness and empire, Mussolini invaded Ethiopia with the secret encouragement of Britain and France who preferred to see him bogged down there rather than creating problems in Europe. Italian trade with Eastern Europe fell rapidly after the Ethiopian affair and Germany replaced it in most Eastern European countries as a major trading partner. Mussolini vacillated between the Western Powers and Germany, coveting Romania's oil and Yugoslavia's non-ferrous metals, blowing hot and cold to annex Croatia with the help of the Croatian separatists. After Italy joined the Axis in 1939, though urged by Hitler to attack Yugoslavia in August 1939 on the eve of the war, Mussolini hesitated until Germany attacked France in 1940. Jealous of Hitler's masterful victories, Mussolini's own imperialist ambitions in the Balkans were in conflict with Germany's for the resources of the region and he tried sub-rosa unsuccessfully to head a coalition of East European powers to check German domination there. Italy and its leader Mussolini gradually degenerated into a docile satellite of Hitler.

Final Conclusions

Clashing imperialist interests of the Great Powers over markets played out in Eastern Europe and Latin America and other global markets. The conflict in interests expressed itself in political and ideological forms over territory, markets and political hegemony. Normally the struggle between the Great Powers would have been almost a replay of the same imperialist conflicts that brought on World War I except for two new factors: fascism and communism. Germany's demands for the return of lost territory merited consideration, viewed from that epoch's purely imperialist context, had Germany not been a fascist country with aspirations to enslave other countries under that virulent ideology. Thus, the Western European and American imperialisms became the lesser of two evils and the peoples of those states had to unite with the Western Powers and the Soviet Union to fight against fascism in a just war for self-preservation. If Nazi Germany had not expanded beyond its borders, its fascist ideology notwithstanding, there never would have been a Second World War.

After the Bolshevik Revolution of 1917 the political equation changed. Besides Nazi Germany, the Soviet Communist state also had to be considered. Unfortunately, the British and French governments, abhorring communism more than fascism, preferred to mollify Hitler, first sacrificing Austria and Czechoslovakia, and to ally with Poland rather than with the Soviet Union, drawing Germany toward the east and conflict with the Soviet Union. The great experiences of the Bolshevik Revolution and its aftermath had not yet been put behind and sufficiently absorbed for the Western Powers to understand that in allying with the Soviet Union they were allying with a country rather than an ideology.

The world market system, Western European colonialism and its North American variant had reached the end of its tether in the 1930s and there needed to be a restructuring of the world economy that would have siphoned off economic stresses by absorbing the era's greatly expanded production since 1914. That restructuring occurred only during and after the Second World War. It is doubtful if this could have been done on a massive enough scale through state supported projects such as those carried out somewhat timidly and insufficiently, it seems to me, by the Roosevelt Administration — but fears of creating a kind of state socialism limited those endeavors. The economic and social stagnation in which the world lay mired for over a decade could not easily be overcome without a redistribution of wealth and the social transformation that this implied would have encountered too many entrenched interests. The deficit spending for rearmament production necessitated by the war vastly expanded the scope and structures of capitalism and solved that problem. Thus, the Second World War occurred not as a stumbling into war by the diplomats and statesmen acting like blind cuttlefish at the bottom of the sea, misreading one another's signs and signals, as A. J. P. Taylor would have us believe, though there was plenty of that. This perverse reading of history as Greek tragedy offers us little more fare than history as accident and ultimately is not satisfying. Nor did the war have mechanistic "programmatic" or "intentionalist" origins with Hitler as demiurge according to *Mein Kampf*. This is too simplistic. Nor was it only internal and institutional problems inside the Third Reich propelling Hitler into adventures abroad as the "functionalists" believed. This would ignore the other states opposing Hitler and their interests and reinvokes Taylor's blind mice thesis, substituting many random and subordinate internal and institutional causes for primary causes, completely ignoring the conflict between the expansionist ambitions of German imperialism and the more sated Western colonial states in general. It was an agenda driven by the struggle for international hegemony on the world market, fought out in Eastern Europe by the Great Powers like ferrets in a hole. In this contest Eastern Europe played its tragic and fateful historic role of apple of discord between the Great Powers.

A Postscript

During the 1930s the exiled German Socialists provided a high level analysis of the Nazi regime's increasingly precarious economic position. Their chief economic specialist, Rudolf Hilferding, who coined the term "finance capital," poured out over 240 articles. Though Hilferding's exegetic and analytic reference and rhetoric were Marxist, he and his party had long since become reformist. His recent excellent biographer, Professor William Smaldone, writes that Hilferding earlier believed the state in the parliamentary era enjoyed a neutral position, independent of class domination.[1] Then, after wavering, he concluded again in exile that the state in the post-war era assumed a dominant position "in which the state apparatus...took possession and restructured society as it saw fit."[2]

Hilferding's analysis of the Nazi state after 1933 is astonishingly accurate and confirms most of my own findings. It was only a matter of time, Hilferding warned, before rearmament either destroyed the economy or resulted in "total war" for the goal of "living space."[3]

In Hilferding's 1936 article, "Schacht's Headache — Raw Materials Problem Unsolved — the Unstable Debt Grows," he describes Schacht's struggle to get raw materials, the growing debt problem, the exhaustion of reserves and the looming inflation.[4] In an August 1936 article, "Hitler's Drive to the Balkans," he describes the Nazi economic expansion toward the Balkans as a hinterland for the German economy, exploiting Balkan copper, bauxite, etc., critical for the war industry.[5] By then, Hilferding notes, the older "finance capital" of the liberal state collapsed, in which capital is used to develop underdeveloped areas and is replaced by a new kind of total state which uses its power to cyclically expand and consolidate, a plunder economy, which can only be maintained by constant expansion.[6] By late 1937 Hilferding noted in "The Prospects for German Exports — The 1936 Export Battle [is] Lost," that the import increase of 1936 over 1935 was only 1.7%, forcing subsidization and dumping of exports and vast debts to foreign creditors. All these contradictions, he concludes, compelled a slowing down of the war economy and an end to a compulsory economy (*Zwangwirtschaft*), impossible because of power-political reasons.[7]

A November 1938 article emphasized that Hitler had achieved Germany's World War I imperialist aims and that Western appeasement to deflect the Nazis to the east will fail and only accelerate the process of conquest. His analysis that the West had totally underestimated the importance of the German position in the Balkans we now know is not correct, as Britain and France did that only to avoid an explosion and war, but later after Munich blocked Hitler's expansion there.[8]

Notes

Abbreviations

BFO	British Foreign Office
CAB	British Cabinet Meetings
CP	British Cabinet Papers
DBFP	Documents on British Foreign Policy
DDF	Documents Diplomatiques Français
DDI	Documenti Diplomatici Italiani
DGFP	Documents on German Foreign Policy
DPFP	Documents on Polish Foreign Policy
DVP	Dokumenty Vneshnei Politiki SSSR
FRUS	Foreign Relations of the United States
IMT	International Military Tribunal
PPA	Prince Paul's Archive
PSF	Roosevelt Library, President's Secretary's File
PRO/BT	Public Record Office, Board of Trade
PRO/T	Public Record Office, Treasury Department
UGFOD	Unpublished German Foreign Office Documents

Introduction

1. Gerhard L. Weinberg, *Germany, Hitler and World War II* (New York, 1995).

2. Rudolf Augstein et al., *"Historikerstreit": die Dokumentation der Kontroverse um die Einzigartigkeit der nationalsozialistischen Judenvernichtung* (Munich, 1987).

3. John Lukacs, *The Hitler of History* (New York, 1997), p. 2.

4. Dietmar Petzina, *Autarkiepolitik im Dritten Reich 1933 bis 1939* (Stuttgart, 1968); Hans-Jürgen Schröder, "Die deutsche Südosteuropapolitik 1929–1936 Zur Kontinuität deutscher Aussenpolitik in der Weltwirtschaftskrise," *Geschichte u. Gesellschaft* 2, no. 1 (1976): 14; and also by Schröder, *Deutschland u. die Vereinigten Staaten 1933–1939* (Wiesbaden, 1970).

5. Timothy W. Mason, *Arbeiterklasse und Volksgemeinschaft: Dokumente und Materiallien zur deutsche arbeiterpolitik 1936–1939* (Opladen, 1975).

6. W. Wheeler-Bennett, *Munich: Prologue to Tragedy* (London, 1948); and L. B. Namier, *Diplomatic Prelude 1938–1939* (London, 1948). For a survey and overview of the numerous studies on appeasement see Paul M. Kennedy, "The Tradition of Appeasement in British Foreign Policy 1865–1939," *British Journal of International Studies* 2 (1976): 195–215; and also by the same author " 'Appeasement' and British Defence Policy in the Inter-war Years," *British Journal of International Studies* 4 (1978): 161–177.

7. Martin Gilbert and Richard Gott, *The Appeasers* (Boston, 1963).

8. William R. Rock, *Appeasement on Trial: The British Foreign Office and its Critics 1938–1939* (Hamden, 1966) and *British Appeasement in the 1930s* (London, 1977).

9. John Charmley, *Chamberlain and the Lost Peace* (London, 1989).

10. R. A. C. Parker, *Chamberlain and Appeasement: British Policy and the Coming of the Second World War* (New York, 1993).

11. Bernd-Jürgen Wendt, *Economic Appeasement: Handel und Finanz in der britischen Deutschlandspolitik 1933–1939* (Düsseldorf, 1971).

12. David Kaiser E., *Economic Diplomacy and the Origins of the Second World War 1930–1939* (Princeton, 1980); and William A. Grenzebach, "Germany's Informal Empire in East Central Europe" (Ph.D. Thesis, Brandeis University, 1980).

Chapter 1

1. For foreign trade and capital exports as a "vent for surplus" and a stimulus to production, see Arthur I. Bloomfield, "British Thought on the Influence of Foreign Trade and Investment on Growth, 1800–1880," *History of Political Economy* 13, no. 1: 95–120. On the problem of unequal trade, see Samir Amin, *Unequal Development* (New York, 1976) and *Imperialism and Unequal Development* (New York, 1977).

2. Karl Polanyi, *The Great Transformation: The Political and Economic Origins of our Time* (paperback ed., Boston, 1957), p. 3, and chaps. 1 and 2, pp. 274ff.

3. Bertil Ohlin, *The Course and Phases of the World Economic Depression* (repr. New York, 1972), p. 28.

4. David Thompson (ed.), *The New Cambridge Modern History: The Era of Violence 1898–1945,* vol. 12 (London, 1960), p. 28. However, in the era from 1923 to 1929 England's exportation of capital is slightly greater than that of the U.S. at $3,133 billion and $2,864 billion. See W. Arthur Lewis, *Economic Survey, 1919–1939* (London, 1969), p. 31.

5. René Erbe, *Die nationalsozialistische Wirtschaftspolitik, 1933–1939 im Lichte der modernen Theorie* (Zurich, 1958), pp. 17–18.

6. *New Cambridge Modern History,* vol. 12, p. 36.

7. This is discussed in great detail in the work of David Abraham, *The Collapse of the Weimar Republic* (New York, 1986). The labor intensive and capital intensive industries conflict that led to Hitler's support by the latter is not a new thesis and is discussed in the 1930s study by Daniel Guérin, *Fascism and Big Business* (repr., New York, 1973), pp. 24ff.

8. Arthur Marwick, *Britain in the Century of Total War: Peace and Social Change 1900– 1967* (Boston, 1968), p. 10.

9. Andrew Glyn and Bob Sutcliffe, *Capitalism in Crisis* (published in England as *British Capitalism, Workers and the Profit Squeeze*) (New York, 1972), p. 19. According to another source which gives a somewhat lower figure, the United Kingdom's total world manufacturing share in 1880 was 22.9% of total world production, shrinking to 13.6% by 1913, while its world trade went from 23.2% in 1880 to 14.1% in 1911–1913. See Paul Kennedy, *The Rise and Fall of the Great Powers* (New York, 1984), p. 228.

10. Glyn and Sutcliffe, *Capitalism in Crisis,* p. 19.

11. Ibid.

12. Ibid., pp. 20–21.

13. Ibid., p. 22.

14. Ibid., p. 24.

15. A. J. H. Latham, *The Depression and the Developing World, 1914–1939* (London, 1981), pp. 15f. Britain in 1914 had about $4,950 million invested in the developing world, 65% of total foreign investment there: India and Ceylon, $1,850 million; China, $600 million; Africa (South Africa and Rhodesia) $1,750 million; with $400 million for the remainder south of the Sahara. Ibid., p. 16.

16. *The New Cambridge Modern History,* vol. 12, pp. 28f.

17. Latham, *The Depression and the Developing World, 1914–1939,* p. 17.

18. Ibid., p. 89.

19. Keith Hutchison, *The Decline and Fall of British Capitalism* (London, 1951, repr. 1966), pp. 251ff.

20. *The New Cambridge Modern History,* vol. 12, p. 33. Production in 1929 equals 100 in each case.

21. Kennedy, *The Rise and Fall of the Great Powers,* pp. 282f.

22. Ibid., p. 283.

23. For national comparisons, see Eckart Teichert, *Autarkie und Grossraumwirtschaft in Deutschland 1930–1939: Aussenwirtschaftspolitische Konzeptionen zwischen Wirtschaftskrise und Zweitem Weltkrieg* (Munich, 1984), p. 15, n. 15.

24. Kennedy, *The Rise and Fall of the Great Powers,* p. 307 and n. 83, citing Williamson Murray, *The Change in the European Balance of Power, 1938–1939: The Path to Ruin* (Princeton, N.J., 1984), p. 15.

25. For the struggle over gold in the 1930s, see Ian M. Drummond, *The Floating Pound and the Sterling Area, 1931–1939* (Cambridge, 1981), passim. See also Polanyi, *The Great Transformation,* pp. 23ff. Polanyi writes: "While at the end of the Great War nineteenth century

ideals were paramount, and their influence dominated the following decade, by 1940 every vestige of the international crisis had disappeared and, apart from a few enclaves, the nations were living in an entirely new international setting.... The root cause of the crisis...was the threatening collapse of the international economic system. It had only haltingly functioned since the turn of the century, and the Great War and the treaties [i.e., the Versailles Treaty and the other treaties for Germany's defeated allies—author] had wrecked it finally." Ibid., p. 23.

26. Drummond, *The Floating Pound and the Sterling Area, 1931–1939*, p. 256.

27. Teichert, *Autarkie und Grossraumwirtschaft in Deutschland 1930–1939: Aussenpolitische Konzeptionen zwischen Wirtschaftkrise und Zweitem Weltkrieg*, p. 33.

28. Ibid.

29. For discussions of Posse's and Schacht's ideas see ibid., pp. 105–128.

30. Andrew J. Crozier, *Appeasement and Germany's Last Bid for Colonies* (New York, 1988), p. 176.

31. Ibid., pp. 68f.

32. Ibid., p. 177.

33. *U.S. State Dept.*, Division of Western European Affairs, memo, Phillip Adams, American consul, Canada, to State Department, March 5, 1930. T-1252/R-1.

34. *U.S. State Dept.*, William Phillips, Undersecretary of State, Memorandum on conversation with Lord Lothian, October 11, 1934. T-1252/711.41/280/0214.

35. *U.S. State Dept.*, Raymond Atherton, Chief of the European Division, to London, February 1932, T-1252/1/711.41/237/0062.

36. *U.S. State Dept.*, Wilson to Sec. of State, October 3, 1932, T-1252/1/711.41/255/0099.

37. *National Archives, Franklin D. Roosevelt Library*, Hyde Park, N.Y., President's Secretarial File, Bullitt Papers, Bullitt to President Roosevelt, June 5, 1934 (hereafter Roosevelt Library *PSF*).

38. *U.S. State Dept.*, Davis from Naval Conference of 1935, November 14, 1934, T-1252/711.4/281/0223.

39. *U.S. State Dept.*, February 9, 1935, T-1252/1/711.41/293.

40. *U.S. State Dept.*, Atherton to Sec. of State, March 20, 1935, T-1252/1/711.41/299.

41. *U.S. State Dept.*, letter to Roosevelt, Charles Strutt, March 13, 1935, T-1252/1/711.41/302/0296.

42. *U.S. State Dept.*, Jay Pierpont Moffat, Chief of Div. of Western European Affairs, May 18, 1935, T-1252/1/711.41/305. Lord Hailsham, Sec. of War, made a similar address to the Canadian Women's Club. *U.S. State Dept.*, London, to Atherton, May 6, 1935, T-1252/1/711.41/305.

43. *U.S. Dept. of State*, London Embassy to Sec. of State, May 28, 1935, T-1252/711.41/306.

44. *U.S. Dept. of State*, American Consul, Darien, China to Edwin L. Neville, American chargé ad Interim, Tokyo, August 21, 1935, T-1252/711.41/306.

45. *U.S. Dept. of State*, Norman Davis, memo, August 8, 1935, conversation between Sir Ronald Lindsay, the British ambassador to the U.S., James Dunn and Davis, T-1252/1/711.41/313.

46. *U.S. Dept. of State*, Jay Pierpont Moffat, memo, to State Department Division of Western European Affairs, July 14, 1934, T-1252/1711.41/275/0193.

47. For details, see Scott Newton, *Profits of Peace: The Political Economy of Anglo-German Appeasement* (Oxford, 1996), pp. 58 ff., 112–113.

48. Ibid., p. 72.

49. Ibid., p. 92.

50. Ibid., p. 98.

51. *U.S. Dept. of State*, Atherton, London, August 20, 1935, T-1252/1/711.41/314.

52. Cordell Hull, *The Memoirs of Cordell Hull* (New York, 1948), p. 530. For a full account of the negotiations surrounding the Anglo-American Trade Agreement of 1938, see Arthur W. Schatz, "The Anglo-American Trade Agreement and Cordell Hull's search for Peace 1936–1938," *Journal of American History* 57 (June 1970): 85–103. See also Richard A. Harrison, "The Runciman Visit to Washington in January 1937," *Canadian Journal of History* 19 (August 1984): 217–239. Others see hegemonial ambition in American commercial policy in the 1930s. See C. A. MacDonald, *The United States, Britain and Appeasement 1936–1939* (New York,

1981). American policy and U.S. commercial rivalry with Britain is covered more fully in chap. 14.

53. *Roosevelt Library, PSF,* Bullitt, Paris, to Hull, January 13, 1937, Doc. 751.62/387.

54. Ibid.

55. *Roosevelt Library, PSF,* Bullitt, Paris, to Hull, April 29, 1937.

56. Ibid.

57. *Roosevelt Library, PSF,* Bullitt, Paris, to Hull, tels. for April 29, 30, May 1, and May 20, 1937, Docs. 740.00/156, sec. 1 and 2, 740.00/158, 740.00/178.

58. *Roosevelt Library, PSF,* Bullitt, Paris, to Hull, April 30 and May 20, 1937. Box 18, Doc. 740.00/157 and 740.00/178.

59. For Mason's defense against his detractors, see Tim Mason, "The Domestic Dynamics of Nazi Conquests" in Thomas Childers and Jane Caplan (eds.), *Reevaluating the Third Reich* (New York, 1993), pp. 161–189. For a final restatement of Mason's position and R. J. Overy's rebuttal, see Tim Mason and R. J. Overy, "Debate: Germany, 'domestic crisis' and war in 1939" in Patrick Finney (ed.), *Origins of the Second World War,* chap. 4, pp. 90–112. This is an edited extract from *Past and Present* 122 (1989): 205–240. Mason cites David Kaiser as arriving at the "conclusion that the Third Reich's foreign trade position became critical in 1939, leaving the regime with a choice between military conquest and a curtailment of the rearmament drive." David E. Kaiser, *Economic Diplomacy and the Origins of the Second World War: Germany, Britain, France and Eastern Europe, 1930–1939* (Princeton, 1980), esp. pp. 258 and 282.

60. Childers and Caplan (eds.), *Reevaluating the Third Reich,* pp. 180f.

61. *Roosevelt Library, PSF,* Bullitt, Paris, to Hull, May 20, 1937, Doc. 740.00/178.

62. *Roosevelt Library, PSF,* Bullitt, Paris, to Hull, September 8, 1937, Doc. 962.00/6401.

63. *Roosevelt Library, PSF,* Bullitt, Paris, to Hull, September 26, 1938. Doc. 760F/62/1124.

64. *Roosevelt Library, PSF,* Bullitt, Paris, to Hull, September 26, 1938. Doc. 760F/62/1125.

65. *Roosevelt Library, PSF,* Bullitt, Paris, to Hull, October 3, 1938, Doc. 760F/62/1429.

66. For the full statement, see G. M. Gilbert, *Nuremberg Diary* (New York, 1947), p. 91. Also quoted in Leonard Mosley, *The Reich Marshal: A Biography of Hermann Göring* (New York, 1974), pp. 276–277.

67. *Roosevelt Library, PSF,* Bullitt, Paris, October 3, 1938, Doc. 700 F.62/1429.

68. John A. Lukacs, *The Great Powers and Eastern Europe* (New York, 1953), p. 133, and note 7; the Harvey quote is cited in Clement Leibovitz, *The Chamberlain-Hitler Deal* (Edmonton, Alberta, 1993), p. 112 citing Oliver Harvey, *The Diplomatic Diaries of Oliver Harvey, 1937–1940* (London, 1958), p. 222.

69. R. A. C. Parker, *Chamberlain and Appeasement: British Policy and the Coming of the Second World War* (New York, 1993), p. 318.

70. Cf. the two opposite conclusions of the British writer Parker who flatly denies that Chamberlain gave Hitler a "free hand in the east" and Leibovitz who believes Chamberlain gave Hitler a green light to expand to the east. See Parker, *Chamberlain and Appeasement: British Policy and the Coming of the Second World War,* pp. 180, 347. See Leibovitz, *The Chamberlain-Hitler Deal* for the period up to and including Munich, on "a free hand in the east" in British policy, see chaps. 10, 11, 12, pp. 223–363.

71. On Williams's arguments quoted here, see William Appleman Williams, *The Tragedy of American Diplomacy* (New York, 1962), pp. 176–192.

72. Larry William Fuchser, *Neville Chamberlain and Appeasement* (New York, 1982), p. 15.

73. Keith Hutchison, *The Decline and Fall of British Capitalism,* p. 256.

74. Ibid., p. 258 quoting Keith Feiling, *The Life of Neville Chamberlain* (London, 1946), p. 229.

75. Kaiser, *Economic Diplomacy and the Origins of the Second World War: Germany, Britain, France and Eastern Europe, 1930–1939,* pp. 84–85.

76. Ibid., pp. 90–92, 98–99.

77. *Documents on British Foreign Policy,* Series 2, vol. 1, Doc. 195 (hereafter *DBFP*).

78. Hans-Jürgen Schröder, "Die deutsche Südosteuropapolitik 1929–1936 Zur Kontinuität deutscher Aussenpolitik in der Weltwirtschaftskrise" *Geschichte u. Gesellschaft* 2, no. 1 (1976): 14.

79. *DBFP*, 2, I, Docs., 189, 193, 195. Earlier, Austin Chamberlain in 1925 described his admiration: "Briand has almost taken my breath away by his liberality, his conciliatoriness, his strong and manifest desire to promote peace" while the German attitude had been "niggling, provocative, crooked." Anthony Adamthwaite, *France and the Coming of the Second World War 1936–1939* (London, 1977), p. 28.

80. Ibid., p. 29.

81. Schröder, "Die deutsche Südosteuropapolitik 1929–1936," p. 8.

82. Dirk Stegmann, "Mitteleuropa, 1925–1934: Zum Problem der Kontinuität deutscher Aussenhandelspolitik" in Dirk Stegmann, et al., *Industrielle Gesellschaft u. Politisches System* (Bonn, 1978), pp. 203–221.

83. Ivan T. Berend and György Ránki, *Economic Development in East-Central Europe in the 19th and 20th Centuries* (New York and London, 1974), p. 232.

84. Ibid., p. 237.

85. Ibid., p. 236.

86. Stegmann, "Mitteleuropa 1925–1934," p. 213.

87. "German economists and industrialists alike were convinced that British, French and American policies were such that Germany would have to depend more on its Danube trade." Abraham, *Collapse of the Weimar Republic*, p. 227.

88. Ibid., p. 224, n. 111.

89. Thomas Parke Hughes, "Technological Momentum in History: Hydrogenation in Germany 1898–1933," *Past and Present* 44 (August 1969): 51, n. 11.

90. Ibid., p. 117, n. 28.

91. Ibid., p. 123.

92. Stegmann, "Mitteleuropa 1925–1934," p. 217.

93. For Hitler's Malthusian rationale for Lebensraum as enunciated in a 1927 statement to the industrialists, see Henry A. Turner, Jr., "Hitler's Secret Pamphlet for Industrialists 1927," *Journal of Modern History* 40, no. 3 (September 1968): 365–374. For Hitler's 1932 Düsseldorf speech to the industrialists voicing similar aggressive expansionist sentiments, see Jeremy Noakes and Geoffry Pridham (eds.), *Documents on Nazism 1919–1945* (New York, 1975), pp. 124f.

94. Schröder, "Die deutsche Südosteuropapolitik u. die Reaktion der Angelsächischen Mächte," p. 357. The Czech leader, Beneš, to counter the German-Austrian union which he rejected, proposed a Central European tariff union of most of the regions' states including Poland for a time. It complemented a French plan, for France and the industrialized states to relieve the agrarian crisis in Eastern Europe, by taking cereals from the small states under a reduced tariff arrangement or some kind of preferential arrangement. But the plan later fizzled out for political and other reasons. For the details, see Piotr S. Wandycz, *The Twilight of French Eastern Alliances, 1926–1936: French-Czechoslovak-Polish Relations from Locarno to the Remilitarization of the Rhineland* (Princeton, 1988), pp. 198–203.

95. Kaiser, *Economic Diplomacy and the Origins of the Second World War*, p. 42.

96. *DBFP*, 2, 7, Doc. 285.

97. Schröder, "Die deutsche Südosteuropapolitik u. die Reaktion der Angelsächischen Mächte," p. 358, citing cabinet session protocol of March 16, 1932, CAB 23/70.

98. Ibid.

99. Erbe, *Die Nationalsozialistische Wirtschaftspolitik, 1933–1939*, p. 94.

100. Timothy W. Mason, *Arbeiterklasse und Volksgemeinschaft: Dokumente und Materialien zur deutschen Arbeiterpolitik 1936–1939* (Opladen, 1975), p. 231.

101. Erbe, *Die Nationalsozialistische Wirtschaftspolitik, 1933–1939*, p. 25.

102. Ibid., p. 54.

103. See also *International Military Tribunal*, Nuremberg Trial, XXXVI, Doc. EC-028 (hereafter *IMT*). Kuczynski cites much higher figures. See Jürgen Kuczynski, *Die Geschichte der Lage der Arbeiter unter dem Kapitalismus* (Berlin, 1963), pp. 128–136. The earlier low findings of Klein have largely been dismissed by most historians. See Burton H. Klein, *Germany's Economic Preparations for War* (Cambridge, Mass., 1959), p. 19. Overy gives somewhat similar

figures based upon public expenditure outlays for rearmament: 1928, 0.7; 1932, 0.7; 1933, 1.7; 1934, 3.0; 1935, 5.4; 1936, 10.2; 1937, 10.9; 1938, 17%. See R. J. Overy, *The Nazi Economic Recovery, 1932–1938,* 2nd ed. (New York, 1996), p. 48, table XIII.

104. Dietmar Petzina, *Autarkiepolitik im Dritten Reich 1933 bis 1939* (Stuttgart, 1968), p. 97; also Ramon Knauerhase, *An Introduction to National Socialism, 1920 to 1939* (Columbus, Ohio, 1972), p. 123.

105. Jürgen Kuczynski, *Germany: Economic and Labor Conditions Under Fascism* (New York, 1945), p. 54.

106. Ibid., p. 60.

107. Petzina, *Autarkiepolitik im Dritten Reich 1933 bis 1939,* p. 31; also Erbe *Die Nationalistische Wirtschaftspolitik, 1933–1939,* pp. 74–75.

108. Ibid., p. 74.

109. Wilhelm Deist et al., *Das Deutsche Reich und der Zweite Weltkrieg: Ursachen und Voraussetzungen der deutschen Kriegspolitik* (Stuttgart, 1979), p. 256.

110. Ibid.

111. Ibid.

112. Ibid., p. 352.

113. Erbe, *Die Nationalsozialistische Wirtschaftspolitik, 1933–1939,* p. 61.

114. Michael Grow, *The Good Neighbor Policy and Authoritarianism in Paraguay: United States Economic Expansion and Great Power Rivalry in Latin America During World War II* (Lawrence, Kans., 1981). See especially chap. 3 "Great Power Rivalry in Southeastern South America, 1933–41," pp. 25–41. Germany increased its foreign trade volume with the region by 137% compared to 41% for the U.S. and 19% for Britain from 1933 to 1938. Ibid., p. 27.

115. Ibid., p. 33. Two naval heavy cruisers were sent to the Rio de la Plata and plans for air-lifting 10,000 troops to Brazil were drawn up.

116. For German intervention in Spain I have relied upon Marion Einhorn, *Die Ökonomis-chen Hintergründe der Faschistischen Deutschen Intervention in Spanien 1936–1939* (Berlin, 1962) and Glenn T. Harper, *German Economic Policy in Spain During the Spanish Civil War 1936–1939* (The Hague, 1967).

117. Harper, *German Economic Policy in Spain,* p. 65.

118. Einhorn, *Die Ökonomischen Hintergründe der Faschistischen Deutschen Intervention in Spanien 1936–1939,* p. 142.

119. The 1936 crisis is described in detail in Berenice A. Carroll, *Design for Total War: Arms and Economics in the Third Reich* (Paris, 1968), chap. 8, pp. 122–139. For the German text of Hitler's secret memorandum on the Four Year Plan, see Walther Hofer, *Der nationalsozialismus Dokumente 1933–1945* (Frankfurt, 1957), pp. 84–86. For German raw material deficiencies on the eve of World War II, see *IMT,* V. XXXVI, Doc. EC-028. Also see Deist, *Das Deutsche Reich und der Zweite Weltkrieg,* vol. 1, pp. 359ff.

120. Dietrich Eichholz, *Geschichte der deutschen Kriegswirtschaft 1939–1945* (East Berlin, 1969), vol. 1, p. 15.

121. William Manchester, *The Arms of Krupp, 1587–1968* (Boston, 1968, pbk. ed.), p. 452.

122. Ibid.

123. Ibid., pp. 439–440.

124. Petzina, *Autarkiepolitik im Dritten Reich,* pp. 27–28.

125. Ibid., p. 123; Eichholz, *Geschichte der deutschen Kriegswirtschaft 1939–1945,* vol. 1, p. 39. See also Peter Hayes, *Industry and Ideology: I. G. Farben in the Nazi Era* (New York, 1987), pp. 170–171 and Hayes's paper delivered at the American Historical Association, December 28, 1985.

126. Eichholz, *Geschichte der deutschen Kriegswirtschaft 1939–1945,* vol. 1, pp. 248ff.

127. Ibid., p. 55.

128. Ibid.

129. Ibid., pp. 55–56.

130. Ibid., pp. 57–58.

131. James Pool, *Hitler and His Secret Partners* (New York, 1997), p. 188, quoting n. 37, Hitler's Reichstag speech, April 28, 1939.

132. Ibid., p. 189, quoting Murray, *The Change in the European Balance of Power, 1938–1939: The Path to Ruin* (Princeton, 1984), p. 292, and Pool, *Hitler and His Secret Partners*, p. 189, n. 40.

133. Eichholz, *Geschichte der deutschen Kriegswirtschaft 1939–1945*, vol. 1, p. 58.

134. For the May 23, 1939, and August 22, 1939, conferences, see *Captured German Documents* of World War II, Washington, D.C., National Archives, *Docs. on German Foreign Policy*, Series D, Vol. VI, Doc. 433 and Vol. VII, Doc. 192 (hereafter *DGFP*).

135. Ibid. and Deist et al., *Das Deutsche Reich und der Zweite Weltkriege*, vol. 1, p. 357.

136. Ibid.

137. Ibid., p. 359.

138. Affidavit of Dr. Anton Reithinger, June 18, 1947, *U.S. National Archives, Nuremberg Trials Affidavits*, RG-238/M-1019/R-57; also Affidavit of Karl Blessing, January 30, 1947. RG-238/M-1019/R-7.

139. *U.S. National Archives,* Hermann Göring Affidavit, Col. Amen interrogation, August 28, 1945, Office of U.S. Chief of Counsel for the Prosecution of Axis Criminality, German Dossiers, Box 18.

140. Pool, *Hitler and His Secret Partners,* p. 202, and n. 19, citing Fritz Fischer, *From Kaiserreich to Third Reich: Elements of Continuity in German History 1871–1945* (London and Boston, 1986), p. 104.

141. Ibid., p. 202.

142. For the details of the looting of Poland by the Nazis, see Ibid., pp. 197–199.

143. John W. Dower, *Embracing Defeat: Japan in the Wake of World War II* (New York, 1999), p. 468.

144. For an excellent interpretive discussion of the role of hegemony in the history of the Great Powers in the first half of the twentieth century and beyond, see Thomas J. McCormick, *America's Half-Century: United States Foreign Policy in the Cold War* (Baltimore and London, 1987), especially chaps. 1 and 2, pp. 1–42.

Chapter 2

1. Hugh Seton-Watson, *Eastern Europe Between the Wars 1918–1941* (Cambridge, 1945), p. 419.

2. Conte Lugo de Voinovitch, *La Dalmatie, L'Italie, L'Unité Yougoslave (1797–1917)* (Geneva, 1917), pp. 78–80.

3. See George Pripić, "French Rule in Croatia: 1806–1813, *Balkan Studies* 5, no. 2 (1964): 221–276.

4. On the Italians in the 1876 Hercegovina revolt, see Grgr Novak, *Italija prema Stvaranju Jugoslavije* (Zagreb, 1925), chaps. 5 and 6, pp. 84–130; also a recent article by Eric R. Terzuolo, "The Garibaldini in the Balkans 1875–1876," *International Historical Review* (February 1982): 110–126.

5. For this confused picture, see Ronald W. Hanks, "Via Victis! The Austro-Hungarian Armee oberkommando and the Armistice of Villa Giusti," *Austrian History Yearbook* 14 (1978): 101–102 and 112.

6. Glen St. J. Barclay, *The Rise and Fall of the New Roman Empire: Italy's Bid for World Power, 1890–1943* (London, 1973).

7. Ibid., p. 114.

8. Cecil J. S. Sprigge, *The Development of Modern Italy* (New Haven, 1944), pp. 190f.

9. See Luigi Sturzo, *Italy and Fascism* (London, 1926), pp. 101, 103.

10. Ibid., p. 101.

11. On the generational conflict I have relied on Bruno Wanrooji, "The Rise and Fall of Italian Fascism as a Generational Conflict," *Journal of Contemporary History* 22 (1987): 401–418.

12. Ibid., p. 413.

13. Herbert L. Matthews, *The Fruits of Fascism* (New York, 1943), p. 56.

14. Ante Mandić, *Fragmenti za istoriju ujedinjenja* (Zagreb, 1956), p. 222, Doc. 149.

15. Ibid.

16. For a description of the diplomatic haggling, see Count Carlo Sforza, *Contemporary Italy* (New York, 1944), chap. 31, pp. 266–280; also Ivo Lederer, *Yugoslavia at the Paris*

Peace Conference (New Haven, 1963); and René Albrecht-Carrie, *Italy at the Paris Peace Conference* (New York, 1938). For the various Adriatic treaties and other documents in Serbo-Croatian, see Ferdo Sišić, *Jadransko Pitanje Na Konferenciji Mira u Parizu. Zbirka Akata i Dokumenata* (Zagreb, 1920). The Treaty of London text is contained in Doc. 1, pp. 5–9. For a detailed summary in English on the Julian Region and Trieste, see Bogdan C. Novak, *Trieste— 1941–1954* (Chicago, 1970), pp. 23–34.

17. See Denis Mack Smith, *Mussolini's Roman Empire* (New York, 1976).

18. Ibid., particularly the chapter on "The Ethiopian War," chap. 6.

19. Paul Kennedy, *The Rise and Fall of the Great Powers* (New York, 1989 edition), pp. 296–297.

20. Seton-Watson, *Eastern Europe Between the Wars 1918–1941,* p. 419.

21. See MacGregor Knox, "Conquest, Foreign and Domestic, in Fascist Italy and Nazi Germany," *Journal of Modern History* 56 (1984): 17–19, and Matthews, *The Fruits of Fascism,* p. 123.

22. Knox, "Conquest, Foreign and Domestic, in Fascist Italy and Nazi Germany," *Journal of Modern History* 56 (1984): 17.

23. Sforza, *Contemporary Italy,* p. 300.

24. Knox, "Conquest, Foreign and Domestic, in Fascist Italy and Nazi Germany," p. 4.

25. For these points, see Edward R. Tannenbaum, "The Goals of Italian Fascism," *American Historical Review* 74, no. 4 (April 1969): 1195–1199.

26. Ibid., p. 1193.

27. For these interpretations, see Smith, *Mussolini's Roman Empire;* MacGregor Knox, *Mussolini Unleashed 1939–1941: Politics and Strategy in Fascist Italy's Last War* (Cambridge and New York, 1986, paperback ed.); and the same writer's "Conquest, Foreign and Domestic, in Fascist Italy and Nazi Germany"; Renzo De Felice's, *Mussolini, il fascista,* vol. 1 (Turin, 1966) and *Mussolini, il Duce,* vol. 3 (Turin, 1974).

28. See, for example, the deprecatory comments of Knox, "Conquest, Foreign and Domestic, in Fascist Italy and Nazi Germany," pp. 43–44.

29. Figures cited in Kennedy, *The Rise and Fall of the Great Powers,* p. 299, table 28.

30. Ibid., p. 330, Table 30.

31. Kennedy, *The Rise and Fall of the Great Powers,* p. 293.

32. For the full statistics, see Cesare Vanutelli, "The Living Standard of Italian Workers" in Roland Sarti, *The Ax Within* (New York, 1974), pp. 139–160.

33. Kennedy, *The Rise and Fall of the Great Powers,* p. 293, n. 46.

34. Vanutelli, "The Living Standard of the Italian Worker," p. 158.

35. Ibid., p. 153.

36. Jon S. Cohen, "Fascism and Agriculture in Italy: Policies and Consequences," *Economic History* 32 (February 1979): 72ff. and Table 4.

37. Ibid., pp. 71–72, n.6.

38. V. Zamagni, "La Dinamica dei salari nel settore industrial," in P. Ciocca and G. Toniolo (eds.), *L'Economia Italiana nel Perioda Fascista,* quoted in Cohen, "Fascism and Agriculture in Italy: Policies and Consequences," p. 70.

39. Ibid., pp. 70–71.

40. Ibid., p. 71 and notes 2 and 3.

41. Ibid., p. 84, Table 5.

42. Roland Sarti, *Fascism and the Industrial Leadership in Italy 1919–1940: A Study in the Expansion of Private Power under Fascism* (Berkeley, 1971), pp. 126–127.

43. The Stresa Agreement was signed in April 1935. Ibid., p. 129.

44. Ibid., pp. 130–131.

45. Ibid., p. 131 and n. 31.

46. Barrington Moore, Jr., *Social Origins of Dictatorship and Democracy* (Boston, 1966), p. 452.

47. Knox, "Conquest, Foreign and Domestic, in Fascist Italy and Nazi Germany," p. 36, and n. 111 citing revelations published in "La Guerra Segreta di Mussolini" in *La Stampa* (January 9, 1982).

48. See the telegrams of Mussolini ordering the killings, in Knox, *Mussolini Unleashed,* pp. 3–4.

49. Ibid.

50. Knox, *Mussolini Unleashed,* pp. 11–12.

51. For figures and statistics, see Enzo Santorelli, "The Economic and Political Background" in Roland Sarti, *The Ax Within,* pp. 170–171.

52. Knox, *Mussolini Unleashed,* pp. 30–32.

53. Ibid., pp. 32–33.

54. *U.S. National Archives,* Riggs, Chargé d'affaires to Sec. of State, September 17, 1934, Doc. 740.00/31.

55. For this see Robert Bigler, "Heil Hitler and Heil Horthy! The Nature of Hungarian Racist Nationalism and its Impact on German-Hungarian Relations 1919–1945," *East European Quarterly* 8, no. 3: 251–273.

56. On Gömbös, see Ibid., passim.

57. Thomas L. Sakmyster, *Hungary, the Great Powers and the Danubian Crisis* (Athens, Ga., 1980), p. 40.

58. Ibid., p. 47.

59. Lukacs, *The Great Powers and Eastern Europe,* p. 58.

60. Hans Roos, *Polen und Europa: Studien zur Polnischen Aussenpolitik, 1931–1939* (Tübingen, 1957), pp. 150–151.

61. Ibid., p. 270; see also Comte Jean Szembek, *Journal 1932–1939* (Paris, 1952), p. 274.

62. Gaines Post, Jr., *Dilemmas of Appeasement: British Deterrence and Defense, 1934–1937* (Ithaca, 1993), p. 84.

63. Smith, *Mussolini's Roman Empire,* pp. 90–91.

64. E. H. Robertson, "Race as a Factor in Mussolini's Policy in Africa and Europe" *Journal of Contemporary History* 23 (1988): 50–52.

65. For details see the excellent article of Esmonde Robertson, "Hitler and Sanctions: Mussolini and the Rhineland," *European Studies Review* 7 (1977): 409–435.

66. Ibid., p. 91.

67. *Papers of John F. Montgomery,* Pierpont Moffat, Washington, D.C., to Montgomery, Budapest, December 20, 1934, Vol. III, Pt. 1, Box 2.

68. For details of Mussolini's Hapsburg flirtations, see Lukacs, *The Great Powers and Eastern Europe,* pp. 62ff.

69. For Mussolini's plans to attack these countries, see especially Knox, *Mussolini Unleashed,* the opening chaps. 1–3, pp. 3–116.

70. Sakmyster, *Hungary, the Great Powers and the Danubian Crisis 1936–1939,* p. 123.

71. Ibid.

72. See Betty Jo Winchester, "Hungary and the 'Third Europe' in 1938," *Slavic Review* 32, no. 4 (December 1973): 755.

73. Thomas Sakmyster, "Hungary and the Munich Crisis," *Slavic Review* 32, no. 4 (December 1973): 731.

74. Ibid., p. 739.

75. Smith, *Mussolini's Roman Empire,* p. 131.

76. Szembek, *Journal 1933–1939,* entry for March 22, 1938, p. 298.

77. For this manifesto, see Knox, *Mussolini Unleashed,* p. 40.

78. Knox, *Mussolini Unleashed,* p. 147.

79. Ibid., p. 42.

80. Ibid., p. 43 and Ciano, *Diary,* entry for August 8, 1939.

81. Knox, *Mussolini Unleashed,* p. 42, n. 203.

82. *Documenti diplomatici Italiani,* 8th Series, Vol. XII, Doc. XII (hereafter DDI); also Count Ciano, *L'Europa verso la catastrofe,* Rome, May 30, 1939, pp. 434–435.

83. DDI, 8, XII, Doc. 59; cf. Mario Toscano, *The Origins of the Pact of Steel* (Baltimore, 1967), pp. 186–188; and *The Trial of the Major War Criminals Before the Military Tribunal,* XXXI, Doc. 2818PS, pp. 156–159.

84. *DDI,* 8, XII, Docs. 6, 206, 235, 268, 289.

85. *DDI,* 8, XII, Docs. 6, 17, 62, 140, 177, 179, 206, 270, 301.

86. *DDI,* 8, XII, Doc. 629, 734.

87. *DDI,* 8, XII, Doc. 216, 368, 425, 548.

88. For Italy's economic problems on the eve of the war, see Smith, *Mussolini's Roman Empire,* pp. 159ff, 203ff.

Chapter 3

1. Lewis B. Namier, *Europe in Decay* (London, 1950), pp. 4–5.

2. This theme has been examined by Jean-Baptiste Duroselle, *La Décadence, 1932–1939* (Paris, 1979, 1985) and Eugen Weber, *The Hollow Years: France in the 1930s* (New York, 1994).

3. For Maritain's statement and numerous essays, in the aftermath of defeat, by intellectuals and historians (Marc Bloch), politicians (Edouard Daladier, Paul Reynaud, Pierre Cot, Pierre Laval), the military specialists and others (A. Rossi on the communists and unions), see Samuel Osgood, *The Fall of France, 1940* (Boston, 1965). See also Piotr Wandycz, *Twilight of French Eastern Alliances, 1926–1936: French-Czechoslovak-Polish Relations from Locarno to the Remilitarization of the Rhineland* (Princeton, 1988).

4. See especially in this respect, Paul Reynaud's citation of the then-War Minister Daladier's defense before parliament in January 1937 and of General Gamelin and the French High Command and its strategy of defense. Ibid., pp. 24f.

5. Among English language studies are the unpublished thesis of George Sakwa, "Franco-Polish Relations 1935–1938" (M.Phil. Thesis, University of London, 1968) and my own study, Paul N. Hehn, "Franco-Polish Relations 1935–1938" (M.A. Thesis, Columbia University, 1954). An older study of Polish foreign policy during a two-year critical period, which tends toward an apologetic vindication of the pre-war Pilsudskist regime, is Anna M. Cienciala, *Poland and the Western Powers 1938–1939* (London, 1968). A recent study in English is Jan Karski, *Poland in World Affairs* (Guilford, Conn., 1980). There is a chapter on France and Poland in Lewis Namier's *Diplomatic Prelude* (London, 1948). The most detailed study of Polish-German relations in a Western language remains the older study of Hans Roos, *Polen und Europa: Studien zur polnischen Aussenpolitik 1931–1939* (Tübingen, 1957). See also a German translation of an important work by Marian Wojciechowski, *Die Polnische-Deutsche Beziehungen, 1933–1939* (Leiden, 1971).

6. For the Upper Silesian problem, see F. Gregory Campbell, "The Struggle for Upper Silesia, 1919–1922," *Journal of Modern History* 42, no. 3 (September 1970): 361–385.

7. Ferdynand Zweig, *Poland Between Two Wars: A Critical Study of Social and Economic Changes* (London, 1944), p. 66. See also Hugh Seton-Watson's scathing comments on the Pilsudski regime, in *Eastern Europe Between the Wars 1918–1941* (Boulder, repr. 1962), chap. 6, pp. 157–412.

8. *The Concise Statistical Yearbook of Poland,* 1937, p. 337.

9. W. J. Rose, *The Rise of Polish Democracy* (London, 1944), p. 247.

10. R. L. Buell, *Poland Key to Europe* (London and New York, 1939), p. 99.

11. For a comprehensive view of the internal political situation, see Edward Wynot, *Polish Politics in Transition: The Camp of National Unity and the Struggle for Power 1935–1939* (Athens, Ga., 1974).

12. This portrait of Beck's career is provided by Hans Roos, *Polen und Europa: Studien zur polnischen Aussenpolitik 1931–1939,* p. 29, n. 6. For a scathing portrait of Beck's personal behavior, see Anthony Read and David Fisher, *The Deadly Embrace: Hitler, Stalin and the Nazi-Soviet Pact, 1939–1941* (New York and London, 1988), chap. 3, "The One and Only Colonel Beck," pp. 32ff.

13. Wandycz, *The Twilight of French Eastern Alliances 1926–1936,* p. 469.

14. Roos, *Polen und Europa,* p. 9, n. 37 and Karski, *Poland in World Affairs,* p. 84.

15. Ibid., p. 85.

16. Ibid.

17. Ibid.

18. Harald von Riekhoff, *German-Polish Relations, 1918–1933* (Baltimore and London, 1971), p. 162, quoting *Reichstag Sten. Berichte, Anlagen,* 442, No. 2138, pp. 85–86.

19. Ibid., p. 171.

20. For a more detailed account of the trade war between Germany and Poland, see Ibid., chap. 6, pp. 161–193.

21. Ibid., p. 189. For Poland's reduced German trade figures, see Harald von Riekhoff, *German-Polish Relations 1918–1933* (Baltimore, 1971), p. 389.

22. For the Gdansk (Danzig) and Gdynia figures from 1924 to 1932, see Hans L. Leonard, *Nazi Conquest of Danzig* (Chicago, 1942), pp. 37–38.

23. Karski, *Poland in World Affairs,* p. 106.

24. Ibid., p. 178, citing *Documents Diplomatiques Français,* Series 1, Tome I, pp. 668–670 (hereafter *DDF*).

25. Anna M. Cienciala and Titus Komarnicki, *From Versailles to Locarno: Keys to Polish Foreign Policy, 1919–25* (Lawrence, Kans., 1984), pp. 29–31.

26. For the squabble over Giraudoux, see Jules Laroche, *La Pologne de Pilsudski: Souvenirs d'une Ambassade, 1926–1933* (Paris, 1953), pp. 175ff.

27. Laroche, *La Pologne de Pilsudski,* pp. 14–15. The text of the accord is in ibid., pp. 229–230. The French military thought Pilsudski an "amateur" and Berthelot thought him to be "an adventurous character" and disliked Polish Catholicism. He had a special regard for Beneš and a rapport with the Czechs. See also Wandycz, *France and her Eastern Allies 1919–1925,* p. 24 and pp. 214–216.

28. Karski states: "From the military standpoint, the alliance was never more than symbolic." Karski, *Poland in World Affairs,* p. 108.

29. Ibid., p. 111, quoting Beck, *Dernier Rapport,* p. 268.

30. For details see Roos, *Polen und Europa,* p. 37 and n. 43; on the danger of a German attack on East Prussia and Upper Silesia, see also my article, Paul N. Hehn, "The National Socialist Revolution and the Rise of Hitler: The View from Moscow and Warsaw, 1923–1933" [The dates are incorrect and should be 1932–1933.], *Polish Review* 25, nos. 3 and 4 (1980): 28–48.

31. Quoted in Taras Hunczak, "Polish Colonial Ambitions in the Inter-War Period," *Slavic Review* 26, no. 4 (December 1967), p. 653.

32. Ibid., p. 655 and n. 45 quoting *DBFP,* 3, IV, Doc. 205.

33. Ibid., p. 656.

34. *DDF,* Series 2, Tome XIV, Doc. 67.

35. For the complicated story of the Madagascar immigration plan, see L. Yahil, "Madagascar — Phantom of a Solution for the Jewish Question," in Bela Vago and George L. Mosse, eds., *Jews and Non-Jews in Eastern Europe 1918–1945* (New York, 1974), pp. 315–329.

36. *DDF,* 2, XIV, Doc. 67.

37. Hubert Ripka, *Munich: Before and After* (London, 1939), p. 335.

38. See Jozef Beck, *Dernier Rapport* (Paris, 1951), pp. 136 ff. According to Leon Surzynski, a deputy marshal of the Seym, Colonel Beck was the first to chart the course of action designed to elevate Poland to a colonial power. Hunczak, "Polish Colonial Ambitions in the Inter-war Period," p. 651.

39. "They are still haunted here by the story of the military alliance offered to France," wrote Dirksen, German ambassador to Moscow. *DGFP,* C, I, Doc. 29. See his memoirs, Herbert von Dirksen, *Moscow-Tokyo-London: Twenty Years of German Foreign Policy* (Norman, Okla., 1952).

40. Bohdan B. Budurowycz, *Polish-Soviet Relations 1932–1939* (New York, 1963), pp. 8–9. Debicki lists the same reasons for the changed Soviet attitude towards Poland. Roman Debicki, *Foreign Policy of Poland, 1919–1939* (New York, 1963), p. 65.

41. Yegorov, then Soviet Chief of Staff, expressed the view of the pro-German section of the Red Army close to Tukhachevsky, when he "implored ... General Kostring (German military attaché to Moscow) to impress upon the German government that Germany would have to make up her mind whether she wanted to align her policy with the East or the West. If she preferred to waver between the two or to take sides with the West, a fundamental change in Soviet policy would be inevitable." Dirksen, *Moscow-Tokyo-London: Twenty Years of German Foreign Policy,* p. 106.

42. Budurowycz, *Polish-Soviet Relations 1932–1939,* p. 23.

43. On the advent of the Hitler government, see Hehn, "The National Socialist Revolution and the Rise of Hitler: The View from Warsaw and Moscow," pp. 28–48.

44. *Documents on Polish Foreign Policy,* Pilsudski Institute, letter, Wysocki, June 23, 1932. No. 2657/12 (hereafter *DPFP*).

45. Ibid.

46. A. A. Gromyko (ed.), *Dokumenty Vneshnei Politiki SSSR,* Moscow, 1969, Vol. XV, 1932. Hunchak to Moscow, November 20, 1932, Doc. 444 (hereafter DVP).

47. *DPFP,* Pilsudski Institute, N.Y.C., Schimitzek, Polish embassy in Berlin, June 13, 1931.

48. *DPFP,* Wysocki, Berlin, June 1, 1933.

49. *DGFP,* C, I, Doc. 63.

50. For some of the leading studies see the article of Henry Roberts, "The Diplomacy of Colonel Beck" in Gordon Craig and Felix Gilbert (eds.), *The Diplomats 1919–1939* (Princeton, 1953), pp. 579–614. Particularly the note on Polish proposals for preventive action against Germany, pp. 612–614; Hans Roos, "Die Präventivkriegspläne Pilsudskis von 1933" in *Vierteljahresheft für Zeitgeschichte* 1, 2 Jahrgang (1955): 90–93; Boris Celovsky, "Pilsudskis Präventivkrieg gegen das Nationalsozialistische Deutschland (Entstehung, Verbreitung und Widerlegung einer Legende)" in *Die Welt als Geschichte* 1 (1954): 53–70; Zygmunt Gasiorowski, "The German-Polish Non-aggression Pact of 1934," *Journal of Central European Affairs* 15, no. 1; and by the same author, "Did Pilsudski Attempt to Initiate a Preventive War in 1933?" *Journal of Modern History,* no. 2 (June 1955). Among the Pilsudskists who have attempted to prove the veracity of the "preventive war" theory, the most prominent is Wladyslaw Pobog-Malinowski, "Niedoszla Wojna z Niemiecami (The War with the Germans which did not Occur," *Orzel Bialy* (White Eagle) 12, no. 506 (March 15, 1952): 5 and 8; Alexander Bregman, "Gdyby w 1933 r. usluchano Jozefa Pilsudskiego (If they had listened to Jozef Pilsudski in 1933)," *Kultura,* no. 15 (1949): 109–117; and by the same writer, A. Bregman, "Legenda czy fakt historyczny (Legend or Historical Fact)," *Dziewnik Polski* (Polish Daily), London, 1954, 1–4. A complete list of those who mention the preventive war proposals of Pilsudski in 1933–1934 is included in Zygmunt Gasiorowski's article, "Did Pilsudski Attempt to Initiate a Preventive War in 1933?," pp. 135–136.

51. *DGFP,* C, I, Docs. 2, 18, 19.

52. *DGFP,* C, I, Doc. 34.

53. Ibid., p. 56.

54. *DGFP,* C, I, Doc. 16. Also Thilo Vogelsang, "Neue Dokumente," *Vierteljahresheft für Zeitgeschichte* 11, no. 4 (1954): 435.

55. Thus, Neurath noted: "We must always bear in mind that revision of the eastern frontier is an indivisible problem and that there will be only one more partition of Poland." *DGFP,* C, I, Doc. 18.

56. Dennis Mack Smith, *Mussolini's Roman Empire,* pp. 49–50.

57. For these French fears see, *DGFP,* C, I, Doc. 24. *Foreign Relations of the United States,* 1933, Vol. II, February 20, 1933, Alfred W. Kliefoth, First Sec., pp. 191–193 (hereafter *FRUS*).

58. See his lengthy memorandum on the eve of German-Italian economic talks at the end of February 1933. *DGFP,* C, I, Doc. 35, Rome, February 23, 1933.

59. *DGFP,* C, I, Doc. 27.

60. *DGFP,* C, I, Doc. 64.

61. Ibid., Doc. 301; for a summary of these discussions, see *DBFP,* Series 2, Vol. IV, Docs. 301, 302, 303, 305, 306, 310, March 14–16, 1933, pp. 526–544.

62. Ibid., Doc. 310, p. 540.

63. *DGFP,* C, I, Doc. 85.

64. *DGFP,* C, I, Doc. 98.

65. *DGFP,* C, I, Doc. 84.

66. *DBFP,* 2, V, Doc. 42.

67. *DDF,* I, III, Doc. 24.

68. *DDF,* I, III, Doc. 42.

69. For a record of the conversations between the British and Mussolini, see *DBFP,* 2, V, Doc. 44, enclosure 4–5, March 18–19, 1933, Palazzo Venezia, pp. 70–76, and in the British embassy in Rome, pp. 76–80. A summary is presented by the British Ambassador Graham, ibid., Doc. 45.

70. Ibid.

71. Ibid., 2, V, Doc. 43.

72. *DBFP,* 2, V, Doc. 52.

73. Ibid., Doc. 53, March 25, 1933.

74. Ibid., Doc. 58, March 29, 1933.

75. Ibid.

76. *British Foreign Office,* Paris, Tyrrel to Sir John Simon, April 4, 1933; also similar sentiments by Titulescu to A. W. A. Leeper, C3374/220/62 (hereafter *BFO*).

77. *DDF,* 1, III, Doc. 82.

78. BFO, Paris, Lord Tyrrel to F.O., May 25, 1933, C4645/2607/62.

79. BFO, London, F.O. to Lord Tyrrel, May 26, 1933.

80. Eduard Beneš, *Memoirs: from Munich to New War and Victory* (New York, 1954), p. 2.

81. BFO, citing *Gazeta Polska* of May 23, 1933, C4645/2607/62.

82. *DDF,* I, III, Doc. 84.

83. *DDF,* I, III, Doc. 320.

84. *DDF,* I, III, Docs. 349 and 429.

85. *DDF,* I, III, Doc. 429.

86. *DDF,* I, III, Docs. 87 and 117.

87. Ibid.

88. *DDF,* 1, III, Doc. 345.

89. *DDF,* 1, III, Doc. 94.

90. *DDF,* 1, III, Doc. 429.

91. Ibid.

92. See Henry Ashby Turner (ed.), *Hitler — Memoirs of a Confidant* (New Haven, 1985), pp. 49–51.

93. Alexandra Pilsudska, *Pilsudski* (New York, 1941), p. 341.

94. Cited in Laroche, *La Pologne de Pilsudski: Souvenirs d'une ambassade 1926–1933,* p. 141, citing tel. of November 24, 1933.

95. *DDF,* 1, V, Doc. 337.

96. *DDF,* 1, VI, Doc. 17.

97. For the Eastern Locarno Pact, see Roos, *Polen und Europa,* pp. 165–170; Laroche, *La Pologne de Pilsudski: Souvenirs d'une ambassade 1926–1933,* pp. 163–173.

98. *DDF,* 1, IX, Doc. 52.

99. *DDF,* 1, IX, Doc. 47, Annex, pp. 71–72.

100. These arguments are reviewed in the French discussions with Pilsudski, Beck and Szembek, in *DDF,* 1, VI, Docs. 139, 473 and 491, and Laroche, *La Pologne de Pilsudski: Souvenirs d'une ambassade 1926–1933,* pp. 167–172.

101. Alfred Sauvy, *Histoire Économique de la France entre les Deux Guerres (1931–1939),* vol. 2 (Paris, 1967), p. 563.

102. Ibid., pp. 572–574; see also Duroselle, *La Décadance,* p. 221.

103. See Duroselle, *La Décadence,* pp. 228f.

104. Ibid., p. 230.

105. Ibid., p. 230.

106. Jacques Néré, *La Troisième République, 1914–1940* (Paris, 1967), p. 87.

107. See Sauvy, *Histoire Économique de la France,* table 4, pp. 566–567.

108. Duroselle, *La Décadence,* p. 222.

109. René Girault, "The Impact of the Economic Situation on the Foreign Policy of France, 1936–1939," in Wolfgang J. Mommsen and Lothar Kettenacker, *The Fascist Challenge and the Policy of Appeasement* (London, 1983), pp. 209–216.

110. See the arguments of Girault in Ibid., pp. 214ff.

111. Duroselle, *La Décadence,* p. 224.

112. While René Girault is somewhat tentative, nevertheless his material makes this conclusion inescapable. See Girault, "The Impact of the Economic Situation on the Foreign Policy of France, 1936–1939," pp. 219–221.

113. Ibid., p. 219.

114. Georges Bonnet, *Défense de la Paix,* vol. 1, p. 55.

115. Ibid., p. 56.

116. Paul A. Gagnon, *France Since 1789* (New York, 1964), pp. 406ff.

117. For an example of this unreasoning fear of bolshevism by François de Wedel of the *Fédération Républicaine* and the right wing parties, see Maurice Vaïsse, "Against Appeasement:

French Advocates of Firmness, 1933–8" in Wolfgang J. Mommsen and Lothar Kettenacker, *The Fascist Callenge and the Policy of Appeasement* (London, 1983), p. 233.

118. Ibid., p. 233.

119. Wojciechowski, *Die Polnische-Deutsche Beziehungen, 1933–1939*, p. 210.

120. E. H. Carr, *Twilight of the Comintern, 1930–1935* (New York, 1982), p. 269, n. 64.

121. Ibid.

122. Ibid., p. 274.

123. Ibid., p. 265.

124. Ibid., p. 269.

125. Damian S. Wandycz, "A Forgotten Letter of Pilsudski to Masaryk," *Polish Review* 9, no. 4 (autumn 1964): 38–54.

126. *DDF*, 1, VIII, Doc. 466.

127. Ibid.

128. *DDF*, 1, VIII, Doc. 73.

129. See his analysis in *DDF*, 1, IX, Doc. 204.

130. See the French ambassador's comments and the Czech arguments in the "Note Annexe" of October 30, 1935, *DDF*, 1, XIII, Doc. 148.

131. *DDF*, 2, III, Docs. 273, 304.

132. *DDF*, 2, III, Doc. 285.

133. See Wojciechowski, *Die Polnische-Deutsche Beziehungen, 1933–1939*, pp. 244–250.

134. Szembek, *Journal 1933–1939*, entry for February 19, 1936; similarly, Moltke's note on the subject; entry for June 19, 1935.

135. Szembek, *Journal 1933–1939*, entry for November 4, 1935.

136. Szembek, *Journal 1933–1939*, entry for January 29, 1935.

137. Szembek, *Journal 1933–1939*, entry for March 23, 1938.

138. See Roos, *Polen und Europa*, pp. 235–239.

139. Szembek, *Journal 1933–1939*, entry for March 7, 1936; Beck, *Dernier Rapport*, p. 113; Leon Noël, *L'Agression Allemande contre la Pologne* (Geneva, 1948), pp. 125–128. For promises of a Polish loan in March 1936, see Wojciechowski, *Die Polnische-Deutsche Beziehungen, 1933–1939*, p. 295.

140. Szembek, *Journal 1933–1939*, entries for October 26, 28, 29, 30, 31 and November 3, 1935.

141. Szembek, *Journal 1933–1939*, entry for December 17, 1935.

142. Szembek, *Journal 1933–1939*, entry for November 4, 1935.

143. Maurice Gamelin, *Servir: Prologue du drame (1930–1939)* vol. 2 (Paris, 1946), p. 232.

144. Beck in his memoir takes a swipe at Śmigły-Rydz: "The conference which I had with Marshal Śmigły-Rydz on these different subjects contributed probably in the reinforcement of my position given the political ambitions the Inspector-General of the Armed Forces now began to show." Beck, *Dernier Rapport*, pp. 124–125.

145. Szembek, *Journal 1933–1939*, entry for August 5, 1936.

146. See George Sakwa, "The 'Renewal' of the Franco-Polish Alliance in 1936 and the Rambouillet Agreement," *The Polish Review* 16, no. 2 (1971): 45–66.

147. This, at least, is Sakwa's opinion. Ibid., p. 52.

148. For the Delbos-Śmigły-Rydz Compte Rendu, see *DDF*, III, Doc. 301.

149. Szembek, *Journal 1933–1939*, entry for September 30, 1936.

150. Gamelin, *Servir: Prologue du drame (1930–1939)*, vol. 3, p. 232.

151. For the detailed story of these French rebuffs to the Soviet's request for a military alliance and military aid, see Michael Jabara Carley, *1939: The Alliance that Never Was and the Coming of World War II* (Chicago, 1999), pp. 18–29.

152. Szembek, *Journal 1933–1939*, entry for May 1, 1936.

153. Sakwa, "The 'Renewal' of the Franco-Polish Alliance in 1936 and the Rambouillet Agreement," pp. 59–60.

154. Ibid.

155. Ibid., p. 61.

156. *Le Temps* (Paris), August 28, 1936; and *Vendredi* (Paris), September 4, 1936.

157. See Roger Massip, "After the trip of General Śmigły-Rydz to Paris," *L'Europe Nouvelle*, September 22, 1936.

158. Szembek, *Journal 1933–1939,* entry for March 8, 1938.

159. Grigore Gafencu, *Les derniers jours d'Europe* (London, 1948), p. 47.

160. Carley, *1939: The Alliance That Never Was and the Coming of World War II,* pp. 44f.; see also Georges Bonnet, *Défense de la Paix* vol. 1 (Geneva, 1948), pp. 131–140. Bonnet gives May 25, 1938, as the date of the Łukasiewicz interview and not May 22, the date Carley gives.

161. Carley, *1939: The Alliance That Never Was and the Coming of World War II,* pp. 45f.

162. For a negative review of Soviet aid to the Czechs during the May 1938 crisis, see Donald N. Lammers, "The May Crisis of 1938: The Soviet Version Considered," *The South Atlantic Quarterly* 69 (1970): 480–503. Another article reaches a similar conclusion. The writer had some access to the Czech archives. See W. V. Wallace, "The Making of the May Crisis of 1938," *The Slavic and East European Review* 41, no. 1: 382–383. See also, Carley, *1939: The Alliance That Never Was and the Coming of World War II,* n. 98.

163. Carley, *1939: The Alliance That Never Was and the Coming of World War II,* p. 65 and n. 98. For an early summary of the question of Soviet support of the Czechs which seems skeptical, see Lukacs, *The Great Powers and Eastern Europe,* pp. 166–189.

164. Carley, *1939: The Alliance That Never Was and the Coming of World War II,* p. 67.

165. Ibid., passim.

166. Szembek, *Journal 1933–1938,* entry for September 30, 1938.

167. Carley, *1939: The Alliance That Never Was and the Coming of World War II,* p. 64.

168. Noël, *L'Agression Allemande contre la Pologne,* pp. 235–236.

169. Carley, *1939: The Alliance That Never Was and the Coming of World War II,* p. 69.

170. For details on Teschen and Oderberg, see Roos, *Polen und Europa,* pp. 354–357.

171. Carley, *1939: The Alliance That Never Was and the Coming of World War II,* pp. 67–69.

172. A Czech journalist and political figure, Hubert Ripka, comments: "It was to a large extent Poland, by her destructive opposition to a policy of collective security, who facilitated the forces of Pan-Germanism in Europe. The Polish attempt to oppose it by the formation of a "neutral bloc" composed of Poland, Hungary, Romania and Yugoslavia is completely futile." Ripka, *Munich, Before and After,* p. 336. For Beck's peregrinations on behalf of his "third Europe" policy, see Roos, *Polen und Europa,* pp. 260–337; see also Beck, *Dernier Rapport,* passim.

173. *Polish White Book (1940),* Doc. 44.

174. Szembek, *Journal 1933–1939,* entries for January 8, 10, 1939, pp. 404 and 407.

175. On this involved subject, see the short, excellent article of Thaddeus V. Gromada, "The Slovaks and the Failure of Beck's 'Third Europe' Scheme," *Polish Review* 14, no. 4 (autumn 1969): 55–64.

176. *Unpublished German Foreign Office Documents,* T-120, October 25, 1938, Warsaw, Moltke to Berlin, R-1741/Fr-445679 (hereafter *UGFOD*).

177. Noël, *L'Agression Allemande contre la Pologne,* p. 253.

178. Robert Coulondre, *De Staline à Hitler: Souvenirs de Deux Ambassades, 1936–1939* (Paris, 1950), p. 147.

179. Szembek, *Journal 1933–1939,* entry for December 20, 1938, p. 395.

180. *German White Paper,* 1940, Doc. 5. Carley seems to have missed this document and dismisses the meeting of Bonnet and Ribbentrop as a typical Bonnet machination.

181. Ibid.

182. Szembek, *Journal, 1933–1939,* entry for July 7, 1938.

183. This point is made in F. Gregory Campbell, *Confrontation in Central Europe: Weimar Germany and Czechoslovakia* (Chicago and London, 1975).

184. Waclaw Jedrzejewicz, *Pilsudski: A Life for Poland* (New York, 1982), p. 336.

185. Beck, *Dernier Rapport,* p. 193.

186. This also is the opinion of Namier. See Namier, *Diplomatic Prelude, 1938–1939,* p. 104.

187. See Len Deighton, *Blitzkrieg: From the Rise of Hitler to the Fall of Dunkirk* (New York, 1980), pp. 164–175. For similar views, See Ernest R. May, *Strange Victory: Hitler's Conquest of France* (New York, 1999).

188. Tim Mason and R. J. Overy, "Debate: Germany, 'domestic crisis' and war in 1939," in Patrick Finney (ed.), *The Origins of the Second World War* (London, 1997), p. 93.

189. Read and Fisher, *The Deadly Embrace,* pp. 67–70.

190. Ibid., p. 190.

191. The Polish negotiations with Britain and France are covered in Anna M. Cienciala, "Poland in British and French Policy in 1939: Determination to Fight — or Avoid War?" in Finney (ed.), *The Origins of the Second World War,* pp. 413–433.

192. See, for example, Cienciala, p. 428; and Andrzej Suchcitz, "Poland's Defense in 1939," in Peter D. Stachura, *Poland Between the Wars, 1918–1939* (New York, 1998), p. 114.

193. Roos, *Polen und Europa,* p. 400.

194. *Roosevelt Library,* PSF, Bullitt, Paris to Washington, D.C., November 23, 1937, encl. no. 1 to dispatch 1267.

195. Ibid., Bullitt, Paris to Sec. State, March 3, 1939, Doc. 751.65/570.

196. Ibid., Bullitt, Paris to Sec. State, June 24, 1939, "Possibilities of a Second Munich," no. 4573, Doc. 760C.62/680.

197. Pool, *Hitler and His Secret Partners,* pp. 197–198, quoting Segal, *The New Order in Poland,* p. 118 and *IMT,* Docs. EC-344–16 and EC-344–17, ND.

Chapter 4

1. For this explanation of Germany's plight in the 1930s see William S. Grenzebach, "Germany's Informal Empire in East Central Europe" (Ph.D. Dissertation, Brandeis University, Boston, 1978), passim.

2. Ibid., p. 83, n.3.

3. *IMT,* V, p. 120, Doc. 3729–PS. For Schacht's role under the Nazi regime see *IMT,* V, pp. 120–151.

4. *Nazi Conspiracy and Aggression,* Doc. EC-457, Vol. 2, p. 740.

5. For data on the decline in the working conditions of the German worker during the 1930s under the National Socialist regime, see Jürgen Kuczynski, *Die Geschichte der Lage der Arbeiter in Deutschland* vol. 2 (Berlin, 1947), pp. 325–326, 329–330.

6. Arthur Schweitzer, *Big Business in the Third Reich* (Bloomington, 1964), p. 226, quoting *Nazi Conspiracy and Aggression* vol. 7, p. 472. For the conflict between the "intransigent" and "imperialist" Nazis, see ibid., chap. 5, "The End of Middle Class Socialism," pp. 197–238.

7. Grenzebach, "Germany's Informal Empire in East Central Europe," p. 76, n. 41 and pp. 81–83, n. 42.

8. Schacht told an official in the American Embassy in Berlin on September 23, 1935, that Germany needed colonies and would seek them through negotiation, if possible, "but if not, we shall take them." *IMT,* V, p. 134, Doc. EC-450.

9. This point is made in Alice Teichova, *An Economic Background to Munich: International Business and Czechoslovakia 1918–1938* (London, 1974), p. 14.

10. L. Berov, "Le capital financier occidental et les pays balkaniques dans les années vingt," *Études Balkaniques* 2–3 (1965): 162.

11. Ibid., pp. 142–143.

12. Ibid., p. 163.

13. See Friedrich Naumann, *Mitteleuropa* (Berlin, 1915).

14. Hans Radandt, "Die IG Farbenindustrie AG und Südosteuropa bis 1938," *Jahrbuch für Wirtschaftsgeschichte* no. 3 (1966): 151.

15. Ibid., p. 153.

16. Ibid., p. 155.

17. Ibid., p. 163.

18. UGFOD, Report of Dr. Adolf Kruemmer, Bergassessor (Mining Assessor) a.d., Berlin, October 13, 1938 T-84/103/1397685–1397758.

19. Ibid.

20. UGFOD, "Die Wehrwirtschaftliche Bedeutung Jugoslawiens für das deutsches Reich," Reichsamt fur Wehrwirtschaftliche Planung, Berlin, August 1938, pp. 24–25. T-84/104/139844.

21. Nuremberg Trials, *Trials of the War Criminals,* Vol. 7, p. 948, Prosecution Exhibit 455.

22. Ibid.

23. William Carr, *Arms, Autarchy and Aggression* (New York, 1972), p. 105.

24. Grenzebach, "Germany's Informal Empire in East Central Europe," p. 74.

25. Ibid., pp. 27, 84.

26. Ibid., pp. 84, 864.

27. Martin L. van Creveld, *Hitler's Strategy 1940–1941: The Balkan Clue* (Cambridge, 1973), p. 4.

28. For the remarks of Ulrich and Ritter on the political aspects of the agreements, see Grenzebach, "Germany's Informal Empire in East Central Europe," p. 124, n. 12; also Hans-Jürgen Schröder, "Südosteuropa als 'Informal Empire' Deutschlands 1933–1939," *Jahresbücher für Osteuropas* 23 (1975): 70–96.

29. V. K. Volkov, *Germano-Jugoslavskie otnoseniia i razval maloi antanty 1933–1938* (Moscow, 1966), p. 139.

30. Ibid.

31. Ibid., pp. 139–140.

32. Carr, *Arms, Autarchy and Aggression,* pp. 40–41; also Arnold Toynbee (ed.), *Survey of International Affairs: 1936* (London, 1937), p. 531.

33. Toynbee, *Survey of International Affairs: 1936,* p. 531.

34. Ibid.

35. Volkov, *Germano-Jugoslavskie otnoseniia i razval maloi antanty 1933–1938,* p. 144 quoting *Politika,* December 29, 1936, March 20, 1937.

36. Ibid., p. 261 quoting *The London Times,* November 18, 1938.

37. Ibid., pp. 146ff.

38. *UGFOD,* Dresden, Ministerial Director Sarnow, note, conversation between Pilja and Clodius, October 12, 1936; *UGFOD,* Berlin, Benzler circular to Austria and Balkan capitals, February 27, 1936.

39. Grenzebach, "Germany's Informal Empire in East Central Europe," p. 190 quoting Wilson (Belgrade) to Sec. of State, June 25, 1936, Doc. NA RG56.600H 6231/66.

40. Ibid., p. 192.

41. Volkov, *Germano-Jugoslavskie otnoseniia i razval maloi antanty 1933–1938,* pp. 147f.

42. Carroll, *Design for Total War: Arms and Economics in the Third Reich,* p. 177.

43. *IMT,* XXXVI, Doc. EC-028.

44. Ibid.

45. *IMT,* XXXVII, Doc. 1301–PS, p. 125.

46. *UGFOD,* Kruemmer Report, October 13, 1938; see also Robert Lee Wolff, *The Balkans in Our Times* (Cambridge, 1956), pp. 180ff.

47. Živko, Avramovski, "Sukob interesa v. britanije i nemačke na balkanu Uoǎi drugog svetskog ratu," *Istorija XX Veka,* pp. 28f.; also *UGFOD,* "Die Wehrwirtschaftlich Bedeutung Jugoslawiens für das Deutsches Reich." Reichsamt für Wehrwirtschaftliche Planung, Berlin, August 1938, T-84/R-104/139844.

48. Ibid. Foreign capital accounted for about one-third of total private investments in Yugoslav stock companies.

49. Sergije Dimitrijević, *Das ausländische Kapital in Jugoslawien vor der zweiten Weltkrieg* (tr. from Serbo-Croatian) (Berlin, 1963), p. 90. The figures listed for the end of 1937 by the Reichsamt für wehrwirtschaftliche Planung show German mining investments in Yugoslavia at less than 1%; Great Britain 40.8%; France 28.7%; Austria 4.7%; Belgium 4.7%; Italy 1.8%; Switzerland 1.0%; Germany 0.9%. By 1940 English and French investment sank to 37.5% and 21.6% respectively and German investments rose to 20% with the addition of Austrian, Czech and other holdings. See T-84/R-104/1398708.

50. Ibid., p. 90.

51. Ibid., p. 226.

52. Ibid., p. 235.

53. For a discussion of this point, see Harry Magdoff, *The Age of Imperialism* (New York, 1969), p. 35.

54. For the sessions of the MWT and SOEG, see Wolfgang Schumann, *Griff nach Südosteuropa* (Berlin, 1973), passim, also for the activities of I. G. Farben's Sudosteuropa Committee and the role of I. G. Farben's representatives Max Ilger and others in the MWT, see Hans Radandt, "Die IG Farbenindustrie AG und Südosteuropa 1938 bis zum Ende des zweiten Weltkrieges," *Jahrbuch für Wirtschaftsgeschichte,* vol. 1 (Berlin, 1967), passim.

55. Schumann, *Griff nach Südosteuropa,* p. 17.

56. Ibid., p. 20.

57. Ibid.

58. Ibid., p. 25.

59. Grenzebach, "Germany's Informal Empire in East Central Europe," pp. 470–471, 474.

60. Ibid., passim.

61. Schumann, *Griff nach Südosteuropa,* pp. 56f., Docs. 15, 20, 21, 23.

62. Grenzebach, "Germany's Informal Empire in East Central Europe," p. 475.

63. *IMT,* XXVII, Doc. 1301–PS.

64. Carroll, *Design for Total War,* p. 128.

65. For Germany's imperialist plundering of Austria, see Maurice Williams, "German Imperialism and Austria, 1938," *Journal of Contemporary History* 14 (1979): 144f.

66. Ibid., p. 151 n. 46.

67. Ibid., p. 145.

68. Grenzebach, "Germany's Informal Empire in East Central Europe," p. 175.

69. Carroll, *Design for Total War,* p. 88.

70. Ibid., p. 173.

71. Allan S. Milward, *The German Economy at War* (London, 1965), p. 13.

72. For the problem of copper in World War I as it affected Austria-Hungary and Germany, see J. Robert Wegs, "The Marshaling of Copper: An Index of Austro-Hungarian Economic Mobilization during World War I," *Austrian History Yearbook* 12–13, part 1 (1976–1977): 189–202.

73. *IMT,* XXVII, Doc. 1301–PS.

74. Milward, *The German Economy at War,* p. 13.

75. Ibid., p. 110.

76. *UGFOD,* Ankara, Mohraht to Berlin, note, January 9, 1940.

77. *UGFOD,* Ankara, Schmidt to Berlin, note, November 25, 1939.

78. *UGFOD,* Berlin, Ribbentrop to Papen, December 16, 1939, tel. No. 495.

79. *UGFOD,* Berlin, Wiehl to Ankara, January 9, 1940, tel. No. 16.

80. *DBFP,* 3, VII, Doc. 340.

81. Grenzebach, "Germany's Informal Empire in East Central Europe," p. 802.

82. Ibid., p. 493.

83. For the October 5, 1939, agreement, see *UGFOD,* Secret protocol of October 5, 1939, signed by Dr. Jur. Friedrich Langfried and State Sec. Milivoje Pilja.

84. Grenzebach, "Germany's Informal Empire in East Central Europe," p. 505, n. 74, citing State Dept. Doc. NA RG660 H.623/122, November 23, 1939.

85. *UGFOD,* Belgrade, von Heeren to Berlin, June 22, 1940, tel. No. 502.

86. *UGFOD,* Belgrade, May 12, 1940, Trade Agreement, signed by Pilja and v. Heeren.

87. *UGFOD,* Berlin, Wiehl note, June 28, 1940.

88. *Nazi Conspiracy and Aggression,* Doc. EC-43, Vol. I, p. 1061, 1079.

89. For the story of the German purchase of the Bor mines, see Roland Schonfeld, "Deutsche Rohstoffsicherungspolitik in Jugoslawien, 1934–1944," *Vierteljahreshefte für Zeitgeschichte* 3, no. 24 (1976): 229ff.

90. Ibid., pp. 230f.

91. Ibid.

92. Carr, *Arms, Autarchy and Aggression,* p. 105.

93. Schonfeld, "Deutsche Rohstoffsicherungspolitik in Jugoslawien 1934–1944," p. 225.

94. Ibid., p. 226.

95. *UGFOD,* I. G. Farbenindustrie AG Volkswirtschaftliche Abteilung, T-84/104/1398338-61.

96. Schonfeld, "Deutsche Rohstoffsicherungspolitik in Jugoslawien 1934–1944," pp. 255f. See also *Trials of the War Criminals,* IX (Krupp case), pp. 1466–1469, Doc. NIK-13383. Extracts from testimony of Krupp, transcript pp. 1499–1559, 11034–11054, and Krupp Director Tilo von Wilmowsky, pp. 5162–5242.

97. *UGFOD,* "Die Wehrwirtschaftliche Bedeutung Jugoslawiens für das Deutsches Reich," pp. 24–25, Berlin, 1938.

98. Schonfeld, "Deutsche Rohstoffsicherungspolitik in Jugoslawien, 1934–1944," p. 224.

99. Ibid., pp. 226, 228.

100. Radandt, "Die IG Farbenindustrie AG und Südosteuropa 1938 bis zum Ende des zweiten Weltkrieges," p. 97, n. 104.

101. *UGFOD*, "Die Wehrwirtschaftliche Bedeutung Jugoslawiens für das Deutsches Reich," p. 21, Berlin, 1938.

102. Ibid.

103. Ibid.

104. Ibid., pp. 24–25.

105. Ibid., p. 23.

106. Carr, *Arms, Autarchy and Aggression,* p. 63.

107. Ibid., p. 99.

108. Ibid.

109. Radandt, "Die IG Farbenindustrie AG und Sudosteuropa 1938 bis zum Ende des zweiten Weltkriegs," p. 80.

110. Ibid.

111. Schweitzer, *Big Business in the Third Reich,* p. 553, citing the speeches of Gustav Krupp von Bohlen and Carl Krauch at Nuremberg which "leave little doubt on this score." IG Farben Prosecution Documents, Vol. VII, Exhibit 29.

112. *Trials of the War Criminals,* IX (Krupp case), pp. 84–85.

113. Ibid., p. 488, Doc. EC-137.

114. Wolff, *The Balkans in Our Time,* p. 180.

Chapter 5

1. I owe this observation to Betty Jo Winchester, "Hungary and the 'Third Europe,'" *Slavic Review* 32, no. 4 (December 1973): 741.

2. Woodruff D. Smith, "Friedrich Ratzel and the Origins of Lebensraum," *German Studies Review* 3, no. 1 (February 1980): 54–55. See also by the same author, *The Ideological Origins of Nazi Imperialism* (New York, 1986), pp. 146–150.

3. Gerhard L. Weinberg, *The Foreign Policy of Hitler's Germany,* vol. 1 (Chicago, 1970), p. 3.

4. See Leo Marx, *The Machine in the Garden* (New York, 1964).

5. Weinberg, *The Foreign Policy of Hitler's Germany,* vol. 1, pp. 2ff. quoting Norman H. Baynes, *The Speeches of Adolf Hitler,* vol. 1, p. 835.

6. Grenzebach, "Germany's Informal Empire in East Central Europe," pp. 31–32.

7. For German notions about a German Monroe Doctrine, Manifest Destiny and *Grossraumordnung,* see Reinhard Frommelt, *Paneuropa oder Mitteleuropa* (Stuttgart, 1977).

8. There is still no adequate study of *Grossraumwirtschaft* with the possible exception of Norman Rich, *Hitler's War Aims: Ideology, the Nazi State and the Course of Expansion,* vols. 1 and 2 (New York, 1973).

9. Peter Stachura, "The Political Strategy of the Nazi Party, 1919–1933," *German Studies Review* 3, no. 2 (May 1980): 274.

10. Klaus Hildebrand, *Das Vergangene Reich: Deutsche Aussenpolitik von Bismarck bis Hitler 1871–1945* (Stuttgart, 1995).

11. Ibid., p. 571.

12. Ibid.

13. Ibid, pp. 570, 573.

14. For the various Czech and French "Danubia" plans, see chap. 6 of this work.

15. Stachura, "The Political Strategy of the Nazi Party 1919–1933," pp. 287–288.

16. For Hitler's *Lebensraum* ideas, see Adolf Hitler, *Mein Kampf* (tr. Ralph Manheim) (Boston, 1943), pp. 137ff.; for the interaction of Hitler's ideology with foreign policy, see Andreas Hillgruber, "England's Place in Hitler's Plans for World Dominion," *Journal of Contemporary History* 9 (1974): 5–22, and Milan Hauner, "Did Hitler Want a World Dominion?" *Journal of Contemporary History* 13 (1978): 15–32. A good study of the options and dilemmas are in P. M. H. Bell, *The Origins of the Second World War in Europe* (New York, 1986), chap. 4, pp. 39–47. See also the older but still important studies of Hitler: Alan Bullock, *Hitler, A Study in Tyranny* (London, 1952); Andreas Hillgruber, *Hitlers Strategie* (Frankfurt, 1965); Hermann Rauschning, *The Voice of Destruction* (London, 1939) and also by the same au-

thor *Hitler Speaks* (London, 1939); Klaus Hildebrand, *The Foreign Policy of the Third Reich* (London, 1973); and Eberhard Jäckel, *Hitlers Weltanschauung* (Middletown, Conn., 1972).

17. See Blair R. Holmes, "Europe and the Hapsburg Restoration in Austria, 1930–1938," *East European Quarterly* 9, no. 2 (summer 1975): 180.

18. Weinberg, *The Foreign Policy of Hitler's Germany,* vol. 1, pp. 17f.

19. Jacob B. Hoptner, *Yugoslavia in Crisis, 1934–1941* (New York, 1963), pp. 35f.

20. Nevile Henderson, *Failure of a Mission* (London, 1940), p. 58; also *DBFP,* 3, 1, Doc. 121.

21. *DBFP,* 3, I, Letter from Henderson to Halifax, Berlin, May 3, 1938, p. 626.

22. *DBFP,* 3, 1, Doc. 101 and n.1.

23. Ibid.

24. *DBFP,* 3, I, Doc. 243; *DBFP,* 3, II, Doc. 627.

25. *DBFP,* 3, II, Doc. 1228; Feiling, *The Life of Neville Chamberlain,* p. 370; Dr. Paul Schmidt, *Statist auf diplomatischer Bühne 1923–1945* (Bonn, 1954), p. 414.

26. *DBFP,* 3, III, Doc. 262.

27. *Public Record Office,* London, Board of Trade 11/1242, "Effects of the Annexation of Czechoslovakia on Germany's Defense" (hereafter *PRO/BT*).

28. Coulondre, *De Staline à Hitler,* pp. 215–16.

29. Ibid., p. 220.

30. Ibid., p. 224.

31. For a discussion of the "Third Europe" see Roos, *Polen und Europa: Studien zur polnischen Aussenpolitik,* chap. 10, pp. 376–397; also the article of Winchester, "Hungary and the 'Third Europe,'" pp. 741–753; and Cienciala, *Poland and the Western Powers,* pp. 149ff.

32. Winchester, "Hungary and the 'Third Europe,'" p. 752; also *DBFP,* D, 4, Doc. 45; and *Nazi Conspiracy and Aggression,* Vol. 6, Doc. 3638, p. 400.

33. *DBFP,* D, 4, Doc. 45; Namier, *Diplomatic Prelude 1938–1939,* pp. 37ff.; Waclaw Jedrzejewicz (ed.), *Diplomat in Berlin, 1933–1939: Papers and Memoirs of Józef Lipski, Ambassador of Poland* (New York, 1968), pp. 454f.; *Les relations polono-allemandes et polono-sovietiques* (Paris, 1940), Docs. 44, 45; Roos, *Polen und Europa,* pp. 382ff.

34. *Nazi Conspiracy and Aggression,* Vol. 34, Docs. 136–C, 138–C.

35. Henderson, *Failure of a Mission,* pp. 207–208.

36. Ibid., p. 210.

37. *DBFP,* 3, IV, Appendix IV, March 29, 1939, p. 615.

38. Namier, *Diplomatic Prelude,* p. 79.

39. Robert Manne, "The British Decision for Alliance with Russia, May 1939," *Journal of Contemporary History* no. 3 (1974): 25f. For a contrary view of Chamberlain's anti-Soviet outlook, see Leibovitz, *The Chamberlain-Hitler Deal,* pp. 480–494. Similarly, a very recent diplomatic study is the already mentioned, Carley, *1939: The Alliance That Never Was and the Coming of World War II.*

40. *DBFP,* 3, IV, Doc. 195.

41. Ibid. Chamberlain also implicitly voiced a similar view in a cabinet session in late November 1938, warning that Britain should avoid entanglement arising out of a possible dispute between Russia and Germany," *Public Record Office,* London, Cabinet Meeting 23/56 (38), November 22, 1938 (hereafter *CAB*).

42. Andrew Crozier, "Prelude to Munich: British Foreign Policy and Germany, 1935–8," *European Studies Review* 6 (1976): 359.

43. Ibid.

44. Ian Colvin, *None So Blind* (pub. in England under the title: *Vansittart in Office*) (New York, 1965), p. 25.

45. A. J. P. Taylor, *The Origins of the Second World War* (London, 1961, sec. ed. pbk.), pp. 234–235.

46. Henderson, *Failure of a Mission,* p. 237.

47. Ibid., p. 260.

48. Crozier, "Prelude to Munich: British Foreign Policy and Germany, 1935–1938," p. 369.

49. For a post-war testimony of Chamberlain's hostility to communism, see the statement of Sir Alex Douglas Home made in 1962. Home was the parliamentary private secretary

of Chamberlain. See Donald N. Lammers, *Explaining Munich* (1966, Hoover Institutional Studies), p. 62, n. 69.

50. CAB 23/56 (38), November 22, 1938.

51. For this important point see Manne, "The British Decision for Alliance with Russia, May 1939," pp. 3, 4, 6, 8, 14, and passim.

52. For Chamberlain's statement to the House of Commons on November 5, 1936, disavowing Britain's traditional balance of power policy in Europe, see Gottfried Niedhart, "Appeasement: Die britische Antwort auf die Krise des Weltreichs und des internationalen Systems vor dem Zweiten Weltkrieg," *Historische Zeitschrift* 226 (1978): 84.

Chapter 6

1. M. Edelstein, "Foreign Investment and Empire 1860–1914," in Roderick Floud and Donald McCloskey (eds.), *The Economic History of Britain Since 1700,* vol. 2 (Cambridge, 1981), pp. 70–72. Lenin, quoting Hobson, notes that in 1893 British capital invested abroad amounted to 15% of the total wealth of the British Empire. V. I. Lenin, *Imperialism, The Highest Stage of Capitalism* (Foreign Language Press, 1975), p. 120.

2. Ibid., p. 74.

3. See Lance E. Davis and Robert A. Huttenback, "The Political Economy of British Imperialism: Measures of Benefits and Supports," *Journal of Economic History* 42, no. 1 (March 1982): 119–130.

4. Ibid., p. 124.

5. Ibid.

6. Ibid., p. 129.

7. See Standish Meacham, "The Sense of an Impending Clash: English Working Class Unrest Before the First World War," *American Historical Review* 77, no. 5 (December 1972): 1343–1364 and 1348, n. 19. For the riots of the poor and unemployed in London in the mid-1880s that sacked parts of the west end and threw the middle class into a panic, see the excellent study of Gareth Stedman Jones, *Outcast London* (Oxford, 1971), pp. 293ff.

8. See Alan E. Booth and Sean Glynn, "Unemployment in the Interwar Period: A Multiple Problem," *Journal of Contemporary History* 10 (1975): 612. See also the sharp exchange between Booth and Glynn and J. D. Tomlinson on the nature and extent of pre-war and inter-war unemployment in "Inter-war Unemployment — Two Views," *Journal of Contemporary History* 17 (1982): 545–555.

9. Quoted in John Stevenson, "Myth and Reality: Britain in the 1930s," in Alan Sked and Chris Cook (eds.), *Crisis and Controversy: Essays in Honour of A. J. P. Taylor* (New York, 1976), p. 91.

10. Ibid., p. 94.

11. Lenin, *Imperialism, The Highest Stage of Capitalism,* p. 105.

12. Margaret George, *The Warped Vision: British Foreign Policy 1933–1939* (Pittsburgh, 1965), p. 9.

13. Anthony Adamthwaite, *France and the Coming of the Second World War* (London, 1977), p. 23 quoting *DBFP,* First Series, XV, Doc. 70.

14. Ibid.

15. *Public Record Office,* Treasury Department, Financial Inquiry Branch, Pinsent's Monthly Reports, Doc. Treasury 208/175 (hereafter *PRO /T*). The important analysis of Harold James seems to corroborate Pinsent. See Harold Jones, "Innovation and Conservatism in Economic Recovery: The Alleged 'Nazi Recovery' of the 1930s," in Childers and Caplan, *Reevaluating the Reich,* pp. 114–138.

16. *PRO /T*-160/729/F-12929/2, "German Competition in World Trade," Appendix 5, p. 42.

17. *PRO /T*-188/81, "German-British 1934 Trade Negotiations." See also Harold James, *The German Slump: Politics and Economics 1924–1936* (Oxford, 1986), pp. 406ff.; CAB 23/77, 3 (34), January 31, 1934, and CAB 23/79, 23 (34), June 13, 1934; and Bernd-Jürgen Wendt, *Economic Appeasement: Handel und Finanz in der Britischen Deutschland Politik 1933–1939* (Düsseldorf, 1971), pp. 157–219.

18. *PRO /T*-180/81.

19. Ibid.

20. *PRO* /T-188/288, October 27, 1934, Letter, Leith-Ross to Schacht.
21. Ibid.
22. Ibid.
23. Ibid. See also Newton, *Profits of Peace,* pp. 63–65.
24. *PRO* /T-160/729/12829/2, "German Competition in World Trade."
25. Ibid.
26. For more details see Ibid.
27. Ibid., Memo, S. D. Waley to Crowe, June 15, 1936.
28. Ibid., Memo, Leith-Ross, June 13, 1936.
29. Ibid.
30. *PRO* /T-208/176, Pinsent, Letter to F.O. (Berlin), June 11, 1936.
31. *PRO* /T-175/208, Pinsent, Memo to F.O., on a lecture of Dr. Blessing of the Reich Economics Ministry, May 14, 1934.
32. *PRO* /T-176, Sir E. Phipps to Eden, on lecture of Dr. Blessing, November 24, 1936. See also Schacht's speech at the Leipzig Spring Fair in 1935 regarding Germany's need for colonies. He observed: "The possession of colonial raw material areas was essential for a modern industrial state as a complement to its home economy. It would facilitate the German transfer problem enormously if she could produce many of her raw materials now paid for in currency exchange, within her currency area." *The London Times,* March 5, 1935. Of course, should Germany receive back her colonies, Britain would then not only face unwelcome trade competition from Germany, but would also be aiding Germany to rearm.
33. *PRO* /T-230/52, "The Economic History of Britain Between the Wars," (1918–1935), p. 34. On this subject Polanyi writes: "In so doing they [the Great Powers –P.N.H.] followed the logic of the self-regulating market. Yet such a course of action tended to spread the crisis; it burdened finance with the unbearable strain of massive economic dislocations, and it heaped up the deficits of the various national economies to the point where a disruption of the international division of labor became inevitable. The stubbornness with which economic liberals, for a critical decade, supported authoritarian interventionism, [i.e., Bruning's deflationary policy, maintaining the gold standard, etc. — the author] merely resulted in a decisive weakening of the democratic forces which might otherwise have averted the fascist catastrophe." Polanyi, *The Great Transformation,* pp. 233f.
34. *PRO* /T-230/56, p. 42.
35. Ibid.
36. Ibid., p. 45.
37. *PRO* /T-208/176, letter of Pinsent to F.O., Berlin, June 11, 1936.
38. I. Drummond, "Britain and the World Economy 1900–1945," in Roderick Floud and Donald McCloskey (eds.), *The Economic History of Britain since 1700,* vol. 2 (Cambridge, 1981), pp. 300f. Compare the much lower surplus for the 1920s cited by György Ránki, *Economy and Foreign Policy: The Struggle of the Great Powers for Hegemony in the Danube Valley, 1919–1929* (Boulder, Colo., 1983), p. 43.
39. *PRO* /T-172/1853, note, Waley, February 5, 1937.
40. Anthony Eden, *Facing the Dictators: The Eden Memoirs,* vol. 1 (London, 1962), p. 137.
41. Albert Speer, *Inside the Third Reich: Memoirs* (New York, 1970), p. 116; also John L. Heinemann, *Hitler's First Foreign Minister: Constantin Freiherr von Neurath, Diplomat and Statesman* (Berkeley and Los Angeles, 1979), p. 161.
42. According to Schacht, Hitler had been more interested in "those fantasies of *Mein Kampf*" or expansion into eastern Europe. See John E. Dreifort, *Yvon Delbos at the Quai d'Orsay: French Foreign Policy during the Popular Front 1936–1938* (Lawrence, Kans., 1973), p. 162. On the discussions between Schacht and the French in 1936, see also Gerhard L. Weinberg, *The Foreign Policy of Hitler's Germany: Starting World War II 1937–1939,* vol. 2 (Chicago, 1980), pp. 68–69; and Adamthwaite, *France and the Coming of the Second World War.*
43. Dreifort, *Yvon Delbos at the Quai d'Orsay,* p. 165, n. 74.
44. On the Chamberlain government's relations with the moderates, see the excellent article of Callum A. MacDonald, "Economic Appeasement and the German 'Moderates' 1937–1939," *Past and Present,* no. 56 (August 1972): 105–131.

45. *Roosevelt Library,* PSF, Morgenthau to Roosevelt, January 15, 1937, reporting Cochran cable of January 12, 1937.

46. *Roosevelt Library,* PSF, Bullitt, Paris, to Sec. of State, January 13, 1937, Doc. 751.62/ /387.

47. The Plymouth committee found the idea of colonial appeasement, "an attractive proposition," but colonies were not likely to satisfy Germany's needs. Imperialists like Amery would not give up an acre of colonial territory and others, the "hard bargainers," did not wish to cede anything without exacting a price from Germany. On the Plymouth report, see A. Edho Ekoko, "The British Attitude Towards Germany's Colonial Irredentism in Africa in the Inter-War Years," *Journal of Contemporary History* 14 (1979): 287–305.

48. On the February 2, 1937, Badenweiler conference, see Leith-Ross's memo in *PRO /T-*188/288. See also the latter's post-war account in Sir Frederick Leith-Ross, *Money Talks: Fifty Years of International Finance* (London, 1968), pp. 238ff.

49. *PRO /T*-188/288, February 2, 1937, Badenweiler Conference.

50. Ibid.

51. Ibid.

52. Ibid.

53. Ibid.

54. *The London Times,* January 3, 1935, p. 11.

55. George C. Peden, *British Rearmament and the Treasury, 1932–1939* (Edinburgh, 1979), p. 81.

56. *PRO /T*-188/288, memo of Leith-Ross conversation with C. Gördeler, July 6, 1937.

57. Leith-Ross, *Money Talks,* p. 245.

58. Ibid.

59. Heinemann, *Hitler's First Foreign Minister,* pp. 163f. On the authenticity of the November 5, 1937, conference, Gerhard Weinberg dismisses the efforts in articles and books to explain away the meeting as "unimportant or meaningless" and as "irrelevant for understanding German military planning since none of those present at the meeting or immediately informed of Hitler's wishes could possibly know that there ever was such a literature; they were too busy trying to carry out what they took to be the dictator's orders." Weinberg points out that those present did not in general disagree with Hitler's long-term or short-term goals, but only the risks involved. In my opinion, equally if not more important were the economic motives, the need for greater *Lebensraum* and the dearth of raw materials, invoked by Hitler at the meeting, as the reason for unleashing the conflict. See Gerhard Weinberg, *Germany, Hitler and World War II* (Cambridge and New York, 1995), pp. 135ff. and n. 18, 19. General Beck was appalled at Hitler's intentions and wrote a detailed commentary on a November 12 copy of the document testifying to the gravity of the meeting. For the Hossbach Memorandum of the conference, see *DGFP,* D, Vol. 1, Doc. 19; also *IMT,* Vol. XXV, pp. 403ff. (Doc. 386–PS). Bell also agrees with Weinberg on the undoubted significance of the memorandum. See Bell, *The Origins of the Second World War in Europe,* pp. 232f. and n. 5.

60. Heinemann, *Hitler's First Foreign Minister,* pp. 160ff.

61. See Lois G. Schwoerer, "Lord Halifax's Visit to Germany: November 1937," *The Historian* 32, no. 3 (May 1970): 353–375.

62. Weinberg, *The Foreign Policy of Hitler's Germany,* vol. 2, p. 125.

Chapter 7

1. *PRO /T*-160/856/F14545/1/68569. See also Wendt, *Economic Appeasement,* pp. 336ff. See also Wendt's summary article "Economic Appeasement — A Crisis Strategie," in Wolfgang J. Mommsen and Lothar Kettenacker (eds.), *The Fascist Challenge and the Policy of Appeasement* (London, 1983), pp. 147–172. See also Gustav Schmidt, *The Politics and Economics of Appeasement: British Foreign Policy in the 1930s* (tr. from German) (New York, 1986), chap. 1, pp. 31–225, for early and mid-1930s appeasement efforts in British government circles.

2. British Cabinet Paper 42/36 (hereafter CP); for a summary of Vansittart's paper see *PRO/T*-160/856/F14545/1/68569.

3. *PRO/T*-160/856/F14545/1/68569.

4. Ibid.

5. Ibid., Harold Butler to Sir Horace Wilson, March 11, 1936.

6. Ibid.

7. Ibid., Phipps (Berlin) to F.O., October 22, 1936.

8. Wendt, *Economic Appeasement,* pp. 316–317.

9. *PRO /T-208/176,* Pinsent, Berlin, British embassy to Treasury Dept.

10. Ibid.

11. Wendt, "Economic Appeasement—A Crisis Strategie," p. 170.

12. Lloyd C. Gardner, *Economic Aspects of New Deal Diplomacy* (Madison, 1964), p. 52.

13. Ibid., p. 106. On the conflict between the "open door" system advocated by the U.S. and the British preferential system of trade, see Callum A. MacDonald, "The United States, Appeasement and the Open Door," and Hans-Jürgen Schröder, "The Ambiguities of Appeasement: Great Britain, the United States and Germany, 1937–1939," in Mommsen and Kettenacker, *The Fascist Challenge and the Policy of Appeasement,* pp. 400–412 and 390–399, respectively.

14. Gardner, *Economic Aspects of New Deal Diplomacy,* p. 106.

15. Ibid., p. 52.

16. For details on the 1938 Anglo-American Commercial Agreement, see Schröder, "The Ambiguities of Appeasement: Great Britain, the United States and Germany, 1937–1939," pp. 394–398.

17. Ibid., pp. 395–396.

18. MacDonald, "The United States, Appeasement and the Open Door," pp. 401f. The Roosevelt administration, according to MacDonald, was divided between the "appeasers" (such as Welles and Berle), who feared that autarchy and rearmament would ultimately drive Germany toward total economic collapse or military expansion to seize new markets and raw materials, and "anti-appeasers" (Messerschmidt and Dodge), who believed that economic collapse in Germany ought to be encouraged and Hitler allowed to stew in his own juice. A deal between Britain and Germany would only strengthen Germany and enable Hitler to further arm and threaten. Ibid., pp. 401–402.

19. Ibid., pp. 404.

20. Ibid.

21. Gardner, *Economic Aspects of New Deal Diplomacy,* pp. 100–101 and 104.

22. On Mexican-American relations and the oil problem, see Octavio Ianni, *El Estado capitalista en la época de Cárdenas* (Mexico City, 1977), especially chap. 7, "Petróleo y Dependencia," pp. 108–121. See also Tzvi Medin, *Ideología y praxis política de Lázaro Cárdenas* (Mexico City, 1972), pp. 129ff.

23. Ianni, *El Estado capitalista en la época de Cárdenas,* p. 193.

24. Beatrice Bishop Berle and Travis Beal Jacobs (eds.), *Navigating the Rapids: From the Papers of Adolph A. Berle* (New York, 1973), entry for June 28, 1939, p. 230.

25. Ibid.

26. Ibid.

27. Ibid.

28. Ibid., entry for April 2, 1939, p. 206.

29. Ibid., entries for April 2 and May 26, 1939, pp. 207, 223f.

30. Ibid., entry for June 28, 1939, p. 230.

31. Gottfried Niedhart, "Appeasement: Die Britische Antwort auf die Krise des Weltreichs und des Internationalen Systems vor dem Zweiten Weltkrieg," *Historische Zeitschrift* 226 (1978): 78.

32. Ibid., pp. 79ff. At the end of December 1937, the British cabinet reviewed its foreign and defense policies and noted that the Chiefs of Staff could not "safeguard [Britain's] territory, trade and vital interests against Germany, Italy and Japan simultaneously. They had urged that our foreign policy must be governed by this consideration and they had made a rather strong appeal to this effect." *British Foreign Office,* December 8, 1937, CAB/23/90A, in Adamthwaite, *The Making of the Second World War,* pp. 176ff., Doc. 44.

33. CAB 23/77 57 (33), October 26, 1933, R-41.

34. Ibid.

35. CAB 23/78 9 (34), March 14, 1934, R-42.

36. Ibid.

37. CAB 23/79 31 (34), July 31, 1934, R-46.

38. CAB 23/77 57 (33), October 26, 1933, R-41.

39. CAB 23/77 66 (33), November 29, 1933, R-41.

40. Ianni, *El Estado capitalista en la época de Cárdenas,* p. 115.

41. Hubert Herring, *A History of Latin America from the Beginnings to the Present* (New York, 1957), p. 638, n. 1 quoting George Wythe, *Industry in Latin America* (New York, 1945), p. 94.

42. Ibid., p. 638.

43. CAB 23/86 56 (36), October 28, 1936, R-50.

44. Ibid.

45. Ibid.; also CAB 23/86 67 (36), November 25, 1936, R-48.

46. CAB 23/77 64 (33), November 22, 1933, R-44.

47. CAB 23/78 2 (34), January 31, 1934, R-41.

48. CAB 23/78 10 (34), March 19, 1934, R-42.

49. CAB 23/78 12 (34), March 22, 1934, R-42.

50. Ibid.

51. CAB 23/79 16 (34), April 18, 1934, R-42.

52. CAB 23/79 23 (34), June 6, 1934, R-42; CAB 23/79 28 (34), July 11, 1934, R-43.

53. CAB 23/79 18 (34), April 30, 1934, R-42.

54. CAB 23/79 31 (34), July 31, 1934, R-43.

55. CAB 23/80 41 (34), November 21, 1934, R-43.

56. CAB 23/80 42 (34), November 26, 1934, R-43.

57. CAB 23/81 2 (35), January 9, 1935, R-44.

58. CAB 23/81 3 (35), January 14, 1935, R-44.

59. Post, *Dilemmas of Appeasement: British Deterrence and Defense 1934–1937,* pp. 106–107.

60. Ibid., p. 107, n. 67, note of March 27, 1935, Liddell Hart Papers, 11/1935/69 (LHCMA).

61. Ibid., p. 271.

62. Ibid., p. 204.

63. Ibid., pp. 204–205.

64. Wendt, *Economic Appeasement,* p. 331.

65. For Eden's impending visit and his account of his meeting with Hitler, see CAB 23/81 16 (35), March 20, 1935, R-44, and C.P. 69 (35), Berlin, March 25, 26, 1935, R-44.

66. CAB 23/83 32 (35), June 5, 1935, R-44.

67. B. R. Tomlinson, "The Political Economy of the Raj: The Decline of Colonialism," *Journal of Economic History* 42, no. 1 (March 1982): 135, n. 7; Wendt, *Economic Appeasement,* pp. 622–623, n. 14, p. 690.

68. Peden, *British Rearmament and the Treasury,* p. 83.

69. Ibid., p. 80.

70. Ibid., pp. 80–81.

71. Ibid., p. 98.

72. Ibid., p. 85.

73. Ibid., p. 104, n. 163.

74. Ibid., p. 8.

75. N. von Tunzelmann, "Britain 1900–1945: a Survey," citing S. Howson, "Domestic Monetary Management in Britain, 1919–1938," in Floud and McCloskey (eds.), *The Economic History of Britain since 1700,* p. 262.

76. On the struggle inside the left, both in and out of the Labor party, see Sabine Wichert, "The British Left and Appeasement: Political Tactics of Alternative Policies," in Mommsen and Kettenacker (eds.), *The Fascist Challenge and the Policy of Appeasement,* pp. 125–141.

77. See G. C. Peden, "Keynes, the Economics of Rearmament and Appeasement," in Mommsen and Kettenacker (eds.), *The Fascist Challenge and the Policy of Appeasement,* pp. 142–156; also Newton, *Profits of Peace,* p. 72.

78. R. C. A. Parker, "Economics, Rearmament and Foreign Policy: The United Kingdom before 1939 — A Preliminary Study," *Journal of Contemporary History* 10 (1975): 638.

79. Ibid., p. 643.

80. Peden, "Keynes, the Economics of Rearmament and Appeasement," p. 151.

Chapter 8

1. Neville Thompson, *The Anti-Appeasers: Conservative Opposition to Appeasement in the 1930s* (Oxford, 1971), p. 163.

2. *DBFP,* 3, I, Doc. 115.

3. *The Economist,* May 14, 1938, p. 356.

4. *BFO,* R 4969/1167/67, Foreign Office, August 17, 1936.

5. Ibid.

6. Ibid.

7. Ibid.

8. Ibid.

9. See memos of Waley and Leith-Ross, June 13, 15, 1936, notes 27, 28, 29.

10. *BFO,* C 3249/772/18, Foreign Office, May 6, 1938, "German Economic Penetration in Central and South-East Europe."

11. Ibid.

12. Ibid.

13. Ibid.

14. *BFO,* C.P. 127 (38), Foreign Office, May 24, 1938, Halifax memo, "British Influence in Central and South-Eastern Europe."

15. Ibid.

16. *The Economist,* January 1, 1938, p. 11.

17. *The Economist,* January 8, 1938, p. 54.

18. *The Economist,* July 2, 1938, p. 3.

19. *The Economist,* July 30, 1938, p. 220.

20. *The Economist,* August 6, 1938, pp. 270–271.

21. *The Economist,* April 21, 1938, p. 9.

22. Ibid.

23. *The Economist,* September 17, 1938, pp. 530f.

24. *The Economist,* August 20, 1938, p. 357.

25. *The Economist,* May 21, 1938, p. 415.

26. *The Economist,* August 20, 1938, p. 365.

27. *The Economist,* August 13, 1938, p. 322.

28. *The Economist,* September 10, 1938, pp. 484f.

29. Ibid.

30. Ibid.

31. *PRO /*T-160/729/F-12829/1.

32. CAB 23/21 (38) 2, April 27, 1938.

33. *PRO /*BT-11/1006, Hawtrey to Wills, memo, May 27, 1938, "Financial Pressure on Germany."

34. Kaiser, *Economic Diplomacy and the Coming of World War II: Britain, France and Germany and the Struggle for Eastern Europe,* pp. 316–318.

35. CAB/27 (38) 6; CAB 23/28 (38), June 15, 1938.

36. CAB/23/96/55 (38) 8, November 16, 1938, Halifax memo.

37. *PRO /*BT-11/901, "Anglo-German Trade Negotiations," minute, signature indecipherable, August 19, 1938.

38. *PRO /*BT-11/901, minute, signature indecipherable, August 29, 1938.

39. *PRO /*BT-11/901, minute, Sir W. B. Brown, B.O.T., August 19, 1938.

40. *PRO /*BT-11/901, November 30, 1938.

41. *PRO /*BT-11/901, December 22, 1938.

42. *PRO /*BT-11/901, minute, signature indecipherable, October 7, 1938.

43. *PRO /*BT-11/901, memo, Guy Locock, to W. Palmer of B.O.T. n.d.

44. Ibid. This "hint" was probably the threat of a subsidy war cited in Newton, *Profits of Peace,* p. 98 and n. 81.

45. *PRO /*T-188/227, n.d., but probably December 1938.

46. *PRO /*T-188/288, letter, Otto Jeidels to Leith-Ross, December 28, 1938.

47. Kaiser, *Economic Diplomacy and the Coming of the Second World War,* p. 150.

48. According to Peterson the 1935 food crisis was solved "when Schacht was over-ruled by Hitler who forced the drastic seizure of German held foreign assets with which to buy

food. The incident was extremely significant in that it determined Hitler not to permit a recurrence." Thereafter, Hitler introduced the Four-Year Plan as "a new answer to the raw material problem." Edward Norman Peterson, *Hjalmar Schacht: For and Against Hitler: A Political-Economic Study of Germany, 1923–1945* (Boston, 1954), p. 225.

49. Ibid.

50. On Schacht's talk with Leith-Ross, see the latter's memo in *PRO* /T-188/227, December 16, 1938. The discussion was actually held on December 1.

51. Ibid. In his 1945 memo about Schacht for the Nuremberg Trial, Leith-Ross described Schacht in the following terms: "He was in a very depressed mood, but warned us against Hitler and said that no agreement with Hitler would be kept longer than suited his convenience." *PRO* /T-180/288, p. 130, dated December 3, 1945.

52. For Gördeler's conversation with Ashton-Gwatkin, see *PRO* /T-227, memo, Ashton-Gwatkin, December 12, 1938. The British Foreign Office official made no comment on Gördeler's proposition.

53. On June 1, 1935, Schacht reportedly collected "voluntarily" from industry 720 million marks, but this was insufficient and by the end of June the export levy was made compulsory. Peterson, *Hjalmar Schacht: For and Against Hitler,* p. 203.

54. *PRO* /BT-11/901, memo, J. J. Wills, CRT Department, B.O.T., November 15, 1938.

55. *PRO* /BT-11/901, memo, J. M. Forsythe to Clutterbuck of the Dominion Office, December 30, 1938.

56. Peterson, *Hjalmar Schacht: For and Against Hitler,* pp. 177–178.

57. Ibid., p. 180. Peterson adds that in 1937 the national income was 71 billion and the debt 47 billion. Until 1938 "the debt in Germany was no serious danger."

58. Ibid., p. 179.

59. Göring told Dr. Rublee that Schacht's dismissal was due "to his refusal to consent to financial measures which he [believed] to be inflationary." *PRO* /T-188/227, Ogilvie-Forbes, Berlin, to Foreign Office, tel. no. 32. Similarly, a note of Per Jacobson to Leith-Ross relates that Schacht "had been very insistent about the magnitude of current expenditure and the methods of financing that it would lead to . . . " *PRO* /T-188/288, note, Per Jacobson to Leith-Ross, February 15, 1939.

60. *PRO* /BT-11/901, letter, Phipps to Halifax, Berlin, January 30, 1939.

61. Ibid.

62. *PRO* /BT-11/901, letter, Pinsent to Ashton-Gwatkin, Berlin, January 31, 1939.

63. Ibid.

64. *PRO* /BT-11/901, letter, Strang to Sir John Simon, January 13, 1939. For similar references to British considerations of a trade war, see Newton, *Profits of Peace,* p. 96. Hudson, among others, believed that just the threat of a subsidy of British goods sold abroad would force the Germans, who did not have the requisite resources to counter, to knuckle under. Ibid.

65. Ibid.

66. *PRO* /T-188/288 memo, Leith-Ross to S. Rowe Dutton, January 25, 1939.

67. For Hitler's January 30, 1939, "Export or Die" speech, see Adolf Hitler, *My New Order* (ed. Raoul de Roussy de Sales) (New York, 1941), pp. 559–594.

68. Grenzebach, "Germany's Informal Empire in East Central Europe," pp. 327–328.

69. Ibid. Similar conclusions were reached by Petzina, Knauerhase and others. Hitler himself gave the failure of the Four Year Plan to secure raw materials as the reason for attacking Poland in his May and August 1939 conferences.

70. *DBFP,* 3, IV, Appendix II, Report by Ashton-Gwatkin on his visit to Germany and interviews with German leaders, February 19, 26, 1939, pp. 596–599.

71. Ibid.

72. Ibid.

73. Ibid.

74. *DBFP,* 3, IV, Doc. 172, memo, Colonel Mason-MacFarlane, "Respecting the Military Point of View as regards Concessions to Germany in the Economic Field," Berlin, February 27, 1939.

75. Ibid.

76. Martin Gilbert and Richard Gott, *The Appeasers* (Boston, 1963), pp. 197f.

77. Ibid.

78. Henderson, *Failure of a Mission*, pp. 191–192.

79. Krupp refused several orders and ultimatums from Hitler in 1938 to cease producing locomotives, bridges, dredging equipment and trucks and switch to tanks. See William Manchester, *The Arms of Krupp 1587–1968* (Boston, 1968, pbk.), p. 433.

80. Newton, *Profits of Peace,* pp. 151ff.

81. This point has been emphasized in the recent work of Parker, *Chamberlain and Appeasement: British Policy and the Coming of the Second World War,* chap. 1, pp. 1–11.

82. Ibid., p. 268. For the various English emissaries to Hitler, see pp. 263–269.

Chapter 9

1. Wendt, *Economic Appeasement,* p. 429.

2. *Westminster Bank Review* no. 288 (February 1938): 3.

3. *Westminster Bank Review* no. 299 (January 1939): 4.

4. *Westminster Bank Review* (January 1939): 3.

5. Ibid.

6. *The Spectator* 163 (July 7, 1939): 5–6.

7. *Westminster Bank Review* no. 303 (May 1939): 3.

8. *Westminster Bank Review* no. 303 (May 1939): 7. For Chamberlain's attempt to avoid curtailing business and trade to pay for the armament program, which cannot be gone into in detail here, see Parker, *Chamberlain and Appeasement,* chap. 13, "Arms and the Economy," pp. 272–293.

9. *Lloyds Bank Monthly Review* 10, no. 109 (March 1939): 75.

10. Ibid., p. 76.

11. Wendt, *Economic Appeasement,* p. 482.

12. Ibid., pp. 482–483.

13. *Lloyds Bank Monthly Review* 6, no. 106: 606.

14. Ibid. In 1936 two-fifths of all world imports were absorbed by the U.S., Britain and the Empire countries, while the U.S. and England alone took one-third of world imports. Hull in his memoirs described the November 1938 agreement the beginning of a bloc that would include 20-odd states at a later date which would hem in further expansion of the fascist states. Some German journalists and foreign office officials spoke of "encirclement," while others thought the agreement primarily a political instrument and not economic, i.e., *"rein handelspolitische"* (purely trade-political). For interesting details of the agreement and its impact on the German, British and American governments, see Hans-Jürgen Schröder, *Deutschland und die Vereinigten Staaten 1933–1939* (Wiesbaden, 1970), pp. 190–199.

15. For German trade statistics, see the Commercial Review of 1938 in *The Economist,* February 18, 1939.

16. *Business Week,* January 14, 1939.

17. Ibid.

18. Ibid., February 4, 1939.

19. *The Economist,* January 28, 1939, p. 166.

20. *The Economist,* January 28, 1939, p. 181.

21. *The Economist,* January 14, 1939, p. 70. For details of the Norman-Schacht talks, see Newton, *Profits of Peace: The Political Economy of Anglo-German Appeasement,* pp. 90f.

22. *The Economist,* February 11, 1939, p. 296.

23. *The Economist,* February 25, 1939, p. 383.

24. *The Economist,* March 4, 1939, p. 441.

25. *The Economist,* March 18, 1939, p. 562.

26. Nuremberg Trial Documents, *Trials of the Major War Criminals,* vol. IX, pp. 84–85. For I. G. Farben's profits to 1936, which are somewhat similar, see Hayes, *Industry and Ideology: I. G. Farben in the Nazi Era,* p. 158.

27. *The Economist,* March 18, 1939, p. 562.

28. Ibid.

29. Ibid.

30. *DDF,* 2, Vol. XII, Doc. 69.

31. Ibid.

32. *DDF,* 2, XIII, Doc. 203.

33. *DDF*, 2, XIII, Doc. 431; see also Newton, *Profits of Peace*, passim.

34. *DDF*, 2, XIII, Doc. 464.

35. Ibid.

36. Robert J. Young, "Reason and Madness: The Axis Powers and the Politics of Economic Disorder, 1938–39," *Canadian Journal of History* 20 (April 1985): 75–79.

37. Ibid., p. 77, quoting Archive Daladier, Bibliothèque Nationale, Paris, 2 DA1, Dossier 5, p. 45, unpub. ms. by Daladier entitled "Munich."

38. Ibid., p. 76.

39. Ibid., pp. 78–79.

40. Ibid., p. 78, Didelet, Deuxième Bureau, March 21, 1939.

41. *DDF*, 2, XV, Doc. 143.

42. *The Economist*, April 1, 1939, p. 14; Overy estimates the German debt at 41.7 billion Rm. See Overy, *The Nazi Economic Recovery 1932–1938*, Table XII, p. 43.

43. Ibid.

44. *DDF*, 2, XVI, Doc. 276.

45. Ibid.

46. *DDF*, 2, XVI, Docs. 120, 121.

47. Ibid.

48. *The Economist*, April 8, 1939, p. 83.

49. For details see *The Economist*, May 13, 1939, pp. 370–371.

50. *The Economist*, June 24, 1939, pp. 710–711.

51. *DBFP*, 3, IV, Doc. 172.

52. See Schmidt, *The Politics and the Economics of Appeasment: British Foreign Policy in the 1930s*, passim, esp. chap. 1, "Economic Appeasement," pp. 31–225.

53. For the Wohltat and Ashton-Gwatkin talks, see *DBFP*, 3, V, Doc. 741.

54. For Wohltat's talks with Hudson and Wilson, see *DBFP*, 2, VI, Doc. 370.

55. *DBFP*, V, Doc. 741.

56. PRO/T-188/288, Leith-Ross to Berkeley Gage, note, July 19, 1939.

57. Leibovitz, *The Chamberlain-Hitler Deal*, pp. 464ff.; also David Dilks (ed.), *The Diaries of Sir Alexander Cadogan* (London, 1971), p. 178.

58. On the press reaction to the British talks with Wohltat, see *DDF*, XVII, Docs. 267, 268, 270, 285, 296.

59. *DDF*, 2, XVII, Doc. 372; see also Martin Gilbert and Richard Gott, *The Appeasers* (London, 1969), pp. 222–224.

60. *DDF*, 2, XVI, Doc. 361.

61. Ibid.

62. In a note to Eden on July 17, 1936, Ramsay MacDonald noted that his policy had been to prevent the "outbreak of war." Schmidt, *The Politics and Economics of Appeasement*, p. 302, n. 498.

63. Ibid., p. 212, n. 535.

64. Ibid., p. 209.

65. On these points Leith-Ross wrote: "I do not believe there is the slightest chance that the totalitarian states would accept such a condition in return for any economic assistance . . . before anything can be done in the way of economic collaboration there must be a better political atmosphere. The German experts like Wiehl, who is over here take the same view." PRO /T-188/288. Leith-Ross to S. Rowe-Dutton, January 25, 1939; see also Schmidt, *The Politics and Economics of Appeasement*, p. 219.

66. Schmidt, *The Politics and Economics of Appeasement*, p. 213.

67. Ibid., p. 219, n. 567.

68. Ribbentrop told Count Ciano, Italian Foreign Minister, in Rome in 1937: "He had to admit frankly that his mission had been a failure. Also some recent British manifestations, the conservative party vote against the cession of colonies to Germany, have proved the irreconcilability of the interests of the two countries." Oswald Hauser, *England und das Dritte Reich, 1936–1938*, vol. 2 (Stuttgart, 1972), pp. 383f., citing Rodolfo Mosca, *L'Europa verso la catastrofe*, vol. 1, p. 236.

69. Hauser, *England und das Dritte Reich*, p. 211. Hitler received the impression from Halifax that if the British were unwilling to join him in an alliance "London would not be

opposed if he moved to solve his problems alone." To the Austrian Chancellor Schuschnigg he declared: "Lord Halifax had completely approved his policy towards Austria and Czechoslovakia." Ibid. Hitler told Halifax that he wanted colonies only for economic reasons, but if Germany's African colonies could not be returned, other areas would be acceptable. Halifax did speak of his willingness to make changes in Austria and the net effect of his visit was to give Hitler the impression that Britain would not object to a closer relationship with Austria if that could be done peacefully. Göring was more specific: Germany wanted to incorporate Austria and the Sudetenland and settle the problems of Danzig and the corridor but he assured Halifax that "We will never use force." Thus, Hauser's conclusion seems to be correct. See Lois G. Schwoerer, "Lord Halifax's Visit to Germany: November 1937," *The Historian* 32, no. 3 (May, 1970): passim.

70. CAB23/100/ 33 (39), June 21, 1939, R-57.

71. CAB23/100/ 36 (39), July 5, 1939, R-57; and C.P. 148 (39), R-57.

72. Ibid.

73. Ibid. The British cabinet paper calculated British and German wage rates on the basis of 1928–1929 as equal to 100. British wage rates were approximately 25% higher. They estimated that, as compared to 1929, German wage rates were down by 20% whereas British were up by 6%. C.P. 148 (39).

74. CAB23/100/ 36 (39), R-57.

75. Ibid.

76. For a masterly analysis of the pyramiding difficulties of the economy, see Tim Mason, "The Domestic Dynamics of Nazi Conquests: A Response to Critics" in Childers and Kaplan (eds.), *Reevaluating the Third Reich,* pp. 161–182.

Chapter 10

1. The arguments are surveyed in the article by Larry Neal, "The Economics and Finance of Bilateral Clearing Agreements: Germany 1934–1938," *The Economic History Review,* Second Series 32, no. 3 (August 1979): 391–404. An older study is Howard S. Ellis, *German Exchange Control in Central Europe* (Cambridge, Mass., 1941). See also articles by various writers from Eastern and Western Europe in the Yugoslav publication, *The Third Reich and Yugoslavia 1933–1945* (Institute for Contemporary History, 1975); also a 1930s study by the Royal Institute of International Affairs, *South East Europe: A Political and Economic Study* (1939). See also P. Friedman, "The Welfare Costs of Bilateralism, German-Hungarian Trade 1933–1938," *Explorations in Economic History* 13, no. 1 (1976). See also Ránki, *Economy and Foreign Policy.*

2. Neal, "The Economics and Finance of Bilateral Agreements: Germany, 1934–1938," pp. 395–396.

3. Ibid.

4. Ibid., citing Charles Kindleberger, *The Terms of Trade: A European Case Study* (New York, 1956), pp. 120–122.

5. Friedman, "The Welfare Costs of Bilateralism, German-Hungarian Trade 1933–1938."

6. See Alan S. Milward, "The Reichsmark Bloc and the International Economy" in Gerhard Hirschfeld and Lothar Kettenacker (eds.), *Der "Führerstaat": Mythe und Realität. Studien zur Struktur und Politik des Dritten Reiches* (Stuttgart, 1981), pp. 377–401. Also his older article, "Der Deutsche Handel und der Welthandel 1925–1939," in Hans Mommsen, Dietmar Petzina, Bernd Weisbrod (eds.), *Industrielles System und politische Entwicklung in der Weimar Republik* (Düsseldorf, 1974).

7. Milward, "The Reichsmark Bloc and the International Economy," p. 383.

8. Ibid., Bernd-Jürgen Wendt, "Südosteuropa in der nationalsozialistischen Grossraumwirtschaft. Eine Antwort auf Alan S. Milward," in Hirschfeld and Kettenacker (eds.), *Der "Führerstaat": Mythe und Realität: Studien zur Struktur und Politik des Dritten Reiches,* p. 419.

9. *Montgomery Papers,* George H. Peck, Special Advisor to the President on Foreign Trade, Washington, D.C., October 31, 1934, to Montgomery, Box 2, Group No. 353, Vol. IV.

10. *Montgomery Papers,* Pierpont Moffat, Washington, D.C., to John F. Montgomery, April 20, 1939, Vol. VI, Box 3.

11. Jozo Tomasevich, *Peasants, Politics and Economic Change in Yugoslavia* (Stanford, 1955), p. 625.

12. Ibid., pp. 627–628.

13. *DDF,* 2, Vol. XVII, Doc. 373, Annex I.

14. Ibid.

15. Ibid.

16. Zdenka Simončić, "The Influence of German Trade Policy on Economic Development in Croatia in the Period from the Great Depression to the Second World War," in *The Third Reich and Yugoslavia,* p. 369.

17. Ibid., 372.

18. Leposava Cvijetić, "The Ambitions and Plans of the Third Reich with Regard to the Integration of Yugoslavia into its So-Called Grosswirtschaftsraum," in *Yugoslavia and the Third Reich, 1933–1945,* p. 195.

19. Ibid., p. 189.

20. Hoptner, *Yugoslavia in Crisis,* p. 113, n. 23 quoting a *New York Times* article.

21. Hans-Joachim Hoppe, *Bulgarien–Hitler's eigenwilliger Verbündeter, eine Fallstudie zur nationalsozialistischen Südosteuropapolitik* (Stuttgart, 1979), p. 50, n. 3, 4, 5, 6, 7.

22. Ivan T. Berend and György Ránki, *The Hungarian Economy in the Twentieth Century* (London and Sydney, 1985), p. 144 and Table 3.28, p. 145.

23. Ivan T. Berend and György Ránki, *Underdevelopment and Economic Growth: Studies in Hungarian Social and Economic History* (Budapest, 1979), p. 222, n. 3, citing Hungarian National Archives, Economic Policy Department of Ministry of Foreign Affairs, German file, Res. 358–1939.

24. Ibid., p. 223, n. 4, citing *Hungarian National Archives,* Foreign Ministry Economic Policy Department. Res. 30–1939.

25. Ibid.

26. Ibid., pp. 222–223.

27. Ibid., p. 224, n. 7, citing *Honi Par (Home Industry),* March 15, April 1, May 1, 1939.

28. Ibid., p. 224, n. 8, citing *Hungarian National Archives,* Orszaggyulesi Bizottsag (Parliamentary Commission) Protocol, vol. 17, p. 84, January 23, 1939.

29. Ibid., p. 226, n. 11, citing *Hungarian National Archives,* Foreign Ministry Economic Policy. Res. 466–1941.

30. Ibid., pp. 226f., n. 12.

31. Ibid., p. 232, n. 29, citing *Hungarian National Archives,* Foreign Ministry Economic Policy Department. Res. 751–1941.

32. Ibid., n. 31, citing *Hungarian National Archives,* Foreign Ministry Economic Policy Department. Res. 402–March 29, 1941.

33. For details see Ibid., pp. 232ff.

34. Ibid., p. 247, n. 78, 79, 80.

35. Ibid., p. 246, n. 76.

36. Ránki, *Economy and Foreign Policy,* p. 191.

37. For Romanian anxieties over Bessarabia, see Dov B. Lungu, *Romania and the Great Powers, 1933–1940* (Durham, 1989), passim.

38. Elizabeth Wiskemann, "The Rumano-German Treaty," *The Spectator,* April 14, 1939 (January–June 1939), 162, p. 626. Grenzebach believes that the major factor in the German-Romanian treaty was the Romanian need for aircraft and other war material. Grenzebach, "Germany's Informal Empire in East Central Europe," p. 784. By granting Germany and the Czech Protectorate 40% of their oil needs for the first six months of 1939, Romania was able to satisfy Germany's aircraft requirements. Ibid., p. 808.

39. Gligor Popi, *Jugoslovensko-Rumunski Odnosi 1918–1941* (Vrsae, 1984), p. 204, citing Romanian Ministry of Foreign Affairs, f. 71/1, vol. 51, tel. no. 7403, Gafencu's report on his Belgrade visit; also Antonia Kuzmanova, *Balkanskata Politika na Rumuniia 1933–1939* (Sofia, 1984), p. 171, n. 98; see also Beck, *Dernier Rapport,* pp. 172–174, and *DGFP,* D, V, Doc. 83, n.1.

40. Popi, *Jugoslovensko-Rumunski Odnosi 1918–1941,* p. 205, citing Romanian Ministry of Foreign Affairs, 7,71/1, Romania, Dosar pe. a 1939, March 18, 1939, report of Romanian minister in Belgrade, Viktor Cadere.

41. Ibid., p. 187.

42. Lungu, *Romania and the Great Powers, 1933–1940*, p. 143, n. 52.

43. Ibid., pp. 148f.

44. Ibid., pp. 160f. and Maurice Pearton, *Oil and the Romanian State* (Oxford, 1971), p. 259. Gafencu's judgment is shared by Pearton as "strictly valid." Ibid., p. 220. My own findings also agree with those of the work of Rebecca Haynes, which appeared too late for analysis, that the March 1939 German-Romanian trade agreement did not give the Germans a monopoly over Romania's exports. See the reviewer's remarks of Frederick Kellogg in the *American Historical Review* 2, no. 1 (2002), pp. 307f.

45. I. Champalov, "K istorii zakluchenie germano-ruminskogo ekonomicheskogo soglashenia 1939 goda," *Novaia i noveisiia istoriia* (1955): 143. On Ashton-Gwatkin's visit to Berlin, Harvey reports that "all he saw there were anxious for more commercial and economic concessions.... All admitted the economic difficulties of Germany, albeit they are as yet far from desperate." John Harvey (ed.), *The Diplomatic Diaries of Oliver Hardy, 1937–1940* (London, 1958), entry for March 9, 1939, p. 259.

46. Champalov, "K istorii zakluchenie...," pp. 144, 146. Maisky, the Soviet minister to London, reported to the British that "Moscow thought [the] Hudson Mission too good to be true and were very mistrustful of us since Munich." Harvey (ed.), *The Diplomatic Diaries of Oliver Hardy, 1937–1940*, entry for March 9, 1939, p. 259.

47. For documentation on the March 23, 1939, German-Romanian economic agreement see *DGFP*, D, V, Docs. 282, 293, 294, 295, 297, 298, 306, and *DGFP*, D, VI, Doc. 131; see also Lungu's account in *Romania and the Great Powers*, pp. 148ff.; also Leo Kunevan, Germany and the Iron Guard (unpublished M.A. thesis, University of Dayton, 1967), pp. 28ff. and Grigore Gafencu, *Prelude to the Russian Campaign* (London, 1945).

48. Ibid. For the text of the German-Romanian agreement see *DGFP*, D, VI, Doc. 78.

49. M. S. Kaser and E. A. Radice (eds.), *The Economic History of Eastern Europe, 1919–1975*, vol. 2 (New York, 1985), p. 402, table 17.3. According to Kaser and Radice's figures, crude oil production fell from 6,610 in 1938 to 3,525 in 1944. Ibid. Writing from Bucharest at the time, Elizabeth Wiskemann noted that Romanian production had been falling since 1936: Some Romanians "are skeptical about Germany's gain because as they are able to point out, the production of oil has been falling off. Whereas 8,704,000 tons of crude oil were produced in 1936, in 1937 production fell to 7,153,000, and in 1938 to 6,600,000." See Wiskemann, "The Rumano-German Treaty," p. 626. Also Pearton, *Oil and the Romanian State*, p. 222. Pearton's figures were 60% of capacity in 1939. Ibid.

50. Ibid., p. 402, table 17.3.

51. Ibid., pp. 161f, n. 42.

52. Ibid., p. 141, n. 34, 35.

53. Ibid., p. 142.

54. Teichert, *Autarkie und Grossraumwirtschaft in Deutschland 1930–1939*, p. 108.

55. Ibid., p. 105.

56. Ibid., p. 172.

57. Ibid., pp. 150f.

58. Ibid., p. 154.

59. Ibid., pp. 191f.

60. Ibid., p. 199.

61. Ibid., pp. 135ff.

62. Dörte Doering, *Deutsche Aussenwirtschaftspolitik, 1933–35* (Berlin, 1969), p. 173.

63. Ibid., p. 347, n. 381.

64. Ibid, p. 180 and n. 410. Gustav Hilger and Alfred G. Meyer, *The Incompatible Allies: A Memoir-History of German-Soviet Relations, 1918–1941* (New York, 1953), pp. 280–284.

Chapter 11

1. Patrick Salmon, "Anglo-German Commercial Rivalry in the Depression Era: The Political and Economic Impact on Scandinavia 1931–1939," in Marie-Luise Recker (ed.), *Von der Konkurrenz zur Rivalität: das britisch-deutsche Verhältnis in den Ländern der europäischen Peripherie* (Stuttgart, 1986), p. 102.

2. For the latest in his studies of U.S.-German trade rivalry, see Hans-Jürgen Schröder, "Widerstände der USA gegen europäische Integrationsbestrebungen in der Weltwirtschaftskrise

1929–1939," in Helmut Berding, *Wirtschaftliche und politische Integration in Europa im 19 und 20 Jahrhundert* (Göttingen, 1984), pp. 169–184.

3. Salmon, "Anglo-German Commercial Rivalry in the Depression Era: The Political and Economic Impact on Scandinavia 1931–1939," pp. 129, 139.

4. Ibid., pp. 116f.

5. Merja-Jiisa Hinkkanen-Lievonen, "Britain as Germany's Commercial Rival in the Baltic States, 1919–1939," in Recker (ed.), *Von der Konkurrenz zur Rivalität: das britisch-deutsche Verhältnis in den Ländern der europäischen Peripherie,* p. 43.

6. Ibid., p. 45 and pp. 46–49, tables on p. 106 for British and German trade with the Baltic states.

7. Zweig, *Poland Between Two Wars,* p. 122; also R. Nötel, chap. 12, p. 272, table 12.46 in Kaser and Radice (eds.), *The Economic History of Eastern Europe 1919–1975.*

8. Zweig, *Poland Between Two Wars,* p. 122; Nötel gives the German share as 18% after 1935, *The Economic History of Eastern Europe,* chap. 12, p. 274, table 12.47.

9. Nötel, chap. 12, p. 274, table 12.47. Zweig gives somewhat different figures: French, 27.1%; American, 19.2%; German, 13.8%; Belgian, 12.5%; Swiss, 7.2%; British, 5.5%; and Austrian, 3.5% for 1977. Zweig, *Poland Between Two Wars,* p. 122.

10. J. Taylor, *The Economic Development of Poland 1919–1950* (Ithaca, N.Y., 1952), p. 121, table 46; Zweig, *Poland Between Two Wars,* p. 99. The figures cited are a composite of the two sources. Similar figures are given in League of Nations, *Europe's Trade, 1941,* p. 52, table 27.

11. Taylor, *The Economic Development of Poland 1919–1950,* p. 121.

12. *The Economist,* March 1938; cf. Taylor, *The Economic Development of Poland,* p. 121, table 45 (in złotys).

13. Svetozar Tskov, "Ekonomichekie pozitsii i protivorechiia mezhdu imperialisticheskimi derzhavami i gretsii nakanuene mirovoi voini," in *Balkanskii Istorskii Sbornik,* vol. 2, Akademiia Nauka Moldavskoi SSR (Kishinev, 1970), pp. 306f.

14. Ibid., p. 308.

15. Ibid., p. 311.

16. Ibid.

17. Ibid.

18. See figures in Ibid.

19. Ibid., p. 314.

20. Ibid.

21. Maurice Williams, "The Aftermath of Anschluss: Disillusioned Germans or Budding Austrian Patriots," *Austrian History Yearbook* 14 (1978): 129–142.

22. Bell, *The Origins of the Second World War in Europe,* p. 155. Cf. J. Jeremy Noakes and Geoffry Pridham (eds.), *Nazism 1919–1945: State, Economy and Society, 1933–39,* vol. 2 (Exeter, 1984), p. 298.

23. Teichert, *Autarkie und Grossraumwirtschaft in Deutschland,* p. 279, n. 53, based upon the calculations of W. G. Hoffmann and J. H. Müller, *Das Deutsche Volkseinkommen 1851–1957* (Tübingen, 1959), table 1.

24. Bell, *The Origins of the Second World War in Europe,* p. 155.

25. Alan Milward comments: "German-Russian trade after 1933 became insignificant and it was clear that a re-ordering of Europe's frontiers to correspond with Germany's economic ambitions would ultimately have to involve large areas of Russian territory. Southeastern Europe, without Russia, could make only a very limited contribution to emancipating Germany from her worldwide network of imports. A war against the Soviet Union seemed to be a necessary vehicle for political and economic gain." Alan Milward, *War, Economy and Society 1939–1945* (Berkeley and Los Angeles, 1977), p. 10.

26. Heinz Pentzlin, *Hjalmar Schacht: Leben u. Wirken einer umstrittenen Persönlichkeit* (Berlin, 1980), p. 252. Hitler had attended a German officer's course on economics in 1918–1919. His attitude toward the subject of foreign trade was that it was "the quintessential domain of the Jew," and a "corruption of the national spirit." Teichert, *Autarkie und Grossraumwirtschaft in Deutschland 1930–1939,* pp. 206, 211. He was unconditionally opposed to the idea of Germany regaining its position of preeminence in the pre–World War I era through economic competition on the world market as "the delusion of a peaceful economic conquest."

This could only be achieved through a policy of power (*Machtpolitk*). Ibid., pp. 210–211. However, Göring's estimate of Hitler's economic knowledge was rather high. See *National Archives*, Göring Interrogation, September 17, 1946, M-1019, R-21, Fr. 0473, p. 4.

27. Bell, *The Origins of the Second World War in Europe*, pp. 151f. and Hayes, *Industry and Ideology: IG Farben in the Nazi Era*, pp. 165f. quoted in Alan Bullock, *Hitler and Stalin, Parallel Lives* (New York, 1992), p. 450.

28. Wilhelm Treue, "Das Dritte Reich u. die Westmächte auf dem Balkan," *Vierteljahreshefte für Zeitgeschichte* 1 (1953): 58.

29. Alfred Kube, "Aussenpolitik und 'Grossraumwirtschaft.' Die deutsche Politik zur wirtschaftlichen Integration Südosteuropas 1933 bis 1939," in Marie-Luise Recker (ed.), *Von der Konkurrenz zur Rivalität: das britisch-deutsche Verhältnis in den Ländern der europäischen Peripherie* (Stuttgart, 1986), pp. 185–211.

30. Hofer, *Der Nationalsozialismus Dokumente 1933–1945*, p. 196; also *IMF*, vol. XXVI, Doc. 789–PS.

31. See Eichholz, *Geschichte der deutschen Kriegswirtschaft 1939–1941*, I, p. 15; also Bell, *The Origins of the Second World War in Europe*, p. 152. On the eve of the German attack on Poland a British source reported "70% against Hitler, party divided and soldiers, etc.," Harvey, *The Diplomatic Diaries of Oliver Hardy, 1937–1940*, entry for August 31, 1939, p. 310.

32. Peter Hayes believes Petzina's figures are somewhat exaggerated; he estimates that in the period of the Plans from 1936 to 1942, IG Farben's share only amounted to 26% of the total Plan. Peter Hayes, Paper, *AHA*, December 28, 1985. However, in his published work he states that if IG's holdings are added it approximates 32.5%, which falls greatly on the high side. Hayes, *Industry and Ideology: IG Farben in the Nazi Era*, p. 170, n. 42. But the figures of Hayes indicate IG Farben's role was still considerable. IG Farben's net profits, according to Hayes, increased fivefold between 1933 and 1943. *AHA*, Paper, December 28, 1985. According to another source it was somewhat more than threefold (74 mill. Rm to 240 mill. Rm). Noakes and Pridham, *Nazism 1919–1945, State, Economy and Society, 1933–1939*, vol. 2, pp. 32, 58.

33. *DGFP*, D, VII, Doc. 192.

34. Hardy notes: the "Polish Finance mission has left in [a] state bordering on despair at [the] attitude of H.M.G. and Treasury towards financial assistance for Poland. They were told we did not regard it 'as of great urgency' and we wished to attach all sorts of conditions." Despite the support of British ambassador Howard Kennard "for really large loans," British Treasury officials, Chamberlain and Halifax, remained niggardly in their financial treatment of Poland. Harvey, *The Diplomatic Diaries of Oliver Hardy, 1937–1940*, entry for July 4, 1939, pp. 301f. For Polish indignation over this flap, see Beck, *Dernier Rapport*, p. 210. Beck ascribes the problem to Leith-Ross and Sir John Simon.

35. Beck noted the "dangerous personality" of the new foreign minister, Ribbentrop, and a "new current" and "new accents" in Hitler's words. Beck, *Dernier Rapport*, p. 182.

36. *National Archives*, Göring Interrogation, by Col. Amen, August 28, 1945, German dossiers, Box 18, pp. 6, 8.

37. Peterson, *Hjalmar Schacht: For and Against Hitler*, p. 238, n. 87.

38. Zdenek Sladek, "L'Industrie Tchécoslovaque et sa lutte contre la concurrence allemande dans les balkans durant les années 30," *Études Balkaniques* nos. 1 and 2 (1990): 59–68 and 3–16, and Zdenek Sladek and Ljuben Berov, "Čehoslovatskii kapital v stranah Jugovostočnoi Evropi v period mezhdu pervoi i vtoroi mirovimi voinami," *Études Balkaniques* no. 4 (1988): 18–40. I am indebted to these two articles by Sladek and Berov for the material in the text on the Czechoslovak struggle against German commercial competition in the Balkans.

39. A. H. Hermann, *The History of the Czechs* (London, 1975), p. 211. Hermann's assessment is concurred in by Victor S. Mamatey and Radomír Luža (eds.), *A History of the Czechoslovak Republic 1918–1948* (Princeton, 1973), p. 197.

40. Ibid.

41. Elizabeth Wiskemann, *Czechs and Germans* (London, 1938), p. 145.

42. The economic and social distress in the Sudeten German populated areas is described in ibid., pp. 166ff.

43. Hermann, *The History of the Czechs*, p. 212.

44. Ibid., p. 216.

45. Ibid., p. 218.

46. Ibid., p. 219; Wiskemann, *Czechs and Germans,* pp. 168 ff.

47. Zora P. Pryor, "Czechoslovak Economic Development in the Interwar Period," in Victor S. Mamatey and Radomír Luža (eds.), *A History of the Czechoslovak Republic 1918–1948,* p. 200.

48. Hermann, *The History of the Czechs,* p. 219.

49. Herbert Gross, "Deutschlands Handelspolitische Einkreisung durch USA," *Wirtschaftsdienst* 41 (October 8, 1937): 1411.

50. Ibid.

51. Ibid.

52. Ibid., p. 1412.

53. Ibid.

54. *UGFOD,* Dresden, Ministerial Director Sarnow, note on conversation between Pilja and Clodius, October 12, 1936; *UGFOD,* Berlin, Benzler circular to Austria and Balkan capitals, February 27, 1936.

55. Schröder, "Südosteuropa als 'Informal Empire' Deutschlands 1933–1939," *Jahresbücher für Osteuropas* 23 (1975): 86–87.

56. For the comments of Addison, see Campbell, *Confrontation in Central Europe: Weimar Germany and Czechoslovakia,* p. 247.

Chapter 12

1. CAB/23/97 2 (39), January 25, 1939, R-55.

2. Ibid.

3. Ibid. For von Krosigk's report to Hitler in September 1938 of Germany's financial problems, see *IMT,* vol. XXXVI, Doc. EC-419, Berlin, September 1, 1938, and for the English translation see *Nazi Crimes and Conspiracy,* vol. 7, pp. 474 ff.; also von Krosigk's account in Lutz Graf Schwerin von Krosigk, *Memoiren* (Stuttgart, 1977), p. 189. Von Krosigk claims he warned Hitler about the possibility of war and that "in order to make an impression" told Hitler that "the day would come when the Czechs can be given the coup de grace" at a later date. This was brought up at Nuremberg and contributed to Krosigk's sentence. Ibid.

4. CAB/23/97 2 (39), January 25, 1939, R-55.

5. Leonidas E. Hill (ed.), *Die Weizsäcker Papiere 1933–1950* (Berlin, 1974) (n.d.), entry for February 1, 1939, p. 149 and n. 7, p. 510.

6. Heinemann, *Hitler's First Foreign Minister: Constantin Freiherr Neurath, Diplomat and Statesman.*

7. Wendt, *Economic Appeasement,* pp. 471f.

8. Hans-Erich Volkmann, "Aussenhandel u. Aufrüstung in Deutschland 1933 bis 1939," in Friedrich Forstmeier and Hans-Erich Volkmann, *Wirtschaft u. Rüstung am Vorabend des Zweiten Weltkrieges* (Düsseldorf, 1975), p. 85.

9. Willi A. Boelcke, *Die deutsche Wirtschaft 1930–1945 Interna des Reichswirtschaftsministeriums* (Düsseldorf, 1983), p. 197.

10. *Hitler's Secret Conversations 1941–1944* (New York, 1961), p. 410.

11. Schmidt, *The Politics and Economics of Appeasement,* p. 244, and n. 69.

12. Wendt, *Economic Appeasement,* p. 487.

13. Ibid. According to an East German writer, Chamberlain held 11,747 shares in Imperial Chemical Industries and Simon 1,512. Moreover, after the First World War Chamberlain was on the Board of the Elliots Metal Company, an affiliate of Imperial Chemical, which had invested £10 million in I. G. Farben, which stood to gain through the seizure of the Czechoslovak chemical industry and the brown coal mines, the basis for many chemical products. To avoid development of the Czechoslovak chemical industry by I. G. Farben, Czechoslovakia invited in Du Pont de Nemours which had no direct connection with Farben. See Albert Norden, *Die Nation und Wir: Ausgewählte Aufsätze und Reden 1933–1964* (Berlin, 1965), vol. 1, pp. 213f. and n. 1, quoting the *Prager Presse,* August 31, 1933, on Du Pont de Nemours.

14. Willi A. Boelcke, *Die Kosten von Hitlers Krieg: Kriegs finanzierung und finanzielles Kriegserbe in Deutschland* (Paderborn, West Germany, 1985), pp. 63–64.

15. For a discussion of the pros and cons of Germany's economic situation on the eve of war in 1939, see Ibid., pp. 51ff. See also Overy, *The Nazi Economic Recovery: 1932–1938.* The latter work stops at 1938 when expansionary pressures really intensified.

16. James, *The German Slump: Politics and Economics 1924–1936*, p. 419.

17. Ibid., pp. 418–419.

18. Ibid.

19. Lutz Graf Schwerin von Krosigk, *Staatsbankrott* (Göttingen, West Germany, 1974), p. 228. Cf. figures cited in Deist et al., *Das Deutsche Reich und der Zeite Weltkrieg*, vol. 1, pp. 247–248. The figure of 60 billion Rm, about 20% of which was covered by the famous secret MEFO bills against future Reich revenues (discontinued after 1937 because they were too inflationary) seems to be the most conservative figure offered and does not include militarily related expenses apart from weaponry, which would make the figure higher. Hitler's inflated figure of 90 billion Rm is generally believed to have been given for propaganda reasons.

20. Maxine Yaple Sweezy, "German Corporate Profits: 1926–1938," *Quarterly Journal of Economics* 54 (1940): 390, table 1. See also the findings of Hoffmann previously stated in chap. 1 corroborating this.

21. Ibid.

22. Hayes, *Industry and Ideology: IG Farben in the Nazi Era*, passim.

23. For the Hermann Göring "Reichswerke" I have relied on R. J. Overy, "Heavy Industry and the State in Nazi Germany: The Reichswerke Crisis," *European History Quarterly* 15 (1985): 322.

24. Ibid.

25. Ibid., pp. 325, 329, 331.

26. Volkmann, "Aussenhandel u. Aufrüstung in Deutschland 1933 bis 1939," p. 86.

27. Ibid., pp. 88f.

28. Ibid., p. 89.

29. Ibid., p. 94.

30. Schröder, *Deutschland u. die Vereinigten Staaten 1933–1939*, p. 130.

31. Volkmann, "Aussenhandel u. Aufrüstung in Deutschland 1933 bis 1939," p. 102, table B.

32. Schröder, *Deutschland u. die Vereinigten Staaten 1933–1939*, p. 142, n. 96. The critical position of trade in the 1930s from the American standpoint may be gauged from the statement of Francis B. Sayre, Assistant Secretary of State and head of the Executive Committee on Commercial Policy: "Every blow at our foreign trade is a direct thrust at our economic and social life." Ibid, p. 240 and n. 31. For the inroads made into U.S. trade in Latin America by Germany and the complaints of U.S. firms like the Sharp Paper Co. and the Goodyear Tire and Rubber Co. to the State Department, see ibid., pp. 243 and 253.

33. Ibid., p. 272. The United States did not accept its gradual exclusion from Southeastern Europe with the equanimity of the British and resented the German bilateral trade system as unfair. See Ibid., especially chap. 6, pp. 265–283.

34. Bernd-Jürgen Wendt, "Strukturbedingungen der britischen Südosteuropapolitik am Vorabend des Zweiten Weltkrieges," in F. Forstmeier and H. Volkmann (eds.), *Wirtschaft u. Rüstung am Vorabend des Zweiten Weltkrieges* (Düsseldorf, 1975), p. 298.

35. Antonin Basch, *The Danube Basin and the German Economic Sphere* (New York, 1943), p. 8.

36. P. L. Cottrell, "Aspects of Western Equity Investment in the Banking Systems of East Central Europe," in Alice Teichova and P. L. Cottrell (eds.), *International Business and Central Eastern Europe* (New York, 1983), p. 310.

37. Ibid., pp. 312 and 372, n. 6.

38. G. Ránki, "The Hungarian General Credit Bank in the 1920s" in Teichova and Cottrell (eds.), *International Business and Central Eastern Europe 1918–1939*, p. 359.

39. Ibid., pp. 358 and 371 n. 5; for Anglo-French rivalries in the 1920s see Ránki, *Economy and Foreign Policy: the Struggle of the Great Powers in the Danube Valley, 1919–1929*, chap. 2, pp. 33–46.

40. Cottrell, "Aspects of Western Equity Investment in the Banking Systems of East Central Europe," p. 344, n. 5.

41. Philippe Marguerat, *Le IIIe Reich et le pétrole roumain 1938–1940* (Leiden, 1977), p. 35.

42. Ibid., p. 66 and n. 3. According to a study made by the Deutsches Institut für Bankwissenschaft u. Bankwesen, in 1938 French and British capital investment made up about 70%

of foreign capital invested in Romania while foreign capital made up about 13 to 14 billion lei out of 49 billion lei, or 25% to 30%. Ibid., p. 29. Cf. Ránki, *Economy and Foreign Policy,* pp. 190–191.

43. Volkov, *Germano-iugoslavskie otnosheniia i razval maloi antanti,* p. 221. Foreign investment capital in southeastern Europe in 1938 totaled more than $2.5 billion of which Britain and France held the lion's share, more than eight times the amount held by Germany. Ibid.

44. *IMT,* Vol. XXVII, Doc. 1301–PS.

45. Volkmann, "Aussenhandel u. Aufrüstung in Deutschland 1933 bis 1939," p. 103. However, of Germany's total foreign trade, the Southeastern European states made up 17%, according to a Yugoslav writer, a somewhat higher figure than usually cited. See Dušan Lukać, *Treći Rajh i Zemlje Jugoistočne Evrope, 1937–1941* (Belgrade, 1982), part 2, p. 26. For a general discussion on the increasing exploitation of the region by Germany see especially pp. 22–48.

46. Ránki, *Economy and Foreign Policy,* p. 191; and see also Lukać, *Treći Rajh i zemlje 1937–1941,* part 2, p. 39.

47. Ibid.

48. L. Berov, "The withdrawing of western capital from Bulgaria on the eve of the Second World War," in *Politikata na Velikite Sili na Balkanite v Navećerieto na vtorata Svetovna voina* (Sofia, 1971), pp. 225–256.

49. Ljudmila Živkova, "The Economic Policy of Germany and Britain in Southeastern Europe on the Eve of the Second World War," *Études Balkaniques* no. 1 (1969): 39.

50. Basch, *The Danube Basin and the German Economic Sphere,* p. 178.

51. Ibid., p. 177.

52. Ibid., p. 200.

53. Lukać, *Treći Rajh i Zemlje Jugoistočne Evrope, 1937–1941,* part 2, p. 35; also Živko Avramovski, "Ekonomičeskie i političeskie celi nemećkogo vvoz vooruzeniia v balkanskie strani nakanune vtoroi mirovoi voini," *Studia Balcanica* 7 (1973): 99–103.

54. Lukać, *Treći Rajh i Zemlje Jugoistočne Evrope, 1937–1941,* part 2, p. 34.

55. Boelcke, *Die deutsche Wirtschaft 1930–1945,* p. 189.

56. Basch, *The Danube Basin and the German Economic Sphere,* pp. 207–208.

57. Avramovski, "Ekonomičeskie i političeskie celi," p. 104.

58. Ibid., p. 105.

59. Ibid., p. 106.

60. Ibid., p. 107.

61. Ibid., p. 108.

62. Ibid., pp. 112–113.

63. Ibid.

64. Ibid., pp. 114–115.

65. See Victor Axenciuc, "La Place occupée par La Roumanie dans la division Mondiale Capitaliste à la veille de la Seconde Guerre Mondiale," *Revue roumanie d'histoire* 4 (1966): 693.

66. Marguerat, *Le IIIe Reich et le pétrole Roumain 1938–1940,* p. 19. Orders of weaponry by the Southeastern countries amounted to 172 million Rm in 1936 (68.5% of German exports of this kind) and 103.8 million Rm in 1937. See Ioan Chiper, "L'Expansion économique de l'Allemagne nazie dans les Balkans: Objectifs, méthodes, résultats (1933–1939)," in *Studia Balcanica* 7 (1973): 125.

67. Avramovski, "Ekonomičeskie i političeskie celi," pp. 115–116.

68. For the Soviet oil delivery schedule, see Marguerat, *Le IIIe Reich et le pétrole Roumain 1938–1940,* pp. 159f.

69. Ibid., p. 76.

70. Živkova, "The Economic Policy of Germany and Britain in southeastern Europe," p. 42; see also Champalov, "K istorii zaklucheniia germano-ruminskogo ekonomicheskogo soglasheniia 1939 goda," *Novaia i noveishaia istoriia* no. 1 (1959): 137. See also Marguerat, *Le IIIe Reich et le pétrole Roumain 1938–1940,* p. 111.

71. See M. J. Rooke, "The Concept of Political Trading in Peacetime: The British Government and Trade with Southeastern Europe, 1938–39," *Rev. Études Sud-Est Europe* 22, no. 2 (1984): 177.

72. CAB 24/277 C.P.127 (38); also Ibid., p. 177.

73. Rooke, "The Concept of Political Trading in Peacetime," p. 178.

74. See Wendt, "Strukturbedingungen der britischen Südosteuropapolitik am vorabend des Zweiten Weltkrieges," pp. 302f.

75. Rooke, "The Concept of Political Trading in Peacetime," pp. 176, 184, 194.

76. Ibid., p. 180.

77. Živkova, "The Economic Policy of Germany and Britain in Southeastern Europe," p. 40.

78. Marguerat, *Le IIIe Reich et le pétrole roumain 1938–1940,* p. 108.

79. CAB/23/96 56 (38), November 22, 1938, R-56.

80. For a detailed analysis of Chamberlain's "free hand in the east" policy toward Hitler, see Leibovitz, *The Chamberlain-Hitler Deal.* A scathing analysis of the "Clivedon set" is given by the British historian A. L. Rowse, who writes: "...there was a fatal confusion in their minds between the interests of their social order and the interests of their country. They did not say much about it, since that would have given the game away and anyway it was thought they did not wish to be too explicit about it even to themselves, but they were anti-Red and that hamstrung them in dealing with the greater immediate danger to their country, Hitler's Germany." On the British leaders of the time: "...a certain superciliousness, a lofty smugness, as well as a superficiality of mind...." "...they were late Victorians by birth, public-spirited and respectable, conventional and unimaginative. Indeed they distrusted imagination and intellectualism." A. L. Rowse, *Appeasement and All Souls: A Study in Political Decline, 1933–1939* (1961), pp. 115, 117.

Chapter 13

1. Schröder, "Südosteuropa als 'Informal Empire' Deutschlands," p. 79.

2. Hoptner, *Yugoslavia in Crisis, 1934–1941,* pp. 74f.; see also *DGFP,* C, 2, Doc. 318; also Weinberg, *The Foreign Policy of Hitler's Germany,* 1, p. 116.

3. Schröder, "Südosteuropa als 'Informal Empire' Deutschlands," p. 79.

4. For German-Yugoslav trade increases, see Ibid., p. 87.

5. Ibid., pp. 88–89.

6. Ibid., p. 89.

7. *Prince Paul's Archive,* Belgrade, Stojadinović to Antić, November 26, 1938 (hereafter *PPA*).

8. *PPA,* Paris, Spaljaković to Prince Paul, July 31, 1935.

9. Ibid.

10. *PPA,* note by Prince Paul, May 4, 1936.

11. *PPA,* Topola, note by Prince Paul on conversation with Beneš, April 6, 1937.

12. *PPA,* note by Prince Paul, May 4, 1936.

13. Ibid.

14. Holmes, "Europe and the Hapsburg Restoration in Austria, 1930–1938," p. 179.

15. *DGFP,* V, Doc. 56; see also Weinberg, *The Foreign Policy of Hitler's Germany,* 1, pp. 116–117.

16. *UGFOD,* Berlin, Benzler, circular note, February 17, 1936.

17. *UGFOD,* Berlin, von Neurath, note of conversation with Cincar-Marković, March 10, 1936; *UGFOD,* Berlin, Bulow note, March 16, 1936; *UGFOD,* Belgrade, von Hassell, March 24, 1936.

18. *UGFOD,* Belgrade, unsigned note, March 24, 1936.

19. J. B. Hoptner, "Yugoslavia as Neutralist: 1937," *Journal of Central European Affairs* 16, no. 11 (July 1956): 172.

20. Hoptner, *Yugoslavia in Crisis, 1934–1941,* p. 40; also Hoptner, "Yugoslavia as Neutralist," p. 173.

21. Ibid., pp. 41f; also Hoptner, "Yugoslavia as Neutralist," pp. 173–174.

22. Ibid., pp. 48–51.

23. Milan Stojadinović, *Ni rat ni Pakt, Jugoslavia izmedju dva rata* (Buenos Aires, 1963), p. 447.

24. *PPA,* note by Prince Paul, May 4, 1936.

25. *PPA*, Purić to Stojadinović, February 15, 1937, conversation between Prince Paul and Mussolini. The document reads 1929, but must refer to 1937.

26. *PPA*, note by Prince Paul, March 25, 1937, conversation between Ciano and Prince Paul.

27. The Bulgarian minister to Berlin reported German enthusiasm over the pact between Bulgaria and Yugoslavia: "In the German Ministry of Foreign Affairs everybody told me they are extremely glad this agreement has been arrived at.... Some functionaries... told me that this was the first gap made in the Balkan Agreement." See Živko Avramovski, "The Yugoslav-Bulgarian Perpetual Friendship Pact of 24 January 1937," *Canadian Slavonic Papers* 11, no. 1 (1959): 304–338. On Yugoslavia's waning influence in Albania, see Živko Avramovski, "Problem albanije u Jugoslavensko-Italijanskom Pakta od 25, III, 1937," *Istorijski Pregled* 1 (Zagreb, 1963): 19–31; and Hoptner, *Yugoslavia in Crisis,* pp. 61–83.

28. *UGFOD*, Berlin, von Erdmannsdorff note, March 25, 1936.

29. *UGFOD*, Rome, Hassell note, April 2, 1937.

30. *UGFOD*, Athens, note, June 4, 1937.

31. *UGFOD*, Athens, unsigned note, May 21, 1937.

32. *PPA*, note by Prince Paul, May 14, 1937, Belgrade conversation with Yvon Delbos.

33. Stojadinović, *Ni Rat ni Pakt,* p. 502.

34. *PPA*, note, May 13, 1938.

35. *PPA*, Stojadinović to Prince Paul, September 22, and 25, 1938.

36. *PPA*, letter, Stojadinović through Nenadović to Prince Paul, September 25, 1938; see also Nicolae Petrescu-Comnen, *Preludi del Grande Dramma* (Rome, 1947), pp. 120f. These sentiments undoubtedly stemmed from Campbell's (the British minister in Belgrade) statement according to Stojadinović, that "England did not want to go to war for two million Sudetens, but England had made her last concession." Ibid.

37. Campbell noted Yugoslavia's change of policy: "For Yugoslavia the Berlin-Rome axis is scarcely a reality since Germany and Italy are competing for her favors." Yugoslavia's momentary course was "in favor of Italy who shares her fear of a German thrust to the Adriatic." *BFO*, Campbell, Belgrade, to F.O., January 13, 1939, 371/R382/383/317/67.

38. *BFO*, Campbell, Belgrade, to F.O., January 19, 1939, 371/R1079/297/67. Also Avramovski, "Sukob interesa V. Britanije i Nemačke na Balkanu uoči drugog svetskog rata," p. 35.

39. *BFO*, Campbell, Belgrade, to F.O., January 19, 1939, 371/R1079/297/67.

40. Ibid.

41. Ibid.; also Alfredo Breccia, *Jugoslavia 1939–1941: Diplomazia della Neutralità* (Milan, 1978), pp. 9ff.

42. *BFO*, Campbell, Belgrade, to F.O., January 19, 1939, 371/R1079/297/67.

43. *PPA*, Foreign Press Reports, Belgrade, November 16, 1937.

44. *BFO*, Campbell, to F.O., Belgrade, January 19, 1939, 371/R1079/297/67.

45. A detailed analysis of Stojadinović's fall is in Breccia, *Jugoslavia 1939–1941,* pp. 1–13. For conflicting views of what Stojadinović told Ciano, see Stojadinović, *Ni Rat ni Pakt,* pp. 56ff. Cf. Ciano, *L'Europa verso la Catastrofe,* pp. 409ff. and *Ciano's Diary, 1939–43* (London, 1947), entries for January 12, 16, 1939. In January 1939 Ciano noted: "There is no doubt about the intentions of Stojadinović with respect to the Axis and full solidarity. Personally he would like to go even further. But I wonder if the present internal situation will allow him to make decisions of such nature."

46. *BFO*, Campbell, to F.O., Belgrade, January 16, 1939, 371/R629/20/92.

47. Ciano, *L'Europa verso la Catastrofe,* p. 411.

48. The Political Director of the French Government told Sir Eric Phipps that Stojadinović "had rather frightened the Prince Regent." *BFO*, Paris, Sir Eric Phipps, to F.O., February 8, 1939, 371/93520/92. See also Stojadinović, *Ni Rat ni Pakt,* pp. 576ff. and Hoptner, *Yugoslavia in Crisis, 1934–1941,* pp. 121ff. In November 1940 Prince Paul told Ugo von Hassell, the former German minister to Belgrade, that he suspected Stojadinović of having intimate conversations with Ciano and of wanting to sacrifice Croatia to Italy. He had to get an accord with the Croats and Stojadinović stood in his way because of his bad relations with them. *UGFOD*, von Hassell, to Berlin, note conversations held in Belgrade, November 25, 1940. Prince Paul also suspected Italy of wanting to get a foothold in Albania through Stojadinović to surround

Yugoslavia with the aid of Bulgaria which was to receive territory on the Aegean through which Italian supplies could be shipped to the Bulgars. See Breccia, *Jugoslavia 1939–1941*, p. 10.

49. Korošec, the Slovenian representative in the government, then feuding with Stojadinović, is reported to have gone to Athens and secured the support of the Greek royal house for his removal. For this story and the role of the British, according to James Joyce, the American Vice-Minister in Belgrade, see Branko Pešelj, "The Serbo-Croatian Agreement of 1939 and American Foreign Policy," *Journal of Croatian Studies* 11–12 (1970–1971): 37. The British were uncertain whether Stojadinović's removal was a pre-condition for the negotiations with the Croats. BFO, Campbell, to F.O., February 13, 1939, 371/R1093/20/92.

50. Prince Paul's analysis of the Axis leaders and their courses of action and other matters were highly prized pieces of information in London. Thus, for example, his confidential notes to Halifax on his visits to Rome and Berlin in June 1939 were carefully scrutinized. See the comments of Halifax and Foreign Office officials and Prince Paul's handwritten note of September 4, 1939, on Italy's attitude in the event of war between Germany and the Western Powers. BFO, Campbell, to F.O., Belgrade, June 14, 1939, 371/7636/409/92. On the June 1939 confidences made through Campbell to Halifax, the British minister stated: "Prince Paul made me once again beg him (Halifax) to observe the strictest discretion. If the Germans, he said, got to know that he had told me (Campbell) everything he had, he might just as well take a revolver and shoot himself." BFO, Campbell, to F.O., Belgrade, June 17, 1939, 371/R5148/202/6409/92. Apropos of Prince Paul's loyalty, Maček noted in June 1939 that the transfer of Yugoslavia's gold to London meant that "Belgrade would adhere to England." Breccia, *Jugoslavia 1939–1941*, p. 42, n. 61.

51. BFO, Wickham-Steed to Vansittart, London, April 7, 1939, F.O., 371/R2704/20/92 and appended letter of R. W. Seton-Watson.

52. The involved story of Maček's coquetting with the Italians cannot be detailed here and may be reviewed in Ciano, *Diaries, 1939–1943*, passim, Hoptner, *Yugoslavia in Crisis, 1934–1941*, pp. 138–141, and Breccia, *Jugoslavia 1939–1941*, passim.

53. IMT, Doc. 1874 PS; Ciano, *Diaries, 1939–1943*, entry for March 15, 1939; Hoptner, *Yugoslavia in Crisis*, pp. 136f. See also the memorandum of the German minister in Belgrade, von Heeren, "The New Direction of Domestic Policy in Yugoslavia and the Effect on our Further Treatment of the Croatian Question." Von Heeren recommended supporting the federalist, autonomist position of the Croats instead of the centralist policy of the fallen Stojadinović because of the cultural and historical ties between Germans and Croats, the danger from Italy and the possibility of a Croatian gravitation to "a leftist democratic direction." However, this was rejected by the German State Secretary who advised a "hands off" policy be adopted toward Croatian separatism. DGFP, D, 5, Doc. 310.

54. UGFOD, v. Mackensen, to Berlin, Rome, March 20, 21, 22, 1939.

55. UGFOD, Berlin, Ribbentrop memo, March 25, 1939.

56. BFO, 371/R2807/R3276/R3417/409/92.

57. Mario Toscano, *The Origins of the Pact of Steel* (Baltimore, 1967), p. 232.

58. Churchill cautioned in the House of Commons against provoking Italy into a war in the Mediterranean. Winston Churchill, *Blood, Sweat and Tears* (New York, 1941), pp. 113f. For similar remarks by Bullitt, see FRUS, II (1939), p. 380. Joseph Kennedy commented on the Italian seizure of Albania: "The striking part is Halifax does not know whether they (i.e., the Yugoslavs) are in on the deal with the Italians or whether they are playing it safe. The English had written off Albania and the Adriatic as an Italian sphere. At a meeting of the Naval Board this morning they dismissed the idea that the Adriatic was of any importance to them; that previous to this time it has all been in Italy's hands anyway." FRUS, II (1939) p. 387. The American minister Lane in Belgrade found the Yugoslav government "weak and cringing toward Germany" and afraid to move against Italy. FRUS, II (1939), p. 377, 379. Cf. Yugoslav Premier Cvetković's claim that Yugoslavia would have fought if assured of British support, in Hoptner, *Yugoslavia in Crisis*, p. 143, n. 21.

59. UGFOD, Heeren, to AA, Belgrade, April 13, 1939; also UGFOD, Schmidt to Ribbentrop, April 14, 1939.

60. UGFOD, v. Erdmannsdorff to AA, Budapest, April 12, 1939.

61. UGFOD, v. Mackensen to AA, Rome, April 24, 1939, tel. 161.

62. *UGFOD,* Clodius memos, Berlin, April 24, 27, 1939. Though still suspicious of Yugoslav intentions, the Italians believed the Yugoslavs were advancing slowly along the prescribed road. *UGFOD,* Mackensen to AA, Rome, May 12, 1939, tel. 187.

63. *DBFP,* III, 5, Docs. *555, 606, 635, 705.* For Turkey's alarm at Italian and German actions in Czechoslovakia and Albania, see the reports of the Italian ministers in Sofia, Bucharest, Athens and Ankara. See *DDI,* VIII, 12, Docs. 6, 179, 206, 235, 265, 268. Turkish Foreign Minister Saracoglu told De Peppo, the Italian minister at Ankara after Hitler's dismemberment of Czechoslovakia, that Hitler "believed himself in direct contact with God" and Mussolini's desire to recreate the Roman Empire including in it Anatolia had created uneasiness in Turkey. *DDI,* VIII, 12, Doc. 289. In July Saracoglu brusquely asked De Peppo: "Why concentrate so many troops in Albania?" *DDI,* VIII, 12, Doc. 513.

64. *DBFP,* III, 5, Doc. 555.

65. *DDI,* VIII, 12, Docs. 129, 140, 177, 362.

66. *UGFOD,* v. Heeren to AA, Belgrade, May 6, 1939, tel. 138.

67. *UGFOD,* Woermann note, May 3, 31, 1939. According to De Peppo at Ankara, the terms of the offer to Bulgaria were: Bulgaria would enter the Balkan Pact; if Bulgaria did not receive southern Dobrudja after two years the matter would be resolved by arbitration. Bulgaria, in turn, would have to renounce its demand for Thrace. *DDI,* VIII, 12, Doc. 217.

68. Potemkin's visit to Sofia is described in *UGFOD,* Bülow to AA, Sofia, May 5, 8, 1939, tels. 50 and 53.

69. *UGFOD,* v. Richthofen to AA, Sofia, May 21, 1939; *UGFOD,* Clodius to AA, Sofia, July 12, 1939, tel. 99; *UGFOD,* Wehl note, Berlin, August 11, 1939.

70. Avramovski, "Sukob Interesa V. Britanije i Nemačke na Balkanu uoči drugog svetskog rata," p. 111, n. 197, citing the letter of the Turkish Minister of Foreign Affairs of August 25, 1939, No. 1453.

71. *UGFOD,* Welczeck to AA, Paris, July 24, 1939, tel. 383.

72. Avramovski, "Sukob Interesa V. Britanije i Nemačke na Balkanu uoči drugog svetskog rata," p. 118, n. 206.

73. Ibid., p. 118, n. 205.

74. *DBFP,* IV, Doc. 393.

75. Raymond Brugère, *Veni, Vedi, Vichy ... et la Suite* (Paris, 1953), p. 12 and annex 1, pp. 161–163 and pp. 13–14; and General Alexandro Papagos, *The Battle of Greece 1940–1941* (Athens, 1949), p. 66.

76. Papagos, *The Battle of Greece 1940–1941,* pp. 60f. These assurances were renewed by General Gamelin to General Papagos, December 27, 1940. Ibid., pp. 145–148.

77. Ibid., p. 64.

78. Ibid., pp. 93–94

79. *UGFOD,* Weizsäcker, memo, Berlin, September 28, 1939.

80. *UGFOD,* Richthofen to AA, Sofia, September 1, 1939, tel. 146.

81. The German historian, Broszat, refers to this period from March 1939 to May 1940 as the "phase of retarded German hegemony." After the Prague coup of March 1939 any plans for the closer cooperation of the states of Southeastern Europe failed, in particular the possibility of a settlement between Romania and Hungary. Martin Broszat, "Deutschland-Ungarn-Rumänien," *Historische Zeitschrift* 206 (1968): 70f.

82. *UGFOD,* Woermann, memo, Berlin, Draganov conversation, October 23, 1939.

83. The British suspected that General Weygand harbored a desire to command the combined Allied forces in any future Balkan theater of operations. See Elizabeth Barker, *British Policy in South-east Europe in the Second World War* (London, 1976), pp. 14–15.

84. René Massigli, *La Turquie devant la guerre: Mission à Ankara 1939–1940* (Paris, 1964), p. 320; General Maxime Weygand, *Recalled to Service* (London, 1952), p. 26.

85. Massigli, *La Turquie devant la guerre,* p. 284; also Read and Fisher, *The Deadly Embrace,* pp. 362–363.

86. Ivan Maisky, *Memoirs of a Soviet Ambassador* (New York, 1967), p. 44.

87. Eloise Engle and Lauri Paananen, *The Winter War: the Russo-Finnish Conflict 1939–1940* (New York, 1973), pp. 132–133; also Lukacs, *The Great Powers and Eastern Europe,* pp. 282–283.

88. For an interesting study of these events, see Charles O. Richardson, "French Plans for Allied Attacks on the Caucasus Oil Fields January–April 1940," *French Historical Studies* 8, no. 1 (spring 1975). Also Sir Llewellyn Woodward, *British Foreign Policy in the Second World War* (London, 1970 and 1976), pp. 101, 104, 110–112.

89. J. A. Bayer, "British Policy Towards the Russo-Finnish Winter War 1939–40," *Canadian Journal of History* 16, no. 1 (April 1981): 27–65. For Richardson's conclusion see Richardson, "French Plans for Allied Attacks on the Caucasus Oil Fields January–April 1940," pp. 155–156.

90. Richardson, "French Plans for Allied Attacks on the Caucasus Oil Fields January–April 1940," p. 156.

91. John Colville, *The Fringes of Power: 10 Downing Street 1939–1955* (New York, 1986), p. 64.

92. Ibid., p. 92.

93. Carley, *1939: The Alliance That Never Was and the Coming of World War II*, pp. 246ff.

94. Ibid., pp. 246ff.

Chapter 14

1. CAB 23//96; also quoted in Ian Colvin, *The Chamberlain Cabinet: How the Meetings in 10 Downing Street, 1937–1939, led to the Second World War* (New York, 1971), p. 158.

2. Murray concludes: "Yet in economic and strategic terms Hitler's move against Prague made sense. In particular it eased the serious difficulties that Germany faced with foreign exchange, the purchase of raw materials and with maintaining the tempo of rearmament. As with the Anschluss the previous year, the occupation of Czechoslovakia gave a major boost to the rearmament effort. Thus, economic problems as well as long range goals led Hitler to make this effort." Murray, *The Change in the European Balance of Power 1938–1939: The Path to Ruin*, p. 281.

3. John Charmley, *Chamberlain and the Lost Peace* (London, 1989), p. 67.

4. *DBFP,* 3, 1, Doc. 157.

5. Rooke, "The Concept of Political Trading in Peacetime. The British Government and Trade with South-Eastern Europe 1938–39," p. 184.

6. Charmley, *Chamberlain and the Lost Peace,* p. 183; also *DBFP,* 3, 5, Letter of Henderson to Cadogan, May 14, 1939, p. 804.

7. *DBFP,* 3, 5, Letter of Henderson to Cadogan, May 14, 1939, p. 804.

8. Ibid., p. 192.

9. *DBFP,* 3, 5, Letter of N. Henderson, Mason-MacFarlane enclosure, May 15, 1939, pp. 806f.

10. Ibid., 3, 5, Doc. 8.

11. Ibid., 3, 5, Doc. 39.

12. Ibid., 3, 5, Doc. 41.

13. Simon Newman, *March 1939: The British Guarantee to Poland* (Oxford, 1976), p. 215.

14. Anita Prazmowska, *Britain, Poland and the Eastern Front 1939* (New York, 1987), p. 43. Bonnet, the French Foreign Minister, reports similar statements, on the occasion of his visit to London, by Halifax. Bonnet, *Défense de la Paix,* vol. 2, p. 162.

15. CAB 27/624 (41), March 27, 1939.

16. Namier, *Diplomatic Prelude, 1938–1939,* p. 104.

17. Phillip V. Cannistraro, Edward D. Wynot, Theodore P. Kovaleff (eds.), *Poland and the Coming of the Second World War: The Diplomatic Papers of A. J. Drexel Biddle, Jr., United States Ambassador to Poland 1937–1939* (New York, 1976), Docs. 17, 18, pp. 30ff.

18. Namier, *Diplomatic Prelude, 1938–1939,* pp. 104ff.

19. Cannistraro, et al., *Poland and the Coming of the Second World War,* p. 17, n. 50.

20. Ibid., Doc. 4, pp. 220f.

21. Ibid.

22. *DBFP,* 5, 3, Doc. 2.

23. Ibid., Doc. 263.

24. Ibid., Doc. 274.

25. Kaiser, *Economic Diplomacy and the Origins of the Second World War,* p. 294.

26. Dilks, *The Diaries of Sir Alexander Cadogan,* entry for October 1, 1938; also Prazmowska, *Britain, Poland and the Eastern Front, 1939,* pp. 35, 43.

27. See Read and Fisher, *The Deadly Embrace: Hitler, Stalin and the Nazi-Soviet Pact 1939–1941,* p. 35. Beck was not liked in Paris by Alexis Leger, Secretary-general of the French Foreign Office, Daladier and others.

28. Namier, *Diplomatic Prelude, 1938–1939,* p. 10. On March 22 Arciszewski told Szembek that "the [foreign] minister leaned toward the conception of a bilateral accord with England, which would leave France and the Soviets aside, in order not to give appearance of following a broad plan for the encirclement of Germany." Lipski had suggested to Beck tying Poland's counter-guarantee to the Franco-Polish Pact. Whether this decision by Beck was fatal is doubtful as Hitler would not have been taken in by such evasions. Namier believes Beck got carried away in London and could not resist playing the role of representative of a "Great Power." Ibid., pp. 112f., and Szembek, *Journal 1933–1939,* pp. 433f.

29. From the floor of the House of Commons Lloyd George — whom Chamberlain heartily disliked for sacking him from his cabinet in 1922 — derided Chamberlain's decision to guarantee Poland and exclude the Soviets. Both the Liberal and Labor leaders thought the Soviet Union and not Poland was the key. See Sidney Aster, *1939: The Making of the Second World War* (London, 1973), p. 115 and Newman, *March 1939: The British Guarantee to Poland,* p. 215. Prazmowska repeats the myth that Beck duped the British into giving him a guarantee. Prazmowska, *Britain, Poland and the Eastern Front, 1939,* p. 61.

30. Lord Halifax, *Fullness of Days* (New York, 1957), pp. 207f.

31. Ibid., p. 208.

32. Ibid., p. 209.

33. Read and Fisher, *The Deadly Embrace,* p. 70

34. Coulondre, *De Staline à Hitler,* p. 105.

35. Ibid., p. 254.

36. For the earliest contacts between Berlin and Moscow leading to the Nazi-Soviet Pact of August 1939, see Read and Fisher, *The Deadly Embrace,* pp. 70ff.

37. Aster, *1939: The Making of the Second World War,* pp. 173–174.

38. Ibid., p. 184.

39. Dilks, *The Diaries of Sir Alexander Cadogan,* p. 182; also quoted in Aster, *1939: The Making of the Second World War,* p. 185. Chamberlain's aversion for and diatribes against the Soviet Union are particularly revealing in his letters to his sisters.

40. Ibid., pp. 179f.

41. R. J. Q. Adams, *British Politics and Foreign Policy in the Age of Appeasement 1935–1939* (London, 1993), p. 149.

42. Sumner Welles, *The Time for Decision* (New York, 1944), p. 55.

43. Alfred Schneider, "Grenzen der Annäherung USA — Südamerika." *Wirtschaftsdienst* 41 (October 8, 1937): 1412.

44. *DBFP,* 3, 2, Docs. 896.

45. For Nazi impressions of the early New Deal and Roosevelt, see John A. Garraty, "The New Deal, National Socialism and the Great Depression," *American Historical Review* 78, no. 4 (October 1973): 907–944.

46. James McGregor Burns, *Roosevelt: The Lion and the Fox* (New York, 1956), p. 179.

47. On Roosevelt's tendency to view Germany and Hitler from his World War I experience in the Wilson government, see Klaus Schwabe, "Die Regierung Roosevelt und die Expansionspolitik Hitlers vor dem Zweiten Weltkrieg" in Karl Rohe, *Die Westmächte und das dritte Reich 1933–1939* (Paderborn, 1982), p. 105.

48. MacDonald, *The United States, Britain and Appeasement, 1936–1939,* pp. 8–9.

49. Ibid., pp. 6–7. See also Arnold A. Offner, *The Origins of the Second World War: American Foreign Policy and World Politics, 1917–1941* (New York, 1975), p. 121.

50. Ibid., p. 5.

51. *U.S. State Department,* Davies to State Department, January 29, 1937, tel. 12, Doc. 862.50.

52. MacDonald, *The United States, Britain and Appeasement, 1936–1939,* pp. 27f.

53. See Schatz, "The Anglo-American Trade Agreement and Cordell Hull's Search for Peace 1936–1938," pp. 89, n. 16., 93ff. Also on the visit of Lord Runciman, see Richard A. Harrison, "The Runciman Visit to Washington in January 1937." *Canadian Journal of History* 19 (August 1984): 217–239. Schatz cites David Reynold's belief that Chamberlain's interest in the trade talks was self-serving and "more cosmetic than real, as the prime minister hoped to advertise an Anglo-American cooperation to whose substance he had no real commitment." Ibid., p. 233, n. 63, citing Reynolds, *The Creation of the Anglo-American Alliance 1937–1941* (London, 1981), p. 286.

54. Ibid., pp. 50–62.

55. Ibid., pp. 22ff.

56. Burns, *Roosevelt: The Lion and the Fox*, p. 352.

57. Rock, *Chamberlain and Roosevelt: British Foreign Policy and the United States, 1937–1940*, p. 71.

58. MacDonald, *The United States, Britain and Appeasement, 1936–1939*, pp. 116, 118.

59. William R. Rock, *Chamberlain and Roosevelt: British Foreign Policy and the United States, 1937–1940* (Columbus, Ohio, 1988), p. 77.

60. These impressions are confirmed by Schwoerer, "Lord Halifax's Visit to Germany: November, 1937," pp. 361–363. See also Charmley, *Chamberlain and the Lost Peace*, pp. 18–21; and *U.S. State Department,* H. Johnson, London, December 10, 1937, Doc. RG59/740.00/253.

61. *U.S. State Department,* Bullitt and Welles, to Sec. of State, February 21 and 25, 1938, Docs. RG59/740.00/2991/2.

62. Ibid., Sayre to State Dept., memo, February 19, 1938, Doc. RG59/740.00/310.

63. For the negotiations of the Anglo-American Trade Agreement of 1938, see *U.S. State Department,* Sayre (London) to State Department, November 16, 1937, R-1252/712.49/365/0532–36; CAB23/96, October 19, 1938, R-54. See also Rock, *Chamberlain and Roosevelt, British Foreign Policy and the United States, 1937–1940,* pp. 137f. and MacDonald, *The United States, Britain and Appeasement,* pp. 110ff.

64. Hull, *The Memoirs of Cordell Hull,* vol. 1, p. 530; also quoted in Schatz, "The Anglo-American Trade Agreement and Cordell Hull's Search for Peace, 1936–1938," p. 103, n. 64.

65. Offner, *The Origins of the Second World War,* p. 107.

66. MacDonald, *The United States, Britain and Appeasement, 1936–1939,* p. 77.

67. Arnold A. Offner, *American Appeasement: United States Foreign Policy and Germany, 1933–1938* (Cambridge, Mass., 1969), p. 279.

68. MacDonald, *The United States, Britain and Appeasement, 1936–1939,* p. 88; Offner, *The Origins of the Second World War,* pp. 86ff.

69. Schwabe, "Die Regierung Roosevelt und die Expansionspolitik Hitlers vor dem Zweiten Weltkrieg," p. 131.

70. Rock, *Chamberlain and Roosevelt: British Foreign Policy and the United States, 1937–1940,* p. 140.

71. Ibid., pp. 173–174.

72. Ibid., p. 176.

73. For Thomsen's analysis of Roosevelt's foreign policy and his numerous fulminations against "an economic war . . . unleashed against Germany," see *DGFP,* D, VI, Docs. 14, 24, 33, 34, 56, 107, 130, 283, 403. See also *FRUS,* 1939, II, pp. 568f., 572–574. Through withdrawal of most-favored-nation status for goods from the former Czech provinces, the additional duty cost the Greater Reich's export trade, hitherto worth 200 million Rm, a cut of approximately 85 million Rm, which would have to be made up with hard currency, according to Wiehl, the economic specialist in the German Foreign Office. *DGFP,* D, VI, Doc. 130.

74. Newman, *March 1939: The British Guarantee to Poland,* p. 204.

75. MacDonald, *The United States, Britain and Appeasement, 1936–1939,* p. 12.

76. Ibid., p. 79.

77. Elliot Roosevelt (ed.), *F.D.R. His Personal Letters, 1928–1945* (New York, 1950), vol. 2, pp. 875–876. Roosevelt's handwritten note for the occasion reads: "Muss. hold key to peace[;] Hitler-bad shape-war as way out[;] Has to have Italy. Then cast her aside." Ibid.

78. Schatz, "The Anglo-American Trade Agreement and Cordell Hull's Search for Peace 1936–1938," p. 101 and n. 57 and 58.

79. Walter LaFeber, *Inevitable Revolutions — the United States in Central America* (New York, 1983), p. 88.

Chapter 15

1. PRO/T-188/231, Leith-Ross Papers.
2. PRO/T-188/297, Leith-Ross to Titulescu, December 28, 1934.
3. Ibid., note on the Anglo-Romanian Payments Agreement of September 2, 1938.
4. PRO/T-188/231, Leith-Ross Papers, Minute of S. D. Waley, June 17, 1938.
5. Ibid., British Minister Sir Reginald Hoare, Bucharest, to Foreign Office, n.d.
6. Ibid., memo, Leith-Ross on Tatarescu talk, June 21, 1938.
7. Ibid., Locock (Federation of British Industries), letter, June 22, 1938, with attached letter of June 13, 1938.
8. Ibid., letter of Leith-Ross to W. Brown, June 24, 1938; Brown to Leith-Ross, June 24, 1938; Leith-Ross to Ashton-Gwatkin, June 21, 1938; Sargent to Leith-Ross, June 27, 1938; Leith-Ross to Sargent, June 28, 1938.
9. Lungu, *Romania and the Great Powers 1933–1940,* p. 123; see also Kaiser, *Economic Diplomacy and the Origins of the Second World War,* p. 256.
10. According to Oliver Hardy, Halifax's cabinet paper, designed to increase financial and commercial assistance in the Balkans, was prompted by Maurice Ingram, an anti-appeaser. Harvey, *The Diplomatic Diaries of Oliver Harvey 1937–1940,* entry for June 5, 1938, p. 148. See also CAB/24/277 and CP (38)127, May 24, 1938.
11. Ion Calafeteanu, "Les Relations Économiques Germano-Roumaines de 1933 à 1944," *Revue d'Histoire 2e Guerre* no. 140 (1985): 29 and n. 20.
12. Ibid., p. 28.
13. Gheorghe Zaharia and Ion Calafeteanu, "The International Situation and Romania's Foreign Policy Between 1938 and 1940," *Revue Roumaine d'Histoire* 18, no. 1 (January–March 1979): 85f.
14. Charmley, *Chamberlain and the Lost Peace,* p. 91.
15. On the Wilson-Kordt episode the British documents are silent. Only a note in Cadogan's diary mentions a meeting with Kordt, but this concerned a warning from Theo's brother Eric working in Ribbentrop's Büro that Hitler intended war on September 20, 1938. Nothing is mentioned about Wilson's discussion of abandoning Southeastern Europe, which could only have been approved by Chamberlain. See Dilks, *The Diaries of Sir Alexander Cadogan 1938–1945,* pp. 94f., entry for September 6, 1938. See also the work by Erich Kordt, which does not mention Southeastern Europe. Eric Kordt, *Nicht aus den Akten: Die Wilhelmstrasse in Frieden und Krieg, Erlebnisse, Begegnungen und Eindrücke, 1928–1945* (Stuttgart, 1950), pp. 279f. The German description of the meeting is in *DGFP,* D, II, Doc. 382. For further details surrounding the discussions, see Kaiser, *Economic Diplomacy and the Origins of the Second World War,* pp. 256f.
16. For the Berchtesgaden and Godesberg conferences, see *DBFP,* 3, II, Docs. 896 and 1033. The British-French conferences are in ibid., Docs. 928 and 1093.
17. Charmley, *Chamberlain and the Lost Peace,* p. 126.
18. Lungu, *Romania and the Great Powers, 1933–1940,* p. 109.
19. Ibid., p. 126.
20. Ibid., p. 129.
21. Szembek, *Journal 1933–1939,* entry for July 1938, pp. 325f.
22. Lungu, *Romania and the Great Powers 1933–1940,* p. 131.
23. *DBFP,* 3, II, Doc. 898 and Kordt, *Nicht aus dem Akten,* p. 237.
24. A. A. Sheviakov, "Vneshniaia politika ruminii v period miunhena," *Voprosi Istorii* 12 (1970): 79, n. 38 citing A. Hillgruber, *Hitler, König Carol und Marschall Antonescu: Die Deutsch-Rumänischen Beziehungen 1938–1944* (Wiesbaden, 1954), p. 22.
25. Bigler, "Heil Hitler and Heil Horthy: The Nature of Hungarian Racist Nationalism and its Impact on German-Hungarian Relations 1919–1945," *East European Quarterly* 8, no. 3: 264. For a good summary of Hungarian foreign policy on the eve of Munich, see also Eric Roman, "Munich and Hungary: An Overview of Hungarian Diplomacy During the Sudeten Crisis," *East European Quarterly* 8, no. 1, pp. 71–94.

26. Anthony Tihamer Komjathy, *The Crisis of France's East European Diplomacy, 1933–1938* (New York, 1976), p. 114.

27. Miklós Szinai and Laszlo Szücs (eds.), *The Confidential Papers of Admiral Horthy* (Budapest, 1965), Doc. 7, pp. 26ff. On these early contacts see Bigler, "Heil Hitler and Heil Horthy," pp. 258ff.

28. Ibid., p. 260.

29. For Hungarian wavering between Hitler and the Western Powers, see both Roman, "Munich and Hungary," passim and Anthony T. Komjathy, "The First Vienna Award (November 2, 1938)," *Austrian History Yearbook* 15–16 (1979–1980): 131–156.

30. Roman, "Munich and Hungary," p. 82 quoting *DGFP*, D, II, Doc. 367.

31. The German account of the Hitler-Horthy meetings is in *DGFP*, D, II, Doc. 383. The best account is pieced together by C. A. Macartney, *A History of Hungary 1929–1945* (New York, 1956), vol. 1, pp. 238ff. Horthy repeated to Macartney in 1945 Hungary's lack of military preparations for war as his reason for declining Hitler's invitation to attack Czechoslovakia.

32. For Horthy's letters to Hitler and Chamberlain asking for restitution of Hungary's claims against Czechoslovakia and Chamberlain's answer, see Szinai and Szücs, *The Confidential Papers of Admiral Horthy,* Doc. 25, pp. 101ff. and Doc. 26, pp. 103ff. Chamberlain's favorable answer is in Doc. 29, pp. 109f.

33. Cienciala, mildly criticizing Beck and the Polish government, predicates their attitude on British and French failure to defend Czechoslovakia. Cienciala, *Poland and the Western Powers 1938–1939: A Study in the Interdependence of Eastern and Western Europe,* chaps. 2, 3, 4, especially pp. 142–148.

34. *DGFP*, D, IV, Docs. 257, 259 and n. 5, 267, 273. See also MacDonald, *The United States, Britain and Appeasement,* p. 109, n. 12. For Leith-Ross's dealings with the Germans, see Kaiser, *Economic Diplomacy and the Origins of the Second World War,* pp. 286ff. Kaiser correctly concludes that Leith-Ross must have had the approval of Chamberlain for such a step and he cooperated in the negotiations with Ashton-Gwatkin, a supporter of Chamberlain's appeasement policy. As Ashton-Gwatkin was the Foreign Office economic expert, it is difficult to see how that department would not have been privy to the offer. What is significant is that there is nothing in the British documents on Leith-Ross's offer which we learn of only through the German documents.

35. Ibid.; see also Reynolds, *The Creation of the Anglo-American Alliance 1937–41: A Study in Competitive Cooperation,* pp. 34, 52.

36. *The Westminster Bank Review,* February 1938, No. 288 and March 1939, No. 301, pp. 4–6.

37. Ibid., April 1939, No. 302, pp. 14–15; *The Chamber of Commerce Journal* 70, no. 999 (June 1939), "Anglo-Romanian Trade."

38. *Lloyd's Bank Monthly Review,* September 1939; *The Spectator,* Vol. 163, July 7, 1939.

39. George F. Kennan, *Memoirs 1925–1950* (Boston, 1967 paperback ed.), pp. 104f.

40. Murray, *The Change in the European Balance of Power, 1939–1939: The Path to Ruin,* pp. 258f. For Göring's fears that the shortages might lead to consumer product cuts, inflation and "the beginning of the end," see Carroll, *Design for Total War,* p. 103.

41. Murray's and Carroll's conclusions are confirmed by Göring's biographer, Alfred Kube, *Pour le Merite und Hakenkreuz: Hermann Göring im Dritten Reich* (Munich, 1986), pp. 182–184, 214, 260–264, 286ff. The annexation of the Czech area gained Hitler much military booty but was, according to his military experts, a disappointment, along with seizing Austria, as a solution to Germany's agrarian and raw material needs. Fearing the adverse effect of further armament expenses on the domestic economy, Hitler ordered that "military expenses in the future will be reduced to an acceptable amount." Ibid., pp. 282, 286.

42. Rooke, "The Concept of Political Trading in Peacetime. The British Government and Trade with Southeastern Europe, 1938–39," pp. 176f.

43. Ibid., p. 183.

44. Ibid., p. 185.

45. Dilks, *The Diaries of Sir Alexander Cadogan 1938–1945,* p. 121, entry for October 17, 1938. On the following day Cadogan again repeated to Halifax his "misgivings about Roumanian wheat," but the subject is not mentioned again in his diary. Ibid., entry for October 18, 1938.

46. Harold Nicolson (ed. Nigel Nicolson), *Diaries and Letters 1930–1939* (London, 1980), p. 376, entry for October 6, 1938.

47. Dilks, *The Diaries of Sir Alexander Cadogan 1938–1945,* p. 120.

48. Ibid., p. 119, n.d. but probably written in October 1938.

49. Nicolson, *Diaries and Letters 1930–1939,* p. 380, entry for November 5, 1938.

50. Newman, *March 1939: The British Guarantee to Poland,* p. 48, n. 2. Higher figures are cited in *The Economist.* For 1937 the trade deficit was £431.3 million and in 1938 it was £387.9 million or a 10.3% decline. See *The Economist,* February 18, 1939, vol. 134, no. 4982, *Commercial History and Review of 1938. The Westminster Bank Review* cites a drop of 11.3% in exports for 1938. *The Westminster Bank Review,* March 1939, No. 301, p. 3.

51. Newman, *March 1939: The British Guarantee to Poland,* pp. 44–45, n. 1.

52. CAB 24/280, R-194 "Central and Southeastern Europe," and attached First Interim Report of the Inter-Departmental Committee of October 26, 1938.

53. Ibid.

54. Ibid.

55. Ibid.

56. The British-Romanian discussions of November 1938 are described in Petrescu-Comnen, *Preludi del Grande Dramma,* pp. 577ff., also *DBFP,* III, 3, Doc. 262.

57. Rooke, "The Concept of Political Trading in Peacetime. The British Government and Trade with Southeastern Europe, 1938–1939," p. 190.

58. Dilks, *The Diaries of Sir Alexander Cadogan, 1938–1945,* entry for October 20, 1938, pp. 121f.

59. Vuk Vinaver, *Jugoslavija i Francuska izmedju dva svetska rata: Da li je Jugoslavija bila francuski "satelit"* (Belgrade, 1985), p. 396.

60. Ibid., pp. 396f.

61. Rooke, "The Concept of Political Trading in Peacetime. The British Government and Trade with Southeastern Europe, 1938–1939," p. 190.

62. For a somewhat different analysis, see Kaiser, *Economic Diplomacy and the Origins of the Second World War,* pp. 288–289.

63. PRO/T-188/297, Leith-Ross to Oliver Harvey, Bucharest, January 19, 1939.

64. Ibid.

65. Kaiser negatively viewed Leith-Ross's chairmanship of the Inter-Departmental Committee and believed that he "would not pursue an aggressively anti-German policy and doubted that Britain could do much to increase trade with Southeastern Europe." See Kaiser, *Economic Diplomacy and the Origins of the Second World War,* p. 254.

66. PRO/T-188/291, Memo, A. E. Overton, Board of Trade, to Leith-Ross, January 19, 1939.

67. PRO/T-188/231 and R-2352/26/37.

68. PRO/BT-11/231, Leith-Ross Papers, Note of Leith-Ross, April 25, 1939.

69. Ibid.

70. Ibid.

71. Ibid.

72. PRO/T-188/244, British Legation, Bucharest, Leith-Ross to Sir W. Brown on agreement between the British Trade mission and the Romanian Government.

73. Ibid.

74. Ibid., Sir W. Brown to Leith-Ross, letter, n.d.

Chapter 16

1. PRO/BT-11/1001.

2. Ibid.

3. Ibid.

4. Ibid.

5. Ibid.

6. Charmley, *Chamberlain and the Lost Peace,* p. 83, and chap. 9, n. 17.

7. PRO/BT-11/1077, memo, conversation between Djuričić, Yugoslav Minister of Finance, and W. Sturrock and C. N. Sterling, May 19, 1939.

8. Ibid., Campbell to Halifax, May 22, 1939.

9. Ibid., minute, June 6, 1939.

10. Ibid., minute, July 5, 1939.

11. Ibid., S. W. Waley, Treasury Dept., to Fraser, Board of Trade, June 8, 1939.

12. Ibid., S. W. Wood, Food Defense Plans Dept., to Fraser, Board of Trade, n.d.

13. Ibid., memo, Leith Ross, June 28, 1939.

14. Ibid., memo, Oliver Stanley to Halifax, June 30, 1939.

15. Ibid., memo, Sargent on conversation with Subbotić, July 3, 1939.

16. Ibid., also *BFO,* Belgrade, Campbell to Halifax, June 5, 1939, R-4808/409/92.

17. Ibid., Belgrade, Campbell to F.O., June 18, 1939.

18. CAB 23 (minutes) 38 (39) 13.

19. PRO/BT-11/1077 and PRO/R-6419/325/92, memo, H. R. MacLean, F.O., August 15, 1939. See also the attached Royal Yugoslav Government note on the bacon issue.

20. Ibid., memo, Campbell to F.O. September 11, 1939.

21. *U.S. State Department,* Belgrade, Lane to State Dept., April 20, 1938, Doc. 660h.6231.

22. For the Cavallero memorandum see *DDI,* 8, 12, Doc. 59. For an analysis of this important document see Toscano, *The Origins of the Pact of Steel,* pp. 376ff.

23. For Hitler's May 23, 1939, Secret Conference in the German Chancellery see *DGFP,* D, VI, Doc. 433; also Toscano, *The Origins of the Pact of Steel,* pp. 371–376.

24. *DGFP,* D, VI, Doc. 438, n. 2.

25. *DGFP,* D, V, Docs. 287.292, 299.

26. *BFO,* Campbell to F.O., Belgrade, April 24, 1939, 371/R3429/20/92.

27. *BFO,* Campbell to F.O., Belgrade, April 14, 1939, 371/R3001/20/92.

28. *BFO,* Campbell to F.O., Belgrade, June 3, 1939, 371/R4824/20/92.

29. Ibid.

30. Ibid.

31. *DGFP,* D, VI, Doc. 948.

32. *BFO,* Campbell to F.O. Belgrade, June 14, 1939, 371/R5148/202/G409/92. Paul conveyed his description of the two dictators to London in unflattering terms: Mussolini was "the murderer of King Alexander," "by comparison with the Duce, Al Capone must be a polished and God-fearing man!" In Rome the Italian leader had talked of Hitler almost with "tenderness" and Paul gained the impression the Axis was "unbreakable." The Regent felt London had not yet realized the moment was "ripe" to extricate Mussolini from the Axis grasp. *BFO,* Campbell to F.O., Belgrade, May 20, 1939, 371/R4494/92. See also Breccia, *Jugoslavia 1939–1941,* pp. 126ff. and *DGFP,* D, VI, Doc. 474.

33. *UGFOD,* v. Richthofen to Berlin, Sofia, July 3, 1939, No. 206.

34. *UGFOD,* v. Heeren to Berlin, Belgrade, July 3, 1939, No. 206.

35. *UGFOD,* Feine to Berlin, Belgrade, July 18, 1939, No. 212.

36. *BFO,* Campbell to State Secretary, Belgrade, July 18, 1939, No. 212.

37. Breccia, *Jugoslavia 1939–1941,* pp. 27f. quoting *Diplomatski arhiv Državnog sekretarijata inostranih poslova,* Subbotić Report, February 1939, n. 14, London Legation Fund, 1939, fasc. 2/1–11.

38. Ibid., p. 30 n. 42 quoting *Statistique du Commerce Exterieur de Yougoslavie,* pp. xx and xxi.

39. Ibid., p. 150, n. 22.

40. Ibid., pp. 122–123.

41. *DBFP,* III, 4, Doc. 420; also quoted in Kuzmanova, *Balkanskata Politika na Rumuniia, 1933–1939,* p. 170, and Breccia, *Jugoslavia 1939–1941,* p. 37.

42. Kuzmanova, *Balkanskata Politika na Rumunia, 1933–1939,* p. 170.

43. For Weizsäcker's testy remarks on the Turks and Gafencu see *UGFOD.* Berlin, Weizsäcker notes of June 13 and 27, 1939, St. Sec. File, Nos. 483, 516.

44. *DGFP,* D, 5, Doc. 310, "The New Directives of Domestic Policy and the Effect on our Further Treatment of the Croatian Question."

45. Ljubo Boban, *Sporazum Cvetković-Maček* (Belgrade, I.D.N., 1965), p. 72.

46. Vladko Maček, *In the Struggle for Freedom* (New York, 1957), pp. 195f.

47. Boban, *Sporazum Cvetković-Maček,* pp. 67f, n. 99.

48. Ibid., p. 69.

49. *UGFOD,* von Hassell, Belgrade, note of conversation with Prince Paul, n.d. but November 1940.

50. *BFO,* unsigned note. July 21, 1939, 371/R4066/92.

51. On Krnjević's visit to the Foreign Office, see *BFO,* unsigned memo, June 23, 1939, and Ingram's attached note, 371/R5341/20/92. Campbell blamed the failure of the negotiations on Maček's stubborn and unyielding attitude. *BFO,* Campbell, to Halifax, Belgrade, May 8, 1939, 371/R4066/20/92.

52. *DGFP,* D, 5, Doc. 310.

53. *UGFOD,* Heeren to Berlin, Belgrade, August 22 and 24, 1939.

54. *UGFOD,* Heeren to Berlin, Belgrade, September 24, 1939.

55. *BFO,* London, Interview of Ivan Subbotić with R. A. Butler, 371/R6939/20/92.

56. *BFO,* Campbell, Belgrade, December 29, 1939, 371/R12201/20/92, and paper "Communism in Yugoslavia."

57. *BFO,* Campbell, December 26, 1939, 371/R12201/29/92.

58. Sava D. Bosnitch, The Foreign Policy Line of the Communist Party of Yugoslavia in the Second Imperialist War, September 1, 1939–June 22, 1941 (unpub. Ph.D. dissertation, McGill University, Montreal, July 1970), pp. 45–46ff.

59. Ibid. At the time the CPY viewed the Balkans as a zone of conflict between British and German capital interests, a view held by Yugoslav historians until the dissolution of that country in 1989–1990. Ibid., quoting *Izraz.*

60. *BFO,* Campbell, December 26, 1939, 371/R12201/29/92. See also Branko Lazitch, *Tito et la Révolution Yugoslave* (Paris, 1957), pp. 36–38.

61. Ibid., citing *Izraz,* II, 1939, pp. 597–606; see also Avramovski, "Sukob Interesa V. Britanije i Nemačke na Balkanu uoči drugog svetskog rata," *Istorija XX veka,* II knjiga.

62. Ibid.

63. *BFO,* R. H. Seton-Watson to F.O., memo, "The Situation in Yugoslavia," November 26, 1939, 371/R11331/29/92.

64. Ciano, *L'Europa verso la Catastrofe,* pp. 451–455.

65. Ciano, *Diaries, 1939–1943,* entry for August 31, 1939; also Ciano, *L'Europa verso la Catastrofe,* pp. 461f. For a tantalizingly brief moment, prodded by Ciano, Mussolini toyed with breaking relations with Hitler. Ciano, *Diaries, 1939–1943,* entries for August 15, 18, 21, 1939.

66. *BFO,* Prince Paul to Halifax, handwritten note, August 25, 1939, 371/R7099/122/37.

67. Ibid.

68. *BFO,* Campbell, Belgrade, September 16, 1939, 371/R7636/409/92.

69. *BFO,* Campbell, Belgrade, June 15, 1939, 371/R5106/790/7. The British ambassador to Ankara, Knatchbull-Hugessen, suggested giving southern Dobrudja to Bulgaria as a bribe in April 1939. *DGFP,* III, 5, Docs. 62, 73, 162, 279, 285, 279.

70. *BFO,* Lord Halifax to Prince Paul, note July 5, 1939.

71. The terms of Jebel Agreement are in Gafencu, *Prelude to the Russian Campaign,* p. 260. See also Breccia, *Jugoslavia, 1939–1941,* pp. 210ff.

72. See Frank Marzari, "Projects for an Italian-Led Balkan Bloc of Neutrals, September–December 1939," *Historical Journal* 13, no. 4 (December 1970): 778, n. 30.

73. For a discussion of these plans see ibid. The plan for a neutral bloc of states headed by Italy was encouraged both in Rome and Bucharest by the British Foreign Office. It was anti-Soviet as well as anti-German but Berlin saw it as a British conspiracy aimed against Germany. See Živko Avramovski, "Attempt to Form a Neutral Bloc in the Balkans (September–December 1939)," *Studia Balcanica* no. 4 (1971): 151. See also Breccia, *Jugoslavia 1939–1941,* pp. 212ff. According to Breccia, the suggestion for the bloc of neutrals came from Ciano to the German ambassador in Rome which would have "a primarily commercial character," p. 213.

74. Marzari, "Projects for an Italian-Led Balkan Bloc of Neutrals," p. 780, citing Eliza Campus, "Der balkanbloc der Neutralen (Sept. 1939–Marz 1940)," *Wissenschaftliche Zeitschrift der Karl Marx Universität* 6 (1956–1957): 15–22.

75. Ibid., p. 781.

76. Ibid., p. 782. *BFO,* Terrance Shone, British Chargé, Belgrade, November 10, 1939, 371/R10517/2613/67.

77. *UGFOD,* v. Papen, Ankara, November 8, 1939, No. 458.

78. *UGFOD,* v. Richthofen, Sofia, October 18, 1939.
79. *BFO,* O'Malley, Budapest, October 13, 1939, 371/C17002.
80. Woodward, *British Foreign Policy in the Second World War,* pp. 23ff.
81. *War Cabinet Meeting,* September 13, 1939, Doc. WM (39). See also Phyllis Auty and Richard Clogg (eds.), *British Policy Towards Wartime Resistance in Yugoslavia and Greece* (London, 1975), p. 96.
82. Woodward, *British Foreign Policy in the Second World War,* p. 29.
83. *BFO,* Campbell, Belgrade, November 1939, and attached "Memorandum for Chiefs of Staff," War Cabinet Meeting.
84. *UGFOD,* v. Heeren, Belgrade, September 30, 1940.
85. *UGFOD,* Berlin, note, September 17, 1939.
86. *UGFOD,* v. Heeren, Belgrade, September 10, 1939, No. 283.
87. *UGFOD,* Berlin, Wiehl note, September 21, 1939; also *UGFOD,* v. Heeren, Belgrade, September 21, 1939.
88. *UGFOD,* Wiehl note, Berlin, February 7, 1940.
89. *UGFOD,* v. Heeren, Belgrade, September 11, 1939, No. 346.
90. *UGFOD,* v. Heeren, Belgrade, September 24, 1939, No. 346.
91. *UGFOD,* v. Heeren, Belgrade, September 28, 1939, No. 362.
92. *UGFOD,* v. Heeren, Belgrade, September 19, 1939.
93. *UGFOD,* Weizsäcker note, September 21, 1939, No. 327.
94. Ciano, *Diaries, 1939–43,* entry for October 23, 1939. Hungarian Foreign Minister Czaky had gotten wind of the plan and warned Ciano of Italian unpopularity in Croatia and the danger of setting the Balkans on fire. Ibid., entry for January 8, 1940, and Ciano, *L'Europa Verso la Catastrofe,* p. 503.
95. For details of this meeting in the house of Ciano in Rome with Pavelić, Bombelles, Maček's confidant and probably a double agent in Belgrade's pay, and Anfuso, chef de cabinet of Ciano, see Ciano, *Diaries, 1939–1943,* entry for January 22, 1940. See also Breccia, *Jugoslavia, 1939–1941,* pp. 239ff.
96. *BFO,* Campbell, Belgrade, to Nichols, January 7, 1940, 371/R544192; also *DDI,* 9, III, Doc. 16.
97. Cvetković's statement, Campbell thought, was "directed to Yugoslavia's powerful neighbors [with] whose good intentions the Minister for Foreign Affairs is not, I think, so satisfied as his words seem to indicate." *BFO,* Campbell, Belgrade to Halifax, January 8, 1940, 371/R621/415/92.
98. Woodward, *British Foreign Policy in the Second World War,* p. 22.
99. *BFO,* Nichols to Cadogan, February 12, 1940, 371/R2457/415/92.
100. *BFO,* Campbell to Cadogan, Belgrade, January 7, 1940, and appended notes of Noble and Phillip Broad.
101. *BFO,* Campbell, Belgrade, April 4, 1940, 371/R4832/415/92.
102. *BFO,* Campbell to Cadogan, Belgrade, January 22, 1940, 371/R1318/5/67.
103. Richardson, "French Plans for Allied Attacks on the Caucasus Oil Fields, January–April 1940," pp. 130–156.
104. Broszat, "Deutschland-Ungarn-Rumänien Entwicklung und Grundfaktoren national-sozialistischer Hegemonial und Bundnispolitik 1938–1941," pp. 44–99.
105. See Barker, *British Policy in Southeastern Europe in the Second World War,* pp. 28–43.
106. Ibid., p. 33.
107. *DGFP,* D, XIII, Doc. 514, memorandum of Keitel to Ribbentrop.
108. *UGFOD,* v. Richthofen, Sofia, May 31, 1940, No. 160.
109. Barker, *British Policy in South-east Europe in the Second World War,* pp. 31.
110. *DGFP,* D, IX, Docs. 191 and 237.
111. *UGFOD,* Ritter, Berlin, to Belgrade, May 4, 1940, Nos. 309, 352.
112. *DGFP,* D, IX, Doc. 442, n. 1.
113. Ciano, *Diaries, 1939–1943,* entry for April 9, 1940.
114. *DGFP,* D. VIII, Doc. 669; *DGFP,* D, IX, Doc. 93; Franz Halder, *Kriegstagebuch des Oberkommandos der Wehrmacht,* vol. 1 (Stuttgart, 1962), passim for March and April 1940.
115. *DDI,* 9, IV, Docs. 137, 181, 186, 258.
116. *DDI,* 9, IV, Doc, 210, 158.

117. See the assurances of Paul Reynaud and R. A. Butler to Mussolini in *DDI,* 9, IV, Docs. 140, 165, 166.

118. *DDI,* 9, IV, Docs. 117, 126, 140, 188.

119. *BFO, War Cabinet Meeting,* April, 1940 WM (40).

120. Ibid.

121. Ibid.

122. *BFO, War Cabinet Meeting,* April 18, 1940, WM 96 (40).

123. *BFO, War Cabinet Meeting,* April 27, 1940, WM 105 (40).

124. Ibid.

125. Ibid.

126. *BFO, War Cabinet Meeting,* May 17, 1940, WM 126 (40).

127. Ibid; also *BFO,* Campbell, Belgrade, May 15, 1940, tel. 211.

128. The Yugoslav Chief of Staff stated in April 1940 that Yugoslavia would resist both an Italian attack on the Dalmatian coast and a German threat on its northern frontier. *BFO,* London, Dominion Office, circular tel. to all Dominion Governments, April 21, 1940, 371/5225/415/92.

129. *BFO,* London, memorandum of R. A. Butler, April 25, 1940, 371/R5278/415/92.

130. Woodward, *British Foreign Policy in the Second World War,* vol. 1, p. 149. Also Winston Churchill, *Their Finest Hour* (Boston, 1949), pp. 128–129, letter of Prime Minister to Secretary for Foreign Affairs (6/6/40).

131. *BFO,* Campbell, Belgrade, to Halifax, April 29, 1940, 371/R719/415/92. Nichol's minute suggested telling Yugoslavia that in the event of an Italian attack England and France, due to geography, would immediately attack Italy.

132. *BFO,* Campbell, Belgrade, March 30, 1940, 371/R4191/415/92.

133. *BFO,* Campbell, Belgrade, May 14, 1940, 371/R6023/415/92.

134. Ibid.

135. Ibid.

136. In September 1939 Prince Paul told the Germans of his fears of Bolshevism, Pan-Slavism and world revolution, and v. Heeren of his belief that Germany had been thrown into the arms of Soviet Russia by English policy. *UGFOD,* v. Heeren, Belgrade, September 28, 1939.

137. *BFO,* Nichols minute, June 12, 1940, 371/R6023/415/92.

138. *BFO,* Campbell, Belgrade, n.d. 371/6023/415/92.

139. *BFO,* Campbell, Belgrade, November 26, and December 9, 1940, 371/R8611/415/92.

140. *BFO,* Campbell, Belgrade June 3, 1940, 371/R6425/5/67.

141. Arnold J. Toynbee, *Survey of International Affairs, Hitler's Europe, 1939–1946* (London, 1954), pp. 288f.; Ciano, *Ciano Diaries, 1939–1943,* entries for June 19, 20, 1940; Ciano, *L'Europa verso la Catastrofe,* pp. 562–565.

142. Raymond J. Sontag and James S. Beddie (eds.), *Nazi-Soviet Relations, 1939–1941; Documents from the Archives of the German Foreign Office* (Washington, D.C., 1948), pp. 165–168; Hoptner, *Yugoslavia in Crisis 1934–1941,* p. 176; Woodward, *British Foreign Policy in the Second World War,* pp. 26, 463–470.

143. *DGFP,* D, X, Doc. 129; Galeazzo Ciano, *Ciano's Diplomatic Papers* (London, 1948), entry for July 7, 1940; *DGFP,* D, X, Doc. 343; *Kriegstagebuch des Oberkommandos der Wehrmacht (1940–1941),* vol. 1, entries for August 14, 15, 1940. Ciano, *Ciano Diaries, 1939–1943,* entries for August 4, 5, 1940; for the Italian flirtations with Moscow, see Toynbee, *Survey of International Affairs, 1939–1946, Hitler's Europe, 1939–1946* (London, 1954), pp. 291–293; also Ilija Jukić, *The Fall of Yugoslavia* (New York, 1974), pp. 32–34.

144. On the Italian attack on Greece, see Ciano, *Ciano Diaries, 1939–1943,* entry for October 12, 1940; *Kriegstagebuch des Oberkommandos der Wehrmacht,* vol. 1, 1940–1941, p. 125; and *Il Process o Roatta* (Rome, 1945), p. 63; Ugo von Hassell, *The von Hassell Diaries* (New York, 1947), p. 172. Mussolini believed that an Italian attack would set off an Albanian revolt in Epirus, but that did not materialize and the Albanians surrendered en masse to the Greeks. *UGFOD,* v. Mackensen, Rome, December 7, 1940, No. 2235. For the revisionist view of Van Creveld that Hitler knew in advance of Mussolini's plans to attack Greece, see van Creveld, *Hitler's Strategy 1940–1941: The Balkan Clue,* chap. 2, pp. 35–51.

145. *BFO,* Campbell, Belgrade, June 3, 1940, 371/R64257/5/67.

146. *FRUS,* I (1940), p. 470; also Woodward, *British Foreign Policy in the Second World War,* pp. 16, 245ff.

147. *Kriegstagebuch des Oberkommandos der Wehrmacht,* (1940–1941), vol. 1, p. 131.

148. *BFO,* Belgrade, British Military Attaché to War Office, October 28, 1940, 371/8144/415/92. The Foreign Office official Dixon minuted: "The attitude of the Chief of General Staff is deplorable and unfortunately of a piece with what we know of the attitude of the Yugoslav government generally."

149. *BFO,* Sir M. Palairet, Athens, October 31, 1940, 371/8144/415/92.

150. Barker, *British Policy in South-east Europe in the Second World War,* p. 97. Nichols observed that the Germans had to extricate the Italians "if they got into a mess. They can hardly afford not to." Cadogan added cannily: "I agree and that is why it is essential to make the mess as bad as possible so as to cause the Germans the maximum of embarrassment." Ibid.

151. *BFO,* Campbell, Belgrade, November 1, 1940, 371/R8181/415/92. On the secret Yugoslav military assistance to Greece, see Hoptner, *Yugoslavia in Crisis, 1934–1941,* p. 191. In the event of a Bulgarian attack on Greece in conjunction with Germany, Cvetković told Campbell: "Yugoslavia would be guided by the situation *de fait.*" C. L. Rose, a southern department official, summarized: "In brief Yugoslavia will in no case oppose Germany but will resist Italy or Bulgaria if they are acting alone." Ibid.

152. The Nedić memorandum is reproduced in Dragiša N. Ristić, *Yugoslavia's Revolution of 1941* (University Park, Pa., 1966), p. 44. Cvetković believed Nedić may have been dismissed for his alleged connections with the rightist Zbor movement. See Dragiša Cvetković, *Dokumenti o Jugoslaviji* no. 10, p. 12. See also Hoptner, *Yugoslavia in Crisis, 1934–1941,* pp. 186f. Breccia states that Nedić was ready to sacrifice Croatia and Dalmatia in exchange for German support for the acquisition of Greek Macedonia and Salonika as a prelude to a political collaboration with Bulgaria once it obtained egress to the Aegean Sea. The former Chief of Staff General Simović, on the other hand, wanted to seize Salonika before the Italians for a Salonika front as in World War I with the Allied forces. Simović also favored removing Prince Paul as too weak and replacing him with a military dictatorship after declaring the majority of King Peter. Both the Germans and Italians got wind of this split between the pro-German group around Nedić and the pro-Allied one around Simović, which later had repercussions in the coup of March 17, 1941, and after. See Breccia, *Jugoslavia 1939–1941,* pp. 356f.

153. *BFO,* Campbell, Belgrade, November 9, 1940, 371/R8490/415/92.

154. *DGFP,* D, XI, Doc. 324. In November 1940 Soviet Foreign Minister Molotov went to see Hitler to try to reactivate the Nazi-Soviet Pact of 1939 which the German occupation of Romania now threatened. The German guarantee to Romania particularly piqued Molotov. ("Against who," he enquired. "Against the British," he was told.) See *DGFP,* D, XII, Docs. 325, 326, 329; Sontag and Beddie, *Nazi-Soviet Relations,* pp. 217–254.

155. *DGFP,* D, XI and XII, Docs. 365, 472.

156. *UGFOD,* Ribbentrop to v. Heeren, November 28, 1940.

157. Ciano, *Ciano Diaries 1939–1943,* entry for November 18, 1940; also Ciano, *Diplomatic Papers,* p. 410 and *DGFP,* XI, Doc. 353.

158. *DGFP,* D, V, Docs. 366, 383.

159. Smiljanić, the Yugoslav Undersecretary, told the Vichy chargé in Belgrade that secret Yugoslav policy was to play for time until May when the U.S. would enter the war and England's growing strength would bring about a change in the war situation. *UGFOD,* Heeren, Belgrade, February 10, 1941, tel. 108.

160. *BFO,* British Naval Attaché, Belgrade, to D.N.I., n.d., 371/8611/415/92. A minute by Dixon summed up the dilemma: "There is little we could offer in the way of support and the Yugoslavs know this." *BFO,* Campbell, Belgrade, November 17–22, 1940, 371/8492/415/92, notes of Dixon and Cadogan.

161. *BFO,* War Cabinet, Yugoslavia, Report of the Chiefs of Staff Committee, CAB/66/13, W.P. (40) 461, also C.O.S. 978, November 24, 1940.

162. *BFO,* British Military Attaché to War Office, February 9, 1941, 371/R947/73/92.

163. Helmuth Greiner, *Die Oberste Wehrmachtführung 1939–1943* (1951), p. 189; also *Kriegstagebuch des Oberkommando der Wehrmacht,* vol. 1, p. 171.

164. Breccia, *Jugoslavia 1939–1941,* p. 336.

165. Ibid., pp. 339–340. Mameli, the Italian representative in Belgrade, noted that "every day the German penetration of this country becomes more intense in every field, but especially in the commercial, industrial, financial and cultural." The German attitude was that "it is preferable not to change the Yugoslav situation in view of the fact that it can be so admirably exploited to our advantage." Ibid., p. 341, n. 81 citing *DDI*, 9, V, Doc. 713.

166. BFO, Letter of King George to Prince Paul, November 15, 1940, 371/8249/415/92; also *BFO*, Campbell, Belgrade, December 13, 1940, 371/8631/415/92.

167. *BFO*, Campbell, Belgrade, n.d., 371/8619/415/92.

168. Macartney, *A History of Hungary 1929–1945*, vol. 1, p. 447. *DGFP*, D, XI, Docs. 431 and n. 5 and 365. The Yugoslavs agreed to give up only the Zenta and Topola districts as the price of the treaty fearing a demand for territorial revisions from its other neighbors.

169. The 1941 pact had as many interpretations as the oracle of Delphi. Bardossy, succeeding Czaky, later minister-president, admitted Germany requested it to draw Yugoslavia to the Axis; the Hungarians told London it was to gain Hungary independence; the Germans were enthusiastic but refused to acknowledge paternity; and Rome saw it as a bridge to bring Yugoslavia into the Axis. See Antal Ullein-Reviczky, *Guerre Allemande Paix Russe: le drame Hongrois* (Neuchatel, 1947), p. 75; Macartney, *A History of Hungary 1929–1945*, vol. 1, p. 449; and Hoptner, *Yugoslavia in Crisis*, pp. 194f. See also *Unpublished Italian Foreign Office Docs.*, Direzione General, Storico Diplomatico, Ungheria, October 19, 1938–December 31, 1939, Quaderno 63.

170. Welles, *The Time for Decision*, pp. 106f. Welles hinted to Hitler the promise of greater trade with the United States in exchange for the spoils of Southeastern and Eastern Europe at a later peace arrangement. Similarly, to Mussolini he alluded to trade with Italy. The Italian leader demanded Germany's right to its "vital interests in central Europe." Mussolini held the Ottawa agreement discriminatory and together with the American tariff policy prior to the Roosevelt Administration it forced Italy to an autarchic system as a "last resort . . . in self-defense." Peace could only come if Germany's demands for her former colonies and territories in Europe were recognized. A plebiscite in Austria could be held which Hitler believed would probably devolve to Germany, but a reconstituted Czech region in Bohemia and Moravia would be independent together with an independent Slovakia under German protection. Poland would have to be restored after population transfers with access to the sea. Ibid., pp. 85ff. and 104ff.

171. BFO, Campbell, Belgrade, December 29–30, 1940 and January 1, 2, 1941, 371/1/1/67; BFO, Campbell, January 6, 1941. In the previous November Ugo v. Hassell arrived in the Balkans to assess the situation. He found the country crackling with tension. Hatred and fear of Italy ran like a red thread through his discussions with Prince Paul, the Croat leaders and Maček. Paul and the Croat leaders feared the Communists and Communism, as a result of the bad economic conditions. Von Hassell concluded: "One can say the most salient element of foreign policy in Yugoslavia is the strong mistrust even hatred of Italy. The Italian thrust against Greece has greatly increased this feeling. This is the case in all parts of the country, the Slovene, Croatian and Serbian. All other inclinations have been thrust into the background. Sometimes I am told that the best way to unite Yugoslavia would be an Italian attack, as they do not feel themselves inferior to the Italians alone.

"Nevertheless, the Slovenes and Croats 'coquette' with the Italians. Some Croats hate Belgrade so much they would prefer a united autonomous Croatia under Italy. Pavelić tries to use this to counter Maček's conciliatory attitude toward Belgrade.

"Serbian hatred of Italy was greater than Croatian. Everywhere there was fear of Italy because of Salonika and Macedonia. Not a few Serbs would sacrifice Croatia and Dalmatia as the price for Greek Macedonia and Salonika. The Serbs, Croats and Slovenes look to Germany to save them from Italy."

Von Hassell found feeling for Germany was neither widespread nor deep. The occupation of Prague was badly received in Yugoslavia, particularly in Slovenia and the Yugoslavs feared economic exploitation as in the case of Romania. See *UGFOD*, note of von Hassell to Berlin, n.d. but November, 1940.

172. *BFO*, Cadogan note, London, January 16, 1941, 371/R434/113/67.

173. Frederick B. Chary, "The Diary of Bogdan Filov," *Southeastern Europe*, vol. 1, pt. 1 (1975), p. 59, entry for January 4, 1941.

174. Ibid., p. 60, entry for January 7, 1941.

175. Ibid., p. 63, entry for January 20, 1941.

176. Ibid., p. 62, entry for January 18, 1941.

177. Ibid., p. 80, entry for February 7, 1941.

178. *BFO,* Campbell, Belgrade, January 22, 1941, 371/542/92.

179. Chary, "The Diary of Bogdan Filov," *Southeastern Europe,* vol. 2, pt. 1 (1975), pp. 76, 80, entries for March 3, 30, 1941.

180. *BFO,* Rendel, Sophia, n.d., and January 10, 1940, 371/R76/32/7 and 371/R184/67.

181. Chary, "The Diary of Bogdan Filov," vol. 1, pt. 1, entry for January 9, 1941.

182. *BFO,* Campbell, Belgrade, January 5, 1941, and Clutter's note of January 8, 1941, 371/181/1/67.

183. *BFO,* Campbell, January 7, 1941, 371/R226/113/67.

184. *BFO,* Campbell, Belgrade, January 5, 1941, 371/R76/32/7.

185. Though the Turks had given a "very satisfactory" reply to their inquiries, Belgrade later learned through the German ambassador at Ankara, who had held discussions with the Turkish authorities, that there was no certainty Turkey would act if the Germans entered Belgrade. *BFO,* Campbell, Belgrade, January 29, 1941, 371/R463/32/7.

186. *BFO,* Campbell, Belgrade, January 7, 1941, 371/226/113/67; *UGFOD,* Ribbentrop to v. Papen, February 27, 1941.

187. *BFO,* Campbell, Belgrade, February 10 and January 22, 1941, 371/542/73/92.

188. See Campbell's interview with "W" in *BFO,* Campbell, Belgrade, January 22, 1941, 371/542/73/92.

189. *BFO,* Campbell, January 29, 1941, 371/R463/32/7 (4).

190. *BFO,* Rendel, Sofia, January 18, 1941, 371/R463/32/7, see also attached notes of Clutter, Bowker, Nichol and Cadogan.

191. *BFO,* Rendel, Sofia, January 22, 1941, Nos. 189, 190. To whip the Turks into line Ribbentrop instructed von Papen: "If the Turks are looking for grounds for war, then you may tell them this: that you want to know whether the statements made signify a threat to Germany and indicate that you might pack your bags.... We believe such talk will clear the air." *UGFOD,* Ribbentrop to Papen, February 27, 1941, No. 111. Von Papen reported Eden's efforts to bring about an accord between Belgrade and Ankara had failed: "The Turks on account of inferior armaments are not in a position to move toward the English sausage and would fight only if attacked." *UGFOD,* von Papen to Berlin, Ankara, February 28, 1941, Nos. 189, 190.

192. *UGFOD,* Heeren, Belgrade, January 30, 1941, No. 72.

193. *UGFOD,* v. Richthofen, Sofia, January 23, 1941, tel. 70. On the German entry into Bulgaria Prince Paul wavered: "It is difficult. I believe we will attack. It encircles us. But my people are not all agreed. The time has come to act on principle, to abandon expediency." See *FRUS,* II, 1941, p. 939. Later in mid-February Washington again tried to shore up Yugoslav resistance to Hitler by a promise from Roosevelt to Prince Paul of lend-lease aid and by a visit of Cordell Hull to the Yugoslav ambassador. Ibid., p. 949.

194. *UGFOD,* v. Richthofen, February 22, 1941, tel. 208. Other attempts to open talks through Milanović, the Yugoslav minister in Sofia, came to nothing. Chary, "The Diary of Bogdan Filov," vol. 2, pt. 1, entry for February 8, 1941 (1975), p. 69.

195. *BFO,* Rendel, Sofia, January 22, 1941, 371/R463/32/7.

196. *DGFP,* D, XII, Docs. 30, 39.

197. Chary, "The Diary of Bogdan Filov," vol. 2, pt. 1 (1975), entry for February 27, 1941.

198. Ibid., entry for March 1, 1941, p. 72.

199. Ibid.

200. Ibid., p. 73.

201. Ibid.

202. *BFO.,* Campbell, February 22, 1941, 371/R1396/73/92, No. 239.

203. Ibid.

204. Sir George Rendel, *The Sword and the Olive* (London, 1957), p. 160.

205. *PPA,* Moscow, Gavrilović to Belgrade, February 14, 1941.

206. Ibid.

207. *PPA,* Gavrilović, Moscow, to Belgrade, February 18, 1941.

208. *PPA,* Gavrilović, Moscow, to Belgrade, March 10, 1941.

209. *PPA,* Cincar-Marković, Belgrade to Moscow, March 14, 1941.

210. Rendel, *The Sword and the Olive,* p. 167.

Chapter 17

1. *BFO,* minutes of conversation between State Secretary and Simović and Ninčić. June 27, 1941, 371/R7011/1195/92.

2. Jukić, *The Fall of Yugoslavia,* p. 43.

3. Hoptner, *Yugoslavia in Crisis, 1934–1941,* p. 209.

4. Ibid.

5. For Hitler's reasons for attacking the Soviet Union, see *TMWC* (Trial of the Major War Criminals), Vol. IX, Göring Testimony, March 15, 1946, pp. 333ff. See also Hitler's reasons given in 1941 and 1945 in Read and Fisher, *The Deadly Embrace: Hitler, Stalin and the Nazi-Soviet Pact 1939–1941,* pp. 545–549.

6. *IMT,* IX, pp. 333ff.

7. Ibid.

8. *DGFP,* D, XII, Doc. 10.

9. *UGFOD,* Belgrade, v. Heeren to Berlin, February 10, 1941, tel. 108.

10. *UGFOD,* Belgrade, v. Heeren to Berlin, February 12, 1940, tel. 121.

11. *DGFP,* D, XII, Doc. 117.

12. For the March 4 meeting between Prince Paul and Hitler see *DGFP,* D, XII, Doc. 130.

13. *Hoptner Collection,* Columbia University, Letter of Cvetković, Paris, February 6, 1953.

14. *Hoptner Collection,* unsigned note but probably from Cvetković, Paris, February 6, 1953.

15. Hoptner, *Yugoslavia in Crisis, 1934–1941,* p. 218.

16. Jukić, *The Fall of Yugoslavia,* p. 51.

17. *DGFP,* D, XIII, Doc. 131.

18. *DGFP,* D, XII, Doc. 144.

19. Hassell, *The Von Hassell Diaries 1938–1944,* p. 176.

20. *DGFP,* D, XII, Doc. 151.

21. *FRUS,* II (Europe), 1941, p. 957.

22. John S. Koliopoulos, *Greece and the British Connection 1935–1941* (Oxford, 1977), p. 139.

23. For British hesitations in aiding the Greeks, see ibid., p. 142, and chap. 6, pp. 169–200.

24. Ibid., p. 180.

25. Ibid., p. 181.

26. For an analysis of Directives 18 and 20 and Hitler's decision to invade Greece, see Van Creveld, *Hitler's Strategy 1940–1941,* pp. 58–59, 92–93.

27. Ibid., chap. 5.

28. *PPA,* Letters of Metaxas to Prince Paul, January 6, 17, 1941.

29. Winston Churchill, *The Grand Alliance* (Boston, 1951), p. 102.

30. Koliopoulos, *Greece and the British Connection 1935–1941,* p. 236.

31. Edgar O'Ballance, *The Greek Civil War 1944–1949* (New York, 1966), p. 40.

32. Koliopoulos, *Greece and the British Connection 1935–1941,* p. 246.

33. John Connell, *Wavell: Scholar and Soldier* (New York, 1964), p. 330.

34. Anthony Eden, *The Reckoning: The Eden Memoirs* (London, 1962), p. 231.

35. Barker, *British Policy in South-east Europe in the Second World War,* p. 108.

36. John O. Iatrides (ed.), *Ambassador McVeagh Reports: Greece 1933–1947* (Princeton, 1980), p. 306.

37. Ibid., p. 308.

38. Eden, *The Reckoning: The Eden Memoirs,* p. 240.

39. Ibid., p. 250.

40. Iatrides, *Ambassador McVeagh Reports: Greece 1933–1947,* p. 306.

41. Ibid., p. 312.

42. *PPA,* Letter of Dragiša Cvetković, Paris, May 17, 1953.

43. Ibid.

44. Eden, *The Reckoning: The Eden Memoirs,* p. 260.

45. Ibid.
46. *BFO*, London, F.O. to Campbell, March 12, 1941, 371/R2387/1195/92.
47. *UGFOD*, Belgrade, v. Heeren to Berlin, March 21, 1941, No. 254.
48. *DGFP*, D, XII, Doc. 192.
49. *UGFOD*, Belgrade, v. Heeren to Berlin, March 15, 1941, No. 231.
50. *UGFOD*, Berlin, Central Sicherheitsdienst Office, Heydrich to Ribbentrop, June 16–17, 1941, memorandum.
51. Ibid.
52. Ristić, *Yugoslavia's Revolution of 1941*, pp. 74ff.
53. Danilo Gregorić, *So Endete Jugoslawien* (Leipzig, 1943), pp. 149f.
54. *FRUS*, II, 1941, p. 957.
55. Ibid.
56. Ibid.
57. *BFO*, Belgrade, Campbell to Eden, March 20, 1941, No. 168.
58. Eden, *The Reckoning: The Eden Memoirs*, p. 262.
59. *BFO*, London, F.O. to Campbell, March 22, 1941, 371/R2987/73/92.
60. *BFO*, Belgrade, Campbell to F.O. March 22, 1941, 371/R2806/114/92.
61. *BFO*, Belgrade, Campbell to Eden March 22, 1941, 371/R2924/3/92.
62. Eden, *The Reckoning: The Eden Memoirs*, p. 263.
63. Ibid., p. 264.
64. David A. T. Stafford, "S.O.E. and British Involvement in the Belgrade Coup d'état of March 1941," *Slavic Review* 36, no. 3 (September 1972): 400, 414ff. See also Jozo Tomasevich, *The Chetniks: War and Revolution in Yugoslavia 1941–1945* (Stanford, 1975) and Barker, *British Policy in Southeast Europe in the Second World War.*
65. See the *Slavic Review* 38, no. 2 (June 1979): 361–362.
66. *BFO*, Washington, Halifax to London, March 23, 1941, 371/R2938/73/92.
67. *BFO*, Belgrade, Campbell to Eden, March 22, 1941, 371/R2924/73/52.
68. Jukić, *The Fall of Yugoslavia*, p. 58.
69. *BFO*, Belgrade, Shone to Eden March 23, 1941, 371/R2925/73/92.
70. Hoptner, *Yugoslavia in Crisis, 1934–1941*, p. 237.
71. *BFO*, Belgrade, Shone to Eden March 23, 1941, 371/R2925/73/92.
72. *FRUS*, II (Europe), 1941, p. 964.
73. For the German notes see *DGFP*, D, XII, Doc. 178.
74. *BFO*, Belgrade, Campbell to F.O., March 24, 1941.
75. *BFO*, London, Butler memo, March 26, 1941, 371/R3193/73/93.
76. *BFO*, Belgrade, Campbell to F.O., March 15, 1941, 371/R2491/73/92; *BFO*, Belgrade, Campbell to F.O., March 24, 1941, 371/R2973/73/92.
77. Ibid., Rose minute.
78. *BFO*, Washington, Lord Halifax to London, March 23, 1941, 371/R3020/73/92.
79. *BFO*, Moscow, Sir Stafford Cripps to London, March 24, 1941, 371/R2980/73/92.
80. *BFO*, Zagreb, Rapp to F.O., March 29, 1941, 371/R3224/73/92.
81. Ibid., Notes of Bowker and Nichol, March 31, 1941.
82. *DGFP*, D, XII, Doc. 208.
83. *UGFOD*, Berlin, note of Hans Kramarz, German Foreign Office, March 27, 1941.
84. Hoptner, *Yugoslavia in Crisis, 1934–1941*, pp. 263.
85. *BFO*, London, Churchill to Campbell and Eden, March 27, 1941, 371/R3090/73/92.
86. Ibid.
87. *BFO*, Belgrade, Campbell to F.O., March 27, 1941, 371/R3081/114/92.
88. *BFO*, Belgrade, Campbell to F.O., March 27, 1941, 371/R3113/73/92.
89. *BFO*, Belgrade, Campbell to F.O., March 27, 1941, minutes of Nichol, F.O. 371/R3090/73/92.
90. *BFO*, Belgrade, Campbell to F.O., March 27, 1941, 371/R3152/73/92.
91. *UGFOD*, Belgrade, v. Heeren to Berlin, October 1940.
92. *DGFP*, D, XII, Doc. 259. Hoptner pictures General Bora Mirković as the behind-the-scenes architect of the coup and Simović as his creature. For Hoptner's account of the coup see Hoptner, *Yugoslavia in Crisis 1934–1941*, pp. 84–94.
93. Maček, *In the Struggle for Freedom*, pp. 217–218.

94. *DGFP,* D, XII, Docs. 215, 216. However, the Magyars declined the offer of Croatia. *DGFP,* D, XII, Doc. 228.

95. Franz von Papen, *Memoirs* (New York, 1953), p. 543.

96. Hassell, *The Von Hassell Diaries 1938–1944,* p. 188.

97. *DGFP,* D, XII, Doc. 217.

98. *UGFOD,* Belgrade, v. Heeren to Berlin, March 27, 1941, tel. 273.

99. *UGFOD,* Belgrade, v. Heeren to Berlin, March 29, 1941, tel. 301.

100. *UGFOD,* Belgrade, v. Heeren to Berlin, March 30, 1941.

101. *UGFOD,* Belgrade, v. Heeren to Berlin, March 27, 1941.

102. *UGFOD,* Belgrade, v. Heeren to Berlin, March 30, 1941, tel. 311; *DGFP,* D, XII, Doc. 235n2. Mussolini informed Rintelen, the German military attaché in Rome, of the incident. *UGFOD,* Rome, von Mackensen to Berlin, n.d., tel. 722.

103. *DGFP,* D, XII, Doc. 235, n2.

104. *UGFOD,* Belgrade, v. Heeren to Berlin, March 30, 1941.

105. *UGFOD,* telephone call from the German military attaché in Bucharest to Auswärtiges Amt, March 30, 1941.

106. *UGFOD,* Bern, Kocher, to Berlin, April 3, 1941, tel. 334.

107. *BFO,* Belgrade, Campbell to F.O., March 27, 1941, 371/R3186/73/92.

108. *UGFOD,* Belgrade, v. Heeren to Berlin, March 29, 1941, tel. 301.

109. Ibid.

110. *UGFOD,* Memorandum of Curt Heinburg, Head of Pol. Div. of Foreign Office, March 29, 1941.

111. *DGFP,* D, XII, Doc. 239.

112. *DGFP,* D, XII, Doc. 241.

113. *UGFOD,* Zagreb, Freundt to Berlin, April 2, 1941, tel. 29.

114. *UGFOD,* Belgrade, v. Heeren to Berlin, March 29, 1941, tel. 301.

115. *UGFOD,* Zagreb, Freundt to Berlin, April 2, 1941, tel. 28.

116. U.S. Dept. of State, Zagreb, Miely to Sec. State, June 13, 1941, Doc. 860H.00/1309.

117. *DGFP,* D, XII, Doc. 262.

118. Ibid.

119. *DGFP,* D, XII, Doc. 270 n2.

120. *UGFOD,* Zagreb, Feine to Berlin, April 5, 1941, tel. 381.

121. *UGFOD,* Zagreb, Vessenmayer and Freundt to Berlin, April 6, 1941, tel. 44.

122. *UGFOD,* Zagreb, Feine to Berlin, April 4, 1941, tel. 35.

123. *UGFOD,* unsigned note, April 5, 1941, No. 385.

124. *PPA,* Belgrade, Cincar-Marković to Gavrilović (Moscow), February 3, 1941.

125. *PPA,* Moscow, Gavrilović to Belgrade, February 8, 1941.

126. *PPA,* Moscow, Gavrilović to Belgrade, February 17, 1941.

127. *PPA,* Moscow, Gavrilović to Belgrade, February 25, 1941.

128. *PPA,* Moscow, Gavrilović to Belgrade, March 6, 1941.

129. *PPA,* Moscow, Gavrilović to Belgrade, March 15, 1941.

130. *PPA,* Moscow, Gavrilović to Belgrade, March 23, 1941.

131. *PPA,* Moscow, Gavrilović to Belgrade, March 23, 1941.

132. *PPA,* Moscow, Gavrilović to Belgrade, n.d. tel. 47.

133. *PPA,* Moscow, Gavrilović to Belgrade, April 1, 1941.

134. *PPA,* Moscow, Gavrilović to Belgrade, April 1, 1941.

135. *PPA,* Moscow, Gavrilović to Belgrade, April 4, 1941.

136. Hoptner, *Yugoslavia in Crisis, 1934–1941,* pp. 278ff.

137. *U.S. State Dept.,* Moscow, Steinhardt to State Dept., May 18, 1941. Doc. 740.0011/11063.

138. *IMT, TMWC,* vol. IX, pp. 333ff.

Conclusion

1. Christopher Hitchens, "The Medals of His Defeats," *Atlantic Monthly,* April 2002.

2. Göring testified that before 1933 very few planes were built for Lufthansa. "At that time I told the airplane industry: You people just pray that we will come to power. We'll give

you so many orders it will make your ears buzz." See *U.S. National Archives,* M-1019, R-21, Göring Interrogation, Interrogator Charmatz, September 18, 1946.

3. See Traian Stoianovich, "Land Tenure and Related Sectors of the Balkan Economy, 1600–1800," *Journal of Economic History* 13 (Fall 1953): 398–411. See also Paul N. Hehn, "Capitalism and the Revolutionary Factor in the Balkans and Crimean War Diplomacy," *East European Quarterly* 18, no. 2 (June 1984): 155–185.

A Postscript

1. For a brief discussion of these ideas, see William Smaldone, *Rudolf Hilferding: The Tragedy of a German Social Democrat* (DeKalb, 1998), pp. 190, 196–197.

2. Ibid., p. 194.

3. Ibid., pp. 195f.

4. *Neuer Vorwärts,* no. 163, January 26, 1936. For the *Neuer Vorwärts* articles, I am indebted to Professor William Smaldone, who generously put them at my disposal.

5. *Neuer Vorwärts,* no. 164, August 2, 1936.

6. *Neuer Vorwärts,* no. 179, November 15, 1936.

7. *Neuer Vorwärts,* no. 191, February 7, 1937.

8. *Neuer Vorwärts,* no. 283, November 20, 1938.

Bibliography

Archival Sources (Unpublished)

German

U.S. National Archives, Washington, D.C., Captured German Documents of World War II, Reichsamt für Wehrwirtschaft Planung, Microfilm Series T-84, Rolls 103, 104, 183; T-71, Serial 3, Rolls 3, 12, 14, 55, 74.

File of Ribbentrop, German Foreign Minister (Microfilm).

File of German State Secretary Weizsäcker (Microfilm).

File of von Heeren, German Minister to Belgrade (Microfilm).

File of von Erdmannsdorff, German Minister to Budapest (Microfilm).

File of Fabricius, German Minister to Romania (Microfilm).

File of von Papen, German Ambassador to Turkey (Microfilm).

File of von Mackensen, German Minister to Rome (Microfilm).

File of von Richtofen, German Minister to Bulgaria (Microfilm).

Affidavits (Microfilm) M-1019, RG-238, Rolls 7, 21, 57, 65. Affidavit of Reichsbank Direktor, Dr. Blessing.

Affidavit of Reichmarshal Hermann Göring, Göring Interrogation, Col. Amen, German Dossiers, Box 18.

Affidavit of Reichsbank Direktor, Dr. Reithinger.

Affidavit of Reichsbank Direktor, Dr. Pohl.

British

Public Record Office, London, Board of Trade, Files BT-11, BT-59.

Treasury Department Files T-160, T-161, T-172, T-188, T-208, T-230.

British Cabinet Meetings (Minutes and Papers) 1930–1939, CAB/23 and CAB/24, Rolls 41, 42, 43, 44, 45, 46, 47, 48, 56, 57, 58, 62, 180, 182.

Foreign Policy Committee Minutes and Memorandums.

British Foreign Office, 1939–1941, various files, including file of Ronald Campbell, British Minister to Yugoslavia 1939–1941 period.

American

National Archives, Washington, D.C., U.S. State Department, Index of World War II Materials, R.G.59/740.00 (microfilm) T-1252, Rolls 1–6.

National Archives, Franklin D. Roosevelt Library, President's Secretary's File, Hyde Park, N.Y.; William Bullitt Papers and various others. (PSF)

Papers of John F. Montgomery, American Ambassador to Hungary, Yale University.

Papers of John Rankin, American Consul at Belgrade, Yale University.

Reports of American Consuls in Poland, 1931–1933. *National Archives,* Washington, D.C.

French

Bibliothèque Nationale, Daladier memoir.

Italian

Captured Italian Documents of World War II, Alexandria, Va.

465

Yugoslav

Archive of Regent Prince Paul of Yugoslavia, Columbia University. (PPA) Hoptner Fund, Columbia University.

Polish

Pilsudski Institute, New York. Correspondence of Marshal Pilsudski and other Polish leaders.

Major Published Document Collections

Documents on German Foreign Policy, Series C, D. Government Printing Office, Washington, D.C. (DGFP).

Documenti diplomatici Italiani, 8th series, vols. XI, XII, XIII; 9th series, vols. III, IV (DDI).

Ferdo Sišić. *Jadransko Pitanje na Konferenciji Mira u Parizu, Zbirka Akata i Dokumenata.* Zagreb, 1920 (DVP).

Gromyko, A. A., ed. *Dokumenty Vneshnei Politiki SSSR,* Moscow, 1969, vol. XV, 1932.

Documents Diplomatiques Français (1932–1939), 1re Série (1932–35), 2e Série (1936–1939), Paris, Imprimerie Nationale (DDF).

Documents on British Foreign Policy, 1919–1939, Series 3, vols., I, II, III, IV, V. HMSO, London, 1949–1950 (DBFP).

Foreign Relations of the United States, published by the State Department for 1919 to 1941, Washington, D.C., 1934–1956. (FRUS)

Trials of War Criminals before the International Military Tribunal, 90 vols., U.S. Government Printing Office, Washington, D.C. (IMT).

Nazi Conspiracy and Aggression, 8 vols., U.S. Government Printing Office, Washington, D.C. (NCC).

Kriegstagebuch des Oberkommandos der Wehrmacht. Vol. I, 1940–1941.

Hofer, Walter. *Der Nationalsozialismus Dokumente,* 1933–1945.

Les Lettres Secrètes Échangées par Hitler et Mussolini. Paris: Editions du Pavois, 1946.

Nazi-Soviet Relations, 1939–1941. Department of State, Washington, D.C.

Colored Books

Les Relations polono-allemandes et polono-sovietique. Paris, 1940.

Polish White Book, Official Documents concerning Polish-German and Polish-Soviet Relations, 1933–39 (English Trans.) London, 1939, Hutchinson.

The French Yellow Book, Diplomatic Documents, 1938–1939. London, 1939, Hutchinson.

German White Book. Documents on the Events preceding the Outbreak of War. The Second German White Book, The German Library of Information, New York, 1939.

M.A. Theses, Ph.D. Dissertations, Conference Papers (Unpublished)

Bosnitch, Sava D. "The Foreign Policy Line of the Communist Party of Yugoslavia in the Second Imperialist War, September 1, 1939–June 22, 1941." Ph.D. Dissertation, McGill University, Montreal, 1970.

Grenzebach, William S. "Germany's Informal Empire in East Central Europe." Ph.D. Dissertation, Brandeis University, Boston, 1978.

Hayes, Peter. "Industry and Ideology: I. G. Farben in the Nazi Era," paper, *AHA,* 1985.

Hehn, Paul N. "Franco-Polish Relations 1936–1939." M.A. Thesis, Columbia University, 1954.

Kunevan, Leo. "Germany and the Iron Guard." M.A. Thesis, University of Dayton, 1967.

Statistics

Banque Nationale de Romanie, Service des Études Économiques, Bulletin d'information et documentation, 1934–1938.

National Bank of Hungary, 1932–1939.

National Bank of Yugoslavia, 1935–1939.

Statistisches Handbuch von Deutschland.
The Concise Statistical Yearbook of Poland, 1937.
The League of Nations, the Network of World Trade, 1937.
The League of Nations, the Network of World Trade, 1942.

Newspapers, Reviews, Journals

The London Times
Westminster Bank Review
The Spectator
Lloyds Bank Monthly
The Economist
Business Week
Le Temps
Vendredi
L'Europe Nouvelle
The New York Times
Voprosi Istorii
Neuer Vorwärts

Autobiographies, Diaries, Papers and Memoirs (Published)

Beck, Colonel Joseph. *Dernier Rapport: Politique Polonaise 1926–1939*. Paris: Baconnière, 1951. [There is also an English language translation.]

Beneš, Eduard. *Memoirs: from Munich to New War and Victory*. New York: Houghton Mifflin, 1954.

Berezhkov, Valentin M. *Diplomaticheskoi Missiei v Berlin, 1940–1941*. Novosti, 1966.

Berle, Beatrice Bishop, and Travis Beal Jacobs, eds. *Navigating the Rapids: From the Papers of Adolph A. Berle*. New York: 1973.

Bonnet, Georges. *Défense de la Paix*. 2 vols. Geneva: Les Éditions du Cheval Ailé, 1948.

Brugère, Raymond. *Veni, Vedi, Vichy… et la Suite*. Paris: Deux-Rives, 1953 and Paris: Témoignages, 1940–1945.

Cannistraro, Phillip V., and Edward D. Wynot and Theodore P. Kovaleff, eds. *Poland and the Coming of the Second World War: The Diplomatic Papers of A. J. Drexel Biddle, Jr., United States Ambassador to Poland 1937–1939*. New York: Columbia, 1976.

Churchill, Winston S. *The Gathering Storm*. London: Penguin, 1948.

———. *Blood, Sweat and Tears*. New York: G. P. Putnam Sons, 1941.

———. *Their Finest Hour*. Boston: Houghton Mifflin, 1949.

———. *The Grand Alliance*. Boston: Houghton Mifflin, 1951.

Ciano, Galeazzo. *Ciano's Diary, 1937–1938*. London: Methuen, 1952.

———. *Ciano's Diplomatic Papers*. London: Adams Press, 1948.

———. *L'Europa verso la Catastrofe*. Milan: Mondadori, 1948.

———. *Ciano's Diary, 1939–1943* (edited by Hugh Gibson). Garden City: Doubleday, 1946.

Colville, John. *The Fringes of Power: 10 Downing Street 1939–1955* (first American edition). London and New York: W. W. Norton, 1986.

Connell, John. *Wavell, Scholar and Soldier*. New York: Harcourt, Brace and World, 1964.

Coulondre, Robert. *De Staline à Hitler: Souvenirs de Deux Ambassades 1936–1939*. Paris: Hachette, 1950.

Dalton, Hugh. *Memoirs II: The Fateful Years 1931–1945*. London: Muller, 1953 and 1957.

Davenport-Hines, Richard P. T. *Dudley Docker: The Life and Times of a Trade Warrior*. New York: Cambridge University Press, 1984.

Dilks, David, ed. *The Diaries of Sir Alexander Cadogan*. London: Cassell, 1971.

Dirksen, Herbert von. *Moscow-Tokyo-London: Twenty Years of German Foreign Policy*. Norman: University of Oklahoma Press, 1952.

Dixon, Piers. *Double Diploma: The Life of Sir Pierson Dixon, Don and Diplomat*. London: Hutchinson.

Dreifort, John E. *Yvon Delbos at the Quai d'Orsay: French Foreign Policy during the Popular Front, 1936–1938*. Lawrence: University of Kansas Press, 1973.

Eden, Anthony (Lord Avon). *Facing the Dictators: The Eden Memoirs.* London: Cassell, 1962.

————. *The Reckoning: The Eden Memoirs.* London: Cassell, 1962.

Feiling, Keith Grahame, Sir. *The Life of Neville Chamberlain.* London: Macmillan, 1946.

François-Poncet, André. *The Fateful Years.* London: Gollancz, 1949.

Gafencu, Grigore. *Les Derniers Jours d'Europe.* London: Yale University Press, 1948.

————. *Prelude to the Russian Campaign* (translated by Fletcher-Allen). London: F. Muller, Ltd., 1945.

Gamelin, Général Maurice. *Servir: Prologue du drame, 1930–1939.* Paris: Plon, 1946.

Gilbert, G. M. *Nuremburg Diary.* New York: Farrar, Straus, 1947.

Gregorić, Danilo. *So Endete Jugoslawien.* Leipzig: W. Goldmann, 1943.

Halder, Franz. *Kriegstagebuch,* 4 vols. Stuttgart: Kohlhammer, 1962.

Halifax, Lord. *Fullness of Days.* New York: Dodd, Mead, 1957.

Harvey, John, ed. *The Diplomatic Diaries of Oliver Harvey 1937–1940.* London: Collins, 1958.

Hassell, Ugo von. *The Von Hassell Diaries, 1938–1944.* London: Hamish Hamilton, 1948.

Heinemann, John L. *Hitler's First Foreign Minister: Constantin Freiherr von Neurath, Diplomat and Statesman.* Berkeley and Los Angeles: University of California Press, 1979.

Henderson, Nevile. *Failure of a Mission.* London: Hodder & Stoughton, 1940.

Hill, Leonidas E., ed. *Die Weizsäcker Papiere 1933–1950.* Berlin: Propyläen, 1974.

Hitler, Adolf. *Mein Kampf* (ed. Raoul de Roussy de Sales, translated by Ralph Manheim). Boston: Houghton Mifflin, 1943.

————. *My New Order* (ed. Raoul de Roussy de Sales). New York: Reynal & Hitchcock, 1941.

Hitler's Secret Conversations 1941–1944. New York: Signet Books, 1961.

Horthy, Admiral Nicholas. *Memoirs.* New York: Robert Speller & Sons, 1957.

Hull, Cordell. *The Memoirs of Cordell Hull,* 2 vols. New York: Macmillan, 1948.

Iatrides, John O., ed. *Ambassador MacVeagh Reports: Greece, 1933–1947.* Princeton: Princeton University Press, 1980.

Jacobsen, Hans-Adolf. *Kriegstagebuch des Oberkommandos der Wehrmacht.* August 1940–December 1941. 1 vol. Frankfurt: Bernard & Graefe, 1965.

Jedrzejewicz, Waclaw, ed. *Diplomat in Berlin, 1933–1939: Papers and Memoirs of Józef Lipski, Ambassador of Poland.* New York: Columbia University Press, 1968.

————. *Pilsudski: A Life for Poland.* New York: Hippocrene, 1982.

————. *Diplomat in Paris, 1936–1939: Papers and Memoirs of Juliusz Łukasiewicz.* New York: Columbia University Press, 1970.

Jukić, Ilija. *The Fall of Yugoslavia* (translated by Darion Cook). New York: Harcourt Brace Jovanovich, 1974.

Kennan, George F. *Memoirs 1925–1950* (paperback). Boston: Bantam Books, 1967.

Krosigk, Lutz Graf Schwerin von. *Staatsbankrott: Die Geschichte der Finanzpolitik des Deutschen Reiches von 1920 bis 1945.* Göttingen: Musterschmidt, 1974.

————. *Memoiren.* Stuttgart: Seewald, 1977.

Kube, Alfred. *Pour le Merite und Hakenkreuz: Hermann Göring im Dritten Reich.* Munich, 1986.

Laroche, Jules. *La Pologne de Pilsudski: Souvenirs d'une Ambassade, 1926–1935.* Paris: Flammarion, 1953.

Leith-Ross, Frederick. *Money Talks: Fifty Years of International Finance: The Autobiography of Sir Frederick Leith-Ross.* London: Hutchinson, 1968.

Maček, Vladko. *In the Struggle for Freedom* (translated by Elizabeth and Stjepan Gazi). New York: Speller, 1957.

Maisky, Ivan. *Memoirs of a Soviet Ambassador.* New York: Hutchinson, 1967.

Massigli, René. *La Turquie devant la Guerre: Mission à Ankara 1939–1940.* Paris: Plon, 1964.

Montgomery, John Flournoy. *Hungary The Unwilling Satellite.* New York: Devin-Adair, 1947.

Mosley, Leonard. *The Reich Marshal: A Biography of Hermann Göring.* New York: Dell, 1974.

Nicolson, Harold. (ed. Nigel Nicolson). *Diaries and Letters, 1930–1939.* London: Collins, 1980.

Noël, Leon. *L'Agression Allemande Contre la Pologne.* Geneva: Flammarion, 1948.

Overy, R. J. *Goering, the "Iron Man."* London: Routledge and Kegan Paul, 1984.

Papagos, General Alexandros. *The Battle of Greece, 1940–1941* (translated by Pat Eliascos). Athens: J. M. Scazikas "Alpha" Editions, 1949.

Papen, Franz von. *Memoirs* (translated by Brian Connell). New York: Dutton, 1953.

Petrescu-Comnen, Nicolae. *Preludi del Grande Dramma: Recordi e Documenti di un diplomatico.* Rome: Edizione Leonardo, 1947.

Pilsudska, Alexandra. *Pilsudski.* New York: Dodd Mead, 1941.

Rendel, Sir George. *The Sword and the Olive.* London: Murray, 1957.

Roosevelt, Elliot, ed. *F.D.R. His Personal Letters, 1928–1945,* 4 vols. New York: Duell, Sloan and Pearce, 1950.

Schacht, Hjalmar. *Abrechnung mit Hitler.* Hamburg: Rowohlt, 1948.

———. *Confessions of "the Old Wizard."* (translated by Diana Pyke). Boston: Houghton Mifflin, 1956.

Schmidt, Paul. *Statist auf diplomatischer Bühne, 1923–45: Erlebnisse des Chefdolmetschers im Auswärtingen Amt mit den Staatsmännern Europas.* Bonn: Athenaum, 1949.

Speer, Albert. *Inside the Third Reich.* New York: Weidenfeld & Nicholson, 1970.

Stojadinović, Milan. *Ni Rat ni Pakt, Jugoslavija izmedju dva rata.* Buenos Aires: 1963.

Szembek, Comte Jean. *Journal 1933–1939.* Paris: Plon, 1952.

Szinai, Miklós, and Laszlo Szücs, eds. *The Confidential Papers of Admiral Horthy.* Budapest: Corvina, 1965.

Turner, Henry Ashby, Jr., ed. *Hitler — Memoirs of a Confidant* (translated by Ruth Hein). New Haven: Yale University Press, 1985.

Weizsäcker, Ernst von. *Memoirs* (translated by John Andrews [pseud.]). London: Gallancz, 1951).

Welles, Sumner. *The Time for Decision.* New York: Harper and Bros, 1944.

Weygand, General Maxime. *Recalled to Service* (translated by E. W. Dickes). London: Heinemann, 1952.

Published Books

Abraham, David. *The Collapse of the Weimar Republic: Political Economy and Crisis* (2nd ed.). New York: Holmes and Meier, 1986.

Ádám, Magda, Gyula Juhasz, and Lajos Kerekes, eds. *Allianz Hitler-Horthy-Mussolini, Dokuments zur Ungarischen Aussenpolitik, 1933–1944.* Budapest: Académiai Kiodó, 1966.

Adams, R. J. Q. *British Politics and Foreign Policy in the Age of Appeasement 1935–39.* Stanford: Stanford University Press, 1993.

Adamthwaite, Anthony. *Making of the Second World War.* London: Allen and Unwin, 1977.

———. *France and the Coming of the Second World War 1936–1939.* London: Cass, 1977.

Albrecht-Carrie, René. *Italy at the Paris Peace Conference.* New York: Columbia University Press, 1938.

Amin, Samir. *Unequal Development* (translated by Brian Pearce). New York: Monthly Review, 1976.

———. *Imperialism and Unequal Development.* New York: Monthly Review, 1977.

Aster, Sidney. *1939: The Making of the Second World War.* London: Deutsch, 1973.

Augstein, Rudolf, et al. *"Historikerstreit": Die Dokumentation der Kontroverse um die Einzigartigkeit der nationalsozialistischen Judenvernichtung.* Munich: R. Piper, 1987.

Auty, Phyllis, and Richard Clogg, eds. *British Policy towards Wartime Resistance in Yugoslavia and Greece.* London: Macmillan, 1975.

Avramovski, Živko. *Balkanske Zemlje i Velike Sile, 1935–1937.* Belgrade: Prosveta, 1968.

Barclay, Glen St. J. *The Rise and Fall of the New Roman Empire: Italy's Bid for World Power, 1890–1943.* London: Sidgwick and Jackson, 1973.

Barker, Elizabeth. *British Policy in South-east Europe in the Second World War.* London: Macmillan, 1976.

Basch, Antonin. *The Danube Basin and the German Economic Sphere.* New York: Columbia University Press, 1943.

Baynes, Norman H. *The Speeches of Adolf Hitler.* New York: H. Fertig, 1969.

Bell, P. M. H. *The Origins of the Second World War in Europe.* New York: Longman, 1986.

Berding, Helmut. *Wirtschaftliche und Politische Integration in Europa im 19 und 20 Jahrhundert.* Göttingen: Vandenhoeck & Ruprecht, 1984.

Berend, Ivan T., and György Ránki. *The Hungarian Economy in the Twentieth Century.* London: Croom Helm, 1985.

———. *Underdevelopment and Economic Growth: Studies in Hungarian Social and Economic History* (translated by Zsuzsa Berend). Budapest: Akadémiai Kiadó, 1979.

———. *Economic Development in East-Central Europe in the 19th and 20th Centuries.* New York: Columbia University Press, 1974.

Boban, Ljubo. *Sporazum Cvetković-Maček.* Belgrade: I.D.N., 1965.

Boelcke, Willi A. *Die deutsche Wirtschaft 1930–1945: Interna des Reichswirtschaftsministeriums.* Düsseldorf: Droste, 1983.

———. *Die Kosten von Hitlers Krieg: Kriegsfinanzierung und finanzielles Kriegserbe in Deutschland.* Paderborn: Schöningh, 1985.

Borkin, Joseph. *The Crime and Punishment of I. G. Farben.* New York: Free Press, 1978.

Breccia, Alfredo. *Jugoslavia 1939–1941: diplomazia della neutralità.* Milan: Giuffre, 1978.

Budurowycz, Bohdan B. *Polish-Soviet Relations 1932–1939.* New York: Columbia University Press, 1963.

Buell, R. L. *Poland: Key to Europe.* London and New York: A. A. Knopf, 1939.

Bullock, Alan. *Hitler and Stalin: Parallel Lives.* New York: Knopf, 1992.

———. *Hitler: A Study in Tyranny.* London: Harper (pbk), 1952.

Burns, James MacGregor. *Roosevelt: The Lion and the Fox.* New York: Harcourt Brace, 1956.

Campbell, F. Gregory. *Confrontation in Central Europe: Weimar Germany and Czechoslovakia.* Chicago and London: University of Chicago Press, 1975.

Carley, Michael Jabara. *1939: The Alliance That Never Was and the Coming of World War II.* Chicago: Ivan R. Dee, 1999.

Carr, E. H. *Twilight of the Comintern, 1930–1935.* New York: Pantheon, 1982.

Carr, William. *Arms, Autarky and Aggression: A Study in German Foreign Policy, 1933–1939.* New York: W. W. Norton, 1972.

Carroll, Berenice A. *Design for Total War: Arms and Economics in the Third Reich.* Paris: Mouton, 1968.

Charmley, John. *Chamberlain and the Lost Peace.* London: Hodder and Stoughton, 1989.

Childers, Thomas, and Jane Caplan, eds. *Reevaluating the Third Reich.* New York: Holmes and Meier, 1993.

Cienciala, Anna M. *Poland and the Western Powers 1938–1939: A Study in the Interdependence of Eastern and Western Europe.* London: Routledge and Kegan Paul, 1968.

———, and Titus Komarnicki. *From Versailles to Locarno: Keys to Polish Foreign Policy, 1919–1925.* Lawrence: University of Kansas Press, 1984.

Colvin, Ian. *None So Blind* (published in England under the title *Vansittart in Office*). New York: Harcourt, Brace and World, 1965.

———. *The Chamberlain Cabinet: How the Meetings in 10 Downing Street, 1937–1939, led to the Second World War.* New York: Taplinger, 1971.

Craig, Gordon A., and Felix Gilbert, eds. *The Diplomats 1919–1939.* Princeton: Princeton University Press, 1953.

Crozier, Andrew J. *Appeasement and Germany's Last Bid for Colonies.* New York: St. Martin's, 1988.

Debicki, Roman. *Foreign Policy of Poland 1919–1939: From the Rebirth of the Polish Republic to World War II.* New York: Einaudi Praeger, 1963.

DeFelice, Renzo. *Mussolini: il Fascista.* Turin: Einaudi, 1966.

———. *Mussolini: il Duce.* Turin: Einaudi, 1974.

Deighton, Len. *Blitzkrieg: From the Rise of Hitler to the Fall of Dunkirk.* New York: Knopf, 1980.

Deist, Wilhelm, et al., eds. *Das Deutsche Reich und der Zweite Weltkrieg: Ursachen Voraussetzungen der deutschen Kriegspolitik,* 1 vol. Stuttgart: Deutsche Verlags-Anstalt, 1979.

Dilks, David, ed. *Neville Chamberlain.* New York: Cambridge University Press, 1984.

Dimitrijević, Sergije. *Das ausländische Kapital in Jugoslawien vor dem zweiten Weltkrieg* (translated from Serbo-Croatian by Martin Zoller) Berlin: Rütten & Loening, 1963.

Doering, Dörte. *Deutsche Aussenwirtschaftspolitik, 1933–1935.* Berlin, 1969.

Dower, John W. *Embracing Defeat: Japan in the Wake of World War II.* New York: W. W. Norton, 1998.

Drummond, Ian M. *The Floating Pound and the Sterling Area 1931–1939.* Cambridge: Cambridge University Press, 1981.

Duroselle, Jean-Baptiste. *La Décadence, 1932–1939.* Paris: I.N., 1979, 1985.

Eichholtz, Dietrich. *Geschichte der deutschen Kriegswirtschaft, 1939–1945,* 1 vol. East Berlin, 1969.

———, and W. Schuman. *Anatomie des Krieges: Neue Dokumente über die Rolle des deutschen Monopolkapitals bei der Vorbereitung und Durchführung des Zweiten Weltkrieges.* East Berlin, 1969.

Einhorn, Marion. *Die Ökonomischen Hintergründe der Faschistischen Deutschen Intervention in Spanien 1936–1939.* Berlin: Akademie, 1962.

Ellis, Howard S. *German Exchange Control in Central Europe.* Cambridge: Harvard University Press, 1941.

Engle, Eloise, and Lauri Paananen. *The Winter War: the Russo-Finnish Conflict 1939–1940.* New York: Scribner, 1973.

Erbe, René. *Die Nationalsozialistische Wirtschaftspolitik 1933–1939 im Lichte der modernen Theorie.* Zürich: Polygraphischer, 1958.

Fenyo, Mario D. *Hitler, Horthy and Hungary: German-Hungarian Relations, 1941–1944.* New Haven: Yale University Press, 1972.

Finney, Patrick, ed. *The Origins of the Second World War.* London: Arnold, 1997.

Fischer, Fritz. *From Kaiserreich to Third Reich: Elements of Continuity in German History 1871–1945.* London and Boston: Allen and Unwin, 1986.

Floud, Roderick, and Donald McCloskey, eds. *The Economic History of Britain Since 1700,* vol. 2. Cambridge: Cambridge University Press, 1981.

Forstmeier, Friedrich, and Hans-Erich Volkmann. *Wirtschaft u. Rüstung am Vorabend des Zweiten Weltkrieges.* Düsseldorf: Droste, 1975.

Frommelt, Reinhard. *Paneuropa oder Mitteleuropa: Einigungsbestrebungen im Kalkül deutscher Wirtschaft und Politik, 1925–1933.* Stuttgart: Deutsche Verlags-Anstalt, 1977.

Fuchser, Larry W. *Neville Chamberlain and Appeasement: A Study in the Politics of History.* New York: Norton, 1982.

Funke, Manfred. *Hitler, Deutschland und die Mächte: Materialien zur Aussenpolitik des Dritten Reiches.* Düsseldorf: Droste, 1976.

Gagnon, Paul A. *France Since 1789.* New York: Harper & Row, 1989.

Gardner, Lloyd C. *Economic Aspects of New Deal Diplomacy.* Madison: University of Wisconsin Press, 1964.

George, Margaret. *The Warped Vision: British Foreign Policy, 1933–1939.* Pittsburgh: University of Pittsburgh Press, 1965.

Gilbert, Martin, and Richard Gott. *The Appeasers.* Boston: Houghton Mifflin, 1963.

———. *The Appeasers.* London, 1969.

Gillingham, John. *Industry and Politics in the Third Reich: Ruhr Coal, Hitler and Europe.* London: Methuen, 1985.

Glyn, Andrew, and Bob Sutcliffe. *Capitalism in Crisis* (published in England as *British Capitalism, Workers and the Profit Squeeze*). New York: Pantheon, 1972.

Greiner, Helmuth. *Die Oberste Wehrmachtführung 1939–1943.* 1951.

Grenzebach, William S. *Germany's Informal Empire in East Central Europe: German Economic Policy toward Yugoslavia and Rumania, 1933–1939.* Stuttgart: F. Steiner Verlag Wiesbaden, 1988.

Grow, Michael. *The Good Neighbor Policy and Authoritarianism in Paraguay: United States Economic Expansion and Great Power Rivalry in Latin America During World War II,* Lawrence, Kans.: Regents, 1981.

Guérin, Daniel. *Fascism and Big Business.* New York: Pathfinder Press, 1973 (reprint).

Harper, Glenn T. *German Economic Policy in Spain During the Spanish Civil War, 1936–1939.* The Hague: Mouton, 1967.

Hauser, Oswald. *England und das Dritte Reich 1936–1938.* Stuttgart: Seewald, 1972.

Hayes, Peter J. *Industry and Ideology: I. G. Farben in the Nazi Era.* New York: Cambridge University Press, 1987.

Henke, Joseph. *England in Hitlers politschen Kalkül 1935–1939.* Boppard am Rhein: H. Boldt, 1973.

Hermann, A. H. *The History of the Czechs.* London: A. Lane, 1975.

Herring, Hubert. *A History of Latin America from the Beginnings to the Present.* New York: Knopf, 1957.

Hildebrand, Klaus. *The Foreign Policy of the Third Reich* (translated by Anthony Foithergill). London: Batsford, 1973.

———. *Das vergangene Reich: Deutsche Aussenpolitik von Bismarck bis Hitler 1871–1945.* Stuttgart: Deutsche Verlag-Anstalt, 1995.

Hilger, Gustav, and Alfred G. Meyer. *The Incompatible Allies: a memoir-history of German-Soviet relations, 1918–1941.* New York: Hafner, 1953 and 1971.

Hillgruber, Andreas. *Hitlers Strategie Politik und Kriegführung, 1940–1941.* Frankfurt: Bernard & Graefe, 1965.

———. *Hitler, König Carol und Marschall Antonescu: die Deutsch-Rumänischen Beziehungen 1938–1944.* Wiesbaden: Franz Steiner, 1954.

Hitchens, Marilyn. *Germany, Russia and the Balkans: Prelude to the Nazi-Soviet Non-Aggression Pact* (Boulder, Colo.: East European Monographs, 1983.

Hofer, Walther. *Der Nationalsozialismus, Dokumente 1933–1945* (pbk.). Frankfurt am Main: Fischer Bucherei, 1957.

Hoffmann, Walther G., and Josef H. Müller. *Das Deutsche Volkseinkommen 1851–1957.* Tübingen: Mohr, 1959.

Hoppe, Hans-Joachim. *Bulgarien, Hitler's eigenwilliger Verbündeter: Eine Fallstudie zur nationalsozialistischen Südosteuropapolitik.* Stuttgart: Deutsche Verlag-Anstalt, 1979.

Hoptner, Jacob B. *Yugoslavia in Crisis, 1934–1941.* New York: Columbia University Press, 1963.

Hutchison, Keith. *The Decline and Fall of British Capitalism.* London: Archon Books, 1951, repr. 1966.

Ianni, Octavio. *El Estado capitalista en la época de Cárdenas.* Mexico City: Ediciones Era, 1977.

Institute for Contemporary History. *The Third Reich and Yugoslavia 1933–1945.* 1975.

Jäckel, Eberhard. *Hitler's Weltanschauung: a Blueprint for Power.* Middletown, Conn.: Wesleyan University Press, 1972.

Jacobsen, H. A. *Nationalsozialistische Aussenpolitik, 1933–1938.* Frankfurt: A. Metzner, 1968.

James, Harold. *The German Slump: Politics and Economics 1924–1936.* Oxford: Clarendon, 1986.

Jones, Gareth Stedman. *Outcast London.* Oxford: Clarendon, 1971.

Juhasz, Gyula. *Hungarian Foreign Policy, 1919–1945.* Budapest: Akdemiai Kiado, 1979.

Kaiser, David E. *Economic Diplomacy and the Origins of the Second World War: Germany, Britain, France and Eastern Europe, 1930–1939.* Princeton: Princeton University Press, 1980.

Karski, Jan. *Poland in World Affairs.* Guilford, Conn.: International, 1980.

Kaser, Michael S., and Edward A. Radice, eds. *The Economic History of Eastern Europe, 1919–1975.* 3 vols. New York: Oxford University Press, 1985.

Kennedy, Paul. *The Rise and Fall of the Great Powers.* New York: First Vintage Books, 1984, 1986, 1989.

Kimmich, Christopher M. *German Foreign Policy 1918–1945: A Guide to Research and Research Materials.* Wilmington, Del.: Scholarly Resources, 1981.

Kindleberger, Charles Poor. *The World in Depression, 1929–1939.* Berkeley: University of California Press, 1973.

———. *The Terms of Trade: A European Case Study.* New York: Technology Press of MIT and Wiley, 1956.

Kiraly, Bela I., Peter Pastor and Ivan Sanders, eds. *War and Society in East Central Europe, Essays on World War I: Total War and Peacemaking, a Case Study on Trianon,* vol. 6. New York: Columbia University Press, 1982.

Klein, B. H. *Germany's Economic Preparations for War.* Cambridge: Harvard University Press, 1959.

Kluge, Dankwart. *Das Hossbach-'Protokoll': Die Zerstörung einer Legende.* Leoni am Starnberge See: Druffel, 1980.

Knauerhase, Ramon. *An Introduction to National Socialism, 1920–1939.* Columbus, Ohio: C. E. Merrill, 1972.

Knox, MacGregor. *Mussolini Unleashed 1939–1941: Politics and Strategy in Fascist Italy's Last War* (pbk.). Cambridge and New York: Cambridge University Press, 1986.

Koliopoulos, John S. *Greece and the British Connection 1935–1941.* Oxford: Clarendon, 1977.

Komjathy, Anthony T. *The Crises of France's East Central European Diplomacy, 1933–1938.* New York: East European Monographs, Columbia University Press and E.E.Q., 1976.

Kordt, Erich. *Nicht aus den Akten: Die Wilhelmstrasse in Frieden und Krieg; Erlebnisse, Begegnungen und Eindrücke, 1928–1945.* Stuttgart: Union Deutsche, 1950.

———. *Wahn und Wirklichkeit: Die Aussenpolitik des Dritten Reiches: Versuch einer Darstellung.* Stuttgart: Union Deutsche, 1948.

Kreider, Carl J. *The Anglo-American Trade Agreement: A Study of British and American Commercial Policies, 1934–1939.* Princeton: Princeton University Press, 1943.

Kuczynski, Jürgen. *Germany: Economic and Labor Conditions Under Fascism.* New York: International, 1945.

———. *Die Geschichte der Lage der Arbeiter unter dem Kapitalismus.* Berlin: Tribune, 1963.

———. *Die Geschichte der Lage der Arbeiter in Deutschland,* vol. 2. Berlin: Verlag Die Freie Gewerkschaft, 1947.

Kuzmanova, Antonia. *Balkanskata Politika na Rumuniia 1933–1939.* Sofia: Izd-vo na Bulgarskata academiia na naukite, 1984.

LaFeber, Walter. *Inevitable Revolutions — the United States in Central America.* New York: W. W. Norton, 1983.

Lammers, Donald N. *Explaining Munich: The Search for Motive in British Policy.* Stanford, Calif.: Hoover Institution on War, Revolution and Peace, 1966.

Latham, A. J. H. *The Depression and the Developing World, 1914–1939.* London, 1981.

Lazitch, Branko. *Tito and the Yugoslav Revolution.* Paris: Fasquelle, 1957.

Lederer, Ivo J. *Yugoslavia at the Paris Peace Conference.* New Haven: Yale University Press, 1963.

Leibovitz, Clement. *The Chamberlain-Hitler Deal.* Edmonton, Alberta: Les Éditions Duval, 1993.

Lenin, Vladmir I. *Imperialism, The Highest Stage of Capitalism.* Foreign Language Press, 1975.

Lewis, W. Arthur. *Economic Survey 1919–1939* (reprint). London: Harper Torchbooks, 1969.

Lukać, Dušan. *Treći Rajh i Zemlje Jugoistočne Evrope, 1937–1941,* 2 vols. Belgrade: Vojnoizdavački zavod, 1982.

Lukacs, John A. *The Great Powers and Eastern Europe.* New York: The American Book Co., 1953.

———. *The Hitler of History.* New York: Knopf, 1997.

Lungu, Dov B. *Romania and the Great Powers, 1933–1940.* Durham: Duke University Press, 1989.

Lyttelton, Adrian, ed. *Italian Fascisms: From Pareto to Gentile.* London: Jonathan Cape, 1973.

Macartney, C. A. *A History of Hungary 1929–1945,* New York: Praeger, 1956.

———. *October Fifteenth: a History of Modern Hungary, 1929–1945.* Edinburgh: University Press, 1957.

———. *Hungary: a Short History.* Chicago: Aldine, 1962.

———, and A. W. Palmer. *Independent Eastern Europe: a History.* London: Macmillan, 1962.

MacDonald, Callum A. *The United States, Britain and Appeasement, 1936–1939.* New York: St. Martin's, 1981.

Magdoff, Harry. *The Age of Imperialism.* New York: Monthly Review, 1969.

Mamatey, Victor S., and Radomír Luža, eds. *A History of the Czechoslovak Republic 1918–1948.* Princeton: Princeton University Press, 1973.

Manchester, William. *The Arms of Krupp 1587–1968* (pbk.). Boston: Little, Brown, 1968.

Mandić, Ante. *Fragmenti za istoriju ujedinjenja.* Zagreb: Jugoslavenska akademija znamosti i umjetnosti, 1956.

Marguerat, Phillipe. *Le IIIe Reich et le pétrole Roumain, 1938–1940.* Leiden: A. W. Sijthoff, 1977.

Marwick, Arthur. *Britain in the Century of Total War: Peace and Social Change 1900–1967.* Boston: Little, Brown, 1968.

Marx, Leo. *The Machine in the Garden: Technology and the Pastoral Ideal in America.* New York: Oxford University Press, 1964.

Mason, Timothy W. *Arbeiterklasse und Volksgemeinschaft: Dokumente und Materialien zur deutschen Arbeiterpolitik 1936–1939.* Opladen: Westdeutscher, 1975.

Matthews, Herbert L. *The Fruits of Fascism.* New York, 1943.

May, Ernest R. *Strange Victory: Hitler's Conquest of France.* New York, 1999.

McCormick, Thomas J. *America's Half-Century: United States Foreign Policy in the Cold War.* Baltimore and London: Johns Hopkins, 1987.

Medin, Tzvi. *Ideología y Praxis política de Lázaro Cárdenas.* Mexico City: Siglo Veintiuno Editores, 1972.

Medlicott, William Norton. *Economic Blockade.* London: Her Majesty's Stationery Office, 1964.

Middlemaes, Robert Keith. *The Strategy of Appeasement: The British Government and Germany.* Chicago: Quadrangle Books, 1972.

Milward, Alan S. *War, Economy and Society, 1939–1945.* Berkeley: University of California Press, 1977.

———. *The German Economy at War.* London: Athlone, 1965.

Mommsen, Hans, Dietmar Petzina, and Bernd Weisbrod, eds. *Industrielles System und politische Entwicklung in der Weimar Republik.* Düsseldorf: Droste, 1974.

Mommsen, Wolfgang J., and Lothar Kettenacker, eds. *The Fascist Challenge and the Policy of Appeasement.* London: G. Allen & Unwin, 1983.

Moore, Barrington, Jr. *Social Origins of Dictatorship and Democracy.* Boston: Beacon, 1966.

Murray, Williamson. *The Change in the European Balance of Power, 1938–1939: The Path to Ruin.* Princeton: Princeton University Press, 1984.

Namier, Lewis B. *Diplomatic Prelude 1938–1939.* London: Macmillan, 1948.

———. *Europe in Decay: A Study in Disintegration, 1936–1940.* London: Macmillan, 1950.

Naumann, Friedrich. *Mitteleuropa.* Berlin, 1915.

Néré, Jacques. *La Troisième République, 1914–1940.* Paris: A. Colin, 1967.

Newman, Simon. *March 1939: The British Guarantee to Poland: A Study in the Continuity of British Foreign Policy.* Oxford: Clarendon, 1976.

Newton, Scott. *Profits of Peace: The Political Economy of Anglo-German Appeasement.* Oxford: Clarendon, 1996.

Noakes, Jeremy, and Geoffry Pridham, eds. *Nazism 1919–1945: State, Economy and Society, 1933–1939,* vol. 2. Exeter: University of Exeter Press, 1984.

———. *Documents on Nazism 1919–1945.* New York: Viking, 1975.

Norden, Albert. *Die Nation und Wir: Ausgewählte Aufsätze und Reden 1933–1964,* vol. 1. Berlin: Dietz, 1965.

Novak, Bogdan C. *Trieste, 1941–1954.* Chicago: University of Chicago Press, 1970.

Novak, Grgr. *Italija prema Stvaranju Jugoslavije.* Zagreb, 1925.

O'Ballance, Edgar. *The Greek Civil War 1944–1949.* New York: Praeger, 1966.

Offner, Arnold A. *The Origins of the Second World War: American Foreign Policy and World Politics, 1917–1941.* New York: Praeger, 1975.

———. *American Appeasement: United States Foreign Policy and Germany, 1933–1938.* Cambridge: Belknap, 1969.

Ohlin, Bertil. *The Course and Phases of the World Economic Depression.* Report Presented to the Assembly of the League of Nations. (reprint). New York: Arno, 1972.

Osgood, Samuel. *The Fall of France, 1940.* Boston, 1965.

Overy, R. J. *The Nazi Economic Recovery: 1932–1938.* 2nd ed. London: Macmillan, 1982 and 1996.

Parker, R. A. C. *Chamberlain and Appeasement: British Policy and the Coming of the Second World War.* New York: St. Martin's, 1993.

Pearton, Maurice. *Oil and the Romanian State.* Oxford: Clarendon, 1971.

Peden, George C. *British Rearmament and the Treasury, 1932–1939.* Edinburgh: Scottish Academic, 1979.

Pentzlin, Heinz. *Hjalmar Schacht: Leben und Wirken einer umstrittenen Persönlichkeit.* Berlin: Ullstein, 1980.

Peterson, Edward Norman. *Hjalmar Schacht: For and Against Hitler: A Political-Economic Study of Germany, 1923–1945.* Boston: The Christopher Publishing House, 1954.

Petzina, Dietmar. *Autarkiepolitik im Dritten Reich 1936 bis 1939.* Stuttgart: Deutsche, 1968.

Peukert, Detlev. *Ruhrarbeiter gegen den Faschismus: Dokumentation über den Widerstand im Ruhrgebiet 1933–1945.* Frankfurt: Roderberg, 1976.

———. *Spuren des Widerstands: Die Bergarbeiterbewegung im Dritten Reich und im Exil.* Munich: Beck, 1987.

———. *Der Deutsche Arbeitswiderstand gegen das Dritte Reich.* Berlin Informationszentrum Berlin, 1980.

Polanyi, Karl. *The Great Transformation: The Political and Economic Origins of Our Time.* Boston: First Beacon, 1957.

Pollard, Sidney. *The Development of the British Economy, 1914–1967* (2nd ed.). New York: St. Martin's, 1969.

Pool, James. *Hitler and His Secret Partners.* New York, 1997.

Popi, Gligor. *Jugoslovensko-Rumunski Odnosi 1918–1941.* Vrsac: Sloboda, 1984.

Post, Gaines. *Dilemmas of Appeasement: British Deterrence and Defense, 1934–1937.* Ithaca: Cornell University Press, 1993.

Prazmowska, Anita. *Britain, Poland and the Eastern Front, 1939.* New York: Cambridge University Press, 1987.

Ránki, György. *Economy and Foreign Policy: The Struggle of the Great Powers for Hegemony in the Danube Valley, 1919–1939.* Boulder, Colo.: East European Monographs, 1983.

Rauschning, Hermann. *The Voice of Destruction.* London, 1939.

———. *Hitler Speaks.* London: T. Butterworth, 1939.

Read, Anthony, and David Fisher. *The Deadly Embrace: Hitler, Stalin and the Nazi-Soviet Pact 1939–1941.* New York: Norton, 1988.

Recker, Marie-Luise, ed. *Von der Konkurrenz zur Rivalität, das britisch-deutsche Verhältnis in den Ländern der europäischen Peripherie, 1919–1939.* Stuttgart: F. Steiner Verlag Wiesbaden, 1986.

Reynolds, David. *The Creation of the Anglo-American Alliance 1937–41: A Study in Competitive Cooperation.* London, 1981.

Ribbentrop, Annelies von. *Deutsche-englische Geheimverbindungen: Britische Dokumente der Jahre 1938 und 1939 im Lichte der Kriegschuldfrage.* Tübingen: Verlag der Deutschen Hochschullehrer-Zeitung 1967.

Rich, Norman. *Hitler's War Aims: Ideology, the Nazi State and the Course of Expansion,* 2 vols. New York: Norton, 1973.

Richardson, J. Henry. *British Economic Foreign Policy* (reprint). New York: Garland, 1983.

Riekhoff, Harald von. *German-Polish Relations, 1918–1933.* Baltimore and London: Johns Hopkins, 1971.

Ripka, Hubert. *Munich: Before and After.* London: V. G. Gollancz, 1939.

Ristić Dragiša N. *Yugoslavia's Revolution of 1941.* University Park: Pennsylvania State University Press, 1966.

Rock, William R. *British Appeasement in the 1930s.* New York: Norton, 1977.

———. *Appeasement on Trial: The British Foreign Office and its Critics 1938–1939.* Hamden: Archon Books, 1966.

———. *Chamberlain and Roosevelt: British Foreign Policy and the United States, 1937–1940.* Columbus: Ohio State University Press, 1988.

Rohe, Karl. *Die Westmächte und das dritte Reich 1933–1939: Klassische Grossmachtrivalität oder Kampf zwischen Demokratie und Diktatur?* Paderborn: F. Schöningh, 1982.

Roos, Hans. *Polen und Europa: Studien zur polnischen Aussenpolitik, 1931–1939.* Tübingen: Mohr, 1957.

Rose, William John. *The Rise of Polish Democracy.* London: G. Bell and Sons, 1944.

Rowse, A. L. *Appeasement and All Souls: A Study in Political Decline, 1933–1939.* 1961.

Royal Institute of International Affairs. *South East Europe: A Political and Economic Study.* 1939.

Sakmyster, Thomas L. *Hungary, the Great Powers and the Danubian Crisis.* Athens: University of Georgia Press, 1980.

Sarti, Roland. *The Ax Within.* New York: New Viewpoints, 1974.

———. *Fascism and the Industrial Leadership in Italy 1919–1940: A Study in the Expansion of Private Power under Fascism.* Berkeley: University of California Press, 1971.

Sauvy, Alfred. *Histoire Économique de la France entre les Deux Guerres (1931–1939),* vol. 2. Paris: Fayard, 1967.

Sayers, Richard S. *Financial Policy, 1939–1945.* London: Her Majesty's Stationery Office, 1956.

———. *The Bank of England, 1891–1944,* vol. 2. Cambridge: Cambridge University Press, 1976.

Schacher, Gerhard. *Germany Pushes South-east.* London: Hurst and Blackett, 1937.

Schlarp, Karl-Heinz. *Wirtschaft und Besatzung in Serbien 1941–1944: Ein Beitrag zur national-sozialistischen Wirtschaftspolitik in Südosteuropa.* Stuttgart: F. Steiner Verlag Wiesbaden, 1986.

Schmidt, Gustav. *The Politics and the Economics of Appeasment: British Foreign Policy in the 1930s* (translated by Jackie Bennett-Ruete). New York: St. Martin's, 1986.

Schröder, Hans-Jürgen. *Deutschland und die Vereinigten Staaten 1933–1939.* Wiesbaden: F. Steiner, 1970.

Schumann, Wolfgang, *Griff nach Südost-Europa.* Berlin: VEB Deutscher, 1973.

Schweitzer, Arthur. *Big Business in the Third Reich.* Bloomington: Indiana University Press, 1964.

Seabury, Paul. *The Wilhelmstrasse: A study of German diplomats under the Nazi regime.* Berkeley: University of California Press, 1954.

Seton-Watson, Hugh. *Eastern Europe Between the Wars, 1918–1941.* Cambridge: The University Press, 1945.

Sforza, Carlo Count. *Contemporary Italy: Its Intellectual and Moral Origins* (translated by Drake and Denise DeKay). New York: E. P. Dutton, 1944.

Šišić, Ferdo. *Jadransko Pitanje na Konferenciji Mira u Parizu: Zbirka Akata i Dokumenata.* Zagreb: Matice hrvatske Izd., 1920.

Smaldone, William. *Rudolf Hilferding: The Tragedy of a German Social Democrat.* DeKalb: Northern Illinois University Press, 1998.

Smith, Denis Mack. *Mussolini's Roman Empire.* New York: Longman, 1976.

Smith, Woodruff D. *The Ideological Origins of Nazi Imperialism.* New York: Oxford University Press, 1986.

Sontag, Raymond J., and James S. Beddie, eds. *Nazi-Soviet Relations, 1939–1941: Documents from the Archives of the German Foreign Office.* Washington, D.C.: Department of State, 1948.

Sprigge, Cecil J. S. *The Development of Modern Italy.* New Haven: Yale University Press, 1944.

Stachura, Peter D., ed. *Poland Between the Wars, 1918–1939.* New York: St. Martins, 1998.

Stegmann, Dirk, and Bernd-Jürgen Wendt and Peter-Christian Witt. *Industrielle Gesellschaft und politisches System.* Bonn: Neue Gesellschaft, 1978.

Strauch, Rudi. *Sir Neville Henderson: Britischer Botschafter in Berlin von 1937 bis 1939.* Bonn: Rohrscheid, 1959.

Sturzo, Luigi. *Italy and Fascism* (translated by Barbara Barclay Carter). London: Faber and Gwyer, 1926.

Tapié, Victor L. *Le pays de Teschen et les rapports entre la Pologne et le Tchécoslovaquie.* Paris: Paul Hartmann, 1936.

Taylor, A. J. P. *The Origins of the Second World War* (2nd ed., paperback). London: Hamilton, 1961.

Taylor, J. *The Economic Development of Poland 1919–1950.* Ithaca: Cornell University Press, 1952.

Teichert, Eckart. *Autarkie und Grossraumwirtschaft in Deutschland 1930–1939: Aussen-wirtschaftspolitische Konzeptionen zwischen Wirtschaftskrise und Zweitem Weltkrieg.* Munich: Oldenbourg, 1984.

Teichova, Alice. *An Economic Background to Munich: International Business and Czechoslovakia 1918–1938.* London: Cambridge University Press, 1974.

Teichova, Alice, and P. L. Cottrell. *International Business and Central Europe 1918–1939.* New York: St. Martin's, 1983.

Thompson, David, ed. *The New Cambridge Modern History: The Era of Violence 1898–1945,* vol. 12. London: Cambridge University Press, 1960.

Thompson, Neville. *The Anti-Appeasers: Conservative Opposition to Appeasement in the 30s.* Oxford: Clarendon, 1971.

Tomasevich, Jozo. *Peasants, Politics and Economic Change in Yugoslavia.* Stanford: Stanford University Press, 1955.

———. *The Chetniks: War and Revolution in Yugoslavia 1941–1945.* Stanford: Stanford University Press, 1975.

Toscano, Mario. *The Origins of the Pact of Steel.* Baltimore: Johns Hopkins, 1967.

Toynbee, Arnold J., ed. *Survey of International Affairs 1935.* London: Oxford University Press, 1936.

———. *Survey of International Affairs 1936.* London: Oxford University Press, 1937.

———. *Survey of International Affairs 1937.* London: Oxford University Press, 1938.

———. *Survey of International Affairs, Hitler's Europe, 1939–1946.* London: Oxford University Press, 1954.

Trias, Vivian. *Imperio Británico en América Latina.* Buenos Aires: South East Europe, 1939.

Ullein-Reviczky, Antal. *Guerre Allemande, Paix Russe: le Drame Hongrois.* Neuchatel: Bacconnière, 1947.

van Creveld, Martin L. *Hitler's Strategy, 1940–1941: The Balkan Clue.* London: Cambridge University Press, 1973.

Vego, Bela, George L., and Mosse, eds. *Jews and Non-Jews in Eastern Europe 1918–1945.* New York: Wiley, 1974.

Vinaver, Vuk. *Jugoslavija i Francuska izmedju dva svetska rata: Da li je Jugoslavija bila francuski "satelit."* Belgrade: Institutza savremenu istoriju, 1985.

Voinovitch, Conte Lugo de. *La Dalmatie, L'Italie, L'Unité Yougoslave (1797–1917).* Geneva: George, 1917.

Volkov, Vladimir K. *Miunkhenskii sgovor i Balkanskie Strany.* Moscow: Nauka, 1978.

———. *Germano-iugoslavskie otnosheniia: razval Maloi Antanty, 1933–1938.* Moscow: Nauka, 1966.

Wandycz, Piotr S. *France and her Eastern Allies, 1919–1925: French-Czechoslovak-Polish Relations from the Paris Peace Conference to Locarno.* Minneapolis: University of Minnesota Press, 1962.

———. *The Twilight of French Eastern Alliances, 1926–1936: French-Czechoslovak-Polish Relations from Locarno to the Remilitarization of the Rhineland.* Princeton: Princeton University Press, 1988.

Watt, Donald Cameron. *How War Came: The Immediate Origins of the Second World War.* London: Heinemann, 1989.

Weber, Eugen. *The Hollow Years: France in the 1930s.* New York, 1994.

Weinberg, Gerhard L. *The Foreign Policy of Hitler's Germany: Diplomatic Revolution in Europe, 1933–1936,* vol. 1. Chicago: University of Chicago Press, 1970.

———. *The Foreign Policy of Hitler's Germany: Starting World War II, 1937–1939,* vol. 2. Chicago: University of Chicago Press, 1980.

———. *Germany, Hitler and World War II.* Cambridge and New York: Cambridge University Press, 1995.

Wendt, Bernd-Jürgen. *Economic Appeasement: Handel und Finanz in der britischen Deutschland-Politik 1933–1939.* Düsseldorf: Bertelsmann Universitätsverlag, 1971.

Werner, Otto. *Englands Kriegspolitik gegen Deutschland.* Munich: Türmer, 1971.

Wheeler-Bennett, W. *Munich: Prologue to Tragedy.* London: Macmillan, 1948.

Williams, William Appleman. *The Tragedy of American Diplomacy.* New York: Dell, 1962.

Wiskemann, Elizabeth. *Czechs and Germans.* London: Oxford University Press, 1938.

Wojciechowski, Marian. *Die Polnische-Deutsche Beziehungen, 1933–1939.* Leiden: Brill, 1971.

Wolff, Robert Lee. *The Balkans in our Times.* Cambridge: Harvard University Press, 1956.

Woodward, Sir Llewellyn. *British Foreign Policy in the Second World War,* 5 vols. London: Her Majesty's Stationery Office, 1970–1976.

Wuescht, J. *Jugoslawien und das Dritte Reich, eine dokumentierte Geschichte der deutsch-jugoslawischen Beziehungen von 1933 bis 1945.* Stuttgart: Seewald, 1945.

Wynot, Edward. *Polish Politics in Transition: The Camp of National Unity and the Struggle for Power 1935–1939.* Athens: University of Georgia Press, 1974.

Zweig, Ferdynand. *Poland Between Two Wars: A Critical Study of Social and Economic Changes.* London: Secker & Warburg, 1944.

Published Articles

Abraham, David. "Conflicts within German Industry and the Collapse of the Weimar Republic." *Past & Present: A Journal of Historical Studies* 88 (August 1980): 88–128.

———. "Review of The Nazi Economic Recovery, 1932–1938. By R. J. Overy." *Journal of Economic History* 45, no. 4 (December 1985): 986–987.

Avramovski, Živko. "Ekonomičeskie i političeskie celi nemečkogo vvoz vooruzeniia v balkanskie strani nakanune vtoroi mirovoi voini." *Studia Balcanica* 7 (1973).

———."Attempt to form a neutral bloc in the Balkans (September–December 1939)." *Studia Balcanica* no. 4 (1971): 123–153.

———. "Sukob Interesa V. Britanije i Nemačke na Balkanu uoči drugog svetskog rata." *Istoriya XX veka* 2: 5–158.

———. "Problem Albanije u Jugoslavensko-Italijanskom Pakta od 25. III 1937." *Istorijski Pregled* 1 (1963): 19–31.

———. "The Yugoslav-Bulgarian Perpetual Friendship Pact of 24 January 1937." *Canadian Slavonic Papers* 11, no. 1 (1969): 304–338.

Axenciuc, Victor. "La Place occupée par la Roumanie dans la Division Mondiale Capitaliste à La veille de la Seconde Guerre Mondiale." *Revue roumanie d'histoire* 4 (1966).

Bariety, Jacques. "Der Tardieu-Plan zur Sanierung des Donauraums (Februar-Mai 1932)." In *Internationale Beziehungen in der Weltwirtschaftskrise 1929–1933,* edited by Hildebrand Becker, et al. Munich: Ernst Vogel, 1980.

Bayer, J. A. "British Policy towards the Russo-Finnish Winter War 1939–40." *Canadian Journal of History* 16, no. 1 (April 1981): 27–65.

Berov, L. "The withdrawing of western capital from Bulgaria on the eve of the Second World War." In *Politikata na Velikite Sili na Balkanite v Navečerieto na vtorata Svetovna voina.* Sofia: 1971.

———. "Le Capital Financier Occidental et les Pays Balkaniques dans les Années Vingt." *Études Balkaniques* 2–3 (1965): 139–169.

Bidwell, Percy W. "Prospects of a Trade Agreement with England." *Foreign Affairs* 16, no. 1 (1937): 103–114.

———. "Latin America, Germany, and the Hull Program." *Foreign Affairs* 17, no. 2 (January 1939): 374–390.

Bigler, Robert M. "Heil Hitler and Heil Horthy! The Nature of Hungarian Racist Nationalism and its Impact on German-Hungarian Relations 1919–1945." *East European Quarterly* 8, no. 3: 251–273.

Bloomfield, Arthur I. "British Thought on the Influence of Foreign Trade and Investment on Growth, 1800–1880." *History of Political Economy* 13, no. 1: 95–120.

Booth, Alan E., and Sean Glynn. "Unemployment in the Interwar Period: A Multiple Problem." *Journal of Contemporary History* 10 (1975): 611–636.

———, and J. D. Tomlinson. "Inter-War Unemployment — Two Views." *Journal of Contemporary History* 17 (1982): 545–555.

Bregman, Alexander. "Gdyby w 1933 r. usluchano Jozefa Pilsudskiego (If they had listened to Jozef Pilsudski in 1933)." *Kultura* no. 15 (1949): 109–117.

———. "Legenda czy fakt historyczny (Legend or Historical Fact)." *Dziewnik Polski* (Polish Daily) London (1954).

Broszat, Martin. "Deutschland-Ungarn-Rumänien Entwicklung und Grundfaktoren national-sozialistischer Hegemonial-und Bundnispolitik 1938–1941." *Historische Zeitschrift* 206 (1968): 45–99.

Calafeteanu, Ion. "Les Relations Économiques Germano-Roumaines de 1933 à 1944." *Revue d'Histoire 2e Guerre* no. 140 (1985): 23–33.

Campbell, F. Gregory. "The Struggle for Upper Silesia, 1919–1922." *Journal of Modern History* 42, no. 3 (September 1970): 361–385.

Campus, Eliza. "Le Bloc des Neutres (septembre-decembre 1939)." *Studia Balcanica* no. 7 (1973): 269–272.

———. "Der Balkanblock der Neutralen (Sept. 1939–Marz 1940)." *Wissenschaftliche Zeitschrift der Karl Marx Universität* 6 (1956–1957): 15–22.

Celovsky, Boris. "Pilsudskis Präventivkrieg gegen das Nationalsozialistische Deutschland (Entstehung, Verbreitung und Widerlegung einer Legende)." In *Die Welt als Geschichte* 1 (1954): 53–70.

Champalov, I. N. "K istorii zakluchenie germano-ruminskogo ekonomicheskogo soglashenia 1939 goda." *Novaia i noveishaia istoriia* no. 1 (1955).

Chary, Frederick B. "The Diary of Bogdan Filov." *Southeastern Europe* 1 and 2 (1975).

Chiper, Ioan. "L'expansion économique de l'Allemagne nazie dans les Balkans: Objectifs, Méthodes, Résultats (1933–1939)." *Studia Balcanica* no. 7 (1973): 121–127.

Cienciala, Anna M. "Poland in British and French policy in 1939: determination to fight — or avoid war?" In *The Origins of the Second World War,* edited by Patrick Finney. London: Arnold, 1997.

Coghlan, F. "Armaments, Economic Policy and Appeasement. Background to British Foreign Policy, 1931–1937." *History* 57 (1972): 205–216.

Cohen, Jon S. "Fascism and Agriculture in Italy: Policies and Consequences." *Economic History* 32 (February 1979).

Cottrell, P. L. "Aspects of Western Equity Investment in the Banking Systems of East Central Europe." In *International Business and Central Europe,* edited by Alice Teichova and P. L. Cottrell. New York: St. Martin's, 1983.

Crozier, Andrew. "Prelude to Munich: British Foreign Policy and Germany, 1935–1938." *European Studies Review* 6 (1976): 357–381.

Cvijetić, Leposava. "The Ambitions and Plans of the Third Reich with Regard to the Integration of Yugoslavia into its So-Called Grosswirtschaftsraum." In *Yugoslavia and the Third Reich, 1933–1945,* Institute for Contemporary History, 1975.

Davidson, Basil. "Germany over Roumania." *Contemporary Review* 156 (August 1939): 182–188.

Davis, Lance E., and Huttenback, Robert A. "The Political Economy of British Imperialism: Measures of Benefits and Supports." *Journal of Economic History* 42, no. 1 (March 1982): 119–130.

Debicki, Roman. "The Remilitarization of the Rhineland and Its Impact on the French-Polish Alliance." *Polish Review* 14, no. 4 (autumn 1969).

Drummond, I. "Britain and the World Economy 1900–1945." In *The Economic History of Britain since 1700,* vol. 2, edited by Roderick Floud and Donald McCloskey. Cambridge: Cambridge University Press, 1981.

Edelstein, M. "Foreign Investment and Empire 1860–1914." In *The Economic History of Britain Since 1700,* vol. 2, edited by Roderick Floud and Donald McCloskey. Cambridge: Cambridge University Press, 1981.

Ekoko, A. Edho. "The British Attitude Towards Germany's Colonial Irredentism in Africa in the Inter-War Years." *Journal of Contemporary History* 14 (1979): 287–307.

Fair, John D. "The Conservative Basis for the Formation of the National Government of 1931." *Journal of British Studies* 19, no. 2 (spring 1980): 142–164.

Fomin, V. T. "Podgotovka Nemetsko-Fashistkoi Aggresii Protiv Yugoslavii (1937–1941 godi)." *Voprosi Istorii* no. 6: 28–49.

Friedman, P. "The Welfare Costs of Bilateralism, German-Hungarian trade 1933–1938." *Explorations in Economic History* 13, no. 1 (1976): 113–125.

Garraty, John A. "The New Deal, National Socialism and the Great Depression." *American Historical Review* 78, no. 4 (October 1973): 907–944.

Gasiorowski, Zygmunt. "The German-Polish Non-Aggression Pact of 1934." *Journal of Central European Affairs* 15, no. 1.

————. "Did Pilsudski Attempt to Initiate a Preventive War in 1933?" *Journal of Modern History,* no. 2 (June 1955).

Girault, René. "The Impact of the Economic Situation on the Foreign Policy of France, 1936–1939." In *The Fascist Challenge and the Policy of Appeasement,* edited by Wolfgang J. Mommsen and Lothar Kettenacker. London: G. Allen & Unwin, 1983.

Goldman, Aaron L. "Sir Robert Vansittart's Search for Italian Cooperation against Hitler, 1933–1936." *Contemporary History* 9 (1974): 93–130.

Gromada, Thaddeus V. "The Slovaks and the Failure of Beck's 'Third Europe' Scheme." *Polish Review* 14, no. 4 (autumn 1969): 55–64.

Gross, Felix. "The State, the Nation and the Party in Poland." *Slavic Review* 32, no. 1 (March 1973): 134–140.

Gross, Herbert. "Deutschlands handelspolitische Einkreisung durch USA." *Wirtschaftsdienst* 41 (October 8, 1937): 1411–1413.

Hanks, Ronald W. "Via Victis! The Austro-Hungarian Armee Oberkommando and the Armistice of Villa Giusti." *Austrian History Yearbook* 14 (1978): 101–112.

Harrison, Richard A. "The Runciman Visit to Washington in January 1937." *Canadian Journal of History* 19 (August 1984): 217–239.

Hauner, Milan. "Did Hitler Want a World Dominion?" *Journal of Contemporary History* 13, no. 1 (January 1978): 15–32.

Hehn, Paul N. "Capitalism and the Revolutionary Factor in the Balkans and Crimean War Diplomacy." *East European Quarterly* 18, no. 2 (June 1984): 155–185.

————. "The National Socialist Revolution and the Rise of Hitler: The View from Moscow and Warsaw, 1923–1933 [the dates cited are incorrect and should be 1932–1933 –P.N.H.]." *Polish Review* 25, no. 3–4 (1980): 28–48.

Hillgruber, Andreas. "England's Place in Hitler's Plans for World Dominion." *Journal of Contemporary History* 9 (1974): 5–22.

————. "Der Hitler-Stalin-Pakt und die Entfesselung des zweiten Weltkrieges — Situationsanalyse und Machtkalkül der beiden Pakt-Partner." *Historische Zeitschrift* 230 (April 1980): 339–361.

————. "England in Hitler's Aussenpolitischer Konzeption." *Historische Zeitschrift* 218 (1974): 65–84.

Hinkkanen-Lievonen, Merja-Liisa. "Britain as Germany's Commercial Rival in the Baltic States, 1919–1939." In *Von der Konkurrenz zur Rivalität, das britisch-deutsche Verhältnis in den Ländern der europäischen Peripherie, 1919–1939,* edited by Marie-Luise Recker. Stuttgart: F. Steiner Verlag Wiesbaden, 1986.

Hoisington, William A. "The Struggle for Economic Influence in Southeastern Europe: The French Failure in Romania, 1940." *Journal of Modern History* 43, no. 3 (1971): 468–482.

Holland, R. F. "The Federation of British Industries and the International Economy, 1929–1939." *Economic History Review* 34 (1981): 287–300.

Holmes, Blair R. "Europe and the Hapsburg Restoration in Austria, 1930–1938." *East European Quarterly* 9, no. 2 (summer 1975): 173–184.

Hoptner, J. B. "Yugoslavia as Neutralist: 1937." *Journal of Central European Affairs* 16, no. 11 (July 1956): 156–176.

Hughes, Thomas Parke. "Technological Momentum in History: Hydrogenation in Germany 1898–1993." *Past and Present* no. 44 (August 1969).

Hunczak, Taras. "Polish Colonial Ambitions in the Inter-War Period." *Slavic Review* 26, no. 4 (December 1967): 648–662.

Huttenback, Robert A. "The Political Economy of British Imperialism: Measures of Benefits and Supports." *Journal of Economic History* 42, no. 1 (March 1982): 119–130.

Jones, Harold. "Innovation and Conservatism in Economic Recovery: The Alleged 'Nazi Recovery' of the 1930s." In *Reevaluating the Third Reich,* edited by Thomas Childers and Jane Caplan. New York and London: Holmes and Meier, 1993.

Juhasz, Gy. "La politique extérieure de la Hongrie à l'époque de la 'drôle de guerre.'" *Acta Historica* 9, no. 3–4: 407–457.

Kennedy, Paul M. "The Tradition of Appeasement in British Foreign Policy 1865–1939." *British Journal of International Studies* 2 (1976): 195–215.

———. " 'Appeasement' and British Defence policy in the Inter-war Years." *British Journal of International Studies* 4 (1978): 161–177.

Kerekes, L. "A. J. P. Taylor: Die Ursprünge des Zweiten Weltkrieges." *Akta Historica* 9, no. 3–4: 476–483, Book Review.

Knox, MacGregor. "Conquest, Foreign and Domestic, in Fascist Italy and Nazi Germany." *Journal of Modern History* 56 (1984): 17–19.

Kolko, Gabriel. "American Business and Germany, 1930–1941." *Western Political Quarterly* 15 (1962): 713–728.

Komjathy, Anthony Tihamer. "The First Vienna Award (November 2, 1938)." *Austrian History Yearbook* 16–17 (1979–1980): 131–156.

Kube, Alfred. "Aussenpolitik und 'Grossraumwirtschaft': Die deutsche Politik zur wirtschaftlichen Integration Südosteuropas 1933 bis 1939." In *Von der Konkurrenz zur Rivalität: das britisch-deutsche Verhältnis in den Ländern der europäischen Peripherie, 1919–1939,* edited by Marie-Luise Recker. Stuttgart: F. Steiner Verlag Wiesbaden, 1986.

Kuzmanova, Antonina. "Sur le Problème de la Restitution de la Dobrudza du Sud à la Bulgarie (septembre 1939–septembre 1940)." *Études Balkaniques* no. 2 (1984): 114–124.

———. "La Roumanie et l'Accord de Salonique." *Études Balkaniques* no. 2 (1980): 42–55.

Lammers, Donald. "From Whitehall after Munich: The Foreign Office and the Future Course of British Policy." *The Historical Journal* 16, no. 4 (1973): 831–856.

———. "Fascism, Communism, and the Foreign Office, 1937–1939." *Journal of Contemporary History* 6 (1971): 66–86.

———. "The May Crisis of 1938: The Soviet Version Considered." *The South Atlantic Quarterly* 69 (1970): 480–503.

Lossowski, Piotr. "Stosunki Polsko-Niemieckie W Latach 1933–1939 a Kleska Wrzesniowa." *Wojskowy Przeglad Historyczny* no. 1 (1963): 132–162.

MacDonald, Callum A. "Economic Appeasement and the German 'Moderates' 1937–1939." *Past and Present* no. 56 (August 1972): 105–135.

———. "The United States, Appeasement and the Open Door." In *The Fascist Challenge and the Policy of Appeasement,* edited by Wolfgang J. Mommsen and Lothar Kettenacker. London: G. Allen & Unwin, 1983.

Manne, Robert. "The British Decision for Alliance with Russia, May 1939." *Journal of Contemporary History* no. 3 (1974): 3–26.

———. "Some British Light on the Nazi-Soviet Pact." *European Studies Review* 11 (1981): 83–102.

———. "The Foreign Office and the Failure of Anglo-Soviet Rapprochement." *Journal of Contemporary History* 16 (1981): 725–755.

Marzari, Frank. "Some Factors Making for Neutrality in the Balkans in August–September 1939." *East European Quarterly* 10, no. 1 (1976): 179–199.

———. "Projects for an Italian-Led Balkan Bloc of Neutrals, September–December 1939." *Historical Journal* 13, no. 4 (December 1970): 767–788.

Mason, Tim. "The Domestic Dynamics of Nazi Conquests: A Response to Critics." In *Reevaluating the Third Reich,* edited by Thomas Childers and Jane Caplan. New York and London: Holmes and Meier, 1993.

———, and R. J. Overy. "Debate: Germany, 'Domestic Crisis' and War in 1939." In *The Origins of the Second World War,* edited by Patrick Finney. London: Arnold, 1997.

Massip, Roger. "After the Trip of General Śmigły-Rydz to Paris." *L'Europe Nouvelle* (September 22, 1936).

Meacham, Standish. "The Sense of an Impending Clash: English Working Class Unrest Before the First World War." *American Historical Review* 77, no. 5 (1972): 1343–1364.

Milward, Alan S. "The Reichsmark Bloc and the International Economy." In *Der "Führerstaat": Mythe und Realität: Studien zur Struktur und Politik des Dritten Reiches,* edited by Gerhard Hirschfeld and Lothar Kettenacker. Stuttgart: Klett-Cotta, 1981.

———. "Der Deutsche Handel und der Welthandel 1925–1939." In *Industrielles System und politische Entwicklung in der Weimar Republik,* edited by Hans Mommsen, Dietmar Petzina, and Bernd Weisbrod. Düsseldorf: Droste, 1974.

Neal, Larry. "The Economics and Finance of Bilateral Clearing Agreements: Germany 1934–1938." *The Economic History Review* (Second Series) 32, no. 3 (August 1979): 391–404.

Niedhart, Gottfried. "Appeasement: Die britische Antwort auf die Krise des Weltreichs und des internationalen Systems vor dem Zweiten Weltkrieg." *Historische Zeitschrift* 226 (1978): 67–88.

Orde, Anne. "France and Hungary in 1920: Revisionism and Railways." In *War and Society in East Central Europe* vol. 6, edited by Bela I. Kiraly, Peter Paitor and Ivan Sandors. New York, 1982.

Overy, R. J. "Heavy Industry and the State in Nazi Germany: The Reichswerke Crisis." *European History Quarterly* 15 (1985): 313–340.

———. "The German Motorisierung and Rearmament: A Reply." *Economic History Review* 2nd series 32 (February 1979): 107–113.

Parker, R. A. C. "Economics, Rearmament and Foreign Policy: The United Kingdom before 1939 — A Preliminary Study." *Journal of Contemporary History* 10 (1975): 637–647.

Peden, G. C. "Keynes, the Economics of Rearmament and Appeasement." In *The Fascist Challenge and the Policy of Appeasement,* edited by Wolfgang J. Mommsen and Lothar Kettenacker. London: G. Allen & Unwin, 1983.

Pešelj, Branko. "The Serbo-Croatian Agreement of 1939 and American Foreign Policy." *Journal of Croatian Studies* 11–12 (1970–1971).

Pobog-Malinowski, Wladyslaw. "Niedoszla Wojna z Niemiecami (The War with the Germans which did not Occur)." *Orzel Bialy* (White Eagle) 12, no. 506 (March 15, 1952).

Prpić, George. "French Rule in Croatia: 1806–1813," *Balkan Studies* 5, no. 2 (1964): 221–276.

Pryor, Zora P. "Czechoslovak Economic Development in the Interwar Period." In *A History of the Czechoslovak Republic 1918–1948,* edited by Victor S. Mamatey and Radomír Luža. Princeton: Princeton University Press, 1973.

Radandt, Hans. "Die IG Farbenindustrie AG und Südosteuropa bis 1938." *Jahrbuch für Wirtschaftsgeschichte* no. 3 (1966): 146–195.

———. "Die IG Farbenindustrie AG und Südosteuropa 1938 bis zum Ende des zweiten Weltkrieges." *Jahrbuch für Wirtschaftsgeschichte* 1 (1967).

Ránki, G. "The Hungarian General Credit Bank in the 1920s." In *International Business and Central Eastern Europe 1918–1939,* edited by Alice Teichova and P. L. Cottrell. New York: St. Martin's, 1983.

Richardson, Charles O. "French Plans for Allied Attacks on the Caucasus Oil Fields January–April, 1940." *French Historical Studies* 8, no. 1 (spring 1975): 130–156.

Roberts, Henry. "The Diplomacy of Colonel Beck." In *The Diplomats 1919–1939,* edited by Gordon Craig and Felix Gilbert. Princeton: Princeton University Press, 1953.

Robertson, E. H. "Race as a Factor in Mussolini's Policy in Africa and Europe." *Journal of Contemporary History* 23 (1988): 50–52.

Robertson, Esmonde. "Hitler and Sanctions: Mussolini and the Rhineland." *European Studies Review* 7 (1977): 409–435.

Roman, Eric. "Munich and Hungary: An Overview of Hungarian Diplomacy during the Sudeten Crisis." *East European Quarterly* 8, no. 1: 71–97.

Rooke, M. J. "The Concept of Political Trading in Peacetime. The British Government and Trade with Southeastern Europe, 1938–1939." *Revue Études Sud-Est Europe* 22, no. 2 (1984): 171–195.

Roos, Hans. "Die Präventivkriegspläne Pilsudskis von 1933." In *Vierteljahresheft für Zeitgeschichte,* 2 Jahrgang. 1 (1955): 90–93.

Sakmyster, Thomas. "Hungary and the Munich Crisis. The Revisionist Dilemma." *Slavic Review* 32, no. 4 (December 1973): 725–740.

Sakwa, George. "The 'Renewal' of the Franco-Polish Alliance in 1936 and the Rambouillet Agreement." *The Polish Review* 16, no. 2 (spring 1971): 45–66.

Salmon, Patrick. "Anglo-German Commercial Rivalry in the Depression Era: The Political and Economic Impact on Scandinavia 1931–1939." In *Von der Konkurrenz zur Rivalität: das britisch-deutsche Verhältnis in den Ländern der europäischen Peripherie, 1919–1939,* edited by Marie-Luise Recker. Stuttgart: F. Steiner Verlag Wiesbaden, 1986.

Santorelli, Enzo. "The Economic and Political Background." In *The Ax Within,* edited by Roland Sarti. New York: New Viewpoints, 1974.

Schacht, Hjalmar. "Germany's Colonial Demands." *Foreign Affairs* 12, no. 2 (January 1937): 223–234.

————. "German Trade and German Debts." *Foreign Affairs* 13, no. 1 (October 1934): 1–5.

Schatz, Arthur W. "The Anglo-American Trade Agreement and Cordell Hull's Search for Peace 1936–1938." *Journal of American History* 57 (June 1970): 85–103.

Schneider, Alfred. "Grenzen der Annäherung USA — Südamerika." *Wirtschaftsdienst* 41 (October 8, 1937): 1413–1415.

Schonfeld, Roland. "Deutsche Rohstoffsicherungspolitik in Jugoslawien 1934–1944." *Vierteljahreshefte für Zeitgeschichte*, 24, no. 3 (1976): 215–258.

Schröder, Hans-Jürgen. "Widerstände der USA gegen europäische Integrationsbestrebungen in der Weltwirtschaftskrise 1929–1939." In *Wirtschaftliche und politische Integration in Europa im 19 und 20 Jahrhundert*, edited by Helmut Berding. Göttingen: Vandenhoeck & Ruprecht.

————. "Südosteuropa als 'Informal Empire' Deutschlands 1933–1939." *Jahresbücher für Osteuropas* 23 (1975): 70–96.

————. "The Ambiguities of Appeasement: Great Britain, the United States and Germany, 1937–1939." In *The Fascist Challenge and the Policy of Appeasement*, edited by Wolfgang J. Mommsen and Lothar Kettenacker. London: G. Allen & Unwin, 1983.

————. "Die deutsche Südosteuropapolitik 1929–1936 Zur Kontinuität deutscher Aussenpolitik in der Weltwirtschaftskrise." *Geschichte u. Gesellschaft* 2, no. 1 (1976).

————. "Die deutsche Südosteuropapolitik u. die Reaktion der Angelsächischen Mächte."

Schwabe, Klaus. "Die Regierung Roosevelt und die Expansionspolitik Hitlers vor dem Zweiten Weltkrieg." In *Die Westmächte und das dritte Reich 1933–1939: Klassische Grossmachtrivalität oder Kampf zwischen Demokratie und Diktatur?*, edited by K. Rohe. Paderborn: F. Schöningh, 1982.

Schwoerer, Lois G. "Lord Halifax's Visit to Germany: November 1937." *The Historian* 32, no. 3 (May 1970): 353–375.

Sheviakov, A. A. "Vneshniaia Politika Ruminii v period Miunhena." *Voprosi Istorii* 12 (1970): 71–83.

Simončić, Zdenka. "The Influence of German Trade Policy on Economic Development in Croatia in the Period from the Great Depression to the Second World War." In *The Third Reich and Yugoslavia*, Institute for Contemporary History (1975).

Sladek, Zdenek. "L'Industrie Tchécoslovaque et sa Lutte contre la Concurrence Allemande dans les Balkans durant les années 30." *Études Balkaniques* no. 1 (1990): 59–68.

————. "L'Industrie Tchécoslovaque et sa Lutte contre la Concurrence Allemande dans les Balkans durant les années 30." *Études Balkaniques* no. 2 (1990): 3–16.

————, and Ljuben Berov. "Čehoslovatskii kapital v stranah Jugovostočnoi Evropi v period mezhdu pervoi i vtoroi mirovimi voinami." *Études Balkaniques* no. 4 (1988): 18–40.

Smith, Woodruff D. "Friedrich Ratzel and the Origins of Lebensraum." *German Studies Review* 3, no. 1 (February 1980).

Spasov, Ljudmila. "L'URSS et les Relations Bulgaro-Turques à l'Époque de 1934 à 1938." *Études Balkaniques* no. 3 (1983): 58–76.

Spenceley, G. F. R. "R. J. Overy and the Motorisierung: A Comment." *Economic History Review* 2nd series 32 (February 1979): 100–106.

Stachura, Peter. "The Political Strategy of the Nazi Party, 1919–1933." *German Studies Review* 3, no. 2 (May 1980).

Stafford, David A. T. "S.O.E. and British Involvement in the Belgrade Coup d'État of March 1941." *Slavic Review* 36, no. 3 (September 1972).

Stegmann, Dirk. " 'Mitteleuropa' 1925–1934: zum Problem der Kontinuität deutscher Aussenhandelspolitik von Stresemann bis Hitler." In *Industrielle Gesellschaft und politisches System*, edited by Dirk Stegmann, Bernd-Jürgen Wendt, and Peter-Christian Witt. Bonn: Verlag Neue Gesellschaft, 1978.

Stevenson, John, "Myth and Reality: Britain in the 1930s." In *Crisis and Controversy, Essays in Honour of A. J. P. Taylor*, edited by Alan Sked and Chris Cook. New York: St. Martin's, 1976.

Stoianovich, Traian. "Land Tenure and Related Sectors of the Balkan Economy, 1600–1800." *Journal of Economic History* 13 (Fall 1953): 398–411.

Suchcitz, Andrzej. "Poland's Defence Preparations in 1939." In *Poland Between the Wars, 1918–1939*. New York: St. Martin's, 1998.

Sweezy, Maxine Yaple. "German Corporate Profits: 1926–1938." *Quarterly Journal of Economics* 54 (1940): 384–398.

Tannenbaum, Edward R. "The Goals of Italian Fascism." *American Historical Review* 74, no. 4 (April 1969): 1195–1199.

Terzuolo, Eric R. "The Garibaldini in the Balkans 1875–1876." *International History Review* (February 1982): 110–126.

Tomlinson, B. R. "The Political Economy of the Raj: The Decline of Colonialism." *Journal of Economic History* 42, no. 1 (March 1982): 133–137.

Tomlinson, J. D. "Inter-war Unemployment—Two Views." *Journal of Contemporary History* 17 (1982): 545–555.

Treue, Wilhelm. "Das Dritte Reich u. die Westmächte auf dem Balkan." *Vierteljahreshefte für Zeitgeschichte* 1 (1953): 45–64.

Tskov, Svetozar. "Ekonomichekie pozitsii i protivorechiia mezhdu imperialisticheskimi derzhavami i gretsii nakanune mirovoi voini." In *Balkanskii Istorskii Sbornik,* vol. 2. Kishinev: Akademiia Nauk Moldavskoi SSR, 1970.

Tunzelmann, N. von. "Britain 1900–1945: A Survey." In *The Economic History of Britain Since 1700,* vol. 2, edited by Roderick Floud and Donald McCloskey. Cambridge: Cambridge University Press, 1981.

Turner, Henry A. "Hitler's Secret Pamphlet for Industrialists 1927." *Journal of Modern History* 40, no. 3 (September 1968): 365–374.

Vaïsse, Maurice. "Against Appeasement: French Advocates of Firmness, 1933–1938." In *The Fascist Challenge and the Policy of Appeasement,* edited by Wolfgang J. Mommsen and Lothar Kettenacker. London: G. Allen & Unwin, 1983.

Vanutelli, Cesare. "The Living Standard of Italian Workers." In *The Ax Within,* edited by Roland Sarti. New York: New Viewpoints, 1974.

Velikov, Stefan. "Les Relations Bulgaro-turques 1934–1939." *Études Balkaniques* no. 1 (1982): 34–51.

Vogelsang, Thilo. "Neue Dokumente." *Vierteljahresheft für Zeitgeschichte* 11, no. 4 (1954).

Volkmann, Hans-Erich. "Aussenhandel u. Aufrüstung in Deutschland 1933 bis 1939." In *Wirtschaft u. Rüstung am Vorabend des Zweiten Weltkrieges,* edited by Friedrich Forstmeier and Hans-Erich Volkmann. Düsseldorf: Droste, 1975.

Wallace, W. V. "The Making of the May Crisis of 1938." *The Slavonic and East European Review* 41, no. 97 (June 1963): 368–389.

Wandycz, Damian S. "A Forgotten Letter of Pilsudski to Masaryk." *Polish Review* 9, no. 4 (autumn 1964): 38–54.

Wanrooji, Bruno. "The Rise and Fall of Italian Fascism as a Generational Conflict." *Journal of Contemporary History* 22 (1987).

Watt, D. C. "Appeasement: The Rise of a Revisionist School?" *Political Quarterly* 36 (1965): 191–213.

Wegs, J. Robert. "The Marshaling of Copper: An Index of Austro-Hungarian Economic Mobilization during World War I." *Austrian History Yearbook* 12–13 (1976–1977): 189–202.

Wendt, Bernd-Jürgen. "Strukturbedingungen der britischen Südosteuropapolitik am Vorabend des Zweiten Weltkrieges." In *Wirtschaft u. Rüstung am Vorabend des Zweiten Weltkrieges,* edited by Friedrich Forstmeier and Hans-Erich Volkmann. Düsseldorf: Droste, 1975.

———. "Economic Appeasement—A Crisis Strategie." In *The Fascist Challenge and the Policy of Appeasement,* edited by Wolfgang J. Mommsen and Lothar Kettenacker. London: G. Allen & Unwin, 1983.

———. "Südosteuropa in der nationalsozialistischen Grossraumwirtschaft, Eine Antwort auf Alan S. Milward." In *Der "Führerstaat": Mythe und Realität Studien zur Struktur und Politik des Dritten Reiches,* edited by Gerhard Hirschfeld and Lothar Kettenacker. Stuttgart: Klett-Cotta, 1981.

Wichert, Sabine. "The British Left and Appeasement: Political Tactics of Alternative Policies." In *The Fascist Challenge and the Policy of Appeasement,* edited by Wolfgang J. Mommsen and Lothar Kettenacker. London: G. Allen & Unwin, 1983.

Williams, Maurice. "German Imperialism and Austria, 1938." *Journal of Contemporary History* 14 (1979): 139–253.

———. "The Aftermath of Anschluss: Disillusioned Germans or Budding Austrian Patriots." *Austrian History Yearbook* 14 (1978): 129–132.

Winchester, Betty Jo. "Hungary and the 'Third Europe.'" *Slavic Review* 32, no. 4 (December 1973).

Wiskemann, Elizabeth. "The Rumano-German Treaty." *The Spectator* (April 14, 1939) 162 (January–June 1939): 626–627.

Yahil, L. "Madagascar — Phantom of a Solution for the Jewish Question." In *Jews and Non-Jews in Eastern Europe 1918–1945*, edited by Bela Vago and George L. Mosse. New York: Wiley, 1974.

Young, Robert J. "Reason and Madness: France, the Axis Powers and the Politics of Economic Disorder, 1938–39." *Canadian Journal of History* 20 (April 1985): 65–83.

Zaharia, Gheorghe, and Ion Calafeteanu. "The International Situation and Romania's Foreign Policy between 1938 and 1940." *Revue Roumaine d'Histoire* 18, no. 1 (January–March 1979): 83–105.

Živkova, Ljudmila. "The Economic Policy of Germany and Britain in South-eastern Europe on the Eve of the Second World War." *Études Balkaniques* no. 1 (1969): 36–54.

A Glossary of Key Names and Diplomatic Agreements

Alexander, King Karadjordjević : ruler of Yugoslavia, assassinated in 1935.

Alphand, Charles: French Ambassador to Moscow.

Andrić, Ivo: Yugoslav Ambassador to Germany; Bosnian Serb novelist and Nobel prize winner.

Anfuso, Filippo: assistant to Count Ciano.

Antonescu, General Ion: later Marshal of the Romanian army, premier 1940–1945. Arrested and executed in 1946.

Antonescu, Victor: Romanian Foreign Minister, 1938.

Ashton-Gwatkin, Frank: Chief of the Economics Section of the British Foreign Office, 1938–1939.

Atherton, Raymond: American State Department, European Division Chief.

Attolico, Bernardo: Italian Ambassador at Berlin.

Badoglio, Count Pietro: General, later Marshal, Chief of Staff of Italian Army.

Baldwin, Stanley: British Prime Minister, 1935–1937.

Balkan Entente: Greece, Romania, Turkey and Yugoslavia.

Barthou, Louis: French Foreign Minister, February–October, 1934, assassinated in 1934.

Beaverbrook, Lord Maxwell Atkin: influential British publisher.

Beck, Colonel Jozef: Polish Foreign Minister, 1932–1939.

Beck, General Ludwig: German Army Chief of Staff.

Beneš, Dr. Eduard: Czech Foreign Minister; President of Czechoslovakia, 1935–1938.

Benzler, Felix: German Foreign Office official, plenipotentiary to Serbia, 1941.

Berle, Adolph: American Undersecretary of State in the Roosevelt administration.

Berthelot, Philippe: Secretary-General of the French Foreign Ministry, predecessor of Alexis Leger.

Bethlen, Count Istvan: Premier of Hungary, 1921–1931.

Biddle, A. J. Drexel Jr.: American Ambassador to Poland, 1937–1939.

Bissolati, Leonida: Italian Socialist politician, editor of *Avanti*, Cabinet Minister, 1916–1918.

Blessing, Dr. Karl: German Reichsbank Director.

Blomberg, Field-Marshal Werner von: Minister of Defense and Wehrmacht Chief of Staff, 1933–1938.

Blum, Leon: Socialist party leader and French Prime Minister, 1936–1937, 1938.

Bonnet, Georges: French Minister of Foreign Affairs in Daladier government, 1938–1939. Held other cabinet posts previously.

Boris, Czar: Ruler of Bulgaria, 1918–1943. Died mysteriously in 1943.

Bosch, Carl: a Director of I. G. Farben.

Brauchitsch, Field-Marshal Walther von: German War Minister and Commander-in-Chief, 1938–1941, suffered heart attack, died in British captivity.

Briand, Aristide: French Premier eleven times, Foreign Minister, 1925–1932.

Brown, Sir William: British Treasury Department official.

Brüning, Heinrich: German Chancellor, 1930–1932.

Bullitt, William C.: American Ambassador to the USSR; later Ambassador to France.

Bülow, Bernard von: German State Secretary in the Foreign Office.

Burckhardt, Karl: League of Nations High Commissioner at Danzig.

Butler, R. A. (Rab): Parliamentary Under-Secretary at the Foreign Office; private secretary to Chamberlain.

Cadere, V.: Romanian minister to Belgrade.

Cadogan, Sir Alexander: British Foreign Office Deputy Under-Secretary; later Permanent Under-Secretary.

Campbell, Ronald Ian: British Minister at Belgrade.

Carol II, King: Romanian ruler, 1930–1940. Driven from Romania by the Iron Guard and Ion Antonescu in 1940.

Chamberlain, Neville: British Chancellor of the Exchequer, 1931–1937; Prime Minister, 1937–1940.

Chautemps, Camille: French Prime Minister, 1937–1938; held many cabinet positions.

Churchill, Winston S.: various cabinet posts before 1940; British cabinet member 1940; thereafter wartime Prime Minister.

Ciano, Count Galeazzo: Mussolini's son-in-law and Italian Foreign Minister, 1936–1943. Executed by order of Mussolini in 1943.

Cincar-Marković, Alexander: Yugoslav Minister in Berlin, 1939–1941; Yugoslav Foreign Minister, 1940–1941.

Clemenceau, Georges: French politician; World War I Premier.

Clodius, Carl.: Director-Minister of Economic Affairs in the German Foreign Office.

Codreanu, Cornelius: Founder and leader of the Romanian fascist Iron Guard; assassinated November 1938.

Collier, Laurence: head of the British Foreign Office Northern Department, 1935–1942.

Cooper, Duff Alfred: British Secretary of State for War, 1935; First Lord of the Admiralty, 1937–1938. Opposed Chamberlain's appeasement policy and resigned after Munich Agreement.

Coulondre, Robert: French Ambassador to Moscow, 1936–1938; Minister to Berlin, 1938–1939.

Cripps, Sir Stafford: British Ambassador to Moscow, 1940–1942.

Cvetković, Dragiša: Minister-President of Yugoslavia, 1939–1941. Headed government which signed the Tripartite Pact in April 1941 and was overthrown.

Csaky, Count Istvan: Hungarian Minister for Foreign Affairs, 1938–1940.

Daladier, Edouard: French Premier, 1938–1940; War Minister, 1936–1940; Minister for Foreign Affairs, 1939–1940.

Delbos, Yvon: French Foreign Minister, 1936–1938.

Dill, General Marshall: British military leader, Vice Chief then Chief of the Imperial General Staff.

Dirksen, Dr. Herbert von: German ambassador to London.

Djuvara: Romanian minister in Berlin.

Dodd, W. E.: American Ambassador in Berlin, 1933–1938.

Dollfuss, Dr. Englebert: Austrian Chancellor, 1932–1934, murdered by Nazis in 1934.

Donovan, Colonel William: President Roosevelt's troubleshooter to the Balkans; later OSS founder.

Draganov, Parvan: Bulgarian Minister to Berlin.

Duisberg, Karl: founder and head of I. G. Farben chemical company.

Eden, Anthony (Earl of Avon): British Foreign Secretary, 1935–1938, later wartime Foreign Secretary.

Erskine, William: British Ambassador to Poland and later Czechoslovakia.

Fabricius, Wilhelm: German Minister at Bucharest.

Feine, Gerhard: German Consul in Zagreb.

Fischer, Sir Warren: British Permanent Secretary of the Treasury Department, 1919–1939.

Fotić, Konstantine: Yugoslav Minister in Washington before and during World War II.

Franco, General Francisco: Head of Spanish Fascist Party and government.

François-Poncet, André: French Ambassador to Berlin, later to Italy.

Freundt, Alfred: German Consul in Zagreb.

Frank, Hans: German Gauleiter of Poland during World War II, hung after Nuremberg trial.

Fritsch, General Werner von: German Commander in Chief of the Army. Framed by Nazis on charges of homosexuality, later killed in Polish campaign.

Funk, Walter: German Economic Minister, 1938–1945, successor of Schacht.

Gafencu, Grigore: Romanian Foreign Minister, 1939–1941.

Gamelin, General Maurice : Chief of French General Staff, 1938–1939; Commander in Chief of French Army, 1939–1940.

Gavrilović, Milan: Yugoslav politician and Minister at Moscow.

George, Lloyd David: British Prime Minister, 1916–1922; Liberal member of Parliament, 1931–1945.

Giolitti, Giovanni: Deputy 1882–1928; Prime Minister four times, 1892–1921, died in 1928.

Gömbös, Gyula: Premier of Hungary, 1932–1935.

Gördeler, Carl: Oberbürgermeister of Leipzig; coup plotter against Hitler; killed by Hitler.

Göring, Reichsmarshal Hermann: head of Four Year Plan rearmament administration; head of German Luftwaffe. Committed suicide in prison after the war.

Graziani, General Rodolfo, later Marschal: Italian military commander.

Grzybowski, Waclav: Polish Minister at Prague; then Moscow.

Guarneri, Felice: Italian Finance Minister under Mussolini.

Halder, Col. General Franz : German Chief of Staff; replaced Beck; resigned in 1942.

Halifax, Viscount Edward (Lord Irwin): British Secretary for War; Lord Privy Seal; Foreign Secretary, 1938–1940.

Harvey, Oliver Charles: private secretary to Eden and Halifax, 1936–1939.

Hassell, Ugo von: German Minister to Belgrade; later to Rome.

Henderson, Sir Nevile: British Minister to Belgrade; later British Ambassador to Berlin, 1937–1939.

Heeren, Viktor von: German Minister to Belgrade.

Herriot, Édouard: French Deputy Premier, 1919–1940; Radical party leader, cabinet minister 1926–1936; Premier, 1932; President of Chamber of Deputies, 1936–1940.

Hoare, Sir Reginald: British Minister to Bucharest.

Hoare, Sir Samuel (Viscount Templewood): British Foreign Secretary, June–December 1935.

Hodža, Milan: Czechoslovak politician.

Horthy, Admiral Nicholas: Regent of Hungary.

Hudson, Robert Spear: Chief of the British Overseas Trade Department, 1937–1940.

Hull, Cordell: American Secretary of State, 1933–1944.

Ickes, Harold: American Secretary of the Interior during the New Deal period.

Ingram, Rex: British Foreign Office official.

Inskip, Sir Thomas: British Minister for Coordination of Defense, 1936–1939.

Jebb, Gladwyn: economic specialist in the British Foreign Office; private secretary to the Permanent Under-Secretary.

Jodl, Lieutenant General Alfred: German General at Führer headquarters, Chief of operations staff OKW, hanged at Nuremberg 1946.

Jukić, Ilija: Croat official in the Yugoslav Foreign Office.

Kanya, Kalman: Hungarian Foreign Minister, later Premier.

Kehrl, Hans: German industrialist and Nazi economic planner.

Keitel, General Wilhelm: Head of OKW, tried and hanged at Nuremberg.

Kennard, Sir Howard W.: British Ambassador to Poland, 1935–1939.

Kennedy, A. L.: *London Times* correspondent in Berlin.

Kennedy, Joseph: American Ambassador in London, a leading appeaser, father of John F. Kennedy.

Kerr, Phillip (Lord Lothian): British pacifist, appeaser.

Keynes, John Maynard: British economist.

Kiosseivanov, George: Bulgarian Foreign Minister and Premier.

Knatchbull-Hugessen, Sir Hugh: Foreign Minister to the Baltic States and later to Turkey.

Knežević, Colonel Živan: one of 1941 Belgrade coup conspirators.

Kordt, Erich: German Foreign Office official.

Kordt, Theodore: chargé d'affaires in the German Embassy in London.

Krauch, Carl: Director of I. G. Farben; on staff of Göring's Four Year Plan Administration.

Krnjević, Juraj: a Croatian Peasant Party official, leader of Peasant Party in exile.

Krosigk, Lutz Graf Schwerin von: German Treasury Minister, 1920–1945.

Krupp, Alfred: son of Gustav Krupp, head of Krupp Armament firm. Tried and sentenced as a war criminal at Nuremberg.

Krupp, Gustav: German industrialist, pre–World War I head of Krupp firm.

Kun, Bela: communist leader of Hungarian Soviet, 1918–1920, fled to Soviet Union, executed during the purges in 1938.

Lane, Arthur Bliss: American Minister to Yugoslavia, and later Poland.

Laroche, Jules: French Ambassador to Poland, 1926–1935.

Laval, Pierre: French Premier, 1931–1932; 1935–1936; Foreign Minister, 1934–1935. Leading Vichy government collaborator.

Lebrun, Albert: President of France, 1932–1940.

Leger, Alexis: Secretary General of French Foreign Ministry. Successor to Berthelot.

Leith-Ross, Sir Frederick: chief economic advisor to the British government, 1932–1939.

Lever, E. H.: a representative of British bondholders in Berlin.

Lindsay, Sir Ronald: British Ambassador in Washington, 1930–1939.

Lipski, Jozef: Polish Ambassador to Germany, 1934–1939.

Little Entente: Czechoslovakia, Romania and Yugoslavia.

Locock, Guy: Director of the Federation of British Industries.

Loraine, Sir Percy: British Ambassador to Ankara; Minister at Rome, 1939–1940.

Lothian, Lord (Phillip Kerr): British pacifist, appeaser.

Łukasiewicz, Juliusz: Polish Ambassador to France, 1938–1939.

Maček, Vladko: Croatian Peasant Party leader.

MacDonald, Ramsay: British Prime Minister, 1929–1935.

Maiskii, Ivan M.: Soviet Ambassador to Britain, 1932–1943.

Malletke, Walter: Nazi Party Foreign Office specialist for Southeastern Europe.

Mandel, Georges: chef de cabinet of Clemenceau, 1917–1919; deputy, 1920–1940; French cabinet member, 1934–1936, 1938–1940.

Mapplebeck, T. G.: British honorary air attaché in Belgrade.

Mason-MacFarlane, Colonel (Sir) Frank: British Military attaché at Berlin, 1937–1939.

Massigli, René: official at French Foreign Office; later Ambassador at Ankara, 1939–1940.

Messersmith, George: American Ambassador to Vienna; Assistant Secretary of State.

Metaxas, General Jihannes: Greek dictator, 1936–1941.

Miely, James : American consul in Zagreb.

Mirković, General Bora: Yugoslav Air Force Chief, purported leader of the March 1941 Belgrade coup.

Moffat, Jay Pierpont: American State Department European Division Chief.

Molotov, Vyacheslav M.: Soviet Minister for Foreign Affairs, 1939–1949.

Moltke, Count Hans-Adolph von: German Ambassador to Poland throughout the 1930s.

Morgenthau, Henry: American Secretary of the Treasury and friend of Roosevelt.

Moscicki, Ignacy: President of Polish Republic.

Mühlstein, Anatol: Polish chargé d'affaires in Paris.

Mussolini, Benito: Fascist Party head; head of Italian government.

Namier, Sir Lewis B.: British historian.

Nedić, Milan: Yugoslav Minister of War, dismissed by Prince Paul; head of wartime Serbian government.

Neuhausen, Franz: German Consul-General in Belgrade.

Neurath, Baron Constantin von: German Foreign Minister, 1932–1938.

Nichols: British Foreign Office official.

Nicolson, Harold: British Foreign Office official; later M.P.; writer.

Ninčić, Momčilo: Yugoslav politician; Foreign Minister in Simović government, 1941.

Noël, Leon: French Ambassador to Poland, 1935–1939.

Norman, Montagu: Governor of the Bank of England.

Ogilvie-Forbes, Sir George Arthur: Counsellor in the British Embassy at Berlin.

O'Malley, Sir Owen St. Clair: British Minister at Budapest.

Otto, Archduke: Hapsburg pretender to the throne.

Palairet, Sir Michael: British Minister in Athens.

Papagos, General Alexandros: Greek military leader.

Papen, Franz von: German Chancellor in 1930s; Ambassador to Turkey.

Pašić, Nikola: Serbian Premier before World War I.

Paul, Prince: Regent of Yugoslavia, 1934–1941, supported Yugoslavia's adherence to Tripartite Pact, overthrown in 1941 and deported to Kenya by Churchill.

Paul-Boncour, Joseph: French Foreign Minister, March–April, 1938.

Pavelić, Dr. Ante: Croatian separatist leader; leader of wartime Independent State of Croatia 1941–1945, died in Spain 1957.

Petrescu-Comnen, Nicolae: Romanian Foreign Minister, 1938.

Phillips, William: American Undersecretary of State, later ambassador to Italy.

Phipps, Sir Eric: British Ambassador at Paris, 1937–1939; formerly at Berlin, 1933–1937.

Pilsudski, Marshal Jozef: Polish Chief of State, 1926–1935.

Pinsent, Michael: British Treasury Department official on loan to the Embassy in Berlin.

Posse, Emile: Director of the Trade and Political Department of the German Economics Ministry; State Secretary for the Economy.

Potemkin, Vladimir: Soviet Undersecretary; Vice Commissar for Foreign Affairs.

Raczynski, Count Edward: Polish Ambassador in London.

Rendel, Sir George: British Minister at Sophia.

Reynaud, Paul: French Premier, 1939–1940.

Ribbentrop, Joachim von: Nazi Foreign Minister; tried and hanged at Nuremberg.

Richthofen: German Minister to Bulgaria.

Rosenberg, Alfred: Nazi theorist; head of Nazi Party Foreign Office.

Rumbold, Horace: British Minister at Berlin. Succeeded by Eric Phipps.

Runciman, Lord Walter: British Minister of Trade.

Sapieha, Prince: Polish Foreign Minister after World War I.

Saracoglu, Sükrü: Turkish Foreign Minister.

Sargent, Sir Orme: Assistant Under-Secretary of State for Foreign Affairs.

Sayre, Francis B.: American Under-Secretary in the Trade Division of the State Department.

Schacht, Hjalmar: German Minister of Economics, 1934–1937; President of Reichsbank, 1923–1930, 1933–1939.

Schlotterer, Gustav: German Economic Ministry Director.

Schulenberg, Friedrich Werner von der: German Ambassador in Moscow, 1935–1941. Executed in 1944 for involvement in plot to assassinate Hitler.

Seeckt, General Hans von: Head of German General Staff to 1926.

Sforza, Carlo Count: Italian Foreign Minister.

Simon, Sir John: British cabinet member, Chancellor of the Exchequer; Foreign Secretary, 1937–1940.

Simović, General Dušan: Yugoslav Army Chief of Staff; Air Force Chief.

Slawek, Colonel Walery: Polish political figure; close friend of Pilsudski, member of his inner circle and Polish premier.

Śmigły-Rydz, Marshal Edward: Head of Polish Army, and follower of Pilsudski.

Smiljanić, Milan: Yugoslav Assistant Foreign Secretary.

Sonnino, Sidney: Italian Prime Minister, 1906, 1909–1910; Foreign Minister, 1915–1919.

Sosnkowski, General: Inspector of the Polish Army; close collaborator of Pilsudski; fell into disfavor after 1926 Pilsudski coup.

Spaljaković: Yugoslav Minister to Paris.

Stanley, Oliver: Head of the British Board of Trade, 1937–1940.

Steinhardt, Lawrence: American Ambassador in Moscow before the war and during the war.

Stinnes, Hugo: German industrialist and steel magnate. Hitler supporter, later fled Germany.

Stojadinović, Milan: Serb, Prime Minister of Yugoslavia.

Strang, William: Head of Central Department of Foreign Office; foreign office representative on ill-fated British mission to Moscow in 1939.

Stresemann, Gustav: German Foreign Minister, negotiated the Locarno Agreement of 1928.

Šubašić, Ivan: pre-war Ban (Governor) of Croatia; Royal Government official during war and after.

Subbotić, Ivan Dr.: Yugoslav Minister to Britain.

Suritz, Jakov: Soviet Ambassador at Paris, 1937–1940.

Szembek, Comte Jean: Polish Vice Minister at Polish Foreign Ministry.

Szentmiklossy, A.: Hungarian chargé d'affaires at Berlin.

Sztojay, Dome: Hungarian Ambassador in Berlin.

Tardieu, André: French Premier, author of the Tardieu Plan for Central and Eastern Europe.

Tatarescu, G.: Romanian Prime Minister.

Teleki, Count Pal: Hungarian Premier; committed suicide in 1941.

Thomas, General Georg: Head of German War Economy and Armaments Office.

Thyssen, Fritz: German industrialist, chairman of Vereingte Stahlwerke (United Steelworks).

Tilea, Viorel: Romanian minister to London, 1939–1940.

Tito, Josip Broz: Yugoslav communist and partisan leader; post-war leader of Yugoslavia.

Titulescu, Nikola: Romanian Foreign Minister; carried out pro-Western foreign policy.

Tripartite Pact: Germany, Italy and Japan.

Trumbić, Ante: post–World War I Croat, one of the founders of the Yugoslav state.

Tyrrel (or Tyrel), Lord William George: British Ambassador in Paris, 1928–1934.

Ulrich, Dr.: economic specialist in German Foreign Office.

Vansittart, Sir Robert Gilbert: British Foreign Office Permanent Under-Secretary.

Veesenmayer, Edmund: official in German Foreign Office for Special Missions.

Vyshinsky, Andrei: Soviet Deputy Foreign Commissar; prosecutor of Moscow trials.

Waley, S. D.: British Treasury Department Official.

Wavell, Field Marshal Archibald Percival: Commander of British forces in North Africa.

Weizsäcker, Ernst von: German State Secretary in Foreign Office.

Welles, Sumner: American Under-Secretary of State and rival of Hull, boyhood friend and confident of Roosevelt.

Weygand, General Maxime: Chief of French Military Forces in 1940; in World War I on Petain's staff.

Wiehl, Emil: Economics specialist in German Foreign Office.

Wildenfeldt, Otto: German Ambassador to the U.S. and former Krupp director.

Wilmowsky, Tilo von: Krupp Director.

Wilson, Sir Horace John: Chancellor of the Exchequer; alter ego and closest adviser of Neville Chamberlain.

Wohltat, Helmuth: German Foreign Office economic specialist and protegé of Göring.

Wysocki, Alfred: Polish Minister in Berlin, 1931–1933; then Ambassador to Rome, 1933–1938.

Zeeland Paul van: Premier of Belgium, 1935–1937, foreign minister in 1947.

List of Tables

Index